BLACKS IN THE NEW WORLD

August Meier, Series Editor

Along the Color Line

Along the Color Line

Explorations in the Black Experience

August Meier and Elliott Rudwick

UNIVERSITY OF ILLINOIS PRESS
Urbana Chicago London

Library of Congress Cataloging in Publication Data

Meier, August, 1923–
    Along the color line, explorations in the Black
experience.

    (Blacks in the New World)
    1. Afro-Americans—History—Addresses, essays,
lectures. 2. Afro-Americans—Civil rights—Addresses,
essays, lectures. I. Rudwick, Elliott M., joint
author. II. Title. III. Series.
E185.M39   973'.04'96073   76-27293
ISBN 0-252-00636-4

FOR FRANK AND MARILYN BYRNE

Contents

Foreword

For some two decades August Meier and Elliott Rudwick have been among the most prolific and protean writers on the history of black America, first in separate books and articles and more recently as collaborators. Seminal monographs, general histories, textbooks, government reports, collections of essays and documents, review essays, and research articles have poured forth from their workshop.

This outpouring suggests an extraordinary energy and creative drive, but perhaps its main focus suggests more clearly its motivation. Though they have written comprehensively of the whole Afro-American history field, and especially of black leadership and ideology, their emphasis has been on the history of the civil rights movement. August Meier has written perceptively of Booker T. Washington, for example, but his real hero is Frederick Douglass, as the essay herein makes clear. Elliott Rudwick began his scholarly career with a biography of W. E. B. Du Bois that did not flinch at pointing out his foibles, and he continues to do so in an article in this volume; but underlying these criticisms is a deep commitment to the cause of racial equality. In Meier's case especially, perhaps because he came to reformism from a parental background of radical Socialism, the commitment to civil rights took an activist form. While a faculty member at Morgan State College in the early 1960's he took part in the student-sponsored department store demonstrations in Baltimore, and to those who attended the civil rights marches Meier was a familiar sight, swinging his heavy briefcase and passing out to any who would take them his perceptive articles on Martin Luther King and on many aspects of the history of civil rights. Rudwick came more indirectly to study of the civil rights movement through academic training in sociology and urban studies. He adds an interdisciplinary dimension to their collaborative essays.

The essays in this volume are by no means all that the two authors have written. Not included are the articles that in another form appeared in Meier's *Negro Thought in America, 1880–1915* (1963), in Rudwick's *W. E. B. Du Bois* (1960) and *Race Riot at East St. Louis* (1964), and in their joint work, *CORE* (1973). Some readers will also miss those timely but perhaps now dated comments on passing events that appeared either in civil rights journals or obscure scholarly journals. I recall vividly, for example, the insights of one of Meier's articles, based partly on his own experience, on the relationships between white and black teachers in black colleges, and at the time of the stall-in at the New York world's fair in 1964 an article by Meier and Rudwick in *The Crisis* (called "Come to the Fair?") on black protest against discrimination at earlier world's fairs.

The authors have decided wisely, I think, to limit this volume to research articles only. In this collection appear all the works which are not already in book form but which have a long-range scholarly significance. In addition, some items not previously published in themselves make the volume worthy of serious attention. Included in "Attorneys Black and White: A Case Study of Race Relations within the NAACP" is fuller biographical information that was abbreviated or omitted when the article on lawyers appeared in the *Journal of American History* in 1976. There is also an original article that upsets many previous assumptions, "The Origins of Nonviolent Direct Action in Afro-American Protest: A Note on Historical Discontinuities." This "note" of nearly one hundred pages, after reviewing direct action tactics over more than a century, concludes that each generation of blacks has had to discover direct action for itself. So Meier and Rudwick continue to enlighten us on the nature of the struggle for human rights.

—Louis R. Harlan

Preface

The title of this book was inspired by W. E. B. Du Bois's column, "Along the Color Line," which appeared monthly in *The Crisis*. As graduate students both of us spent much time studying the career of this sociologist, historian, and protest leader, and ever since then our research interests and writing have been devoted to an exploration of the black experience and black-white relations in America.

In selecting articles for this anthology we have excluded any that have been reprinted virtually verbatim in our published books. Three of the essays appearing here were prepared especially for this volume. (These are the analysis of the rise of the black secretariat in the NAACP, the comparison of the responses made by NAACP and CORE to the Black Power thrust of the late 1960's, and the analysis of the origins of nonviolent direct action.) In one case—the article dealing with the NAACP and its lawyers—when the essay was originally published it was not feasible to include all of the detailed supporting data about the various lawyers involved; this material has here been added in the footnotes. All of the other essays are reprinted in their entirety as they originally appeared, except for corrections of spelling and typographical errors. No attempt has been made to eliminate the occasional redundancy that results, or to make changes in the light of later events and more recent scholarship. (In a very few cases where it has seemed particularly advisable we have updated factual information by the use of a phrase or sentence inserted in brackets, but in these cases nothing in the original has been deleted.) Throughout, footnotes have been made to conform to the University of Chicago Press's *Manual of Style*.

We wish to acknowledge with warm appreciation the help of Professor Louis R. Harlan and Richard L. Wentworth, associate director of the University of Illinois Press, whose advice in the selection of articles and whose encouragement made this volume's appearance possible. We also wish to thank our old friend Benjamin A. Quarles for his helpful reactions and suggestions.

We wish to express our appreciation to people who were helpful in the preparation of individual essays, particularly the previously unpublished ones. A number of persons who graciously agreed to be interviewed are cited in the footnotes, but we want to single out certain individuals for special mention.

NAACP officials Roy Wilkins, Gloster Current, the late John Morsell, and Bobbie Branche; Bayard Rustin, chairman of the A. Philip Randolph Institute; and the late Judge William H. Hastie have all been unfailingly helpful, no matter how many times we have called upon them for assistance. Professor Gary T. Marx of M.I.T. read an earlier version of our essay on the NAACP and its lawyers; his comments opened up a whole new area of research for us, and the generalizations we developed about the characteristics of the black and white lawyers resulted from his suggestion. Similarly, the critique of an earlier version of "Integration vs. Separatism: The NAACP and CORE Face Challenge from Within" by Professor William Yancey of Temple University was enormously stimulating and greatly influenced the rewriting of the essay.

Howard Smead of the Washington *Post* Library was exceedingly helpful on a number of occasions in supplying citations to articles in that newspaper. Clifton H. Johnson, director of the Amistad Research Center, Dillard University, New Orleans, promptly and diligently ran down our requests for information that filled vital gaps in our knowledge.

Among the many people interviewed for our article on the origins of nonviolent direct action, we are particularly indebted to Professors Mark Solomon of Simmons College and Mark Naison of Fordham University for generously sharing with us their intimate knowledge of Communist involvement in the black community during the 1930's. Charles Chatfield of Wittenberg College clarified for us elusive aspects of the development of pacifist thought and vocabulary during the 1930's. Our colleague at Kent State University, James P. Louis, provided us with data that made clear the connection between the tactics of the feminist movement and those of the black protest movement in the World War I era. Professor Louis Ruchames, of the University of Massachusetts at Boston, was helpful when we sought to explore the possible connections between early direct-action protests in Massachusetts and Garrisonian ideology. Discussions with Professor Kenneth Kusmer of Temple University and Christopher Wye of Washington, D.C., were valuable in explaining the durability of the Future Outlook League in Cleveland. Professor Arthur O. White of the University of Florida kindly supplied us with copies of his published and unpublished essays on nineteenth-century school boycotts, while Professor Michael W. Homel of Eastern Michigan University elucidated recondite aspects of the history of the educational struggles in Chicago. John A. Hague of Stetson University helped us unravel the subtleties in the thought of Charles Nagel and kindly allowed us to consult sections of his manuscript on the subject. Thomas Webster, formerly head of the Kansas City Urban League, went out of his way to search out information for us. We are most appreciative of the diligent search made by William D. Barnard of the Alabama Commission on Higher Education for information about the elusive Anniston lawyer, Charles D. Kline. Jonathan Gottlieb of Rye, New York, who studied the careers of Bayard Rustin and A. Philip Randolph for his senior thesis at Brown University, called our attention to material that lent documentary support to information about their relationship which we had secured previously from interviews.

We wish to thank the staff of the Kent State University Library, especially Jane Benson, Sally Osgood, Linda Burroughs, and Helen Peoples, for aiding in many ways the preparation of the new articles in the book. Jefferson Kellogg and Kenneth Zinz wrote master's theses on the Don't-Buy-Where-You-Can't-Work Campaigns that were helpful in our exploration of that topic. Threasa Gainer checked numerous bibliographical citations. Barbara Hostetler prepared the manuscript for the publisher with her usual thoroughness and efficiency. And to Eugene P. Wenninger, director of the Kent State University Center for Urban Regionalism, and to his administrative assistant, Carol Toncar, we are deeply indebted for the many ways in which our connection with the Center has facilitated the preparation of the book.

Finally, we acknowledge financial assistance from various sources—the Kent State University Center for Urban Regionalism, which supports all of our research efforts; the John Simon Guggenheim Memorial Foundation, which granted fellowships in 1971–72, permitting us to do most of the research for the two articles dealing with the NAACP lawyers and secretariat; and from the National Endowment for the Humanities for a research grant that facilitated the completion of these two articles and most of the research and writing of the essay on the origins of nonviolent direct action. Of course, the findings and conclusions do not necessarily represent the view of any of these sources of financial assistance.

Washington, D.C.   — AUGUST MEIER
March 24, 1976   ELLIOTT RUDWICK

PART I

On Afro-American Leadership: From Frederick Douglass to Martin Luther King

The essays in this section deal with selected aspects of black leadership from the mid-nineteenth to the mid-twentieth century. Throughout our careers as scholars we have been interested not in portraying heroes or villains, but in seeking to understand how black leaders functioned and how they tried to cope with the problems stemming from white racism in the different times and varied milieus in which they lived.[1]

Typically historians have highlighted the very evident contrasts among the best-known of the black leaders—militants like Frederick Douglass and W. E. B. Du Bois being contrasted with the accommodating Booker T. Washington; the charismatic A. Philip Randolph, Martin Luther King, and Malcolm X, with skillful bureaucrats like Walter White and Roy Wilkins in the NAACP, or ambassadors to white elites like Whitney Young of the National Urban League; the nationalists Marcus Garvey and Malcolm X with outspoken integrationists like Douglass, King, and the NAACP leaders. Yet from Douglass and Washington through Du Bois and Garvey to King and Malcolm X there runs an underlying similarity that suggests much about the nature of American race relations and the exclusion of blacks from the levers of political power in our society. For all of these men have been primarily spokesmen, symbolic leaders, and propagandists, rather than individuals with a solid organizational base. This was true even of Garvey and King, whose organizations were essentially extensions of their charismatic leadership and declined to virtual impotence after the founder had left the scene. It was equally true of Du Bois, who at the outset of his career sought to bring about social change not as an activist but as a scholar, and who as editor of the NAACP's *Crisis* magazine largely isolated himself from the building and running of the Association. Nor did Washington, for all his influence among Negroes, have an organizational base in the black community. The so-called Tuskegee Machine was nothing more than a handful of people at Tuskegee skillfully manipulating the wires of influence that Washington possessed because of his standing among white elites, and the vogue that a man of his international fame enjoyed among black elites as well. (And as the essay on "Booker T. Washington and the Negro Press" suggests, it is difficult to evaluate how influential the Tuskegee machine really was in shaping the ideological expression of black newspapers, in a period when accommodation was in the ascendancy quite independently of Booker T. Washington's role.) It is an irony of history that in the case of the NAACP, which did develop a strong organizational mechanism and deep roots in the black community, leaders like James Weldon Johnson,[2] Walter F. White, and Charles Hamilton Houston, while prominent in their day, have been relegated to the sidelines in the pantheon of famous Afro-Americans.

Given the racist context in which they worked, one of the issues with which black spokesmen and protest leaders had to grapple was the extent to which they should utilize white assistance and cooperation. Paradoxically, in the early part of the century it was the accommodator Booker T. Washington who espoused a program of black self-help, while the militant founders of the NAACP believed in the value of interracial action. Two of the essays in this section analyze the changing roles of whites and blacks in the NAACP during the first quarter-century of its history, and describe how the Association's work came increasingly under black control.

1. We have chosen to reprint here the essay on Du Bois's early career as a sociologist rather than some of our other articles about him, since these have all appeared as part of our previously published books. See the discussions in Rudwick, *W. E. B. Du Bois: A Study in Minority Group Leadership* (Philadelphia, 1960), reprinted with a new epilogue under the title *W. E. B. Du Bois: Propagandist of the Negro Protest* (New York and Philadelphia, 1968); and Meier, *Negro Thought in America, 1880–1915* (Ann Arbor, 1963), ch. 11.

2. Johnson is celebrated as a writer rather than as the builder of the NAACP.

ONE

Frederick Douglass's Vision for America: A Case Study in Nineteenth-Century Negro Protest

BY AUGUST MEIER

The most distinguished Negro in nineteenth-century America was Frederick Douglass. His fame rests chiefly upon his work as a brilliant antislavery orator and newspaper editor. Yet Douglass was also deeply concerned with developing a program to secure full citizenship rights and acceptance in American society for the free Negroes—both for the minority who were free before the Civil War and for the great masses after emancipation. With his thinking rooted in the principles of American democracy and Christianity—in the Declaration of Independence and the Sermon on the Mount—Douglass's life was a moral crusade for the abolition of slavery and racial distinction, the attainment of civil and political rights and equality before the law, and the assimilation of Negroes into American society. However his specific tactics and programs for racial elevation might vary—and they did undergo significant changes over the years—Douglass was ever the militant agitator, ever the forthright editor and orator, who consistently worked toward these goals through his half-century (1841–95) of leadership.

Douglass's antislavery career has received detailed treatment at the hands of other scholars,[1] but his ideologies concerning the advancement of free Negroes have not yet been the subject of systematic analysis. This paper, therefore, is limited to a

From Harold M. Hyman and Leonard W. Levy, eds., *Freedom and Reform: Essays in Honor of Henry Steele Commager* (New York: Harper & Row, 1967), pp. 127–48. © 1967 by Harold M. Hyman and Leonard W. Levy.

discussion of the programs he advocated for the achievement of full racial equality, and the relationship of these programs to the dominant patterns in nineteenth-century Negro thought.

Today Negro protest is expressed in the form of demands rather than appeals, in terms of power as well as justice, and is identified with a strategy of direct action rather than one of oratory and propaganda. The character of modern Negro protest is founded on the international pressures raised in behalf of American Negroes, the growing support for civil rights in the white population, and the increasing power of the Negro vote, which now acts as a balance of power in national elections. Throughout the nineteenth century, however, Negroes lacked leverage of this sort. They utilized the written and spoken word as their major vehicle of protest, combining denunciation of the undemocratic and unchristian oppression under which they lived with pleas directed at awakening the conscience of white Americans in order to secure redress of these grievances and recognition of their constitutional rights. Instances of what we would today call direct action did occur, but they were rare. Where conditions warranted it—as in those states where the antebellum Negroes could vote, and especially during Reconstruction—advocacy of political activity, in itself the central constitutional right which Negroes asked, was a leading theme, supplementing and lending weight to written and oral agitation, to conventions and meetings, to petitions and resolutions.

On the other hand, articulate Negroes in that era ordinarily gave nearly equal emphasis to urging Negroes to cultivate good character, to be thrifty and industrious, and to acquire as much property as possible. It was believed that by thus achieving middle-class moral and economic respectability, Negroes would earn the respect of the whites, counteract prejudice, and ease the way toward recognition of their manhood and their citizenship.

Many nineteenth-century advocates of thrift, industry, and economic accumulation placed special emphasis on the value of industrial education or training in mechanical trades. Most prominently associated with the accommodating ideology of Booker T. Washington at the end of the century, industrial education had been seriously advocated by prominent Negroes as early as the 1830's. Many Negro and white abolitionists viewed manual-labor schools, where the students earned their way through the productive work they performed while learning a useful trade, as an instrument for uplifting the lowly of both races and assimilating them into the mainstream of American middle-class society. Such schools, it was believed, would inculcate the values of thrift and industry at the same time that they provided the students with the means of making a living. At mid-century the economic crisis facing unskilled Negro workers fostered a resurgence of interest in industrial training.

Underlying the moral and economic program was a theme of individual and racial self-help that in turn overlapped with an ideology of racial solidarity—of racial cooperation and racial unity. This ideology of racial solidarity was one that caused considerable division and argument among articulate nineteenth-century Negroes. While a few went so far as to question the advisability of Negro churches and social organizations, the debate raged chiefly over whether or not Negroes should form their own protest organizations and establish and support their own protest publications, rather than rely solely upon cooperation with sympathetic whites. This division of opinion was due to more than the attitudes and policies of the many white abolitionists who failed to concern themselves with the Negroes' citizenship rights, who objected to employing Negroes in other than menial positions, and who even refused to allow Negroes to participate fully in the decision-making process of the antislavery societies. It was more than an argument over the question of whether or not it was consistent for Negroes to ask for integration and for acceptance into the mainstream of white society, and at the same time segregate themselves into separate organizations. Beyond these matters the debate was rooted in a fundamental ethnic dualism—an identification with American society on the one hand, and the persecuted Negro group on the other. This dualism arose out of the contradiction in American culture as Negroes experienced it: the contradiction between the American dream of equality for all and the reality of American race prejudice and discrimination.

Racial solidarity and self-help were always most characteristically associated with the advocacy of morality and economic accumulation, and, like these doctrines, tended to be especially popular in periods of greatest discouragement, particularly during the 1850's and again at the end of the century. During the decade before the Civil War, the passage of the Fugitive Slave Law of 1850, the decline of the antislavery societies, the increasing competition of Irish immigrants for menial and laboring jobs, and the southern ascendancy in the national government which culminated in the *Dred Scott* decision all made the outlook appear increasingly hopeless. Later, after the overthrow of Reconstruction, the increasing disfranchisement, segregation, and mob violence in the South and, by the 1890's, the growing evidence of prejudice and discrimination in the North, again "forced the Negro back upon himself," as contemporaries expressed it. In the latter period, protest efforts declined sharply, and the advocacy of racial solidarity, self-help, and economic and moral uplift tended to be most often coupled with an ideology of accommodation, especially in the South. This combination of ideas received its most notable expression in the philosophy of Booker T. Washington.

Proposals for racial union, self-help, and solidarity are generally recognized as a variety of Negro "nationalism." It was a form of nationalism which insisted upon the Negro's American citizenship, and viewed the cultivation of race pride and unity as a prerequisite for Negroes organizing themselves for the struggle to obtain equality and integration in American society. Related to this kind of ideology, though eschewing ethnic dualism and the notion that Negroes could ever hope to achieve freedom and equal rights in the United States, was the philosophy of emigration or colonization. Its advocates held that the only solution to the problems facing American Negroes was to emigrate and create a national state of their own, either in the Caribbean area or in Africa. Such proposals, especially popular during the 1850's, cropped up with varying intensity throughout the century. Actually the function of colonization as an ideology is ambiguous. While its advocates protested vigorously against race discrimination in America, they nevertheless favored a form of withdrawal that was in effect an escapist accommodation to the American race system, rather than an assault upon it.

Except for colonization, Douglass enunciated all of these ideologies—agitation, political action, the practice of morality and economy, the acquisition of property, self-help, and racial cooperation. Like other Negroes he shifted his emphasis as the changing situation seemed to warrant. Yet Douglass's views are not simply a reflection of what Negroes generally were saying. Ever the independent thinker, he was willing at times to diverge widely from the patterns of thought ascendant among his friends and contemporaries.[2]

The Antebellum Era

While in the latter part of the century Douglass was a symbol rather than a man of broad influence, during the years prior to the Civil War he was undoubtedly the most powerful leader in the northern Negro community, and his views roughly paralleled the ascendant ideologies among the antebellum free people of color.

Because there was an interrelationship between his program for securing the emancipation of the slaves and his proposals for advancing the status of free Negroes, a brief recapitulation of his antislavery career is in order. Born a slave on the eastern shore of Maryland, Douglass succeeded in escaping from his Baltimore master in 1838. By 1841 he had entered the ranks of Massachusetts abolitionist orators. His public career during the abolitionist period may be fairly neatly divided into two parts: the 1840's, when he followed the moral suasion tactics of the Garrisonians, and the 1850's, when he espoused the cause of political abolition. The four years following the establishment of his weekly newspaper, *North Star*, in Rochester, were a period of transition during which, influenced by western abolitionists like Gerrit Smith, he reexamined his views and finally came to support political abolition, openly breaking with Garrison in 1851.[3] From then on, agitation for political rights and stress upon the value of political activity became one of the most important themes in his thinking, and one which he articulated consistently for the rest of his life. Moreover, it was probably from his abolitionist role that Douglass derived a belief in the value of verbal agitation, and a social philosophy which saw the world in essentially moral terms, explaining social institutions and social change as based on the good and evil propensities in human nature. To Douglass the solution of America's race problem lay not in any fundamental institutional changes beyond the destruction of slavery. Rather, the solution lay in a sincere effort to apply the moral principles upon which the Republic was founded. How to activate these moral principles was his major lifelong concern.

In the years from the founding of *North Star* to the election of Lincoln, Douglass's program for the advancement of free Negroes consisted of three principal elements: a major emphasis on protest and citizenship rights, and secondary emphases on self-help, race pride, and racial solidarity on the one hand, and economic development on the other. First and foremost, he regarded Negroes as Americans: "By birth, we are American citizens; by the principles of the Declaration of Independence, we are American citizens; within the meaning of the United States Constitution, we are American citizens; by the facts of history . . . by the hardships and trials endured, by the courage and fidelity displayed by our ancestors in defending the liberties and in achieving the independence of our land, we are American citizens."[4] Only on the rarest of occasions did his alienation and anger lead him to declare that "I have no love for America," that he could feel no patriotism for a country like the United States,[5] or to warn that the oppressed black men might some day rise up and "become the instruments of spreading desolation, devastation, and death throughout our borders."[6]

Douglass constantly condemned the prejudice and discrimination which Negroes met daily: the segregation, the lack of economic opportunity, the exclusion from churches and schools, from juries and armed forces, and above all the disfranchisement. He denounced the "shameful" and "diabolical" Black Laws of Ohio as "the servile work of pandering politicians." He called upon the white people of Ohio to repeal the Black Laws and enfranchise the Negro, thus wiping out "a most foul imputation" upon their character and making Ohio "the paragon of all the free States."[7] In 1860, in the midst of a campaign to abolish the discriminatory franchise qualifications of the New York state constitution, he declared:

> It is a mockery to talk about protection in a government like ours to a class in it denied the elective franchise. The very denial of that right strips them of "protection," and leaves them at the mercy of all that is low, vulgar, cruel, and base in the community. The ballot box and the jury box both stand closed against the man of color. . . . The white people of this country would wade knee-deep in blood before they would be deprived of either of these means of protection against power and oppression.[8]

Not satisfied with mere resolves and declarations, Douglass was constantly in active rebellion against segregation and discrimination in all its forms, and was one of the few men of his time who engaged in what today would be regarded as nonviolent direct action. While residing in Massachusetts in the early 1840's he refused to ride on the Jim Crow railroad car, and was forcibly removed from the white coach.[9] He withdrew his daughter from school rather than permit her to attend segregated schools in Rochester, and agitated for their elimination until he was successful.[10] As his biographer says, "He made it a point to go into hotels, sit down at tables in restaurants, and enter public carriers."[11] A well-known incident was his insistence upon being admitted to the reception President Lincoln held on the eve of his second inauguration, even though the guards tried to keep him out.[12]

Douglass was interested in more than protesting against discrimination and agitating for citizenship rights. Firmly in the American middle-class tradition, he also campaigned for "education, that grand lever of improvement," and for moral elevation and economic independence.[13] While "not insensible" to the "withering prejudice" and "malignant and active hate" that placed obstacles in the Negro's pathway to respectability "even in the best parts of the country," he nevertheless believed: "The fact that we are limited and circumscribed ought rather to incite us to a more vigorous and persevering use of the elevating means within our reach, than to dishearten us." What Negroes needed, he went on, was character, and this they could only obtain for themselves through hard toil. "A change in our polit-

ical condition would do very little for us without this. . . . Industry, sobriety, honesty, combined with intelligence and a due
self-respect, find them where you will, among black or white,
must be looked up to." With character would come power, in the
sense that with it "we may appeal to the sense of justice alive in
the public mind, and by an honest, upright life, we may at least
wring from a reluctant public the all-important confession that
we are men, worthy men, good citizens, good Christians, and
ought to be treated as such."[14] True, hostility was directed not
at the lower-class Negroes whom whites found acceptable in
their subordinate status, but against respectable Negroes; but
this, he asserted, was only because color had for so long been
associated in the public mind with the degradation of slavery. If
Negroes generally acquired middle-class ways, whites would
cease to couple undesirable qualities with a black skin.[15]

Along with this emphasis on Negroes helping themselves
through moral elevation and the cultivation of good character
went a decided interest in economic matters—an interest
greatly intensified by the growing competition from immigrants who threatened the Negroes' hold upon even the unskilled and service occupations. Accordingly, Douglass emphatically urged the acquisition of skilled trades to stave off impend-
ing disaster. Dramatically he called upon Negroes to "Learn
Trades or Starve." In phraseology that was remarkably similar
to that which Washington employed a half-century later, Douglass insisted:

> We must become valuable to society in other departments of
> industry than those service ones from which we are rapidly being
> excluded. We must show that we can *do* as well as *be*; and to this
> end we must learn trades. When we can build as well as live in
> houses; when we can *make* as well as *wear* shoes; when we can
> produce as well as consume wheat, corn and rye—then we shall
> become valuable to society. Society is a hard-hearted affair. With
> it the helpless may expect no higher dignity than that of paupers.
> The individual must lay society under obligation to him, or so-
> ciety will harbor him only as a stranger. . . . *How* shall this be
> done? In this manner: Use every means, strain every nerve to
> master some important mechanic art.[16]

Neither classical education nor "holding conventions and passing strong resolutions" could prevent the "degradation of Ne-

groes. . . . The fact is . . . the education of the hand must precede that of the head. We can never have an educated class until we have more men of means amongst us."[17] Negroes could not become merchants or professional men "in a single leap," but only "when we have patiently and laboriously . . . passed through the intermediate gradations of agriculture and mechanic arts."[18] Backed by an offer of financial assistance (later withdrawn) from Harriet Beecher Stowe, Douglass presented a proposal for a manual-labor school to the national convention of Negro leaders which met at Rochester in 1853. The conferees, convinced that a strong emphasis on racial solidarity and economic accumulation was essential to the securing of citizenship rights, enthusiastically endorsed Douglass's plan.[19]

The hopes of the Rochester Convention proved illusory. Nevertheless, it is significant that over a generation before industrial education became a major plank in Booker T. Washington's platform of accommodation, arguments almost identical to those later employed by the Tuskegeean had been utilized by the noted protest leader Frederick Douglass to justify emphasis on training for the trades over education for the learned professions.

For Douglass, of course, the advocacy of character development and economic accumulation was no substitute for agitation for citizenship rights. When Horace Greeley in 1855 urged Negroes to stop agitating for the vote and instead direct their energies toward achieving the economic standing necessary for them to meet the discriminatory franchise qualifications of New York State, Douglass replied:

> Why should we be told to break up our Conventions, cease "jawing" and "clamoring," when others equally "*indolent, improvident, servile and licentious*" (all of which adjectives we reject as untruthful . . .) are suffered to indulge . . . in similar demonstrations? In a word, why should we be sent to hoeing, and planting corn, to digging potatoes, and raising cabbages, as the "*preferable and more effective*" method of abrogating the unjust, anti-Republican and disgraceful race restrictions imposed upon us, in the property qualification?[20]

Thus for Douglass the acquisition of morality and property was a supplemental instrument in the struggle for equal rights.

Character and wealth certainly did not take precedence over protest and agitation, or an appeal to the conscience of white America, based upon its democratic and egalitarian values.

Deteriorating conditions also led Douglass to place considerable emphasis on self-help and racial solidarity. *North Star* in fact was founded in a period when the advocacy both of these ideas and of colonization was on the rise. In fact, in the very first issue Douglass urged his "oppressed countrymen" to "remember that we are one, that our cause is one, and that we must help each other, if we would succeed. . . . We are indissolubly united, and must fall or flourish together."[21] He criticized Negroes for depending too much on whites to better their condition. True, he counselled Negroes to "Never refuse to act with a white society or institution because it is white, or a black one, because it is black. But act with all men without distinction of color. . . . We say avail yourselves of *white* institutions, not because they are white, but because they afford a more convenient means of improvement."[22] Nevertheless, he maintained that "the main work must be commenced, carried on, and concluded by ourselves. . . . Our destiny, for good or evil . . . is, by an all-wise God, committed to us. . . . It is evident that we can be improved and elevated only just so fast and far as we shall improve and elevate ourselves."[23]

Douglass perceived that race prejudice produced among Negroes what in today's terms would be called an awareness of a separate identity. He held that while all men were brothers, and were "naturally and self-evidently entitled to all the rights, privileges and immunities common to every member of that family," nevertheless "the force of potent circumstance" made it proper for him to address Negroes as "our own people."[24] Indeed, he referred to Negroes as an oppressed "nation within a nation," slave and free alike united in a "destiny [that] seems one and the same."[25] He proposed a "Union of the Oppressed for the Sake of Freedom," to organize Negroes in order to obtain their rights and elevate themselves through collective effort.[26] His propaganda bore fruit when the Rochester Convention of 1853, which marked the high tide of enthusiasm for racial solidarity among the antebellum Negro conventions, organized an abortive Protective Union to coordinate race interests and efforts.

Douglass defended his plans for racial union against charges that such a segregated organization would create a "complexional issue." It was not the colored men but whites who, by their policy of discrimination, had created a "complexional issue." As he put it in 1855, in roundly criticizing that class of abolitionists who kept Negroes subservient to whites in the movement: "Every day brings with it renewed evidence of the truthfulness of the sentiment, now . . . gaining the confidence and sympathy of our oppressed People, THAT OUR ELEVATION AS A RACE, IS ALMOST WHOLLY DEPENDENT UPON OUR OWN EXERTIONS. . . . The history of other oppressed nations will confirm us in this assertion . . . the oppressed nation itself, has always taken a prominent part in the conflict."[27]

Douglass, with his feeling that prejudice and discrimination made Negroes a "nation within a nation," resembled many other articulate Negroes of this period in exhibiting strong ethnocentric tendencies. Yet he never went as far as did a number of others who completely rejected American society and advocated colonization. It is not unlikely that a majority of Negro leaders at one time or another in the 1850's espoused emigration,[28] but Douglass consistently affirmed that "Nothing seems more evident to us, than that our destiny is sealed up with that of the white people of this country, and we believe that we must fall or flourish with them. We must banish all thought of emigration from our minds, and resolve to stay just where we are . . . among white people, and avail ourselves of the civilization of America."[29] Born in America, Negroes had fought and bled for the country: "We are here; . . . this is *our* country; . . . The white man's happiness cannot be purchased by the black man's misery. . . ."[30] Even during the 1850's, when colonization sentiments were making strong inroads into the thinking of articulate Negroes, he opposed them. Writing to Henry Highland Garnet, the eminent Presbyterian minister and abolitionist who had become an emigrationist, Douglass maintained that the emigrationists actually weakened the efforts to elevate Negroes in this country, since they channeled their energies, which might have helped Negroes in the United States, into visionary colonization schemes.[31]

Yet the pressure for expatriation was exceedingly strong. As the decade drew to a close, conditions seemed to grow worse. Lincoln's policy after his inauguration appeared to Douglass to be one of appeasing the slaveholders, and he was bitterly disappointed.[32] Discouraged, he finally lent an open ear and eye to emigration, and agreed to undertake a trip to Haiti; not with the intention of settling there himself, but to obtain information that might be useful to those who, alarmed at the persecution and hardships that were becoming "more and more rigorous and grievous with every year," were "looking out into the world for a place of retreat," and were "already resolved to look for homes beyond the boundaries of the United States."[33]

Even before this editorial appeared in print the attack on Fort Sumter occurred. To Douglass this was a welcome event and one which completely changed his plans. To him the war presaged both the emancipation of the slaves and the attainment of racial equality. As he said in a speech in Philadelphia in 1863, "The Mission of the War" was twofold: "the utter extirpation of slavery from every facet of American soil, and the complete enfranchisement of the entire colored people of this country."[34]

Reconstruction and After

Douglass's wartime efforts to secure the emancipation of the slaves, and the admission of Negro soldiers to the Union armies, have been amply described by other scholars.[35] Both of these activities were, in his view, but a prelude to the larger task of securing full citizenship rights and ending all forms of race discrimination. Speaking at the thirtieth anniversary meeting of the American Anti-Slavery Society in December, 1863, Douglass warned that the struggle was not over; "that our work will not be done until the colored man is admitted a full member in good and regular standing in the American body politic."[36] Merely to abolish slavery was no solution to the race problem. Rather, "the question is: Can the white and colored peoples of this country be blended into a common nationality . . . and enjoy together in the same country, under the same flag, the inestimable blessings of life, liberty, and the pursuit of happiness, as neighborly citizens of a common country."[37]

Over the course of the next two decades, during Reconstruction and the years immediately following, Douglass's philosophy retained the broad scope of the pre–Civil War decade, but with some differences in emphasis. Basically, Douglass demanded the immediate and complete integration of Negroes into American society. He held to a vision of the United States as a "composite nation," in which all races of men participated without discrimination. "In whatever else other nations may have been great and grand," Douglass explained, "our greatness and grandeur will be found in the faithful application of the principle of perfect civil equality to the people of all races and creeds."[38] Addressing the Massachusetts Anti-Slavery Society in the spring of 1865, he called for the " 'immediate, unconditional and universal' enfranchisement of the black man." He pointed out that Negroes wanted the suffrage

> because it is our right, first of all. No class of men can, without insulting their own nature, be content with any deprivation of their rights. . . . Again, I want the elective franchise . . . because ours is a peculiar government, based upon a peculiar idea, and that idea is universal suffrage. If I were in a monarchical government, or an aristocratic government, where the few ruled and the many were subject, there would be no special stigma resting upon me because I did not exercise the elective franchise. . . . But here, where universal suffrage . . . is the fundamental idea of the Government, to rule us out is to make us an exception, to brand us with the stigma of inferiority, and to invite to our heads the missiles of those about us.

Later, when men hitherto friendly toward the Negroes became critical of their stress on political rights, alleging that their interest in politics was "far more lively than is consistent" with their welfare, he conceded that no intelligent person could want to see the Negroes "look to politics" as their proper vocation, or to government as their only means of advancement. But he also insisted that "scarcely less deplorable would be the condition of this people, if among them there should be found no disposition . . . for political activity. That man who would advise the black man to make no effort to distinguish himself in politics will advise him to omit one of the most important levers that can be employed to elevate his race."[39]

Meanwhile, Douglass placed greater emphasis on the gospel

of wealth and racial cooperation than did most of his articulate contemporaries, though these ideas were less prominent in his ideology than formerly. As president of the national conventions held by Negro leaders at Syracuse in 1864 and at Louisville in 1883, he replied to critics of the idea of holding a race convention by calling attention to the prejudice and discrimination which Negroes still encountered, in spite of the Emancipation Proclamation and in spite of the legislation and constitutional amendments enacted during Reconstruction.[40] When he and others established a newspaper known as *The New Era* in 1870, he appealed for Negro support for a race journal on the basis of self-help and racial solidarity: "Our friends," he declared, "can do much for us, but there are some things which colored men can and must do for themselves." Later he grew irate when Negroes failed to support the publication, and he criticized them because they were "not conscious of any associated existence or a common cause."[41]

On economic matters his thought remained unchanged. In 1864 he advised the freedmen "to shape their course toward frugality, the accumulation of property, and above all, to leave untried no amount of effort and self-denial to acquire knowledge, and to secure a vigorous moral and religious growth." Sixteen years later, in a rhetoric typical of the age, and in words that Booker T. Washington would have fully approved, he was still uttering the standard pieties of middle-class Americans:

Neither we, nor any other people, will ever be respected till we respect ourselves, and we will never respect ourselves till we have the means to live respectably. . . . A race which cannot save its earnings, which spends all it makes . . . can never rise in the scale of civilization. . . .

. . . This part of our destiny is in our own hands. . . . If the time shall ever come when we shall possess in the colored people of the United States, a class of men noted for enterprise, industry, economy and success, we shall no longer have any trouble in the matter of civil and political rights. The battle against popular prejudice will have been fought and won. . . . The laws which determine the destinies of individuals and nations are impartial and eternal. We shall reap as we shall sow. There is no escape. The conditions of success are universal and unchangeable. The nation or people which shall comply with them will rise, and those which violate them will fall.[42]

Douglass's basically middle-class orientation toward the solution of the problems facing American Negroes is revealed in the way in which he expressed his very genuine concern with the problems of the Negro working classes. Basically he believed that the ordinary person, of whatever race, should strive to become an entrepreneur. He admitted that "the disproportionate distribution of wealth certainly is one of the evils which puzzle the greatest national economists," but thought that attacking capital was to attack a "symptom" rather than a cause. "Real pauperism," he continued, existed only in those states "where liberty and equality have been mere mockeries until lately." Workers had the right to strike, but Douglass thought it "tyranny" when they tried to prevent others from working in their places.[43] Douglass's attitudes were perceptibly reinforced by a personal experience—the exclusion of his son from the typographical society of Washington.[44] Yet on occasion he could express a vague consciousness of the identity of interest between white and black workers, as when he argued in 1883 that the white labor unions should not isolate themselves and "throw away this colored element of strength." Labor everywhere, regardless of race, wanted the same thing: "an honest day's pay for an honest day's work." Unity among black and white workers was desirable, he concluded, because "Experience demonstrates that there may be a slavery of wages only a little less galling and crushing in its effects than chattel slavery, and this slavery of wages must go down with the other."[45]

After the failure of Radical Reconstruction and the restoration of white supremacy in the South, Douglass's philosophy did not change; if anything, he became more vigorous in his denunciations of caste and oppression and proscription. Writing in the *North American Review* in 1881, he denounced the growing repression in the South in scathing terms: "Of all the varieties of men who have suffered from this feeling [of race prejudice] the colored people of this country have endured most. . . . The workshop denies him work, and the inn denies him shelter; the ballot-box a fair vote, and the jury-box a fair trial. He has ceased to be the slave of an individual, but has in some sense become the slave of society. . . ." Ridiculing the inconsistencies of the color line, he pointed out that the Chinese were hated because they were industrious, the Negroes because they were thought to be lazy. Southerners thought the Negro so deficient in "intellect and . . . manhood, that he is but the echo of the designing white man," and yet so strong and clearheaded "that he cannot be persuaded by arguments or intimidated by threats, and that nothing but the shotgun can restrain him from voting. . . . They shrink back in horror from contact with the Negro as a man and a gentleman, but like him very well as a barber, waiter, coachman or cook." Two years later, when the Supreme Court declared the Civil Rights Act of 1875 unconstitutional, Douglass, speaking at an indignation meeting in Washington, called the decision a "shocking" sign of "moral weakness in high places," a "calamity" resulting from the "autocratic" powers of the Court that embarrassed the country before the world. If the Civil Rights Act was "a bill for social equality, so is the Declaration of Independence, which declares that all men have equal rights; so is the Sermon on the Mount, so is the Golden Rule . . . ; so is the Apostolic teaching that of one blood, God has made all nations . . . ; so is the Constitution. . . ." Douglass became so bitter that in 1884 he suggested that Negroes might resort to retaliatory violence. Unfortunately the "safety valves" provided by American institutions for the peaceful expression and redress of grievances—free speech, a free press, the right of assembly, and the ballot box—did not exist in the South. Only such institutions made violence and insurrection, daggers and dynamite, unnecessary for an oppressed people; and he warned the South that ideas were contagious, and that the black man was aware of the example set by revolutionists in European countries. Such statements were extremely rare in Douglass's speeches; that he made them at this juncture reveals the depth of his disillusionment and anger as he observed the worsening situation of southern Negroes.[46]

Meanwhile, Douglass had developed misgivings about the compromising course of the Republican party in regard to protecting the rights of southern Negroes, even though Presidents Hayes, Garfield, Arthur, and Harrison appointed him to politi-

cal office.[47] Sharply criticized for his supposed support of the
Compromise of 1877, Douglass, at the Louisville Convention in
1883, felt it necessary to defend himself from charges of indifference to the Compromise. He described himself as "an un-
easy Republican" who had opposed Hayes's policy. He was
quoted as saying that "Parties are made for men and not men
for parties. . . . Follow no party blindly. If the Republican
Party cannot stand a demand for justice and fair play it ought to
go down. . . ." Six years later, in a widely circulated address
delivered before the Bethel Literary and Historical Society of
Washington, the most celebrated forum in the American Negro
community, Douglass defended the favorable comments he
had made about Cleveland in 1885, and argued that even
though the Republican party had recently returned to power in
Washington, "past experience makes us doubtful" that anything would be done for Negro rights. To Douglass the question was purely a moral one: the Republican defeat in the congressional elections of 1890, like Blaine's defeat in 1884, was
due to the fact that the party had deserted the Negro's cause.
"The success of the Republican Party," he averred, "does not
depend mainly upon its economic theories. . . . Its appeal is to
the conscience of the Nation, and its success is to be sought and
found in firm adhesion to the humane and progressive ideas of
liberty and humanity which called it into being."[48]

Douglass had traveled a long road indeed from 1872 when
he had uttered his famous phrase, "The Republican Party is the
deck, all else is the sea."[49] Yet he never deserted the party, and
during the eighties campaigned vigorously on its behalf. "I am
sometimes reproached," he once wrote, "[for] being too much
addicted to the Republican Party. I am not ashamed of that
reproach." Negroes, he continued, owed a great deal to the
party, and to desert it would be to ignore both this debt and the
atrocities suffered at the hands of southern Democrats.[50] Indeed, in the final analysis the situation in the South, where the
Democrats dominated, demanded loyalty to the Republicans,[51]
and at election time he expressed nothing but contempt for
those Negroes who were Democrats—men whose talks were
"rank with treason to the highest and best interest of the Negro
race."[52] Yet continued loyalty was not rewarded, and by 1892

Douglass confessed that he was only lukewarm in his support of the party.[53]

The Final Decade

It is a noteworthy fact that during the 1880's and 1890's, as conditions grew worse, as Negro thought veered from emphasis on political activity and immediate attainment of equal rights to doctrines of self-help, racial solidarity, and economic advancement, Douglass's thought moved in an opposite direction to a position more consistently assimilationist than at any time since the founding of *North Star* in 1847. More than ever he stressed assimilation and amalgamation as the solution to the race problem, and he constantly asserted that it was not a Negro problem, to be solved largely by the Negro's efforts to acquire morality and wealth, but the problem of the nation and the whites who had created the situation. It should be stressed that these ideas were not new in Douglass's philosophy; what is notable is the shift in emphasis, for in the last years of his life he discarded almost completely the idea of self-help, ignored the theme of race solidarity, declaimed against race pride, and said little of the gospel of wealth.

One may surmise that this shift came about as a result of one or both of two factors. Undoubtedly he was deeply concerned about the rising ascendancy of an accommodating ideology which accepted white stereotypes of Negroes as ignorant, immoral, lazy, and thriftless; blamed Negroes themselves for this state of affairs and for the white prejudice they suffered; placed the principal burden of Negro advancement upon Negroes themselves; accepted segregation; depreciated agitation and politics; and stressed self-help, character-building, the frugal virtues, and the acquisition of wealth as a program for achieving the respect of the white man and thus ultimately, it was implied, "earning" the "privilege" of enjoying citizenship rights. Accordingly Douglass may well have decided to cease stressing those aspects of his philosophy which had been appropriated by the accommodators.

More likely his ideological change was due largely to the influence of his second wife, a white woman, Helen Pitts, whom he married in January, 1884. Douglass had earlier expressed the view that race intermixture would increase,[54] and in the year preceding his second marriage he had declared: "There is but one destiny, it seems to me, left for us, and that is to make ourselves and be made by others a part of the American people in every sense of the word. Assimilation and not isolation is our true policy and our national destiny."[55] The marriage caused quite an uproar among many Negroes, who accused Douglass of lacking race pride. As he wrote to his friend and supporter, George L. Ruffin: "What business has any man to trouble himself about the color of another man's wife? Does it not appear violently impertinent—this intermeddling? Every man ought to try to be content with the form and color of his own wife and stop at that."[56] Two years later he explicitly predicted that amalgamation of the races would be the "inevitable" solution of the race problem.[57]

In a widely reprinted address, originally delivered before the Bethel Literary Association in 1889, Douglass summarized the views he held during the last decade of his life. In the first place, he said, the problem was not one for Negroes to solve themselves: "It is not what we shall do but what the nation shall do and be, that is to settle this great national problem." Admittedly Negroes could in part combat discrimination "by lives and acquirements which counteract and put to shame this narrow and malignant" prejudice. Indeed, "we have errors of our own to abandon, habits to reform, manners to improve, ignorance to dispel, and character to build up."

Douglass then went on to specify, even though he ran "the risk of incurring displeasure," other errors committed by Negroes which contemporaries usually listed as virtues—race pride, race solidarity, and economic nationalism (or the advocacy of Negro support of Negro business). First among them was the "greater prominence of late" being given to the "stimulation of a sentiment we are pleased to call race pride," to which Negroes were "inclining most persistently and mischievously. . . . I find it in all our books, papers and speeches." Douglass could see nothing to be either proud or ashamed of in a "gift from the Almighty," and perceived "no benefit to be derived from this everlasting exhortation to the cultivation of race pride. On the contrary, I see in it a positive evil. It is building on a false

foundation. Besides, what is the thing we are fighting against
. . . but race pride . . . ? Let us away with this supercilious
nonsense."

A second error was the doctrine "that union among ourselves
is an essential element of success in our relations with the white
race." Douglass held that "our union is our weakness," that the
trouble was that when assembled together "in numerous numbers" rather than scattered among whites, "we are apt to form
communities by ourselves." This, in turn, "brings us into separate schools, separate churches, separate benevolent and literary societies, and the result is the adoption of a scale of manners, morals and customs peculiar to our condition . . . as an
oppressed people." Moreover, "a nation within a nation is an
anomaly. There can be but one American nation . . . and we
are Americans." Negroes should yield as little as humanly possible to the circumstances that compelled them to maintain
separate neighborhoods and institutions. "We cannot afford to
draw the line in politics, trade, education, manner, religion, or
civilization." Douglass then went on to ridicule as "another
popular error flaunted in our faces at every turn, and for the
most part by very weak and impossible editors, the alleged
duty of the colored man to patronize colored newspapers . . . because they happen to be edited and published by
colored men." Though he continued to believe that an "able"
Negro paper was "a powerful lever for the elevation and advancement of the race," colored journals, like colored artisans,
should be supported only on the basis of the "character of the
man and the quality of his work."[58]

In short, during his last years, Douglass was the protest and
assimilationist leader epitomized.

Yet interestingly enough he was on friendly terms with
Booker T. Washington. In 1892 he gave the commencement
address at Tuskegee Institute, and two years later he obtained a
substantial gift for the school from an English friend.[59] At the
same time he proudly recalled his earlier advocacy of industrial
education.[60]

There is no reason to believe that Douglass would have favored Washington's ascendancy as a race leader, which began a
few months after Douglass's death with Washington's famous

address at the Atlanta Exposition in September, 1895. It is true that during the 1850's, and even for some years after the Civil War, Douglass had frequently expressed himself in terms that were remarkably similar to those that Washington enunciated at the end of the century. Like Washington, and using the same arguments and clichés, Douglass had stressed the middle-class virtues and middle-class respectability; the importance of trades and industrial education; the necessity for self-help and racial solidarity. But unlike Washington, Douglass was always clear and explicit about his desire for full equality. In fact he always subordinated these aspects of his philosophy to his advocacy of agitation and political activity. He never employed the flattering and conciliatory phraseology of the Tuskegeean; he never put the principal blame on Negro shoulders, nor did he make Negro self-improvement a panacea for the solution of the race problem. Finally, unlike Washington, he never permitted his ends to be obscured by his emphasis on the means.

We have pointed out that as the constellation of ideas which Washington epitomized was achieving ascendancy in Negro thought during the years after Reconstruction, Douglass's writings and speeches moved in an opposite direction. Integration, assimilation, protest against segregation and all other forms of oppression, and spirited advocacy of political rights and political activity were the hallmarks of his creed. Washington's ascendancy symbolized Negro acquiescence in segregation and disfranchisement and a soft-pedaling of political activity. And if there was one thing which Douglass had emphasized consistently, from midcentury on, it was the importance of political rights and political activity as essential for protecting Negroes and advancing their status in American society.

To raise Negroes to the highest status in American society, to secure their inclusion in the "body politic," to make them integrally a part of the American community, had been Douglass's aim, his vision, his dream. In constructing his program he naturally stressed and utilized the basic values and ideologies of American culture. If whites treasured political and civil rights, Negroes as a minority group treasured them even more. If white Americans valued self-help, independence, virtuous character, and the accumulation of property, these things would also be of inestimable aid to Negroes in their struggle for

advancement. If white Americans were proud of their nationality and what they had achieved by the collective effort of the
nation, Negroes also needed to be proud of themselves and
cooperate with each other in order to advance and progress.
Douglass, like his friends and associates, thus fashioned the
basic ideologies of American civilization into a program for the
elevation of a minority group that would secure its acceptance
into the larger society. Beyond all else Douglass was the
moralist, constantly appealing to the democratic and Christian
values of brotherhood, equality, and justice—values which
Americans cherished but which, for Negroes, remained un-
fulfilled. As Douglass put it in 1889: "The real question is
whether American justice, American liberty, American civilization, American law and American Christianity can be made to
include and protect alike and forever all American citizens.
. . . It is whether this great nation shall conquer its prejudices, rise to the dignity of its professions and proceed in the
sublime course of truth and liberty [which Providence] has
marked out for it."[61]

1. See the two biographies, Philip S. Foner, *Frederick Douglass: A Biography* (New
York, 1964), and esp. Benjamin Quarles, *Frederick Douglass* (Washington, 1948).
   2. On Negro thought in the nineteenth century, see esp. Carter G. Woodson, ed.,
The Negro Mind as Reflected in Letters Written during the Crisis, 1800–1860 (Washington,
1926); Howard H. Bell, "A Survey of the Negro Convention Movement, 1830–1861"
(Ph.D. dissertation, Northwestern University, 1953); August Meier, *Negro Thought in
America, 1880–1915* (Ann Arbor, 1963), chs. 1–7.
   3. Quarles, *Frederick Douglass*, chs. 1–5, 7–9; Foner, *Frederick Douglass*, pts. 1 and 2;
Quarles, "Abolition's Different Drummer: Frederick Douglass," in Martin Duberman,
ed., *The Antislavery Vanguard: New Essays on the Abolitionists* (Princeton, 1965), pp. 123–
34.
   4. Frederick Douglass, "The Claims of Our Common Cause," Address to the 1853
Colored National Convention, in *Proceedings of the Colored National Convention . . . 1853*
(Rochester, 1853), p. 11.
   5. Frederick Douglass, "The Right to Criticize American Institutions," Speech before the American Antislavery Society, May 11, 1847, reprinted in Philip S. Foner, ed.,
The Life and Writings of Frederick Douglass (New York, 1950–55), I, 236.
   6. *North Star*, Nov. 9, 1849.
   7. Frederick Douglass to Sidney Howard Gay, Sept. 17, 1847, in Foner, ed., *Life and
Writings*, I, 265.
   8. *Douglass' Monthly*, Oct., 1860.
   9. Frederick Douglass, *Life and Times of Frederick Douglass* (Hartford, 1882), pp.
250–51.
   10. *Ibid.*, pp. 298–99; Quarles, *Frederick Douglass*, p. 108.
   11. Quarles, *Frederick Douglass*, pp. 101–2.
   12. *Ibid.*, p. 219; Foner, *Frederick Douglass*, pp. 231–32; Douglass, *Life and Times*, pp.
402–4.

13. *North Star*, Jan. 19, 1849.
14. *Ibid.*, July 14, 1848.
15. *Ibid.*, June 13, 1850.
16. *Frederick Douglass' Paper*, Mar. 4, 1853. See also Douglass and others, "Address to the Colored People of the United States of the Colored National Convention of 1848," *North Star*, Sept. 29, 1848; and *Proceedings of the National Convention of Colored People . . . 1847* (Troy, N.Y., 1847), pp. 37–38.
17. *Frederick Douglass' Paper*, Mar. 11, 1853.
18. Douglass to Harriet Beecher Stowe, Mar. 8, 1853, in *Proceedings of the Colored National Convention, 1853*, pp. 33–38.
19. *Ibid.*, pp. 22–40. On the 1853–55 movement for industrial education generally, see Bell, "Survey of the Negro Convention Movement," pp. 171–75.
20. *Frederick Douglass' Paper*, Oct. 5, 1855.
21. *North Star*, Dec. 3, 1847.
22. "Address to the Colored People of the United States, 1848 National Convention," in *North Star*, Sept. 29, 1848.
23. *Ibid.*, July 14, 1848.
24. *Ibid.*, Jan. 19, 1849.
25. Douglass, "The Present Condition and Future Prospects of the Negro People," Speech at Annual Meeting of the American and Foreign Anti-Slavery Society, New York, May, 1853, reprinted in Foner, ed., *Life and Writings*, II, 243, 246.
26. *North Star*, Aug. 10 and Oct. 29, 1849.
27. *Ibid.*, Dec. 14, 1849; *Frederick Douglass' Paper*, Apr. 13, 1855.
28. Bell, "Survey of the Negro Convention Movement."
29. *North Star*, Jan. 19, 1848.
30. *Ibid.*, Nov. 16, 1849.
31. *Douglass' Monthly*, Feb., 1859.
32. *Ibid.*, Apr., 1861.
33. *Ibid.*, May, 1861.
34. Douglass, "The Mission of the War," 1863, MS, Frederick Douglass Papers, at the Frederick Douglass Home, Washington, D.C.; available on microfilm at the Schomburg Collection, New York Public Library, Reel 13.
35. Quarles, *Frederick Douglass*, chs. 11, 12; Foner, *Frederick Douglass*, pt. 3; James M. McPherson, *The Negro's Civil War* (New York, 1965), pp. 17–18, 37–40, 161–63.
36. Douglass, "Our Work Is Not Done," Speech delivered at the Annual Meeting of the American Anti-Slavery Society, Philadelphia, Dec. 3–4, 1863, reprinted in Foner, ed., *Life and Writings*, III, 381. See also Quarles, *Frederick Douglass*, pp. 214–15; Douglass, *Life and Times*, p. 418.
37. *Douglass' Monthly*, June, 1863.
38. Douglass, "A Composite Nation," Lecture, 1867, MS, Douglass Papers, Microfilm Reel 13.
39. Douglass, "What the Black Man Wants," in William D. Kelley, Wendell Phillips, and Frederick Douglass, *The Equality of All Men Before the Law* (Boston, 1865), pp. 36–37; *New National Era*, Aug. 24, 1871.
40. *Proceedings of the National Convention of Colored Men . . . 1864* (Boston, 1864), pp. 13–14; Douglass, "Address to the People of the United States," Delivered at National Convention of Colored Men, Louisville, 1883, in *Three Addresses on the Relations Subsisting between the White and Colored People of the United States* (Washington, 1886), pp. 4–6.
41. *The New Era*, Jan. 27, 1870; Douglass to Gerrit Smith, Sept. 26, 1873, cited in Quarles, *Frederick Douglass*, p. 110.
42. *Proceedings of the National Convention of Colored Men, 1863*, p. 5; Appendix to Douglass, *Life and Times*, pp. 561–62.
43. *New National Era*, Apr. 20, 1871.
44. *Ibid.*, Feb. 2, 1871.
45. Douglass, "Address to the People of the United States," Louisville Convention, 1883, in *Three Addresses*, pp. 12–13.

46. Douglass, "The Color Line," *North American Review*, 132 (June, 1881), 568–75; *Proceedings of the Civil Rights Mass-Meeting . . . Washington, October 22, 1883* (Washington, 1883), pp. 5, 7, 8, 14; Douglass, "Address on American Civilization" (1884), MS, Douglass Papers, Microfilm Reel 13.

47. Hayes made Douglass marshal of the District of Columbia; Garfield and Arthur appointed him recorder of deeds of the District of Columbia; and Harrison made him minister to Haiti.

48. Alexandria, Va., *People's Advocate*, Oct. 6, 1883; New York *Globe*, Sept. 29, 1883; Douglass, "The Future of the Race," *African Methodist Episcopal Church Review*, 6 (Oct., 1889), 232–33; Douglass, *Life and Times* (Hartford, 1891 ed.), p. 559; Douglass, "The Cause of Republican Defeat" (1890), MS, Douglass Papers, Microfilm Reel 12.

49. Quarles, *Frederick Douglass*, p. 260.

50. Douglass to C. N. Bliss, Oct. 5, 1887, Douglass Papers, Microfilm Reel 1.

51. Cleveland *Gazette*, Oct. 30, 1886.

52. Douglass to D. A. Straker, Aug. 2, 1888, Douglass Papers, Microfilm Reel 1.

53. Quarles, *Frederick Douglass*, p. 354.

54. For example, *New National Era*, Sept. 27, 1870.

55. Douglass, *Address . . . on the Twenty-first Anniversary of Emancipation in the District of Columbia* (Washington, 1883), p. 16.

56. Francis J. Grimké, "The Second Marriage of Frederick Douglass," *Journal of Negro History*, 19 (July, 1934), 324–29; Douglass to George L. Ruffin, Jan. 28 [1884], photostatic copy, Ruffin Papers, Howard University Library. Ruffin, a Massachusetts lawyer, was the first Negro appointed to a judgeship in the North.

57. Douglass, "The Future of the Colored Race," *North American Review*, 142 (May, 1886), 438–39.

58. Douglass, "The Future of the Race," pp. 225–36.

59. Samuel R. Spencer, Jr., *Booker T. Washington and the Negro's Place in American Life* (Boston, 1955), p. 108; Washington to Douglass, Apr. 2, 1894, Douglass Papers, Microfilm Reel 7.

60. Douglass, "Oration" delivered at Manassas Industrial School, Va., Sept. 3, 1894, MS, Douglass Papers, Microfilm Reel 13.

61. Douglass, "The Future of the Race," pp. 225–26.

TWO

W. E. B. Du Bois as Sociologist

BY ELLIOTT RUDWICK

The works of several of the most prominent black sociologists—E. Franklin Frazier, St. Clair Drake, and Horace
Cayton—reveal their indebtedness to W. E. B. Du Bois. Frazier,
for example, dedicated *The Negro in the United States* to Du Bois
and said his efforts were "the first attempt to study in a scientific
spirit the problems of the Negro in American life."[1] Drake and
Cayton, in their classic *Black Metropolis*, noted that Du Bois's *The
Philadelphia Negro*—written nearly a half-century earlier—was
the "first important sociological study of a Negro community in
the United States."[2] Ironically, their teachers, the influential
Robert Park and Ernest Burgess, were aware of Du Bois's writ-
ings and cited him in their texts; they did not mention his
Philadelphia Negro, while they did cite sources such as Charles
Booth's *Life and Labour of the People in London* (1889, 1891), *Hull
House Maps and Papers* (1895), plus other social surveys.[3]

Du Bois, in fact, is best known as the most prominent propagandist of the Negro protest during the first half of the twentieth century, largely because he was one of the principal
founders of the National Association for the Advancement of
Colored People and for almost twenty-five years editor of the
NAACP's official publication, *The Crisis*. Yet from the time he
received his Ph.D. from Harvard in 1895 until shortly before
World War I, Du Bois was responsible for impressive pioneering research on black Americans. In both his training and the
quality of his published scholarship, Du Bois compares favorably with other sociologists.

From James E. Blackwell and Morris Janowitz, eds., *Black Sociologists: Historical and
Contemporary Perspectives* (Chicago: University of Chicago Press, 1974). pp. 25–55. Re-
printed with permission of the University of Chicago Press. ©1974 by the University of
Chicago.

At the turn of the century, sociology was just emerging as an academic discipline from the more generalized field of "social science" that included political economy, government, social problems, and even history.[4] The first formal department of sociology was organized in 1892 at the University of Chicago, the second at Columbia in 1894.[5] Moreover, the American Sociological Society was not founded until 1905, when sociologists separated from the American Economic Association.[6]

Thus, in the 1890's, sociology, economics, the study of social problems, and the field of social ethics were closely intertwined and often not distinguished. Many scholars were interested in using social science to improve human society. Much of their work was imbued with a reformist spirit more akin to the study of social ethics than to scientific sociology. We should emphasize that the concern of these scholars with problems of the criminal and the poor did not involve a belief that society needed fundamental change. Their interest was reformist rather than radical and was closely related to the developing field of social work. In fact, during the early twentieth century the most important studies of American blacks, done by contemporaries of Du Bois like John Daniels, Mary White Ovington, and George Edmund Haynes, were all explicitly directed toward providing knowledge for social work programs.[7]

Reflecting this faith of an important segment of America's social scientists that knowledge would lead to the solution of social problems, Du Bois, during his early career, passionately believed that research could supply the basis for achieving a racially equalitarian society. He contended that race prejudice was caused by ignorance and that social science would provide the knowledge to defeat injustice. Sociology was not recognized as a separate discipline at Harvard when he studied there; Du Bois took his Ph.D. in history, but also earned many credits in the social sciences. He recalled that "my course of study would have been called sociology."[8] Among the courses he took was "Ethics of Social Reform," taught by F. G. Peabody, who in the 1880's had been one of the pioneers in teaching academic courses in "social science." Peabody was interested in applying knowledge of society to the treatment of its ills.[9] From his advisor, Albert Bushnell Hart, Du Bois imbibed an emphasis on careful empirical research. Du Bois himself largely credited Hart's research methods with having "turned me back from the lovely but sterile land of philosophic speculation, to the social sciences as the field for gathering and interpreting that body of fact which would apply to my program for [advancing] the Negro."[10]

In 1892, during his graduate work at Harvard, Du Bois went to the University of Berlin for a more concentrated program in the social sciences. He examined Prussian state reform under Rudolph von Gneist and "Industrialism and Society" under Adolph Wagner. For Gustav von Schmoller's seminar, Du Bois wrote on "The Plantation and Peasant Proprietorship System of Agriculture in the Southern United States." Probably more than any other professor under whom Du Bois had studied, Schmoller stressed the value of a hard-nosed empiricism and the faith that a systematic body of knowledge could be used to shape national policy.[11]

With his zeal for collecting "facts," Du Bois had only impatience for the armchair generalizing of such social theorists as Herbert Spencer or Franklin H. Giddings. He commented: "The biological analogy, the vast generalizations, were striking, but actual scientific accomplishment lagged. For me an opportunity seemed to present itself. I could not lull my mind to hypnosis by regarding a phrase like 'consciousness of kind' as a scientific law. . . . I determined to put science into sociology through a study of the condition and problems of my own group. I was going to study the facts, any and all facts, concerning the American Negro and his plight, and by measurement and comparison and research, work up to any valid generalization which I could."[12]

Du Bois's opportunity came in 1896, when municipal reformers in the Philadelphia settlement-house movement invited him to describe and analyze black participation in local politics and other social institutions. Familiar with Booth's *Life and Labour of the People in London* as well as with the *Hull House Maps and Papers*, Du Bois and his sponsors believed that a painstaking study of Philadelphia's Negroes could provide a guideline for improving their social conditions.[13] Accordingly, in addition to writing a rigorous empirical monograph, Du Bois set forth specific proposals for racial advancement. In *The Philadelphia Negro*, which Gunnar Myrdal described as a model "of what a study of a Negro community should be,"[14] Du Bois enthusiastically played his dual role of social scientist and social reformer.

Philadelphia in the mid-1890's had over 45,000 blacks, the largest Negro population of any city in the North. For over a year Du Bois was a participant-observer in the Seventh Ward, "the historic centre of Negro settlement in the City," where about one-fifth of the community's blacks lived.[15] His study area was appropriate not only because the Seventh Ward contained the largest concentration of Negroes in Philadelphia, but also because it was the chief locus of black community institutions such as the church and, as Du Bois put it, because all social classes, with their "varying conditions of life," were represented there. Using a lengthy questionnaire, he did a house-to-house survey of all the black families in the ward. He compiled voluminous data on patterns of migration into and within the city, family structure, income, occupations, property holdings, social stratification, black community institutions, politics, pauperism. The data gave a dismal portrait of unemployment, job discrimination by both employers and trade unions, wretched housing, family breakdowns, substantial criminality, and widespread health and hygienic problems. On the other hand, Du Bois's monograph was a brilliant description of the contours and functioning of the black community, its institutions, and its mechanisms for racial survival and advancement.

His interviews revealed that three-fourths of the black workingmen of the Seventh Ward were "laborers and servants" and that about the same proportion of the women were employed as "day laborers and domestic servants." The color bar in Philadelphia's many manufacturing plants was especially striking—about 8 percent of the blacks had factory jobs.[16] Du Bois commented that, in the Seventh Ward, "the mass of Negroes are in the economic world purveyors to the rich—working in private houses, in hotels, large stores, etc." Most blacks were thus engaged in low-paying jobs, and many could obtain only irregular work. "Stevedores, hod-carriers and day-laborers are especially liable to irregular employment, which makes life hard for them sometimes. . . . The mass of men . . . meet their greatest difficulty in securing work. The competition in ordinary laboring work is severe in so crowded a city. The women day-laborers are, on the whole, poorly paid, and meet fierce competition in laundry work and cleaning."[17]

However, about one-fourth of the men were employed in skilled trades, in the professions, and as small businessmen, providing the economic base for what Du Bois termed the city's small black "aristocracy." Yet even the most successful black entrepreneurs—the barbers and caterers—labored under serious difficulties. Barbering had once been "an almost exclusively Negro calling" but, by the end of the century, competition by white immigrants was driving blacks out of the lucrative white market. Changes in fashion and "the application of large capital to the catering business" had destroyed the position of the nationally famous black caterers who had dominated this business in Philadelphia throughout much of the nineteenth century. Du Bois noted: "If the Negro caterers of Philadelphia had been white, some of them would have been put in charge of a large hotel, or would have become co-partners in some large restaurant business, for which capitalists furnished funds."[18]

The black man's economic plight was, of course, reflected in the various "social problems"—illiteracy, "pauperism," crime, and family disorganization—which had initially prompted the white philanthropists and social workers to ask Du Bois to undertake his study. The Philadelphia Negro includes trenchant descriptions of the overcrowded squalor in which the city's black poor were forced to live. It discusses extensively how such poverty, exacerbated by the new influx of many penniless and illiterate Southerners and by the serious economic depression of the 1890's, accounted for black criminality. More important for long-range sociological interests, however, was Du Bois's pioneering examination of black family life.

Du Bois described the direct connection between economic status and family structure. He contrasted the conventional middle-class family life of the "well-to-do," a group that E. Franklin Frazier later termed the "Black Puritans," with the temporary cohabitation and common-law marriages among the very poor. Du Bois noted the difficulties of sustaining a cohesive family life, even for workers with regular employment. He was the first sociologist to indicate the disproportionately numerous female-headed households among the black poor. The substantial number of women describing themselves as "widowed and separated indicates widespread and early breaking up of family life. . . . The number of deserted wives . . . of unmarried mothers . . . is astoundingly large and presents many intricate problems."[19] The situation, he explained, resulted partly from the heritage of slavery and even more from harsh economic realities in the cities. As he observed, "economic difficulties arise continually among young waiters and servant girls"; having married, they "soon find that the husband's income cannot alone support a family; then comes a struggle which generally results in the wife's turning laundress, but often results in desertion or voluntary separation."[20] The role of the black woman as breadwinner, both when the husband was absent and when he was present, was revealed in the statistics: where 16 percent of the native white women were employed, 43 percent of the black women were breadwinners. Thus, even among the "great mass of the Negro population" characterized by households headed by men with regular employment, the minimal income of these men, combined with the relatively high rents families had to pay, often involved serious problems. "The low wages of men make it necessary for mothers to work and in numbers of cases to work away from home several days in the week. This leaves the children without guidance or restraint for the better part of the day."[21] Forced to rent part of their dwellings to lodgers in order to pay the landlords, "38 percent of the homes of the Seventh Ward have unknown strangers admitted freely into their doors. The result is, on the whole, pernicious, especially where there are growing children. . . . The lodgers are often waiters, who are at home . . . at the very hours when the housewife is off at work, and growing daughters are thus left unprotected. . . . In such ways, the privacy and intimacy of home life is destroyed, and elements of danger and demoralization admitted."[22]

Du Bois identified three factors responsible for this "pressing series of social problems": slavery, which left so many of its victims untrained, uneducated, and impoverished; the enduring prejudice of white Americans; and the influx of migrants from the South. In slavery, with its "attendant phenomena of ignorance, lack of discipline, and moral weakness," and in migration, with its increased competition, lay two basic causes of the urban blacks' condition. "To this must be added a third as great—and possibly greater influence than the other two, namely the environment in which a Negro finds himself—the world of custom and thought in which he must live and work, the physical surroundings of house and home and ward, the moral encouragements and discouragements which he encounters."[23] Though *The Philadelphia Negro* was written in scholarly tones and during an era of widespread accommodation to white supremacy, Du Bois's indictment of white prejudice was unmistakable. He stressed that blacks lived in a different environment from whites, that the basis of the difference was "the widespread feeling all over the land, in Philadelphia as well as in Boston and New Orleans, that the Negro is something less than an American and ought not to be much more than what he is."[24]

He found discrimination pervasive, but devoted his attention particularly to the barriers in the way of the black man's economic development. Regardless of ability, a black man did not have the same opportunity to work as a white man. "There is no doubt that in Philadelphia the centre and kernel of the Negro problem so far as the white people are concerned is the narrow opportunities afforded Negroes for earning a decent living."[25] His examples ranged from the school system, which refused to appoint black graduates of its own normal school to positions outside the few all-black schools, to the trade unions, whose policies of exclusion drove blacks from the foothold they once had in the building trades. Not only were caterers and barbers losing their white customers, but Negro shopkeepers were also unable to attract white patronage. Black pharmacists, clerks, and unskilled workers of all kinds found it difficult to get employment in the fields for which they were trained. Even butlers, coachmen, and janitors were being displaced by whites.[26] Blacks were forced into poverty, and the black paupers became objects of philanthropic assistance. Even though many charitable institutions were discriminating against blacks,

Du Bois concluded ironically, "the class of Negroes which the prejudices of the city have distinctly encouraged is that of the criminal, the lazy and the shiftless; for them the city teems with institutions and charities . . . for them, Philadelphians are thinking and planning; but for the educated and industrious young colored man who wants work and not platitudes, wages and not alms, just rewards and not sermons—for such colored men Philadelphia apparently has no use."[27]

Du Bois also emphasized the impact of discrimination on the personalities and aspirations of black men and women and their children. Foreshadowing the interest of scholars like Frazier, Charles S. Johnson, and Allison Davis, who in the early 1940's would explore the impact of segregation and discrimination on blacks, and especially on Negro youth, Du Bois observed: "when one group of people suffer all these little differences of treatment and discriminations and insults continually, the result is either discouragement, or bitterness, or over-sensitiveness, or recklessness. . . . The Negro finds it extremely difficult to rear children in such an atmosphere and not have them either cringing or impudent: if he impresses upon them patience with their lot, they may grow up satisfied with their condition; if he inspires them with ambition to rise, they may grow up to despise their own people, hate the whites and become embittered with the world."[28]

In stressing the importance of migration, Du Bois also prefigured a subject that would interest later sociologists studying black urban communities. The "Great Migration" began during World War I, nearly two decades after Du Bois did the research for *The Philadelphia Negro*, yet throughout his book he displayed a keen awareness of the significance for urban Negro life of the movement of southern blacks to the cities. Like Johnson, Frazier, and the others to come, Du Bois emphasized the fact that the desire to escape from oppression in the South motivated the migration. He reported that most of the blacks in the Seventh Ward were migrants, the majority having arrived during the preceding decade. Only one-third were born in Philadelphia; more than half had been born in the South.[29] These young, impoverished, often illiterate Southerners settle "in pretty well-defined localities in or near the slums, and thus get the worst possible introduction to city life." Constantly, Du Bois related the problems of urban Negroes to their southern rural and small-town origins—whether in examining literacy, pauperism, crime, or family life. For example, in discussing criminality, he observed that while arrests among blacks "after the war . . . decreased until the middle of the seventies," after that, "coincident with the new Negro immigration to cities," they rose steadily.[30] This migration, he explained, accounted for "much that is paradoxical about the Negro slums," which had long remained at the same locations. "Many people wonder that the mission and [reform] agencies at work there for so many years have so little to show by way of results." In large part the reason was "that this work has new material continually to work upon," as those who moved up economically moved away and left the poor behind.[31]

Du Bois's generalizations about social problems later became standard in sociology. But when *The Philadelphia Negro* was written, they contrasted strongly with the racist assumptions held by most sociologists and by the general public. Du Bois rejected explanations based on biological differences or inherent inferiority, emphasizing instead the critical importance of historical and environmental factors. In describing his method of studying black Philadelphians, Du Bois stated that the student of the social problems affecting ethnic minorities must go beyond the group itself. He "must specially notice the environment: the physical environment of city, sections and houses, the far mightier social environment—the surrounding world of custom, wish, whim, and thought which envelops this group and powerfully influences its social development."[32] Discounting notions of innate differences between classes and peoples, he observed: "We rather hasten to forget that once the courtiers of English kings looked upon the ancestors of most Americans with far greater contempt than these Americans look upon Negroes—and perhaps, indeed, had more cause. We forget that once French peasants were the 'Niggers' of France, and that German princelings once discussed with doubt the brains and humanity of the *bauer*."[33]

But *The Philadelphia Negro* would scarcely be an important contribution to sociology if it had been confined to describing social problems and discussing their causes. This book lives because it is a well-rounded study of a local black community—its social strata, its institutions, and its varying lifestyles. It was thus a forerunner of the holistic community case studies that culminated in Drake and Cayton's *Black Metropolis*.

Especially important was Du Bois's emphasis on the complexity and variety in the black community, most notably in the differentiation among the social classes and their varying lifestyles. This was directed partly at countering white stereotypes of blacks. More important, his discussion of social class was functional in terms of understanding the black community. Finally, his class analysis was at the heart of his proposals for race advancement.

Du Bois observed, "There is always a strong tendency . . . to consider the Negroes as composing one practically homogeneous mass. This view has of course a certain justification: the people of Negro descent in this land have had a common history, suffer to-day common disabilities, and contribute to one general set of social problems." Yet, if the numerous statistics supplied in the volume "have emphasized any one fact it is that wide variations in antecedents, wealth, intelligence, and general efficiency have already been differentiated within this group."[34]

Du Bois's analysis of social stratification in Philadelphia's black community reflected the moral standards of the social reformers of that period. While his conceptualization was not so refined as that employed by social scientists today, he used criteria that included income, occupation, and lifestyle. He described four general social "grades" or classes. At the top, constituting about one-tenth of the population, was an upper class or "aristocracy," "families of undoubted respectability earning sufficient income to live well; not engaged in menial service of any kind; the wife engaged in no occupation save that of housewife . . . the children not compelled to be breadwinners, but found in schools; the family living in a well-kept home." Primarily entrepreneurs and professional people, they were largely Philadelphia-born, often descended from domestic servants, and included many mulattoes. This was the class most assimilated to American middle-class culture. Its members usually felt compelled, as the elite of the race, to spend more than their white neighbors on clothes and entertainment.

The next group, about half of the whole, was "the respectable working class; in comfortable circumstances, with a good home, and having steady, remunerative work, the younger children in school." This group consisted of "the mass of the servant class, the porters and waiters, and the best of the laborers." Ambitious and anxious to rise in the world, they were hard-working and beginning to accumulate property. While they usually had lodgers and their wages were low compared to those of whites, they had neatly furnished homes. "The best expression of the life of this group is the Negro church where their social life centers." Their greatest difficulty was finding suitable careers for their children; the lack of "congenial occupation, especially among the young," produced widespread disappointment and discouragement.

Below this group of strivers came "the poor; persons not earning enough to keep them at all times above want; honest, although not always energetic or thrifty, and with no touch of gross immorality or crime." About one-third of the population, they were "the poor and unfortunate and the casual laborers"; many lived in slums or on back streets. "They include immigrants who cannot get steady work; . . . unreliable and shiftless persons who cannot keep work or spend their earnings thoughtfully; those who have suffered accident and misfortune . . . many widows and orphans and deserted wives. . . . Some correspond to the 'worthy poor' of most charitable organizations and some fall a little below that class." The children of the very poor tended to go to school irregularly and, through poverty and sometimes parental neglect, became "the feeders of the criminal classes."

At the bottom of Du Bois's classification was the group with criminal records—about 6 percent, which loomed large in the eyes of white Philadelphians.[35]

As in *Black Metropolis* and other works of the Warner school, the theme of social class was used in *The Philadelphia Negro* as an integrating device, although not so explicitly as later scholars like Allison Davis and Drake and Cayton would use it. Yet, as Drake and Cayton have noted, "All serious students of Negro

communities since Du Bois have been concerned with the nature of social stratification."[36] In *The Philadelphia Negro*, occupation, property-holding, literacy, and income, on the one hand,
and style of family life, on the other, are all related to social
class. Similarly, the institutional structure of the black community—notably the church—was clearly integrated with
the class structure. The well-to-do mostly attended either St.
Thomas Episcopal Church, representing the most educated
and economically secure of the black Philadelphians, or the
Central Presbyterian Church, representing "the older, simpler
set of respectable Philadelphians." Their style of worship was
formal and reserved; the aristocracy "shrink from the free and
easy worship of most of the Negro churches." The great mass
of "respectable" working-class people attended the large African Methodist Episcopal and Baptist churches. Thus at Mother
Bethel A.M.E. Church, one found "the best of the great laboring class—steady honest people," while at Union Baptist "one
may look for the Virginia servant girls and their young men."
The very poor largely did not have a church, but some tended
to fill "a host of noisy missions."[37]

Du Bois emphasized that the church performed a number of
important social functions, some latent, that served as an integrative force in the black community. Black Philadelphia
churches were the center of social life "to a degree unknown in
white churches." They also offered opportunities for status,
recognition, and office-holding that made them "almost political." Their forums, lyceums, and musical events were important in the community's cultural life. Their publishing houses
and newspapers gave them a significant place in the black
economy of the city. Finally, "all movements for social betterment are apt to centre in the churches."[38] Many beneficial
societies, building and loan associations, and secret societies
were organized in churches. Ministers frequently served as
employment agents, and considerable charitable work was conducted by churches.

Du Bois stressed the importance and integrative functions of
the secret and beneficial societies and of other forms of
cooperative endeavor—ranging from building and loan associations, through organizations of waiters, coachmen, and bar-

bers, to social welfare institutions such as the Home for Aged and Infirmed Colored Persons and the Frederick Douglass Hospital and Training School. These organizations showed "how intimately bound together the Negroes of Philadelphia are."[39]

Another important contribution in *The Philadelphia Negro* was Du Bois's implicitly functional analysis of black participation in city politics. At the time, Philadelphia was one of the most notoriously corrupt American cities, dominated by a powerful Republican machine. In Du Bois's words, most blacks were the machine's "willing tools." While personally critical of its venality, Du Bois attempted to show the machine's functions for blacks. In that era Negroes, of course, were traditionally loyal to the Republican party because of its role in the Civil War and Emancipation and because the Irish, the blacks' chief competitors and antagonists in the labor market, were Democrats. In fact, Du Bois demonstrated that the Republican machine functioned for blacks as the Democratic party did for the Irish. On a very practical level, the machine offered protection to those engaged in vice and minor crime and to a larger body of noncriminal migrants harassed by the police. It provided clubhouses where the poor could come for drinking, gambling, and sociability. City Hall, although dispensing only token jobs as schoolteachers, policemen, and clerks, was nonetheless the largest employer of blacks in nonmenial positions in Philadelphia. Given the highly limited economic opportunities for blacks, these few white-collar jobs were extremely important and were ordinarily filled by well-qualified blacks of high ability and education.

Du Bois made the earliest analysis of the relationship of turn-of-the-century municipal "good government" movements to the Negro population, in an illuminating discussion of "The Paradox of Reform." The reform movement promised "efficiency" and "honesty" in government and condemned the corrupt machine's relationships to poor immigrants and blacks, but it failed to recognize the important needs that the machine filled for the minority communities. A few economically secure Negroes did support the reformers; but, as Du Bois perceived, their victory was likely to be dysfunctional for blacks, depriving them of the few benefits they received from political participation.[40]

The Philadelphia Negro was a conscientious and perceptive sociological study. But Du Bois undertook the research as more than description and analysis. In the final section of his monograph, Du Bois the social scientist and fact-gatherer became the social reformer recommending solutions for the problems he had highlighted. He criticized whites for offering platitudes and sermons rather than providing jobs and extensive financial aid for racial advancement. Discrimination, which Du Bois called "morally wrong, politically dangerous, industrially wasteful and socially silly," was to be eliminated by the whites: "It is the duty of the whites to stop it."[41] "A radical change in public opinion" was needed to give blacks equal opportunity to forge ahead. Such a change "would inspire the young to try harder; it would stimulate the idle and discouraged, and it would take away from this race the omnipresent excuse for failure: prejudice. Such a moral change would work a revolution in the criminal rate during the next ten years."[42]

However, Du Bois insisted that much of the responsibility for the race's advancement lay with blacks themselves. "That the Negro race has an appalling work of social reform before it need hardly be said," he observed. Despite the history of oppression and discrimination, Du Bois contended that modern society had the right to demand "that as far as possible and as rapidly as possible the Negro bend his energy to the solving of his own social problems." Blacks had the "right to demand freedom for self-development" and substantial aid from whites for schools, relief, and preventive agencies, "but the bulk of the raising [of] the Negro must be done by the Negro himself. . . . Against prejudice, injustice and wrong the Negro ought to protest energetically and continuously, but he must never forget that he protests because those things hinder his own efforts, and that those efforts are the key to his future."[43]

Du Bois believed that this key required the development of the cooperative economic and social endeavor which he had described. Economically, while advancement must come largely from a change in white attitudes and behavior, cooperation among Philadelphia's blacks would provide many job opportunities in black-owned establishments. The hope of blacks was in "the mastery of the art of social organized life." In pushing the race forward, the black "aristocracy" would play the crucial role, but it was the duty of whites to support their efforts. In a foreshadowing of Frazier's *Black Bourgeoisie*, Du Bois unhappily reported that the black upper class felt considerable alienation from the masses and had a pronounced tendency to remain aloof. Fearing that they might be mistaken for the masses, many of the elite isolated themselves and rationalized their not acting as race leaders by arguing that they refused to draw "the color line against which they protest." Although the rise of Philadelphia's tiny number of business and professional black men had been so difficult that "they fear to fall if now they stoop to lend a hand to their fellows," Du Bois reiterated their "duty toward the masses." They should establish more social services, such as day nurseries and sewing schools. They should develop more building and loan associations, newspapers, labor unions, and industrial enterprises. In short, foreshadowing his famous theory of the "Talented Tenth," Du Bois preached an ideology of Negro self-help and solidarity, a program of racial self-elevation under the leadership of an educated black elite.[44]

Du Bois conceived of *The Philadelphia Negro* as the start of a larger research program in which Negroes in other key American cities and in selected rural areas would be similarly studied. Discovering that many black Philadelphians had migrated from rural Virginia, he went there in the summer of 1897 and gathered material for a social study that the United States Bureau of Labor published as *The Negroes of Farmville, Virginia*. That autumn, he returned to Philadelphia to address the American Academy of Political and Social Science, where he urged support for his ideas about an extensive program of research among blacks. From the standpoints of pure science and of practical social need, he argued, the study of more than eight million Americans of African descent should be a matter of the highest priority. Unfortunately, the research thus far done had been "lamentably unsystematic and fragmentary" and, "most unfortunate of all," had been superficial and racially biased. "The most baneful cause of uncritical study of the Negro is the manifest and far-reaching bias of writers.

. . . When such men come to write on the subject, without technical training, without breadth of view, and in some cases without a deep sense of the sanctity of scientific truth, their testimony, however interesting as opinion, must of necessity be worthless as science."[45] Du Bois maintained that, because Negroes were readily identifiable and segregated, they provided especially valuable subjects for historical, anthropological, and sociological inquiry that would contribute substantially to the advancement of human knowledge. At the same time, the importance of scientific knowledge as a prerequisite for social understanding and the solution of social problems remained an important consideration: "The sole aim of any society is to settle its problems in accordance with its highest ideals, and the only rational method of accomplishing this is to study those problems in the light of the best scientific research."[46] Accordingly, he proposed a research plan far more ambitious than merely encouraging small-scale studies by independent, individual scholars. The necessary work would be difficult and expensive and would require decades to complete. Only a venture involving cooperation between a black college and the major universities would be sufficient to carry it out. "The first effective step toward the solving of the Negro question will be the endowment of a Negro college which is not merely a teaching body, but a centre of sociological research, in close connection and cooperation with Harvard, Columbia, Johns Hopkins, and the University of Pennsylvania."[47]

There was no interest in his appeal, and Du Bois attempted to implement the proposal on his own. He accepted a teaching position at Atlanta University in 1897. There, building on a modest research program already inaugurated by President Horace Bumstead and trustee George Bradford,[48] Du Bois unveiled a grandiose one-hundred-year plan for a comprehensive investigation of various aspects of black community life, such as business, education, the church, welfare organizations, family life, and criminality. He envisioned "ten-year cycles" in which data on each topic were to be published. During each decade, such research projects were to be continued simultaneously. After a century, enough would be known about Negro life to be of inestimable benefit to the entire society.[49] As he explained, "The method employed is to divide the various aspects of his [the black American's] social condition into ten great subjects. To treat one of these subjects each year as carefully and exhaustively as means will allow until the cycle is completed. To begin then again on the same cycle for a second ten years. So that in the course of a century, if the work is well done we shall have a continuous record on the condition and development of a group of 10 to 20 millions of men—a body of sociological material unsurpassed in human annals."[50] In presenting this program, Du Bois used arguments similar to those used at the American Academy of Political and Social Science. Sociology had to move from the broad abstractions and unsystematic fact-gathering that "have neither permanently increased the amount of our own knowledge nor introduced in the maze of fact any illuminating system or satisfying interpretation" to "the minute study of limited fields of human action, where observation and accurate measurement are possible and where real illuminating knowledge can be had. The careful exhaustive study of the isolated group, then, is the ideal of the sociologist of the 20th century—from that may come . . . at last careful, cautious generalization and formulation."[51] A study of American blacks provided "a peculiar opportunity . . . never in the history of the modern world has there been presented . . . so rare an opportunity to observe and measure and study the evolution of a great branch of the human race as is given to Americans in the study of the American Negro. Here is a crucial test on a scale that is astounding and under circumstances peculiarly fortunate. By reason of color and color prejudice the group is isolated—by reason of incentive to change, the changes are rapid and kaleidoscopic; by reason of the peculiar environment, the action and reaction of social forces are seen and can be measured with more than usual ease." Denouncing the racist bias of contemporaries, he called for a dispassionate, scientific attitude: "We urge and invite all men of science into the field, but we plead for men of science—not for . . . men with theories to sustain or prejudices to strengthen. We sincerely regret that there has been a tendency for so many men without adequate scientific knowledge and without conscientious study to pronounce public opinions and put gratuitous slurs on me and my people which were as insulting to us as they were to their own scientific reputations." [52]

Since Atlanta University was a struggling and impoverished institution that could not afford to support Du Bois's research adequately for one year—much less for a decade or a century—it is a tribute to his determination that he actually supervised the preparation of sixteen Atlanta University sociological monographs between 1897 and 1914. Obliged to use only unpaid part-time investigators, Du Bois was limited in the breadth and extensiveness of the study projects. He has described the method he was forced to use: "work in sociology was inaugurated with the thought that a university is primarily a seat of learning and that Atlanta University, being in the midst of the Negro problems, ought to become a centre of such a systematic and thoroughgoing study of those problems. . . . It goes without saying that our ideals in this respect are far from being realized. Although our researches have cost less than $500 a year, yet we find it difficult and sometimes impossible to raise that meagre sum. We lack proper appliances for statistical work and proper clerical aid; notwithstanding this, something has been done. The plan of work is this: a subject is chosen; it is always a definite, limited subject covering some phase of the general Negro problem; schedules are then prepared, and these with letters are sent to the voluntary correspondents, mostly graduates of this and other Negro institutions of higher training. They, by means of local inquiry, fill out and return the schedules; then other sources of information, depending on the question under discussion, are tried, until after six or eight months' work a body of material is gathered." [53]

Considering the limited resources at Du Bois's disposal, it is not surprising that the Atlanta monographs do not compare with *The Philadelphia Negro* as a contribution to sociology. They were uneven in quality, planning, methods, and content. At the less successful end of the spectrum were *Some Efforts of Negroes for Their Own Social Betterment*, done in 1898 and repeated in 1909, and *Economic Cooperation among Negro Americans*, produced in 1907 and dealing partly with the same kind of material found in the other two monographs. "Mathematical accuracy in these studies is impossible; the sources of information are of varying degree of accuracy and the pictures are woefully incomplete."[54] In attempting to examine the charitable work of churches, secret societies, and other organizations that blacks were establishing for themselves, Du Bois in 1898 selected several southern cities. The college graduates who collected the data were asked to record "typical examples." He was fortunate to obtain the services of these interviewers, but he gave them few instructions beyond telling them to submit limited descriptions of some benevolent organizations within their own communities. Du Bois recognized that he could not check the material he would receive for reliability or validity. He succeeded in amassing an encyclopedic array of facts, often having little connection to each other, and he simply added them up where he could. There is list after list of services and societies, with little or no comment except an indication of what could be accomplished through greater collective action. The local church questionnaire, for example, included such items as: number of enrolled members, number of active members, value of real-estate indebtedness, number of religious meetings weekly; entertainments per year; lectures and literary programs per year; suppers and socials per year; concerts and fairs per year; number of literary and benevolent and missionary societies; annual income, annual budget, disbursements for charity, number of poor helped, and so on. Du Bois considered his presentation as a significant "scientific" contribution which demonstrated that Negroes were not "one vast unorganized, homogeneous mass." However, race prejudice had isolated the group and caused the accelerated formation of racial institutions for which no adequate preparation had been made. He believed that more inquiries like his would establish the extent of white aid which the race required.[55]

This Atlanta monograph, and all the others as well, offered Du Bois considerable opportunity to play the role of social reformer. At the conclusion of each year's project, he and Atlanta University hosted a conference that brought educated Negroes and a sprinkling of sympathetic whites to the campus for a discussion of the relevance of the research topic to the future advancement of the Negro. Du Bois usually served on the resolutions committees of these conclaves and was influential in composing exhortations and admonitions about ways to improve living conditions among blacks. The resolutions printed in the annual monographs generally did not grow out of the inductive studies and typically failed to suggest specific techniques to accomplish the desired ends. Thus in 1898 Du Bois's resolutions committee urged black churches to cut their operating expenses and use the money to increase charitable work. Funerals were criticized as too extravagant—blacks were urged to make them simple and inexpensive, and to eliminate tawdry display. Similarly, black secret societies were told to "be careful not to give undue prominence to ritual, regalia, and parade." [56] Obviously, Du Bois and his fellow counselors of austerity failed to appreciate the integrative and status functions of expensive rituals here. In this, of course, they were imbued with the Puritan ethic of reform that characterized much of sociology in the Progressive era.

The 1907 *Economic Cooperation among Negro Americans* was to be "a continuation and enlargement" of the 1898 account. In his treatment of the black church in 1907, Du Bois did not use the 1898 material on individual churches. Instead, he discussed the income, expenses, mission work, and many other details of the larger religious denominations. In this later study, he did not refer to his handling of the beneficial and insurance societies in 1898. The 1898 monograph had contained a catalogue of various local secret societies, giving the usual data on membership, income, and expenses. The 1907 work included the history and purposes of some of the larger societies, such as the Masons. The two treatments were not related to each other. The 1898 monograph had mentioned several cooperative businesses and described a few in some detail. One, a North Carolina cotton mill called the Coleman Manufacturing Company, was also discussed in 1907, but no connection was made between these examinations of the same company. Nothing was said about its development in the intervening nine years. Du Bois mentioned that the founder had died "and a white company bought the mill and is running it with white help." An excellent opportunity for a case study of how a race enterprise failed—but not enough data had been gathered and related.

The 1907 conference resolutions committee, in urging more

cooperative effort among blacks, noted a "crisis." The Negro
race was "at the crossroads—one way leading to the old trodden
ways of grasping individualistic competition, where the shrewd,
cunning, skilled and rich among them will prey upon the ignorance and simplicity of the mass of the race and get wealth at
the expense of the general well being; the other way leading to
co-operation in capital and labor, the massing of small savings,
the wide distribution of capital and a more general equality of
wealth and comfort."[57] This conclusion was not developed
from the data presented in the monograph. Two years later
Efforts for Social Betterment among Negro Americans was published,
and it too presented a cornucopia of facts without making any
connections to material in the earlier volumes.

The best monographs in the series were two dealing with *The
Negro Artisan* (1902 and 1912), which made a more thorough
and ordered contribution to our knowledge of blacks. Du Bois
realized that he faced a "peculiar difficulty," since much of his
data came from "interested persons," although to some extent
part of the material could be checked by "third parties." For
instance, in some cases the word of the workers was validated by
making inquiries of their fellow workers and their employers.
The 1902 research was based upon many sources. A questionnaire was distributed to hundreds of black artisans, most residing in Georgia, who described their work experiences in comparison with those of white artisans in the same occupations.
Another was sent to "correspondents" in many states, who sur-
veyed skilled workers in their own communities. One man described the trades Negroes entered in Memphis and whether
they belonged to the same labor unions as whites. Independent
unions and those affiliated with the American Federation of
Labor received a questionnaire on the black worker. Another
was distributed to the central labor bodies in a number of cities.
Inquiries were also made of state federations.

Du Bois was thus able to determine which unions admitted
Negroes and the relative proportions of blacks to the total
membership. He could pinpoint the trades in which Negroes
encountered hostility. He appended the views of labor leaders
on race relations in industry. Industrial schools submitted information on their courses of study. Educational leaders in all

southern states were asked about the kinds of manual training included in their curricula and requested to comment upon the results. Employers in various parts of the South were asked to appraise Negro efficiency in relation to that of whites. Comparative data were secured on the wages paid to blacks and whites in various trades. In the 1912 survey, similar questionnaires were sent to some of the same groups. Comparisons of census data for the two periods were made, to estimate whether blacks were holding their own in the various trades.

Although the Atlanta University studies clearly had their limitations, their value and importance should not be ignored. At a time when serious study of the black community was otherwise absent, Du Bois amassed a body of data that not only compared quite favorably with the social survey research being done at the time but has provided a valuable storehouse of information to his successors. Du Bois himself modestly evaluated the significance of his worth: "When we at Atlanta University say that we are the only institution in the United States that is making any serious study of the race problems . . . we make no great boast because it is not that we are doing so much, but rather that the rest of the nation is doing nothing."[58] In short, the real importance of the Atlanta University monographs lies in the fact that, in them and in *The Philadelphia Negro*, Du Bois singlehandedly initiated serious empirical research on blacks in America.

Despite the depth of Du Bois's commitment to sociology, he was in the main ignored by the elite in the profession. It is interesting that Albion W. Small, a founder of America's first department of sociology in 1892, of the *American Journal of Sociology* in 1895, and of the American Sociological Society a decade later, had, like Du Bois, been trained in Germany by Schmoller.[59] In spite of this similarity in professional background and although the *American Journal of Sociology*, in addition to publishing theoretical articles, devoted many pages to social welfare problems, Small clearly considered Du Bois's work of minor importance. Yet books by known racists were reviewed and often warmly praised. In 1906, Thomas Nelson Page's *The Negro: The Southerner's Problem* was glowingly lauded by Charles Ellwood, who had been Small's graduate student.[60]

In another review, Ellwood gratuitously commented, "it is only through the full recognition that the average negro is still a savage child of nature that the North and the South can be brought to unite in work to uplift the race."[61]

The *American Journal of Sociology* never published a single one of Du Bois's many articles on the Negro. On one occasion, however, the *Journal* included his remarks at a 1908 symposium on "Is Race Friction between Blacks and Whites in the United States Growing and Inevitable?" In this address he restated his "dream . . . that we could . . . begin at a small Negro college a movement for the scientific study of race differences and likenesses which should in time revolutionize the knowledge of the world. . . . As I have said [whether blacks are an inferior race] is primarily a scientific question, a matter of scientific measurement and observation; and yet the data upon which the mass of men, and even intelligent men, are basing their conclusions today, the basis which they are putting back of their treatment of the Negro, is a most ludicrous and harmful conglomeration of myth, falsehood, and desire. It would certainly be a most commendable thing if [the American Sociological Society] and other learned societies would put themselves on record as favoring a most thorough and unbiased scientific study of the race problem in America."[62]

Under Small's editorship, though the *American Journal of Sociology* included such articles as "Has Illinois the Best Laws in the Country for the Protection of Children?" "A Decade of Official Poor Relief in Indiana," "Boston's Experience with Municipal Baths," and "Sanitation and Social Progress," articles about black Americans were relatively few. It is true that the *Journal* did carry articles by a man like W. I. Thomas, who criticized racist theories, but other items displayed the racial biases of their authors. The September, 1903, issue included an article by H. E. Berlin entitled "The Civil War as Seen through Southern Glasses," in which the author described slavery as "the most humane and the most practical method ever devised for 'bearing the white man's burden.' "[63] In 1908 the *Journal* carried a piece by the same author on "A Southern View of Slavery."[64] The publication of such views in the *American Journal of Sociology* reflected theories about race held in the profession at the time. Sociological theory on race prevalent before World War I generally stressed the biological superiority of the white race and the "primitiveness" of the "inferior" black's "racial temperament," which predisposed him toward "shiftlessness and sensuality," rendering him basically unassimilable.

As Frazier has described the situation, the "general point of view" of the first sociologists to study the black man was that "the Negro is an inferior race because of either biological or social heredity or both; that the Negro because of his physical characteristics could not be assimilated; and that physical amalgamation was bad and therefore undesirable." These conclusions were generally supported by the marshaling of a vast amount of statistical data on the pathological aspects of Negro life. In short, "The sociological theories which were implicit in the writings on the Negro problem were merely rationalizations of the existing racial situation."[65]

Thus, ironically, Du Bois, who by training and research orientation toward both empiricism and reform was part of the mainstream of American sociology as it evolved at the turn of the century, found himself relegated to the periphery of his profession.

The Chicago school of urban sociology that began about the time of World War I did not consider Du Bois's work significant, even though its leader, Robert Park, was deeply interested in the study of race relations. The social survey movement sensitized sociologists to the importance of studying the urban community and urban problems.[66] Indeed, Park and his colleagues recognized the value of Booth's internationally famous research on London, Chicago's *Hull House Maps and Papers*, and the noted Pittsburgh Survey of 1909–12. Yet they and almost every commentator since, while mentioning these and other case studies of communities, failed to include *The Philadelphia Negro*. (For some examples, see works by Elmer, Taylor, and Steiner.)[67] Among those who have written of the origins of modern sociology and social research, only Nathan Glazer appears to have recognized *The Philadelphia Negro*'s contribution.[68] As Frazier said, "It appears that there was a feeling, perhaps unconscious and therefore all the more significant, that since the Negro occupied a low status and did not play an important role in American society, studies of the Negro were of less significance from the standpoint of social science." [69] The neglect of Du Bois's work appears all the more remarkable when his work is compared with other products of the social survey movement. *The Philadelphia Negro* was, in fact, one of the finest monographs inspired by Booth's study of London. It was superior to *Hull House Maps and Papers* and antedated by ten years the elaborate and influential Pittsburgh Survey. But in the United States of the early twentieth century, white sociologists were not likely to recognize the contribution made by a study of a black community.

Yet times would change, and the *American Journal of Sociology* would soon be publishing many serious articles on the Negro. Under Park's leadership, the University of Chicago's sociology department became a major center for the study of race relations in America. [70] Blacks like Charles S. Johnson and E. Franklin Frazier became students in sociology at Chicago and began producing work that owed much to Du Bois's influence. But by then Du Bois had ceased to think of himself primarily as a sociologist. He had become deeply aware of the seething and often erupting anti-Negro forces in America. After being confronted with situations, like lynchings, that "called—shrieked —for action," he concluded that social research was futile. [71] Almost completely in vain, he had made public appeals for money to finance the annual Atlanta studies. In despair, he remarked, "If Negroes were lost in Africa, money would be available to measure their heads, but $500 a year is hard to raise for Atlanta." [72] He had become less sure that social science could seriously effect social reform. Increasingly, he turned his attention to writing propaganda that aggressively and unconditionally demanded the same civil rights for blacks that other Americans enjoyed—a theme absent from the Atlanta studies. In 1909 he became a founder of the National Association for the Advancement of Colored People. In 1910 he left Atlanta University to work for the new organization. For a brief period he continued the Atlanta studies, but his basic interests now lay elsewhere.

Although Du Bois himself thus left the field of sociology, his influence on students of the black community was profound.

His was more than the obvious model for the surveys of Negroes in New York and Boston by Ovington, Haynes, and
Daniels in the period before World War I. His pioneering
work also bears important similarities to such later studies as
Johnson's *The Negro in Chicago*, Frazier's *Negro Youth at the
Crossways*, Davis and Gardner's *Deep South*, and Drake and
Cayton's *Black Metropolis*. In their holistic approach to the study
of black urban communities, in their attention to the importance of social class, and in their painstaking scholarship and
quest for scientific knowledge, their likeness to Du Bois is evident. Like Du Bois, they clearly showed the social problems
arising from white oppression and discrimination and at the
same time described the richness and diversity of black life and
the inventiveness which Negroes displayed in creating institutions and life styles that enabled them to cope and survive.
Finally, like Du Bois, they all hoped that their research and
published works, by reaching an influential white audience,
would promote beneficial changes for blacks in American society.

1. E. Franklin Frazier, *The Negro in the United States*, rev. ed. (New York: Macmillan,
1957).
2. St. Clair Drake and Horace Cayton, *Black Metropolis* (New York: Harcourt, Brace,
1945), p. 787.
3. Robert Park, "The City as a Social Laboratory," in T. V. Smith and Leonard D.
White, eds., *Chicago: An Experiment in Social Science Research* (Chicago: University of
Chicago Press, 1929), pp. 4–7; Ernest Burgess, "The Social Survey: A Field for Constructive Service by Departments of Sociology," *American Journal of Sociology*, 21 (Jan.,
1916), 493.
4. L. L. Bernard and Jessie Bernard, *Origins of American Sociology* (New York:
Crowell, 1943), pp. 559–644.
5. *Ibid.*, p. 657; Harry Elmer Barnes and Howard Becker, *Social Thought from Lore to
Science* (Boston: Heath, 1938), II, 976–79.
6. Bernard and Bernard, *Origins of American Sociology*, p. 559.
7. John Daniels, *In Freedom's Birthplace: A Study of the Boston Negroes* (Boston:
Houghton Mifflin, 1914); Mary White Ovington, *Half a Man: The Status of the Negro in
New York* (New York: Longmans, Green, 1911); George Edmund Haynes, *The Negro at
Work in New York City: A Study in Economic Progress* (New York: Longmans, Green, 1912).
8. W. E. B. Du Bois, *Dusk of Dawn* (New York: Harcourt, Brace, 1940), p. 39.
9. Bernard and Bernard, *Origins of American Sociology*, pp. 614–16.
10. W. E. B. Du Bois, *The Autobiography of W. E. B. Du Bois* (New York: International, 1968), p. 148.
11. Francis L. Broderick, "The Academic Training of W. E. B. Du Bois," *Journal of
Negro Education*, 27 (Winter, 1958), 16.
12. Du Bois, *Dusk of Dawn*, p. 51.
13. W. E. B. Du Bois, *The Philadelphia Negro: A Social Study* (Philadelphia: University
of Pennsylvania, 1899), p. x; Allen F. Davis, *Spearheads for Reform* (New York: Oxford
University Press, 1967), p. 96.

14. Gunnar Myrdal, *An American Dilemma* (New York: Harper, 1944), p. 1132.

15. Du Bois, *Philadelphia Negro*, p. 58.

16. *Ibid.*, pp. 101–2, 108.

17. *Ibid.*, pp. 296, 133.

18. *Ibid.*, p. 120.

19. *Ibid.*, pp. 66–68.

20. *Ibid.*, p. 67.

21. *Ibid.*, pp. 113–14.

22. *Ibid.*, pp. 193–94.

23. *Ibid.*, p. 284.

24. *Ibid.*

25. *Ibid.*, p. 394.

26. *Ibid.*, pp. 89, 128, 326–32.

27. *Ibid.*, p. 352.

28. *Ibid.*, pp. 324–25.

29. *Ibid.*, pp. 74–79.

30. *Ibid.*, pp. 81–243.

31. *Ibid.*, p. 306.

32. *Ibid.*, p. 5.

33. *Ibid.*, p. 386.

34. *Ibid.*, p. 309.

35. *Ibid.*, pp. 311–18.

36. Drake and Cayton, *Black Metropolis*, p. 787.

37. Du Bois, *Philadelphia Negro*, pp. 172, 177, 198, 203–4, 220.

38. *Ibid.*, pp. 201–3, 207.

39. *Ibid.*, p. 227.

40. *Ibid.*, pp. 372–84; Du Bois, "The Black Vote of Philadelphia," *Charities*, 15 (Oct. 7, 1905), 619–22.

41. Du Bois, *Philadelphia Negro*, p. 394.

42. *Ibid.*, p. 395.

43. *Ibid.*, pp. 389–90.

44. *Ibid.*, pp. 233, 389–96.

45. Du Bois, "The Study of the Negro Problems," *Annals of the American Academy of Political and Social Science*, 11 (Jan., 1898), 22.

46. *Ibid.*, p. 16.

47. *Ibid.*, p. 22.

48. Du Bois, "The Atlanta University Conferences," *Charities*, 10 (May 2, 1903), 436.

49. *Ibid.*, pp. 435–39.

50. Du Bois, "The Atlanta Conferences," *Voice of the Negro*, 1 (Mar., 1904), 88.

51. *Ibid.*, p. 85.

52. *Ibid.*, pp. 86, 89.

53. Du Bois, "The Laboratory in Sociology at Atlanta University," *Annals of the American Academy of Political and Social Science*, 21 (May, 1903), 162.

54. Du Bois, *Efforts for Social Betterment among Negro Americans* (Atlanta: Atlanta University Press, 1909), pp. 5–6.

55. Du Bois, *Some Efforts of American Negroes for Their Own Social Betterment* (Atlanta: Atlanta University Press, 1898).

56. *Ibid.*, pp. 47–48.

57. Du Bois, *Economic Cooperation among Negro Americans* (Atlanta: Atlanta University Press, 1907), p. 4.

58. Du Bois, "Race Friction between Black and White," *American Journal of Sociology*, 13 (May, 1908), 835–36.

59. Barnes and Becker, *Social Thought*, II, 766–92.

60. *American Journal of Sociology*, 11 (1905–6), 698–99; Barnes and Becker, *Social Thought*, II, 853–55.

61. *American Journal of Sociology*, 12 (1906–7), 275.

62. Du Bois, "Race Friction," pp. 835–36.

63. *American Journal of Sociology*, 9 (Sept., 1903), 266.

64. *Ibid.*, 13 (Jan., 1908), 513–22.

65. E. Franklin Frazier, "Race Contacts and the Social Structure," *American Sociological Review*, 14 (Feb., 1949), 2; and Frazier, "Sociological Theory and Race Relations," *ibid.*, 12 (June, 1947), 268.

66. James F. Short, Jr., *The Social Fabric of the Metropolis* (Chicago: University of Chicago Press, 1971), p. xvi; Ernest Burgess and Donald Bogue, *Contributions to Urban Sociology* (Chicago: University of Chicago Press, 1964), p. 3.

67. Manuel C. Elmer, *Social Surveys of Urban Communities* (Menasha, Wisc., 1914); Carl C. Taylor, *The Social Survey: Its History and Methods* (Columbia, Mo., 1919); and J. F. Steiner, "The Sources and Methods of Community Study," in L. L. Bernard, ed., *The Field and Methods of Sociology* (New York: Long and Smith, 1934).

68. Nathan Glazer, "The Rise of Social Research in Europe," in Daniel Lerner, ed., *The Human Meaning of the Social Sciences* (Cleveland: World, 1959), p. 64.

69. Frazier, "Race Contacts," p. 2.

70. Peter I. Rose, *The Subject Is Race* (New York: Oxford University Press, 1968), p. 3.

71. Du Bois, *Darkwater* (New York: Harcourt, Brace, and Howe, 1920), pp. 21–22.

72. Du Bois, "The Laboratory in Sociology," p. 162; "The Atlanta Conferences," pp. 85–90.

THREE

Booker T. Washington and the Negro Press

BY AUGUST MEIER

Perhaps the most sensational charge leveled at Booker T. Washington during his score of years as a leader of national importance was that he subsidized newspapers and magazines in order to silence criticism of himself and his policies, and in effect seriously curtailed freedom of the press. Washington's own correspondence[1] reveals his far-reaching influence among Negro editors and publishers. In what ways was this influence maintained, and to what extent was Washington able to direct the editorial policies of individual journals?

Washington achieved his considerable degree of control over the Negro press by a variety of methods. Some editors were genuinely friendly to Washington and his point of view. Certainly his prestige and power played a large role in attracting support in the press as elsewhere. Indirectly, he worked through R. W. Thompson's National Press Bureau in Washington, and through the Negro press organizations[2] which were dominated by Tuskegee supporters. Tuskegee itself sent out news items and often paid for the cost of printing them. Advertisements were freely placed in a number of journals. Several were assisted by the purchase of great quantities of certain issues for distribution, or by payments for subscriptions to be sent to a large group of selected individuals. Occasionally Tuskegee helped to subsidize a special Tuskegee issue of a journal. A few, closer in their relations with Washington, received suggestions and even actual copy for editorials.

From *The Journal of Negro History*, 38 (Jan., 1953), 67–90. Reprinted with permission of *The Journal of Negro History*. © 1952 by The Association for the Study of Negro Life and History.

And then there were at least five or six periodicals which Washington aided by sustained cash contributions. These were the New York *Age*, the Washington *Colored American*, the Boston *Colored Citizen*, the *Colored American Magazine*, *Alexander's Magazine*, and perhaps the Washington *Bee*. Two of these—the New York *Age* and the *Colored American Magazine*—were, for a time, partly owned by Washington.

In order to obtain a closer view of how Washington worked, let us take the *Colored American Magazine* as a specific example for investigation. Published from 1900 to 1909, during the period of Washington's greatest popularity and influence, it was founded in Boston by the Colored Co-Operative Publishing Company, whose leading figure was the postal superintendent, civic leader, and businessman William H. Dupree. Though the data are meagre, it is evident that Washington owned a few shares of stock in the company in 1901, but disposed of them when it was charged that he was attempting to control this and other journals.[3] The editors aimed to publish a literary magazine that would foster racial solidarity and advancement.[4] Though in an early issue they published a vigorous attack on Washington and his philosophy written by George Washington Forbes, co-editor of the Boston *Guardian* (Washington's most bitter newspaper critic),[5] the editors themselves were friendly toward Washington.[6] And while at first there were some articles supporting protest organizations, as time went on the magazine veered more and more toward an emphasis upon economic advancement and Negro support of Negro business—two important themes in the philosophy of Booker T. Washington. By 1904, however, the Colored Co-Operative Publishing Company was suffering serious financial difficulties, and in its last months was enabled to continue only through the philanthropy of a New York publisher, John C. Freund.[7]

It was at this point, during the spring of 1904, that Washington again became interested in the *Colored American Magazine*. In March, Freund was corresponding with him about the possibility of establishing the magazine in New York, and Washington went so far as to put Freund in touch with his close friend, William H. Baldwin, president of the Long Island Railroad.[8] Freund dropped out of the picture shortly thereafter, but before he did so Washington had decided to arrange for the magazine's purchase and to move it to New York, and had selected an editor.

The man whom Washington chose for this task was Fred R. Moore, later better known as editor and publisher of the New York *Age*. To assist Moore Washington selected his wife's nephew, Roscoe Conkling Simmons, who left the magazine after misunderstandings with Moore in 1906.[9] While not one of Washington's most intimate associates, Moore was one in whom the Tuskegean placed important trusts. At the time he took over the magazine Moore was national organizer and recording secretary of Washington's National Negro Business League, and he had been placed on the *Age* to assist T. Thomas Fortune. Later he became editor of the *Age* when the Tuskegee group bought the paper in 1907.[10]

In April, 1904, after conferring with Freund, Moore went to Boston to look over the situation personally.[11] In May he assured Washington that the latter would not be publicly connected with the magazine.[12] However, it is clear that from the first Washington was interested in the finances of the journal.[13] Among other things, he secured advertisements from Doubleday, Page and Company.[14] During the summer Washington made an unsuccessful attempt to get the philanthropist Robert C. Ogden to invest money in the journal.[15] Finally, according to Moore, Washington personally invested $3,000 in the magazine.[16]

But Washington's financial involvement did not stop here. Moore's first issue was in June, 1904, and by October he was making requests for money. Everything was going smoothly, he wrote on October 25, except that he was worried about the $750 note due the original publishers on November 16. Washington replied that he hoped to have some advice by about November 10. By that time Moore was able to inform Washington that he had arranged for an extension of the notes.[17] In April, 1905, Moore wrote that he needed assistance, as the magazine was incurring a deficit of about $100 each month, and Washington wrote in reply that he would discuss the matter when he came to New York.[18] Later, in October,

1905, it appears that of $476 due, Washington paid $275.[19] Again, on March 2, 1906, Moore wrote that he needed $75 by April 1, in order to pay a $225 note, and $100 by May 3. On March 27 Washington sent him the $75 immediately necessary.[20] And a year and a half later Moore asked Emmett Scott, Washington's private secretary, to be sure that Washington would send him $100 by the end of the week.[21] Evidence in the papers does not indicate whether or not Washington acceded to all of these requests for money. It is likely that, as in the case of other editors, Washington contributed only in emergencies.

So, while in true Washingtonian fashion, Moore's optimism as to the magazine's ultimate success persisted through all of its vicissitudes, it remained a losing proposition.[22] By 1909 Washington indicated that he was unable to contribute any more funds to the magazine's support.[23] And later in the same year the magazine, now edited by George W. Harris, was discontinued in connection with a reorganization of the New York Age.[24]

In addition to his financial involvement, Washington maintained an active interest in editorial affairs, often making specific suggestions which were usually followed. Indeed, from the first, Moore welcomed the advice of both Scott and Washington.[25] In characteristic fashion in May and again in June, 1904, Washington was suggesting that Moore secure permission to reprint particular articles from other journals, and Scott secured the illustrations for one of them.[26] In July Washington practically offered R. L. Stokes an editorial position under a plan for the joint management of the Age and the Colored American Magazine.[27] Specific suggestions continued to come frequently from Tuskegee until well into 1905.[28] There were also many letters from Washington commenting on the quality and appearance of the magazine.[29] Though it took less interest as time went on, Tuskegee did maintain an active role. For example, Scott helped to prepare a form letter and printed circular in 1906, which paradoxically asserted that the magazine would not take sides in the ideological controversies then raging.[30] And toward the end of the next year Moore wrote Scott that he wanted to discuss the magazine's affairs with him.[31]

In spite of all this activity, Washington was anxious to see that the journal was not too closely identified with himself and Tuskegee. Ostensibly Washington had no connection with the Moore Publishing Company which put out the magazine. Furthermore, he objected to too many articles on himself or Tuskegee, and he directed that advertisements connected with the work of the school be kept to a minimum.[32]

Now, just why was it that Washington showed so much interest in the *Colored American Magazine*? He was not one to spend his money without good reason, as an examination of the publications which he subsidized shows. The *Age*, for example, was the leading Negro newspaper of the period. Its editor, T. Thomas Fortune, for years a close friend of Washington, proved unstable and broke with Washington several times. Washington gave generously to Fortune for the paper's support, made strong but unsuccessful efforts to purchase it in 1903–4, and finally obtained control over the majority of its stock in 1907. Washington was especially interested in the *Age* because of his friendship with Fortune, because of the paper's importance and influence, and because he feared that it might be sold to his enemies.[33] In Boston, where the fiery Monroe Trotter published his critical *Guardian*, Washington heavily subsidized two organs—first the Boston *Colored Citizen* and later *Alexander's Magazine*. He was especially intimate in the affairs of the *Colored Citizen* during the stormy days of 1903 (when the "opposition" first became a more or less organized revolt against Washington's leadership), giving advice, criticism, money, and editorial copy.[34] Business in "radical" Boston was so poor, however, that by 1905 Washington came to see the futility of subsidizing the paper further. Consequently editor Charles Alexander took Washington's advice and replaced the newspaper with a monthly, *Alexander's Magazine*.[35] Alexander continued to appeal to Washington for funds, and Washington at times acceded to his requests,[36] the magazine failing in 1909. In the nation's capital, where W. Calvin Chase used the powerful and influential *Bee* to sting Washington and denounce his policies, Tuskegee assisted E. E. Cooper's struggling Washington *Colored American* (newspaper) until its demise in 1904.[37] Later, in 1906, Chase became an ardent supporter of

Washington. While the Washington papers shed very little light on the Tuskegean's relationships with Chase, it is evident that in 1908, at least, Chase asked for and did receive some funds.[38] In Chicago, where the *Conservator* was attacking him, Washington toyed with the idea of subsidizing a rival organ. While he gave some money to Allison Sweeney, Washington seems to have given up the project because he could not find a dependable editor.[39] The evidence concerning the *Colored American Magazine* is less clear, but it is certain that by late 1905, at least, Washington was frankly viewing it as a rival of the "radical" *Voice of the Negro*, one of whose editors, J. Max Barber, was a member of the Niagara Movement.[40]

Washington's subsidization of the *Colored American Magazine* and other journals is, then, clearly indicated in his own correspondence. Yet he consistently denied that he was doing this. His basic argument was that if he subsidized one, he would have to subsidize all, and, as this was manifestly impossible, it was easily apparent that he couldn't support any. He declared that advertisements were not intended to influence editorial policy in any way.[41] Yet his own letters contradict such assertions as that made to Francis J. Garrison in May, 1905, when he said that he was not subsidizing any publication—specifically that he had no connection with the *Colored American Magazine*.[42]

Furthermore, Washington unquestionably attempted to use his influence with the press in his fight with the "radical" opposition, and to a considerable degree he succeeded. He was able, for example, to get many or most of the Negro journals to ignore the Niagara Movement. Even more striking evidence is available on Washington's treatment of James H. Hayes and the National Negro Suffrage League. He urged newspapers either to ignore the organization or, as in the case of the *Age*, to attack it. He worked indirectly through a mutual friend, J. C. Asbury of the *Oddfellows Journal*, who tried to convince Hayes that Washington's more tactful approach was the better one. After Hayes had come around to Washington's way of thinking, Washington showed his hand in an unusual letter in which he regretted his inability to stop Fortune's criticism, but pointed out that, as he had promised, the other journals had ceased their attacks.[43]

So much, then, for Washington's techniques of influencing the press. Less dramatic but equally significant are conclusions to be drawn from a study of the editorial policies of the journals of the Washington orbit. Before turning to an analysis of the ideological content of the *Colored American Magazine*, however, it will be well to review briefly Washington's own social philosophy.

Undoubtedly the impression which emerges most clearly from a careful study of Washington's public statements is that of the accommodating and ingratiating tone which he adopted toward the white South. He appeared to abjure social equality and to accept, at least temporarily, disfranchisement and segregation. He emphasized instead economic advancement, self-help, and industrial education. This program was especially appealing to whites because in effect Washington was transmuting the currently dominant social ideologies of economic individualism and the gospel of wealth into the key to racial salvation. But, even disregarding certain highly secret efforts against segregation and disfranchisement[44] which were unknown to his contemporaries, one can observe contradictions in his thought and activities. Washington's tone was accommodating, but there was a peculiar militancy about his emphasis on self-help, economic advancement, and moral improvement, his concern with developing manhood and race pride, and his espousal of Negro support for Negro business. While he denied any interest in social equality, Washington was at home in northern and foreign social circles which few southern whites could enter. While he emphasized industrial education, he sometimes asserted that he would place no limitations on the educational development of any race. Nor would he, as he often pointed out, deny Negroes their constitutional rights. Personally he was deeply involved in politics, and publicly he urged not disfranchisement, but literacy and property qualifications that would apply equally to both races. And shortly after he died there appeared his *New Republic* article opposing segregation laws. In short, Washington believed that material advancement achieved through thrift, hard work, Christian character, and economic chauvinism would bring recognition of the Negro's constitutional rights and break down oppression

and segregation. Nevertheless, his disarming flattery of southern whites, his emphasis upon economic development and
moral uplift rather than on oppression and injustices, his soft-
pedaling of civil and political rights and higher education, and
his placing the chief responsibility for the Negroes' difficulties
and the burden of their advancement upon Negroes themselves, make his thought characteristically accommodating in
tone. His ultimate goals were mentioned relatively seldom, and
when they were, they were carefully and tactfully—and often
vaguely—expressed. In short, his felicitous manner of expression decidedly masked the protest content of his thought and
effectively bridged the contradictions in his philosophy.

Let us now turn to a discussion of the ideological content of
the *Colored American Magazine* under Fred R. Moore. The editor
succinctly stated his basic aims concerning the magazine when
he told his readers that "It seeks to publish articles showing the
advancement of our people along material lines, believing that
the people generally are more interested in having information
of the doings of the members of the race, rather [than] the
writings of dreamers or theorists." Moore was frank to admit
his admiration for Booker T. Washington, but wanted "it
frankly understood that he [Moore] alone is responsible for the
Magazine. . . . We have always been known," he added, perhaps prophetically, "to do our own thinking when it comes to
policies to be followed. . . ."[45] In general Moore emphasized
the things closest to his heart—the virtues of Tuskegee and its
founder, and the achievements of Negro businessmen and business enterprises. Articles appeared which bitterly attacked
higher education. And Moore agreed enthusiastically when
Ben J. Davis, editor of the Atlanta *Independent*, declared that the
"civilization of a race must rest upon economic fundamentals
and not politics," and that "thrift, industry, intelligence and
economy must precede control."[46] Moore also shared Washington's spirit of optimism and declared: "The inspiration of a
healthy optimism is abroad in the thought and effort of the
Afro-American people, who are more disposed to look on the
bright side than on the dark side of life; and this is a sufficient
reason for the faith that they will ultimately come into all that is
good in this land which is theirs."[47]

Other strands in Washington's social philosophy that appealed to Moore were the concepts of race pride, racial self-help, racial solidarity, and economic chauvinism—that is, Negro support for Negro business. "Let the Negro alone," he declared. "The Negro should awake to the necessity of relying more on his own resources as an impetus to race progress. The race cannot expect the whites to do for it what it can do for itself. . . . We must learn to walk alone. If race prejudice shuts the door of hope in our face, we must turn our face in other directions. If opportunities do not come, let us make opportunities. How can this be done better than by patronizing race enterprises? . . . How can we expect to ever be anything but 'hewers of wood and drawers of water,' " unless "we . . . stand together in this matter of race patronage. Go out of your way to help the colored business and professional man. . . . Patronize your own is the new watch cry!"[48]

Moore, then, enthusiastically supported Washington's program of self-help, racial solidarity, and economic development. But only once did he adopt Washington's characteristically accommodating phraseology toward the white South.[49] On the contrary, he was sometimes moved to vigorous criticism, couched in language Washington never employed. Once, for example, he militantly declared: "The American people have stood by and allowed the Negro to be 'jim-crowed' in politics, in religion, in education, in business, on the railroads, and in the theatres and hotels, without a ripple of dissent. . . . Congress might help us, but it has been silent in seven different languages. The Supreme Court might help us, but has evaded the issue." In short, Congress and the Supreme Court "are playing 'hide and seek' with us, and in the meantime the great horse leech of prejudice cries out for more Negro blood. Where will this thing stop?" The South "has repressed the Negro in almost every . . . conceivable way in the states and now its aim is at the national bulwark of Negro citizenship"—the Fourteenth and Fifteenth Amendments. Nor did Moore mince words on the psychological impact of segregation: "The 'Jim-Crow' system is a constant proclamation to the Negro people that they are an inferior race. . . . To have this sting constantly flaunted in our faces all the time is likely to breed in us a self-contempt that will dwarf our aspirations and make us hate those whom we inevitably must consider our oppressors."[50]

In spite of occasional statements of this nature, however, the magazine did not stray too far from Washington's point of view. Moore devoted most of its pages to booming the economic and material advancement of the race, and the development of a Negro bourgeoisie. The contradictions in his thinking are especially well revealed in a comment which he made on the Niagara Movement. "All this," he said, "has the true abolitionist ring. It is a good thing that there are some abolitionists among the members of the Negro race. . . . It is, however, a fortunate thing that the great mass of the Negro people are willing to toil on and up, by the slow process of industry, thrift [and] sobriety. . . . The aggressive attitude of the Niagara Movement lessens the number of the friends of the Negro, it intensifies the antagonism between the races, it discourages any solution of the racial problem along industrial or economic lines, but it keeps the issue clear, and if the South really proposes to settle the contest in blood, it brings the final catastrophe nearer."[51]

Furthermore, Moore's very espousal of race pride, racial solidarity, and economic chauvinism was couched in militant terms. Yet, as he himself realized, there was an important difference between his militancy and that of the so-called radicals. Commenting on the *Horizon* magazine, organ of the Niagara Movement, which had criticized the *Colored American Magazine* for a lack of editorial vigor, Moore declared that the race needed something other than "*vigorous* talk and loudmouthed railings in newspapers," and he urged the *Horizon* to "spend its energies in urging Negroes to buy homes and educate their children." Instead of fighting each other, Negroes should "punch" the white man "back either directly or indirectly. . . . When the race gets property and education this will go a long way to relieve us from our enemies in this country. We insist that emphasis at this time should be placed upon doing and being rather than talking and writing so-called vigorous editorials."[52] To Moore, race salvation lay primarily in economic development; to the *Horizon*, it lay basically in civil and political rights. The *Colored American Magazine* felt that Negroes should work through self-help and racial solidarity to improve themselves so that they would be worthy of the rights of citizens, while the *Horizon* demanded the immediate enforcement of those rights. Both were militant, but in different ways.

Nevertheless, the strain of militant protest running through the pages of the *Colored American Magazine*, and its failure to adopt an accommodating tone toward the white South, present something of a problem in view of its close relations with Booker T. Washington. This protest tendency was of course deeply rooted in the basic thinking of American Negroes. The matter assumes a larger significance because other journals of the Washington orbit, such as the Washington *Colored American*, the St. Paul and Chicago *Appeal*, the Indianapolis *Freeman*, and the A.M.E. *Christian Recorder*, exhibited similar tendencies and expressed themselves forcefully on political and civil rights. T. Thomas Fortune of the New York *Age* was known to be "independent," and Washington could not always depend upon him. Even more striking was Ben J. Davis, editor of the Atlanta *Independent*, who was an object of ridicule to his inimical contemporaries and has been something of a puzzle to modern scholars[53] because of his continual oscillation between abject subservience and dynamic militance. Characteristic was the statement of the Tuskegee-dominated Afro-American Press Association, which in 1903 went on record as vigorously opposed to disfranchisement, lynching, and inequality in education, and reaffirmed its "unalterable determination to contend in all lawful ways for every civil and political right which is ours under the Federal Constitution, and which is enjoyed without dispute by all other ethnic elements of the national State."[54] Consequently two pertinent questions arise: Why did Washington permit the tone of militant protest to assume the importance it did in journals of his orbit, and why did these journals with their militant protest outlook support Booker T. Washington?

Either or both of two hypotheses may explain the paradox of Washington supporting militant newspapers carrying a strong message of protest. In the first place, Washington may have been quite willing to support a journal that ordinarily did not adopt an accommodating tone, but did agitate in what he called "a manly way" and "without whining" for political and civil rights, as long as that organ supported him personally. On the other hand it is also possible that Washington was aware that he had to work with people as he found them, and could not expect his supporters to always agree with him. There is evidence to support both of these hypotheses.

In the first place Washington's papers do show that he was simply unable to command rigid adherence from the editors of his orbit. A striking case is seen in the activities of Fred R. Moore as editor and later owner of the New York *Age*. Several times Washington urged Moore to stop discussing "political" matters, and to treat instead the economic advancement of the race.[55] On one occasion in particular he protested to Moore that he was giving too much attention to lynchings.[56] Moreover, Washington was unable to prevent Moore from engaging in certain injudicious activities. Moore was friendly with the Tammany Hall Negro politicians, and, although Washington supported Taft, Moore opened the pages of the *Age* to anti-Taft writers in 1908, and was severely berating the national administration as late as 1911. Furthermore, Moore was on close terms with some of Washington's ex-associates and opponents like A.M.E. Zion Bishop Alexander Walters, who as president of the Afro-American Council swung that organization out of the Washington orbit in 1907.[57] Moore also appeared to be a great friend of the Niagara Movement's famous orator, the Reverend Reverdy C. Ransom, and boomed him for a bishopric in the A.M.E. Church at the very time that Washington was trying to head off this effort. Even worse, perhaps, certain of Moore's actions, instead of solidifying Washington's support, were making enemies for him among Negroes. In the face of all these things all that Washington did was to chide Moore occasionally and urge him to attack others less and be more constructive in his editorial policies.[58] On one occasion Washington wrote that there was little he could do to control *Age* policies unless he was willing to pay the bills. He added that he would not hesitate to direct the editorial expression of the *Age*, if he had the cash to support his demands.[59] Washington, however, remained convinced of Moore's personal loyalty to him.[60]

Washington, of course, was slow to criticize journals less close in their relationships with him. Yet occasionally he became rather irked. Once he complained angrily that the trouble with the Indianapolis *Freeman* was that it lacked a well-defined editorial outlook.[61] On another occasion he wrote sharply to a western supporter, Nick Chiles of the Topeka *Plaindealer*. Chiles replied vigorously that Washington's program was all right for the South, but not for the country as a whole. "We think," he said, "you will finally come to realize that it is not only wealth and education that are needed by the Negro . . . but a little manhood and courage to go along with it." Washington replied in somewhat chastened tones, that while he feared southern reaction to Chiles's editorial (which had been distributed widely over the South), he agreed that agitation and protest had their uses, and that his and Chiles's differing methods were necessary to the solution of the race problem.[62]

Though they were relatively rare, admissions of this nature were made also to Charles W. Chesnutt and others. But these seemed to be the sense of the matter to the majority of Washington's journalistic supporters. A good example of the supporters' point of view was given in 1903 by Cyrus Field Adams, editor of the Chicago *Appeal*. At the time Adams was one of the leading figures in the Washington orbit, being transportation agent of the National Negro Business League, secretary of the Afro-American Council, and president of the National Afro-American Press Association. In reviewing Du Bois's *Souls of Black Folk*, Adams praised the author for "an earnest . . . eloquent . . . and sincere appeal," but thought he had misunderstood Washington and done him a "great injustice. There is no contradiction," he said, "between the Washington theories and the words of the cultured advocate of higher education. . . . Nowhere . . . has Mr. Washington advised his people to give up their rights."[63] Undoubtedly most of the editors of the Washington orbit would have agreed with W. H. Lewis, assistant attorney general of the United States under Taft, when he described Washington as simply trying to bring the wooden horse inside the walls of Troy.[64]

It becomes apparent then that there were several reasons why various journals supported Booker T. Washington. A few editors perhaps agreed with his philosophy of accommodation. The majority were sympathetic with his emphasis upon economic development as the basic solution to the race prob-

lem. The sincerity of some of the editors who supported
Washington is not to be doubted. It should also be remembered
that Washington's ascendancy coincided with the period of
greatest oppression Negroes have faced since the Civil War.
The resulting discouragement and frustration explain much of
the instability in the ideologies of many individuals, and a great
deal of the support Washington received. Many editors stressed
the protest strands in his thinking and felt that his accommodating tendencies were necessary in view of his position in the
South. There were also, of course, some editors who joined the
Washington bandwagon from selfish calculations, and for
whatever Washington's cash, prestige, and influence might
bring them. In many cases, the motives were undoubtedly
largely mixed.

On the other hand, it is also clear that Washington had more
than one motive for allowing the journals in his orbit to carry a
message of militant protest. The evidence indicates that
Washington saw some value in agitation and protest, and was
willing to let his supporters use these techniques as long as they
supported him personally. Furthermore, the evidence is clear
that Washington was simply unable to control the activities of
even certain of his closest associates—most notably T. Thomas
Fortune and Fred R. Moore. In short it is apparent that
Washington could not exercise a dictatorial policy in regard to
the Negro press. While powerful, he needed the support of the
press as much as certain journals needed him. In such a situation, and given the dynamics of American society, a large
amount of compromise was necessary. It is difficult to see how it
could have been otherwise.

So, while Washington's influence over the Negro press was
enormous, it was not absolute—not even over those journals
which he subsidized heavily and, in part, owned. While it is true
that Washington used his influence over the Negro press to
squelch movements opposed to him, it is also true that most of
the leading journals in his orbit did not adopt his accommodating phraseology. The *Colored American Magazine* and other
journals undoubtedly expressed the outlook of the militant rising Negro bourgeoisie—the forerunner of the postwar New
Negro. Like Washington, this educated, prosperous, race-

conscious bourgeoisie viewed economic success as the key to social, cultural, and political advancement. Its members emphasized race pride and race solidarity as important ingredients in racial advancement along all lines. Significantly, they emphasized business development and not agricultural advancement, though the latter was the main objective of the Hampton-Tuskegee philosophy. They believed that their economic and cultural status entitled them then and there to the rights which Washington indicated as his goal. Washington's emphasis upon self-help, race pride, business development, and economic solidarity, and his undoubted goal of full citizenship rights, made, all in all, a program that squared well with the experience and self-interest of the Negro bourgeoisie. Like the other journals, the *Colored American Magazine* was basically militant in its outlook. It seized upon those elements in Washington's thought that were congenial with the point of view of the new Negro bourgeoisie. In this way in effect, the journals of the Washington orbit unwittingly made explicit the contradictions implicit in the Tuskegean's social philosophy. And indeed, their ideologies of racial solidarity, militant self-help, and economic advancement were transmutations of the philosophies of modern nationalism and bourgeois individualism into techniques for racial advancement leading to ultimate integration into American society. In conclusion, it is significant to note that the editors of the journals in the Washington orbit, and indeed Washington himself, shared in the basic desire of American Negroes throughout their history—the goal of assimilation and the rights of citizenship.

Thanks are due to John Hope Franklin, and to Marquis James and his research assistants Helena Hooker, Suzanne Carson, and Margaret Ells for helpful suggestions and information in the preparation of this article.

1. The Booker T. Washington Papers, Library of Congress.

2. The National Afro-American Press Association, and later the National Negro Press Association.

3. Washington Papers: Robert W. Taylor to Washington, Jan. 17, 1901; also a circular letter announcing a stockholders' meeting of the Colored Co-Operative Publishing Company to be held Dec. 30, 1901. See also Washington to Francis J. Garrison, May 17, 1905, in the Washington-Garrison Correspondence, Schomburg Collection, New York Public Library.

4. *Colored American Magazine*, 1, no. 1 (May, 1900), 3, 6. Copies at the Cleveland Public Library, and at the Moorland Foundation Room of the Howard University Library, Washington, D.C., together provide a fairly complete file of this periodical.

5. *Ibid.*, 1, no. 2 (June, 1900), 111–13.

6. *Ibid.*, 1, no. 1 (May, 1900), 61–62. The editor declared: "Much has been said about Mr. Washington's plans or methods. . . . His plans may not be yours, but I believe, if they reach the many poor boys and girls . . . of the South, you nor I could take exception to them. Complaint has often been made that he caters too much to the opposite race at the expense of his own, but we have failed . . . to discover any expression or sentence that would, in any way, convey such a thought. . . . Loyal to the welfare of the race . . . he is a benefactor . . . [who] does not deserve censure, criticism and calumny."

7. Fred R. Moore to Washington, Apr. 25, 1904. The *Colored American Magazine*, 7, nos. 1–2 (Jan.–Feb., 1904), 6; and no. 3 (Mar., 1904), 151–60. Freund was publisher of the magazine *Music Trades*. Moore wrote Washington that Freund contributed almost a thousand dollars to the *Colored American Magazine* while it was in Boston

8. John C. Freund to Washington, Mar. 26, 28, 1904; Washington to Freund, Mar. 27, 1904. Washington to W. H. Baldwin, Apr. 23, 1904.

9. See correspondence between Moore and Washington, and Washington and Simmons, 1906.

10. Moore in 1910 pointed out to Washington that he had assumed the editorship of the *Colored American Magazine*, and the office of national organizer of the National Negro Business League, at Washington's suggestion. Moore to Washington, Mar. 23, 1910.

11. Moore to Washington, Apr. 25, 1904.

12. Moore to Washington, May 20, 1904.

13. Moore to Washington, July 19, 1904. Moore asked Washington not to discuss the magazine's finances in the presence of T. Thomas Fortune, editor of the *Age*.

14. Washington to Moore, May 25, 1904.

15. Washington to Robert C. Ogden, July 16, 1904; Ogden to Washington, Aug. 9 and Sept. 24, 1904; Ogden to Moore, Sept. 24, 1904. Ogden, an executive of Wanamaker's department stores, was a member of the Tuskegee Institute Trustee Board, and chairman of the Board of Hampton Institute. He was also the chief promoter of the Southern Education Board, forerunner of the General Education Board of which he became chairman. Ogden declined to invest in the *Colored American Magazine* because he felt that it was not a sound venture.

16. Moore to Washington, Mar. 23, 1910. Moore stated that he himself invested $5,000 in the magazine.

17. Moore to Washington, Oct. 25 and Nov. 10, 1904. Washington to Moore, Oct. 29 1904.

18. Moore to Washington, Apr. 7, 1905; Washington to Moore, Apr. 21, 1905.

19. See telegraphic exchange: Washington to Moore, Oct. 4, 17, and 18, 1905, and Moore to Washington, Oct. 6 and 18, 1905; and letter from Moore to Washington, Oct. 18, 1905.

20. Moore to Washington, Mar. 2, 1906.

21. Moore to Scott, Nov. 5, 1907.

22. Washington to Moore, Sept. 8, 1908. Washington chided Moore for advertising the magazine's stock as bringing 6% interest, when it was losing money each month.

23. Washington to Moore, Mar. 9, 1909.

24. Memorandum dated 1909 (no day or month) "Copy for Mr. Moore," entitled "Decisions reached with regard to the New York Age." The provisions of this memorandum stated that the magazine would be discontinued if not sold within sixty days.

25. Moore to Washington, May (n.d.) and June 1, 1904; Moore to Scott, June 1, 1904; Scott to Moore, June 4, 1904.

26. Washington to Moore, May 17 and June 15, 1904; Moore to Scott, July 13, 1904; Scott to Moore, July 15, 1904.

27. Washington to R. L. Stokes, July 8, 1904.

28. *E.g.*, Moore to Scott, Aug. 16, 1904; Moore to Washington, Oct. 26, 1904; Washington to Moore, Oct. 31 and Nov. 30, 1904.

29. *E.g.*, Washington to Moore, Oct. 6, 1905. On one occasion Moore made a detailed explanation of his faults: Moore to Washington, May 24, 1905.

30. Undated manuscripts, 1906.

31. Moore to Scott, Nov. 5, 1907.

32. Washington to Roscoe Conkling Simmons, May 13, 1905. On one occasion Scott had to withdraw an arrangement for an exchange advertisement between the *Colored American Magazine* and the *Tuskegee Student*, after Washington found out about it. Scott to Moore, June 28, 1905.

33. The correspondence with and concerning Fortune is extensive and complex, and is scattered throughout the papers.

34. See, *e.g.*, correspondence with Peter J. Smith, Oct. and Nov., 1903. That was the year of the publication of Du Bois's *Souls of Black Folk*; of the concerted effort of the "radicals" (especially the Boston contingent) to oust Washington from his control of the Afro-American Council; and especially of the dramatic "Boston Riot," when Trotter's attempts to heckle Washington and break up a meeting at which he spoke landed the editor in jail.

35. See, *e.g.*, Alexander to Washington, Feb. 19 and Apr. 2, 1905, and telegram from Washington to Alexander, Apr. 2, 1905, for examples of appeals for funds. See Washington to Alexander, Apr. 8, and Alexander to Washington, Apr. 15, 1905, for Alexander changing the newspaper into a magazine at Washington's suggestion.

36. *E.g.*, correspondence between Scott and Washington, and Alexander, Sept. to Dec., 1907.

37. See esp. Scott to Washington, Dec. 16, 1904, regarding Tuskegee's financial support of E. E. Cooper.

38. W. Calvin Chase to Scott, Jan. 22, 1908; Chase to Washington, Feb. 7 and 24, 1908; Washington to Chase, Feb. 23, 1908. [Subsequent scholarship by Louis R. Harlan has revealed more details on Washington's relations with Chase and the *Bee*.]

39. See correspondence with Allison Sweeney from Apr. to Aug., 1903. Also T. Thomas Fortune to Washington, July 16 and 21, 1903. For Washington's mistrust of Sweeney, see Washington to Scott, July 29, 1903. On May 16, 1903, Washington sent Sweeney $50 for the purpose of improving the *Monitor*. Later Sweeney became editor of the *Conservator*, which changed hands (and consequently editorial policy) several times.

40. Washington to Moore, Oct. 12, 1905, March 21, April 8, 1906. The story of Washington's relationships with the *Voice of the Negro* is a complicated one. It was subsidized by Hertel, Jenkins and Company, publishers of certain of Washington's books. Washington at first contributed several articles to it, and Scott served on the editorial board. Tensions between Barber and Tuskegee existed from the very first, however, and Scott finally resigned angrily in 1905. The other editor, J. W. E. Bowen, tried to conciliate both sides. Later, in 1906, Washington was to be of assistance to Bowen in his successful bid for the presidency of Gammon Theological Seminary in Atlanta (Bowen to Washington, Nov. 2, 1906).

41. There can be little doubt, however, that in spite of Washington's disclaimers, the judicious use of advertising exerted a significant influence. Judge Robert H. Terrell once commented how easy it was to influence the Negro press with a little tact and diplomacy and by small advertisements. On the other hand, certain journals carried advertisements of Tuskegee free of charge (Terrell to Washington, Mar. 20, 1906).

42. Washington to Francis J. Garrison, May 17, 1905, in Washington-Garrison Correspondence, Schomburg Collection. See also Washington to J. C. Asbury, Feb. 22, 1904; and Washington to Alton H. Blake, Nov. 2, 1907, Washington Papers.

43. Washington to W. H. Steward, Jan. 10, 1904; Washington to Fortune, Jan. 12, 1904, and Fortune to Washington, Jan. 21, 1904; J. C. Asbury to William H. Hayes, Jan. 23, 1904; Washington to Hayes, Feb. 2, 1904.

44. Among the most interesting and surprising materials in the Washington papers are those dealing with his secret activities in opposition to Jim Crow and disfranchisement. While publicly he defended the disfranchisement amendments to the state con-

stitutions, on the grounds that they would encourage Negroes to obtain property and education, he personally spent thousands of dollars to test their constitutionality in the federal courts. So secret was the correspondence on the Alabama test cases involving disfranchisement and jury discrimination, that Emmett J. Scott and the lawyer Wilford H. Smith corresponded under the pseudonyms R. C. Black and J. C. May, respectively. (See correspondence between R. C. Black and J. C. May, 1903. Curiously enough, some of the correspondence relating to the court case against Monroe Trotter was conducted under the same pseudonyms. For Washington's participation in the Louisiana test case, officially sponsored by the Afro-American Council, see his correspondence with Jesse Lawson, 1901–3.) Washington was also interested in test cases with reference to peonage. And working through Archibald Grimké and Kelly Miller as intermediaries, he employed ex-Senator Henry W. Blair (noted for his espousal of federal aid to education) as a lobbyist to defeat the Warner-Foraker amendment to the Hepburn Act. This amendment, if passed, would have permitted or encouraged segregation on northern railroads. (Archibald H. Grimké to Washington, May 25 and June 10, 1906; Washington to Grimké, June 2, 4, and 18, 1906; Kelly Miller to Washington, May 22, 1906. Grimké before 1904 had been one of Washington's most extreme opponents. Kelly Miller was then professor of mathematics at Howard University, and was to become dean about a year later. Miller and Grimké acted as intermediaries, paying the necessary fees to Blair.) It is interesting to note that both the Afro-American Council and the Niagara Movement claimed credit for defeating the amendment by arousing public opinion.

45. *Colored American Magazine*, 7 (Nov., 1904), 693.

46. *Ibid.*, 13, no. 6 (Dec., 1907), 454. These sentiments did not, however, prevent Moore and Davis from being avid dabblers in politics.

47. *Ibid.*, 7, no. 8 (Aug., 1904), 530.

48. *Ibid.*, 13, no. 5 (Nov., 1907), 327–28. See also, 10, no. 1 (Jan., 1906), 640–42, where Moore urged Negroes to be like the Jews—a theme iterated often by Washington and others; 14, no. 1 (Jan., 1908), 8–9; 15, no. 3 (Mar., 1909), 133, etc.

49. *Ibid.*, 13, no. 6 (Dec., 1907), 413. Late in 1907, the famous clubwoman, Mary Church Terrell, first president of the National Association of Colored Women, whose husband, Judge Robert H. Terrell, had been named municipal judge in Washington, D.C., on the recommendation of Booker T. Washington, strayed too far from the Tuskegee line in her criticisms of the South. Considerable commotion resulted in the Washington circle, and the magazine declared: "While she was talking that way, Southern men were paying many thousand dollars in taxes to support Negro schools. Women employed in white homes know that their best friends are their employers, and that race peace and good feeling prevail throughout the South. Such intemperate utterances, based upon exceptions to the general rule, will be deplored by the thoughtful people of both races." Mrs. Terrell had particularly criticized the white South for plotting against Negro education, and for not protecting Negro domestic workers from the sexual advances of their employers.

50. *Ibid.*, 12, no. 5 (May, 1907), 327, 331.

51. *Ibid.*, 11, no. 4 (Oct., 1906), 217.

52. *Ibid.*, 13, no. 6 (Dec., 1907), 409.

53. Interview with Clarence A. Bacote of Atlanta University, Apr., 1952.

54. Address of the National Afro-American Press Association, adopted at its 24th annual meeting, Louisville, June 29, 1903. In Washington Papers.

55. Washington to Moore, *e.g.*, July 7, Nov. 8, 1908, and Feb. 28, 1909.

56. Washington to Moore, Aug. 29, 1908.

57. The Afro-American Council, founded in 1898 by Alexander Walters and T. Thomas Fortune (a resurrection of the earlier Afro-American League founded by T. Thomas Fortune in 1890), was the leading organization among Negroes in the early years of the twentieth century. It is clear from the Washington Papers that the Tuskegean deliberately attempted and was successful in dominating the activities of the Council, in spite of its militant ideological outlook. His control was seriously threatened

by the radicals at the Louisville Convention in 1903, but he retained his grasp. In 1906 he was able to keep the Council from making extreme statements on the Atlanta Riot and the Brownsville affair. (See, *e.g.*, Washington to Fortune, Nov. 3, 1903, and Washington to Anderson, Oct. 4, 1906.) Washington, of course, denied to outsiders that he was trying to control the Council (Washington to Francis J. Garrison, May 17, 1905, Schomburg Collection).

58. This information is contained in a stream of letters written between 1907 and 1913 by Charles W. Anderson, collector of internal revenue in New York, and one of Washington's most intimate friends and loyal supporters. Washington's replies substantiate, in guarded form, the truth of the charges. See, *e.g.*, Anderson to Washington, Sept. 28, 1907; Feb. 24, 1908; Jan. 3 and Apr. 12, 1909; Oct. 24, 1910; Jan. 17, 25, Feb. 20, Mar. 28, Apr. 4, May 4, June 5, and Sept. 29, 1911; Mar. 9, 1912; Sept. 11, 1913. Washington to Anderson, Apr. 15 and Oct. 27, 1910; Jan. 23, June 9, and an undated letter, 1911. Anderson to Scott, Apr. 2, 1913. Washington to Moore, Mar. 6 and Apr. 12, 1908.

59. Washington to Anderson, Apr. 7, 1910.

60. Calvin Chase of the Washington *Bee* once remarked: "It has been a common saying that 'God could not make Fred Moore an editor, but Booker Washington did.'" Washington *Bee*, Dec. 21, 1912.

As amazing as Moore was Charles Alexander. Advertisements, articles, and editorial comments in both *Alexander's Magazine* and the *Horizon* indicate a friendly relationship between the editors of the two journals. Alexander carried advertisements, quotations, and favorable comments on the works of Du Bois. For months his magazine carried a full-page advertisement urging readers to buy Du Bois's *Souls of Black Folk* through him. Through much of 1907 and 1908 Alexander strongly opposed Taft. And just when Tuskegee was doing its level best to hush up the agitation over the Brownsville affair, *Alexander's* reprinted *twice* "The Black Battalion," Foraker's famous defense of the Brownsville soldiers.

61. Washington to Scott, July 9, 1904.

62. Nick Chiles to Washington, Nov. 12, 1906; Washington to Chiles, Nov. 19, 1906. On support and advertisements previously given by Washington to Chiles, see Chiles to Washington, Oct. 27 and Nov. 8, 1905, and Washington to Chiles, Nov. 28, 1905.

63. Cyrus Field Adams to Washington, July 24, 1903, and accompanying clipping from the Chicago *Appeal*. H. T. Kealing expressed an almost identical viewpoint in an editorial in the A.M.E. *Church Review*, 20, no. 1 (July, 1903), 97–101.

64. Cited in J. C. Asbury to William H. Hayes, Jan. 23, 1904.

FOUR

Booker T. Washington and the Rise of the NAACP

BY AUGUST MEIER

The story of the birth of the National Association for the Advancement of Colored People, and of Booker T. Washington's relations with it, properly begins some years before the Association was organized in 1909–10. Among Negroes, opposition to the accommodating philosophy of the Tuskegean achieved organized form by 1903. In the spring of that year appeared W. E. B. Du Bois's *Souls of Black Folk*, with its critical essay, "Of Booker T. Washington and Others." In July, Monroe Trotter and other "radicals" from Boston—long a center of "Anti-Bookerite" sentiment—noisily and unsuccessfully attempted to unhorse "The Wizard" (as Washington was often called) from his control of the Afro-American Council, at that time the leading Negro rights organization. A few weeks later Trotter precipitated the "Boston Riot" by heckling Washington at a public meeting and trying to ask him a few pertinent questions. During 1903 and 1904, first the National Negro Suffrage League, and then the New England Suffrage and Georgia Equal Rights Leagues proved troublesome to Washington. Certain well-established journals, like the Chicago *Conservator* and the Washington *Bee*, had consistently criticized Washington, and in 1904 there appeared *The Voice of the Negro*, easily the most outstanding Negro magazine of the period, but one which soon proved to be something less than a friend to Tuskegee. Then, in 1905, came the Niagara Movement.

Washington viewed "the opposition" as a threat to the success of his program, and probably also as a threat to his power and

From *The Crisis*, 61, no. 2 (Feb., 1954), 69–76, 117–23. Reprinted with permission. © 1954 by the Crisis Publishing Company.

prestige. A study of the Washington Papers reveals that the Tuskegean had for his goals full equality and citizenship rights. He sincerely believed that an approach stressing economic development and vocational education, attacking mob violence tactfully and only occasionally, and flattering southern upper-class whites and northern industrialists, would eventually accomplish the ends desired by both himself and his critics. At the very time when he publicly minimized the importance of the franchise, he was deeply involved in the politics of the Roosevelt administration, exerted tremendous influence over political patronage dispensed to Negroes and certain southern whites, fought a desperate and losing action against the encroachments of the lily-white Republicans, and secretly financed the Alabama and Louisiana test cases against southern disfranchisement. He was instrumental in taking to the Supreme Court cases involving peonage and the exclusion of Negroes from juries. He did not complain about segregation and he abjured "social equality," yet he secretly employed a lobbyist to defeat a congressional bill that would have encouraged railroad segregation in the North; and he traveled in social circles in the North and abroad that few southern whites could enter.

Nor, for the most part, did those Negro newspapers which supported Washington adopt his accommodating tone. H. T. Johnson of the A.M.E. *Christian Recorder*, for example, was on cordial terms with Washington and wrote strong editorials in his favor. But he wrote equally strong ones against southern outrages and discrimination. Even an organ like the New York *Age*, which was heavily subsidized and for a time partly owned by Washington, was militant in its outlook. Again, Washington was friendly with the author Charles Chesnutt, who, though in ideological agreement with the "radicals," entertained a sincere admiration for the Tuskegean. In short, what appeared to bother Washington about his critics was not "whining and complaining," or their outspoken attacks upon the South and their demands for the ballot and civil rights, but their equally outspoken criticism of him and his program.

Undoubtedly he felt that their attack upon his leadership jeopardized the success of the only program he thought would

win Negroes their full rights. At the same time his papers lead
one to suspect that, subconsciously at least, he feared the loss of
his own ascendancy. In view of his tactful manipulation of most
situations, his bitter and often vindictive battle with his critics
can hardly be otherwise explained. Indeed, the evidence
suggests that Washington was frightened by the attacks made
upon him. He never questioned the sincerity or good will of the
"better class" of southern whites, or of the northern industrialists who supported him, or of Presidents Roosevelt and Taft,
with all their shilly-shallying on the race problem; but he found
it almost impossible to credit the integrity of his liberal critics,
who were more interested in the advancement of colored
people than many of his supporters. There is no reason to
doubt Washington's sincerity. So thoroughly did he identify his
success with that of his program that he was unable to ascribe
any but selfish motives to his opponents.

Even before the Louisville Convention of the Afro-American
Council, Washington had taken steps to undercut "the opposition." Early in 1902 Roscoe Conkling Bruce, son of Reconstruction Senator Blanche K. Bruce, was a student at Harvard; he
later became head of Tuskegee's academic department. The
younger Bruce was attempting to wean Clement Morgan away
from the other "radicals," and trying to obtain the dismissal of
George Washington Forbes, co-editor of Trotter's *Guardian*,
from his post in the Boston Library. Again, early in 1903,
A.M.E. Zion Bishop Alexander Walters was in Boston to prevent "the opposition" from using a public meeting to denounce
Washington. During the agitated spring and summer of 1903
Washington bent his efforts, especially through his contacts
with the Negro press, to quiet the calls for conventions, and to
keep the Afro-American Council, which he controlled, as the
sole organization of Negro action. In August he asked his secretary, Emmett J. Scott, to have certain trustworthy journals publish a Tuskegee-prepared attack on the "radicals" as coming
from a "Boston correspondent." Washington vigorously pressed
the prosecution of Trotter for his role in the "Boston Riot," and
it was at the behest of the Tuskegee group that William Pickens,
then a student at Yale, sued Trotter's *Guardian* for libel.

Meanwhile, Washington had been working for a meeting with

"the opposition" in an attempt at conciliation. Such a conference met at Carnegie Hall in New York in January, 1904. Though the meeting was secret, it appears that Washington clarified his stand on ultimate goals and temporarily convinced most of his critics of his sincerity and loyalty to the cause of Negro advancement. But the pot was almost immediately merrily boiling again. Trotter, though not a member of the conference, tried to have his version of the proceedings published in the daily press—an effort neatly foiled by the Washington group. E. H. Morris, member of the Illinois legislature, past Grand Master of the Odd Fellows, and a member of the conference, violently denounced Washington in an address titled "Shams" before the noted Bethel Literary and Historical Association in Washington. The Tuskegean himself immediately made an extended tour to present his view to Negro audiences, and for the next two years he made numerous addresses emphasizing the necessity of stressing industrial education and economic development, but also recognizing the importance of higher education and political and civil rights.

Nor did Washington discard less overt maneuvers. In fact, a rising crescendo of criticism undoubtedly made further astute measures appear imperative. Disliking the tactics of the National Negro Suffrage League and its president, Richmond lawyer James H. Hayes, he urged that papers friendly to his own position ignore the movement, and sent T. Thomas Fortune editorial copy with which to subtly attack the League in the New York *Age*. Fortune and others, nevertheless, hammered away at Hayes. Working through a mutual friend, Washington temporarily convinced Hayes of the error of his ways, and of the value of cooperation with the Tuskegean. Once Hayes had come around, Washington wrote him an unusually revealing letter, apologizing for being unable to stop Fortune's attacks, but noting that—as he had promised—the other papers had ceased to disturb Hayes.

This incident shows how Washington employed one of his most effective instruments—the Negro press—against his critics. Through the influence of strategically placed friends, by judicious use of advertisements and subscriptions and subsidies for special issues, through control over the Negro press associations, in some cases by supplying actual editorial copy, in half a dozen instances by substantial cash contributions, and in two cases by securing part ownership in a journal, Washington exercised wide influence. In Boston he subsidized first the *Colored Citizen* and later *Alexander's Magazine* to offset Trotter's *Guardian*. In Washington he assisted E. E. Cooper's struggling *Colored American* against Calvin Chase's *Bee*, later apparently obtaining Chase's support by a similar method. In Chicago he toyed with the idea of subsidizing a rival to the hostile *Conservator*, but was unable to find a dependable editor. After many efforts the Tuskegee group in 1907 finally succeeded in buying the leading journal of the time—the New York *Age*—from Washington's undependable friend, T. Thomas Fortune. The evidence also suggests that in 1904 Washington and Fred R. Moore acquired the *Colored American Magazine* so as to have an effective rival to the *Voice of the Negro*.

Throughout 1904 and 1905 steps were taken to squelch "the opposition." In September, 1904, Washington directed his close associate, Charles W. Anderson, collector of internal revenue in New York, to thwart Trotter's efforts to get a campaign subsidy from the Connecticut Republican Committee. More significant was Washington's infiltration of the New England Suffrage League, formed under Trotter's leadership in October, 1904. At this meeting Clifford H. Plummer, posing as an opponent of Washington, worked successfully in the resolutions committee and on the floor to eliminate any expression of anti-Washington sentiment, and secured a place on the organization's executive committee.

The Niagara Movement formed in July, 1905, called forth similar tactics. While in letters to each other the Tuskegee group dismissed the movement as consisting of selfish notoriety seekers, "unmoneyed patriots" whose very stinginess would lead to failure, actions belied this whistling in the dark. Collector Anderson immediately suggested that a way be found to oust L. M. Hershaw, later an editor of the Niagara Movement's *Horizon* magazine, from his government position. Acting on a telegram from Washington, Scott asked R. W. Thompson of the National Press Bureau not to mention the movement in his dispatches, and to influence various journals to the same effect.

Only one journal "heretofore favorable" to Washington seemed equivocal in its attitude, and Washington, expressing concern lest he "lose" any "friends," suggested that its editor be invited to Tuskegee "at our expense" for a conference. Yet in spite of all these efforts, Washington found it "puzzling" that some of his supporters had "discussed" the Niagara Movement on the assumption that its members were "honest." In later years he planted materials in the New York *Age* deprecating the movement's influence.

Washington also tried to infiltrate the new movement. At the end of 1905 he urged his trusted confidant, Charles Anderson, to find someone who could enter the "inner circles" of the organization and secure information about its "operations." Whether or not Anderson was able to do so, it is certain that by the time of the Niagara Movement's Harpers Ferry meeting in August, 1906, Washington had secured the services of Richard T. Greener, the first Negro graduate from Harvard and the consul at Vladivostok from 1897 to 1901. Informing Greener that the aim of the Niagara Movement was "to defeat" all that he did, and that he had tried to work with Du Bois, who had "been fooled" by Trotter and others into believing himself a "leader," Washington asked Greener to make every effort to enter into "the inside of things."

Meanwhile, opposition to Washington's program was developing among liberal whites. Originally supporters of Washington, men like John E. Milholland and Oswald Garrison Villard eventually became impatient with his tactics and moved over into the opposition.

John E. Milholland, a Republican politician and president of the Batcheller Pneumatic Tube Company, manufacturers of equipment for rapid underground mail transit in large cities, was interested in a variety of reform movements. He was on cordial terms with Washington during the stormy days of 1903, contributing substantially to what appears to have been the Alabama test case. About 1904 he took the lead in organizing the Constitution League, whose purpose was to attack disfranchisement, peonage, and mob violence by court action, legislation, and propaganda. As an interracial protest organization it, like the Niagara Movement, was one of the precursors of the NAACP. League secretary Andrew M. Humphrey made an early effort to enlist the tacit support of Washington for its activities. In view of Washington's peculiar position in the South, he disclaimed any hope of close cooperation, but welcomed Washington's cordial assurance to help in furthering the "common cause." Nor was it long before the Tuskegean had recourse to the League. In characteristic indirect fashion he had Humphrey submit—as the views of representative colored men—strongly worded planks on Negro rights to the platform committee of the 1904 Republican national convention.

Affairs ran fairly smoothly between Washington and Milholland until the summer of 1905. An unfortunate error which prevented Milholland's speaking at the convention of Washington's National Negro Business League in August brought forth an apology from Washington, who hoped he had not lost the friendship of one so courageous and "generous" in working for Negro rights. Though Milholland accepted the apology, it was only a short time before he and Washington had reached a fundamental disagreement over the Platt bill, which proposed to end disfranchisement by reducing the congressional representation of discriminating states in accordance with the Fourteenth Amendment. Washington consistently opposed such measures on the ground that the South would accept reduction in representation and thus stamp disfranchisement with the seal of constitutionality. And so Milholland found that the League's efforts for the bill were always met with the same reply, from the President on down, that Booker Washington was opposed to it. Probably because of Washington's attitude, Milholland turned to others like Trotter and Du Bois. Although Milholland expressed continued friendliness toward Washington, the latter was distinctly nettled, and came to believe that Milholland was merely a " 'professional' friend" of Negroes, using them to further his own ends. Relationships remained edgy through most of 1906. And then came the Brownsville affair to precipitate new crises and a permanent break.

Undoubtedly Washington did all he could to stay Roosevelt's hand from dishonorably discharging the members of the 25th U.S. Infantry, stationed at Fort Brown, Texas, on charges of "shooting up" nearby Brownsville. But once Roosevelt and Secretary of War Taft had taken their action, Washington remained loyal to them, feeling that they had made a sincere though unfortunate mistake. Most Negroes and liberal whites felt otherwise. Immediately upon receipt of news of Roosevelt's order of November 5, 1906, Milholland sent Mary Church Terrell to see Secretary Taft. Mrs. Terrell, first president of the National Association of Colored Women, was the wife of District of Columbia Judge Robert H. Terrell, who owed his appointment to the influence of Washington. At her request, Taft delayed the execution of the order thirty-six hours until President Roosevelt returned to Washington. The League held a series of indignation meetings in various cities and sent Gilchrist Stewart, a Tuskegee graduate, to Texas to make an investigation. Upon Stewart's return he and Mrs. Terrell had an interview with the President, who merely promised to send their evidence to the War Department.

Washington perceived the fine hand of the Constitution League in all this agitation. Early in 1907 he informed Postmaster General Cortelyou that it was Milholland, who derived most of his income from selling pneumatic tube equipment to the post office department, who, as the mainstay of the Constitution League, was mainly responsible for stirring up the Brownsville agitation. Washington, indeed, was so closely associated with the national administration that it was only natural that opposition to him should be practically identical with opposition to Roosevelt and Taft. As Washington worked to swing Negro support behind Taft in the election of 1908, he found his chief difficulty to be the Constitution League. Undoubtedly the Tuskegee group's most remarkable effort in this direction was a famous editorial in the New York *Age*, entitled "The Brownsville Ghouls." Written by the auditor of the navy, Ralph W. Tyler, who was active in lining up the Negro press behind Taft, this piece—without calling names—pictured the opposition as "human ghouls, worthless parasites who represent nothing save selfish avarice," who had led "the race into ambush" by preying upon the misfortunes of the Brownsville soldiers in their greedy desire for personal advancement.

Tyler was also directed to inform a Washington *Post*

correspondent—who was gathering material on anti-Taft sentiment among Negroes—that such feelings emanated entirely from a small group associated with the Constitution League. Further steps against the opposition included exerting pressure to prevent the election of the Niagara Movement's famous orator, A.M.E. minister Reverdy C. Ransom, to the post of editor of the *Christian Recorder*, and of the Reverend S. L. Corrothers to a bishopric in the A.M.E. Zion Church. But all in all it was a difficult time for Washington. Gilchrist Stewart and others were playing both sides, claiming friendship with Washington and yet working on salary for the League, and informing the League of Washington's "political moves." Washington came to feel that the initiative had passed out of his hands, and that the League's offices were the "headquarters" of all the opposition to him. He now judged Milholland to be a "dangerous" person, jealous of any Negro of prominence, a man who was playing the "old carpet-bag game" of using supposed Negro support as a bargaining point at Republican conventions, and one who would battle Washington until the "Blacklegs" and "schemers" on the League's payroll had squandered all his money. (Washington said this group included W. A. Sinclair, author and field secretary of the League, Ransom, Bishop Walters, Trotter, and J. Max Barber, formerly editor of *The Voice of the Negro*.) In spite of all the concern the League caused Washington, the majority of Negroes remained loyal to the Republican ticket in 1908. Only a few like Bishop Walters and Du Bois supported Bryan that year.

With Oswald Garrison Villard, wealthy capitalist, philanthropist, and publisher of the New York *Evening Post*, Washington maintained a closer relationship than he had with Milholland. During the exciting summer of 1903 Villard had addressed the National Negro Business League at its meeting in Nashville. When the *Post* supported the Platt bill for reducing southern representation in Congress, Washington worked through eminent men like his own close friend William H. Baldwin, president of the Long Island Railroad; Wallace Buttrick, agent of the General Education Board; and the liberal Southerner of New York, Walter Hines Page, to change Villard's views. From 1905 to 1909 there was a continual flow of cordial correspondence about various matters, including the Manassas Industrial School in which Villard was deeply interested, Villard's address at the twenty-fifth anniversary of Tuskegee in 1906, and especially Villard's campaign to raise $157,000 as the William H. Baldwin Memorial Fund for the Tuskegee endowment. Once Washington asked Villard for two or three hundred dollars for a legal fight against the practice of sentencing to the chain gang colored farm tenants who had violated their contracts. On one occasion Villard referred to Washington as a man with a "rare and pure spirit."

But Villard was not entirely isolated from the opposition. He and his uncle Francis J. Garrison displayed considerable concern over charges that Washington was subsidizing various journals. In a lengthy letter in 1905 Washington denied that he subsidized or possessed shares in any newspaper or magazine, or that he deliberately exercised control over any Negro organizations. Though at variance with the facts, Washington's denials were so convincingly stated that Villard declared to his uncle that Washington's letter was "absolutely satisfactory," and that he wished he might show it to Du Bois "and shut him up."

Yet Villard was not entirely satisfied with current efforts for the advancement of colored people. Neither Washington's indirection, nor the agitation of the declining Niagara Movement and Afro-American Council, nor the noisy Constitution League were effectively stemming the seemingly irresistible tide of segregation, disfranchisement, and race riots. The remedy lay, Villard wrote Washington in 1908, in a "strong central defense committee" which would secure land, bring cases of lynching to court, agitate for Negro rights, and maintain a publications bureau.

Others too were thinking of the necessity of an effective rights organization. The story of how William English Walling, Mary White Ovington, and Dr. Henry Moskowitz prevailed upon Villard to issue a call for a conference on the Negro to be held on May 30, 1909, and how their meeting resulted in the NAACP, has been frequently told. Washington declined Villard's invitation to attend the conference and in tactful terms clearly stated his position. He denied that he was afraid to attend, but felt that his presence might deter free discussion and might harm the cause of Negro education and interfere with the work which he alone could do in the South. He agreed that "agitation and criticism" were valuable, but felt that they were not a "cure-all." The NAACP, incorporated in 1910, never formally united with the Niagara Movement, or with the remnants of the Afro-American Council which its president, Bishop Walters, had brought out of Washington's orbit in 1907, or with the Constitution League, which maintained an independent existence for some time. But most of their members joined the new movement. In short, the NAACP was the climax of a rising protest movement among Negroes and whites against race discrimination and the Washington tactics. It was the most effective instrument of agitation and protest for Negro rights formed since slavery times, and by the same token was the most effective combination of forces against Washington's methods yet organized.

In the first months following the conference of 1909 Collector Anderson in New York did his best by speeches and personal influence to counteract the "anti-Bookerites" like Du Bois, Walters, and Ransom, though Villard and Washington remained on cordial terms. Then, in April, 1910, Anderson, recalling his consistent dislike of Villard, called to Tuskegee's attention a new and critical note in the editorial policy of the *Post*. He also informed Washington that Villard and Milholland were discussing a merger of the Constitution League and the committee formed at the 1909 conference, with Du Bois to be a paid executive. These developments, he said, strengthened his opinion that "certain" whites were trying to "lessen" Washington's influence. Washington took immediate steps to "lessen" the influence of the NAACP, which had been incorporated in May, 1910. The evidence suggests, for example, that at Washington's request H. T. Kealing, editor of the *A.M.E. Church Review*, declined to serve on the NAACP executive board. When it was definitely ascertained that Du Bois would take charge of publicity and research for the NAACP, Washington directed Anderson to enlarge his Republican Club so as to include representatives of all Negro groups in the city, and thus put the collector in "control" of the "situation." Yet Washington remained friendly with Villard, who addressed the

Negro Business League convention in 1910 with an appeal on behalf of the NAACP.

Meanwhile, Robert Russa Moton, commandant of cadets at Hampton Institute, was working for an understanding with the opposition. Of all the members of the Tuskegee circle he was the one who maintained the most friendly relations with Washington's critics. He was on especially good terms with Atlanta Baptist (later Morehouse) College president John Hope, who was a member of the Niagara Movement and an intimate of Du Bois. During the summer of 1910 Moton conferred with Villard and received the latter's assurances that the NAACP was not attacking Hampton, Tuskegee, or Booker T. Washington. He also tried—unsuccessfully—to secure a conference between Washington and Du Bois through the mediation of John Hope.

Moton's efforts received a rude setback in October, 1910, during Washington's lecture tour in England. NAACP treasurer Milholland distributed a circular in London attacking Washington's optimistic utterances and asserting that the *Post* had turned against the Tuskegean. Shortly afterwards a group of Negroes headed by Du Bois circulated an attack upon Washington in the same city. Giving their address as "Headquarters, National Negro Committee, 20 Vesey Street, New York" (the address of the NAACP), this circular denied that "the Negro problem in America is in process of satisfactory solution," and declared that "Washington's large responsibilities have made him dependent on the rich charitable public and that, for this reason, he has for years been compelled to tell, not the whole truth, but that part of which certain powerful interests in America wish to appear as the whole truth." "In flat contradiction to the pleasant pictures" depicted by Washington, the circular enumerated the grievances suffered by American Negroes, and appealed for "the moral support of . . . Europe in this crusade for the recognition of manhood. . . . It is," the signers concluded, "one thing to be optimistic . . . and forgiving, but it is quite a different thing, consciously or unconsciously to misrepresent the truth." Meanwhile Washington had been attacked at an NAACP meeting in Chicago, and by Du Bois in Washington, D.C. To Booker T. Washington all this was evidence of Villard's insincerity in claiming that neither he nor the NAACP were against Washington or Hampton and Tuskegee. At Washington's request, Moton wrote Villard and John Hope about the situation, asking for frankness and reiterating his desire for conciliation between the two groups.

In replying to both Moton and Washington, Villard insisted that the NAACP was not fighting Hampton and Tuskegee or Booker T. Washington, and explained that it was not responsible for Milholland's or Du Bois's statements. Yet he frankly admitted substantial agreement with their views. He pointed out, however, that his philanthropic activities in behalf of Manassas and Tuskegee certainly showed him to be no foe of industrial education, and that he never failed to speak hopefully of Washington at NAACP meetings. Negroes had taken forward steps under Washington's "leadership," but "prejudice and discrimination" had increased even more rapidly, and Washington had done little to stop them. Villard respected Washington's sincerity, but felt that he had been led "astray" by his "optimism," that he was not speaking out against the many "evils" needing correction, but was saying what the South liked to hear; and that, indeed, certain of Washington's activities had been "most hurtful" to the Negroes.

Moton expressed discouragement at ever being able to do anything with the NAACP group, and dismissed the claim that the NAACP was not responsible for the activities of its officials as "moonshine." But Washington replied to Villard, defending his course and citing quotations from recent speeches to show that he did speak out on "public questions." He thought Villard had mistaken views because he associated with "sour" and "unhappy" northern Negroes, failures in life who were not in a position to observe actual conditions in the South. In turn Villard defended Milholland as an "unselfish" "friend of liberty" whom Washington had once found useful. Washington, he said, presented only the pleasant side, and remained silent about "increasing prejudice and injustice." He resented Washington's aspersions upon his friends, pointing out that acquaintances like Mary Church Terrell were not unhappy, and that Du Bois could hardly be called unsuccessful. He assured Washington that objections raised by his critics were not personal, but were concerned solely with ideological matters. Meanwhile Washington kept supplying Villard with clippings showing good race relations in the South, and Villard wrote editorials about some of them.

During the winter of 1910/11 Charles Anderson was in his "shirt-sleeves," working "day and night"—making numerous speeches, manipulating situations, talking to people—so as ·to keep down the influence of the NAACP. In order to "monopolize" the public speaking in New York, he devised a plan whereby each of Washington's friends in the city prepared two speeches, setting forth the "proper doctrine," for use at any time. Particularly trying were defections from the Washington circle. Anderson worked hard to counteract the unfortunate influence of *Age* editor Fred R. Moore, who consorted with radicals and Democrats like Ransom and Walters and antagonized Washington's supporters, though it was Washington who had made him editor. When Villard informed Washington that the Constitution League and the NAACP would not merge, and asked him not to hold the NAACP "liable" for the League's actions, Washington skeptically thought that Villard and Milholland either had come to a parting of the ways or had decided to let the League do the "dirty work," while the NAACP would "inveigle" Washington's friends into its program. That the NAACP was "inveigling" Washington's friends was evident, for in January, 1911, Anderson reported that some of them had attended a reception for Du Bois arranged by Walters, and complained that most of them were "loyal" only when Washington was close by.

The success of Du Bois, Walters, and others was evident also in the disconcerting number of Negroes who voted for the Democrats in 1910. Washington was able to help Anderson but little in his struggle to keep their ranks intact. Terribly busy, and with the opposition steadily "hammering" at him, he found himself mentally and physically unable .to cope with such "details." Yet he maintained an eager interest in Anderson's activities, directed him to have Moore write an editorial that would "'burn [William English] Walling up,'" and personally did all he could to wean the eminent financier Jacob Schiff away from his interest in the NAACP.

In the midst of these efforts Washington was severely beaten in New York in March, 1911, for allegedly approaching a white woman. All factions rushed to his defense, and an era of good feelings followed. Anderson reported that almost everyone but Du Bois was now "talking right." Individuals ranging from Ransom to Anderson addressed a mass meeting at Ransom's Bethel A.M.E. Church. At Villard's request Washington sent a message of greeting to the NAACP's annual meeting. He and Anderson agreed that since all but Du Bois had "softened" toward Washington, not to adopt a "conciliatory course" would lay Washington open to the charge of narrowness and furnish a weapon for "the scoundrels" of the opposition. In his telegram to the NAACP Washington pledged his "friendly cooperation," and declared that he was "convinced" that the time had come to put away "personal bickerings" and to work with "mutual understanding," though along different lines. The NAACP passed a resolution regretting the assault upon Washington, and, at the Tuskegean's suggestion, appointed two fraternal delegates to the next Business League meeting. For his part Washington soon informed Villard that the wealthy drug manufacturer William Jay Schieffelin had agreed to serve on the NAACP educational committee, and that efforts were being made to stop Fred R. Moore from attacking the Association in the *Age*. In his forthcoming book, *My Larger Education*, Washington, though critical of the "intellectuals," gave favorable mention to Villard. And Moton, who attended the Races Congress in London the next summer in order to counteract NAACP action, was pleasantly surprised at the moderate statements of Du Bois and Milholland.

The only sour note in this love feast was their relationship between Tuskegee and Du Bois. Washington felt that Du Bois was the only one who had not "softened" toward him, and both he and Anderson hoped that the revival of general friendliness toward Washington would isolate Du Bois. Anderson was still suspicious of the "crocheteers in Vesey Street," but for Washington's sake he had done the "strange" thing of acquiring a large number of "olive branches," and was "maintaining" a "precautionary respect . . . just now" toward the "Vesey Street crowd." At Washington's request the collector made representations to the administration against Milholland's attempt to secure Du Bois a place on the Haytian Commission. Even Moton finally came to feel that it was hopeless to expect any "co-operation" from Du Bois, and that it would be a waste of time to try working with any movement in which he was active. Furthermore, to Washington's pleasure, Anderson secured the dismissal of the Socialist lecturer and pamphleteer Hubert H. Harrison from his place in the postal service because of anti-Washington articles he had written.

Villard and Washington remained on friendly terms until 1913. New tensions then arose in regard to Villard's sponsorship of an association of Negro industrial schools. Villard was naturally interested in such a project because of his connection with Manassas. But Washington was suspicious because the first meeting was to be held in the same building in which the NAACP had its offices. Denying that he was "too fearful," he wrote Villard that it would be unfortunate to "confuse the work" of the NAACP with southern education, but that he would send a representative if the conference were held elsewhere. To Scott he expressed the view that "the real purpose" of the new organization was to create the impression that Washington was working with the National Association. Villard, writing to Moton, called Washington's refusal "cowardly," but changed the meeting place. Moton however agreed with Washington, and thought it would be most unwise to meet in "Du Bois' . . . office," and that Washington had shown real courage to reply as he had. Villard went ahead anyhow, but he and Washington never agreed on the matter, and it was only a question of time before the organization died.

Moton continued, in spite of discouragements and a growing pessimism, to mediate between Washington and the NAACP. In March, 1914, he wrote Villard that while he "appreciated" the work of the Association, he questioned some of its methods and was especially disturbed by criticisms which Joel Spingarn, chairman of the Association's executive board, had made at a Chicago meeting. Villard did not agree with Spingarn, but he still felt that Washington was in a "pitiful position"—"like Nero, fiddling while Rome burns," and silent, while Negroes were being deprived of "one right after another." He felt that Washington was becoming "anathema" to educated Negroes and was losing his position as a "real leader." He was especially pained because he had always been a "loyal supporter" of Washington and Tuskegee, raising the Baldwin Fund, and rushing to Washington's defense after the New York incident of 1911.

Moton didn't appreciate Villard's description of the Tuskegean, but he still thought Villard sincere and wishing to "help," though misguided and "deceived" by others. While Scott thought it was hopeless to make more attempts to convince Villard, Moton arranged a conference between Villard and Moore in order to iron out difficulties between the *Age* and the Association, and to give Moore an opportunity to convince Villard of the erroneousness of his views. Nothing fruitful was accomplished, however, and Washington resignedly wrote Moton that he would not become "bitter" just because certain "good friends" like Villard did not "understand" him. He went on to say that outrages and injustices "pained" him just as much as they did others, but that in the long run he felt his program the more constructive.

Yet Washington resented what he thought was Villard's attempt to dominate him. Effecting a rapprochement with Walters early in 1914, he and the Bishop entered upon a campaign to influence the press to emphasize the importance of Negro leadership. Such leadership would welcome the "advice" of "disinterested" individuals like Dr. Frissell of Hampton, but would not be dominated by any single white man — that is, Washington meant, by Villard. It is curious that Washington put such faith in paternalistic do-gooders like Frissell, who were skeptical of any ultimate full equality for racial minorities in the United States, yet was suspicious of genuine liberals like Villard.

Truly cordial relationships were not reestablished before Washington died late in 1915. In March of that year Charles Anderson thought it advantageous to play a petty trick on the NAACP. Spingarn, Du Bois, Villard, Fred R. Moore (!), and others had obtained a hearing before the mayor of New York in order to protest the showing of *The Birth of a Nation*. Anderson promptly cut the ground from under them by seeing the mayor first, so that the delegation must have felt foolish when informed by the mayor that he had already censored the picture.

Washington was delighted that Anderson had forestalled the NAACP "crowd" and taken "the wind out of their sails."

But in spite of all that Washington did, the NAACP continued to grow. Du Bois's *Crisis* proved a phenomenal success. A number of important figures friendly to Washington had come over to the Association. The election of Moton instead of Emmett Scott to the Tuskegee presidency after Washington's death meant that a moderate who had long tried to find a meeting ground with the opposition, and who in 1918 said he was a friend of Du Bois, now led the Hampton-Tuskegee group. In 1916 Joel Spingarn sponsored the Amenia Conference, attended by representatives of all points of view ranging from Emmett Scott to Monroe Trotter. Even Scott was softened by this conference into friendly feelings for Spingarn. And then in 1917 the NAACP played an ironic master stroke in selecting one of the most talented and capable individuals in the Washington orbit—James Weldon Johnson—as its field secretary.

In his autobiography, *Along This Way*, written after fourteen years as field secretary and executive secretary of the NAACP, James Weldon Johnson recalled how his good friend Charles Anderson put him in charge of the local Republican Club, and then arranged for his consular appointments, first to Venezuela and then to Nicaragua. What Johnson does not tell us is that it was through Booker T. Washington, the arbiter of Roosevelt's appointments for all Negroes, that Anderson obtained these positions for Johnson. Johnson felt "deeply indebted" to Washington for the "invaluable service" he had done in recommending Johnson to the President and the secretary of state, and from time to time he wrote the Tuskegean long, chatty letters about life in Porto Cabello and Corinto. Washington was quite taken with Johnson and pushed his promotion with the Roosevelt and Taft administrations.

Johnson in later years referred to Washington's noted Atlanta Exposition Address as "illogical," but in the early part of the century the shrewd writer and diplomat was clearly a member of the Washington group. A man who referred to the opposition as "the enemy," who was a close friend of Collector Anderson, and whom Washington considered "a first class man" could not have been anything else. Yet Johnson was acutely aware of discrimination and indignities, and his novel, *The Autobiography of an Ex-Colored Man* (1912), described them effectively. Undoubtedly Johnson would have agreed with William H. Lewis, assistant attorney general under Taft, when he described Washington's indirect approach as simply bringing the wooden horse inside the walls of Troy. It was Joel Spingarn who had the perspicacity to propose the *"Coup d'état,"* as he put it, of securing Johnson as field secretary for the NAACP. Du Bois, when consulted, also thought that he was "entirely desirable." One suspects that Johnson's "desirability" may have been enhanced by his middle-of-the-road position and his earlier identification with the Tuskegee group.

And so in spite of all that Washington did, the opposition had triumphed. Nothing Washington could have done would have prevented the rise of the NAACP, and all of Anderson's feverish and brilliant tactics went for naught. Washington's prominence and position of leadership had been due to conditions at the turn of the century, when even many Negroes, discouraged at the increasing oppression, thought his program contained some hope. But conditions steadily deteriorated during Washington's ascendancy, and this fact, coupled with the reform currents set loose during the Progressive Era, made inevitable the rise of protest organizations which culminated in the NAACP. Nothing could illustrate better than did Johnson's selection as field secretary of the NAACP the large shift in public sentiment that had taken place in the dozen years following the formation of the Niagara Movement in 1905 and Johnson's appointment as consul at Porto Cabello in 1906. It simply remains a pleasant irony that the eventual success of the NAACP was due, in no small degree, to the most versatile, and one of the very ablest, of the men in the whole Booker T. Washington orbit.

This article was prepared under a grant from the American Council of Learned Societies and is based mostly on materials in the Booker T. Washington Papers at the Library of Congress. The Spingarn Papers at Howard, the F. J. Garrison Papers at the Schomburg Collection, the Chesnutt Papers at Fisk, and a few printed sources also proved helpful. Because of space limitations, footnotes were eliminated in the original article.

FIVE

The Rise of the Black Secretariat in the NAACP, 1909–35

BY ELLIOTT RUDWICK AND AUGUST MEIER

Studies of Negro-white relations in movements for black advancement have highlighted the paradox of interracial tensions within organizations dedicated to creating an egalitarian society. Not only did many white abolitionists manifest racism and paternalism, but "color-line" problems also arose in organizations like CORE and the NAACP, whose founders believed intensely in both racial equality and interracial action.

Nancy Weiss has traced the shift at the turn of the century from an all-black to an interracial protest movement which developed with the founding of the NAACP and Urban League in 1909–11.[1] Given the impotence of black protest in that period of extreme racism, and given the resources and legitimization that prominent whites could provide, an interracial movement appeared essential to blacks like W. E. B. Du Bois. In analyzing the broad sweep of twentieth-century civil rights activism that followed, one finds a transition from interracial leadership back to black leadership and control. The process was complex and varied in different organizations; an understanding of this phenomenon in the NAACP alone requires research in several topics. This paper is restricted to an analysis of the Association's bureaucracy.[2]

The NAACP began as a Board-dominated organization, with policy chiefly made by a few white Progressives and one distinguished black—W. E. B. Du Bois. And although Du Bois was uniquely influential, in practice he ran *The Crisis* magazine autonomously and largely removed himself from other activities. Two decades after its founding, however, the Association had become dominated by a black bureaucracy. This transition involved two interrelated trends: a shift in power from the Board to the expanding staff, especially into the hands of the secretary; and the change from a white to a black secretariat. A Negro was not appointed secretary on a permanent basis until 1920. This paper will focus on the two most important of the four whites who occupied the post before 1920—May Childs Nerney and John R. Shillady—and the two black secretaries who followed—James Weldon Johnson and Walter White.[3]

The minutes of Board meetings and correspondence of its leading members suggest that at first they operated upon two assumptions in choosing a secretary. Wishing to dominate policy-making, the Board sought an administrator to carry out its decisions rather than to exercise much initiative. Second, the Board, having secured Du Bois for the other principal salaried post, sought a symbolic racial balance; as Du Bois once put it, "I've tried to see if we could not have two branches of the work, one with a white head and one with a colored, working in harmony and sympathy for one end."[4] Although from the beginning bookkeeping, clerical, and field personnel were practically always Negroes, NAACP policy regarding the secretaryship contrasted with that of the Urban League, where from its inception the white-dominated Board employed only black executives.[5]

The most effective of the four white secretaries was May Childs Nerney, a young librarian hired in 1912. Selected for her "obvious executive ability,"[6] she had the responsibility for securing new members, developing and supervising branches, handling publicity, raising money, coordinating legal work, and carrying out campaigns against *The Birth of a Nation* and segregation in the federal civil service.[7] A prodigious worker, she was also temperamental, tactless with colleagues, and inept at organizational infighting. Dedicated to black advancement, she was nevertheless acutely aware of the anomaly of a white person like herself helping to lead the struggle—a sensitivity that paradoxically caused her to resent charges that racial paternalism disqualified her, and simultaneously to insist that blacks should fill all the key offices in the organization.[8]

Nerney's chief accomplishment was developing the NAACP's branches. Though without a regular field worker, in four years she increased the number of branches from three to sixty-three and the membership from 300 to nearly 10,000, arranging speaking tours for national leaders, visiting the branches herself, and conducting an extensive correspondence.[9] Although nearly all large donations continued to come from well-to-do whites, by 1914 Negroes constituted 80 percent of the membership, and when Nerney resigned in January, 1916, Board chairman Joel Spingarn praised her foresight in encouraging the Association to move toward funding its work through building a Negro membership base.[10]

Nerney approached the national office's other two functions—publicity and legal work—with comparable vigor. She handled routine press releases herself, unhesitatingly called upon prominent NAACP members for help in publicizing important events, and did not shrink from clashing with Board chairman Villard in her efforts to obtain good publicity.[11] Responsible for coordinating the legal work throughout most of her tenure, Nerney was disconsolate when financial setbacks compelled the Board to terminate the services of a full-time attorney whose appointment had been made possible by her diligent fund-raising.[12] She handled preliminary correspondence concerning cases, occasionally traveled to make on-the-spot investigations, assembled relevant documents, consulted with NAACP lawyers on cases to be taken, and at times forcefully recommended action which she thought appropriate. For example, during the struggle against residential segregation ordinances, Nerney was sent to Richmond to investigate the viability of a test case. Her assessment of the lawyers and the divisiveness among Richmond's blacks led the Association to take instead a Louisville case, which in 1917 brought a landmark Supreme Court victory.[13] The procedures which Nerney and legal committee chairman Arthur Spingarn thus created became standard operations in the NAACP's growing legal work that flowered during the 1920's in the close cooperation between Spingarn and assistant secretary Walter White.[14]

Nerney's vigorous leadership was also evident in the NAACP's campaigns against the segregation of federal clerks in Washington in 1913. Although Villard, a personal acquaintance of the President, was the one who first went to Washington to intercede with Wilson, thereafter Nerney managed the campaign. Personally making two trips to Washington, she secured confidential information from frightened black clerks and talkative government guides unaware of her background. Nerney wrote a hard-hitting report which received widespread publicity, and enthusiastically directed a letter-writing campaign to pressure the President and Congress.[15] Again, two years later, when concerned Association officials sought to combat *The Birth of a Nation* by having it banned, or at least by forcing the producers to cut the worst scenes, Nerney plunged in with characteristic energy. She prodded Villard to try to secure the help of one of the film's investors to have the movie refilmed. Working closely with Board leaders, she pushed and coordinated the campaign in New York and aroused branches across the country into action. At Columbus, for example, she galvanized discouraged Negroes into a protest that led the governor to pledge that the movie would be kept out of Ohio.[16] On both projects she spent endless hours, and, even after others had become discouraged, vigorously opposed giving up.[17]

As the preceding discussion indicates, Nerney was a hard-driving executive of considerable initiative, rather than one who quietly administered Board policies. She neither hesitated to push branches into activity, nor shrank from the difficult task of resolving factional fights within them. At times she felt her authority failed to match her responsibilities. Asked to investigate a conflict in Washington, where a dissident majority sought to overthrow branch president J. Milton Waldron because he was seeking political office under Wilson, she recommended that he be replaced with the rebellious faction's candidate, Archibald Grimké. Unhappy when the Board, following the more temperate counsel of Joel Spingarn, simply ordered a new election, she wrote him frankly: "I have a strong feeling that the Secretary should be given absolute power in matters like the Washington case. . . . after all, things have to be run by one person if we are to get anything done."[18] In her insistent efforts to influence Board decisions she worked primarily through Spingarn and a few important black branch leaders who were also Board members. Even before Spingarn became chairman, she found him a responsive leader who would at least listen sympathetically.[19] Thus when the Board was losing interest in the federal segregation issue, it was not to Chairman Villard but to Spingarn whom she wrote urging renewed action.[20] Second, during her fieldwork she had developed close ties with Grimké, his close friend president Francis Cardozo of the Baltimore branch, and Charles Bentley of Chicago. The key figure in this alliance was Grimké, who had come to know Nerney when she sided with him in the Waldron controversy; as president of the largest and most active branch, he enjoyed a stature among Board members that made him a most valuable ally. Thus when the first Spingarn Award Committee recommended Robert Moton of Hampton Institute, Nerney, appalled that the first medal should go to a friend of Booker T. Washington rather than to a scholar or scientist "so that white people would be impressed by the fact that colored people are really doing things," urged Grimké and Bentley to intervene in behalf of the young Howard University biologist Ernest Just. In the end Just was the first recipient of the Spingarn Medal.[21]

Both Nerney's desire to shape policy and get things done and her querulous, argumentative style embroiled her in conflicts with Villard, Mary White Ovington, and Du Bois. Du Bois, who resented her questioning of his judgment about how NAACP news should be presented in *The Crisis*, declared with considerable justification, "Miss Nerney, while of excellent spirit and indefatigable energy, has a violent temper and is depressingly suspicious of motives."[22] She was sometimes sarcastic even with Spingarn; she had no compunction about criticizing the distinguished lawyer and NAACP president Moorfield Storey to an outsider,[23] and she freely attributed cynical motivations to those with whom she disagreed.[24] Nerney was aware of her weaknesses; as she confided to Grimké, "Really this job requires more tact and patience than I possess."[25] From one viewpoint the resulting conflicts were simply a universal fact of organizational life, with factions vying for resources and power. Thus both Nerney and Du Bois struggled with Board leaders for greater authority and autonomy in their respective spheres, and part of Nerney's problem in fact was that she got drawn into Du Bois's disputes with the two successive Board chairmen, Villard and Spingarn. Yet within the NAACP such conflicts had racial overtones. Du Bois saw them as the old story of white attempts to dominate blacks, and in the ensuing battles Nerney deliberately sought black allies to undercut the *Crisis* editor.

While in February, 1913, she actually submitted her resignation over the alleged insolence of Du Bois's secretary and his support of her, at first Nerney envied how Du Bois resisted Villard's attempt to subordinate the *Crisis* editor to his authority.[26] As she wrote Spingarn justifying her own desire for greater power, "I am beginning to understand better every day Mr. Du Bois' attitude in regard to the *Crisis*."[27] In November Villard found himself challenged by both of the executives. Nerney, irritated at what she deemed his interference,[28] undermined his attempts to handle publicity, even killing releases sent by him and substituting her own. Convinced that Villard "is determined to dominate everything," Nerney, like Du Bois, whose battle with Villard had also reached a showdown, favored stripping the chairman of all power, thus allowing the two almost complete control of their respective departments.[29] But Villard resigned before such a proposal could be considered.

Ovington was "sick at heart" over this "confession to the world that we cannot work with colored people unless they are our subordinates."[30] As her comment indicates, the interracial character of the Association was important to NAACP leaders. There had been a studied effort to make the branches, as well as the Board, interracial, to secure both prominent whites and influential black spokesmen for NAACP meetings.[31] Yet some blacks resented white prominence in the organization and sometimes felt that certain white officers were prejudiced or paternalistic. Du Bois accused Villard of outright racism, and Nerney's questioning of his judgment led him to conclude that "she hasn't an ounce of conscious prejudice, but her every step is unconsciously along the color line." At the NAACP's 1914 annual meeting, complaints about the prominence of white leadership were, in fact, publicly voiced.[32]

On the other hand many, if not most, blacks in the NAACP welcomed white participation. Spingarn's militant speaking tours found a warm response in black communities.[33] Grimké, whose commitment to interracial action reached back to his

many years as a Boston civic leader, was the one at the 1914
annual meeting who rose to challenge those questioning the
role of whites. While predicting that ultimately a great Negro
would emerge to lead the NAACP, he singled out Villard,
Spingarn, and Nerney for praise and insisted: "Let us never
hear of drawing the color line in this association. . . . To put
somebody against somebody else simply because he is colored
would be a fatal mistake." Nerney, already stung by suspicions
directed against her whiteness, was deeply appreciative: "No
one else could have given such an eloquent and tactful rebuke
to the attempt, always fatal, to put all our difficulties on the
grounds of race prejudice. To me this is always dreadful but a
charge before which every sincere white man or woman must
always feel helpless remembering that the colored people have
little cause to trust white people." In Grimké she found one
who "remember[s] only that I am human and do[es] not make
me constantly uncomfortable by reminding me I am white."[34]
The high regard was mutual, and Grimké became Nerney's
most effective supporter; ultimately when Grimké switched to
Du Bois her resignation would be inevitable.

Joel Spingarn was a skillful interpersonal leader,[35] but his
accession to the chairmanship did not bring an end to the personality conflicts. Nerney's relationships with Du Bois were
permanently ruptured in January, 1914. At a time when the
NAACP was fighting the mushrooming efforts to enact anti-
intermarriage laws, Du Bois, writing for the *Survey* magazine,
had composed a statement of the black man's goals which he
represented as official NAACP policy and which included a
demand for the right to intermarry. Given the highly sensitive
nature of the issue, *Survey* editor Paul Kellogg asked Nerney if
the Association endorsed this demand, and she urged him not
to publish the statement as NAACP policy. Although Du Bois
agreed to omit the reference to the Association, the *Survey* rejected his manuscript, and the angered editor penned a sting-
ing editorial condemning the magazine. Although Nerney
maintained that she had kept Du Bois fully informed, the
editor claimed that both she and Villard had "discredited me
behind my back."[36] Afterward Nerney concluded that Du Bois
was using *The Crisis* as a personal weapon and developing a

machine to take over the NAACP. Determined that "no one person colored or white shall dominate it [the NAACP] . . . [and] that more than one member of the colored race shall occasionally be heard," she proposed to control Du Bois by creating a three-man executive committee, on which Grimké would be the black representative. Spingarn seemed receptive, and Nerney urged the D.C. Branch president to tell him that Negroes also objected to Du Bois's behavior.[37] The Board failed to act, however, and Nerney's suggestion had an ironic denouement a few months later when Du Bois counterattacked by proposing a similar body, but with himself as a member. Du Bois also attempted to undermine Nerney by recommending that any new departments which the Board created would, like *The Crisis*, be excluded from the secretary's supervision. The upshot was a new compromise set of by-laws which, while creating an executive committee, ratified Du Bois's autonomous position but left Nerney's sphere of authority undisturbed.[38]

By late 1914 it was evident that these arrangements would not resolve Du Bois's relationship with either the secretary or the chairman.[39] Embarrassment caused the Association by his editorial attacks on black editors, ministers, and educators, and his demands upon the Association's finances in the face of fiscal difficulties, produced a new crisis. Although the recession of 1914 sharply reduced NAACP income, Spingarn and the Board reluctantly acceded to Du Bois's demands for more staff and office space.[40] Yet Nerney, with a small staff and office room but with responsibility for money-raising, was forced to accept budget cuts which seriously curtailed the activities of the national office: "To give up our legal bureau is a bitter blow after we have worked so hard to get it. . . . Meanwhile the *Crisis* goes gaily on expanding merrily while the N.A. is forced to retrench and retrench to help the *Crisis* expand." Nerney was particularly upset because Du Bois, in resisting a budget cut, charged racial discrimination: ". . . when we are ordered to cut down expenses," she explained to Grimké, "the N.A. complies but Du Bois refuses and says we are trying to discriminate against him, a colored man. . . ." Highly sensitive to this kind of charge, Nerney decided that the best way to fight Du Bois would be for Grimké to replace her and thus "absolutely eliminate the race issue. . . . That is the . . . only way this Association is to come into its own—under a colored leader . . . who has the . . . confidence of the colored people. . . . The colored people will never come into their own until *they do it for themselves.*"[41]

It is doubtful that Nerney actually thought Grimké would entertain such a suggestion, but she took other steps to expand his influence in the Association. She urged him and Cardozo to attend Board meetings;[42] she got Spingarn to allow her to withdraw from the all-white branch committee if Grimké could be persuaded to become its chairman, since for a long time "we have felt that there should be a colored member on this committee but it seemed most important that we should have a member in whose judgment we could place complete confidence."[43] And in order "to avoid the play to race prejudice made at the last annual meeting," she prevailed upon Spingarn to take the unprecedented step of appointing an all-black nominating committee headed by Grimké, and then urged Grimké to nominate "as many colored members on the Board as possible." She was pleased when two blacks were named to positions vacated by whites.[44]

By then Spingarn, reluctantly concluding that executive authority should be centered in the board chairman, frankly wrote Du Bois about the problems that the latter's personality created. Defending himself, Du Bois charged Villard and Nerney with racism; his relationships with them, he insisted, were actually part of the historic problem of securing satisfactory black-white cooperation in race advancement organizations.[45] In November a tense board meeting (which Grimké and Cardozo both attended at Nerney's urging) voted to abolish the executive committee and give the chairman "full authority over all officials and employees of the Association."[46] Due to the bitter opposition of Du Bois and Ovington, however, a final decision was postponed until December. At that time, following an impassioned address by Grimké, the Board rejected Du Bois's substitute motion completely exempting him from the chairman's control, and instead adopted a compromise providing that Du Bois and a special *Crisis* committee, rather than Spingarn alone, would supervise the magazine. An infuriated

Ovington proposed that if there wasn't enough money "to support the *Crisis* in its present style," Nerney should resign and allow the office to be run by volunteers. Ultimately Spingarn's tact prevailed, and the 1915 annual meeting of the Association duly ratified the new constitution and by-laws.[47]

Over the following months Du Bois accommodated to the new arrangements, while Nerney absorbed herself in the branch and legal work. By year's end, however, Nerney was becoming disillusioned with the Association's effectiveness and the editor aroused renewed controversy, now centering over the limited time he devoted to NAACP business. Nerney, irritated for months at Du Bois's failure to prepare NAACP pamphlets, judged that he "has built up a very perfect machine . . . which enables him to get out the *Crisis* with very little trouble to himself except writing of editorials," leaving him ample time for outside activities. After considerable debate the Board in November asked a committee headed by Spingarn to define once again the duties of the executive officers.[48] Soon after, Nerney returned from a midwestern field trip with an attitude highly critical of the branches. "Nowhere are we even beginning to cope with the undeniable increase in prejudice and discrimination," she informed the Board. The seemingly hopeless uphill struggle for constitutional rights convinced her that the Association would die unless the branches initiated an economic and social welfare program similar to the Urban League's. Believing furthermore that deeper roots in the black community were essential, she urged the Association to work more closely with the black churches, have local legal cases "handled by a colored lawyer if possible," and, most important, employ a full-time organizer.[49]

Responding to the issues raised by the two executives, the Spingarn Committee recommended that the Board secure an organizer on the one hand, and, on the other, prohibit Du Bois from undertaking extraneous duties without specific authorization.[50] Du Bois, resolving to fight this issue, precipitated the most serious internal crisis the NAACP had ever faced. To Grimké, with whom he had recently effected a temporary rapprochement, he wrote that if the committee's proposal passed he would "of course resign."[51] When the Board, arguing with unprecedented intensity at its December meeting, voted that it was "inexpedient" to approve the Spingarn committee's report, it was the anguished chairman who announced his resignation instead.[52]

Du Bois, championed by Ovington and Grimké, now proposed that if the NAACP wanted to retain *The Crisis*, it should either make him secretary as well as editor, or, preferably, name his close friend Ovington as chairman and "a young colored man" as secretary.[53] Either arrangement would have gotten rid of Nerney. Actually, by then, as Spingarn sensed, Nerney was unlikely to remain much longer. As for himself, the Board chairman, having reconciled with Grimké, decided, as Nerney had under similarly trying circumstances a year earlier, that blacks should assume full responsibility for the Association and that Grimké was the logical candidate to succeed him. By the time of the annual meeting in January, 1916, Spingarn had been prevailed upon to remain as chairman, but Nerney resigned.[54] While she did not state her reasons, Grimké's desertion and Du Bois's victory at the December meeting must have been bitter blows, and clearly the strain of the conflict had taken its toll. Moreover, discouraged over the paucity of branch achievement, she must have been unhappy when Spingarn rejected her proposals for new directions in branch work.

In resigning, Nerney recommended that her successor be a Negro.[55] The Board, however, disagreed; evidently still committed to splitting the work into two divisions, one headed by a white and the other by a black, it selected as secretary Roy Nash, a white writer who had formerly led the Northern California NAACP branch. Nash proved singularly ineffective. The disappointing character of his administration was epitomized by a meeting with Villard in November, 1916. Villard concluded that Nash "made a very poor showing indeed. . . . I asked him what he was doing; he said it took him most of his time to answer his mail. . . . When I asked what his program for the winter's work was, he said he had none. . . ."[56] Obviously the Board was not unhappy when Nash soon left to join the army.

Yet during Nash's administration the Board finally solved the fieldwork problem by creating the post of field secretary and organizer, and filling it with a fortunate choice—James Weldon

Johnson.[57] The Board, which considered only Negroes for the position, obtained in Johnson a person well known both in the black community and in white literary and Republican party circles. Urbane and sophisticated, he could move easily in almost any group. As a man who had become U.S. consul in Venezuela and Nicaragua through the intervention of Booker T. Washington, and more recently as an editorial writer for the Bookerite New York *Age*, Johnson was identified with the Tuskegee circle. Yet his writings contained an unmistakably protest strain; he had maintained cordial relations with Du Bois, and he even joined the New York NAACP in 1915.[58] His standing among Negroes generally was of prime importance, since his chief responsibility was to develop the NAACP's black constituency, and his ties with the Washingtonians legitimized the NAACP among many blacks previously suspicious of the organization. His political connections helped the NAACP's efforts to influence Republican party policy and national legislation, while his numerous contacts and his image of "responsible" militance made him an excellent emissary to white philanthropists. These qualities, combined with impressive skills in public speaking and an extraordinary tact and diplomacy, provided the foundation for his achievements both as field organizer and subsequently as secretary.

Johnson was the first black other than Du Bois to serve the Association in an administrative capacity. He embarked at once on a strikingly successful organizing trip that firmly established the NAACP for the first time in the hostile South. Du Bois stated enthusiastically: "the organization of a dozen lusty, young branches . . . in the heart of the South marks the beginning of a new era in the history of the NAACP."[59] Subsequent tours across the country were characterized by enthusiastic meetings before both blacks and influential whites.[60] By the end of 1919, three years after Johnson began work, the membership had risen to almost 100,000.[61] Johnson's work was facilitated by the prosperity and increased black militancy accompanying World War I, but the major credit for "building up the strong chain of branches"[62] belongs to the field secretary himself. The new income enabled the NAACP to substantially increase its national office staff, and by 1920 the Association was employing two full-time field secretaries in addition to Johnson.

While both Johnson in his field reports and the NAACP in its publicity referred proudly to his successes in securing memberships among prominent whites, the new members were overwhelmingly black.[63] In fact, Johnson, who envisioned the NAACP as the vehicle for harnessing into united action the collective forces of the Negro community,[64] made a concerted effort to develop NAACP roots in key black institutions. The NAACP's close connection with the black church and lodge began during his tenure as field secretary. During his first year with the Association he compiled "a directory of colored ministers, heads of schools and secret and fraternal organizations throughout the country" as the first step in a campaign to bring them "into cooperation with the Association."[65] In his travels he "eagerly" seized opportunities to speak before black professional groups.[66] In the summer of 1919 he spent two days at the annual convention of the Knights of Pythias, journeyed to St. Louis to address the annual gathering of the National Negro Business League, and urged Board Chairman Ovington: "We must not overlook a single opportunity to have a representative at these national gatherings. The national convention of the Elks meets . . . next week; I wish we could have someone present. The national convention of the Baptist Church meets next week . . . we *must* have somebody there. We must, of course, be represented at the doctor's convention in Newark."[67]

Given Johnson's abilities and the smoothness with which he substituted for Nash when the latter resigned, it seems surprising that the Board did not name him secretary on a permanent basis. But, continuing its previous policy of maintaining a racial balance in the top executive positions, the Board did not even consider any blacks and instead appointed a fairly prominent white social worker, John R. Shillady.[68] Yet at the same time the Board acted to increase black representation at the top administrative levels. Upon Johnson's recommendation it appointed the young Atlanta Negro civic leader, Walter White, to the new post of assistant secretary.[69] Surviving evidence contains no explicit indication that race was considered in either appointment, but there can be little doubt that such was the case. Significantly, White's appointment, made by the Board unilaterally without first consulting Shillady, showed that Board leaders still intended to handle basic decisions.

Essentially an office man carrying out the Board's directives and smoothly administering the growing staff, Shillady was almost the opposite of Nerney. Lacking her drive and initiative, he proved to be an ineffective fund-raiser, failed to push Board members into action, preferred to leave contacts with public officials to others, and avoided internal organizational conflicts. He was well liked by everybody, but the real accomplishments of his administration were due to two black executives, Johnson and White, to whom he willingly delegated authority.[70]

Shillady had little to do with the dramatic rise in NAACP income and membership during his administration. He did coordinate the first large-scale membership drive in the NAACP history,[71] but he himself was a lackluster speaker,[72] and credit for the organization's growth belongs to Johnson and White. They and the other field secretaries organized and developed the branches, which by 1919 supplied half of the Association's revenue. Shillady's effectiveness in raising money from philanthropists was limited; the larger donations actually declined in number,[73] and lengthy negotiations with Julius Rosenwald proved inconclusive until Johnson prevailed upon the Chicago mail-order house magnate to renew his annual $1,000 contribution.[74] Moreover, Shillady had relatively little personal contact with outside agencies and influentials after his first several months in office.[75] As time went on, lobbying in Washington fell almost entirely to Johnson and White. Mostly Shillady thrived on office routines. He thought his paperwork so important that he wrote a lengthy *Crisis* article describing in loving detail "A Day's Work at the National Office." Ovington recalled, "Shillady's correspondence soon required two stenographers, for he was meticulous in clearing up his desk before his day was done."[76] Publicity work particularly benefited from his interest; he expanded the system of news releases and in 1919 secured the employment of the Association's first full-time publicity director.[77] On the other hand, he avoided factional conflicts, and, when forced to face such issues, grew discouraged. For example, in May, 1919, with Du Bois having characteristically stirred up a couple of bitter rows, Shillady informed Grimké that he was seriously thinking of resigning "if there is to be a drawing of lines and hostile forces lined up permanently to hamper the work."[78]

Epitomizing the way in which Shillady functioned and how, despite his titular leadership, the black executives carried the principal burden of the Association's program were the roles played by each in the intensive campaign against mob violence. White, who was originally regarded by Shillady as essentially part of the clerical staff,[79] quickly became the man who investigated lynchings.[80] Shillady, operating in the office, supervised the preparation of extensive publicity literature and, more important, handled the bulk of the correspondence connected with the NAACP's ambitious national anti-lynching conference of 1919.[81] Perhaps nothing illustrated Shillady's propensity for attempting to redress inequities through paperwork more clearly than his proud recital of his numerous letters to southern governors, the President, the executive committee of the American Bar Association, and the attorney general.[82] Significantly, Johnson and White thought that the practice of writing southern governors requesting action in individual lynchings was fruitless.[83] In the case of the President, the memoranda submitted by him were unavailing, but Shillady inspired a letter-writing campaign from the branches and influential citizens that finally led Wilson in July, 1918, to issue a statement against lynching.[84]

Yet even here Johnson and White performed important duties that Shillady seemed unwilling to assume. They were the ones who lobbied with congressmen, senators, and cabinet members and bore the chief responsibility for representing the Association in Washington and Chicago after the 1919 riots in those cities. White was assigned the task of enlisting the support of Secretary of Interior Franklin K. Lane and Attorney General A. Mitchell Palmer for the anti-lynching conference, while White and Johnson handled the negotiations involved in securing Charles Evans Hughes as principal speaker.[85] When Congressman Dyer first introduced an anti-lynching bill in 1918, Shillady coordinated matters with the NAACP's anti-lynching committee, but it was White who dealt with Dyer.[86] When the

Washington riot erupted, Shillady characteristically dictated a letter to Attorney General Palmer charging that the Washington *Post* incited whites to violence. Having done this, and having sent Johnson and publicity director Herbert Seligmann to investigate the riot, he departed on a vacation.[87] When the Chicago riot broke out shortly afterward, Shillady did go to the scene; but he quickly returned to Saranac Lake, and it was White, following him to the violence-torn city, who really galvanized the local NAACP branch and other racial advancement groups into action.[88]

In the aftermath of that "Red summer," Johnson emerged as the Association's chief lobbyist in Washington. While investigating the riot there, he spoke with local editors about their inflammatory news coverage[89] and prevailed upon Senator Curtis of Kansas to introduce a resolution calling for a congressional investigation of mob violence.[90] In the following months Johnson lobbied vigorously both for this resolution and for the new Dyer Bill, and against a sedition bill which, it was feared, might silence militant black periodicals like *The Crisis*. In January, 1920, Johnson made at least three trips to Washington to lobby before congressional committees on these matters, and while other NAACP people joined him in these appearances, the major responsibility for carrying out the Association's congressional work was his.[91]

Despite what in retrospect appear to have been serious limitations in Shillady's leadership, the Board and his colleagues were not unhappy with him. His departure resulted from his own disillusionment, not from any sentiment to force him out. Deeply depressed after he was violently assaulted while investigating harassment of the NAACP branch in Austin, Texas, late in 1919, Shillady never recovered his earlier enthusiasm. Submitting his resignation effective in May, 1920, he informed the Board that "I am less confident than heretofore . . . of the probability of overcoming within a reasonable period the forces opposed to Negro equality by the means and methods which are within the Association's power to employ."[92]

Johnson's accomplishments would seem to have made him a logical successor to Shillady. He had been acting secretary for seven months after Nash left, and his interpersonal talents and growing political contacts were demonstrated during the 1920 presidential campaign. Attending the national Republican convention, he both addressed the resolutions committee on behalf of an anti-lynching plank and privately obtained a commitment from the committee's chairman to work for such a plank. Moving with his usual self-assurance, Johnson also spoke with Republican National Committee chairman Will Hays and met "quite a number of men prominent in party councils." Subsequently he secured a conference with Warren Harding at which he presented NAACP desires on a number of issues to the Republican candidate.[93]

Nevertheless, when Shillady resigned the Board seemed reluctant to promote Johnson, and he once more filled in as acting secretary. Surviving evidence offers no real explanation, but does suggest that Board Chairman Ovington was the major barrier. She had originally vigorously opposed Johnson's appointment as field secretary, perhaps because of his previous connection with Booker T. Washington and because she, as a Socialist, considered him "hopelessly reactionary on labor and other problems."[94] A year later, recognizing that "in his quiet way [he] accomplishes a good deal," she conceded that Spingarn had been right in pressing the Board to hire Johnson. But she still felt that "we need . . . someone to keep Mr. Johnson stirred up a little more." Not surprisingly, therefore, upon Shillady's resignation, she wanted to "go very slowly" in finding a replacement.[95] Perhaps because of her influence, the search committee deliberated very carefully before proposing a successor, although there is no evidence that any other candidate was considered. Du Bois, who had helped Spingarn recruit Johnson as field secretary in the first place, championed his candidacy on the basis of Johnson's experience and because "the new secretary should be a colored man." Nevertheless, in July the committee, unable to reach agreement, postponed action until January. Shortly afterward a curiously worded press release announced that Johnson had been appointed acting secretary, "pending final action by the Board of Directors." If someone was trying to force the Board's hand, the tactic succeeded. Although the Board in September concurred in the recommendation to postpone a decision until the new year, the public announcement galvanized sentiment among Negroes. Field Secretary Robert Bagnall "found every branch I visit clamoring for the ratification of Johnson as Executive Secretary." With such support, and with no other contender in sight, the Board delayed no longer and confirmed Johnson as secretary in November.[96] Though there may have been a lingering commitment to a biracial bureaucracy among certain board members, by 1920 Johnson's accomplishments in building the Association in the black community had made his choice practically inevitable.

As suggested earlier, in addition to administrative skills, there were two main attributes for a successful NAACP secretary: a broad appeal to the black community, and an ability to legitimize the Association's program among white elites. Johnson, the NAACP's first successful secretary, performed both functions superbly. While Johnson did value the interracial character of the NAACP leadership,[97] basically he believed that the Association must consciously build "power" through the united might of blacks themselves. Thus in 1921 he asserted that while the Association, since its founding, always "had many able and enthusiastic white members, its work is mainly to be done by colored men," and he proudly pointed out that over 95 percent of the NAACP's "support" came from Negroes. Moreover, Johnson continued to cultivate all the leading black interest groups.[98] Thus, when he led a delegation to President Harding to urge a pardon for the soldiers allegedly involved in the Houston Riot of 1917, the committee included prominent editors, heads of major church organizations, and important fraternal leaders.[99]

As this conference indicated, the day was past when the Association would be represented at the White House or in Congress by a white NAACP leader, as had happened when Villard had served as the NAACP spokesman, personally going to Washington on the civil service segregation issue.[100] Johnson had, in fact, become the Association's lobbyist par excellence. His personal charm, his political contacts, and the fact that he indisputably represented black America made him ideal for this task. Almost singlehandedly managing the lobbying for the Dyer antilynching bill, he split his time between New York and

Washington in 1921–22 and successfully shepherded the bill through the House, only to see it killed in the Senate.[101] Johnson also served the Association well in fund-raising. Thus when he became secretary, Johnson capitalized on his personal relationship with the man who managed Julius Rosenwald's philanthropies: "The responsibility of the organization is now resting upon my shoulders. . . . I am writing this letter both from the official and personal point of view . . . asking that you use your influence with Mr. Rosenwald." As Walter White expressed it after Johnson left the secretaryship, the latter had "raised a great deal of money through his personal efforts, especially from such organizations as the Garland, Rockefeller, and Rosenwald Funds."[102]

The roles of the Board and the staff in the organization's decision-making process underwent fundamental changes during the Johnson administration. Ovington later recalled that Johnson's succession had marked a definite shift of responsibility,[103] and the cumulative impression that emerges from the Board minutes, reports of executives, and correspondence of NAACP leaders is one of power passing from the Board to the secretariat.[104] Because whites were still the most influential figures on the Board, even though that body was about half black in membership, this change also marked the clearcut ascendancy of black influence within the Association. There were several reasons for the Board's new deference to the salaried black officers. The very growth in size and complexity of operations made it increasingly difficult for volunteer Board members to exercise close supervision. The most they could do was to help formulate Board policy, and, since there was a basic consensus on this matter, it was easy for the Board to follow the secretary's leadership. Second, Johnson was the first secretary whose influence derived less from the authority delegated to him by the Board than from the broad base of support he enjoyed in the black community, in effect providing him with an outside constituency quite independent of the Board of Directors.

Then, too, the very effectiveness with which Johnson and White ran the organization encouraged the Board to rely upon their judgment. The two men complemented each other well, and together they made a remarkably successful team. Johnson functioned as the Association's ambassador to white and black America, symbolizing the Association's unalterable insistence on first-class citizenship for Afro-Americans, while his interpersonal skills made him an effective administrator. A man who commanded loyalty and respect from colleagues, Johnson, like Shillady, knew how to delegate authority, and he gave unusual latitude to his principal staff members. His tact, sensitivity to others, and skillful leadership were epitomized by his relations with Du Bois. Although Du Bois was constantly at odds with the Board, Johnson, on all but one occasion, was able to remain on cordial terms with the *Crisis* editor.

Not only did Johnson have an influence and autonomy unprecedented for a NAACP secretary, but the Board also found itself delegating greater responsibility to White. Possessed of enormous drive and ambition, a quick mind and a passion for detail, White soon made himself indispensable. By the 1920's it was evident that the organization's most important activities would lie in the courts, and by then White had become the liaison between the staff and the Board in legal work. This was supervised by legal committee chairman Arthur Spingarn, who advised which cases should be selected. White proved adept at mastering complicated legal matters and, working closely with Spingarn, screened requests for legal aid, handled negotiations with local lawyers, and carried out much of the committee's routine business. Basically he and Spingarn coordinated the legal program, with Johnson and the Board accepting their recommendations. By the mid-1920's all important decisions regarding legal work were in practice made jointly by the two men—and, in fact, as time passed, Spingarn tended to allow White greater authority in deciding what actions to take.[105]

Thus more and more policy decisions were made by staff with the Board tending to concur, rather than charting the NAACP program itself. It is of course difficult to pinpoint the emerging network of informal relations that supplemented and modified the formal structure defined in the constitution and by-laws. Certainly, as in any voluntary organization, even the most powerful executive secretary cannot adopt policies that would arouse serious objections among a substantial segment of the Board. On the other hand, the secretary's influence could sometimes be felt very directly. For example, though the nominating committee's records for this period do not survive, there is evidence indicating that the secretary influenced the choice of new members of the Board.[106]

Meanwhile, the role of the handful of influential white Board members who had been crucial in the Association's early days was undergoing important changes. President Moorfield Storey had never taken a hand in internal administration but continued to serve as legal counsel for important cases. Villard had withdrawn from active participation in 1918. Joel Spingarn was in semi-retirement, and while as treasurer he directed the investment of NAACP funds, he influenced no policy decisions during Johnson's administration. Meanwhile the role of Board Chairman Ovington became more peripheral; by the end of the 1920's she summed up her situation to Arthur Spingarn: ". . . But I am not much use except as a cheerer on." She found the staff "always pleasant and friendly," but reluctant to adopt her suggestions. "I have wasted an awful lot of time sitting around there [in the office], enjoying little talks, signing checks, but really doing nothing constructive."[107] On the other hand, Arthur Spingarn came to play a more crucial role than any other Board member, white or black. Given the salience of the legal program, the legal committee chairman was a central figure. His importance is suggested by the fact that he was often asked to join in staff meetings. Yet his correspondence indicates that even he rarely took the initiative in offering advice. Rather, he functioned as "a wise counselor" who gave help only when asked.[108]

By 1929 Johnson, finding himself completely exhausted, took a year's leave and then resigned. White was the obvious choice to succeed him in 1931.[109] The new secretary would bring the Association through the critical Depression years so that it emerged with greater prestige than ever. At the same time, White emerged with unprecedented personal control of the organizational machinery and a degree of power in the Association that no single person had ever before enjoyed.

The Association's serious financial problems during the early 1930's produced organizational crises that were resolved with the consolidation of the secretary's power over the staff. White, who spent considerable time raising money among white philanthropists to shore up a disastrous membership decline,[110] recommended a substantial reduction in salaries and staff. This produced an unprecedented rebellion, with the department heads sharply criticizing the secretary to the Board. That body, though recognizing White's own extravagances, nevertheless sided with him, and, except for Du Bois, the staff withdrew their protest. A few, most notably the director of branches, were dismissed, and White now had undisputed control over all departments except for *The Crisis*.[111]

White and Du Bois, though both of strong ego, would likely have tolerated each other if the Depression had not produced serious competition for scarce funds. Through the 1920's Du Bois's editorial independence had continued to bring periodic conflicts with the Board, but his personal eminence had prevented an open break. Now, however, with *The Crisis* running a serious deficit,[112] Du Bois's espousal of a black separatist position precipitated a clash between the two men that ended in the editor's resignation. Management of *The Crisis* came under White's jurisdiction, with the appointment of the new assistant secretary, Roy Wilkins, as editor.[113]

The relationship between White and Wilkins was quite different from the one which White had sustained with Johnson.[114] White exercised a tighter rein over the staff than Johnson, and he did not imitate his predecessor's policy of permitting the assistant secretary a virtually independent sphere of operations. For example, Wilkins assumed the task of handling the routine administration of the legal work, but unlike Johnson, White very directly involved himself in important cases, continuing to make key decisions with Arthur Spingarn.

White's relationships with the Board during the first half-decade of his administration largely revolved around the Spingarn brothers. Ovington resigned as chairman at the end of 1931 because White refused to consult her.[115] Joel Spingarn, who succeeded her, shared with White a basic consensus about the Association's direction, but at times forcefully injected himself into the running of the organization, clamping down on what he regarded as unnecessary expenditures, and encouraging White to broaden the Association's program to cope with the economic catastrophe of the 1930's.

Although the NAACP led the attack on the discriminatory economic policies of the New Deal agencies, critics complained that the Association was dominated by a concern for the interests of the black bourgeoisie. Not entirely new, this criticism achieved greater salience during the Depression when young intellectuals like Abram Harris and Ralph Bunche of Howard University denounced the oligarchic character of the NAACP Board, charged that whites had undue influence, and insisted that the Association encourage the unionization of black workers. The critics correctly judged that both White and influential Board members like Joel Spingarn believed that the NAACP should not depart from the battle to secure the Negro's constitutional rights. Yet Spingarn deemed it essential that the Association open a dialogue with its critics, and successfully pushed a reluctant White to hold a conference with a cross-section of these young intellectuals. Subsequently both White, the astute bureaucrat, and Spingarn, the skillful interpersonal leader, realizing that the organization would have to respond to the agitation, encouraged the Board to appoint a Committee on Future Plan and Program, chaired by Abram Harris. The committee's report urged the Association to democratize Board elections and to encourage Negroes "to view their special grievances as a natural part of the larger issues of American labor as a whole." White lauded the report but doubted that funds could be obtained to carry out its recommendation that the Association create workers' councils to educate the masses for economic and political action.[116] Certainly implementation of this proposal would have drastically altered the organization and curtailed the struggle against disfranchisement and segregation. Although changes did follow, with the branches receiving some voice in electing Board members and the Association forging an alliance with the CIO, both the organizational structure and program remained essentially unaltered.

Meanwhile, hurt by all the criticism, Joel Spingarn had quit as Board chairman in 1935; he was succeeded by White's close friend, the distinguished black surgeon Louis Wright. Although there had been no pressure on Spingarn to resign, his withdrawal symbolized the ending of the crucial role which white leaders had played in the Association since its founding, and served to further consolidate White's control. Spingarn and White had always been in basic agreement about goals and strategies, but Wright deferred to the secretary's judgment even more.

White's relationship with Dr. Wright reveals the way in which the organization's informal structure was changing, so that while the Board was still the legal governing body, the chief locus of power was shifting decisively to the secretary. During his first years as the chief salaried officer White had exerted weight through his warm relationship with Arthur Spingarn, who, besides continuing to perform his legal functions, had also served in other key roles, including membership on the nominating and budget committees. The other busy Board members found it easy to ratify the recommendations of the able and increasingly celebrated Walter White and his conscientious ally, Arthur Spingarn.[117] White's influence became so pervasive that he frequently suggested to the nominating committee candidates which it chose for Board membership. Through his friendship with Board Chairman Louis Wright he was even able to largely decide on appointments to key Board committees.[118] And prior to the monthly meetings White and an inner circle of Board members would meet at Wright's apartment to caucus on strategy for the next day.[119]

Moreover, in the same year that Wright became chairman, both the work of the Association and the role of the staff were strengthened by the creation of a legal department headed by the noted Negro lawyer Charles Hamilton Houston. In its early years the NAACP had usually employed prestigious white lawyers who offered their services without remuneration to conduct its most important cases, a policy to which Walter White fully subscribed. Because of the extreme racism of the period, black lawyers were at a disadvantage in the courts. Yet Walter White had long wished to see Negro counsel utilized at the highest levels of the NAACP's legal work. During the early 1930's, assisted by pressures from black lawyers who wanted to lead the legal struggle for the race's freedom, White pushed in this direction. He secured both Houston and his law partner,

William H. Hastie, for key NAACP cases in 1933 and 1934, and was finally successful in arranging for a foundation grant to enable the NAACP to hire Houston in 1935.[120] This appointment, coming almost simultaneously with Joel Spingarn's withdrawal, marked the final consolidation of black dominance in the NAACP. And even though the legal staff exhibited greater autonomy than any other department, its establishment was another step in enhancing the organization's bureaucracy, since it greatly diminished the significance of the legal committee chairman. Arthur Spingarn welcomed these developments, and upon his brother's death in 1939 he gracefully assumed the ceremonial post of Association president. Finally, Houston's appointment solidified the NAACP's ties to the black community. It increased support for the Association in the Negro bar, and Houston's subsequent victories in the struggle against southern educational discrimination raised enormously the NAACP's standing and gained for it thousands of members.

Thus by the mid-1930's the NAACP had come under completely black control and the secretary had emerged as the clearly dominant figure. There had been a certain irony in the process. The NAACP had been formed in a period when black protest had proven ineffective, and this interracial organization had been founded just because the wealth and prominence of sympathetic whites were needed. Yet in less than a decade the NAACP discovered that it would have to base its income and membership primarily on the black community. Its real growth began with the fieldwork of Johnson. What followed was a circular process; as membership grew, pressures for a Negro secretary also grew, both because blacks wanted one and because having a black secretary would increase support in the Negro community. The rise of Johnson and White marked the advent of a black bureaucracy within the NAACP which not only gave Negroes a key voice in policy-making, but also tied the national office more closely to the branches and to local Negro communities. Consequently, the Association grew rapidly under their administration and became the dominant racial advancement organization. At the same time this growth and increased income inevitably brought a more complex structure and a broader program. And as this happened the Board had to rely more and more on the secretary and the staff. Even though the Depression temporarily forced a cutback in staff, the NAACP, in meeting the challenges of the 1930's, further concentrated power in the hands of its bureaucracy.

One striking feature of the process described is that each of the bureaucracy's major functions—fieldwork, administration, and litigation—came under black control during different stages in the organization's history. As the sociologists Gary Marx and Michael Useem have suggested, when members of a majority group are involved in movements for minority rights, there is a tendency for the minority group to demand control of the organization and even to force out majority group members.[121] In the early stages majority group members are valued for their wealth, prominence, and expertise. In the NAACP, the main contribution of the early white Board members was to give greater legitimacy to the black protest. In addition Arthur Spingarn, Storey, and the other prominent lawyers provided a legal expertise virtually lacking in the black community at the time. Accordingly, blacks took over first the fieldwork, and then the administration, since in these areas success depended upon personal qualities rather than highly specialized knowledge; not until the 1930's did the legal program come under black control, following the appearance of a group of talented black constitutional lawyers trained at prestigious law schools.[122] The consolidation of the NAACP's bureaucratic structure, including the creation of the legal department, in a sense marked the end of an era. Although he would ultimately lose control of the bureaucratic mechanism he had done so much to create, Walter White had built the structure that provided the basis for the NAACP's wartime and postwar growth and legal victories that culminated in *Brown* v. *Board of Education* in 1954 and paved the way for the civil rights revolution of our own time.

Although this paper is based almost entirely on the written and printed record, confidential interviews with NAACP Executive Director Roy Wilkins, NAACP Director of Branches Gloster Current, and the late Judge William H. Hastie provided illuminating supplementary observations for the period of Walter White's administration. An abbreviated version of this paper was read by Rudwick at the American Historical Association meeting in 1974.

1. Nancy J. Weiss, "From Black Separatism to Interracial Cooperation: The Origins of Organized Efforts for Racial Advancement, 1890–1920," in Barton J. Bernstein and

Allen J. Matusow, eds., *Twentieth-Century America: Recent Interpretations*, rev. ed. (New York, 1972), pp. 52–87.

2. For a general overview of this development in the twentieth-century civil rights movement as a whole, see August Meier, Elliott Rudwick, and Francis Broderick, eds., *Black Protest Thought in the Twentieth Century*, rev. ed. (Indianapolis, 1971), "Introduction." For detailed discussion of the Congress of Racial Equality, see Meier and Rudwick, *CORE: A Study in the Civil Rights Movement, 1942–1968* (New York, 1973). For brief discussions of the role of whites in the Student Nonviolent Coordinating Committee, see Howard Zinn, *SNCC: The New Abolitionists* (Boston, 1964), ch. 9, and Allen J. Matusow, "From Civil Rights to Black Power: The Case of SNCC, 1960–1966," in Bernstein and Matusow, eds., *Twentieth-Century America*, pp. 494–519. B. Joyce Ross analyzes the role of the NAACP's white Board chairman Joel Spingarn and the decline in influence of the white Board members during the 1930's in her *J. E. Spingarn and the Rise of the NAACP* (New York, 1972). The role of whites in a different kind of race advancement organization is discussed in Nancy Weiss, *The National Urban League, 1910–1940* (New York, 1974). References to the limited role played by whites in the Southern Christian Leadership Conference will be found in David L. Lewis, *King: A Critical Biography* (New York, 1970). For a discussion of whites in the NAACP, contending that the white leaders were tainted by racism and paternalism, see Victor M. Glasberg, "The Emergence of White Liberalism: The Founders of the NAACP and American Racial Attitudes" (Ph.D. dissertation, Harvard University, 1971).

3. The first secretary, Frances Blascoer, 1910–11, served only a year and had no significant impact on the Association's development. Roy Nash, the third secretary, is dealt with briefly below. For further discussion of both individuals, see Charles Flint Kellogg, *NAACP: A History of the National Association for the Advancement of Colored People, Volume I, 1909–1920* (Baltimore, 1967).

4. W. E. B. Du Bois to Joel E. Spingarn, Oct. 28, 1914, Spingarn Papers, Beinecke Library, Yale University.

5. Weiss, "From Black Separatism to Interracial Cooperation," p. 72.

6. Oswald Garrison Villard to Francis J. Garrison, Mar. 21, 1912, Villard Papers, Houghton Library, Harvard University.

7. See esp. secretary's duties listed in NAACP, *Annual Report for 1914* (New York, 1915), pp. 15–16. (The titles of the NAACP Annual Reports vary, and for convenience we have adopted the short form employed here.)

8. Examples of this will be given below.

9. J. E. Spingarn, Report of the Chairman; and May Childs Nerney, Report of the Secretary, in Minutes of NAACP Annual Meeting, Jan. 3, 1916, Box A 8, NAACP Archives, Library of Congress.

10. NAACP, *Annual Report for 1914*, p. 15; J. E. Spingarn, Report of the Chairman, in Minutes of NAACP Annual Meeting, Jan. 3, 1916, Box A 8, NAACP Archives.

11. For a good discussion of her publicity work, see Report of National Secretary to 1914 NAACP Annual Conference, Box B 1, NAACP Archives. For her clash with Villard, see below.

12. Nerney to Archibald Grimké, n.d. [Oct., 1914], Box 26, Archibald Grimké Papers, Howard University.

13. Board of Directors' Minutes, July 7, 1914, Box A 8, NAACP Archives; Nerney to W. N. Colson, June 12, 1914, Box G 210, *ibid.*; Nerney to Eugene Kinkle Jones, June 29, 1914, Box C 384, *ibid.*; Nerney to Arthur B. Spingarn, Sept. 15, 1915, Box 1, A. B. Spingarn Papers, Library of Congress. For another example of her forceful involvement in the legal work, see correspondence regarding *McCabe* v. *Santa Fe Railway* case: Moorfield Storey to Nerney, Aug. 8 and 27, 1913, Storey Letterbooks, Massachusetts Historical Society; [Nerney] to Storey, Aug. 11, 1913, Box 1, A. B. Spingarn Papers; [Chapin Brinsmade] to Storey, Nov. 12, 1913, *ibid.*

14. On her work with Arthur Spingarn, see esp. Nerney, Report of Secretary, in Minutes of the Annual Meeting, Jan. 3, 1916, Box A 8, NAACP Archives; Nerney to Grimké, Feb. 5, 1915, Box 27, Grimké Papers.

15. There is extensive material on this campaign in the NAACP Archives. See esp. Box C 403, and Nerney, "Segregation in the Government Departments in Washington," Sept. 30, 1913, Box C 70.

16. See extensive correspondence in NAACP Archives, Boxes C 299, C 300, and C 301; J. E. Spingarn to Nerney, Mar. 10, 17, Apr. 20, and May 3, 1915, Box C 75; Nerney to J. E. Spingarn, Mar. 13, May 15 and 19, 1915, Box C 70; Nerney to Villard, Mar. 9 and 11, 1915, *ibid.*; Nerney to Storey, Apr. 17 and 21, 1915, *ibid.*; also *The Crisis*, 9 (Dec., 1915), 85.

·17. Nerney to J. E. Spingarn, Dec. 1, 1913, Box C 403, and May 19, 1915, Box C 70, NAACP Archives.

18. *The Crisis*, 6 (Aug., 1913), 190, (Sept., 1913), 242, and 7 (Nov., 1913), 342–43; Nerney to J. E. Spingarn, July 2, 1913, Box 3, J. E. Spingarn Papers, Howard University; Nerney to J. E. Spingarn, July 7, 1913, Box G 34, NAACP Archives; Mary White Ovington to J. E. Spingarn, July 29, 1913, *ibid.*; Board of Directors' Minutes, Aug. 5, 1913, Box A 8, *ibid.*; Nerney to Grimké, Sept. 17 and Oct. 28, 1913, Box 26, Grimké Papers; Nerney to J. E. Spingarn, Jan. 20, 1914, Box C 70, NAACP Archives. On her efforts to heal branch factionalism in Philadelphia, Pittsburgh, and Louisville, see Nerney to K. E. Evans, June 27, 1913, Box G 186, NAACP Archives; Villard to F. J. Garrison, Mar. 14, 1913, Villard Papers; Board of Directors' Minutes, July 12, 1915, Box A 8, NAACP Archives.

19. Nerney to J. E. Spingarn, July 2, 1913, Box 3, J. E. Spingarn Papers, Howard University.

20. Nerney to J. E. Spingarn, Dec. 1, 1913, Box C 403, NAACP Archives.

21. Nerney to Charles E. Bentley, Dec. 31, 1914, Box 26, Grimké Papers; Nerney to Grimké, Jan. 22, 1915, Box 27, *ibid.*; *The Crisis*, 9 (Apr., 1915), 281.

22. Du Bois to J. E. Spingarn, Oct. 28, 1914, J. E. Spingarn Papers, Yale University.

23. Nerney to George Packard, July 28, 1913, Box C 403, NAACP Archives.

24. See her letters to Archibald Grimké in Grimké Papers, Boxes 26 and 27.

25. Nerney to Grimké, Nov. 2 and 6, 1913, Box 26, *ibid.*

26. Villard to Garrison, Feb. 7 and 20, 1913, Villard Papers.

27. Villard to Garrison, Feb. 7, 1913, *ibid.*; Du Bois to Villard, Mar. 18, 1913, *ibid.*; Nerney to J. E. Spingarn, July 2, 1913, J. E. Spingarn Papers, Yale University.

28. Nerney to Grimké, Nov. 2 and 6, 1913, Box 26, Grimké Papers. On Nerney's conflict with Villard, see also her letter to Charles T. Hallinan, Jan. 9, 1914, Box C 416, NAACP Archives.

29. Nerney to Grimké, Dec. 4, 1913, Box 26, Grimké Papers.

30. Mary White Ovington to Villard, Nov. 23, 1913, Villard Papers.

31. See, *e.g.*, Board of Directors' Minutes, Feb. 4, 1913, Box A 8, NAACP Archives; Nerney to V. Morton-Jones, Oct. 31, 1912, Box C 1, *ibid.*; Nerney to Addie W. Hunton, Nov. 1 and 4, 1912, Box C 70, *ibid.*; Nerney to R. W. Bagnall, Dec. 29, 1913, Box C 416, *ibid.*; Bagnall to Nerney, Jan. 12, 1914, Box C 412, *ibid.*; C. W. Allinson to Nerney, Jan. 15, 1914, *ibid.*; NAACP, *Annual Report for 1913* (New York, 1914), p. 36, Nerney to Coralie F. Cook, July 9, 1913, Box C 1, NAACP Archives; Nerney to Villard, July 29, 1913, *ibid*; Nerney to Grimké, Mar. 31, Nov. 24, 1913, Feb. 11, 1914, and n.d. [Apr., 1914], Box 26, Grimké Papers.

32. Du Bois to J. E. Spingarn, Oct. 28, 1914, J. E. Spingarn Papers, Yale University; Nerney to Grimké, n.d. [Oct., 1914], Box 26, Grimké Papers.

33. Bagnall to Nerney, Jan. 12, 1914, Box C 412, NAACP Archives; F. E. Young to Nerney, Jan. 25, 1914, Box C 416, *ibid.*; Solomon Porter Hood to J. E. Spingarn, Jan. 6, 1913, Box 2, J. E. Spingarn Papers, Howard University; Lelia Walters to J. E. Spingarn, Jan. 14, 1913, Box 4, *ibid.*; Jessie Fauset to J. E. Spingarn, Feb. 12, 1913, Box 2, *ibid.*; Garnet C. Wilkinson to J. E. Spingarn, Feb. 14, 1913, Box 4, *ibid.*; Butler Wilson to J. E. Spingarn, Mar. 18, 1913, J. E. Spingarn Papers, New York Public Library; Charles Bentley to Nerney, n.d. [Jan., 1914], Box C 416, NAACP Archives.

34. *The Crisis*, 7 (Feb., 1914), 193; Nerney to Grimké, n.d. [Jan., 1914], Jan. 26, 1914, Box 26, Grimké Papers.

35. For discussion of the character of Spingarn's leadership in the NAACP, see Ross, *J. E. Spingarn and the Rise of the NAACP*.

36. *The Crisis*, 7 (Feb., 1914), 186–87, and (Mar., 1914), 240–41; Paul Kellogg to Du Bois, Dec. 17, 1913, printed in Herbert Aptheker, ed., *The Correspondence of W. E. B. Du Bois*, I (Amherst, Mass., 1973), pp. 186–87; *Survey*, 31 (Mar. 28, 1914), 810–11; Nerney to Grimké, Jan. 24, Mar. 26, 1914. Box 26, Grimké Papers; Villard to Garrison, Mar. 1, 1914, Villard Papers; Du Bois to J. E. Spingarn, Oct. 28, 1914, J. E. Spingarn Papers, Yale University.

37. Nerney to Grimké, Jan. 26, 1914, Box 26, Grimké Papers.

38. Board of Directors' Minutes, Apr. 17 and July 7, 1914, Box A 8, NAACP Archives; Florence Kelley to J. E. Spingarn, June 8, 1914, Box 2, J. E. Spingarn Papers, Howard University.

39. Nerney to Grimké, Oct. 20, 1914, Box 26, Grimké Papers.

40. Ross, *J. E. Spingarn*, pp. 70–74; Kellogg, *NAACP*, pp. 97–99; Rudwick, *W. E. B. Du Bois*, pp. 168–71. For discussion of staff size and office arrangements, see *The Crisis*, 7 (Feb., 1914), 189, and 9 (Apr., 1915), 297; Report of Chairman in NAACP, *Annual Report for 1914*, p. 5.

41. Nerney to Grimké, Sept. 2, 1914, n.d. [Sept., 1914], n.d. [Oct. 11 (?), 1914], and n.d. [Oct. 15 (?), 1914], Box 26, Grimké Papers.

42. *E.g.*, Nerney to Grimké, Oct. 20, 1914, n.d. [Oct. 15 (?), 1914], and telegram, Nov. 2, 1914, *ibid*.

43. Nerney to Grimké, Oct. 22, 1914, *ibid*.

44. Nerney to Grimké, n.d. [Oct. 11 (?), 1914], Oct. 17, 20, 21, 22, 1914, *ibid*.; Board of Directors' Minutes, Nov. 4, 1914, Box A 8, NAACP Archives.

45. J. E. Spingarn to Du Bois, Oct. 24, 1914, and Du Bois to J. E. Spingarn, Oct. 28, 1914, J. E. Spingarn Papers, Yale University.

46. Board of Directors' Minutes, Nov. 4, 1914, Box A 8, NAACP Archives; Ovington to J. E. Spingarn, Nov. 7, 1914, Box 3, Spingarn Papers, Howard University; Nerney to Grimké, Oct. 20, 21, and telegram, Nov. 2, 1914, Box 26, Grimké Papers.

47. Board of Directors' Minutes, Nov. 4, Dec. 1, 1914, Box A 8, NAACP Archives; Nerney to Grimké, n.d. [Dec. 6 (?), 1914], Dec. 21, 1914, n.d. [ca. Dec. 28, 1914], Box 26, Grimké Papers; Minutes of NAACP Annual Meeting, Feb. 12, 1915, Box A 8, NAACP Archives.

48. Nerney to Grimké, Sept. 16, Oct. 12, 1915, Box 27, Grimké Papers; Board of Directors' Minutes, Oct. 11, Nov. 8, 1915, Box A 8, NAACP Archives.

49. Nerney, untitled memorandum, Dec. 6, 1915, filed with NAACP Board of Directors' Minutes, Box A 8, NAACP Archives; see also her pessimistic statements in Minutes of NAACP Annual Meeting, Jan. 3, 1916, *ibid*.

Nerney's disillusionment at this point prompted her to make a statement which, while ambiguous in its attitude, comes closer than any of her other remarks to suggesting the possibility that she harbored elements of condescension and paternalism: "In our work with branches we have successfully dealt with the problem of working with groups of people who have no habits of cooperation. How difficult this is cannot be understood except by those who have tried it. One must take advantage of the few instances in which a group emerges from the welter of personal and factional fights, and that the results should sometimes seem crude and unsatisfactory is not strange. Learning to work together and to think together, however, has been invaluable to our branches and to the cause they represent. They understand the rudiments of organized effort; they wear our emblem and are beginning to read and think of the race question in terms of democracy" (Minutes of Annual Meeting, Jan. 3, 1916, *ibid*.). Of course, complaints about black disunity and the opportunism of some branch leaders were common. Moreover, Du Bois himself displayed an elitist attitude toward the masses, sometimes referred to blacks as a "backward race," and editorially pointed to the narrowness and selfishness of black leaders. In *Souls of Black Folk*, for example, he wrote that "while it is a great truth to say that the Negro must strive and strive mightily to help himself, it is equally true that unless his striving be . . . aroused and encouraged, by the initiative of the richer and wiser environing group, he cannot hope for great success," and that "the separation [of the races] is so thorough and deep that it absolutely precludes for the present between the races anything like that sympathetic and effective group-training and leadership of the one by the other, such as the American Negro and all backward peoples must have for effectual progress" (Du Bois, *Souls of Black Folk* [reprint, Greenwich, Conn., 1961], pp. 53, 79). In writing of the black clergy Du Bois maintained: "The trouble is, however, this: there are too few such ["pure-minded, efficient, unselfish"] men. The paths and the higher places are choked with pretentious ill-trained men and in far too many cases with men dishonest and otherwise immoral. Such men make the way of upright and businesslike candidates for power extremely difficult. . . . Having thus a partially tainted leadership, small wonder that the 30,000 colored ministers fall as a mass far below expectations. There are among them hustling business men, eloquent talkers, suave companions and hale fellows, but only here and there does one meet . . . burning spiritual guides . . . utterly devoted to a great ideal of righteousness" (Du Bois, editorial, "The Negro Church," *The Crisis*, 4 [May, 1912], 24).

50. J. E. Spingarn, Florence Kelley, and Charles Studin, untitled menorandum, Dec. 6, 1915, filed with Board of Directors' Minutes, Box A 8, NAACP Archives.

51. Du Bois to Grimké, Dec. 10, 1915, Box 27, Grimké Papers; on Du Bois's rapprochement with Grimké, see reference in J. E. Spingarn to Grimké, Dec. 14, 1915, *ibid.*, and three-page feature devoted to Grimké in *The Crisis*, 10 (Oct., 1915), 288–90.

52. Board of Directors' Minutes, Dec. 13, 1915, Box A 8, NAACP Archives; Ovington to J. E. Spingarn, Dec. 13 [1915], Box 3, J. E. Spingarn Papers, Howard University.

53. Du Bois to J. E. Spingarn, A. B. Spingarn, and Ovington, Dec. 16, 1915, Box 21, A. B. Spingarn Papers. This letter is erroneously cited as Nov., 1913, by Kellogg and Ross on the basis of undated copies in the Johnson and Du Bois papers. On Du Bois's preference, see implications in letters of Ovington to J. E. Spingarn, Dec. 20, 1915, J. E. Spingarn Papers, New York Public Library, and of Du Bois to Grimké, Dec. 23, 1915, Box 27, Grimké Papers.

54. J. E. Spingarn to Grimké, Dec. 16, 1915, Box 27, Grimké Papers; Minutes of NAACP Annual Meeting, Jan. 3, 1916, Box A 8, NAACP Archives; Nerney to Board of Directors, Jan. 6, 1916, Box 21, A. B. Spingarn Papers.

55. Nerney to J. E. Spingarn, Jan. 6, 1916, Box 3, J. E. Spingarn Papers, Howard University; Nerney to Board of Directors, Jan. 6, 1916, Box 21, A. B. Spingarn Papers.

56. Villard to J. E. Spingarn, Nov. 20, 1916, Box 4, J. E. Spingarn Papers, Howard University.

57. On candidates and negotiations involved in finding a field organizer, see John Hope to J. E. Spingarn, Oct. 21, 1916, with annotation by Spingarn to R.N. [Roy Nash], Box 2, J. E. Spingarn Papers, Howard University; R.F.N. [Roy Nash] to [J. E. Spingarn], Oct. 27 [1916], originally attached to preceding letter but now detached and in Box 3, *ibid.*; J. E. Spingarn to Johnson, Oct. 28, Nov. 6, 1916, James Weldon Johnson Papers, Beinecke Library, Yale University; Du Bois to Johnson, Nov. 1, 1916, *ibid.*; Johnson to J. E. Spingarn, Nov. 5, 1916, *ibid.*; Ovington to J. E. Spingarn, Nov. 24, 1916, Box 3, J. E. Spingarn Papers, Howard University; Board of Directors' Minutes, Dec. 11, 1916, Box A 8, NAACP Archives; George F. Cook to J. E. Spingarn, Box 1, J. E. Spingarn Papers, Howard University. See also discussions in Ridgely Torrence, *The Story of John Hope* (New York, 1947), pp. 198–200; and Eugene Levy, *James Weldon Johnson: Black Leader, Black Voice* (Chicago, 1973), pp. 184–87.

58. For a good survey of Johnson's early contacts with the NAACP, see Levy, *James Weldon Johnson*, pp. 178–83. See also Johnson's correspondence with Du Bois, 1905, in Aptheker, ed., *The Correspondence of W. E. B. Du Bois*, I, 115, 116. There are interesting complimentary references to Johnson in *The Crisis*, 5 (Feb., 1913), 171–72, 173.

59. *The Crisis*, 14 (May, 1917), 18–19. When Johnson began his trip there were only two branches in the South.

60. See esp. account of West Coast trip in Report of the Field Secretary, July 8,

1919, NAACP Board of Directors' Minute Books, NAACP National Office, New York. Citations to materials in these Minute Books refer to items not photoduplicated for the Library of Congress, and will be hereafter cited as in NAACP Minute Books, New York.

61. NAACP, *Annual Report for 1919* (New York, 1920), p. 9.

62. NAACP Press Release, Aug. 18, 1920, Box C 6, NAACP Archives.

63. In 1920 the NAACP estimated that 90% of its membership was black. *The Crisis*, 19 (Mar., 1920), 243.

64. *E.g.*, Johnson, "Our Aim," *The Crisis*, 13 (Feb., 1917), 169; Johnson's column in the New York *Age*, Oct. 11, 1917; Johnson, "The Negro's Place in the New Civilization," speech delivered Aug. 12, 1920, Box C 429, NAACP Archives. This was a consistent theme of Johnson's thinking. See esp. his *Negro Americans, What Now?* (New York, 1934). His views were particularly well expressed in a letter written during the 1921 membership campaign: "I repeat again the text of all my talks to our people throughout the country—what we need and what we must have is power. Nothing short of power will accomplish our purpose. It is time for colored men and women of clear brain and red blood to discredit the weak-kneed, compromising teachings that have been so long foisted on the race. We must put up a bold front and let this country realize that we know the things we want, we know the things we are entitled to, and we are determined to have them at any cost" (Johnson to Julian St. George White, Apr. 1, 1921, Box C 7, NAACP Archives.

65. Board of Directors' Minutes, Sept. 17, 1917, Box A 8, NAACP Archives.

66. July 9, 1917, *ibid*.

67. Johnson to Ovington, Aug. 12, 20, 21, 1919, Box C 66, NAACP Archives, and Board of Directors' Minutes, Sept. 8, 1919, Box A 9, *ibid*. The care with which Johnson cultivated key black professionals and businessmen is revealed in his reaction to the complaint of Robert Abbott, publisher of the Chicago *Defender*, that *The Crisis* had ignored his paper: "Whatever may be our opinion . . . [of] the type of journalism practiced by the Defender," he confided to his office diary, "it is true that the splendid achievements of the Defender are worthy of especial notice by the Crisis and it is a matter of wise policy for us to take greater recognition. . . . I shall do small article for Crisis" (Johnson, office diary, entry dated Nov. 9, 1921, Box C 101, *ibid.*).

68. For discussion of persons considered for the job, see Kellogg, *NAACP*, p. 114. In his discussion Kellogg correctly mentions that Roger Baldwin and Owen Lovejoy were among the candidates considered, but he fails to mention the fact that negotiations were seriously undertaken with Ernest Gruening, more recently the well-known senator from Alaska. See Board of Directors' Minutes, Dec. 10, 1917, Box A 8, NAACP Archives.

69. Levy, *James Weldon Johnson*, p. 194; Walter White, *A Man Called White* (New York, 1948), p. 35.

70. For favorable recollections of Shillady, emphasizing his administrative skills, see Johnson, *Along This Way* (New York, 1933), p. 329; White, *A Man Called White*, p. 44; Ovington, *The Walls Came Tumbling Down* (New York, 1947), ch. 5. See also Du Bois's evaluation of Shillady in Du Bois to the Chairman of the Board and the Committee on Secretary, June 28, 1920, Box C 64, NAACP Archives.

71. White, *A Man Called White*, p. 44; Johnson, *Along This Way*, p. 329; Ovington, *The Walls Came Tumbling Down*, p. 149.

72. See, *e.g.*, George A. Towns to Johnson, Feb. 12, 1919, Box C 2, NAACP Archives.

73. Shillady to Storey, Apr. 19, 1919, Box C 74, *ibid*.

74. Shillady to Julius Rosenwald, May 7, July 11, 1918, *ibid*.; Shillady to Ovington, July 16, 1918, *ibid*.; Johnson to William C. Graves, Dec. 4, 1918, Feb. 21, 1919, Box C 333, *ibid*.; Shillady to Graves, May 23, 1919, Jan. 9, 1920, Box C 74, *ibid*.; Johnson, Report of Field Secretary, Mar. 3, 1920, NAACP Minute Books, New York.

75. For Shillady representing the NAACP with government agencies and social work organizations in the early part of his administration, see Board of Directors'

Minutes, Mar. 11, Apr. 8, Oct. 14, Nov. 11, Dec. 9, 1918, Jan. 6, 1919, Boxes A 8 and A 9, NAACP Archives.

76. Shillady, "A Day's Work at the National Office," *The Crisis*, 17 (Dec., 1918), 69–72; Ovington, *The Walls Came Tumbling Down*, p. 149.

77. For a good summary of Shillady's work in this area, see Kellogg, *NAACP*, pp. 148–49.

78. Shillady to Grimké, May 10, 1919, Box 29, Grimké Papers.

79. See outline of White's duties in Board of Directors' Minutes, Feb. 11, 1918, Box A 8, NAACP Archives, and listing of White as a clerical worker in the 1919 salary schedule, at a rate of pay less than certain others on the clerical staff: Jan. 13, 1919, Box A 9, *ibid*.

80. White, *A Man Called White*, pp. 40–42, and White's reports on his early investigations in *The Crisis*, 16 (May, 1918), 16–20, and (Sept., 1918), 221–23.

81. See correspondence in NAACP Archives, Boxes C 332 to C 334, and letters in Box C 74, esp. Shillady to Storey, Feb. 15 and 24, 1919.

82. Shillady, "Finances of the NAACP," *The Crisis*, 17 (Nov., 1918), 19.

83. White, *A Man Called White*, p. 40.

84. Board of Directors' Minutes, July 8, 1918, Box A 8, NAACP Archives.

85. E. G. S. [Ethel G. Stow] to Franklin K. Lane, Feb. 27, 1919, Box C 333, *ibid*.; White to James P. Lowder, Mar. 14, 1919, *ibid*.; White to Will H. Hays, Feb. 20, 1919, *ibid*.; "Memo to be Attached to Diary of Mr. White, Friday, April 11 [1919]," Box C 76, *ibid*.

86. Shillady, Memoranda to Anti-Lynching Committee regarding Dyer Bill, Nov. 14 and 20, 1919, NAACP Minute Books, New York; Minutes of the Conference of Executives, Jan. 19, 1920, Box C 5, NAACP Archives; correspondence regarding Dyer Bill, Apr.-Sept., 1918, Box C 242, *ibid*.; see also correspondence between Walter White and Moorfield Storey on antilynching legislation, May-July, 1918, Boxes C 75 and C 76, *ibid*.

87. Shillady to A. Mitchell Palmer, July 25, 1919, Box G 34, NAACP Archives; Shillady to Ovington, July 25, 1919, *ibid*.

88. *The Crisis*, 18 (Sept., 1919), 244; White to Ovington, Aug. 7, 11, 13, 1919, Box C 76, NAACP Archives; Board of Directors' Minutes, Aug. 26, 1919, Box A 9, *ibid*.; and the following from materials no longer in the NAACP Archives, photocopies of which were supplied through the courtesy of William Tuttle: White to Ovington, Aug. 21, 1919; Shillady to Ovington, Aug. 4, 1919; White to Shillady, Aug. 26, 1919; and White, "Memorandum re Chicago Riots Situation," Sept. 8, 1919. These items were among a file of NAACP archival materials dealing with the 1919 race riot that were detached from the main body of the Association's archives while they were still in New York, and have since disappeared. It is fortunate that Mr. Tuttle was able to consult these documents before they were lost.

89. Johnson to Ovington, Aug. 12, 1919, Box C 66, NAACP Archives; Board of Directors' Minutes, Sept. 8, 1919, Box A 9, *ibid*.

90. Board of Directors' Minutes, Oct., 1919–Feb., 1920, Box A 9, *ibid*.; Reports of the Field Secretary, Sept., 1919–Feb., 1920, NAACP Minute Books, New York.

91. Reports of the Field Secretary, Jan. 12 and Feb. 9, 1920, NAACP Minute Books, New York; NAACP, *Annual Report for 1920* (New York, 1921), p. 44; correspondence between Johnson and Storey, Dec., 1919, and Jan., 1920, in Boxes C 66 and C 75, NAACP Archives, and in Storey Letterbooks, Massachusetts Historical Society; Minutes of Conference of Executives, Jan. 19, 1920, Box C 5, NAACP Archives. On Graham Sedition Bill, see also Johnson's editorial on the subject in the New York *Age*, Dec. 20, 1919.

92. Johnson, *Along This Way*, pp. 342–43; White, *A Man Called White*, pp. 46–47; Ovington, *The Walls Came Tumbling Down*, pp. 171–75; Board of Directors' Minutes, Sept., 1919–Mar., 1920, Boxes A 8 and A 9, NAACP Archives; Ovington to Johnson, Apr. 9, 1920, Johnson Papers; Shillady to Chairman of Board of Directors, Apr. 1, 1920, Box A 19, NAACP Archives.

93. Reports of Field Secretary, Feb. 9, June 14, 1920, NAACP Minute Books, New York; untitled minutes of meeting between Johnson and other NAACP officials, Aug.

2, 1920, Box C 6, NAACP Archives; "Report of the Field Secretary on Interview with Senator Warren G. Harding, Marion, Ohio August 9, 1920," Box C 64, *ibid.*

94. Ovington to J. E. Spingarn, Nov. 24, 1916, Box 3, J. E. Spingarn Papers, Howard University; quotation from R.F.N. [Nash] to [J. E. Spingarn], memorandum, n.d., attached to Hope to Spingarn, Oct. 27, 1916, now detached and *ibid.*

95. Ovington to J. E. Spingarn, Sept. 26, 1917, *ibid.*; Ovington to Johnson, Apr. 9, 1920, Johnson Papers.

96. Board of Directors' Minutes, June 14, Sept. 13, Nov. 8, 1920, Box A 9, NAACP Archives; Minutes of Meeting of Committee on Secretary, July 20, 1920, Box 46, A. B. Spingarn Papers; Du Bois to Chairman of the Board and Committee on Secretary, June 28, 1920, Box C 64, NAACP Archives; press release, Aug. 18, 1920, Box C 6, *ibid.*; Bagnall to Ovington, Nov. 8, 1920, Box C 62, *ibid.* For Du Bois's role in securing Johnson as field secretary, see citations in note 57, above.

97. For example, in 1921 Storey volunteered to resign as president in favor of a younger person, but Johnson would not hear of it. See Storey to Johnson, Dec. 28, 1921, Box C 76, NAACP Archives; Johnson to Storey, Dec. 30, 1921, Box C 66, *ibid.*

98. Johnson, "The Negro's Place in the New Civilization," Aug. 12, 1920, Box C 429, *ibid.*; Johnson, "Organizing 250,000 Colored People to Improve American Race Relations" [April, 1921], Box C 7, *ibid.*; Johnson to Dear Friend, Apr. 26, 1921, Box G 95, *ibid.*

99. NAACP, *Annual Report for 1924* (New York, 1925), pp. 36–37.

100. Villard to Garrison, July 21, Aug. 8, 15, and 30, 1913, Villard Papers; Villard to Storey, Sept. 10, 1913, *ibid.*; Villard to Woodrow Wilson, Sept. 29, 1913, Box 1, A. B. Spingarn Papers.

101. For a full account of Johnson's activities, see Robert L. Zangrando, "The Efforts of the National Association for the Advancement of Colored People to Secure Passage of a Federal Anti-Lynching Law, 1920–40" (Ph.D. dissertation, University of Pennsylvania, 1963), ch. 3. On Johnson's methods, see a particularly illuminating letter, Johnson to White, Jan. 4, 1922, Box C 66, NAACP Archives.

102. Johnson to William C. Graves, Sept. 17, 1920, *ibid.*; White to Eugene M. Martin, Sept. 17, 1929, Box C 97, *ibid.*

103. Ovington, *The Walls Came Tumbling Down*, p. 176.

104. Because the discussion in the following pages consists of generalizations based upon study of voluminous archival and manuscript materials, it is not feasible to supply the usual kinds of detailed citations.

105. August Meier and Elliott Rudwick, "Attorneys Black and White: A Case Study of Race Relations within the NAACP," in this volume.

106. Neval Thomas to NAACP Board of Directors, Dec. 3, 1928, NAACP Minute Books, New York; [Johnson], "The Charges of Mr. Neval H. Thomas," Dec. 24, 1928, *ibid.*; Board of Directors' Minutes, Jan. 10, 1921, Box A 9, NAACP Archives. For further discussion of the matter, arriving at conclusions similar to ours, see Levy, *James Weldon Johnson*, pp. 226–27.

107. Ovington to A. B. Spingarn, June 28, 1929, Box 4, A. B. Spingarn Papers.

108. This description of Spingarn's style of leadership was suggested in an interview with Judge William H. Hastie, Philadelphia, Oct. 17, 1973, and it confirmed the conclusions which we had reached on the basis of research in the NAACP Archives and the Arthur Spingarn Papers. For discussion of Spingarn's legal role, see Meier and Rudwick, "Attorneys Black and White," and in general see the voluminous correspondence with him in NAACP Archives and his own papers at the Library of Congress and the frequent references to him in the Board of Directors' Minutes.

109. Although Du Bois many years later charged that Walter White had forced Johnson out (Du Bois, *The Autobiography of W. E. B. Du Bois* [New York, 1968], pp. 293–94), we have not found any real evidence to confirm this interpretation. Johnson's biographer, carefully examining the evidence and the relationship between Johnson and White, also arrives at the same conclusion as we do (Levy, *James Weldon Johnson*, pp. 292–95).

110. See esp. Walter White's correspondence with William Rosenwald, Boxes C 74, C 77, and C 78, NAACP Archives; with Jacob Billikopf, Boxes C 63 and C 77, *ibid.*; and with Herbert Lehman, Boxes C 156 and C 78, *ibid.*

111. Du Bois and others to the Board of Directors, Dec. 21, 1931, Box A 21, *ibid.*; J. E. Spingarn to A. B. Spingarn, n.d. [Jan., 1932], Box 5, A. B. Spingarn Papers; J. E. Spingarn, "Confidential Memorandum Re: Status of the NAACP," Nov. 11, 1932, Box 46, *ibid.*; Wilkins to F. M. Turner, June 14, 1932, Box C 146, NAACP Archives; untitled statement [1933], *ibid.*; J. E. Spingarn, Remarks to Annual Meeting of NAACP, Jan. 9, 1933, Box A 24, *ibid.*; Board of Directors' Minutes, Dec. 21, 1931, Jan. 4, Feb. 8, Mar. 14, Apr. 11, 1932, Jan. 9, 1933, Box A 10, *ibid.*; Du Bois to J. E. Spingarn, Dec. 31, 1931, J. E. Spingarn Papers, New York Public Library; untitled memorandum, n.d. [1932], *ibid.*, [J. E. Spingarn], "Information for the Committee on Administration," n.d. [ca. 1932], *ibid.*; [J. E. Spingarn], Statement of the Chairman, n.d. [ca. Feb., 1932], *ibid.*; see also correspondence in Budget Committee Files, 1931–32, Box A 26, NAACP Archives, and detailed account in Ross, *J. E. Spingarn and the Rise of the NAACP*, pp. 133–34, 136, 142.

112. Board of Directors' Minutes, Mar. 9, 1931, Box A 10, NAACP Archives.

113. This conflict has been treated several times. See Rudwick, *Du Bois*, pp. 266–85; Ross, *J. E. Spingarn and the Rise of the NAACP*, pp. 198–216; Raymond Wolters, *Negroes and the Great Depression* (Westport, Conn., 1970), ch. 11.

114. This conclusion is based upon correspondence too extensive to be cited here.

115. Ovington to J. E. Spingarn, Dec. 15 [1931], J. E. Spingarn Papers, New York Public Library.

116. On the work of the Committee on Future Plan and Program of the NAACP, see esp. Box A 28 and A 29, NAACP Archives; for an especially good critique of the NAACP by one of the younger black intellectuals, see Ralph J. Bunche, "The Programs, Ideologies, Tactics and Achievements of Negro Betterment and Interracial Organizations," unpublished memorandum for the Carnegie-Myrdal Study of the Negro in America, Schomburg Collection, New York Public Library, pp. 25–52, 155–67. For White's response, see White, Memorandum from the Secretary to the Board of Directors, Oct. 6, 1934, Box 7, A. B. Spingarn Papers; White to Ovington, Oct. 1, 1934, Box C 78, NAACP Archives; and esp. White to Charles H. Houston, Sept. 21, 1934, *ibid.* For an interpretation of Spingarn's role somewhat different from the one we have given, see Ross, *J. E. Spingarn and the Rise of the NAACP*, pp. 231–41.

117. This conclusion regarding the relationship between Walter White and Arthur Spingarn is based upon the very extensive correspondence between the two men. In fact, Arthur Spingarn was far more important than Joel Spingarn when it came to the day-to-day operations of the organization.

118. *E.g.*, White to Lillian Alexander, Nov. 9, 1933, Box A 28, NAACP Archives; White to Charles H. Houston, Oct. 23, 1934, *ibid.*; White to Johnson, Oct. 26, 1934, *ibid.*; White to Arthur Spingarn, Jan. 30, 1937, Box C 79, *ibid.*; White and Houston, "Memorandum from the Secretary and the Special Counsel to the Committee on Nominations," Nov. 10, 1936, Box A 28, *ibid.* By the mid-1930's White was regularly attending the meetings of the nominating committee. See scattered minutes of the Nominating Committee, *ibid.*

119. Confidential interviews.

120. Detailed discussion of this subject will be found in Meier and Rudwick, "Attorneys Black and White."

121. Gary Marx and Michael Useem, "Majority Involvement in Minority Movements: Civil Rights, Abolition, Untouchability," *Journal of Social Issues*, 27 (1972), 424–39.

122. We are indebted to Gary Marx for suggesting that the rate at which blacks move into various positions in an interracial action organization is a function of the specific kinds of skills and training required for those jobs (Gary Marx to authors, Mar. 30, 1974).

SIX

Attorneys Black and White:
A Case Study of Race Relations
within the NAACP

BY AUGUST MEIER AND ELLIOTT RUDWICK

The civil rights revolution of the 1960's has stimulated scholarly research into the history of organizations for black advancement, and a critical reevaluation of the roles of whites and blacks in the struggle for racial equality in America. Much of the recent literature has emphasized the cleavages and tensions between Negroes and whites in these organizations, the ambivalences in the relations between members of the two races, and the blacks' thrust for a greater voice in, or control of, the movement for their freedom.[1] Recently the sociologists Gary Marx and Michael Useem have drawn upon these historical studies in an effort to establish generalizations about the participation of individuals from privileged groups in movements for the emancipation of oppressed minorities. They concluded that intergroup tensions arise within such movements for several reasons: divergent competencies and cultural backgrounds; paternalistic attitudes among members from the privileged majority; and the oppressed minority's distrust of even the best-intentioned people in the majority group. Marx and Useem observe that over time "latent conflict" within these movements becomes more visible, with the minority group attempting to assert control over organizations dedicated to its advancement, and in most instances, ultimately pushing out people from the majority group.[2]

Reprinted, with additions, from *Journal of American History*, 41 (Mar., 1976), 913–46. © 1976 by the Organization of American Historians.

The Charles H. Houston Papers, now at Howard University, are currently being processed and should provide additional illumination on the question discussed here.

In the following pages, the issues raised by this scholarship will be examined through a study of the role of lawyers in the National Association for the Advancement of Colored People. The principal tactic of this organization, which for half a century dominated the racial protest movement, was a legal campaign to secure enforcement of the black man's constitutional rights. Accordingly, an analysis of black and white participation in its legal program illuminates the whole question of black-white interaction in biracial organizations formed to fight for racial equality in America.

The NAACP was founded in 1909 during the most oppressive period which blacks had faced since the Civil War, a time when black protest organizations like the Niagara Movement were all but ignored by whites and enjoyed only meager support among Negroes. Accordingly the interracial character of the NAACP, providing contacts with influential white leaders and a degree of legitimacy in the eyes of white elites, performed a vital function. At first W. E. B. Du Bois was the only Negro in the Association's inner circle, but within a decade the organization had built a black field staff, and since 1921 the top administrative post of secretary has been held by a Negro—first James Weldon Johnson, then Walter White, who was promoted to the post in 1931, and most recently Roy Wilkins. In 1935 both the important position of Board chairman and the chief responsibility of the legal program passed in Negro hands.

For purposes of our discussion, the NAACP's legal work falls into two periods, with the early 1930's a decisive turning point in the Association's use of white and black lawyers. Prior to 1930 prominent white lawyers carried the principal burden of the national office's legal activity. By 1920 this work had come under the joint supervision of the chairman of the National Legal Committee, a white New York lawyer, Arthur Spingarn, and the black assistant secretary, Walter White.*

*The NAACP's very first cases in 1910 were administered on an ad hoc basis by Board chairman Oswald Garrison Villard. The NAACP's legal committee, established in February, 1911, was headed first by Thomas Ewing, Jr., of the prominent New York law firm, Ewing and Ewing, and then in 1912–13 by William M. Wherry, Jr., a corporation lawyer who was counsel for Villard's New York *Evening Post*. Wherry also doubled as the volunteer "Attorney for the Association," while much of the routine correspondence was handled by the secretary. In a reorganization of the legal work at the end of 1913, Arthur Spingarn became chairman of the

Meanwhile, cases undertaken by NAACP branches in the southern states were ordinarily—though not always—handled by white lawyers, while in the northern and border states the usual practice of local branches was to employ black lawyers who on frequent occasions associated themselves with white counsel.

Some would argue that this prominence of white lawyers was evidence of paternalism among the Association's early white leaders. Yet black leaders in the NAACP themselves emphatically favored using prominent white attorneys. Actually this policy was rooted in two very practical considerations— the problems besetting the black legal profession, and the NAACP's ability to secure the services of certain highly distinguished white attorneys.[3]

During the first part of the century there were very few black lawyers. In 1910, at the time when the NAACP was founded, out of about 114,000 lawyers in the country, only 795, or 0.7 percent, were black. Twenty years later the situation was no better—Negroes formed only about 0.8 percent of the country's attorneys. In the South conditions were even worse. In 1910, when 90 percent of the Negroes lived in that region, over half of the black lawyers were in the North and West. And in the next thirty years the number of Negro lawyers declined in nearly every southern state—in Georgia from 18 to 8; in South Carolina from 17 to 5; and in Mississippi from 21 to 3.[4] The situation in Mississippi, indeed, was revealing. By the opening of the century it was becoming increasingly difficult for blacks to be admitted to the bar there, and judges in many parts of the state would not allow Negroes to practice in their courtrooms. And even in cases involving one black man against another, the black attorney often found it wise to associate himself with a white lawyer when the opposing counsel was white. Not surpris-

legal committee, and Chapin Brinsmade, a recent graduate of Harvard Law School, was secured as a salaried staff attorney to investigate cases and handle routine correspondence. Financial exigencies forced the elimination of this fledgling legal department a year later, and until after World War I the staff attorney's duties were carried out by the secretary under the supervision of Arthur Spingarn and his law partner and NAACP Board member, Charles Studin. Both Spingarn and Studin had originally become involved in NAACP work as lawyers for cases conducted by the Association's New York branch in 1911–12. Studin substituted for Spingarn as chairman of the NAACP's legal committee when the latter served in the army during World War I, but thereafter played a minor role in NAACP affairs.

ingly, Mississippi blacks concluded that "the employment of a white lawyer was necessary for a Negro to get justice."[5]

Mississippi was an extreme case of what was true throughout the South and, to a lesser degree, in other parts of the country. Studies undertaken at the end of the 1920's by Carter G. Woodson, the leading black historian, and Charles H. Houston, one of the most prominent members of the Negro bar, revealed that black lawyers generally had an education inferior to that of white lawyers,[6] experienced widespread hostility from courtroom and jury, and faced a Negro public skeptical of their abilities. Even in New York, Negro attorneys reported that most of the patronage of blacks went to white lawyers.[7] Negro businessmen complained that black attorneys lacked competence. As Woodson pointed out, "Most of the large Negro business enterprises employ white lawyers. Some of them may retain a Negro lawyer for minor matters, but for any question involving serious decisions and consequences they resort to the better known and more influential lawyers of the other race."[8] Even highly race-conscious men like Marcus Garvey and more especially A. Philip Randolph occasionally employed prominent white lawyers to handle important legal work.[9] In the face of such handicaps, the Negro lawyer was often highly restricted in his practice, with his work, as Houston noted, involving "only a few, very definite stereotyped situations: the errant spouse, the parent abandoning the children, administration of small estates comprised of a little money in the bank, life insurance policies, and the family residence, and petty criminal offences. As long as the cases run true to type he makes a fairly brave showing. But shunted ever so little off the beaten path, he becomes befuddled."[10] Moreover, because of limited experience and expertise, and the skepticism of black businessmen and other clients, black lawyers frequently adopted the practice of associating themselves with white lawyers in important cases.[11]

There were certain highly successful Negro lawyers—but at the beginning of the NAACP's history almost none of these engaged in NAACP litigation. They were located almost entirely in the North, where their careers were based not on serving the black community but upon the patronage of well-to-do whites. Although several of these men had been members of the Niagara Movement, their expertise lay in areas other than civil rights cases or constitutional law. E. H. Morris of Chicago, among the most distinguished of them, was a corporation lawyer and tax specialist.[12]

Thus the racist context in which the NAACP was born not only created the need for the Association, but with most black lawyers caught in a vicious circle of discrimination and inexperience, their usefulness to the Association was also limited. According to William Hastie, who later became the first black federal judge, in 1930 "there were not ten Negro lawyers, competent and willing to handle substantial civil rights litigation, engaged in practice in the South."[13] Nor were there many white lawyers who would handle the NAACP's civil rights cases. Yet the Association was able to secure the help of some distinguished white attorneys. Most notable among them were two constitutional lawyers of national prominence—Moorfield Storey, the NAACP president and a former president of the American Bar Association, and Louis Marshall, the tireless attorney for Jewish rights organizations.[14] Storey, Marshall, or both supervised the NAACP briefs and presented oral arguments in all five of the cases which the national office argued before the Supreme Court between 1913 and 1927. Both were wealthy men who served without remuneration.

Illuminating both the limited opportunities open to young blacks aspiring to a career in law, and the resulting racial differences in the qualifications of the black and white lawyers available to the NAACP, is an analysis of their legal training.* Through the 1930's the great majority of southern Negro lawyers were graduates of Howard University Law School,[15] although occasionally one finds a leading NAACP attorney of an older generation who had read law in the office of a prominent white attorney.[16] Howard, easily the best of the handful of black institutions granting a law degree, was a night school[17] that remained unaccredited until the 1930's. The training it offered was not unlike that provided by the many average law

*Information supporting the generalizations made in the following paragraphs about the characteristics of the NAACP's black and white lawyers is too extensive for inclusion in the body of this paper. The relevant notes contain detailed empirical evidence.

schools across the country that similarly held part-time evening programs for men too poor to attend the more prestigious institutions. Howard produced nearly all of the most distinguished black lawyers in the two generations following the Civil War; indeed, from the NAACP's beginning, its alumni carried an important share of the Association's local litigation, especially in the border states.[18] Black lawyers in the northern and western NAACP branches, on the other hand, were largely trained in the smaller and less well-known northern white law schools.[19] Few blacks were able to attend the leading white law schools in this period,[20] though it is significant that a tiny handful of black men actively associated with NAACP cases in the 1920's were graduates of such law schools as Harvard, Yale, and the University of Wisconsin.[21] In contrast, white lawyers participating in the national office's legal program or involved in local NAACP cases—even where they were enlisted directly by the branches—were with few exceptions graduates of the finest law schools in the country.[22] Often prominent in politics,[23] typically referred to as being the leading lawyers in their communities or as partners in some of the most prestigious law firms in the country,[24] they were a distinctly elite group.[25] Three, including Storey, served as presidents of the American Bar Association during the course of their careers.[26]

It is striking that the NAACP was able to obtain such eminent white counsel, even in the South, where pressures inhibited white lawyers from taking cases on behalf of Negro rights. The NAACP did pay local counsel, black and white, but the financial remuneration could scarcely have been a significant motivating factor for the prominent white lawyers, since the NAACP seldom paid the usual fee charged by such men. Nor—with the exception of Clarence Darrow, a few of the New York lawyers, and one or two others—can they be classified as turn-of-the-century "Progressives" or post–World War I "Liberals."[27] Moorfield Storey, for example, was an anti-imperialist as well as an advocate of the black man's rights, but Walter White after Storey's death correctly described him as belonging to "the ultra conservative group."[28] For the most part, the prestigious white lawyers whose services the NAACP secured were essentially conservative men, characterized either by a degree of aristocratic noblesse oblige toward blacks or by a conservative's concern with due process, law and order, and the protection of an individual's constitutional rights to life and property. Thus, while we have examined only major cases taken by the NAACP, the social, professional and sometimes political prominence of most of the southern lawyers involved in the litigation discussed below suggests that the NAACP was able to enlist men whose standing was so impeccable in their communities that they could undertake such work without serious criticism or harm to their practices. For certain cases involving mob violence or a flagrant denial of individual liberty and a citizen's rights before the courts, the NAACP was able to obtain attorneys who would certainly oppose much of the Association's broader program.[29] Indeed, it is not entirely surprising that the NAACP could secure such counsel even in the Deep South, for its cases there involved the issue of guaranteeing a fair trial to blacks accused of serious crimes, a position with which even highly conservative lawyers often agreed. In cities like New Orleans, Richmond, Louisville, and El Paso, where white lawyers participated in litigation directly challenging disfranchisement and segregation, the social environment was less repressive, and the white lawyers working with the NAACP were less likely to be subjected to community censure. In Louisville, which was of course hardly typical of the South, the law firm which represented the NAACP in the fight against residential segregation actually consisted of politically prominent Republicans, one of whom was elected mayor a few years after the NAACP won its case before the Supreme Court.[30]

NAACP leaders consciously sought to obtain lawyers of distinction and high reputation—and this usually meant white counsel. Thus Storey often mentioned two essential attributes for lawyers taking NAACP cases—"ability" and "standing." "Standing" meant a community reputation for high status and integrity which would impress judges, an attribute which few Negroes possessed in the minds of judges and community influentials. Epitomizing the low "standing" which blacks had in the eyes of the white legal fraternity was the fact that the American Bar Association excluded them from membership—a policy which Storey had unsuccessfully opposed.[31] Storey's viewpoint on the importance of "standing" was evident in the first brief which he wrote for the NAACP—a brief *amicus curiae* submitted to the Supreme Court in 1913 in the Oklahoma Grandfather Clause case, *Guinn and Beal* v. *the United States*, which the Justice Department was prosecuting. Unable to present it personally, Storey arranged for a prominent white Washington lawyer to file the brief, because this man "would command the respect of the Court. . . ." And when the Court upheld the blacks two years later, Arthur Spingarn noted how fortunate the Association was to have so prestigious a man as Storey to author a brief in its behalf.[32] Again in 1919, when the Memphis NAACP sought assistance in fighting a school bond issue for which it had engaged a biracial legal team, Storey characteristically advised: "I should like to have some assurance that the counsel who propose to undertake it are men of standing and ability, for in a case of this kind so much depends on the standing of the counsel in the community where the suit is brought."[33]

Storey's views were shared by other NAACP leaders. Spingarn and White constantly operated on this principle throughout the 1920's. Du Bois once editorially criticized an Oklahoma Negro attorney, William Harrison, for failing to obtain expert legal advice in an early challenge to the Jim Crow transportation laws, *McCabe* v. *the Atchison, Topeka and Santa Fe Railroad*. Only when Harrison was about to go before the Supreme Court did he request assistance, but Storey, finding that "the case was not properly drawn," declined to participate. When the Court, as Storey feared, decided against the Negroes, Du Bois bitterly wrote:

> It has happened time after time, in case after case. The Negro has taken his cause before the courts half prepared. He has been warned of this. He ought to have learned by bitter experience but he has not yet learned. Law is not simply a matter of right and wrong—it is a matter of learning, experience and precedents. A colored lawyer may go before a court with a just case. . . . In nine cases out of ten he cannot bring experience because the color line in the legal profession gives him little chance for experience. . . . Attorney Harrison . . . was warned . . . frankly by lawyers of wide experience to associate with himself the best legal talent of the country so that his case might be

adequately presented. He refused this aid. He succumbed to the temptation of trying to bear the whole burden himself under circumstances where it was no dishonor but ordinary carefulness to call to his aid other and more experienced attorneys. . . . How many times [asked the *Crisis* editor] are we going to repeat this foolish mistake?[34]

In actual practice there was of course considerable variation in the ways in which the NAACP handled its cases, and black attorneys certainly did not play a negligible role. Even in the South there were a few attorneys like A. T. Walden of Atlanta, N. J. Frederick[35]* of Columbia, South Carolina, and S. D. McGill of Jacksonville who at substantial personal risk for years handled NAACP work in their localities.[36] Yet they too had to operate within the constraints of a social system which devalued their abilities; in South Carolina the NAACP relied on white attorneys for the majority of its cases; McGill, in one long fight to reverse a murder conviction, associated himself with a local white attorney, and eventually prevailed upon Louis Marshall to write the brief for the appeal to the state supreme court.[37] In certain northern and border cities like Baltimore,[38] Cleveland, Indianapolis, Philadelphia, Detroit, Chicago, and Los Angeles, black attorneys managed branch cases, rarely appealing to white lawyers for assistance. On the national level the black lawyer most often consulted by the NAACP was James A. Cobb of Washington, D.C. Cobb, who had received his law degree from Howard University and had served from 1907 to 1915 as special assistant to the U.S. attorney general, brought to the NAACP both an expertise in civil rights law and wide-ranging personal contacts in the nation's capital.[39] Although he

*Frederick's most noted work came in the late 1920's. In one instance handling the case himself, he secured the release of a black landowner who had served thirteen years in prison after being convicted on false charges of raping a white woman. The case, involving a pardon issued and then revoked by the governor, was settled in a dramatic 1929 *en banc* session of all the state circuit and supreme court judges who upheld the pardon. Earlier, Frederick had undertaken the defense of a family of sharecroppers who, falsely charged with making whiskey, had become involved in an altercation with the Aiken County sheriff and his deputies. One deputy shot the mother dead, and in self-defense one of the children killed the sheriff. Outraged at the unjust trial proceedings which followed, Frederick successfully appealed to the state supreme court for a reversal and a new trial. In this new trial Frederick, at his own expense, secured the assistance of a Spartanburg white lawyer, and the two won a directed verdict of acquittal for one of the defendants. Thereupon a mob overpowered the jailer and lynched all three of the children charged with the crime.

lacked the distinction of a Storey or a Marshall, Cobb was nevertheless very valuable to the Association during the 1920's, when he was associated with most of the Association's major litigation against disfranchisement and residential segregation. It was a measure of the respect in which he was held by the national office that Spingarn and James Weldon Johnson urged him to become the NAACP's full-time staff counsel in 1922. Cobb, however, preferred to remain in Washington.[40]

Examples drawn from several outstanding legal redress cases and from the organization's two major long-range campaigns against residential segregation and the Texas white primaries will illustrate the NAACP's policy of using black lawyers where practicable, but relying primarily upon prominent white counsel in important litigation. In the Association's very first case in 1910 involving Pink Franklin, a black sharecropper sentenced to death for shooting a white constable who sought to arrest him for breaking his "agricultural contract," the NAACP, dissatisfied with the competence and standing of the black lawyers engaged by the defendant, resorted to prominent South Carolina white attorneys. Seeking clemency for Franklin, NAACP Board Chairman Oswald Garrison Villard prevailed upon President Taft to intercede with the governor, while other officers of the Association secured the help of influential local white lawyers who obtained a commutation in Franklin's sentence to life imprisonment.[41] In 1917, when black soldiers stationed at Houston were summarily courtmartialed for rioting in the face of harassment from local whites, the NAACP was able to secure the services of a noted attorney who was the son of Sam Houston.[42] In the northern and border states, where black lawyers were more numerous, they were more likely to be retained in such cases, but nearly always as associates of prominent white counsel. After the 1917 East St. Louis riot the NAACP arranged to have the legal defense supervised by "one of the Midwest's most successful lawyers," Charles Nagel of St. Louis, secretary of commerce and labor under President Taft. The cases were argued by two prominent East St. Louis white attorneys—Samuel W. Baxter, a well-known railroad attorney, and Thomas M. Webb, "the leading criminal lawyer of Southern Illinois." Homer G. Phillips, the most outstanding black attorney in St. Louis, assisted in the cases. In addition, when it came to handling the appeals the NAACP also engaged the white president of the Chicago branch, former judge Edward O. Brown.[43] Similarly, after the Chicago riot of 1919, the NAACP arranged to hire distinguished white counsel, notably S. S. Gregory, a former president of the American Bar Association, with members of the local Negro bar lending their assistance.[44] In contrast, after the Washington riot of the same year, the defense of blacks arrested during the riot was handled by the branch's legal committee, headed by James A. Cobb.[45]

Most of the 1919 riots were urban, but in October one occurred in Phillips County, Arkansas, that produced a celebrated NAACP case in which, despite its southern locale, a courageous local Negro attorney, Scipio A. Jones, played a leading role. An attempt by black sharecroppers to form a union precipitated a violent confrontation with a band of armed whites that was followed by a massacre of Negro farmers. In a hasty court trial twelve Negroes were sentenced to death.[46] The NAACP attempted to reverse these convictions and to prevent the extradition of union leader Robert Hill, who had fled to Kansas. Hill was saved after the Association secured the intervention of Senator Arthur Capper, former president of the Topeka branch, who prevailed upon the governor to allow the NAACP time to present its case, and secured as Hill's chief counsel Shawnee County attorney H. T. Fisher, who served without fee. Associated with Fisher were three black attorneys of Topeka, most notably Elisha Scott, who handled a number of other NAACP cases. After Hill was freed the Association noted in its annual report: "Here we have an illustration of the value of influential white members to the organization and of the uniquely effective work that can be done by them."[47]

For chief counsel in its attempt to reverse the death sentences, the NAACP adopted the suggestion of the union's white attorney, U. S. Bratton, and engaged the prominent Little Rock white criminal lawyer, Colonel George W. Murphy. Associated with him was Scipio Jones, who had been active in the black citizens committee organized to help the defendants.[48] When Murphy died Jones took charge of the litigation, but even then he clearly considered it of strategic importance to continue working with prominent white attorneys. He sought unsuccessfully to obtain assistance from Storey, and associated himself with two Arkansas white law firms even though they charged exorbitant fees.[49] When the case was to be appealed to the Supreme Court, all agreed, as Jones put it, that the NAACP should "secure the ablest constitutional lawyer possible," and Walter White approached Storey again. The aging lawyer, hoping to retire from practice, was reluctant to accept, and White toyed with the idea of approaching some other lawyer of Storey's "standing," such as George W. Wickersham, attorney general under Taft. Other NAACP leaders like James Weldon Johnson personally pressed Storey: "No name that we could mention would have such significance to the colored people of the country in arguing these cases before the Supreme Court as your own," he informed the NAACP president. Eventually Storey accepted.[50] Jones worked with him on preparing the written brief, but he did not participate in the oral argument because Storey felt that Bratton, as a southern white, would make a greater impression on the Court.[51] After the Supreme Court reversed the conviction and remanded the case to the lower courts, Jones urged that Storey or someone of equal stature be sent to Arkansas to help him. "I don't see how we can succeed . . . without [his] assistance," he pleaded.[52] The NAACP, however, decided to leave the case in the hands of Jones, who was able to secure discharges or commutations of sentences to short prison terms for the twelve defendants.[53]

The NAACP's Supreme Court victory in the Arkansas cases in 1923 had been based on the contention that the original trial was dominated by a "mob spirit." Impressed, Louis Marshall, who had unsuccessfully used the same argument before the Supreme Court in the celebrated *Leo Frank* case, congratulated the NAACP on its great achievement.[54] NAACP officials, who had been trying for four years to involve Marshall in their crusade against mob violence, welcomed his interest and as soon as a vacancy occurred, placed him on the Board.[55] Marshall subsequently became a central figure in the Association's legal battle against disfranchisement and residential segregation, proving even more willing than Storey to involve himself deeply in the NAACP's work.

For the NAACP, whose first years coincided with the passage of a rash of municipal segregation ordinances, residential segregation had been an issue of high priority from the start. In Baltimore, one of the key cities in this struggle, the fight was led by Ashbie Hawkins, a black attorney who worked independently of white lawyers in the many civil rights cases which he undertook. But in this instance, following his request for assistance, the national office provided the help of prestigious New York lawyers during 1912 and 1913.[56] However, it was the Louisville ordinance which the national office chose to take to the Supreme Court. The Louisville branch employed "one of the best firms in the city," with the branch's black attorney assisting "from time to time." After the state court of appeals upheld the ordinance, Storey in 1916–17 joined with the white Louisville law firm in the appeal to the Supreme Court which ruled in favor of the NAACP.[57]

Subsequently, in their successful battles against several municipal laws enacted to circumvent this decision, NAACP branches still depended primarily on white lawyers. The Indianapolis NAACP employed "one of the most prominent white law firms of Indiana," along with two of the city's black attorneys.[58] In Richmond, Virginia, local citizens engaged a biracial legal team which in turn secured Louis Marshall's aid in preparing the brief.[59] The New Orleans branch relied principally on a white attorney, Loys Charbonnet, who despite NAACP urging was loath to consult with Cobb and Marshall. Cobb amusingly reported a change in Charbonnet's manner when the latter visited Washington to docket the case with the Supreme Court: "Fortunately he had gone to the Clerk's Office of the Supreme Court before coming to mine and was advised that he was on the right course in working with me. Hence, he came in a very pleasant and agreeable mood."[60]

By the mid-1920's the real threat came from restrictive covenants rather than municipal ordinances, and it was in the struggle against this device that Louis Marshall first became actively engaged in the NAACP's legal program. Cobb launched an attack on restrictive covenants in Washington early in 1923, an enterprise in which he secured substantial advice from Spingarn and the white New York lawyer and NAACP

Board member Herbert K. Stockton.[61] After the case had been lost in the lower courts Marshall volunteered to help take it to the Supreme Court,[62] and the octogenarian Storey willingly let Marshall take chief responsibility for the case. Cobb meanwhile associated himself with a prominent white Washington lawyer, Henry Davis, and together they drafted the brief under Marshall's supervision.[63] Cobb, who sought no personal fame in the case, informed Spingarn that "no especial pride is to be mine in arguing the case before the Supreme Court. I shall be happy to have Messrs. Marshall and Davis, or Mr. Storey, if you please, to present it." It was decided that Marshall, assisted by Storey, would make the oral argument in January, 1926: "Two of the most prominent lawyers in the United States will present the argument," proudly announced the NAACP. This array of talent notwithstanding, the Supreme Court decided that it lacked jurisdiction to pass on the merits of the matter.[64]

By then the NAACP was also engaged in *Nixon* v. *Herndon*, its first case in the long struggle against the Texas white primary. The El Paso branch, in casting about for an attorney, had chosen Fred Knollenberg, a local white title-lawyer well regarded in the black community. When the branch, defeated in federal district court, sought help from the national office, Storey and Cobb were asked to supervise the brief, to "see that no slips are made in the record."[65] The ailing Storey proved unable to appear before the Supreme Court,[66] and unfortunately Knollenberg failed to properly prepare himself for the oral argument, not even examining material Cobb had compiled for him. The result was disastrous.[67] Luckily, the Court agreed to Texas's request for reargument. At Cobb's suggestion Louis Marshall was brought into the case, and the latter's masterful presentation probably did much to account for the unanimous decision of March, 1927, against the Texas law.[68]

Marshall and Storey had thus played a central role in the NAACP's legal program, and when both died within a few months of each other in 1929, White lamented: "It is going to be almost impossible to replace these two men who were our greatest legal assets as well as immensely helpful through the prestige which each had."[69] Yet their passing marked a turning point, not only because it removed from the scene "the Association's two great legal champions,"[70] but also because it came at a time when the NAACP's legal work was reaching a crossroads due to several other developments: a rising feeling among black lawyers that they should undertake the major responsibility in the fight for Negro rights; the appearance of an elite nucleus of black lawyers trained in constitutional law at Harvard and other leading institutions; the upgrading and accreditation of Howard University Law School and the creation there of a special curriculum in civil rights law; and a $100,000 grant to the NAACP from the American Fund for Public Service (usually referred to as the Garland Fund after its founder, Charles Garland) for a long-range program of civil rights litigation.

Unhappiness over the Association's reliance on white lawyers, which had been latent in the early years,[71] surfaced during 1925–26 in the celebrated case of Dr. Ossian Sweet, who had moved into a hostile white neighborhood in Detroit. Sweet and ten others were charged with first-degree murder when someone inside his home shot at a threatening mob which surrounded the house, killing one of the whites on the street. When Walter White arrived in Detroit, he learned that the defendants had already engaged three black attorneys. White indicated to the three men that, in keeping with "the position of the National Office," "a [white] lawyer of the very highest standing should be retained at once . . . inasmuch as public sentiment even among the fairest-minded white citizens of Detroit was certain . . . that Dr. Sweet and his ten codefendants had without provocation . . . killed an innocent bystander." To the black attorneys' contention that a white lawyer would be a detriment since he could not "understand Negro psychology," White countered that the judge, the jury, and the "larger court of public opinion which influences the court" would all be white.[72] Privately he expressed a low opinion of these Negro lawyers. One he thought "a man of no personality" who "commands no respect"; another, "a blustering, noisy, pompous individual with a very inflated opinion of his own ability." Of the three, he thought only one was worth retaining because "the other two are trying to gobble all the fees and credit."[73] White's views had considerable support. Oscar Baker of Bay City, one of the most successful black attorneys in Michigan, urged that "the very best white *criminal* lawyer in the State should be engaged," and Mose L. Walker, the black vice-president of the Detroit branch, advised that "the [Negro] public demands that we take action at once to get a white attorney." Although two of the lawyers had threatened to quit the case publicly if a white lawyer was brought in, both Walker and White were certain that they were bluffing, since a considerable amount of money had been raised for the defense.[74] Under pressure the three finally accepted the national office's decision that a white attorney would not only enter the case, but that he would have complete charge. The Association selected Clarence Darrow as the "ablest attorney of national prestige that we can possibly secure."[75]

Just as White recognized that from the point of view of the NAACP's relationship to the black community it was essential to have at least one black lawyer, so Darrow, with an eye on local white opinion, insisted that a white Detroit lawyer should also be retained.[76] In actuality Darrow and his associate Arthur Garfield Hays completely handled the defense, using the local counsel, both white and black, only for symbolic purposes— much to the latter's dissatisfaction. The three Negro lawyers, supported by a number of Detroit blacks, felt that at the very least "a brief statement by a Negro lawyer might have had a good influence."[77] But White complained that the Negro lawyers were demanding the full $4,500 fee tentatively agreed upon, even though they "were of practically no use" in the trial, having been "nothing except ornaments," "due to the fact that we had more capable counsel who did the work."[78] Darrow and Hays received $8,000, a fraction of their usual fee.[79] Yet the black attorneys were fully paid, since failure to do so would have damaged the NAACP's reputation among Negroes.[80]

After the first trial ended in a hung jury, White suggested that in the second trial only one black attorney be used, and that one "solely for the effect upon public opinion." Julian Perry, whom Dr. Sweet preferred, was chosen. As James Weldon Johnson said later, "We wanted a colored lawyer in the case for appearance sake if for nothing more." To save money, White wished to dispense with a local white attorney, but both Darrow and Detroit blacks agreed that one was essential for public relations reasons.[81] In the second trial each defendant was to be tried separately; Darrow and Thomas F. Chawke, one of the top criminal lawyers in Michigan, secured the acquittal of Dr. Sweet's brother, and the following year the other cases were dismissed.[82]

The Sweet case was not an isolated instance. Late in 1924 the Indianapolis NAACP, seeking to fight the erection of a Jim Crow high school, secured the services of three local black attorneys. When the branch appealed to the national office for assistance, Spingarn found that their brief was weak and advised that a prominent Indiana lawyer be consulted. White thereupon unsuccessfully tried to interest ex-Senator Albert J. Beveridge.[83] In the following months the national office grew increasingly unhappy with the Indianapolis black lawyers, who asked for very high fees. White consulted F. B. Ransom, another Negro attorney in Indianapolis, who informed him that "not one of the three lawyers was competent to handle the case properly."[84] Accordingly the national office withdrew from the litigation.[85] Undoubtedly it was the national office's action in this case that led the branch's lawyers to associate with a prestigious white firm in their successful challenge to the residential segregation ordinance that occurred soon after.[86]

If the Sweet and Indianapolis cases revealed resentments on the part of some older black lawyers, a different kind of pressure came from a small but growing elite of brilliant young black men educated at Ivy League law schools during the 1920's.[87] Preeminent among them were a few Harvard graduates who had studied constitutional law under Felix Frankfurter—Jesse Heslip of Toledo, president of the black National Bar Association from 1931 to 1933, and two Washingtonians who had served on the *Harvard Law Review*, William H. Hastie and Charles H. Houston. Frankfurter described Hastie, who received his LL.B. in 1930, as "not only the best colored man we have ever had but he is as good as all but three or four outstanding white men that have been here during the last twenty years."[88]

At this juncture the NAACP was seeking a full-time staff counsel to handle the campaign that was to be financed by the Garland Fund.[89] Hastie was among those considered, with

Frankfurter strongly recommending that a place be found for him "somewhere in your set-up."[90] Although the job went to a man who had an even stronger recommendation from Frankfurter—a more experienced white lawyer named Nathan Margold[91]—and although the Depression forced the Garland Fund to scale down its appropriation, nevertheless it was this grant which ultimately made it possible for the NAACP to appoint Charles Houston as its staff counsel.

Houston, who had worked with Margold on the *Harvard Law Review*, had become dean[92] of the Howard University Law School in 1929. Acutely aware of the limitations of the Negro bar, Houston in the next half-dozen years turned Howard Law School from an unaccredited institution into a respected law school preparing well-qualified black lawyers to lead the race's fight against social injustice.[93] This was a vision shared by Houston's associates in the National Bar Association. As President Heslip told the black lawyers' convention in 1932:

> We are learning the real necessity of race pride and are willing to make the necessary sacrifices to sustain it. . . . We must become thoroughly grounded in constitutional law; we must be ready to face the nation's highest tribunal in search of justice for ourselves. It is more apparent each day that white men of the type of Moorfield Storey, Louis Marshall, Hays, and Darrow are rapidly fading away; they extend to us, Negro lawyers, the torch of able service, and only we, Negro lawyers, can accept it and carry on the battle for justice.

Houston's most famous student, Thurgood Marshall, recalled that as teacher and dean Houston "instilled in the student body the necessary drive to become the best lawyer possible." By 1935 Houston was able to tell the NAACP convention that "the most hopeful sign about our legal defense is the ever increasing number of young Negro lawyers, competent, conscientious, and courageous, who are anxious to pit themselves [without fee] against the forces of reaction and injustice. . . . The time is soon coming when the Negro will be able to rely on his own lawyers to give him every legal protection in every Court."[94]

Given these developments, it is not surprising that the question of using black lawyers was meanwhile growing in salience for the NAACP. The convention of the National Bar Association in 1931 condemned "the unworthy and sinister practices" of black preachers and physicians who recommended people to white lawyers, and criticized unnamed legal defense organizations for not employing Negro attorneys. The delegates pointedly voted to send copies of their resolution to both the NAACP and the Communist-backed International Labor Defense.[95]

Simultaneously the whole issue was being thrown into bold relief for the NAACP by two disfranchisement cases—an abortive attack upon the "understanding" clause of the Louisiana constitution and, more important, the second Texas white primary case, *Nixon* v. *Condon*, which the Supreme Court heard in January, 1932.

For the assault upon the Louisiana law, the New Orleans branch in the spring of 1931 employed a white lawyer, Henry Warmoth Robinson. This was done over the spirited objections of a group of young Negro professional men headed by Alexander P. Tureaud, a 1925 graduate of Howard University Law School who would later become a distinguished civil rights lawyer for the NAACP in Louisiana. Tureaud's friends, picturing the branch's choice as an "old broken down white man," appealed to New York; but the national office, not wishing to meddle in local branch squabbles, declined to intervene and assign the case to Tureaud. Accordingly Robinson handled it, though White and Spingarn insisted that he consult closely with Margold.[96] Tureaud and his friends must have felt themselves vindicated when two years later Robinson, having lost in the Louisiana courts, appealed to the U.S. Supreme Court for a writ of *certiorari*, which was denied.[97]

Meanwhile the national office had been pressing the new *Nixon* case. In the summer of 1931 James Marshall, substituting for his deceased father in the litigation,[98] received a letter from the Houston black law firm of Nabrit, Atkins and Wesley which had been involved in previous legal work against the white primary, and now requested permission to file a brief and join with the NAACP in the oral argument. Marshall did not find their proposed brief helpful, and he advised that while the Texas lawyers were free to seek permission to file a brief *amicus curiae*, the NAACP would use its own attorneys.[99] Replying on behalf of the black firm was J. Alston Atkins, a former member of the editorial board of the *Law Journal* at Yale, where his professors considered him the law school's "most brilliant Negro graduate."[100] He indicated dissatisfaction with Marshall's suggestion and then proceeded to propose changes in Marshall's brief. Atkins added, "but for the effect of the decision . . . upon all Negroes we would not be so presumptuous." The national office nevertheless arranged to have the oral argument delivered by Marshall and Margold.[101] A few months later Atkins, who was not easily repressed, asked to participate in the reargument, and the NAACP received supporting communications from Charles Houston and from Texas civic leaders. A prominent fraternal officer informed White that a man of Atkins's ability should be employed, since he "is of our own nationality and from that fact, is more vitally interested in what Negroes of the South desire."[102] The national office still refused to budge, and though it carefully mentioned Atkins's *amicus curiae* brief in its press release, the Houston attorneys were not mollified.[103]

With Margold bearing the major responsibility for NAACP litigation, White undertook to blunt criticism by increasing the number of blacks on the national legal committee which during the 1920's had averaged about five members who worked closely with Spingarn, all of them, except Cobb, being New Yorkers.[104] As early as 1929, after the deaths of Storey and Marshall, White had prevailed upon Spingarn to add Marshall's son and Felix Frankfurter; at the same time, concerned that no blacks had served since Cobb's resignation in 1926, White urged Spingarn to appoint two Negroes: Francis E. Rivers,[105] a young New Yorker, and the veteran West Virginia legislator and branch president T. G. Nutter. Spingarn readily agreed to Nutter, but felt that Rivers "is too young and unproved." Now, in the fall of 1931, following the Bar Association's resolution and the request from the Houston attorneys, White raised the issue again, urging the appointment of Jesse Heslip and Charles Houston. Spingarn, however, was still skeptical of adding young men who as yet lacked a national reputation, and accordingly at his suggestion the Board added to the legal committee the elderly E. H. Morris and two prominent white

New York civil liberties attorneys, Morris Ernst and Arthur Garfield Hays.[106]

The matter was not pursued further until the following spring when White, evidently spurred both by Atkins's renewed campaign to participate in the *Nixon v. Condon* case, and by further conversations with Houston about promoting cooperation between the NAACP and the Bar Association,[107] brought it up again. White had been invited to address the National Bar Association convention in August, 1932, and wanted several more Negro attorneys to be appointed before then. In June four were added—Houston; Heslip; Louis Redding of Wilmington, Delaware, another Harvard graduate; and the older South Carolina lawyer N. J. Frederick.[108] The legal committee was now nearly equally divided between the races, eight being white and six black.

The response to these new appointments was generally enthusiastic. The Houston *Informer*, of which Atkins served as editor, welcomed this "step forward,"[109] and a Cleveland black attorney wrote, "This recognition is very gratifying, I am sure, to every Negro lawyer in the country and not any less so because it has not been done sooner." Some black lawyers were still critical, however. Thus in November, 1932, NAACP field secretary William Pickens, speaking before a group of black professional and business men in Chicago, received intense criticisms about the Association's failure to make greater use of black lawyers.[110] Accordingly the NAACP found it necessary to work further to consolidate its position. For example, White asked Assistant Secretary Roy Wilkins to prepare a feature on the services of Negro attorneys connected with NAACP cases. A year later, in another effort to defuse such criticism, White successfully promoted the addition of Pittsburgh branch president Homer Brown to the legal committee: "He is able, self-sacrificing and intensely loyal to the NAACP. . . . It will have not only fine reactions so far as Mr. Brown and the Pittsburgh Branch are concerned but. . . . It will also be a definite answer to some of the less able and more ambitious lawyers who for selfish reasons want to use the Association."[111]

White's plans to involve black lawyers more closely in the NAACP were facilitated by the resignation of Margold in the spring of 1933 to become solicitor in the Department of Interior, and White turned to Houston and Hastie for important NAACP cases. Both men served without fee—an important consideration in view of the organization's poverty during the depths of the Depression and the acrimonious, though false, charges which were being made that men like Storey and Marshall had been paid handsomely for their services.[112]

Houston's first case for the Association involved George Crawford, a young Negro charged with murdering two white women in Virginia. With Crawford claiming to have been in Boston at the time of the crime, the black attorney and Boston branch president Butler Wilson and a prominent white Boston lawyer named J. Weston Allen sought to prevent Crawford's extradition from Massachusetts on the traditional grounds that he would not get a fair trial. White consulted Houston and two of his associates, Edward P. Lovett and James G. Tyson, who suggested fighting the extradition on the novel grounds that blacks had been systematically excluded from Virginia grand juries. After a federal judge accepted their reasoning, White expressed his gratitude: "You . . . caused us to see the profound implications of the case. . . . I am perhaps happiest because three young Negro lawyers played the decisive part in the victory."[113] When the judge was overruled and Crawford was extradited to Virginia, White assigned Houston the task of handling the defense, but for strategic reasons he thought it also desirable to hire a white Virginia lawyer. Houston disagreed: "The men [at Howard] feel if Crawford could be defended by all Negro counsel it would mark a turning point in the legal history of the Negro."[114] But when White conferred in Richmond with prominent whites and blacks like newspaper editors Douglas S. Freeman of the *News-Leader*, Virginius Dabney of the *Times-Dispatch*, and Alphonse Norrell of the black journal, the Richmond *Planet*, he found "absolute unanimity among them all and especially strong feeling on the part of the colored people" that "there should be bi-racial counsel."[115] Thus pressed, White and Houston began seeking a prominent white Virginian to serve as co-counsel, but a few days later Houston finally decided that "as Dean of Howard University Law School for Negroes it would not be consistent for him to

serve with white counsel in the Crawford case."[116] His hand
had undeniably been strengthened by the showing that he,
Lovett, and Tyson had made at the hearing to quash the indictment, for even though the court denied the motion, "Dean
Houston's dignity in the court, his thorough grasp of the law,
his courtesy, his firmness in pressing his contentions, his handling of witnesses," had impressed the court and the press alike.
The NAACP informed the public that while "It is not a new
thing for the NAACP to use colored lawyers," this was "the first
time all-Negro counsel have been used in such an important
case," and the attorneys' conduct had been so impressive that it
"finally decided the question of mixed or all-colored counsel" in
the case.[117] In the end Houston discovered that Crawford was
involved in the crime, but the black lawyer's defense was credited with having spared the youth's life. To White, the trial had
been a milestone: "for here was a case of a Negro guilty, under
the law, of a most brutal murder of two white women, tried in
the South and defended by all-Negro counsel and saved from
the electric chair. Equally . . . significant is the fact that without
yielding one iota of principle, fighting on the jury issue and for
every other point, yet the Negro counsel won the respect and
admiration of court, opposing counsel and of everybody in the
courtroom."[118]

At the very time that Houston was taking up the *Crawford*
case, Hastie represented the Association in its first suit to compel a southern university to admit Negroes to its professional
schools. The national office responded to a request from two
Durham black attorneys, Conrad Pearson and Cecil McCoy, for
assistance in helping Thomas R. Hocutt obtain admission to the
University of North Carolina School of Pharmacy.[119] Although
the case was lost on a technicality, given the context of the times
the court proceedings were impressive. Here were young black
lawyers facing distinguished counsel headed by the state's attorney general, and attacking the exclusionary policies of a
major southern university at a time when most black leaders in
North Carolina feared to challenge the status quo. Hastie,
McCoy, and Pearson created a sensation when they proceeded
to obtain subpoenas for everyone, white and black, connected
with the case. According to Pearson's report, before a standing-

room-only audience that included judges, members of the local bar and the North Carolina and Duke University law faculties, and enthusiastic local Negroes, Hastie "swept the entire court-room off its feet with his ability and demeanor. It was immediately rumored among the whites that Mr. Hastie was an 'Ex-D.A. for the District of Columbia.' He is reputed by them to be the smartest of the 'young niggras.' The White Bar was unanimous in its praise . . . and a millionaire white lawyer extended his hand to Mr. Hastie and congratulated us with feeling, on the way the case was conducted." In a press release the NAACP also emphasized that "the hearings were marked with the utmost courtesy between all parties, except that the whites, by one method or another, dodged the use of 'Mister' in addressing the colored attorneys. Mr. Hastie, a Harvard graduate, chatted with Harvard men on the university faculty and with Duke University students who wanted to ask about Harvard Law School."[120]

For Walter White, the *Crawford* and *Hocutt* cases together constituted a turning point in the NAACP's employment of black lawyers.[121] Hastie immediately began working on another phase of the NAACP's campaign against educational discrimination, preparing for a teachers' salary equalization suit in North Carolina.[122] Houston, though still dean at Howard, rapidly became involved in a number of NAACP matters, including a wide range of non-legal concerns. He suggested candidates for the board and legal committee, advised on NAACP relations with the Roosevelt administration and Congress, and helped to shape the Association's direction as it sought to meet the challenge of the Depression and the criticisms of younger black intellectuals. He developed the NAACP's campaign against racial discrimination in education, and in early 1935 his legal redress work came to a climax in the first case appealed by the NAACP to the Supreme Court that was handled exclusively by black counsel. This case involved an Oklahoma Negro, Jess Hollins, who had been sentenced to death for criminal assault on a white girl. Houston submitted a brief claiming that the trial was illegally conducted because blacks were excluded from the jury, and in May, 1935, the Court declared Hollins's conviction unconstitutional.[123]

Although Houston did not play a central role in the continuing struggle against the Texas white primary, he did help to strengthen the participation of black lawyers in the matter. When the Texas Democratic party circumvented the *Nixon* v. *Condon* decision, the El Paso branch on the one hand and the Atkins group on the other sought to mount a court challenge. The national office felt subjected to pressures from both parties. Having a low estimate of Knollenberg's talents, it engaged him reluctantly and also seriously considered inviting Atkins into the case, even though unimpressed by his *amicus curiae* brief in the second *Nixon* case.[124] Knollenberg still had the consummate admiration of the El Paso branch, whose president argued that in the face of criticism from whites Knollenberg had undertaken cases "when we could not find anyone else to do so," never turning down a request from the branch, and serving without compensation. On the other hand White, aware of the volatility of the Negro lawyer issue and anxious to "forestall a case being filed which may take precedence over ours," thought of retaining Atkins as "junior counsel." A black lawyer, he reminded Spingarn, "will have an excellent psychological effect upon colored people."[125] In the end the decision was made to stick with Knollenberg, whose work was to be carefully supervised by James Marshall.[126] A year later, in mid-1934, with proceedings at a standstill, the NAACP cooperated with the National Bar Association in urging the justice department to intervene to protect the voting rights of Texas blacks. In September White (on behalf of the NAACP) and Houston (representing the black lawyers' organization) conferred with assistant attorney general Joseph B. Keenan, but at the end of the year the Negro leaders were still futilely trying to get him to act.[127]

Meanwhile the Atkins group, operating independently of the NAACP, had taken their own white primary case to the U.S. Supreme Court. In *Grovey* v. *Townsend* the Court decided against Atkins in what black Texans regarded as a humiliating reversal of their earlier victories in the two *Nixon* cases. NAACP officials were incensed at Atkins's handling of the case, and even Atkins's former law partner, James Nabrit, later conceded that *Grovey* v. *Townsend* had been a "hasty law suit," not thoroughly prepared.[128]

On the heels of the *Grovey* decision came Houston's victory in the *Hollins* case. Atkins congratulated his good friend and added, "Now that the NAACP has had a Negro lawyer for the first time in its history to handle one of its important cases before the Supreme Court, I trust that this will be the beginning of a new policy, under which no case in the future will be presented in that tribunal without a Negro lawyer at the counsel table. . . ." Houston basically agreed. The NAACP, he replied, "should be the great laboratory for developing Negro leadership wherever possible. . . . I do not know the facts surrounding the choice of lawyers [in the Texas primary cases], but I know that it is the general policy of the Association to appoint Negro lawyers in all cases where considerations are otherwise equal."[129]

This, of course, conformed with Houston's own practice. Thus when the influential Oklahoma newspaper editor and NAACP leader Roscoe Dunjee urged that Houston conduct the retrial of the Hollins case in the state courts, assisted by an Oklahoma white attorney, Houston insisted that local black counsel be included. Recalling the precedent set in the *Crawford* case, he reiterated, "My position as head of the Law School makes it inconsistent for me not to use Negro lawyers whenever possible." As he informed Roy Wilkins, "It may be necessary to have a white lawyer along, but a Negro lawyer is indispensable," particularly "in view of the many competent Negro lawyers in Oklahoma some of whom are Howard graduates." Although the press of other business prevented Houston from assuming an active role in the case, Dunjee did retain a former Houston student, Cecil Robertson, to work with the white firm, until ultimately Hollins's sentence was commuted to life imprisonment.[130]

Meanwhile the issue of the NAACP's use of black lawyers was being resolved with the appointment of Houston as NAACP special counsel in 1935. At the 1934 convention of the National Bar Association, Walter White had angered many delegates when, upon being asked why the NAACP did not employ more Negro lawyers, he replied that his organization would do so when there "are more Charlie Houstons."[131] Actually, at that very time Houston and the joint committee of the NAACP and Garland Fund were engaged in final negotiations regarding his employment. The previous summer, as soon as the Fund's most influential official, Roger Baldwin, had advised White that $10,000 was being released to the NAACP, the delighted secretary had immediately proposed hiring Houston.[132] When Baldwin threw cold water on the idea by expressing doubt that a dean "is the man to argue cases unless he's had a lot of court experience," White added Hastie's name for consideration. Baldwin countered by suggesting three whites.[133] There was considerable discussion over whether a white lawyer or a black one "could best do the job," since whoever was hired would be working mainly in the South. White argued that, given the intense southern animosity toward northern white lawyers engendered by the Communist attorney in the Scottsboro case, "a colored lawyer with the dignity, ability and tact" of Houston or Hastie "would encounter far less hostility than a white lawyer."[134] With Baldwin skeptical of Houston, White pushed Hastie's candidacy vigorously until the latter joined Margold's staff as assistant solicitor in the interior department in November. All that the discomfited White could do was to arrange for Hastie's appointment to the legal committee.[135]

Stymied by the turn of events, White reluctantly concluded that he would have to settle for a top-notch white lawyer, and with the consent of the joint committee he approached the Columbia University law professor Karl Llewellyn, who turned the job down.[136] White thereupon brought up Houston's name again. Although Baldwin approved only reluctantly, the joint committee offered Houston the position, and he joined the staff at the end of the school year in the summer of 1935.[137]

With the accession of Houston to the post of special counsel, the transition from white preeminence to black control of the NAACP's legal work was essentially complete. Arthur Spingarn's participation in the administration of the Association's litigation gradually declined. In 1939 he succeeded his deceased brother in the largely honorific role of NAACP president, while Hastie became chairman of the legal committee. By then, although Houston had returned to Washington, the work of special counsel was being carried on by Thurgood Marshall.

The foregoing analysis of the NAACP's legal work indicates that the roles of whites and blacks in the organization, and the way in which these changed over time, were a function of the shifting social milieu in which the NAACP operated. Neither white paternalism nor black distrust of whites—though both existed to some extent in the NAACP—appears to have exerted a significant influence in determining the NAACP's choice of lawyers. On the one hand, in the early years NAACP leaders of both races believed that, given the limitations of the black lawyers as a group and the extreme racism of white public opinion and the white bar, the use of distinguished white counsel was imperative if the Association was to mount a successful battle for the black man's constitutional rights. On the other hand, blacks involved in the controversies we have analyzed did not express distrust of whites. Those who criticized the NAACP's policies did not question the motivations of men like Moorfield Storey, Louis Marshall, or Arthur Spingarn. Rather, they argued from a position of racial pride. In effect, it was an admission of inadequacy, and an implied criticism of the black bar, to accept the idea that blacks had to depend upon whites to fight their legal battles. Negro lawyers ranging from J. Alston Atkins to Charles Houston emphatically believed that Negroes could fight their own battles successfully, and that the NAACP should shape its practice accordingly.

Basic to the differential roles played by black and white lawyers was the issue of different competencies. Given the nature of the legal profession, competence involves not only the expertise which a lawyer brings to a case, but also how he is regarded by the courts. As pointed out, these two factors are interrelated, since discrimination by the courts made it difficult for black lawyers to develop competencies in areas like constitutional law. In any event, the NAACP's early policy of choosing prestigious white lawyers recognized the fact that "reputation and standing" were important elements in a lawyer's competence before the courts. Significantly, the NAACP's change in policy came at a time when southern judges were beginning to show greater respect for black lawyers, and when a cadre of Negro civil rights lawyers trained at the Ivy League schools and the revamped Howard University Law School was emerging.

As Marx and Useem point out, black demand for control of a biracial movement paradoxically tends to occur in two very different contexts: either when the movement is gaining strength, or when it fails to achieve its goals. Our research on CORE suggested a complex interweaving of both types of factors during the 1960's: the thrust for black control stemmed both from pride in the victories of the nonviolent direct action movement, and from disillusionment arising from the realization that an enormous gap still existed between social reality and complete racial justice. For the NAACP a generation earlier, operating in a context of much slower social change, it was the movement's gradually rising strength and significant, though limited, accomplishments which set the stage for the irresistible thrust for a shift in legal leadership.

It would seem clear that whites played an important role in the early years of the NAACP because the black members felt that the whites were needed. As the movement gained strength and achieved victories, and as the external society accorded greater legitimacy to the Negroes' demands, the usefulness of whites declined, and their role within the organization become constricted. Thus the experience of the NAACP prefigured the developments in the civil rights revolution of the 1960's and the dramatic shift from "Black and White Together" in the struggle for racial equality to black separatism and "Black Power."

1. Historical analyses of the relationship between blacks and whites in the abolitionist movement are best represented by Leon Litwack, Jane and William Pease, and James McPherson. Litwack and the Peases stress the evidences of paternalistic and sometimes racist attitudes and actions among the antebellum white abolitionists. McPherson, on the other hand, has stressed the equalitarian ideology of the white abolitionists and their contribution to the Negro struggle for equal rights during the Civil War and Reconstruction. Leon Litwack, *North of Slavery* (Chicago, 1961), ch. 7; William H. and Jane H. Pease, "Antislavery Ambivalence: Immediatism, Expediency, Race," *American Quarterly*, 17 (Winter, 1965), 682–95; James M. McPherson, *The Struggle for Equality* (Princeton, 1964), ch. 6. See also essays by Litwack and McPherson in Martin Duberman, ed., *The Antislavery Vanguard: New Essays on the Abolitionists* (Princeton, 1965), and two works by the Peases: "Boston Garrisonians and the Problem of Frederick Douglass," *Canadian Journal of History*, 2 (Sept., 1967), 29–48, and *They Who Would Be Free: Blacks' Search for Freedom, 1830–1861* (New York, 1974).

A systematic analysis of race relations in the twentieth-century civil rights movement remains to be done. Many scholars, however, have noted the important role which whites played in founding the NAACP—a subject best treated in Nancy J. Weiss, "From Black Separatism to Interracial Cooperation: The Origins of Organized Efforts for Racial Advancement, 1890–1920," in Barton J. Bernstein and Allen J. Matusow, eds., *Twentieth Century America: Recent Interpretations*, 2nd ed. (New York, 1972), pp. 52–87. Two of the early white leaders in the NAACP are treated in William B. Hixson, *Moorfield Storey and the Abolitionist Tradition* (New York, 1972), and B. Joyce Ross, *J. E. Spingarn and the Rise of the NAACP* (New York, 1972). Meier and Rudwick deal in detail with black and white relations in the Congress of Racial Equality in *CORE: A Study in the Civil Rights Movement, 1942–1968* (New York, 1973). The behavioral science literature on black-white relations in the civil rights movement of the 1960's is quite substantial, the most notable items being Inge Powell Bell's empirical study, *CORE and the Strategy of Nonviolence* (New York, 1968), and the synthesis and analysis offered by Gary T. Marx and Michael Useem, "Majority Involvement in Minority Movements: Civil Rights, Abolition, Untouchability," *Journal of Social Issues*, 27, no. 1 (1971), 81–104.

2. Marx and Useem, "Majority Involvement in Minority Movements," pp. 81–104.

3. The most vigorous portrayal of the early white leaders of the NAACP as paternalistic individuals, tinged with a racist streak, is to be found in Victor M. Glasberg's unpublished dissertation, "The Emergence of White Liberalism: The Founders of the NAACP and American Racial Attitudes" (Ph.D. dissertation, Harvard University, 1971). A functional explanation of the NAACP's early utilization of white and black lawyers, prefiguring the interpretation developed in this paper, is suggested briefly in Weiss, "From Black Separatism to Interracial Cooperation," p. 81.

4. *Thirteenth Census of the United States*, IV: *Population: Occupation Statistics* (Washington, 1914); *Fourteenth Census of the United States*, IV: *Population: Occupations* (Washington, 1923); *Fifteenth Census of the United States*, IV: *Population: Occupations by States* (Washington, 1933); *Sixteenth Census of the United States*, III: *Population: The Labor Force* (Washington, 1943), pts. 2, 3, 4, 5.

The situation was actually even worse than the raw figures indicate. A survey made in the late 1920's revealed that half of the Negroes listed as lawyers in the census were "not actively engaged in the practice of law," but earned their living at other occupations. In 1947 Alexander Tureaud was the only black lawyer in Louisiana. Charles H. Houston, "Cooperation between the National Bar Association and the N.A.A.C.P.," Remarks given at the NAACP Annual Conference, May 20, 1932, Box B 8, NAACP Papers, Library of Congress; obituary of Tureaud in *The National Bar Bulletin*, 4 (Jan.–Mar., 1972), 6.

5. Irvin C. Mollison, "The Negro Lawyer in Mississippi," *Journal of Negro History*, 15 (Jan., 1930), 43–54, 59.

6. Carter G. Woodson, *The Negro Professional Man and the Community: With Special Emphasis on the Physician and the Lawyer* (Washington, 1934), pp. 186, 222; Charles H. Houston, "Findings on Negro Legal Education," May 2, 1928; and "Report of Preliminary Survey on the Negro and His Contact with Administration of Law," May 15, 1928, pp. 9–12, both at Rockefeller Foundation Archives, New York. These were portions of a report on "The Negro and His Contact with the Administration of Law," prepared by Houston in late 1927 and 1928 under a grant from the Laura Spelman Rockefeller Memorial. Woodson's discussion of black lawyers is largely based on this report, as is that of Charles S. Johnson, in *The Negro College Graduate* (Chapel Hill, 1938), ch. 21.

7. Woodson, *The Negro Professional Man*, pp. 231–33.

8. For discussion of relations of Negro business and Negro lawyers, see Houston, "Tentative Findings re Negro Lawyers," Jan. 1928, pp. 7–9, Rockefeller Foundation Archives; Houston, "Report of Preliminary Survey on the Negro and His Contact with the Administration of Law," pp. 11–12; and Woodson, *The Negro Professional Man*, pp. 225–26, 236–38. The quotation is from the Woodson book, pp. 225–26.

9. On Garvey, see Chicago *Defender*, June 26, 1920. On Randolph, see Chandler Owen to James Weldon Johnson, Apr. 21, 1926, James Weldon Johnson Papers, Beinecke Library, Yale University, and Houston *Informer*, May 10, 1930.

10. Houston, "Tentative Findings re Negro Lawyers," pp. 11–12; quoted with the permission of the Rockefeller Foundation.

11. Woodson, *The Negro Professional Man and the Community*, p. 236; G. Franklin Edwards, *The Negro Professional Class* (Glencoe, Ill., 1959), p. 135; Houston, "Tentative Findings re Negro Lawyers," p. 15.

12. Houston, "Tentative Findings re Negro Lawyers," pp. 6–7; Houston, "Report of Preliminary Survey on the Negro and His Contact with the Administration of Law," p. 8; Johnson, *The Negro College Graduate*, pp. 333–34.

13. William H. Hastie, "Toward an Equalitarian Legal Order, 1930–1950," *Annals of the American Academy of Political and Social Science*, 407 (May, 1973), 21.

14. On Storey and Marshall, see esp. Hixson, *Moorfield Storey and the Abolitionist Tradition*, and Morton Rosenstock, *Louis Marshall: Defender of Jewish Rights* (Detroit, 1965).

15. Houston noted that few southern black lawyers were trained in northern schools, and he estimated that as of 1928 approximately a thousand lawyers had graduated from southern black law schools, over 700 of them from Howard. Houston, "Report of Preliminary Survey on the Negro and His Contact with the Administration of Law," p. 9, and "Findings on Negro Legal Education," p. 5.

16. The best examples of NAACP attorneys of this type are Scipio Jones of Little Rock, the lawyer in the celebrated Arkansas riot cases, and Nathaniel J. Frederick of Columbia, S.C., who for years handled much NAACP litigation in South Carolina. This kind of lawyer was rarer in the North, although as distinguished a figure as E. H. Morris of Chicago received his training in this way. For discussion of the successful southern black lawyers trained in the offices of prominent white attorneys, see Houston, "Findings on Negro Legal Education," p. 3. On Jones reading law in the offices of Judges Robert J. Lea, John Martin, and Henry C. Caldwell, the last a U.S. district judge, see Tom Dillard, "Scipio A. Jones," *Arkansas Historical Quarterly*, 31 (Autumn, 1972), 204.

17. On Negro law schools, see Houston, "Findings on Negro Legal Education," pp. 4–8. Of the seven black law schools known to have been founded, four still existed in the 1920's. Of these only Howard offered respectable training.

18. The list of Howard Law School alumni prominently involved in NAACP litigation through the 1920's would include Charles Houston's father, William L. Houston, and James A. Cobb of the Washington, D.C., branch's very active legal committee; R. L. Brokenburr, prominent for years in civil rights litigation in Indianapolis; Ashbie W. Hawkins, easily the leading civil rights attorney in Maryland; T. G. Nutter, who led the struggle before the courts of West Virginia; J. T. Settle, the leading black attorney in Memphis; and J. R. Pollard, who for over two decades was active in the most significant NAACP cases in Virginia. Lawyers mentioned in this article who were associated more briefly with NAACP legal work and who were also graduates of Howard University Law School were Homer G. Phillips, the most important Negro lawyer in St. Louis, and A. A. Andrews of Louisville, a junior counsel in the fight against residential segregation in that city. Only rarely did the NAACP utilize the services of a lawyer trained at one of the lesser law schools connected with black colleges in the South. The only example in the cases examined in this paper was Frank Bernard Smith, a graduate of the law school at Straight University in New Orleans, who played a minor role in the New Orleans residential segregation case.

On William Houston, see Richmond *Planet*, Aug. 24, 1912; on Cobb, *Who's Who in Colored America, 1928–1929* (New York, 1928), p. 82; on Brokenburr, *Who's Who in Colored America, 1950* (Yonkers, 1950), p. 56; on Hawkins, *Who's Who of the Colored Race* (Chicago, 1915), p. 132, and obituary of Hawkins in Baltimore *Afro-American*, Apr. 5, 1941, copy supplied courtesy of Professor Bettye Thomas, University of Maryland Baltimore County; on Nutter, *The Crisis*, 17 (Jan., 1919), 123; on Settle, *ibid.*, 11 (Dec., 1915), 67; on Pollard, Richmond *Planet*, Feb. 20, 1937; on Phillips, *The Crisis*, 39 (Jan., 1932), 466; on Andrews, *Who's Who of the Colored Race*, p. 10; on Smith, see "Straight Law Graduates Admitted to Louisiana Bar," in Alexander P. Tureaud Papers, Amistad Research Center, Dillard University, New Orleans (information supplied courtesy of Clifton H. Johnson, director).

19. Typical examples of men with this type of training who were active in NAACP cases in their respective states on a sustained basis were E. Burton Ceruti of Los Angeles, who had his law degree from St. Lawrence University; G. Edward Dickerson of Philadelphia, trained at Temple University Law School; Chester K. Gillespie of Cleveland, who had a degree from Baldwin-Wallace College Law Department; R. L. Bailey of Indianapolis, trained at Indiana Law School; and Elisha Scott, the NAACP's leading attorney in Kansas, who graduated from Washburn University Law School in

Topeka. Houston's broader survey of northern black attorneys also concludes that the majority of them were trained in northern white law schools.

On Ceruti, see *Who's Who in Colored America, 1927* (New York, 1927), p. 40; on Dickerson, *Who's Who in Colored America, 1928–1929*, p. 109; on Gillespie, *ibid.*, p. 146; on Bailey, *ibid.*, p. 18; on Scott, *Who's Who in Colored America, 1950*, p. 456. Houston, "Report of Preliminary Survey on the Negro and His Contact with the Administration of Law," p. 9.

20. Houston did not attribute this paucity of blacks in prominent northern white law schools to discrimination; in fact, he observed that admissions policies of northern schools had not been discriminatory. He did, however, note that those who attended such institutions usually operated at a disadvantage because of an inferior pre-legal education, and a precarious financial status that forced them to work long hours earning a living. Houston, "Findings on Negro Legal Education," pp. 1–2.

21. These included two southern lawyers active in NAACP work over long periods—A. T. Walden of Atlanta, LL.B., University of Michigan, and S. D. McGill of Jacksonville, LL.B., Boston University; an occasional northern branch lawyer like Butler Wilson, the long-time leader of the Boston NAACP, who also obtained his law degree from Boston University; and a handful of lawyers in New York whom Arthur Spingarn tried to involve, with only modest success, in litigation sponsored by the national office. This last group consisted of two men who served for a few years on the National Legal Committee—Philip M. Thorne, LL.B., Yale University, and member of the national legal committee for a brief period beginning in 1914, and Aiken A. Pope, LL.B., Harvard University, and member of National Legal Committee, 1921–24—and William T. Andrews, LL.B., Columbia University, who served as a salaried special legal assistant from 1927 until 1932. Pope, a recluse who specialized in research work for Wall Street corporate lawyers, handled a few NAACP cases in the early 1920's. In one of them he was associated with another black lawyer, James C. Thomas, LL.B., Cornell University. Spingarn originally had high hopes for Andrews, but both he and Walter White were disappointed in the young attorney's performance.

On Walden, see *Who's Who in Colored America, 1928–1929*, p. 376; on McGill, *ibid.*, p. 249; on Wilson, Clarence G. Contee, "Butler R. Wilson and the Boston NAACP Branch," *The Crisis*, 81 (Dec., 1974), 346; on Thorne, New York *Age*, Sept. 7, 1911; on Pope, *Who's Who in Colored America, 1928–1929*, p. 295; on Thomas, *ibid.*, p. 361, and, on case he handled with Pope, *The Crisis*, 23 (Dec., 1921), 71–72; on Andrews, see Andrews to White, Dec. 2, 1930, Box C-99, NAACP Papers. Spingarn's view of Andrews and a description of Pope from confidential interviews.

22. The list would include Thomas Ewing, Jr., the first chairman of the national legal committee, Georgetown University, Louis Marshall and Arthur Spingarn, Columbia University; Charles Studin, Yale University; Herbert K. Stockton, national board and national legal committee member, Harvard University; Benjamin Adger Hagood, the South Carolina lawyer who represented the NAACP in the *Pink Franklin* case, Georgetown University; Edward Osgood Brown, Chicago lawyer involved in the appeals of the East St. Louis riot defendants, Harvard University; S. S. Gregory, who headed the defense of the Chicago riot defendants, University of Wisconsin; Clayton B. Blakey, senior counsel in the Louisville segregation case, and Fred Knollenberg, local counsel in the Texas white primary cases, both University of Michigan; Alfred E. Cohen, senior counsel in the Richmond franchise and residential segregation cases, University of Virginia; Loys Charbonnet and Henry W. Robinson, the lawyers employed by the New Orleans branch in its franchise and residential segregation cases, both Tulane University; Henry E. Davis and William Leahy, counsel in the Washington, D.C., segregation cases, George Washington and Georgetown University Law Schools, respectively; Arthur Garfield Hays, a counsel in the *Sweet* case, Columbia University; J. Weston Allen, counsel in the *Crawford* extradition case, Harvard University. A few were from lesser, though very respectable law schools. William M. Wherry, Jr., the second national legal committee chairman, obtained his degree from the Cincinnati Law School; Charles A. Boston, who served for a few years on the national legal committee

and helped in the Baltimore residential segregation case, had an LL.B. from the University of Maryland; H. T. Fisher, counsel in a major extradition case growing out of the Elaine, Arkansas, riots, was an alumnus of the University of Kansas Law School; Charles Nagel, who supervised the defense in the East St. Louis riot cases, was a graduate of the St. Louis Law School, which subsequently affiliated with Washington University; Charles D. Kline, the Anniston, Alabama, attorney who was chief counsel in the Caldwell case (see note 39), received his LL.B. from the University of Georgia.

On the other hand, certain very prominent white lawyers who worked with the NAACP either received their degrees from obscure institutions or never obtained them at all. Samuel D. Miller, attorney in the Indianapolis segregation case, had studied at Columbia University, but, because he accepted a political position in the administration of Benjamin Harrison, he obtained his degree from the National University Law School. Thomas Chawke, the Detroit criminal lawyer who assisted Clarence Darrow in the second *Sweet* case, was trained at the Detroit College of Law. Both Darrow and Colonel George Murphy, chief counsel for the Elaine, Arkansas, defendants, had read law. Storey, who began studying law at the Harvard Law School, in the end prepared for the bar under the direction of Charles Sumner.

On Ewing, see *New York Times*, Dec. 8, 1942; on Marshall, *ibid.*, Sept. 12, 1929; on Spingarn, *ibid.*, Dec. 2, 1971; on Studin, *ibid.*, March 7, 1950; on Stockton, *ibid.*, Jan. 3, 1939; on Hagood, Charleston *News and Courier*, Nov. 10, 1946; on Brown, *Who's Who in America, 1916–1917* (Chicago, 1916), pp. 303–304; on Gregory, *Who Was Who in America, I: 1897–1942* (Chicago, 1943), p. 486; on Blakey, Louisville *Post*, Oct. 31, 1922; on Knollenberg, telephone interview with his daughter, Mrs. Robert Roy, Apr. 18, 1974; on Cohen, Richmond *Times-Dispatch*, Sept. 4, 1950; on Charbonnet, William M. Deacon, comp., *Reference Biography of Louisiana Bench and Bar* (New Orleans, 1922), p. 77; on Robinson, *Encyclopedia of American Biography* (New York, 1957), XXVII, 34; on Davis, *Who Was Who in America, I*, p. 300; on Leahy, *Who Was Who in America, III: 1951–1960* (Chicago, 1960), p. 506; on Hays, *Times*, Dec. 15, 1954; on Allen, *ibid.*, Jan. 2, 1942; on Wherry, telephone interview with University of Cincinnati Law School records office, Jan. 30, 1975; on Boston, *Times*, Mar. 9, 1935; on Fisher, Walt Markley, *Builders of Topeka* (Topeka, 1934), p. 91; on Kline, Thomas McAdory Owen, *History of Alabama and Dictionary of Alabama Biography* (Chicago, 1921), III, 989; on Nagel, St. Louis *Post-Dispatch*, Jan. 6, 1940; on Miller, Indianapolis *Star*, Sept. 7, 1939; on Chawke, telephone interview with registrar's office, Detroit College of Law, Jan. 26, 1975; on Darrow, *Who's Who in America, 1926–1927* (Chicago, 1926), pp. 558–59; on Murphy, Little Rock *Arkansas Gazette*, Oct. 12, 1920 (copy supplied courtesy of Professor Walter L. Brown, University of Arkansas).

23. With few exceptions they were Republicans, and certain ones held very high office. Charles Nagel had been secretary of commerce and labor and a member of the Republican National Committee during the presidency of William Howard Taft. Samuel Duncan Miller had served as private secretary to Redfield Proctor and Stephen Elkins, both secretaries of war during the Benjamin Harrison administration, 1891–93. Thomas Ewing, a Democrat, served as commissioner of patents under Wilson. (As patent commissioner he proved a notable exception to the Wilsonian policies of discrimination against blacks in the civil service). Two had served as attorneys general for their respective states: J. Weston Allen, a member of the Massachusetts House of Representatives, 1915–18, and attorney general, 1920–22; and Colonel George W. Murphy, a southern Democrat who was Arkansas's attorney general from 1901 to 1905, and subsequently ran for governor on the Bull Moose ticket in 1913. Others held political appointments from the U.S. Department of Justice—Benjamin Hagood, as a young lawyer, had been an assistant U.S. attorney in South Carolina; Henry E. Davis was assistant attorney for the District of Columbia, 1885–89, and U.S. attorney, 1897–99; and William E. Leahy was assistant U.S. attorney, 1915–19, and would subsequently enjoy several other important appointive positions. Several were prominent in local politics. Clayton Blakey was city attorney for Louisville, 1908–12 and 1921–22, and his law partner and close political associate Huston Quin was judge of the Kentucky Court of Appeals during

1919–21 and mayor of Louisville from 1921 to 1925. In Illinois, Edward O. Brown, a Democrat, had been a circuit court judge in 1903–9, and an appellate court judge in 1910–15. The two lawyers from southern Illinois who participated in the East St. Louis riot cases were both prominent in local political circles; one, Samuel W. Baxter, was a Republican, while the other, Thomas N. Webb, was a Democrat who at one point was slated for appointment to the state supreme court. John J. Barbour, who figured prominently in the defense of the Chicago riot cases, had been a state senator. Surprisingly enough, this pattern of political activity held even for Louisiana. Loys Charbonnet was a Democrat who in 1900–1904 had served in the state legislature, while Henry W. Robinson was active in the Republican party, being prominent in its lily-white faction! (Ironically enough, his contact with local NAACP leaders seems to have come through a Negro prominent in the black-and-tan faction, Walter L. Cohen, who had been Booker T. Washington's closest ally in the state.) And even in Alabama, Charles D. Kline of Anniston had formerly been a state senator.

On Nagel, St. Louis *Post-Dispatch*, Jan. 6, 1940; on Miller, Indianapolis *Star*, Sept. 7, 1939, and Jacob P. Dunn, *History of Greater Indianapolis* (Chicago, 1910), II, 1234; on Ewing, *Who's Who in America, 1914–15* (Chicago, 1914), pp. 751–52, and *The Crisis*, 14 (Oct., 1917), 315–16; on Allen, *Who's Who in America, 1930–1931* (Chicago, 1930), p. 170; on Murphy, Little Rock *Arkansas Gazette*, Oct. 12, 1920, and, regarding gubernatorial nomination, June 25, 1913; on Hagood, Charleston *News and Courier*, Nov. 10, 1946; on Davis, *Who Was Who in America*, I, 300; on Leahy, *ibid.*, III, 506; on Blakey and Quin, Louisville *Courier-Journal*, Nov. 1, 1922, and Aug. 15, 1938, respectively; on Brown, *Who's Who in America, 1916–1917*, pp. 303–304; on Baxter, East St. Louis *Journal*, Oct. 25, 1904, Aug. 16, 1905, and June 30, 1913; on Webb, *ibid.*, Feb. 4, 1915; on Barbour, *Times*, Mar. 30, 1946; on Charbonnet, *Who's Who in Louisiana and Mississippi* (New Orleans, 1918), p. 49; on Robinson, telephone interview with his son, Henry M. Robinson, May 20, 1974; on Kline, Owen, *History of Alabama*, p. 990.

24. The first two chairmen of the legal committee were exceedingly prominent in their specialties: Thomas Ewing was a leading patent lawyer, and William Wherry was a highly successful attorney for utilities. Spingarn, who specialized in helping wealthy families manage their affairs, and his partner Studin were less prominent, though Studin was widely known in the artistic and intellectual community for handling important contracts in the musical, publishing, and theatrical fields. Louis Marshall was a partner in the celebrated firm of Guggenheimer, Untermyer, and Marshall; the most famous member of the firm was Samuel P. Untermyer, wealthy corporate lawyer and counsel for the Pujo Commission. Arthur Garfield Hays has gone down in history as a noted civil liberties attorney, but he made his millions representing Wall Street brokers. Herbert Stockton, who specialized in admiralty law, belonged to the well-known firm of Haight, Griffin, Deming and Gardner. Charles A. Boston belonged to the noted law firm of Hornblower, Miller and Potter, whose senior partners included New York Governor Nathan L. Miller; subsequently he became "a foremost champion of legal ethics." Benjamin Hagood belonged to the prominent Charleston firm of Mordecai, Gadsden, Rutledge and Hagood, known for "representing important corporations"; later his stature and the nature of his practice led to his serving on the boards of directors of South Carolina utility companies and other important businesses, including the two Charleston daily newspapers. A few—George W. Murphy, Thomas F. Chawke, and Thomas Webb—were leading criminal lawyers; William Leahy was a defense attorney for Secretary of the Interior Albert B. Fall in the Teapot Dome scandal. Samuel W. Baxter was such a successful railroad attorney that in 1925 he moved from East St. Louis to Cincinnati as general counsel for Big Four Railroad. Finally, Samuel Duncan Miller was a partner in the most prominent Indianapolis law firm, Miller, Dailey and Thompson, whose founder had been former president Benjamin Harrison.

On occasion the national office of the NAACP found itself burdened with a white lawyer who was less than prominent, even in his local community. A case of this nature arose with Fred Knollenberg, the El Paso attorney who was popular with the black leadership of the local NAACP branch. Knollenberg willingly undertook NAACP work, but he lacked the standing of white lawyers the NAACP was able to obtain in most other places.

On Ewing, see *Times*, Dec. 8, 1942; on Wherry, *ibid.*, May 8, 1960; on Spingarn, confidential interviews; on Studin, *Times*, Mar. 7, 1950; on Marshall and Untermyer, *ibid.*, Sept. 12, 1929, and Mar. 17, 1940; on Hays, *ibid.*, Dec. 15, 1954; on Stockton, *ibid.*, Jan. 3, 1939; on Boston, *ibid.*, Mar. 9, 1935; on Hagood, Charleston *News and Courier*, Nov. 10, 1946; on Leahy, M. R. Werner and John Starr, *Teapot Dome* (New York, 1959), p. 230; on Baxter, East St. Louis *Daily Journal*, Dec. 22, 1924; on Miller, Indianapolis *Star*, Sept. 7, 1939. In the case of Knollenberg, careful checking with his daughter, with the widow of Dr. L. A. Nixon (plaintiff in the Texas white primary cases), and with the reference department of the El Paso Public Library confirmed the impression that emerges from correspondence in the NAACP legal files: Knollenberg, while competent in his specialty, was not a leading member of his local bar.

25. Certain of the lawyers came from exceedingly distinguished families. The grandfather of Thomas Ewing, Jr., Thomas Ewing, had been secretary of the treasury under President William Henry Harrison, and in 1849 became the first secretary of the interior. His father, also named Thomas, had been a private secretary to President Zachary Taylor, the first chief justice of the supreme court of Kansas, a brigadier general during the Civil War, and afterward a prominent Ohio lawyer and Democratic politician, serving in Congress from 1877 to 1881. Thomas Ewing, Jr., was himself a nephew of General W. T. Sherman, and his wife's family was also prominent socially. An heiress, Mrs. Ewing was the extremely wealthy granddaughter of Alexander Smith, founder of the Alexander Smith Carpet Company. Samuel Miller's family had also had close connections with the Harrison family. His father, William Henry Harrison Miller, had read law in the Toledo office of future Supreme Court Justice Morrison R. Waite, and served as attorney general in the cabinet of his law partner President Benjamin Harrison.

Others besides Ewing were descended from men with high posts in the military services. The father of William Wherry, Jr. was a professional soldier whose career lasted through the battle of San Juan Hill, and who had also been a brigadier general since the Civil War. Herbert Stockton was the son of Admiral Charles H. Stockton, formerly head of the Naval War College at Newport, an authority on international law, and also formerly president of George Washington University.

Only a few of the lawyers utilized by the national NAACP were Jews—Marshall and his son James, Spingarn, Alfred E. Cohen, and Arthur Garfield Hays—but all of these were wealthy and most were prominent socially or in civic life. Marshall was one of the most important leaders of the American Jewish community. Cohen, descended from a prominent Sephardic family of New York City, was a well-to-do lawyer who moved in important Christian social circles in Richmond. His second wife was the former Mrs. Virginia Person Darden, stepmother of Colgate W. Darden, Jr., ex-governor and ex-president of the University of Virginia.

Other socially prominent lawyers involved in NAACP cases were J. Weston Allen, who proudly traced his ancestry back to the *Mayflower*; George Murphy, a former Confederate colonel who married into a prominent Arkansas planter family; Henry Warmoth Robinson (son of a Massachusetts carpetbagger who had become city editor of the New Orleans *Times-Picayune*), who belonged to the socially exclusive Pickwick and Boston clubs; and Charles Nagel, a leading figure in the St. Louis German community and the city's civic life.

On the Thomas Ewing family, see obituaries for Ewing's father, Ewing himself, his wife, and their son, in *Times*, Jan. 22, 1896, Dec. 8, 1942, May 5, 1943, and Feb. 9, 1933, respectively. On Miller's family, see Dunn, *History of Greater Indianapolis*, p. 1234, Indianapolis *News*, Sept. 7, 1939, and esp. sketch of Miller compiled by the Citizens Historical Association of Indianapolis, Aug. 6, 1938 (copy supplied courtesy of the Indianapolis Newspapers Inc. Library). On Wherry's family, see *Times*, May 8, 1960, and esp. entry for Wherry, Sr., in *Who's Who in America, 1910–1911* (Chicago, 1910), p. 2057; on Stockton family, *Times*, Jan. 3, 1939; on Marshall, Rosenstock, *Louis Marshall*, and lengthy first-page obituary in *Times*, Sept. 12, 1929; on Cohen, sketch of family background and early life in *The Owl*, 14 (Oct., 1902), n.p. (photocopy supplied courtesy of Samuel V. Troy of Richmond), Richmond *News-Leader*, Sept. 4, 1950, and telephone interviews with Cohen's nephew, Philip N. Schock of Mobile, Apr. 23, 1974, Cohen's grand-niece, Mrs. Joseph Cohn of Richmond, Mar. 31, 1975, and Colgate W. Darden, Jr., of Richmond, Apr. 25, 1974. On Allen, see *Times*, Jan. 2, 1942; on Murphy, Little Rock *Arkansas Gazette*, Oct. 12, 1920; on Robinson, *Encyclopedia of American Biography*, XXVII, 34–35; on Nagel, *Times*, Jan. 6, 1940, William Hyde and Howard L. Conard, *Encyclopedia of the History of St. Louis* (New York, 1899), III, 1612, W. B. Stevens, *Centennial History of Missouri* (St. Louis, 1921), III, 446–47, St. Louis *Post-Dispatch*, Jan. 6, 1940, and telephone interview with Nagel's daughter, Hildegaard Nagel of South Norwalk, Conn., Feb. 18, 1975.

26. S. S. Gregory was president of the American Bar Association in 1911–12, and Charles A. Boston held the same post in 1930–31. In addition, J. Weston Allen served as vice-president of the ABA in 1935–36.

For Gregory, see James Grafton Rogers, *American Bar Leaders 1878–1928* (Chicago, 1932), pp. 165–69; for Boston, *Times*, Mar. 9, 1935; for Allen, *Who's Who in America*, *1938–1939*, p. 165.

27. Exceptions would include E. O. Brown, who listed himself in *Who's Who* as a "radical Democrat" and a Single-Taxer; the noted civil liberties lawyer Arthur Garfield Hays, who, among other things, served as the New York state chairman of the Progressive party campaign in 1924; probably William M. Wherry, Jr., who had been counsel to the liberal New York *Evening Post* and was a prime mover in the creation of the Lawyers' Referral Service which was intended to provide inexpensive advice to moderate income people; and undoubtedly Arthur Spingarn, whose brother Joel had been actively identified with the Theodore Roosevelt wing of the Republican party and had supported the Bull Moose ticket in the election of 1912. Charles D. Kline, though the son of an Alabama and Georgia railroad executive, was a lawyer for labor and farmer groups. When he entered the Alabama senate in 1915 he wrote: "I have never embraced the policy in life that the strong should prosper off of the weak. . . . This has lead me to work in sympathy with the Organized Labor and Farmer's Union movement. I have given a great deal of time and service to both of these organizations. . . . I believe that our State and federal governments have been many times perverted into exploiters of the weak and submerged classes by the strong and wealthy. [I] Have fought this tendency in all of my political activities. . . ." This list should also perhaps include Charles Nagel. Nagel is sometimes referred to as a "Liberal"; for example, he briefly supported the abortive movement of Progressives and liberal Democrats known as the "Committee of 48" in the election of 1920. He then toyed with the idea of endorsing La Follette in 1924, and through the years he sustained a warm friendship with men like Oswald Garrison Villard and Roger Baldwin. However, he had a reputation for hostility toward organized labor, and despite his leanings toward "political independence," he always voted for Republican presidential candidates. His liberalism was limited to his strong civil libertarianism, his opposition to immigration restriction, and his lifelong interest in black Americans.

On Brown, see *Who's Who in America*, *1916–1917*, pp. 303–304; on Hays, *Who's Who in America*, *1926–1927* (Chicago, 1926), p. 918; on Wherry, *Times*, May 8, 1960; on Joel Spingarn, Ross, *J. E. Spingarn and the Rise of the NAACP*, ch. 1 and p. 67; on Kline, William D. Bernard of Montgomery to authors, July 17, 1975, and Kline, Biographical memorandum [1915], Alabama Department of Archives and History, Montgomery; on Nagel, St. Louis *Post-Dispatch*, Jan. 6, 1940, an unpublished biography of Nagel by John A. Hague of Stetson University, entitled "Charles Nagel: A Study in American Conservatism," and Nagel, "Remarks Before the Convention of Negro Baptists," 1906, in Otto Heller, ed., *Charles Nagel: Speeches and Writings 1900–1928* (New York, 1931), I, 30–32.

28. White to Arthur B. Spingarn, July 10, 1930, Box C-77, NAACP Papers. White also classed Allen as in this group, but thought that made him all the more desirable as a possible member of the legal committee. Most conservative of all appears to have been

Samuel Duncan Miller of Indianapolis, who served as the chairman of the executive committee of the Indianapolis chapter of the extreme right-wing, nativist American Protective League during the World War I period (Indianapolis *Star*, Sept. 7, 1939). For discussion of the American Protective League, see esp. John Higham, *Strangers in the Land: Patterns of American Nativism 1860–1925* (New Brunswick, N.J., 1955), pp. 211–12.

29. For example, S. S. Gregory as president of the American Bar Association actually supported the move to exclude Negroes from the organization. See account in Hixson, *Moorfield Storey and the Abolitionist Tradition*, p. 118, and, for more details, New York *Age*, Aug. 29, 1912. It is interesting to note, however, that Gregory had protested the execution of the Haymarket anarchists, and he always considered his participation with Clarence Darrow in the defense of Eugene V. Debs in the criminal conspiracy charges resulting from the Pullman strike to be one of the outstanding events in his career. See Rogers, *American Bar Leaders, 1878–1928*, p. 168; *Times*, Oct. 26, 1920, and entry in *Who Was Who in America*, I, 486. In the Chicago race riot cases he volunteered his services without fee (*The Crisis*, 19 [Nov., 1919], 340).

30. See discussion of Huston Quin in note 23 above.

31. For discussion of the American Bar Association's policy and Storey's struggle against it, see Hixson, *Moorfield Storey and the Abolitionist Tradition*, pp. 117–19, and Charles Flint Kellogg, *NAACP: A History of the National Association for the Advancement of Colored People, I: 1909–1920* (Baltimore, 1967), 199–201. Although a face-saving compromise was worked out, in practice blacks were completely excluded from the organization after 1912. See Houston, "Tentative Findings on the Negro Lawyers," p. 13.

32. Storey to May Childs Nerney, Sept. 19, Oct. 7, 1913, Moorfield Storey Letterbooks, Massachusetts Historical Society; *Guinn and Beal* v. *the United States*, 238 U.S. 347 (1915); NAACP Board of Directors Minutes, July 12, 1915, Box A-1, NAACP Papers.

33. Oswald Braithwaite to John R. Shillady, May 20, 1919, Box C-270, NAACP Papers; Storey to Shillady, May 31, 1915. Box C-75, *ibid.*

34. *The Crisis*, 10 (Aug., 1915), 199–200; [Nerney] to William Harrison, Apr. 17, 1913, Box 1, Arthur B. Spingarn Papers, Library of Congress; [Nerney] to Storey, Aug. 11 and 25, 1913, *ibid.*; Chapin Brinsmade to Storey, Nov. 12 and 15, 1913, *ibid.*; Brinsmade to W. T. Ferguson, Dec. 17, 1913, *ibid.*; Storey to Nerney, Dec. 19, 1914, Storey Letterbooks; *McCabe* v. *the Atchison, Topeka and Santa Fe Railroad*, 235 U.S. 15 (1914); *The Crisis*, 9 (Jan., 1915), 133–34. Harrison, an aggressive individual who was also active in the early stages of litigation against the Oklahoma grandfather clause, had formal legal training that was weaker than most of the other important black lawyers of the period, having received his LL.B. from the tiny law department at Walden University, Nashville, in 1902. Subsequently he moved to Chicago, where he had an active political career, serving as assistant attorney general of Illinois from 1925 to 1928. For Harrison's career, see *Who's Who in Colored America, 1928–1929*, p. 166, and Harold F. Gosnell, *Negro Politicians: The Rise of Negro Politics in Chicago* (Chicago, 1935), pp. 81, 182, 215, 216. *Who's Who in Colored America* mistakenly indicates that Harrison received his LL.B. from Livingstone College, which never had a law department; further checking revealed that he received both his liberal arts and law degrees at Walden University (information from 1917–18 catalogue of Walden University supplied by James P. Brawley, president emeritus of Clark College, Atlanta, in letter dated Feb. 5, 1975).

35. See esp. *The Crisis*, 37 (Jan., 1930), 17, and *Seventeenth Annual Report of the National Association for the Advancement of Colored People for 1926* (New York, 1927), pp. 15–18, for descriptions of two of Frederick's cases. For an evaluation of the importance of the work of this "able and courageous Negro attorney," see Morris Ernst, Lewis Gannett, and James Weldon Johnson, "Memorandum from the Committee on Negro Work to the Directors of the American Fund for Public Service," May 28, 1930, Box 46, Spingarn Papers.

36. See esp. Houston, "Findings on the Negro Lawyer," p. 10. As Houston observed, these men were individuals who did not follow the usual practice of southern black lawyers in associating with white lawyers. Yet, as will be seen, our research re-

vealed that even McGill and Frederick occasionally felt compelled to adopt this strategy.

37. NAACP Board of Directors Minutes, July 11, Oct. 10, 1927, Box A-2, NAACP Papers; *Eighteenth Annual Report of the National Association for the Advancement of Colored People for 1927* (New York, 1928), p. 15. The Florida Supreme Court unfortunately upheld the conviction, and the U.S. Supreme Court refused to hear the case. See Marshall to McGill, Feb. 26, Mar. 26, 1928, Box 1600, Louis Marshall Papers, American Jewish Archives, Cincinnati; Secretary's Report to the Board of Directors, May 9, 1928, NAACP Collection, National Office of NAACP, New York; and Marshall to White, Oct. 9, 1928, Box C-69, NAACP Papers.

38. Houston was especially impressed with the quality of the black bar in Baltimore, and with their commitment to handling civil rights cases. Houston, "Tentative Findings Re Negro Lawyers," p. 3.

39. Illustrative of Cobb's services to the Association were his efforts in 1919 to persuade federal officials to intercede on behalf of a black army sergeant, Edgar C. Caldwell, who had been sentenced to die for killing a streetcar motorman in Alabama. Cobb appealed to President Wilson's secretary Joseph Tumulty, and to high officials in the advocate general's office and the Department of Justice. Convincing them that the soldier should have been tried by a military court, he was influential in getting the case to the U.S. Supreme Court, which heard arguments in 1920. The Court, however, ruled that proper procedures had been followed and thus affirmed the death sentence. *Tenth Annual Report of the National Association for the Advancement of Colored People for the Year 1919* (New York, 1920), pp. 53–54; NAACP Board of Directors Minutes, Dec. 8, 1919, Box A-1, and March 8, 1920, Box A-2, NAACP Papers; Spingarn to Cobb, March 10, 1920, Box 2, Spingarn Papers; *Eleventh Annual Report of the National Association for the Advancement of Colored People for the Year 1920* (New York, 1921), pp. 19–20; correspondence on case in Box D-49, NAACP Papers.

40. Cobb to Spingarn, June 14, 1922, and Spingarn to Cobb, June 15, 1922, Box 2, Spingarn Papers.

41. Thomas E. Miller to Frances Blascoer, July 29, Aug. 5, Oct. 27, Dec. 5, 1910; William D. Sinclair to Blascoer, Aug. 3, 1910; Charles J. Bonaparte to Blascoer, July 30, 1910; Ed Wallace to Whitefield McKinlay, Oct. 10, 1910; Blascoer to Oswald Garrison Villard, Nov. 7, 1910, and other correspondence, all in Box D-55, NAACP Papers. Minutes of Executive Committee, Nov. 29, 1910, in NAACP Board of Directors Minutes, Box A-1, *ibid.*; Villard to Booker T. Washington, Aug 4, 1910, Washington to Villard, Aug. 9, 1910, and Villard to Wherry, Oct. 21, 1910, Oswald Garrison Villard Papers, Houghton Library, Harvard University; Nerney to Storey, Aug. 11, 1913, Box 1, Spingarn Papers; Nerney, Memorandum on Pink Franklin Case, Oct. 25, 1915, *ibid.*; *Tenth Annual Report of the National Association for the Advancement of Colored People for the Year 1919*, p. 54; *The Crisis*, 1 (Nov., 1910), 14, and (Feb., 1911), 15, 17.

42. "Memorandum of Activities of NAACP in the Houston, Texas, riot cases since their inception, 1917–21" [1921], Box C-1, NAACP Papers; NAACP Board of Directors Minutes, Dec. 10, 1917, Box A-1, *ibid.*

43. *The Crisis*, 15 (Apr., 1918), 283, and 25 (Nov., 1922), 17; correspondence with Charles Nagel and others concerning cases growing out of the East St. Louis riots in Box 1, Arthur B. Spingarn Papers; NAACP Board of Directors Minutes, Mar. 11, Oct. 14, 1918, Box A-1, NAACP Papers. On standing of Baxter and Webb, see East St. Louis *Daily Journal*, Apr. 3, 1925, and Dec. 22, 1927, respectively. Quotation on Nagel from his obituary in *Times*, Jan. 6, 1940.

44. [John R. Shillady], "Memorandum Re Conference in Chicago with Legal and Executive Committees of the Chicago Branch, N.A.A.C.P., with Representatives of the Chicago Peace and Protective Association and the Cook County Bar Association (Colored Lawyers), Concerning the Legal Defense of Colored Men Indicted in Chicago as a Result of the Race Riots" [Sept., 1919], Box 27, Spingarn Papers; *Tenth Annual Report*, p. 50; *The Crisis*, 19 (Nov., 1919), 340. On Gregory, see note 29, above.

45. District of Columbia Branch Executive Committee, "To Our Members," leaflet, July 23, 1919; [James A. Cobb ?], untitled memorandum, July 28, 1919; [William L.

Houston ?], untitled memorandum [July 26, 1919 ?], regarding events of July 21, 1919; and Cobb to Mary White Ovington, Dec. 3, 1919, all in Box G-34, NAACP Papers. Also *The Crisis*, 19 (Jan., 1920), 130, and 20 (May, 1920), 41–42.

46. "Arkansas Riot Cases," Oct. 4, 1929, Box C-196, NAACP Papers.

47. Secretary's Report to the Board, Feb. 6, Mar. 3, May 5, July 8, Nov. 8, 1920, NAACP Collection; "Arkansas Riot Cases," Oct. 4, 1929, Box C-196, NAACP Papers; *Eleventh Annual Report*, p. 17.

48. Antilynching Committee Minutes, Nov. 14, 1919, in NAACP Board of Directors Minutes, Box A-1, NAACP Papers; NAACP Board of Directors Minutes, Nov. 24, 1919, *ibid.*; E. L. McHaney to Spingarn, June 18, 1920, Box D-44, *ibid.*; Secretary's Report to the Board, May 5, 1920, NAACP Collection. For Bratton's role in choice of Murphy, see Arthur I. Waskow, *From Race Riot to Sit-In, 1919 and the 1960's* (Garden City, N.Y.), p. 154. Unfortunately, the NAACP correspondence which Waskow used was detached from the Archives and appears to be no longer available.

49. Spingarn to Storey, Oct. 26, 1920, Box 2, Spingarn Papers; Storey to Spingarn, Nov. 1, 1920, Storey Letterbooks; Storey to Spingarn, Nov. 4, 1920, Box 2, Spingarn Papers; Secretary's Report to the Board, Oct. 4, 1922, NAACP Collection; *Fourteenth Annual Report, NAACP for the Year 1923* (New York, 1924), p. 12.

50. Scipio Jones quoted in Secretary's Report to the Board, Nov. 19, 1921, NAACP Collection; Walter White to Storey, Oct. 24, 1921, Box 2, Moorfield Storey Papers, Library of Congress; Storey to White, Oct. 25, 1921, Box 63, Spingarn Papers; White to Jones, Oct. 26, 1921, *ibid.*; James Weldon Johnson to Storey, Nov. 2, 1921, Box 2, Storey Papers; Secretary's Report to the Board, July 8, 1922, NAACP Collection.

51. Storey to White, Dec. 1, 1922, Storey Letterbooks; Waskow, *From Race Riot to Sit-In*, p. 164, citing several letters no longer in the NAACP Papers; Secretary's Report to the Board, Feb. 7, 1923, NAACP Collection; NAACP Board of Directors Minutes, Feb. 14, 1923, Box A-2, NAACP Papers.

52. *Moore* v. *Dempsey*, 261 U.S. 86 (1923); Jones to Robert W. Bagnall, Apr. 30, 1923, Box 2, Storey Papers; Jones to White, May 8, 1923, Box 63, Spingarn Papers; Storey to White, May 7, 1923, *ibid.*; Jones to White, May 24, 1923, Box 16, *ibid.*

53. NAACP Board of Directors Minutes, May 14, Nov. 12, 1923, Box A-2, NAACP Papers; *The Crisis*, 26 (Aug., 1923), 163, and 27 (Jan., 1924), 124–25.

54. Louis Marshall to White, June 24, 1923, Box C-69, NAACP Papers.

55. Ovington to Spingarn, Oct. 24, 1923, Box 2, Spingarn Papers; NAACP Board of Directors Minutes, Dec. 10, 1923, Box A-2, NAACP Papers. On efforts over the years to secure Marshall's active participation in NAACP work there is correspondence, too extensive to be cited in detail here, scattered through both the NAACP Papers and the Marshall Papers, and probably more readily accessible in the latter. See esp. Marshall to Storey, Feb. 25, 1919, Box 1589; Herbert J. Seligmann to Marshall, Oct. 14, 1920, Box 57; and correspondence with White, Johnson, Stockton, and Storey, 1921–23, scattered in Boxes 62, 156, and 1594. Marshall's value in the eyes of Association leaders is indicated by their view that his acceptance of the invitation to join the Board would provide a "tower of strength" to the Association. See Spingarn to Ovington, Oct. 25, 1923, Box 2, Spingarn Papers; Johnson to Marshall, Nov. 7, 1923, Box 67, Marshall Papers.

56. *The Crisis*, 4 (May, 1912), 22, (Aug., 1912), 177–79, and 6 (June, 1913), 91, (July, 1913), 144; NAACP Board of Directors Minutes, July 1, 1913, Box A-1, NAACP Papers; NAACP, *Fourth Annual Report* (New York, 1914), pp. 22, 41; Nerney to Spingarn, July 2, 1915, Box 1, Spingarn Papers.

57. NAACP Board of Directors Minutes, Feb. 3, July 7, 1914, May 10, July 12, 1915, Apr. 9, 1917, Box A-1, NAACP Papers; NAACP, *The Fifth Annual Report 1914* (New York, 1915), p. 8; Spingarn to Nerney, Nov. 30, 1915, Box 1, Spingarn Papers; *The Crisis*, 10 (Aug., 1915), 198–99, (Sept., 1915), 244, and 12 (May, 1916), 37, and 14 (June, 1917), 67–70; *Report of the National Association for the Advancement of Colored People for the years 1917 and 1918* (New York, 1919), pp. 7–8.

58. *The Crisis*, 33 (Jan., 1927), 142. Victory in this case (*Gaillard* v. *Grant*) was secured in the Indiana courts. See correspondence in Box D-60, NAACP Papers.

59. White, Memorandum for the Files, Feb. 25, 1929, Box D-67, NAACP Papers; Marshall to William T. Andrews, Apr. 13, 1929, Box C-69, *ibid.*; Marshall to Andrews, May 15, 1929, Box 1601, Marshall Papers; Johnson to Marshall, May 27, 1929, Box C-66, NAACP Papers; Report of Legal Committee to Board, in NAACP Board of Directors Minutes, July 8, 1929, Box A-2, *ibid.* After Marshall died, the two Richmond attorneys took the case to the Supreme Court and won. See Reports of Acting Secretary, Feb. 6, Mar. 5, June 4, 1930, NAACP Collection; and *City of Richmond* v. *Deans*, 281 U.S. 704 (1930).

60. Cobb to Johnson, Apr. 28, 1926, Box C-413, NAACP Papers. Other correspondence relating to this case will be found there and in Box D-62. The case was won before the Supreme Court in 1927. *Harmon* v. *Tyler*, 273 U.S. 668 (1927).

61. NAACP press release, Apr. 20, 1923, Box G-34, NAACP Papers; and the following correspondence in Box 2, Spingarn Papers: Cobb to Spingarn, May 14, June 13, Aug. 23, Nov. 26, Dec. 9, 1923, Jan. 2, June 7, 1924; Stockton to Spingarn, June 15, Nov. 12, 1923; Spingarn to Stockton, Aug. 23, Nov. 10 and 15, 1923; Spingarn to Cobb, Nov. 15, 23, and 28, 1923.

62. Marshall to Johnson, Sept. 13, 1924, and Johnson to Marshall, Sept. 16, 1924, Box C-414, NAACP Papers; Spingarn to Marshall, Sept. 17, 1924, Spingarn to Cobb, Sept. 17, 1924, and Spingarn to Johnson, Sept. 17, 1924, Box 3, Spingarn Papers; Johnson to Spingarn, Sept. 19, 1924, Box C-414, NAACP Papers.

63. Johnson to Storey, Sept. 13, 1924, Box C-414, NAACP Papers; Storey to Marshall, Sept. 24, 1924, Storey Letterbooks; Storey to Johnson, Sept. 24, 1924, and Cobb to Spingarn, Sept. 18 and 26, 1924, Box 3, Spingarn Papers; White to Cobb, Sept. 25, 1924, Box C-414, NAACP Papers; Marshall to Spingarn, Sept. 30, 1924, Box 3, Spingarn Papers; Secretary's Report to the Board, Oct. 9, 1924, NAACP Collection; Marshall to Storey, Dec. 12, 1924, Box 1596, Marshall Papers; Marshall to Storey, Apr. 23, 25, May 7, June 23, Sept. 24, Oct. 2, 1925, Box 1597, *ibid.*; Marshall to Cobb, June 25, Oct. 3, 1925, *ibid.*; Cobb to Johnson, Oct. 7, 10, 1925, Box G-35, NAACP Papers; Spingarn to Cobb, Oct. 26, 1925, Box 3, Spingarn Papers; Johnson to Cobb, Oct. 27, 1925, Box G-35, NAACP Papers.

64. Cobb to Spingarn, Sept. 18, 1924, Box 3, Spingarn Papers; Marshall to Johnson, Oct. 19, 1925, and press release, Oct. 23, 1925, Box G-35, NAACP Papers; *Corrigan* v. *Buckley*, 271 U.S. 323 (1926). Subsequently the NAACP mounted a second attack on restrictive covenants in the District of Columbia. Cobb, appointed municipal judge in mid-1926, arranged for his law partner, George E. C. Hayes, to work with prominent white Washington lawyers, again under Marshall's supervision. In June, 1929, however, the Supreme Court declined to review two cases which had been decided unfavorably in the District of Columbia Court of Appeals. NAACP Board of Directors Minutes, June 14, 1926, Mar. 12, 1928, Box A-2, NAACP Papers; Cobb to Johnson, June 26, 1926, March 28, 1927, Box G-35, *ibid.*; Marshall to Cobb, Nov. 23, 1927, Box 1599, Marshall Papers; George E. C. Hayes to Johnson, Mar. 2, 1928, Box G-35, NAACP Papers; Marshall to W. T. Andrews, Apr. 12, 1928, and Marshall to Hayes and Harry Davis, Aug. 28, 1928, Box 1600, Marshall Papers; Hayes to Marshall, Dec. 14, 1928, Box G-35, NAACP Papers; NAACP press releases, Aug. 3, Sept. 28, 1928, *ibid.*; NAACP press release, Jan. 11, 1929, Box G-36, *ibid.*; Marshall to Johnson, Apr. 30, June 4, 1929, Box 1601, Marshall Papers; Acting Secretary's Report to the Board, Nov. 8, 1928, May 9, 1929, NAACP Collection; Marshall to W. T. Andrews, Feb. 6, 1929, Box G-37, NAACP Papers; press release, May 3, 1929, *ibid.*; *Cornish* v. *O'Donoghue*, 58 App. D.C. 359, *certiorari* denied; *Russell* v. *Wallace*, 58 App. D.C. 357, *certiorari* denied.

Marshall also gave advice in connection with the litigation against the restrictive covenants in California. See the following in the NAACP Papers: White to Storey, Apr. 17, May 5, May 7, 1925, Box C-77; Storey to White, May 6, 1925, Box C-76; Marshall to Andrews, Aug. 30, 1928, and Marshall to White, July 30, 1928, and Marshall to Robert W. Bagnall, Oct. 23, 1928, Box C-69.

65. L. W. Washington to Bagnall, Dec. 18, 1924, Box D-63, NAACP Papers; Washington to White, Jan. 31, 1925, *ibid.*; Spingarn to White, Jan. 6, 1925, Box 3, Spingarn Papers; Storey to White, Jan. 10, 1925, Box D-63, NAACP Papers; White to Storey, Mar. 16, 1925, Box C-77, *ibid.*; White to Cobb, Mar. 13, 1925, Box D-63, *ibid.*

66. Johnson to Knollenberg, Dec. 20, 1926, Box D-63, NAACP Papers; Storey to Johnson, Dec. 13, 1926, Box C-76, *ibid.* His name, however, did appear on the brief as one of the attorneys of record. NAACP press release, Dec. 17, 1926, Box D-63, *ibid.*

67. Marshall to Johnson, Jan. 13, 1927, and Cobb to Johnson, Jan. 8, 1927, Box D-64, *ibid.* As White observed, Cobb was "one of the best informed men of the country on Southern election laws, having made a special study of them." White to Knollenberg, Mar. 13, 1925, Box D-63, *ibid.*

68. Cobb to Johnson, Jan. 8, 1927, and Johnson to Cobb, Jan. 12, 1927, and Johnson to Marshall, Jan. 12, 1927, Box D-64, *ibid.*; *The Crisis*, 34 (May, 1927), 82; NAACP press release, Mar. 8, 1927, Box D-64, NAACP Papers; *Nixon v. Herndon*, 273 U.S. 536 (1927). Marshall was also involved in advising the NAACP on litigation against the white primary in Florida (*Goode v. Bell*) and Virginia (*West v. Bliley*). On Florida case, see esp. correspondence, 1928, in Box D-58, NAACP Papers, and Marshall's correspondence with Andrews, in Box C-69 of the NAACP Papers and Box 1600 of the Marshall Papers. On Virginia case, see esp. correspondence in 1928, Box D-67, NAACP Papers.

69. White to George N. White, Oct. 29, 1929, Box C-97, NAACP Papers.

70. *Twentieth Annual Report of the National Association for the Advancement of Colored People for 1929* (New York, 1930), p. 4.

71. As far as the extant evidence indicates, the issue had been raised with national officers of the Association at least once before, in 1915, in the form of a communication from the black Indianapolis lawyer R. L. Bailey, objecting to remarks made by a national officer or staff member on the subject. Spingarn reassured the Indiana attorney of the Association's "deep sympathy with every effort of colored men to assume the duties and responsibilities of the learned professions. There are many colored lawyers for whom I personally have the highest regard and I feel certain that my views are shared by every member of the Association." (Spingarn to Bailey, Nov. 24, 1915, Box 1, Spingarn Papers). Perhaps other branch attorneys were expressing similar feelings; at any rate, the white secretary, May Childs Nerney, energetically proceeded to push for the use of Negro lawyers at the local level as a matter of national Association policy: see esp. Nerney, untitled Report to Board of Directors, Dec. 6, 1915, in NAACP Papers Directors Minutes, Box A-1, NAACP Papers. An effort was actually made to develop such a committee of Negro attorneys to handle cases in New York on a contingency basis: Nerney to Spingarn, Dec. 10, 1915, and Spingarn to Nerney, Dec. 13, 1915, Box 1, Spingarn Papers. Evidently nothing ever came of it.

72. White to Oscar Baker, Oct. 5, 1925, Box D-86, NAACP Papers.

73. White to Johnson, Sept. 16, 1925, Box D-85, *ibid.*

74. Baker to White, Oct. 7, 1925, and Mose L. Walker to White, Sept. 22, 1925, and White to Johnson, Sept. 16, 1925, all *ibid.*

75. White to Robert L. Bradby, Sept. 25, 1925, *ibid.*; "Memorandum of conversation between Arthur B. Spingarn and Walter White," Oct. 1, 1925, and Johnson to Clarence Darrow, telegram, Oct. 7, 1925, Box D-86, *ibid.*

76. White to Johnson, Sept. 16, 1925, Box D-85, *ibid.*; NAACP Board of Directors Minutes, Oct. 13, 1925, Box A-2, *ibid.* The man retained was Walter Nelson, a well-known labor lawyer.

77. White to Darrow, Dec. 24 and 28, 1925, Jan. 8, 1926, and quotation in William Pickens to Ira Jayne, Dec. 29, 1925, all in Box D-86, *ibid.* The later recollections of two of the black attorneys in the case confirm their irritation with the stance of the NAACP national office, and the fact that once Darrow entered the case their participation was negligible. See transcripts of Alex Baskin's interviews with Charles Mahoney, Aug., 1960, and with Cecil L. Rowlette, Aug. 1, 1960, Michigan Historical Collections, University of Michigan.

78. White, memorandum for the files, Nov. 30, 1925, and White to Johnson, Feb. 1, 1926, both in Box D-86, NAACP Papers.

79. NAACP press release, Oct. 30, 1925, *ibid.*

80. Walker to White, Jan. 28, 1926, and Bagnall to Johnson, Feb. 18, 1926, *ibid.*

81. White to Baker, Mar. 5, 1926, Johnson to Jayne, Apr. 9, 1926, White to Darrow, Dec. 24, 1925, and Pickens to Jayne, Dec. 29, 1925, all *ibid.*

82. Darrow to Johnson, Apr. 5, 1926, *ibid.*; NAACP press release, May 14, 1926, and Johnson to Darrow, July 21, 1927, Box D-87, *ibid.*; transcript of Alex Baskin's interview with Thomas F. Chawke, Aug. 4, 1960, Michigan Historical Collections. It is interesting to note that, in their interviews with Baskin, Rowlette and Mahoney made the point that they had from the first proposed holding separate trials; they felt that Darrow had not adopted the best strategy for the first trial. See Baskin interviews cited in note 77, above.

83. Spingarn to White, July 28, 1934, Box 3, Spingarn Papers; Report of Secretary to the Board, Sept. 8, 1924, NAACP Collection; White to Spingarn, Sept. 12, 1934, Box 3, Spingarn Papers; "Archie Greathouse vs. Board of School Commissioners, Indianapolis," Jan., 1925 (a summary of actions taken in the case), Box D-11, NAACP Papers.

84. White to W. S. Henry, Jan. 22, 1925, Box 16, Spingarn Papers; White to Spingarn, Nov. 22, 1924, Box 3, *ibid.*; White to Spingarn, Jan. 9 and 17, 1925, *ibid.*

85. White to Henry, Jan. 22, 1925, Box 16, *ibid.*; White to Henry, Feb. 17, 1925, and White to Spingarn, Mar. 10, 1925, Box 3, *ibid.*; *The Crisis*, 30 (May, 1925), 36.

86. See above, p. 140.

87. For emergence of this elite group of lawyers, see Houston, "Findings on Negro Legal Education," p. 2.

88. Felix Frankfurter to Morris Ernst, June 5, 1930, James Weldon Johnson Papers, Beinecke Library, Yale University.

89. See esp. Morris Ernst, Lewis Gannett, and James Weldon Johnson, "Memorandum to the Directors of the American Fund for Public Service from the Committee on Negro Work," May 28, 1930, Box 46, Spingarn Papers.

90. Frankfurter to Ernst, June 5, 1930, Johnson Papers; White to Spingarn, July 15, 1930, and White to James Marshall, July 17, 1930, Box C-77, NAACP Papers; White to Spingarn, Aug. 19, 1930, Box 4, Spingarn Papers; White to Houston, Sept. 4, 1930, Box C-196, NAACP Papers; Houston to White, Sept. 3, 1930, Box 17, Spingarn Papers.

91. Frankfurter to Ernst, June 5, 1930, Johnson Papers; Houston to White, Sept. 3, 1930, Box 17, Spingarn Papers; Acting Secretary's Report to the Board, Oct. 8, 1930, NAACP Collection.

92. Technically Houston's title was "vice-dean," but he was the highest administrative officer of the law school, where he both taught and performed the functions of a dean.

93. Hastie, "Charles Hamilton Houston, 1895–1950," *Journal of Negro History*, 35 (July, 1950), 356; Hastie, "Toward an Equalitarian Legal Order," p. 22. For Houston's views on the problems of the black bar, see above, p. 131. The Howard University Law School was accredited in 1931 (Rayford W. Logan, *Howard University: The First Hundred Years, 1867–1967* [New York, 1969], p. 267).

94. National Bar Association, *Proceedings of the 7th Annual Convention and 8th Annual Convention, 1931 and 1932* (Chicago, [1933]), pp. 69, 71, copy in possession of Elmer C. Jackson of Kansas City; Thurgood Marshall to Geraldine Segal, Feb. 27, 1963, quoted in Geraldine R. Segal, "A Sketch of the Life of Charles Houston" (M.A. thesis, University of Pennsylvania, 1963), p. 23; Houston, "To the Officers and Delegates of the 26th Annual Conference, NAACP, June 24, 1935," Box C-87, NAACP Papers.

95. National Bar Association, *Proceedings*, pp. 49, 53.

96. See extensive correspondence on this case, *Trudeau* v. *Barnes*, in New Orleans Branch files, 1931, Box G-82, NAACP Papers. See also Margold to Robinson, Oct. 3, 1931, and Robinson to Margold, Oct. 1, 1931, Box C-196, *ibid.* For quotation, see William R. Adams to Andrews, July 10, 1931, Box G-82, *ibid.*

97. Robinson to Joel E. Spingarn, Oct. 18, 1933, Box G-82, *ibid.* There is some doubt

about Robinson's competency in handling this case. He followed Margold's advice, but James Marshall, consulted when Robinson was preparing the petition to the Supreme Court, "thought the appeal was doomed to failure because the client had failed to avail himself to certain avenues of relief prescribed by the Louisiana law . . ." (Roy Wilkins to James Marshall, Aug. 25, 1933, *ibid*).

98. On Louis Marshall's role in *Nixon* v. *Condon*, supervising work of Knollenberg, see Andrews to Marshall, Aug. 30, Nov. 8, 1928, Feb. 4, 1929, Box A-20, NAACP Papers; Marshall to Knollenberg, Mar. 11, and 19, April 8 and 17, 1929, and Marshall to White, Mar. 14, 1929, Box 1601, Marshall Papers; Spingarn to Margold, Oct. 16, 1930, Box 5, Spingarn Papers.

99. White, "Memorandum Re Phone Conversation with James Marshall," Sept. 18, 1931, Box D-11, NAACP Papers; James Marshall to Nabrit, Atkins & Wesley, Sept. 17, 1931, Box 64, Spingarn Papers. Atkins's brief was presented to the Supreme Court by his good friend Charles Houston. See *Houston Informer and Texas Freeman*, Dec. 12, 1931.

100. Walter Nelles to Ernst, June 9, 1930, Johnson Papers. (Atkins, listed as Jasper A. Atkins, was book review editor of the *Yale Law Journal* in 1920.) His partners, James M. Nabrit and Carter G. Wesley, were both graduates of Northwestern University Law School (*ibid.*, May 21, 1932). Nabrit was later an important attorney in national NAACP cases, and president of Howard University.

101. J. Alston Atkins to James Marshall, Oct. 26, 1931, Box 65, Spingarn Papers; White to E. O. Smith, Nov. 3, 1931, Box D-62, NAACP Papers.

102. Atkins to James Marshall, Feb. 9, 1932, and Marshall to Spingarn, Feb. 12, 1932, Box 65, Spingarn Papers; Nathan Margold to Houston, Mar. 1, 1932, Box D-63, NAACP Papers; L. D. Lyons *et al.*, telegram to White, Jan. 28, 1932, Box 65, Spingarn Papers; James T. Ewing to White, Feb. 11, 1932, Box D-63, NAACP Papers.

103. NAACP press release, Mar. 11, 1932, and Herbert J. Seligmann to Nabrit, Atkins & Wesley, May 20, 1932, Box D-63, NAACP Papers. The NAACP was also victorious in this case, *Nixon* v. *Condon*, 286 U.S. 73 (1932). For Atkins's report on the briefs submitted by his firm, see J. Alston Atkins, *The Texas Negro and His Political Rights* (Houston, 1932). Additional details on the history of this case from the perspective of Atkins and his colleagues are to be found in the *Houston Informer and Texas Freeman*, esp. Sept. 5, Dec. 12, 1931, Jan. 23, May 7, and July 2, 1932. Atkins was editor of this newspaper while Wesley and Nabrit were officials of the publishing company that owned it.

104. The legal committee rarely if ever met formally as a group, and its individual members worked directly with Spingarn. In addition to Cobb, blacks had been included from time to time in this small group. D. Macon Webster and Philip Thorne had each served one term at the beginning of Spingarn's tenure as chairman. Studin and Spingarn, who were the sole members of this committee following World War I, were evidently desirous of involving black attorneys, and Cobb and Aiken A. Pope were added in 1921. (See lists of NAACP committee members in the NAACP's published annual reports [title varies] for 1913, 1914, 1919, 1920, and 1921.) Thorne and Pope are discussed in note 21 above, but Webster, whose name does not appear in the standard biographical reference sources, has proven to be a more elusive figure. It has not been possible to ascertain anything about his legal training; he was, however, quite clearly a man of some prominence, a leading figure in Negro fraternal circles (see Charles H. Wesley, *History of the Improved Benevolent and Protective Order of Elks of the World 1898–1954* [Washington, 1955], pp. 119, 120, 133, and New York *Age*, June 20, 1912), and among black Democrats in New York City, being appointed to the staff of the state attorney general's office in 1911 (see New York *Age*, Sept. 11, 1911).

105. Rivers, Phi Beta Kappa, Yale University class of 1915, and LL.B., Columbia University, 1922, became the first black member of the Association of the Bar of the City of New York in 1929. In the same year he was elected to the state legislature (*The Crisis*, 36 [June, 1929], 198, and 37 [Jan. 1930], 15). Louis Marshall was the man who had proposed Rivers for membership in the Bar Association, and Spingarn was one of

his endorsers (Report of the Secretary to the Board, Mar. 7, 1929, NAACP Collection). Subsequently Rivers served for many years as a municipal judge in New York.

106. Spingarn to James Marshall, Oct. 15, 1929, Box 4, Spingarn Papers; Spingarn to Frankfurter, Nov. 12, 1929, Felix Frankfurter Papers, Library of Congress; White to Spingarn, Oct. 30, Nov. 2, 1929, Box C-77, NAACP Papers; Spingarn to White, Nov. 1, 1929, Box C-64, *ibid.*; NAACP Board of Directors Minutes, Nov. 11, 1929, Box A-2, *ibid.*; White to Spingarn, Oct. 17, 1931, Box D-11, *ibid.*; NAACP Board of Directors Minutes, Nov. 9, 1931, Box A-3, *ibid.*

107. White to Spingarn, June 15, 1932, Box A-27, NAACP Papers. See also discussion by Houston at NAACP 1932 Annual Conference: "Cooperation Between the National Bar Association and the N.A.A.C.P.," May 20, 1932, Box B-8, *ibid.*

108. White to Spingarn, June 3, 1932, Box 5, Spingarn Papers; White to Spingarn and Spingarn to White, both June 15, 1932, Box A-27, NAACP Papers.

109. *Houston Informer and Texas Freeman*, July 16, 1932. The editorial observed: "These men are well trained. . . . They have every requisite to make fine constitutional lawyers. Negroes were beginning to wonder why the NAACP used only white lawyers to present its cases in the Supreme Court. . . . It was, of course, because Negroes were not experienced and prepared for that type of practice. But the NAACP is now taking steps to remedy that lack . . . by taking Negro lawyers who will get the experience. . . ." The NAACP's action would benefit the race "because it will give Negroes their own constitutional lawyers. No one can prepare or present Negroes' cases as well as a trained Negro. . . ."

110. Charles W. White to White, July 6, 1932, Box G-159, NAACP Papers; Pickens to Ovington, Nov. 27, 1929, Box C-72, *ibid.*

111. Roy Wilkins to White, Feb. 2, 1933, Box D-11, *ibid.*; White to Spingarn, Oct. 25, 1933, Box 6, Spingarn Papers; Spingarn to White, Oct. 27, 1933, Box A-27, NAACP Papers.

112. For references to debate between Walter White and black lawyers over charges that NAACP was paying high fees to white attorneys, see, *e.g.*, White's address to the National Bar Association convention, 1932, in National Bar Association, *Proceedings*, 73; White to Pickens, Nov. 29, 1932, Box C-78, NAACP Papers. For discussion of complaints that Negro lawyers seldom were willing to take meritorious but needy cases without fee, see Houston, "Cooperation Between the National Bar Association and the N.A.A.C.P.," Box B-8, *ibid.*

113. White to Houston, Apr. 25, 1933, Box D-52, NAACP Papers. To the president of an NAACP black college chapter White wrote, "In all my years with the Association, nothing has given me greater pleasure than to help in the arrangements to have Crawford defended by all-Negro counsel" (White to Elwyza Dingind [*sic*], Nov. 15, 1933, Box G-210, *ibid.*).

114. White to Houston and Houston to White, both Oct. 17, 1933, Box D-52, *ibid.*

115. Wilkins to White, Oct. 18, 1933, *ibid.*; "Memorandum on Conference Held Sunday, October 22, 1933 . . . at Home of Arthur B. Spingarn," Box A-27, *ibid.*; White to Edward P. Lovett, Leon Ransom, and James Tyson, Oct. 30, 1933, and White to Houston, Oct. 25, 1933, both Box D-52, *ibid.*

116. White to Houston and White to Douglas S. Freeman, both Oct. 31, 1933, and Virginius Dabney to White, Nov. 3, 1933, all in Box D-52, *ibid.*; "Memo from Mr. White re Long Distance Telephone Conversation with Mr. Charles H. Houston," Nov. 1, 1933, Box C-64, *ibid.*

117. Press release, Nov. 10, 1933, Box D-52, *ibid.*

118. White to Ralph Harlow, Dec. 19, 1933, Box C-104, *ibid.*; see also White, "George Crawford—Symbol," *The Crisis*, 41 (Jan., 1934), 15. For detailed review of the case, and NAACP's reply to Communist charges that Crawford was actually innocent and that Houston had mishandled the litigation, see [Houston], "The George Crawford Case—a Statement by the N.A.A.C.P.," *The Crisis*, 42 (Apr. and May, 1935), 104–5, 116–17, 125, 143, 150–51, 156.

119. Conrad O. Pearson and Cecil A. McCoy to White, Feb. 6, 1933, Box C-84,

NAACP Papers; White to Hastie, Mar. 21, 1933, Box G-159, *ibid.*; White, Memorandum for the files, Mar. 22, 1933, Box D-96, *ibid.*

120. Secretary's Report to the Board, Apr. 6, 1933, NAACP Collection; Pearson to White and NAACP press release, both Mar. 31, 1933, Box D-96, NAACP Papers.

121. White to Spingarn, July 8, 1933, Box C-78, NAACP Papers.

122. Hastie to White, Sept. 15, 16, 22, and 25, 1933, Box C-281, *ibid.*; Secretary's Report to the Board, Oct. 5 and Nov., 1933, NAACP Collection. For discussion of NAACP strategy in campaign against discrimination in public education, see Houston, "Educational Inequalities Must Go." *The Crisis*, 42 (Oct., 1935), 300–301, 316, and Houston, "Cracking Closed University Doors," *ibid.*, (Nov., 1935), 364, 370, 372.

123. NAACP press release, May 17, 1935, Box D-60, NAACP Papers; *Hollins* v. *State of Oklahoma*, 295 U.S. 394 (1935). The first black lawyer to win a case before the U.S. Supreme Court is reputed to have been Wilford H. Smith, a Galveston attorney who in 1900 also won a reversal of a criminal conviction on the jury exclusion issue (*Carter* v. *State of Texas*, 177 U.S. 442 [1900]). Not long afterward Smith moved to New York, where he was when Booker T. Washington secured his services for the unsuccessful test cases against disfranchisement in Alabama. Though Smith in 1919 volunteered to help the NAACP in the Elaine, Arkansas, riot cases, he never seems to have worked with the Association. Emma Lou Thornbrough, "The National Afro-American League, 1887–1908." *Journal of Southern History*, 27 (Nov., 1961), 508–9; Louis R. Harlan to authors, Jan. 22 and 23, 1975; August Meier, *Negro Thought in America, 1880–1915* (Ann Arbor, 1963), p. 111; Ovington to Spingarn, Dec. 3, 1919, Box 2, Spingarn Papers. The first Negro to argue an NAACP case in the Supreme Court seems to have been Cobb, who appeared before the high tribunal along with Henry E. Davis and the white Alabama attorney Charles D. Kline in the Caldwell case in 1920. See note 39, above.

124. On opinion regarding Atkins's brief, see "Memorandum re Meeting of Legal Committee, November 10, 1932," Box A-27, NAACP Papers.

125. L. W. Washington to White, Nov. 2, 1932, White to Margold, Aug. 8, 1932, and White to Spingarn, Jan. 4, 1933, all in Box D-63, NAACP Papers. On consideration being given to securing Atkins, see also the following: "Memorandum re Meeting of Legal Committee, November 10, 1932," Box A-27, and White to Washington, Nov. 11, 1932, Box D-63, *ibid.*

126. James Marshall to Knollenberg, Apr. 18, 1933, Box 17, Spingarn Papers; Spingarn to Marshall and Spingarn to Knollenberg, both Feb. 3, 1934, Box 64, *ibid.*

127. R. D. Evans to Houston, July 20, 1934, and Houston to White and E. Washington Rhodes, July 21, 1934, both Box C-64, NAACP Papers; White to Rhodes, July 30, 1934, Box C-285, *ibid.*; White to Spingarn and James Marshall, Aug. 7, 1934, Box D-34, *ibid.*; White to Spingarn, Sept. 10, 1934, Box 64, Spingarn Papers; Spingarn to James Marshall, Sept. 23, 1934, and White to Joseph B. Keenan, Oct. 2, 1934, and White to Spingarn, James Marshall, Houston and Hastie, Jan. 26, 1934, all in Box C-285, NAACP Papers.

128. *Grovey* v. *Townsend*, 295 U.S. 45 (1935); James Marshall to White, Apr. 15, 1935, White to Evans, May 23, 1935, Pickens to Norman Barton, Dec. 27, 1935, and James Nabrit to Thurgood Marshall, Dec. 1, 1938, all in Box D-92, NAACP Papers.

129. Atkins to Houston, May 12, 1935, and Houston to Atkins, May 15, 1935, Box D-92, NAACP Papers.

130. Wilkins to White, May 18, 1935, Houston to White, May 31, 1935, Roscoe Dunjee to White, June 30, 1935, Cecil Robertson to Houston, July 19, Oct. 4, 1935, Dunjee to Oklahoma Branches [Nov., 1935], NAACP press release, Feb. 29, 1936, all in Box D-60, *ibid.*; quotation from Houston to Wilkins, May 22, 1935, Box C-64, *ibid.*

131. Washington *Tribune*, Sept. 1, 8, 1934, clippings, Box C-64, *ibid.*, Houston to White, Sept. 13, 1934, *ibid.*; White to Houston, Sept. 17, 1934, Box C-78, *ibid.*

132. Roger Baldwin to White, July 17, 1933, Box C-196, NAACP Papers; White to Baldwin, July 8, 1933, Box 6, Spingarn Papers; White to Spingarn, July 8, 1933, Box C-78, NAACP Papers.

133. Baldwin letter quoted in White to Spingarn, July 17, 1933, Box 6, Spingarn Papers; minutes of Joint Committee on Negro Work, Sept. 13, 1933, Box 46, *ibid.*

134. White to Margold, May 22, 1934, Box C-196, NAACP Papers.

135. White to Spingarn, Sept. 23, 1933, Box 6, Spingarn Papers; White to Baldwin, Sept. 25, 1933, Box 17, *ibid.*; White to Spingarn, Oct. 30, 1933, Box 6, *ibid.* For Hastie's appointment to legal committee, see Secretary's Report to Board, Dec. 7, 1933, NAACP Collection. Baldwin's position seems curious, and thus far we have found no satisfactory explanation for it.

136. White to Spingarn, April 3, 1934, Box C-78, NAACP Papers; Spingarn to White, Apr. 5, 1935, Box 6, Spingarn Papers; White to members of Committee on Negro Work, Apr. 11, 1934, Johnson Papers; White to Spingarn and White to Karl Llewellyn, both Apr. 13, 1934, Box 7, Spingarn Papers; White to Margold, May 22, 1934, Box C-196, NAACP Papers.

137. White to Spingarn, May 14 and 22, 1934, Box 7, Spingarn Papers; on negotiations with Houston, see White to Houston, May 28, 1934, Box C-196, NAACP Papers; White to Houston, Aug. 10, 1934, Box C-78, *ibid.*; Houston to White, Aug. 20, Sept. 19, 1934, Box C-64, *ibid.*; White to Houston, Oct. 1, and telegrams of Oct. 2 and 3, 1934, Box C-78, *ibid.*; White to Board of Directors, NAACP, Oct. 6, 1934, Johnson Papers.

SEVEN

On the Role of Martin Luther King

BY AUGUST MEIER

The phenomenon that is Martin Luther King consists of a number of striking paradoxes. The Nobel Prize winner is accepted by the outside world as *the* leader of the nonviolent direct action movement, but he is criticized by many activists within the movement. He is criticized for what appears, at times, as indecisiveness, and is more often denounced for a tendency to accept compromise. Yet in the eyes of most Americans, both black and white, he remains the symbol of militant direct action. So potent is this symbol of King as direct actionist that a new myth is arising about his historic role. The real credit for developing and projecting the techniques and philosophy of nonviolent direct action in the civil rights arena must be given to the Congress of Racial Equality, which was founded in 1942—more than a dozen years before the Montgomery bus boycott projected King into international fame. And the idea of mass action by Negroes themselves to secure redress of their grievances must, in large part, be ascribed to the vision of A. Philip Randolph, architect of the March on Washington Movement during World War II. Yet, as we were told in Montgomery on March 25, 1965, King and his followers now assert, apparently without serious contradiction, that a new type of civil rights strategy was born at Montgomery in 1955 under King's auspices.

In a movement in which respect is accorded in direct proportion to the number of times one has been arrested, King appears to keep the number of times he goes to jail to a minimum. In a movement in which successful leaders are those who share in the hardships of their followers, in the risks they take, in the

From *New Politics*, 4, no. 1 (Winter, 1965), 1–8. © 1965 by the New Politics Publishing Co.

beatings they receive, in the length of time they spend in jail, King tends to leave prison for other important engagements, rather than remaining there and suffering with his followers. In a movement in which leadership ordinarily devolves upon persons who mix democratically with their followers, King remains isolated and aloof. In a movement which prides itself on militancy and "no compromise" with racial discrimination or with the white "power structure," King maintains close relationships with, and appears to be influenced by, Democratic presidents and their emissaries, seems amenable to compromises considered by some half a loaf or less, and often appears willing to postpone or avoid a direct confrontation in the streets.

King's career has been characterized by failures that, in the larger sense, must be accounted triumphs. The buses in Montgomery were desegregated only after lengthy judicial proceedings conducted by the NAACP Legal Defense Fund secured a favorable decision from the U.S. Supreme Court. Nevertheless, the events in Montgomery were a triumph for direct action and gave this tactic a popularity unknown when identified solely with CORE. King's subsequent major campaigns—in Albany, Georgia; Danville, Virginia; Birmingham, Alabama; and St. Augustine, Florida—ended as failures or with only token accomplishments. But each of them, chiefly because of his presence, dramatically focused national and international attention on the plight of the southern Negro, thereby facilitating overall progress. In Birmingham in particular, demonstrations which fell short of their local goals were directly responsible for a major Federal Civil Rights Act. Essentially, this pattern of local failure and national victory was recently enacted at Selma, Alabama.

King is ideologically committed to disobeying unjust laws and court orders, in the Gandhian tradition, but generally he follows a policy of not disobeying federal court orders. In his recent Montgomery speech he expressed a crude, neo-Marxist interpretation of history, romanticizing the Populist movement as a genuine union of black and white common people, ascribing race prejudice to capitalists playing white workers against black. Yet, in practice, he is amenable to compromise with the white bourgeois political and economic establishment. More important, King enunciates a superficial and eclectic philosophy, and by virtue of it he has profoundly awakened the moral conscience of America.

In short, King can be described as a "conservative militant." In this combination of militancy with conservatism and caution, of righteousness with respectability, lies the secret of King's enormous success.

Certain important civil rights leaders have dismissed King's position as the product of publicity generated by the mass communications media. But this can be said of the successes of the civil rights nonviolent action movement generally. Without publicity it is hard to conceive that much progress would have been made. In fact, contrary to the official nonviolent direct action philosophy, demonstrations have secured their results not by changing the hearts of the oppressors through a display of nonviolent love, but through the national and international pressures generated by the publicity arising from mass arrests and incidents of violence. And no one has employed this strategy of securing publicity through mass arrests and precipitating violence from white hoodlums and law enforcement officers more than King himself. King abhors violence; as at Selma, for example, he constantly retreats from situations that might result in the deaths of his followers. But he is precisely most successful when, contrary to his deepest wishes, his demonstrations precipitate violence from southern whites against Negro and white demonstrators. We need only cite Birmingham and Selma to illustrate this point.

Publicity alone does not explain the durability of King's image, or why he remains, for the rank and file of whites and blacks alike, the symbol of the direct action movement, the nearest thing to a charismatic leader that the civil rights movement has ever had. At the heart of King's continuing influence and popularity are two facts. First, better than anyone else, he articulates the aspirations of Negroes who respond to the cadence of his addresses, his religious phraseology and manner of speaking, and the vision of his dream for them and for America. King has intuitively adopted the style of the old-fashioned Negro Baptist preacher and transformed it into a new art form; he has, indeed, restored oratory to its place among the arts. Second, he communicates Negro aspirations to white America more effectively than anyone else. His religious terminology and manipulation of the Christian symbols of love and nonresistance are partly responsible for his appeal among whites. To talk in terms of Christianity, love, and nonviolence is reassuring to the mentality of white America. At the same time, the very superficialities of his philosophy—that rich and eclectic amalgam of Jesus, Hegel, Gandhi, and others as outlined in his *Stride Toward Freedom*—make him appear intellectually profound to the superficially educated middle-class white American. Actually, if he were a truly profound religious thinker, like Tillich or Niebuhr, his influence would of necessity be limited to a select audience. But by uttering moral clichés, the Christian pieties, in a magnificent display of oratory, King becomes enormously effective.

If his success with Negroes is largely due to the style of his utterance, his success with whites is a much more complicated matter. For one thing, he unerringly knows how to exploit with maximum effectiveness their growing feeling of guilt. King, of course, is not unique in attaining fame and popularity among whites through playing upon their guilt feelings. James Baldwin is the most conspicuous example of a man who has achieved success with this formula. The incredible fascination which the Black Muslims have for white people, and the posthumous near-sanctification of Malcolm X by many naive whites (in addition to many Negroes whose motivations are, of course, very different), must in large part be attributed to the same source. But King goes beyond this. With intuitive but extraordinary skill he not only castigates whites for their sins but, in contrast to angry young writers like Baldwin, he explicitly states his belief in their salvation. Not only will direct action bring fulfillment of the "American Dream" to Negroes, but the Negroes' use of direct action will also help whites to live up to their Christian and democratic values; it will purify, cleanse, and heal the sickness in white society. Whites will benefit as well as Negroes. He has faith that the white man will redeem himself. Negroes must not hate whites, but love them. In this manner King first arouses the guilt feelings of whites, and then relieves them—though always leaving the lingering feeling in his white listeners that they should support his nonviolent crusade. Like a Greek tragedy, King's performance provides an extraordinary catharsis for the white listener.

King thus gives white men the feeling that he is their good friend, that he poses no threat to them. It is interesting to note that this was the same feeling that white men received from Booker T. Washington, the noted early twentieth century accommodator. Both men stressed their faith in the white man; both expressed the belief that the white man could be brought to accord Negroes their rights. Both stressed the importance of whites recognizing the rights of Negroes for the moral health and well-being of white society. Like King, Washington had an extraordinary following among whites. Like King, Washington symbolized for most whites the whole program of Negro advancement. While there are important similarities in the functioning of both men vis-à-vis the community, needless to say, in most respects, their philosophies are in disagreement.

It is not surprising, therefore, to find that King is the recipient of contributions from organizations and individuals who fail to eradicate evidence of prejudice in their own backyards. For example, certain liberal trade union leaders who are philosophically committed to full racial equality, who feel the need to identify their organizations with the cause of militant civil rights, although they are unable to defeat racist elements in their unions, contribute hundreds of thousands of dollars to King's Southern Christian Leadership Conference (SCLC). One might attribute this phenomenon to the fact that SCLC works in the South rather than the North, but this is true also for SNCC, which does not benefit similarly from union treasuries. And the fact is that ever since the college students started their sit-ins in 1960, it is SNCC which has been the real spearhead of direct action in most of the South and has performed the lion's share of work in local communities, while SCLC has received most of the publicity and most of the money. However, while King provides a verbal catharsis for whites, leaving them feeling purified and comfortable, SNCC's uncompromising militancy makes whites feel less comfortable and less beneficent.

(The above is not to suggest that SNCC and SCLC are responsible for all, or nearly all, the direct action in the South.

The NAACP has actively engaged in direct action, especially in Savannah under the leadership of W. W. Law, in South Carolina under I. DeQuincy Newman, and in Clarksdale, Mississippi, under Aaron Henry. The work of CORE— including most of the direct action in Louisiana, much of the nonviolent work in Florida and Mississippi, and the famous Freedom Ride of 1961—has been most important. In addition, one should note the work of SCLC affiliates, such as those in Lynchburg, Virginia, led by the Reverend Virgil Wood; in Birmingham, by the Reverend Fred Shuttlesworth; and in Savannah, by Hosea Williams.

(There are other reasons for SNCC's lesser popularity with whites. These are connected with the great changes that have occurred in SNCC since it was founded in 1960, changes reflected in the half-jocular epigram circulating in SNCC circles that the Student Nonviolent Coordinating Committee has now become the "Non-Student Violent Non-Coordinating Committee." The point is, however, that even when SNCC thrilled the nation in 1960–61 with the student sit-ins that swept the South, it did not enjoy the popularity and financial support accorded to King.)

King's very tendencies toward compromise and caution, his willingness to negotiate and bargain with White House emissaries, and his hesitancy to risk the precipitation of mass violence upon demonstrators further endear him to whites. He appears to them a "responsible" and "moderate" man. To militant activists, King's failure to march past the state police on that famous Tuesday morning outside Selma indicated either a lack of courage or a desire to advance himself by currying presidential favor. But King's shrinking from a possible bloodbath, his accession to the entreaties of the political establishment, his acceptance of face-saving compromise in this, as in other instances, are fundamental to the particular role he is playing and essential for achieving and sustaining his image as a leader of heroic moral stature in the eyes of white men. His caution and compromise keep open the channels of communication between the activists and the majority of the white community. In brief: King makes the nonviolent direct action movement respectable.

Of course, many, if not most, activists reject the notion that the movement should be made respectable. Yet American history shows that for any reform movement to succeed, it must attain respectability. It must attract moderates, even conservatives, to its ranks. The March on Washington made direct action respectable; Selma made it fashionable. More than any other force, it is Martin Luther King who impressed the civil rights revolution on the American conscience and is attracting that great middle body of American public opinion to its support. It is this revolution of conscience that will undoubtedly lead fairly soon to the elimination of all violations of Negroes' constitutional rights, thereby creating the conditions for the economic and social changes that are necessary if we are to achieve full racial equality. This is not to deny the dangers to the civil rights movement in becoming respectable. Respectability, for example, encourages the attempts of political machines to capture civil rights organizations. Respectability can also become an end in itself, thereby dulling the cutting edge of its protest activities. Indeed, the history of the labor movement reveals how attaining respectability can produce loss of original purpose and character. These perils, however, do not contradict the importance of achieving respectability—even a degree of modishness—if racial equality is ever to be realized.

There is another side to the picture: King would be neither respected nor respectable if there were not more militant activists on his left, engaged in more radical forms of direct action. Without CORE and, especially, SNCC, King would appear "radical" and "irresponsible," rather than "moderate" and "respectable."

King occupies a position of strategic importance as the "vital center" within the civil rights movement. Though he has lieutenants who are far more militant and "radical" than he is, SCLC acts, in effect, as the most cautious, deliberate and "conservative" of the direct action groups because of King's leadership. This permits King and the SCLC to function—almost certainly unintentionally—not only as an organ of communication with the establishment and majority white public opinion, but as something of a bridge between the activist and more traditionalist or "conservative" civil rights groups as well. For example, it appears unlikely that the Urban League and NAACP, which supplied most of the funds,* would have participated in the 1963 March on Washington if King had not done so. Because King agreed to go along with SNCC and CORE, the NAACP found it mandatory to join if it was to maintain its image as a protest organization. King's identification with the March was also essential for securing the support of large numbers of white clergymen and their moderate followers. The March was the brain child of the civil rights movement's ablest strategist and tactician, Bayard Rustin, and the call was issued by A. Philip Randolph. But it would have been a minor episode in the history of the civil rights movement without King's support.

Yet curiously enough, despite his charisma and international reputation, King thus far has been more a symbol than a power in the civil rights movement. Indeed, his strength in the movement has been derived less from an organizational base than from his symbolic role. Seven or eight years ago, one might have expected King to achieve an organizationally dominant position in the civil rights movement, at least in its direct action wing. The fact is that in the period after the Montgomery bus boycott King developed no program and, it is generally agreed, revealed himself as an ineffective administrator who failed to capitalize upon his popularity among Negroes. In 1957 he founded SCLC to coordinate the work of direct action groups that had sprung up in southern cities. Composed of autonomous units, usually led by Baptist ministers, SCLC does not appear to have developed an overall sense of direction or a program of real breadth and scope. Although the leaders of SCLC affiliates became the race leaders in their communities—displacing the established local conservative leadership of teachers, old-line ministers, businessmen—it is hard for an observer (who admittedly has not been close to SCLC) to perceive exactly what SCLC did before the 1960's except to advance the image and personality of King. King appeared not to direct but to float with the tide of militant direct action. For example, King did not supply the initiative for the bus boycott in

*Actually the March on Washington was financed largely through the philanthropist Stephen Currier, whose Taconic Foundation had also made possible the voter registration campaigns in the South in 1962–64.

Montgomery, but was pushed into the leadership by others, as he himself records in *Stride Toward Freedom*. Similarly, in the late 1950's and early 1960's, he appeared to let events shape his course. In the last two years this has changed, but until the Birmingham demonstrations of 1963 King epitomized conservative militancy.

SCLC under King's leadership called the Raleigh Conference of April, 1960, which gave birth to SNCC. Incredibly, within a year the SNCC youth had lost their faith in the man they now satirically call "De Lawd," and had struck out on their own independent path. By that time, the spring of 1961, King's power in the southern direct action movement had been further curtailed by CORE's stunning Freedom Ride to Alabama and Mississippi.

The limited extent of King's actual power in the civil rights movement was illustrated by the efforts made to invest King with the qualities of a messiah during the recent ceremonies at the state capitol in Montgomery. The Reverend Ralph Abernathy's constant iteration of the theme that King is "our Leader," the Moses of the race, chosen by God, and King's claim that he originated the nonviolent direct action movement at Montgomery a decade ago, are all assertions that would have been superfluous if King's power in the movement was very substantial.

It is, of course, no easier today than it has been in the past few years to predict the course of the Negro protest movement, and it is always possible that the current state of affairs may change quite abruptly. It is conceivable that the ambitious program that SCLC is now projecting—both in southern voter registration and in northern urban direct action programs—may give it a position of commanding importance in civil rights. As a result of the recent demonstrations in Selma and Montgomery, King's prestige is now higher than ever. At the same time, the nature of CORE and NAACP direct action activities at the moment has created a programmatic vacuum which SCLC may be able to exploit. Given this convergence of circumstances, SCLC leaders may be able to establish an organizational base upon which to build a power commensurate with the symbolic position of their president.

It is indeed fortunate that King has not obtained a predominance of power in the movement commensurate with his prestige. For today, as in the past, a diversity of approaches is necessary. Needed in the movement are those who view the struggle chiefly as a conflict situation, in which the power of demonstrations, the power of Negroes, will force recognition of the race's humanity and citizenship rights, and the achievement of equality. Equally needed are those who see the movement's strategy to be chiefly one of capitalizing on the basic consensus of values in American society by awakening the conscience of the white man to the contradiction between his professions and the facts of discrimination. And just as necessary to the movement as both of these are those who operate skillfully, recognizing and yet exploiting the deeply held American belief that compromise among competing interest groups is the best *modus operandi* in public life.

King is unique in that he maintains a delicate balance among all three of these basic strategy assumptions. The traditional approaches of the Urban League (conciliation of the white businessmen) and of the NAACP (most preeminently appeals to the courts and appeals to the sense of fair play in the American public) basically attempted to exploit the consensus in American values. It would of course be a gross oversimplification to say that the Urban League and NAACP strategies are based simply on attempting to capitalize on the consensus of values, while SNCC and CORE act simply as if the situation were purely a conflict situation. Implicit in the actions of all civil rights organizations are both sets of assumptions—even where people are not conscious of the theoretical assumptions under which, in effect, they operate. The NAACP especially encompasses a broad spectrum of strategies and types of activities, ranging from time-tested court procedures to militant direct action. Sophisticated CORE activists know very well when a judicious compromise is necessary or valuable. But I hold that King is in the middle, acting in effect as if he were basing his strategy upon all three assumptions described above. He maintains a delicate balance between a purely moral appeal and a militant display of power. He talks of the power of the bodies of Negro demonstrators in the streets, but, unlike CORE and

SNCC activists, he accepts compromises at times that consist of token improvements and calls them impressive victories. More than any of the other groups, King and SCLC can, up to this point at least, be described as exploiting all three tactical assumptions to an approximately equal degree. King's continued success, I suspect, will depend to a considerable degree upon the difficult feat of maintaining his position at the "vital center" of the civil rights movement.

Viewed from another angle King's failure to achieve a position of power on a level with his prestige is fortunate, because rivalries between personalities and organizations remain an essential ingredient of the dynamics of the movement and a precondition for its success as each current tries to outdo the others in effectiveness and in maintaining a good public image. Without this competitive stimulus, the civil rights revolution would slow down.

I have already noted that one of King's functions is to serve as a bridge between the militant and conservative wings of the movement. In addition, by gathering support for SCLC, he generates wider support for CORE and SNCC as well. The most striking example is the recent series of demonstrations in Selma, where SNCC had been operating for nearly two years with only moderate amounts of publicity before King chose that city as his own target. As usual, it was King's presence that focused world attention on Selma. In the course of subsequent events, the rift between King and SNCC assumed the proportions of a serious conflict. Yet people who otherwise would have been hesitant to support SNCC's efforts, even people who had become disillusioned with certain aspects of SNCC's policies during the Mississippi Summer Project of 1964, were drawn to demonstrate in Selma and Montgomery. Moreover, although King received the major share of credit for the demonstrations, it seems likely that in the controversy between King and SNCC the latter emerged with more power and influence in the civil rights movement than ever before. It is now possible that the administration will, in the future, regard SNCC as more of a force to be reckoned with than it has heretofore.

Major dailies like the *New York Times* and the *Washington Post*, basically sympathetic to civil rights and racial equality, though more gradualist than the activist organizations, have congratulated the nation upon its good fortune in having a "responsible and moderate" leader like King at the head of the nonviolent action movement (though they overestimate his power and underestimate the symbolic nature of his role). It would be more appropriate to congratulate the civil rights movement for *its* good fortune in having as its symbolic leader a man like King. The fact that he has more prestige than power; the fact that he not only criticizes whites but also explicitly believes in their redemption; his ability to arouse creative tension, combined with his inclination to shrink from carrying demonstrations to the point where major bloodshed might result; the intellectual simplicity of his philosophy; his tendency to compromise and exert caution, even his seeming indecisiveness on some occasions; the sparing use he makes of going to or staying in jail himself; his friendship with the man in the White House—all are essential to the role he plays, and invaluable for the success of the movement. It is fortunate, of course, that not all civil rights leaders are cut of the same cloth—that King is unique among them. Like Randolph, who functions very differently, King is really an institution. His most important function, I believe, is that of effectively communicating Negro aspirations to white people, of making nonviolent direct action respectable in the eyes of the white majority. In addition, he functions within the movement by occupying a vital center position between its conservative and radical wings, by symbolizing direct action and attracting people to participate in it without dominating either the civil rights movement or its activist wing. Viewed in this context, traits that many activists criticize in King actually function not as sources of weakness, but as the foundations of his strength.

PART II

On Black Nationalism and Black Power

In the late 1960's, when the cry for "Black Power," the ghetto riots, and the surge of black nationalism largely displaced the integrationist, nonviolent activism of the first half of the decade, it was quite coincidental that our earlier researches enabled us to treat these developments in historical perspective.

Meier's interest in black nationalism, going back to his earliest writing in Negro history, was informed by reading done as an undergraduate at Oberlin College, where Professor Frederick B. Artz introduced him to the classic works on European nationalism by Carlton J. H. Hayes and Hans Kohn. The early article, "The Emergence of Negro Nationalism: A Study in Ideologies," based on his master's thesis at Columbia University, in fact deliberately sought to apply the conceptualization developed by these pioneer studies of Western nationalism to the history of black nationalist thought in America prior to the Garvey movement. At the time, black intellectuals were highly assimilationist, and, with the Garvey movement dead, Negro nationalism was to a considerable extent identified with the Communist espousal of a forty-ninth all-Negro state in the southern black belt.[1] While he no longer subscribes to the unilinear evolution of Afro-American nationalism assumed in that article, and while subsequent research has unearthed much additional information on nearly all aspects of the subject from antebellum emigration to the thought of Alexander Crummell

and W. E. B. Du Bois, he would still largely stand by the conceptualization and conclusions of this early analysis of nationalist
trends in Afro-American ideologies. In addition, this article
provided much of the foundation for his subsequent research
into black thought in the Age of Booker T. Washington. Any
analysis of nationalist tendencies in that period must include
attention to the all-Negro towns. We reprint here a specialized
article on this subject: "Booker T. Washington and the Town of
Mound Bayou."

The article on "Black Violence in the Twentieth Century: A
Study in Rhetoric and Retaliation" is an outgrowth of Rudwick's interest in the field of collective behavior and his earlier
monograph on *Race Riot at East St. Louis, July 2, 1917* (Carbondale, 1964). The insights and conceptualizations developed
there provided the basis for our collaborative effort which,
stimulated by the ghetto riots of the late 1960's, sought to place
these in the perspective of the whole history of black/white riots
in America.

The final essay in this section, "Integration vs. Separatism:
The NAACP and CORE Face Challenge from Within," previously unpublished, is also the fruit of our collaborative efforts.
Growing out of our long-range research interest in the history
of the NAACP and CORE, it seeks to explain why it was that the
two organizations, both originally dedicated to working for an
integrated society, responded in such contrasting ways to the
black nationalist thrust of the late 1960's.

1. The interest of Communist scholars in the subject is best seen in Herbert Aptheker's early essay, "Consciousness of Negro Nationality to 1900," written about the
time of Meier's early research and reprinted in Aptheker, *Toward Negro Freedom* (New
York, 1956), pp. 104–11.

EIGHT

The Emergence of Negro Nationalism: A Study in Ideologies

BY AUGUST MEIER

The social philosophy expressed by the Garvey movement had its roots deep in the past. Like all extreme nationalist ideologies, its basic tenets were drawn from diverse strands of thought that had emerged over the years—strands of thought that were finally crystallized out of their larger frame of reference, and synthesized into a new and dynamic configuration. In this article we shall be concerned, not with the sources of the thinking of Garvey personally, but with the general character of nationalism among American Negroes, and more particularly with the development of this nationalism as a social philosophy down to the emergence of the Garvey movement after World War I.

Nationalism is a peculiarly modern form of ethnocentrism, marked by loyalty to a group characterized by a common cultural experience which differentiates it from other groups, thus giving the members of said group a feeling that they belong together. Among the factors which frequently or usually serve to delimit national groups and form a basis of national feeling are language, religion, a glorious past of great achievement, a common past (and present) of suffering and tribulation, the idea of a national homeland, and a sense of mission for the future. Historically, nationalism has had a long development, varying greatly from time to time and place to place. For example, the humanitarian nationalism of certain eighteenth- and early nineteenth-century thinkers, with their cosmopolitan belief that each national culture has something to contribute to

From *Midwest Journal*, 4, no. 1 (Winter, 1951–52), 96–104, and no. 2 (Summer, 1952), 95–111.

the sum total of civilization, and their warm interest in the freedom of oppressed nationality groups, is in marked contrast to the violent nationalism of German Fascism; and this in turn is hardly in the same class with the contemporary nationalism of Great Britain and of the United States.

For the purposes of analysis we may distinguish certain types of nationalistic manifestation, though they are not mutually exclusive: 1) The cosmopolitan and humanitarian nationalism of a number of eighteenth- and nineteenth-century thinkers, which recognizes and welcomes the existence of various national groups, and emphasizes the contributions of each. 2) A cultural nationalism which emphasizes the achievements— intellectual, military, or otherwise—in the past, present, or even the future—of a particular group. Not necessarily of the exclusive variety, it frequently results in exaggerated claims and questionable historiography, often asserting the superiority of a particular nationality over all others. 3) Political nationalism— the desire of a nationality for its own political state. 4) Economic nationalism—usually aiming to create a self-sufficient national economy. 5) An integral or exclusive nationalism—combining in an extreme form the elements of cultural, economic, and political nationalism. This sort of nationalism ordinarily asserts the superiority of one particular nationality over all others, and often attains its ends by war and violence, and by preaching hatred of other groups.

Negro social thought in the United States has been characterized by a great range of ideologies. At one extreme are those, like Frederick Douglass, with a consistent philosophy of total assimilation; at the other are those who have advocated complete withdrawal from the United States. In between have been a great variety of dualistic philosophies—recognizing Negroes as American citizens, yet emphasizing their independence as an ethnic group—such as eschewing social equality while insisting on political and economic equality; philosophies of self-help and economic cooperation; the idea of all-Negro communities, or an all-Negro state: in general, tendencies toward self-segregation of economic and social institutions. This dualism— this dual identification with both America and the Negro group—characteristic of so much Negro thought, is, of course, the result of the disparity between American ideal and practice, of the contradiction between American democratic philosophy on the one hand, and the discriminatory treatment accorded Negroes on the other. Paradoxically, it is this very contradiction that has led to ethnocentric tendencies among American Negroes, and yet has discouraged the emergence of a full-fledged, deeply rooted, extreme nationalism.

Just as the European ultranationalism of the twentieth century was the fruition of a movement which had roots deep in the past, and which had had a number of manifestations varying in type and intensity, so the basic ideologies of the Garvey movement had been present—at least in embryo—in Negro thought for a long time. It is the object of this article to investigate the origins of Negro nationalism, carrying the story down to the Great Migration of World War I, which formed the immediate backdrop of the Garvey movement. For over a hundred years there had been interest in a homeland for American Negroes; there had been talk and effort moving in the direction of a segregated racial economy; and there had been interest in proving and creating a respectable and glorious racial past. And these three lines of thought were the fundamental elements of Garvey's philosophy.[1]

Like European nationalism, then, these early expressions of nationalism took different forms, and like the nationalism of the minority groups in Eastern and Central Europe, nationalistic tendencies provided an escape from the oppression suffered. But unlike European nationalism, there has been another basic tendency in Negro thought working in an entirely different direction. Indeed, it is not too much to say that the basic desire of American Negroes, influenced by the ethos of American democracy, has been toward integration into American society, rather than toward an exclusive nationalism.[2]

Political Nationalism: Emigration and Colonization

The period between the Revolution and the Civil War was marked by a growing interest among free Negroes in emigration as a solution to the generally worsening situation in which they found themselves. As early as 1789 the Free African Society of Newport, Rhode Island, went on record as favoring a return to Africa as an escape from the conditions in the United States,[3] but it was not until 1815 that Paul Cuffe, prosperous New England Negro shipowner, merchant, and Quaker, took thirty-eight free Negroes to Sierra Leone at his own expense. Cuffe, while interested primarily in Christianizing and civilizing the natives and in destroying the slave trade, also believed that emigration would relieve the oppression of Negroes in the United States. There are glimmerings of nationalist sentiment in a letter written by some of the emigrants in May, 1818, singing the praises of Africa: "Be not fearful to come to Africa, which is your country by right. . . . Though you are free that is not your country. Africa, not America, is your country and your home."[4]

However, the majority of free Negroes remained opposed to colonization right down to the Civil War, though worsening conditions, especially after the Fugitive Slave Law of 1850, increased sentiment for emigration. Even many of those favoring colonization looked with disfavor upon the American Colonization Society, created by leading figures in American public life in 1817. Martin R. Delany referred to it in 1852 as "anti-Christian in its character, and misanthropic in its pretended sympathies," calling its leaders "arrant hypocrites, seeking every opportunity to deceive" the free Negroes.[5] However, Daniel Coker (first bishop of the African Methodist Episcopal Church, who later resigned in favor of Richard Allen) sailed for the American Colonization Society with about ninety free Negroes in 1820. In his *Journal* he waxes romantic about his arrival in Africa: "Who could refrain from tears to see afflicted Africa receiving her sons on her own soil?" And in his letters to the United States he urged Negroes to come to Africa, where they could do much better than in America.[6] As early as 1826 a convention of Negroes at Baltimore expressed the view that Negroes should take an interest in the efforts of the Colonization Society. Since Negroes were strangers to the United States and could never enjoy full rights there, the convention regarded emigration to Africa as the only way to obtain freedom.[7] John B. Russwurm, co-editor with Samuel Cornish of *Freedom's Journal*, the first Negro newspaper, after Cornish's retirement changed from a militant anti-colonizationist to a pro-colonizationist line in 1829, and subsequently emigrated himself.

Letters to the American Colonization Society indicate that for the most part those Negroes who were interested in the Society's activities viewed it either as a means to gain freedom from slavery, as a means of escaping the caste pressures faced by free Negroes, or as an aid in the Christianization of Africa. A few showed signs of an awakening nationalism, as did a free Negro of Charleston who wrote to the Society in 1832, praising Liberia as a place where Negroes could enjoy full freedom, the right of self-government, the emoluments of office, and the protection of their property. Liberia, he hoped, would soon become a "distinguished nation."[8] Augustus Washington, who later emigrated to Liberia, wrote to the Society in 1851 that in view of the hostility of the American government and people, he had long favored emigration and the creation of a Negro state. Liberia, in his opinion, seemed to be the only suitable place. "And hence," he said, "we are driven to the conclusion that the friendly and mutual separation of the two races is not only necessary to preserve the peace, happiness and prosperity of both, but indispensable to the preservation of the one and the glory of the other. While we would thus promote the interests of two great continents, and build up another powerful Republic, as an asylum to the oppressed, we would at the same time gratify national prejudices."[9] A national state would be erected, with the mission and destiny of showing the capabilities of the Negro and redeeming Africa. Others had similar viewpoints. S. Wesley Jones of Tuscaloosa, Alabama, long active in stimulating emigration, wrote in 1851:

> I trust my brethren will think of this matter, and arouse themselves, and let national pride be kindled up in their hearts, and . . . make us a great nation of our own, build our own cities and towns, make our own laws, collect our own revenues, command our own vessels, army and navy, elect our own governors and lawmakers, have our own schools and colleges, our own lawyers and doctors, in a word, cease to be "hewers of wood and drawers of water," and be men.[10]

The Negro Convention movement of the 1830's expressed determined opposition to African colonization. The most eminent of the free Negro leaders opposed emigration, with Henry Highland Garnet [who later did become a prominent colonizationist] declaring in 1848:

> We must cherish and maintain a national and patriotic senti-
> ment. . . . Some people of color say that they have no home, no
> country. I am not among that number. It is empty declamation.
> It is unwise. It is not logical—it is false. . . . America is my home,
> my country, and I have no other. I love whatever of good there
> may be in her institutions. I hate her sins. I loathe her slavery,
> and I pray Heaven that ere long she may wash away her guilt in
> tears of repentance. I love the green hills which my eyes first
> beheld in my infancy. I love every inch of soil which my feet
> pressed in my youth, and I mourn because the accursed shade of
> slavery rests upon it. I love my country's flag, and I hope that
> soon it will be cleansed of its stains, and be hailed by all nations as
> the emblem of freedom and independence.[11]

Sentiment in favor of colonization increased under the worsening conditions of the 1850's. Conventions at Dayton in 1848 and at Cincinnati in 1850 favored emigration. In the latter year the free Negroes of New York organized the New York and Liberia Emigration Society to cooperate with the American Colonization Society. A convention held in Baltimore in 1852 declared that Negroes were capable of conducting their own affairs, that evidence showed that Negroes and whites could never get along in the same country, and that therefore "A separation of ourselves from our white neighbors . . . is an object devoutly to be desired."[12]

Capable and thoughtful leaders, like clear-thinking, Harvard-educated Dr. Martin Robison Delany, who in 1852 published *The Condition, Elevation, Emigration and Destiny of the Colored People of the United States, Politically Considered*, were impressed by emigration as a solution to their problems. Better than anyone else during the antebellum period, Delany exemplifies the dual loyalties of the American Negro, and the instability of his ideologies. On the one hand he considered himself a citizen of the United States:

> Our common country is the United States. Here were we born,
> here raised and educated; here are the scenes of childhood; . . .

the loved enjoyments of our domestic and fireside relations, and the sacred graves of our departed fathers and mothers, and from here will we not be driven by any policy that may be schemed against us.

We are Americans, having a birthright citizenship—natural claims upon this country—claims common to all others of our fellow-citizens, which may, by virtue of unjust laws, be obstructed, but never can be annulled.[13]

He pointed out that Negroes did much of the physical work necessary to build the country; that they were the mainstay of the southern economy; that they had fought with distinction in all the nation's wars; and that they had made significant contributions to its medical, business, religious, and intellectual life. Yet while the Negro deserved full rights in America, Delany was pessimistic about ever attaining them. Negroes in America, he declared, were a "nation within a nation,"[14] comparable to but worse off than national minorities of Europe. Elevation of the Negro, he felt, was possible within the United States through thrift, industry, and economic activity. He also implied that Negroes should use the segregated Negro community as the basic market for their economic development.[15]

But while "elevation" was possible, the only real solution to the Negro's problem lay in emigration. Earlier, he had written an unpublished *Project for an Expedition to the Eastern Coast of Africa*, in which he wrote: "WE must MAKE an ISSUE, CREATE an EVENT, AND ESTABLISH A NATIONAL POSITION FOR OURSELVES. . . ."[16] But meanwhile his mind had turned to the American continents, and the Caribbean area he felt was "evidently the ultimate destination and future home of the colored race." "God himself . . . has presented these measures to us. Our race is to be redeemed; it is a great and glorious work, and we are the instruments by which it is to be done."[17]

In spite of this desire to establish a national state for Negroes, we must remember that Delany regarded himself as a part of the American nationality. To Garrison he penned the following on May 14, 1852:

I am not in favor of caste, nor a separation of the brotherhood of mankind, and would as willingly live among white men as black, if I had an *equal possession* and enjoyment of privileges. . . . If there were any probability of this, I should be willing to remain in the country, fighting and struggling on. . . . But I must admit, that I have no hopes in this country—no confidence in the American people—with a few excellent exceptions—therefore I have written as I have done. Heathenism and Liberty, before Christianity and Slavery.[18]

As the National Convention of 1853 opposed emigration, a dissatisfied minority issued a call for a National Emigration Convention, which met in 1854, 1856, and 1858. Its leading spirits were Martin R. Delany, James Whitfield, and James Theodore Holly, who respectively favored emigration to Nigeria (Delany had changed his mind again), Central America, and Haiti. All three possibilities were investigated, but only the last amounted to anything, with the Haitian government agreeing to encourage migration on generous terms.[19]

In support of Haitian emigration Holly wrote *A Vindication of the Capacity of the Negro Race for Self-Government, and Civilized Progress.* . . . His object was, by tracing Haitian history, to arouse American Negroes "to a full consciousness of their own inherent dignity; and thereby increasing among them that self-respect which shall urge them to the performance of those deeds which the age and the race now demand at their hands." American Negroes have a "weighty responsibility . . . to contribute to the continued advancement of the Negro nationality of the New World, until its glory and renown shall overspread and cover the whole earth, and redeem and regenerate by its influence in the future, the benighted Fatherland of the race of Africa." This Negro nationality of the New World was Haiti, whose mission was "to regenerate and disenthrall the oppression and ignorance of the race, throughout the world." While immediate colonization in Africa would be "premature" and "Utopian," Africa shall have its day, for God "in permitting the accursed slave traffic to transplant so many millions of the race, to the New World, and educing therefrom such a Negro nationality as Hayti, indicates thereby, that we have a work now to do here in the Western World, which in his own good time shall shed its orient beams upon the Fatherland of the race." American Negroes, with their knowledge and skills, should go to Haiti to help her prepare for her great work. And so he concludes: "Then let us boldly enlist in this high pathway of duty, while the watchwords that shall cheer and inspire us in our noble and glorious undertaking, shall be the soul-stirring anthem of GOD and HUMANITY."[20] Here, indeed, is a clear-cut statement of Negro nationalism.

While the Haitian venture finally collapsed, and while few American Negroes went to Africa, colonization died hard. Alexander Crummell, later to become an eminent Episcopalian minister in the United States, had gone to Africa as a missionary during the antebellum period, and was advocating colonization during the Civil War as a means of Christianizing Africa and because Negroes could enjoy in Africa advantages and opportunities not possible in the United States, though he apparently never advocated emigration of the entire Negro population of this country.[21] And even after the war Edward W. Blyden, conscious of the great past of the Negro race in Africa, and criticizing American Negroes for not emigrating when they could have liberty in Africa, saw a magnificent future for the Negro race in its African fatherland. "We . . . repeat with undiminished earnestness the wish we have frequently expressed elsewhere, *that the eyes of the blacks may be opened to discern their true mission and destiny*; that making their escape from the house of bondage, *they may betake themselves to their ancestral home, and assist in constructing a Christian* AFRICAN EMPIRE."[22]

With this emigration movement, then, there came to be associated feelings of real nationalism. Confined to a handful of individuals, and against the main current of American Negro thinking, but gaining strength under the pressures of the 1850's, there was a growing vision of a place where Negroes could establish their own state, enjoy liberty and self-government, and redeem the African fatherland. This nationalism had a strong sense of the past—especially in Holly and Blyden—a sense of mission and future destiny, and the desire for a political state, as well as consciousness of a unity born of prejudice, discrimination, and persecution. It was not, however, until Garvey arrived on the scene that this nationalism became a mass movement. Meanwhile the hopes of Civil War and Reconstruction led to a decline in schemes of emigration, except for minor efforts late in the nineteenth century.

This early Negro nationalism did not assert the superiority of the Negro race to other races, but emphasized its equality with other races. It insisted that Negroes had made a contribution to world civilization, and were to make one in the future, in redeeming and Christianizing Africa. Like English and American nationalism, it was grounded in the ideals of liberty, freedom, equality, self-government, and Christianity—a national state to these early nationalists was, above all, a place where Negroes could enjoy these things, and so feel loyal to the state for what it offered to them. Perhaps Alexander Crummell summed it up best when he described Liberia as "this spot dedicated to nationality, consecrated to freedom, and sacred to religion."[23]

But behind it all, and thwarting these nationalistic endeavors, was the American democratic creed. A man like Delany would obviously have preferred to stay in the United States if he thought he could achieve liberty, equality, security, and the rights of citizenship that way. The majority of free Negro Americans would have agreed with Robert Purvis when he declared in 1862: "Sir, we were born here, and here we choose to remain. . . . A few may go, as a few went to Hayti, and a few went to Liberia, but the colored people as a mass will not leave the land of their birth. . . . I feel confident that I only express their sentiment as a body, when I say that your project of colonizing them . . . with or without their consent, will never succeed."[24]

Cultural Nationalism: The Development of Negro History

The Convention movement, the development of the Negro church and fraternity, the emigration and colonization efforts, and abolitionist activities were all evidence of a rising racial consciousness and solidarity to advance the status of the Negro. At the same time, Negroes found it necessary to assert and prove their equality with whites, and to give a sense of dignity and pride of race to themselves in order to offset the inferiority doctrines of whites. The result was what we might call a cultural nationalism which fostered and was fostered by a series of books and pamphlets intended to vindicate the Negro. While the development of a national history, and of pride in the national past, is a universal element in nationalism, it is important to note the essential dualism of the school of vindicators and historians to be discussed. On one hand, these men looked upon their work as necessary to give Negroes dignity in their own eyes, and to solidify the Negro group in its fight for equality, and at the same time to convince whites of the equality of races, and of the accomplishments of Negroes in order to remove their prejudices and open the door to full integration in America. In most cases, except for those individuals who viewed amalgamation as the ultimate solution of the race problem, this point of view may be called a cosmopolitan nationalism—all groups had, it was felt, something to contribute to the totality of American culture, and should therefore be accorded full participation in American democracy. On the other hand, such arguments always have a tendency both to act as a substitute for integrationist action, and to encourage group separatism by emphasizing the glory of the Negro group and the necessity for maintaining its integrity, and to feed such nationalistic movements as those of Holly, Blyden, and Garvey (each of whom had a strong sense of the past). These two points of view of course overlap, and it is frequently difficult to distinguish between them.

The arguments used were almost entirely scriptural and historical. Inasmuch as they were fully developed by the 1830's, when the earliest available evidence appears, it will be well to summarize them as follows: Negroes are not of pre-Adamic stock (*i.e.*, animals lower than man, as some whites asserted), but are indeed descended from Ham (as almost everyone believed at the time). However, contrary to white thinking, Negroes inherit no curse from Ham, as is shown by several biblical arguments. Now, since Ham was Negro, it follows that all his descendants were—and these included most of the civilized peoples of the ancient Near East: Cushites or Ethiopians, Egyptians, Phoenicians, Babylonians, and Assyrians; and even the Hebrews intermarried with the Cushites, so that Jesus is a descendant of Ham, and therefore a Negro. The oldest civilizations in the world are those of Ethiopia and Egypt, and European civilization is ultimately derived from them through Greece and Rome. Some viewed the Greeks as being of African descent; and all great men of antiquity born in Africa and a number of others are Negroes—including (to name a few) Hannibal, Plato, Cyrus, Caesar, Pompey, and Augustine. Africa lost her ascendancy because she forgot the worship of the true God and turned heathen. God then punished her by destroying her civilization and instituting the slave trade. But Africa gave civilization to the world, and what is more does not the Bible say that Ethiopia shall stretch forth her hands unto God? The future as well as the past is assured.

But what of the recent past and present? Evidence of Negro ability is presented by such men as the ex-slave Juan Latino, sixteenth-century professor at the University of Grenada; Anthony Amo, who took his Ph.D. at the University of Wittenberg; and El Capitein, who in 1742 received his at Leyden (with a thesis defending slavery). Toussaint L'Ouverture and the history of Haiti prove the Negro's capacity for self-government. Later on there were such Europeans as Pushkin and Alexandre Dumas. In America were Thomas Fuller, eighteenth-century illiterate slave who was a "lightning calculator"; Dr. Derham of New Orleans, from whom the celebrated Dr. Benjamin Rush learned things; the fabulous Thomy Lafon of the same city, who before the Civil War amassed a fortune of half a million dollars; and Benjamin Banneker, Phillis Wheatley, Richard Allen, and a large group of talented ministers and abolitionist leaders. And Negroes had fought with valor and distinction in all the nation's wars.

Of course, this summary is a composite picture. As early as 1825 an anonymous article containing many of the above arguments appeared in the Colonization Society's *African Repository*. In 1837 appeared *A Treatise on the Intellectual Character, and Civil and Political Condition of the Colored People of the U. States . . .*, by Hosea Easton, a leader in the Convention Movement. Tracing the Negroes' descent from Ham, he notes that the earliest civilizations were in Africa, and that from Egypt, through Greece and Rome, came the source of all Western civilization. African civilizations were destroyed because they were too peaceful; and the continually warring Europeans had very likely not yet achieved the level of ancient African civilization. Slavery was the cause of the Negroes' relatively slight achievement in America. Conscious of the separateness of the Negroes in America, proud of their African past, he nevertheless expressed in his last chapter the feeling that the Negroes' home is in America, and that they should be accorded full rights as American citizens.

R. B. Lewis's *Light and Truth* was published in 1844 "with a determination that a correct knowledge of the Colored and Indian people . . . may be extended freely, unbiased by any prejudicial effects. . . . In this country, where the former are subjected to the deepest degradation . . . it is highly expedient that 'Light and Truth' should be promulgated, in order that oppressors shall not consider it an indispensable duty to trample upon the weak and defenseless."[25] For the most part the book was an extreme statement of the part played by Negroes in ancient civilizations. There was the usual material on the descendants of Ham, while the Jews, Greeks, Romans, Phoenicians, and American Indians were classed as Negroid peoples. The Ethiopians once held sway over most of Asia, and were the original inhabitants of Spain. Tiglath-Pileser, Sennacherib, Nebuchadnezzar, and Belshazzar; Cyrus; Moses, David, Solomon, and the Hebrew Prophets; Hamilcar, Hannibal, Scipio Africanus, Pompey, and Julius Caesar; Thales, Socrates, Euclid, and Plato; Boethius, Seneca, and Epictetus; Terence, Cato, Cyprian, Origen, and St. Augustine; and Jesus Christ— all were of Ethiopian descent. Lewis's use of more contemporary materials was pale in comparison.

Less extreme were two ministers, leaders in the Convention movement: James W. C. Pennington, author of *Text Book of the Origin and History of the Colored People* (1841), and Henry Highland Garnet, whose *Past and Present Condition, and the Destiny of the Colored Race*, appeared in 1848. Both drew their materials from ancient civilization and prominent Negroes of more recent date, and both were integrationists. Pennington believed that the race problem would be solved by the application of Christian principles,[26] while Garnet declared that "*this western world is destined to be filled with a mixed race*," and that full integration was to be achieved by "peace and temperance, industry and frugality, and love to God, and to all men, and by resisting tyranny in the name of Eternal Justice."[27] Also clearly favoring assimilation, though he did participate in the Emigration Convention movement of the 1850's, was William C. Nell, whose *Colored Patriots of the American Revolution* (1855), a series of accounts of Negro soldiers interspersed with sketches of Negroes prominent in other fields was written with the purpose of rescuing "from oblivion the name and fame of those who, though 'tinged with the hated stain,' yet had warm hearts and active hands in the 'times that tried men's souls.'"[28] To Nell, history was an instrument in the fight for full equality and the full rights of citizenship; he favored a single antislavery organization instead of Negroes having their own conventions, he unhesitatingly said that the United States was the homeland of the American Negro, and he expressed himself as opposed to segregated schools and churches (thus placing himself squarely behind men like Frederick Douglass, whom he quoted with approval on the subject, and against those who stood in the tradition of men like Richard Allen).

Three important post-Emancipation historians, William Wells Brown, George Washington Williams, and William T. Alexander, were interested primarily in the Negro in American history. In three works, culminating in *The Rising Son; or the Antecedents and Advancement of the Colored Race* (1874), Brown, escaped slave and antebellum abolitionist, discussed ancient African civilizations, contemporary Africa, Haiti, and especially the Negro in American history, with emphasis upon individuals of achievement. His aim, outside of writing a popular account of Negro history, was to provide an argument for integration into American society. G. W. Williams, minister, lawyer, and legislator, wrote the first scholarly history of the American Negro—the significant two-volume *History of the Negro Race in America* (1883), "in the hope that the obsolete antagonisms which grew out of the relation of master and slave may speedily sink as storms beneath the horizon; and that the day will hasten when there shall be no North, no South, no Black, no White,—but all be American citizens, with equal duties and equal rights."[29] More popular and less profound, Alexander's *History of the Colored Race in America* ran through several editions in the 1880's and '90's; his aim, as stated in the preface, was to stimulate racial solidarity through the study of history, for "it is only by a thorough knowledge of the past history of the race that the colored people will be better able to avail themselves of the blessings the future has in store for them."

The older school of writers, who emphasized scriptural and ancient history, continued to flourish. Baptist minister Rufus L. Perry, in *The Cushite, or the Decendants of Ham* (1893), repeated the old arguments of the antebellum writers; his underlying philosophy was expressed by the statement: "If it be here shown, beyond reasonable doubt . . . that the ancient Egyptians, Ethiopians and Libyans . . . were the ancestors of the present race of Ham, then the Negro of the nineteenth century may point to them with pride; and with all who would find in him a man and brother, cherish the hope of a return to racial celebrity, when in the light of a Christian civilization, Ethiopia shall stretch out her hands unto God."[30]. An African Methodist Episcopal minister, Joseph E. Hayne, repetitively stated his point of view in several works. He was opposed to colonization on the one hand; on the other, he felt that amalgamation of the races would be for the Negro "a confession of inferiority as to himself, and superiority as to the white," and that "that steady growth of race pride, that determination of the Negro to be the weaver of his own fortune, the carver of his own image, and the fashioner of his own destiny, that spirit in him that grows more rapidly as time passes, utterly precludes the possibility of such a solution."[31] Naturally such race pride and the elevation of the Negro would be stimulated through the study of Negro history. Hayne used the usual theological and historical materials, and in his last work claimed not only the Greeks, but also the newly discovered Cretans, and the Celts (*i.e.*, especially the British) as being of Negroid stock, which accounts for their achievements. In the same work he urged Negroes to be like the Jews (also of Negro ancestry), who had great "race pride," were "industrious and frugal," "never fail to stand by each other," and "never fail in business enterprise for lack of *courage* or push."[32]

By the turn of the century Negroes were manifesting considerable interest in their past, and a large number of minor works appeared, including (among others) the Reverend C. H. Walker's *Appeal to Caesar* (1900), which emphasized the Americanism of the Negro; a pamphlet, *Jesus Christ had Negro Blood in his Veins*, by W. L. Hunter, a Brooklyn physician, which went through nine editions between 1901 and 1913; Harvey Johnson's *The Nations from a New Point of View* (1903), which wasn't new at all, but contained the well-rehearsed materials regarding ancient civilizations; Pauline Hopkins's *Primer of Facts* (1905), which looked to the restoration of Africa through acquainting American Negroes with African history; James Morris Webb's *The Black Man the Father of Civilization* (1910), and William H. Ferris's *The African Abroad* (1913). Less ephemeral, because based on better scholarship, were William A. Sinclair's *Aftermath of Slavery* (1905), notable for its defense of the Negro in Reconstruction; James W. Cromwell's *The Negro in American History* (1914), a series of essays concerning principally Negroes of achievement; and Du Bois's *The Negro* (1915), with an important discussion of the culture of medieval and contemporary Africa. And Du Bois's *Crisis* magazine also showed interest in the Negro's past and the Negro's achievement.

As the lines of caste hardened in the opening years of the twentieth century, as discrimination increased and racial friction deepened, there was a tendency to use Negro history to foster race pride and group solidarity for the purpose of advancing the Negro group by collective action, and as an antidote to prejudice and discrimination. Dr. C. V. Roman, for example, in his pamphlet *A Knowledge of History is Conducive to Racial Solidarity* (1911), declared that "racial solidarity and not amalgamation is the desire and desirable goal of the American Negro." Knowledge of history would "stimulate race pride and promote racial solidarity sufficiently to enable us to spurn as poor relations those unfortunate members of our race who are ashamed of our lineage,"—*i.e.*, those who do "not wish to attend a Negro church, buy from a Negro merchant, consult a Negro lawyer or doctor, deposit in a Negro bank, or live in a Negro neighborhood, or send his children to a Negro school." Negro children should be taught the "glorious deeds of Negro men and Negro women first"—before they learn of the deeds of the national heroes of white America. And he concluded: "A diffusion of such knowledge among the masses of our people will stimulate race pride, strengthen their consciousness of kind without lessening their patriotism, and furnish an atmosphere of mutual cooperation and helpfulness that will change the winter of our discontent into the glorious summer of racial solidarity, that magic alembic in which most of our racial difficulties will disappear."[33] This message is significant, because it represented a sizeable and growing group.

The Negro history movement took on organized form with the creation of the Negro Society for Historical Research in 1911, and the Association for the Study of Negro Life and History in 1915. The former, led by John Edward Bruce (a later Garveyite) and the famous bibliophile Arthur A. Schomburg, set forth its underlying philosophy in a series of occasional papers. In one, York Russell expressed the sentiment that Negroes should "rescue from oblivion, the hidden treasures" of their past. Reciting the glories of Africa, he stated that "all existing nations who are great in the present, either have had or may claim to have had a great past"; apparently viewing Negroes as a nation, he declared that "when Africa of the present is great, Africa of the past will loom into prominence, for then we shall become arbiters of our own destinies, write our own histories, make our own researches, organize our own libraries, establish our own colleges, create our own monuments." The Society deserved loyalty and support, as an "effort" to "form an effective breakwater against the ever increasing and cumulative tide of prejudice and discrimination."[34] Schomburg, in a speech entitled *Racial Integrity*, pleaded for the study of Negro history and intellectual achievement. He desired "to awaken the sensibilities, to kindle the dormant fires in the soul, and to fire the racial patriotism by the study of the Negro books." The educational curriculum must be enlarged to include Negro history, for "it is the season for us to devote our time in kindling the torches that will inspire us to racial integrity." Therefore, "we need a collection . . . of books written by our men and women. If they lack style, let the children of tomorrow correct the omission of their sires."[35] Note that here is no word of Negro history as a means of convincing whites of Negro capabilities—the purpose is to instill race pride and race solidarity into the Negro himself.

Less propagandistic, and very clearly characterized by the dualism of which we have spoken several times, has been the work of the Association for the Study of Negro Life and History, whose declared objectives are to collect documents, promote historical studies, and further interracial harmony. As founder, editor of the *Journal of Negro History*, and active spirit of the organization, the late Carter G. Woodson has exercised a profound influence on both Negro and white thought. His underlying philosophy is succinctly summed up in the oft-repeated idea of "saving and popularizing the records of the race, that it may not become a negligible factor in the thought of the world." Woodson's own work emphasized individual achievements, and has the tone of apologetics and defense rather than being an integrated study of the Negro in American history. Evidence of the dualism in Negro thought are evident in the activities of the Association. On the whole, the emphasis has been on the integrationist side; articles and financial support by whites have been encouraged from the beginning. The articles of the first two years covered a wide variety of subject matter, including a few on Negro achievement in medicine, invention, and the Revolution; most of them were factual and scholarly. In a series of two articles John R. Lynch, formerly speaker of the Mississippi House of Representatives, wrote a spirited defense of the Negro during Reconstruction. Articles on Africa were published also, including (in vol. 2, no. 3) an unsigned piece entitled "The African Origin of Grecian Civilization," which traced all the principal civilizations of antiquity to Negroid origins, and the roots of the Renaissance to contact with African Mohammedans.

If Woodson did not speak in terms of racial solidarity, others did. A letter from a high school principal (published in vol. 1, no. 4) advocated increasing the *Journal's* circulation, so as to "disseminate historical knowledge of the race so necessary to give it self-respect and pride." More revealing were two speeches made at the Association's 1922 convention and reprinted in the *Journal* issue of April, 1923. J. W. Ball, speaking on "The Teaching of Negro History," stated that "the teaching of Negro history will serve the two-fold purpose of informing the white man and inspiring the Negro," and that "the teaching of Negro history to the Negro youth is necessary to inspire racial pride and arouse racial consciousness"; while Paul W. L. Jones, speaking on "Negro Biography," neglected the aspect of

educating whites and asserted that "every race that has counted
for much in history has its heroes." "No race, no nation, no
people," who lack "ideals of manhood and patriotism . . . can
hope to be accorded full recognition by the world. The Negro's
ideal must be a Negro if he is to appreciate keenly his own
particular stock. The Negro's examples of achievement and
devotion must be found within his own group, if he is to serve
the race faithfully and intelligently. Its sages, its patriots, its
heroes must all be persons of color, men whose faces show the
mark of Africa, if the Negro youth is to develop that essential
feeling commonly known as race pride."

The influence of the Association has been complex and is
therefore difficult to evaluate. On one hand, there can be no
question that it has been a potent force in stimulating race pride
and race consciousness; on the other, it has stimulated scholarly
and critical research into the field of Negro history, and has
been effective in making whites aware of Negro history. At any
rate, as far as this article is concerned, its organization and
activities were indicative of the growing interest Negroes were
showing in their history during the first decade of the twentieth
century.

Economic Nationalism: Booker T. Washington and the National Negro Business League

After Emancipation, Negroes held high hopes of achieving full
equality as American citizens, and the dominant ideologies of
the Reconstruction era, represented best by Frederick Douglass, were integrationist, favoring political activity and striving
toward assimilation. The worsening conditions from the 1870's
on, and the desertion of many white supporters, forced the
Negro back upon himself and fostered a growing tendency
toward philosophies of self-help and racial solidarity. We have
already seen the role which some thought history should play in
this development. Extreme forms of isolation and withdrawal
were attempted. All-Negro communities such as Mound Bayou,
and even an attempted all-Negro state were founded in the late
1880's and '90's—and these communities fostered a zealous
race pride, and accepted and encouraged segregation in order

to promote the development of Negro community life, and to offer Negroes opportunities not otherwise available. Emigration was also proposed—notably by Bishop Henry M. Turner, who, encouraged by Alabama's Senator Morgan, advocated settlement in Africa.

More significant was the philosophy of Booker T. Washington. Largely blaming Negroes themselves for their situation because they sought "higher education" and neglected "working with the hands," Washington advocated a policy of conciliation and gradualism, which involved accepting segregation and disfranchisement, and emphasized economic and material advancement through the agency of industrial education. He was opposed to colonization, believing that the Negro must work out his salvation in the United States; on the other hand, he did not think amalgamation, as some were "so bold as to predict," a solution.[36] Rather, the Negro should cast down his bucket in the South, and cooperating with the "best white men," but relying mostly on himself, advance in economic and material well-being until he would be prepared to participate fully in the political and cultural life of the nation. "I do not," he wrote, "favour the Negro's giving up anything which is fundamental and which has been guaranteed to him by the Constitution."[37] And in the last year of his life he wrote a posthumously published article against segregation.[38] Industrial education and advance in business, accomplished by thrift, industry, and Christian character, would help the Negro achieve a better status by showing the white man that the Negro has capabilities and can lead a refined and useful life, and because the white man would find it to his economic advantage and to the well-being of the community to trade with Negroes and hire them as skilled workers. Thus did Washington transmute the laissez-faire individualism of the Gilded Age into the key for racial salvation.

Washington spoke in terms of interracial harmony, cooperation, and good will. Yet just as he reflected the dominant philosophy of white America, so also he reflected the growing emphasis upon racial solidarity and self-help in the Negro community. Even though he hoped for white support of Negro enterprise, from a practical point of view he realized that the

Negro business group would have to depend very largely upon the patronage of the Negro community. "Now, if we wish to bring the race to a point where it should be, where it will be strong and grow and prosper, we have got to, in every way possible, encourage it. We can do this in no better way than by cultivating that amount of faith in the race which will make us patronize its own enterprises wherever those enterprises are worth patronizing." Race pride and solidarity were important to Washington: "The race that would grow strong and powerful must have the element of hero-worship in it that will . . . make it honour its great men. . . . I think we should be ashamed of the coloured man or woman who would not venerate . . . Frederick Douglass"—in spite of the fact that Washington was opposed to intermarriage, and attacked those who looked for salvation in political activity. "I speak of this, not that I want my people to regard themselves in a narrow, bigoted sense . . . but because I wish that it may have a reasonable pride in . . . its history."[39] Washington himself wrote the two-volume *Story of the Negro* and *The Negro in Business* as an antidote to prejudice and discrimination, as a means of stimulating race pride and race consciousness and giving the Negro support and inspiration in his struggle for advancement, and to acquaint whites with Negro achievement. He urged Negroes to be like the Jews, "who have clung together. They have had a certain amount of unity, pride and love of race; and, as the years go on, they will be more and more influential in this country—a country where they were once despised. . . . Unless the Negro learns more and more to imitate the Jew in these matters . . . he cannot expect to have any high degree of success."[40] To Washington, then, race pride, race unity, and racial solidarity were to be instruments in the fight for the achievement of the Negro's salvation in America, including the rights of citizenship and the respect of the white man.

The optimism and dualism of Washington's philosophy were well reflected in the thinking and activities of the National Negro Business League, which he founded in 1900 for the purpose of stimulating Negro business enterprise. The annual conventions were pretty much the same year after year. The tone of the 1904 convention, for example, was set by Washington's annual address, which viewed business enterprise as vital for the eventual removal of prejudice; the higher things of life, while important, depend upon a secure economic foundation. Fred R. Moore, organizing secretary, realized that Negro business depended on the exploitation of the segregated market, for he emphasized racial solidarity in this matter and urged that all League members be required to support "all worthy enterprises managed by men and women of the race," on pain of dismissal from the organization if they did not.

> All business enterprises should be supported; how else can we expect to be respected by the world at large and be representative of something if we do not begin to practice what a great many of us preach? . . . Some would say that this was drawing the color line. I do not believe it. Jews support Jews; Germans support Germans; Italians support Italians, until they get strong enough to compete with their brothers in the professions and trades; and Negroes should now begin to support Negroes.

> We are constantly appealing to the whites to hold open the door of opportunity, but we are not doing it for ourselves, as we should. We must begin to recognize the true principle . . . —believe in your race and practice it by giving the race proper support in all proper undertakings. What a mighty power we shall be when we begin to do this, and we shall never be a mighty power until we do begin.

Various delegates presented their experiences and views as an inspiration to others: Philip A. Payton, Jr., founder of the Afro-American Realty Company, showed how he turned prejudice to profit (the white exodus from Harlem lowered property prices), but looked forward to the day when prejudice would disappear; while T. Thomas Fortune, editor of the New York *Age*, viewed Negroes as an integral part of the American nation, and viewed industrial education and business activity as the way to achieve full citizenship and eliminate prejudice. S. H. Hart, president of the Capital Trust Company of Jacksonville, proudly pointed to the white depositors in his bank—"some of the most influential members of the white race"—but felt that "it is just as necessary to have our own banks and trust companies as it is to have our own physicians, lawyers, and teachers." Fannie Barrier Williams felt that "within the last few years we have learned to feel a new pride and a strong sense of confidence in the future of the colored race, because of the fine courage and wonderful success our men are gaining everywhere as men of business," and understood the signifiance of the League to be that "the Negro race in its increasing business relationships with the white race is opening up new and respected ways of contact. . . . If you can obtain and hold the acquaintance and confidence of the business world, you will be in a position to conquer more prejudices than we have yet been able to estimate." Idleness she termed immoral. A. C. Howard of Chicago felt that the way to succeed was to "find something the people wanted and they would want you," and said that "we cannot expect to be counted among the strong people until we can buy our commodities from Negro firms, or white firms who give the Negro their percentage of employment according to their trade and population." If Negroes would take care of themselves, prejudice would be eliminated. Throughout there was emphasis on optimism and success; on thrift, industry, economy, invention, and initiative; and usually (by implication if not overtly) exploitation of the segregated Negro market—all providing that Negroes have business capabilities and can work out their own salvation.[41]

In spite of all the talk and theory about better relations between the races being the ultimate objective of the League and its efforts to stimulate Negro business, practically speaking most attention centered upon the short-range objective of achieving Negro support of Negro business. This was of course due to the very nature of the situation—a situation compounded by economic discrimination by whites, and the lack of capital and business training necessary to really compete with white business. And this economic necessity was greatly reinforced by the whole general ideology of Negro advancement through racial solidarity and cooperation. What Ralph Bunche calls the "racial chauvinism" of the League[42] and the institution of National Negro Trade Week are then perfectly natural developments. As Gunnar Myrdal points out, the conflict between the desire for full integration in American society and the short-range advantages of exploiting the segregated Negro market, have placed the Negro middle and upper classes in an ideological dilemma.[43]

In general, as one digs into materials written in the generation before World War I, the importance of what we may call these ideologies of withdrawal and solidarity and self-help emerges clearly. In a way this was the climax of the movement begun by men like Richard Allen and Prince Hall, who were instrumental in creating segregated Negro institutions because of discriminatory practices in the white ones. At the turn of the century this development was evident not only in the tendency toward economic nationalism, and in the writings of historians and propagandists, but in the creation of such organizations as the Negro college fraternities and the American Negro Academy, whose objective was to foster Negro intellectual life and Negro culture. All of these reflected and were part of the larger ideology of the necessity of racial solidarity and racial self-help. Broadly speaking, this philosophy was the dominant nationalistic ideology among Negroes in the years before World War I, in the same way that emigration tendencies were the dominant nationalistic ideology in the years before the Civil War. Both were present in germ in Martin R. Delany, and both were incorporated into the dynamic mass movement of Marcus Garvey. Of course it must be remembered that this sentiment did not envisage rejection of America—rather, its aim was to achieve economic and political and civic equality, though it frowned upon social intermingling and encouraged segregated institutions such as school and church. And indeed, the promise of the American ideal continued to operate in a contrary direction, and the early years of the new century saw the short-lived race-conscious and integrationist Niagara Movement, and the beginning of the NAACP—both standing squarely in the tradition of Frederick Douglass with their emphasis upon full equality and full integration into American life.

World War I came at a time when race consciousness and racial solidarity were rapidly becoming augmented and strengthened. The Business League was becoming a potent force in Negro life, and the NAACP was beginning to focus effectively the Negro protest, while Negroes were becoming more and more aware of their past and developing a compensatory race pride. All of this seemed to bring forth a new type of Negro—the New Negro, as he was soon called—race conscious and militant. And the Great Migration created compact Negro ghettoes in northern cities, which made possible not only the segregated Negro community and economy which could be exploited by the business and professional class, but also a fertile field in which to sow the seeds of a mass organization. It was here that the ideologies of the upper classes seeped down to the masses, and that the Negro masses became truly race conscious. These conditions, interacting with the shock of the race riots of 1917–19, created a situation easily exploited by Garvey, with his ultra-nationalistic movement and ideology of economic self-sufficiency, race pride, and a return to Africa. Consciously or unconsciously, in effect what Garvey did was to strip the ideologies of the preceding century of their dualism and overtones of integrationism, and appropriate them to his extremely chauvinistic ideology.

The 1920's marked the high point of Negro nationalism. The Harlem Renaissance, or New Negro movement in literature and art, while fostered by whites, was a race-conscious movement with overtones of nationalism. It emphasized pride of the Negro in Africa and his past, and took its themes from Negro life. Alain Locke compared the movement to the national awakenings in European and Asiatic countries, and regarded it as the fulfillment of the message of race pride, race consciousness, and race solidarity developed during the opening years of the century.[44] And the period was the heyday of the Garvey movement. In a very real sense these two movements were the legacy of the thinking and ideologies of the preceding century discussed in this paper.

The evidence presented in this article indicates the existence of a very definite ethnocentrism among American Negroes. It is the product of the caste pressures to which the Negro is subjected. There is the consciousness of a common suffering in the past and present. There is the consciousness also of a past of achievement, even glory, and in many there is the hope of a wonderful future destiny as a racial group: these form not only a basis for group solidarity, but a psychological escape from prejudice and discrimination—as is true of oppressed nationalities the world over. Negro thinking, too, illustrates the full range of nationalist ideologies discussed earlier in this article. There is the cultural nationalism of the New Negro movement, and of the historical propagandists; there is an economic nationlism chiefly exemplified by the National Negro Business League; there is the political nationalism of the various emigration and colonization projects with the objective of creating a Negro state; and there is the extreme, exclusive nationalism of the Garvey type, which flowered after World War I, and included the ideologies of cultural, economic, and political nationalism which had been formulated in the preceding century and were now finally integrated into a dynamic mass movement.

But always in the background there was the opposite ideology of the American democratic creed, and the desire for integration into American life. Race pride has been encouraged as a means for attaining status in the American society. Not only economic and cultural nationalism, but also the ideologies of racial solidarity and racial unity in general have usually been formulated in terms of ultimate integration into American life. And so one must not overlook the fact that undoubtedly the basic American Negro nationalism is what may be called a cosmopolitan nationalism. In the same way that many eighteenth- and nineteenth-century thinkers felt that each nation should maintain its identity but make its contribution as a member of a peaceful family of nations, so the basic desire of the majority of Negroes is for the Negro group, proud of its past and achievements and contributions, to take its place among the other ethnic groups of American society and enjoy the basic rights of American citizenship and freedom, without legal segregation, without political and economic and civil discrimination. We can do no better than to quote Du Bois's *Souls of Black Folk*:

> The history of the American Negro is the history of this strife,— this longing to attain self-conscious manhood, to merge his double self into a better and truer self. In this merging he wishes neither of the older selves to be lost. He would not Africanize America, for America has too much to teach the world and Africa. He would not bleach his Negro soul in a flood of white

Americanism, for he knows that Negro blood has a message for the world. He simply wishes to make it possible for a man to be both a Negro and an American, without having the doors of Opportunity closed roughly in his face.[45]

The character of this cosmopolitan nationalism is best expressed perhaps in the song "Lift Every Voice and Sing"—commonly known as the Negro National Anthem—written in 1900 and popular by the time of World War I. Not once mentioning the Negro by name, it shows a consciousness of the suffering of the past, hopefulness for the future, a belief in liberty, and faith in God and America. As such it is truly characteristic of Negro thought.

1. The major sources for the frame of reference of this article are Ralph J. Bunche, "Conceptions and Ideologies of the Negro Problem," unpublished memorandum for the Carnegie-Myrdal Study of the Negro in America, 1940; Carlton J. H. Hayes, *Essays on Nationalism* (New York: Macmillan, 1926) and *The Historical Evolution of Modern Nationalism* (New York: Richard R. Smith, 1931); and Hans Kohn, *The Idea of Nationalism* (New York: Macmillan, 1944).

2. Such an outlet was not possible to the repressed minorities of Eastern and Central Europe. Note, however, the essential similarity of American Negro thought to that of Western European and American Jews since the eighteenth century.

3. Charles H. Wesley, *Richard Allen, Apostle of Freedom* (Washington: Associated Publishers, 1935), pp. 66–67.

4. Henry N. Sherwood, "Paul Cuffee," *Journal of Negro History*, 8, no. 2 (1923), 227; and Henry N. Sherwood, "Paul Cuffee and His Contribution to the American Colonization Society," *Proceedings of the Mississippi Valley Historical Association*, 4 (1912–13), 393.

5. Martin Robison Delany, *The Condition, Elevation, Emigration and Destiny of the Colored People of the United States, Politically Considered* (Philadelphia: By the Author, 1852), pp. 31–32.

6. Daniel Coker, *Journal of Daniel Coker, a Descendant of Africa . . . in the Ship Elizabeth, on a Voyage for Sherbro in Africa* (Baltimore: Edward J. Coale, 1820), pp. 24, 43–44.

7. "Memorial from the Free People of Colour to the Citizens of Baltimore," *African Repository*, 2, no. 10 (Dec., 1826), 295–98.

8. Carter G. Woodson, ed., *The Mind of the Negro as Reflected in Letters Written During the Crisis, 1800–1860* (Washington: Association for the Study of Negro Life and History, 1926), p. 7.

9. *Ibid.*, p. 141

10. *Ibid.*, pp. 70–71.

11. Henry Highland Garnet, *The Past and the Present Condition, and the Destiny of the Colored Race* (Troy, N.Y.: J. C. Kneeland, 1848), p. 29.

12. Louis R. Mehlinger, "The Attitude of the Free Negro toward Colonization," *Journal of Negro History*, 1, no. 3 (1915), 298; and "Proceedings of the Convention of Free Colored People of the State of Maryland, 1852," *ibid.*, pp. 334–36.

13. Delany, *Condition, Elevation*, pp. 48–49.

14. *Ibid.*, p. 12.

15. *Ibid.*, chs. 3 and 4.

16. *Ibid.*, "Appendix," p. 215.

17. *Ibid.*, pp. 178, 183.

18. Woodson, *Mind of the Negro*, p. 293.

19. See John W. Cromwell, *The Early Negro Convention Movement*, American Negro

Academy, Occasional Paper no. 9 (Washington, 1904); and Martin R. Delany, *Official Report of the Niger Valley Exploring Party* (New York: Thomas Hamilton, 1861).

20. James Theodore Holly, *A Vindication of the Capacity of the Negro Race for Self-Government, and Civilized Progress, as Demonstrated by Historical Events of the Haytian Revolution* . . . (New Haven: Afric-American Printing Company, 1857), pp. 44–46.

21. Alexander Crummell, "Manuscript Sermons," MS 317, Schomburg Collection, New York Public Library. See also his *Future of Africa* (New York: Charles Scribner, 1862) and *Africa and America* (Springfield, Mass.: Wiley, 1891) for typical sermons expressing his Liberian nationalism during the antebellum period.

22. Edward W. Blyden, *The Negro in Ancient History* (Washington: M'Gill & Witherow, 1869), p. 28.

23. Alexander Crummell, *The Duty of A Rising Christian State to the World's Well-Being and Civilization* (Massachusetts Colonization Society, 1857), p. 31.

24. Robert Purvis, *Speeches and Correspondence* (n.p.: n.d.), pp. 21–22.

25. R. B. Lewis, *Light and Truth; Collected from the Bible and Ancient and Modern History, Containing the Universal History of the Colored and Indian Race* (Boston: Benjamin F. Roberts, 1844), p. iii.

26. James W. C. Pennington, *Text Book of the Origin and History of the Colored People* (Hartford: L. Skinner, 1841), pp. 86ff.

27. Garnet, *Past and Present Condition*, pp. 26 and 28.

28. William C. Nell, *The Colored Patriots of the American Revolution, with Sketches of Several Distinguished Colored Persons, to which is Added a Brief Survey of the Condition and Prospects of Colored Americans* (Boston: Robert F. Wallcut, 1855), p. 9.

29. George W. Williams, *History of the Negro Race in America* (New York: G. P. Putnam's Sons, 1883), I, x.

30. Rufus L. Perry, *The Cushite, or the Descendants of Ham* (Springfield, Mass.: Wiley, 1893), p. x.

31. Joseph E. Hayne, *The Negro in Sacred History, or Ham and His Immediate Descendants* (Charleston, S.C.: Walker, Evans & Cogswell, 1887), p. 7.

32. Joseph E. Hayne, *The Ammonian or Hamitic Origin of the Ancient Greeks, Cretions, and All the Celtic Races*, 2nd ed. (Brooklyn: Guide Printing and Publishing, 1905), p. 156.

33. C. V. Roman, *A Knowledge of History is Conductive to Racial Solidarity* (Nashville: Sunday School Union Printers, 1911), pp. 25–26, 30, 33.

34. York Russell, *Historical Research*, Negro Society for Historical Research, Occasional Paper no. 1 (Yonkers, N.Y., 1912).

35. Arthur A. Schomburg, *Racial Integrity, A Plea for the Establishment of a Chair of Negro History in Our Schools and Colleges*, Negro Society for Historical Research, Occasional Paper no. 3 (Yonkers, N.Y., 1913), pp. 5, 6, and 7.

36. Booker T. Washington, *The Future of the American Negro* (Boston: Small, Maynard & Co., 1899), pp. 157–63, 200.

37. *Ibid.*, p. 141.

38. Booker T. Washington, "My View of Segregation Laws," *The New Republic*, 5, no. 57 (Dec. 4, 1915), 113–14.

39. Washington, *Future of the American Negro*, pp. 179–81.

40. *Ibid.*, p. 183.

41. *Report of the Fifth Annual Convention of the National Negro Business League*, 1904, pp. 17, 46–47, 59, 62, 69–75, 99.

42. Ralph J. Bunche, "Extended Memorandum on the Programs, Ideologies, Tactics, and Achievements of Negro Betterment and Interracial Organizations," unpublished memorandum for Carnegie-Myrdal Study of the Negro in America, 1940, II, 314.

43. Gunnar Myrdal, *An American Dilemma* (New York: Harper & Brothers, 1944), I, 29.

44. Alain Locke, *The New Negro* (New York: Albert and Charles Boni, 1925), pp. xi and 7–8.

45. W. E. B. Du Bois, *The Souls of Black Folk* (Chicago: A. C. McClurg, 1903), p. 4.

NINE

Booker T. Washington and the Town of Mound Bayou

BY AUGUST MEIER

In the face of markedly increasing racial discrimination and proscription, North and South, during the generation follow-ing Reconstruction, Negroes tended to turn from philosophies of political activity and agitation for immediate integration and constitutional rights to ideologies of economic advancement, self-help, and racial solidarity. It is in the all-Negro com-munities founded during the late nineteenth and early twen-tieth centuries (most extensively in Oklahoma)[1] that we find this latter cluster of ideas institutionalized in its most radical form.

Easily the most famous of these settlements was Mound Bayou, Mississippi, even though its eminence was due less to its material prosperity than to the favor of Tuskegee Institute, the beneficence of northern philanthropy, and the fame of its col-orful inhabitants. In its struggles and vicissitudes, it well repre-sented both the ideological outlook of the all-Negro towns and the grave difficulties inherent in the application of this philosophy. The town was established in 1887 by Isaiah T. Montgomery (who later became famous—or infamous—for his defense of disfranchisement in the Mississippi Constitutional Convention of 1890), on an isolated piece of fertile Yazoo-Mississippi Delta land, whose chief advantage lay in its location along the railroad from which it was acquired. The communi-ty's other leading citizen was Charles Banks, one of the chief figures in Booker T. Washington's National Negro Business League, a man described by Washington as "not, by any means,

From *Phylon*, 15 (Fourth Quarter, 1954), 396–401. Reprinted with permission from *Phylon*. © 1953 by Atlanta University.

the wealthiest, but I think I am safe in saying . . . the most influential, Negro business man in the United States" and "the leading Negro banker in Mississippi."[2] The town boomed with a sawmill, a bank, a Farmers' Co-Operative Mercantile Company, real estate ventures, a cottonseed oil mill, and other enterprises.

In a manner characteristic of the Tuskegee group, Banks and Montgomery asserted the philosophy of salvation through economic development and bourgeois virtues with the help of the "best white people," and through self-help and racial cooperation and "taking advantage of the disadvantages" of segregation, rather than through the exercise of the franchise and the defense of civil rights. But overtly and covertly they were involved intimately in political matters. Indeed, as J. Saunders Redding suggests, there was something paradoxical about Montgomery founding a town where Negroes might manage their own affairs, and yet three years later acting as the apologist for disfranchisement.[3] This gentleman, in fact, for some years enjoyed a political plum in the federal land office in Jackson. Banks, endorsed by local whites, was appointed supervisor of the census for the third district of Mississippi in 1900,[4] and various letters in the Booker T. Washington Papers reveal that he was involved deeply in Mississippi Republican politics—as interested, for example, in the distribution of patronage and in fighting the lily-whites.[5]

Tuskegee was intimately concerned with Mound Bayou. Washington's private secretary, Emmett J. Scott, invested in the town's bank.[6] Washington himself thought of Mound Bayou not as a mere town, but as a "place where a Negro may get inspiration by seeing what other members of his race have accomplished . . . [and] where he has an opportunity to learn some of the fundamental duties and responsibilities of social and civic life."[7] Indeed, he once declared that outside of Tuskegee, there was "no community in the world" in which he was "so deeply interested" as Mound Bayou.[8]

During the last seven years of Washington's life, moreover, Tuskegee exerted every effort to get northern philanthropy interested in Mound Bayou. During 1908, "the Wizard" tried to maneuver either Rockefeller or Carnegie to finance a school or a library (respectively) for the community. On December 2, for example, Scott advised Banks to write to the two philanthropists, informing them of President Roosevelt's favorable comments on the town and telling them that Washington had visited Mound Bayou and could give them further information. This, said Scott, would pave the way for "the Doctor" to approach them. In February of the next year Washington did discuss the matter with Carnegie, who donated $4,000 for a library on condition that Mound Bayou appropriate $400 annually for its maintenance.[9] Having obtained the building, however, the wily Mound Bayouans failed to live up to their end of the agreement, for in 1912 we find Scott complaining of reports that the library was housing not books, but Masonic headquarters.[10] Nevertheless, in the latter year the town received a thousand-dollar gift from the Rosenwald Fund for a school.[11]

Furthermore, apparently at Washington's suggestion, the leaders of Mound Bayou tried to attract northern capital into the community in order to develop the surrounding rural area and further the prosperity of the town. For one thing, they hoped that philanthropically minded capitalists might invest in agricultural lands, selling modest plots to prospective farmers on reasonable terms.[12] In 1912, Montgomery was in New York appealing to prospective investors with a six-page pamphlet entitled *Introduction to Mound Bayou.* Whatever other success he may have had (and it is not clear that he had any), it is certain that Montgomery, with Washington's assistance, was able to interest Julius Rosenwald in the cotton oil mill, the most ambitious undertaking at Mound Bayou. The mill, opened with impressive ceremonies (including an address by Washington himself) on November 26, 1912, was reportedly valued at $100,000 and was advertised as being entirely owned and constructed by Negroes.[13]

Even before its opening, Montgomery had been busy discussing financial propositions with Rosenwald; but it was not until February, 1913, that Banks and Rosenwald, conferring at Tuskegee, arranged for the latter to take $25,000 of the $40,000 worth of bonds to be issued at 6 percent interest, the whole to be secured by a first mortgage on the entire property, half of the sum to be guaranteed personally by Banks.[14] The remaining bonds were bought by B. B. Harvey, a white man from Memphis, who leased the mill. By February, 1914, all but $20,000 of the $100,000 stock issue of the Mound Bayou Oil Mill and Manufacturing Company had been sold, and Montgomery was trying to dispose of the remainder in Chicago.[15]

Rosenwald's investment in the mill soon proved to be more philanthropic than profitable. For one thing, the times were not propitious, in view of the depression of 1914. For another, B. B. Harvey proved a scoundrel, though Rosenwald was not informed of this fact until much later. By February, 1915, however, Banks deemed it advisable to suggest to Washington that Rosenwald might send an agent to Mound Bayou to look over the situation and put it "on a paying basis," as a little extra assistance might prevent a failure. He felt constrained to turn down an offer from a Procter and Gamble subsidiary to run the mill, he said, because it would involve "the loss of our identity as a race with the Oil Mill."[16] It appeared that part of the difficulty lay in the failure of Harvey's Memphis mill, and Banks was hoping to force Harvey out of the Mound Bayou establishment and operate it entirely under Negro direction.[17] Furthermore, it developed that the mill's financial agent had sold some stock under false pretenses, and indeed had been pocketing much of the money himself.[18] Finally, late in 1915, the mill's attorney informed Rosenwald of the real state of affairs. Harvey, it seemed, had leased the mill for five years, on the understanding that he would use Rosenwald's $25,000 as a fund for operating purposes, and pay the outstanding debts from the remaining $15,000 of bonds. At the close of the first year, however, Harvey refused to submit any financial statement, and Banks, Montgomery, and others were compelled to pay the arrears of interest, taxes, and insurance. It was later charged in fact that Harvey had illegally obtained possession of the bonds and negotiated them. During the second year the mill ran only half-time until January, 1915, when it suspended operations entirely. Harvey had been able to delay legal action to cancel his contract by obtaining a change of venue. The attorney concluded by recommending that the mill remain idle for the rest of the season.[19] Then, in order to keep Rosenwald's good will, Scott, at Banks's request, spoke to the philanthropist of the heroic efforts of the leaders of Mound Bayou to forestall the evil designs of certain local white men who wanted to see the mill confiscated. Rosenwald assured Scott that he still retained his confidence in Banks and the oil mill company, though he thought that the small size of the town and the current depression had caused serious difficulties. He wished to see his own interests protected, but Scott was sure that he had spoken so effectively to Rosenwald as to prevent any "disposition on his part to be unduly exacting or oppressive."[20]

Meanwhile, Rosenwald had proven of assistance also to the Bank of Mound Bayou. This institution, founded in 1904 with Charles Banks as cashier, shared the difficulties common to Negro banks in this period[21] and encountered serious difficulties during the depression of 1914. In response to an anxious inquiry from Scott, who had invested substantially in the bank's stock, one of its officials replied that "Frankly, the Bank is in a Hell of a Fix." It appeared, he continued, that a large part of the difficulty lay (as in the case of many Negro banks[22]) in the fact that its "ample assets" could "not be converted into cash."[23] By May, Banks was appealing to Tuskegee for funds to save the bank; in June, Washington met him in Chicago, and Rosenwald came to the rescue with a loan of $5,000.[24] Nevertheless, the state banking authorities soon forced the bank to close.[25] The situation looked bleak indeed for the citizens of Mound Bayou and its environs in the fall of 1914. Cotton prices were low; and white banks in nearby towns, no longer competing with the Mound Bayou institution, raised their interest charges, and even began dictating to landowners how much they should charge for rent and insisting that cotton be brought to their towns for ginning. Heroic efforts were made, therefore, to rehabilitate the bank.[26] Washington was delighted that Montgomery and Banks, who apparently had been at odds, were working together in this situation.[27]

The bank situation improved slowly during 1915, though, as we have seen, the oil mill matter was growing steadily worse. An effort to indict the bank officials failed. Banks complained that there had been no evidence of a criminal act, or even of irregularities, or shortages. The examiners' charge that the bank's securities were worthless was false, he said, because it was based upon the fact that the securities represented Negro properties in a Negro town. He looked forward to opening a new Mound Bayou State Bank in June, 1915.[28] The state banking authorities, however, created further obstructions, and it was not until September that they "backed down" and approved "a proposition for the opening of the bank."[29] To Washington's delight, the bank finally opened on October 21.[30] Banks was not a stockholder or officer in the new bank, but he did furnish $11,000 of the $12,000 which the state banking authorities had required the bank officials to raise.[31]

Thus it is apparent that behind the facade of optimism and self-assurance, behind the assertions of prosperity and success, there lay a story of vicissitudes and indeed ultimate failure, even with the whole-hearted support of Tuskegee and the substantial aid of northern philanthropy. Mound Bayou never fulfilled its expectations, and visitors during the last twenty years have found a sleepy, dilapidated town, declining in population, but nevertheless still aggressively proud of its mission and justifying the "advantages of the disadvantages" in segregation.[32]

Mound Bayou was then chiefly noteworthy as an effort to implement or institutionalize ideologies of self-help, economic development, and racial solidarity that were widespread and rather popular during the Age of Booker T. Washington. Yet it appears that in the case of Mound Bayou, at least, the attempt to create a segregated community within the larger American society, an *imperium in imperio*, as contemporaries sometimes called it, was doomed to failure—even, as in this case, with the support of northern philanthropy. The evidence in the Booker T. Washington Papers is especially significant because it documents so clearly the gulf between ideology and practice at Mound Bayou. Self-help and racial solidarity were not, as even Banks and Montgomery realized, a sufficient base upon which to erect a successful economy and community.[33]

1. Mozell C. Hill, "The All-Negro Communities of Oklahoma: The Natural History of a Social Movement," *Journal of Negro History*, 31, no. 3 (July, 1946), 254–68.

2. Booker T. Washington, *My Larger Education* (Garden City, N.Y., 1911), pp. 207–8.

3. J. Saunders Redding, *No Day of Triumph* (New York, 1942), p. 299.

4. Washington, *My Larger Education*, p. 210.

5. *E.g.*, Charles Banks to Booker T. Washington, Mar. 12, Apr. 5, 1909, etc.; Banks to Washington, Oct. 25, 1915. All letters referred to in this article are in the Booker T. Washington Papers, Library of Congress.

6. See esp. Emmett J. Scott to W. P. Kyle, Mar. 30, 1914.

7. Washington, *My Larger Education*, p. 209.

8. Washington to Isaiah T. Montgomery, Jan. 23, 1915.

9. Washington to Banks, Feb. 10, 1909; Banks to James Bertram, Carnegie's secretary, Feb. 16, 1909.

10. Scott to Banks, Jan. 20, 1912.

11. Banks to Washington, Sept. 2, 1912.

12. Banks to Scott, Jan. 13, 1911.

13. Correspondence of Washington and Banks, 1912, *passim*.

14. Banks to Rosenwald, May 13, 1912; Washington to Banks, July 8, 1912; Rosenwald to Banks, Feb. 25, 1913.

15. Banks to William C. Graves, Rosenwald's secretary, Feb. 14, 1914.

16. Banks to Washington, Feb. 15, 1915.

17. *Ibid.*, Apr. 14, 1915.

18. *Ibid.*, Sept. 30, 1915.

19. T. W. Owens to William C. Graves, Oct. 5, 1915.

20. Scott to Banks, Nov. 13, 1915.

21. Abram L. Harris, *The Negro as Capitalist* (Philadelphia, 1936).

22. *Ibid.*, pp. 54–60.

23. Scott to W. P. Kyle, Mar. 30, 1914; Kyle to Scott, Apr. 14, 1914.

24. Banks to Washington, May 9, June 14 and 16, 1914, and Feb. 15, 1915. Scott to Kyle, June 8, 1914.

25. Form letter to bank depositors, Aug. 22, 1914.

26. Montgomery to Washington, Jan. 20, 1915.

27. Washington to Montgomery, Jan. 25, 1915.

28. Banks to Washington, Apr. 14, 1915.

29. Banks to Washington, July 14 and Sept. 30, 1915.

30. Washington to Banks, Oct. 7, 1915, and Banks to Washington, Oct. 22, 1915.

31. Banks to Scott, Oct. 25, 1915.

32. Charles S. Johnson, *Growing Up in the Black Belt* (Washington, 1941), p. 250; Redding, *No Day of Triumph*, pp. 281–301; and "Negro Die Hards," Editorial, *Ebony*, 9, no. 6 (Apr., 1954), 76.

33. See also Harris, *Negro as Capitalist*, ch. 9, for critique of the ideology of a segregated economy.

TEN

Black Violence in the Twentieth Century: A Study in Rhetoric and Retaliation

BY ELLIOTT RUDWICK AND AUGUST MEIER

For most Americans, the increasingly overt talk of retaliatory violence among Negro militants, and the outbreaks in the urban ghettos over recent summers, signify something new and different in the history of Negro protest. Actually, retaliatory violence has never been entirely absent from Negro thinking. Moreover, advocacy of retaliatory violence, and actual instances of it, have tended to increase during periods of heightened Negro protest activity.

Thus the past decade of rising Negro militance has been no stranger to the advocacy of retaliatory violence. For example, as far back as 1959, Robert F. Williams, at the time president of the Monroe, North Carolina, branch of the NAACP, came to public attention when the Union County Superior Court acquitted two white men of brutal assaults on two Negro women, but sentenced a mentally retarded Negro to imprisonment as a result of an argument he had with a white woman. Williams angrily told a reporter, "We cannot take these people who do us injustice to the court, and it becomes necessary to punish them ourselves. If it's necessary to stop lynching with lynching, then we must be willing to resort to that method." The NAACP dismissed Williams as branch president, but he remained a leader of Monroe's working-class Negroes, who for several years had been using guns to protect their homes from white

From Hugh Davis Graham and Ted Robert Gurr, eds., *Violence in America: Historical and Comparative Perspectives*, A Staff Report to the National Commission on the Causes and Prevention of Violence (Washington, D.C.: U.S. Government Printing Office, 1969), pp. 307–16.

Klansmen. In 1961, falsely charged with kidnaping a white couple, he fled the country. Williams became the most famous of that group of militants existing at the fringe of the civil rights movement, who in their complete alienation from American society articulated a revolutionary synthesis of nationalism and Marxism.[1] From his place of exile in Havana, Cuba, Williams undertook the publication of a monthly newsletter, *The Crusader*. In a typical issue he declared:

> Our only logical and successful answer is to meet organized and massive violence with massive and organized violence. . . . The weapons of defense employed by Afro-American freedom fighters must consist of a poor man's arsenal. . . . Molotov cocktails, lye, or acid bombs [made by injecting lye or acid in the metal end of light bulbs] can be used extensively. During the night hours such weapons, thrown from roof tops, will make the streets impossible for racist cops to patrol. . . . Yes, a minority war of self-defense can succeed.[2]

Subsequently Williams was named chairman in exile of an organization known as the Revolutionary Action Movement (RAM),[3] a tiny group of college-educated people in a few major northern cities, some of whose members have been recently charged with plotting the murder of Roy Wilkins and Whitney Young.

Williams, RAM, and the better-known Black Muslims[4] were on the fringes of the Negro protest of the early 1960's. More recently violence and the propaganda for violence have moved closer to the center of the race relations stage. Well over 200 riots have occurred since the summer of 1964. The incendiary statements of the Rap Browns and the Stokely Carmichaels became familiar TV and newspaper fare for millions of white Americans. The Oakland, California, Black Panthers and other local groups espousing a nationalist and revolutionary rhetoric thrived and received national publicity. As has been often pointed out, there is no evidence that the race riots of the 1960's have any direct relations to the preachings of Williams, of these various groups, even of the SNCC advocates of armed rebellion and guerrilla warfare. Yet both the statements of these ideologists, and the spontaneous actions of the masses, have much in common. For both are the product of the frustra-

tions resulting from the growing disparity between the Negroes' status in American society and the rapidly rising expectations induced by the civil rights revolution and its earlier successes.

Historically, this doctrine of retaliatory violence has taken
various forms. Some have advocated self-defense against a
specific attack. Others have called for revolutionary violence.
There are also those who hopefully predicted a general race
war in which Negroes would emerge victorious. Though seldom articulated for white ears, and only rarely appearing in
print, thoughts of violent retaliation against whites have been
quite common. For example, Ralph Bunche, in preparing a
memorandum for Gunnar Myrdal's *American Dilemma* in 1940,
noted that "there are Negroes, too, who, fed up with frustration
of their life here, see no hope and express an angry desire 'to
shoot their way out of it.' I have on many occasions heard
Negroes exclaim, 'Just give us machine guns and we'll blow the
lid off the whole damn business.' "[5]

In surveying the history of race relations during the twentieth century, it is evident that there have been two major
periods of upsurge, both in overt discussion by Negro intellectuals concerning the desirability of violent retaliation against
white oppressors, and also in dramatic incidents of actual social
violence committed by ordinary Negro citizens. One was the
period during and immediately after World War I. The second
has been the period of the current civil rights revolution.

W. E. B. Du Bois, the noted protest leader and a founder of
the NAACP, occasionally advocated retaliatory violence and
somewhat more often predicted intense racial warfare in which
Negroes would be the victors. In 1916, inspired by the Irish
Rebellion, in an editorial in the NAACP's official organ, *The
Crisis*, he admonished Negro youth to stop spouting platitudes
of accommodation and remember that no people ever achieved
their liberation without an armed struggle. He said that "war is
hell, but there are things worse than hell, as every Negro
knows."[6] Amid the violence and repression that Negroes experienced in the postwar world, Du Bois declared that the
holocaust of World War I was "nothing to compare with that
fight for freedom which black and brown and yellow men must

and will make unless their oppression and humiliation and insult at the hands of the White World cease."[7]

Other intellectuals reflected this restless mood. The postwar years were the era of the militant, race-conscious New Negro of the urban North, an intellectual type who rejected the gradualism and conciliation of his ancestors. The tone of the New Negro was recorded by Claude McKay, who in 1919 wrote his well-known poem, "If We Must Die": "If we must die/let it not be like hogs; hunted and penned in an accursed spot!/. . . If we must die; oh, let us nobly die/dying but fighting back." A. Philip Randolph, editor of the militant socialist monthly, *The Messenger*, organizer of the Brotherhood of Sleeping Car Porters, and later leader of the March on Washington Movements of 1941 and 1963, also advocated physical resistance to white mobs. He observed that "Anglo-Saxon jurisprudence recognizes the law of self-defense. . . . The black man has no rights which will be respected unless the black man enforces that respect. . . . We are consequently urging Negroes and other oppressed groups concerned with lynching or mob violence to act upon the recognized and accepted law of self-defense."[8]

The legality of retaliatory violent self-defense was asserted not only by A. Philip Randolph, but also by the NAACP, which Randolph regarded as a moderate if not futile organization, wedded to the interest of the Negro middle class. In 1925, half a dozen years after the *Messenger* article, the NAACP secured the acquittal of Dr. Ossian Sweet and his family. The Sweets were Detroit Negroes who had moved into a white neighborhood and fired on a stone-throwing mob in front of their home, killing one white man and wounding another.[9] More than a quarter of a century later, at the time of the Robert Williams episode, the NAACP in clarifying its position reiterated the stand that "The NAACP has never condoned mob violence but it firmly supports the right of Negroes individually and collectively to defend their person, their homes, and their property from attack. This position has always been the policy of the NAACP."[10] The views of intellectuals like Du Bois, McKay, and Randolph during World War I and the early postwar years paralleled instances of Negro retaliatory violence which actually triggered some of the major race riots of the period.

The East St. Louis riot of 1917, the bloodiest in the twentieth century, was precipitated in July when Negroes, having been waylaid and beaten repeatedly by white gangs, shot into a police car and killed two white detectives. On the darkened street a Negro mob of 50 to 100 evidently mistook the Ford squad car for the Ford automobile containing white "joyriders" who had shot up Negro homes earlier in the evening. The following morning the riot began.[11]

In Houston, several weeks later, about a hundred Negro soldiers broke into an army ammunition storage room and marched on the city's police station. The troops, mostly Northerners, were avenging an incident which occurred earlier in the day, when a white policeman used force in arresting a Negro woman and then beat up a Negro soldier attempting to intervene. A Negro provost guard was pistol whipped and shot at for asking the policeman about the wounded soldier. Even before these events, the Negro soldiers nursed a hatred for Houston policemen, who had attempted to enforce streetcar segregation, frequently used the term "nigger," and officiously patrolled the Negro ghetto. The Houston riot was unusual not only because it involved Negro soldiers, but also because white persons constituted most of the fatalities.[12]

By 1919 there was evidence that the Negro masses were prepared to fight back in many parts of the country, even in the Deep South. In an unpublished report to the NAACP Board of Directors, a staff member, traveling in Tennessee and Mississippi during early 1919, noted that "bloody conflicts impended in a number of southern cities." Perry Howard, the leading colored attorney in Jackson, and R. R. Church, the wealthy Memphis politician, both reported that Negroes were armed and prepared to defend themselves from mob violence. Howard detailed an incident in which armed Negroes had prevented a white policeman from arresting a Negro who had become involved in a fight with two white soldiers after they had slapped a colored girl. In Memphis, R. R. Church, fearing armed conflict, privately advised the city's mayor that "the Negroes would not make trouble unless they were attacked, but in that event they were prepared to defend themselves."[13]

The Chicago race riot of 1919 grew out of Negro resentment

of exclusion from a bathing beach dominated by whites. One Sunday, while Negroes and whites scuffled on the beach, a colored teenager drowned after being attacked in the swimming area. That attack was the most recent of a long series of assaults against Negroes. A white policeman not only refused to arrest a white man allegedly involved in the drowning, but actually attempted to arrest one of the two complaining Negroes. The officer was mobbed and soon the rioting was underway.[14]

The Elaine, Arkansas, riot of 1919 was precipitated when two white law officers shot into a Negro church; the Negroes returned the fire, causing one death. The white planters in the area, already angered because Negro cottonpickers were seeking to unionize and obtain an increase in their sharecropping wages, embarked upon a massive Negro hunt to put the black peons "in their place."[15]

The Tulsa riot of 1921 originated when a crowd of armed Negroes assembled before the courthouse to protest the possible lynching of a Negro who had just been arrested for allegedly attacking a white girl. The Negroes shot at white police and civilians who attempted to disperse them.[16]

In each of these conflagrations, the typical pattern was initial Negro retaliation to white acts of persecution and violence, and white perception of this resistance as an organized, premeditated conspiracy to "take over," thus unleashing the massive armed power of white mobs and police. In the southern communities, Negro resistance tended to collapse early in the riots. After the church incident in the rural Elaine area, most Negroes passively accepted the planters' armed attacks on their homes. At Tulsa, Negroes retreated from the courthouse to the ghetto, and throughout the night held off by gunfire the assaults of white mobs. But after daybreak many Negroes fled or surrendered before the white onslaught burned down much of the ghetto.[17] One exception to this pattern was the Washington riot of 1919, where it appears that Negroes did not retaliate until the third and last day of the riot.[18]

Negro resistance generally lasted longer in northern riots than in southern ones, but even in East St. Louis and Chicago the death toll told the story: in East St. Louis, nine whites and at least thirty-nine Negroes were killed. In Chicago, fifteen whites and twenty-three Negroes lost their lives. Negroes attacked a small number of whites found in the ghetto or on its fringes. Negro fatalities mainly occurred when victims were trapped in white-dominated downtown areas or residential sections. Negroes were also attacked on the edges of their neighborhood in a boundary zone separating a colored residential district from a lower-class white area.[19] In the face of overwhelming white numerical superiority, many armed Negroes fled their homes, leaving guns and ammunition behind. In East St. Louis, for example, there was a constant rattle of small explosions when fire enveloped a small colored residential district. Perhaps psychological factors contributed to the terrified inactivity of some Negroes. Despite the wish to meet fire with fire, over the years they had become so demoralized by white supremacy and race discrimination that effective armed defense could exist only in the realm of psychological fantasy.

During World War II, the most important race riot erupted in 1943 in Detroit, where nine whites and twenty-five Negroes were killed. In many respects the riot exhibited a pattern similar to East St. Louis and Chicago. The precipitating incident involved an attack on whites at the Belle Isle Amusement Park by several Negro teenagers who, a few days earlier, had been ejected from the white-controlled Eastwood Park. In the mounting tension at Belle Isle, many fights between Negroes and whites broke out, and the violence spread to the Negro ghetto, where patrons at a nightclub were urged to "take care of a bunch of whites who killed a colored woman and her baby at Belle Isle." Although there had been no fatalities at the park, the nightclub emptied and vengeful Negroes stoned passing cars driven by whites. They began smashing windows on the ghetto's main business street, where the mob's major attention was directed to destroying and looting white-owned businesses.[20]

It was this symbolic destruction of "whitey" through his property that gave the Detroit holocaust the characteristic of what we may call the "new style" race riot. It may be noted that in all the riots discussed above, there were direct clashes between Negroes and whites, and the major part of the violence was perpetrated by the white mobs. The riot pattern since the summer of 1964, however, has involved Negro aggression mainly against white-owned property, not against white people. This "new style" riot first appeared in Harlem in 1935 and 1943.[21] The modern riot does not involve white mobs at all, and policemen or guardsmen constitute most of the relatively small number of casualties.

One can identify perhaps two major factors responsible for this contrast between the old and the new-style riot. One is the relatively marked shift in the climate of race relations in this country over the past generation. On the one hand, whites have become, on the whole, more sensitive to the Negro's plight, more receptive toward Negro demands, and less punitive in their response to Negro aggression. The black masses, on the other hand, have raised their expectations markedly and, disillusioned by the relatively slow pace of social change which has left the underprivileged urban Negro of the North scarcely, if at all, better off than he was ten or fifteen years ago, have become more restless and militant than before.

In the second place, there is an ecological factor. From South to North, the migration of the World War I period was a mere drop in the bucket compared to what it later became. The migration to the North in each of the decades since 1940 has been equal to or greater than the migration of the whole thirty-year period from 1910 to 1940. At the same time, owing to the Supreme Court's outlawing of the restrictive covenant in 1948, and the tearing down of the older slums through urban renewal, the Negro population has been dispersed over a wider area, thus accentuating the trend toward the development of vast ghettos. Indeed, compared to the enormous ghettos of today, the Negro residential areas of the World War I period were mere enclaves. Today, of course, Negroes are close to becoming a majority in several of the major American cities.

The character of American race riots has been markedly affected by these demographic changes. Even if white mobs were to form, they would be unable to attack and burn down the Negro residential areas; even in the nineteenth and early twentieth-century riots, white mobs did not usually dare to invade the larger Negro sections, and destroyed only the smaller areas of Negro concentration. Nor, since the Negroes are such a large share of the population of the central city areas, would white mobs today be in a position to chase, beat, and kill isolated Negroes on downtown streets. More important, from the Negroes' point of view, the large-scale ghettos provide a relatively safe place for the destruction and looting of white-owned property. It is impossible for local police forces to guard business property in the farflung ghettos; even state police and federal troops find themselves in hostile territory where it is difficult to chase down rioters beyond the principal thoroughfares.

It is notable that during the twentieth century, both the overt discussion of the advisability of violent retaliation on the part of Negroes, and also actual incidents of violence were prominent in the years during and after World War I, and again during the 1960's. While there have been significant differences between the outbreaks characteristic of each era, there have been also important similarities. In both periods retaliatory violence accompanied a heightened militancy among American Negroes—a militancy described as the "New Negro" in the years after World War I, and described in the 1960's with the phrase, "the Negro Revolt." In neither case was retaliatory violence the major tactic or the central thrust, but in both periods it was a significant subordinate theme. However, in both periods a major factor leading Negroes to advocate or adopt such a tactic was the gap between Negro aspiration and objective status. The rapid escalation of the aspirations of the Negro masses who shared Martin Luther King's "dream" and identify vicariously with the success of the civil rights revolution, while their own economic, housing, and educational opportunities have not improved, is a phenomenon of such frequent comment that it requires no elaboration here.

A comparable situation occurred during and shortly after World War I. The agitation of the recently founded NAACP, whose membership doubled in 1918–19, the propaganda of fighting a war to make the world safe for democracy, and especially the great Negro migration to the northern cities which southern peasants and workers viewed as a promised land, all created new hopes for the fulfillment of age-old dreams, while Negro soldiers who had served in France returned with new expectations. But the Negro's new hopes collided with increasing white hostility. Northern Negroes assigned to southern army camps met indignities unknown at home. They rioted at Houston and came so close to rioting in Spartanburg, South Carolina, that the army hastily shipped them overseas. In the northern cities like East St. Louis and Chicago, Negroes found not a promised land, but overcrowded ghettos and hostile white workers who feared Negro competition for their jobs. The Ku Klux Klan was revived beginning in 1915 and grew rapidly in the North and South after the war ended. By 1919 economic opportunities plummeted as factories converted to peacetime operations. For a while Negroes resisted, protested, fought back, in the South as well as the North; but the superior might of the whites proved overpowering and the southern Negroes retreated into old paths of accommodation, where they generally remained until the momentous events of the past decade.

There has been no systematic research on Negro advocacy of violence prior to World War I, but the available evidence supports the thesis that increased overt expression of this tendency accompanies peaks in other kinds of protest activity. For example, it appears likely that Negro resistance to white rioters was minimal in the riots at the turn of the century—at Wilmington, North Carolina, in 1898, and at New Orleans, Akron, and New York in 1900[22]—which took place in a period when the sentiment of accommodation to white supremacy, epitomized by Booker T. Washington, was in the ascendancy.

Again, during the antebellum period, one can cite two noted cases of incendiary statements urging Negroes to revolt—*David Walker's Appeal* of 1829, and the Reverend Henry Highland Garnet's suppressed *Address to the Slaves of the United States of America*, delivered at the national Negro convention of 1843.[23] Both coincided with periods of rising militant protest activity on the part of the northern free Negroes. *Walker's Appeal* appeared on the eve of the Negro Convention Movement, and at the time of intensified Negro opposition to the expatriation plans of the American Colonization Society.[24] Garnet's speech was made at a time when free Negro leaders were disturbed at the prejudiced attitudes of white abolitionists who refused to concern themselves with obtaining rights for the free people of color, or to allow Negroes to participate in the inner circles of the leadership of the antislavery societies. Consequently they had revived the Negro national convention movement which had been inactive since 1836. (Garnet's speech was also in part a product of disillusionment with the lack of actual progress being made by the antislavery societies toward achieving abolition.)

We lack any careful analysis of race riots during the nineteenth century. Some certainly were pogrom-like affairs, in which the Negroes were so thoroughly terrorized from the beginning that they failed to fight back. (Perhaps the Draft Riots, and some of the Reconstruction riots as in Mississippi in 1876 were of this sort.) Yet other riots were characterized by some degree of Negro retaliatory violence, such as the Snow Hill riot in Providence in 1831, and the Cincinnati riots of 1841. Both appear to have been, like the Chicago and East St. Louis riots, the climaxes to a series of interracial altercations. In the Providence riot, a mob of about a hundred white sailors and citizens advanced on a small Negro section; a Negro shot a sailor dead, and within a half-hour a large mob descended upon the neighborhood, damaging many houses.[25] In the Cincinnati riot, a pitched battle was fought on the streets; the blacks had enough guns and ammunition to fire into the mob such a volley that it was twice repulsed. Only when the mob secured an iron six-pounder and hauled it to the place of combat and fired on the Negroes were the latter forced to retreat, permitting the rioters to hold sway for two days without interference from the authorities.[26] A careful study of interracial violence during Reconstruction will undoubtedly produce evidence of comparable situations. These riots occurred at a time of high Negro expectations and self-assertiveness, and seem to have been characterized by a significant amount of fighting back on the part of Negroes.

One period of marked and rising Negro militance, however, was not accompanied by a significant increase in manifestations of Negro retaliatory violence. This was the one following World War II. Indeed, that war itself witnessed far less Negro violence than did World War I. The reason for this would appear to be that the 1940's and early 1950's were years of gradually improving Negro status, and a period in which the expectations of the masses did not greatly outrun the actual improvements being made. In fact, from 1941 until the mid-1950's the relative position of the Negro workers, as compared to the white wage-earners, was generally improving; it was not until the recession of 1954–55, for example, that the Black Muslims, with their rhetoric of race hatred and retaliatory violence, began to expand rapidly.

It would appear that both in the World War I period and today—and indeed, during the antebellum era and at other times when manifestations of violence came to the fore—there has been a strong element of fantasy in Negro discussion and efforts concerning violent retaliation. Robert Williams talked of Molotov cocktails and snarling up traffic as devices for a largely poverty-stricken ethnic minority to engineer a revolution. The Black Muslims talk of violence, but the talk seems to function as a psychological safety valve; by preaching separation, they in effect accommodate to the American social order and place racial warfare off in the future when Allah in his time will destroy the whites and usher in an era of black domination. Similarly, in view of population statistics and power distribution in American society, Du Bois and others who have spoken of the inevitability of racial warfare and Negro victory in such a struggle were engaging in wishful prophecies. And Negroes have been nothing if not realistic. The patterns of Negro behavior in riots demonstrate this. In earlier times, as already indicated, those who bought guns in anticipation of the day when self-defense would be necessary usually did not retaliate. And Negro attacks on whites occurred mainly in the early stages of the riots before the full extent of anger and power and sadism of the white mobs became evident.

Negroes of the World War I era resisted white insults and attacks only as long as they had hopes of being successful in the resistance. It should be emphasized that one of the remarkable things about the riots since 1964, in spite of their having been marked by particular resentment at police brutality, is the fact that Negro destruction was aimed at white-owned property, not white lives, even after National Guardsmen and policemen killed scores of Negroes. And in those cases where retaliatory violence has been attempted, Negroes have retreated in the face of massive white armed force. Economically impoverished

Negroes press as far as they realistically can; and one reason for the explosions of recent years has been the awareness that whites are to some degree in retreat, that white mobs in the North no longer organize to attack, and that to a large degree the frustrated Negroes in slums like Watts, Detroit, Washington, or Newark can get away with acts of destruction.

It is impossible of course to make any foolproof predictions for the future. Yet, judging by past experience and present conditions, it is our view that, despite all the rhetoric of engineering a social revolution through armed rebellion and guerrilla warfare, of planned invasions of downtown business districts and white suburbs, the kind of violence we are likely to witness will, at most, continue to be the sort of outbreaks against the property of white businessmen such as those we have witnessed in recent years. The advocacy and use of violence as a deliberate program for solving the problems of racial discrimination remains thus far, at least, in the realm of fantasy; and there it is likely to remain.

1. For accounts, see Julian Mayfield, "Challenge to Negro Leadership," *Commentary*, 31 (Apr., 1961), 297–305; "The Robert F. Williams Case," *The Crisis*, 66 (June-July, Aug.-Sept., 1959), 325–29, 409–10; Robert F. Williams, *Negroes with Guns* (New York: Marzani & Munsell, 1962).

2. *The Crusader*, 5 (May-June, 1964), 5–6.

3. See the RAM publication *Black America* (Summer-Fall, 1965); *The Crusader*, 6 (Mar., 1965).

4. C. Eric Lincoln, *The Black Muslims in America* (Boston: Beacon Press, 1961)

5. Ralph Bunche, "Conceptions and Ideologies of the Negro Problem," memorandum prepared for the Carnegie-Myrdal Study of the Negro in America, 1940, p. 161.

6. *The Crisis*, 12 (Aug., 1916), 166–67; 13 (Dec., 1916), 63.

7. W. E. B. Du Bois, *Darkwater* (New York, 1920), p. 49.

8. A. Philip Randolph, "How to Stop Lynching," *Messenger*, 3 (Apr., 1919), 8–9.

9. Walter White, "The Sweet Trial," *The Crisis*, 31 (Jan., 1926), 125–29.

10. "The Robert F. Williams Case," p. 327.

11. Elliott M. Rudwick, *Race Riot at East St. Louis* (Carbondale: Southern Illinois University Press, 1964), pp. 38–39.

12. Edgar A. Schuler, "The Houston Race Riot, 1917," *Journal of Negro History*, 29 (Oct., 1944), 300–338.

13. *NAACP Board Minutes*, Secretary's Report, June, 1919 (NAACP office, New York).

14. *The Negro in Chicago* (Chicago, 1922), pp. 4–5.

15. *The Crisis*, 19 (Dec., 1919), 56–62.

16. Allen Grimshaw, "A Study in Social Violence: Urban Race Riots in the U.S." (Ph.D. dissertation, University of Pennsylvania, 1959), pp. 42–47.

17. *Ibid.*

18. Constance M. Green, *Washington, Capital City, 1879–1950* (Princeton: Princeton University Press, 1962), pp. 266–67; John Hope Franklin, *From Slavery to Freedom* (New York: Knopf, 1947), p. 473; *New York Times*, July 20–22, 1919.

19. Rudwick, *Race Riot*, pp. 226–27; *Negro in Chicago*, pp. 5–10.

20. Alfred McClung Lee and Norman D. Humphrey, *Race Riot* (New York, 1943), pp. 26–30.

21. Roi Ottley, *New World A-Coming* (Boston: Beacon Press, 1943), pp. 151–52; Harold Orlansky, *The Harlem Riot: A Study in Mass Frustration* (New York, 1943), pp. 5–6, 14–15; New York *Age*, Mar. 30, 1935, and Aug. 7, 1943.

22. In the New York riot, however, the precipitating incident was a physical altercation between a white policeman and a Negro; see Gilbert Osofsky, *Harlem: The Making of a Ghetto* (New York: Harper & Row, 1966), pp. 46–52.

23. Herbert Aptheker, *A Documentary History of the Negro People in the United States* (New York: Citadel, 1951), pp. 93–97, 226–33.

24. Founded in 1817 by a group of prominent white Americans, the American Colonization Society officially encouraged colonization as a means of furthering the cause of antislavery. Most Negroes, even most of those who themselves at one time or another advocated emigration to Africa or the Caribbean as the only solution for the Negro's hopeless situation in the United States, denounced the Society as a cloak for those attempting to protect slavery by deporting free Negroes.

25. Irving H. Bartlett, "The Free Negro in Providence, Rhode Island," *Negro History Bulletin*, 14 (Dec., 1950), 54.

26. Carter G. Woodson, "The Negroes of Cincinnati prior to the Civil War," *Journal of Negro History*, 1 (Jan., 1916), 13–15.

ELEVEN

Integration vs. Separatism: The NAACP and CORE Face Challenge from Within

BY ELLIOTT RUDWICK AND AUGUST MEIER

The pace both of black activism and of social change in race relations quickened during the early 1960's. Heightened black militancy was most evident in the widespread use of nonviolent direct action tactics which replaced the legalism of the NAACP as the dominant strategy of black protest. The organizations most closely identified with direct action tactics—the Southern Christian Leadership Conference (SCLC), the Student Nonviolent Coordinating Committee (SNCC), and the Congress of Racial Equality (CORE)—seized the headlines. By 1965 public accommodations in the South had been desegregated, and a new law had been passed with enforcement mechanisms upholding the southern blacks' right to vote. Across the North, picketing and sit-ins had also succeeded in opening up many new job opportunities for blacks. Yet, like the earlier strategy of legalism, direct action and legislation that flowed from it proved to be limited instruments for advancing the black man's status in America. The problems of urban police brutality, slum housing, and inferior schooling seemed impervious to attack, and the economic status of the unskilled low-income blacks, North and South, seemed virtually unchanged.

Ironically, although the protest movement had brought blacks closer to the mainstream of American society than ever

This essay is based in part on two articles of ours which originally appeared in *Social Science Quarterly*, 51 (June, 1970): "Organizational Structure and Goal Succession: A Comparative Analysis of the NAACP and CORE, 1964–1968," and "NAACP and CORE: Some Additional Theoretical Considerations." We acknowledge with thanks permission from *Social Science Quarterly* to reprint sections of those articles in this essay.

before, expectations had rapidly outdistanced social change. For many civil rights demonstrators and ghetto-dwellers, the new gains seemed to have been largely token. The euphoria of "Freedom Now" of 1963 was replaced in the more radical sectors of the movement with disillusionment, a loss of faith in the possibility of reforming white racist attitudes, and a belief that blacks alone must find their own salvation. At the same time, the successes of the protest movement had strengthened black pride and the feeling that to fight their battles blacks did not need the help of whites. In this context, there was a rising nationalist sentiment which to the general public suddenly seemed to achieve salience after Stokely Carmichael of SNCC electrified the country during the summer of 1966 with the slogan of "Black Power."

The black community's diverse—and spirited—responses to the cry for "Black Power" revealed that the underlying consensus that had existed among the black protest organizations during the early 1960's had now broken down. Although engaging in lively rivalry and often differing in strategy and tactics, SNCC, SCLC, CORE, and the NAACP—not to mention the National Urban League—had formerly been united in striving for racial integration. Each of these organizations still sought racial equality for black people in the United States, but where the NAACP and SCLC remained committed to integration and to Martin Luther King's dream of "Black and White Together" in a "Beloved Community," CORE and SNCC now announced that they had lost their faith in such a vision and instead took the road of black nationalism and black separatism. Nor was there unity among the apostles of Black Power. Both SNCC and CORE stressed the theme that blacks must control their own destiny, but where SNCC took an anticapitalist revolutionary stance, CORE adopted a reformist position. Without advocating fundamental changes in the American social structure, CORE urged the development of all-black protest organizations, of black capitalism, and of black control of police, education, and other services in ghetto communities. While the organization's leaders sometimes explained that such a separatist program was prerequisite to any long-range integration on a basis of equality, the thrust of their rhetoric was that integration had become an irrelevant issue. In practice they substituted for the goal of integration the goal of black community control over local institutions and the maintenance of a separate Negro community.

This paper seeks to shed light on the varying responses of the different protest organizations to the Black Power thrust through an examination of two of them—the NAACP, which did not change its ideology, and the Congress of Racial Equality, which became radically transformed. At the opening of the 1960's the NAACP and CORE were in fundamental agreement about struggling for an integrated society, assimilating blacks into American life, and fulfilling the democratic, equalitarian values which Gunnar Myrdal has called the American Creed. They differed however, in a number of key respects: tactics, organizational structure, style of leadership, and nature of membership. These differences will be examined in an effort to understand the contrasting ways in which the two organizations responded to the black nationalist thrust a half-dozen years later.

Impressed by the striking contrasts in the structures of CORE and NAACP, we initially assumed that their reactions to "Black Power" largely stemmed from this difference. Structurally, the NAACP and CORE respectively corresponded to what sociologists have called the "corporate-type" and the "federation-type" of voluntary organization. The "corporate-type" is centralized and bureaucratic, consisting of a national headquarters and subordinate local units; the "federation-type" consists of semi-autonomous local affiliates and a weak national structure.[1] On the basis of much sociological literature, one would anticipate that the centralized, rather highly bureaucratic NAACP would be relatively stable in ideology and goals. Similarly, one would expect that CORE, a decentralized organization with a weak national headquarters, only an incipient bureaucracy, and local chapters exhibiting a high degree of autonomy and anti-bureaucratic tendencies, would prove unstable and more easily undergo a radical transformation. However, the situation was more complex, and other factors must be taken into account—notably, the nature of each organization's constituency and leadership. The NAACP and CORE attracted very different kinds of people, both as leaders and as rank-and-file members. Moreover, the nucleus of active people in the NAACP has been far more stable than that in CORE, which was characterized throughout its history by a rapid turnover.

The character of both the NAACP and CORE—and thus the nature of their response to the challenge facing black America and the civil rights movement in the mid-1960's—was rooted in their historical development. Accordingly, a survey of certain key trends in the evolution of each organization is essential to analyzing the problem posed by this paper.[2]

The NAACP was founded in 1909 by a small number of distinguished blacks and reform-minded whites. The black founders were among the most prominent Negroes in the country, even though they represented a minority viewpoint in that period of accommodation known as the Age of Booker T. Washington. The list included leading ministers, lawyers, and editors, the most notable among them being W. E. B. Du Bois. The white leadership ranged from prominent Socialists like William English Walling to the conservative constitutional lawyer and former president of the American Bar Association, Moorfield Storey. Its core consisted of well-to-do, highly distinguished professionals visibly identified with the Progressive movement, the most important of them being Oswald Garrison Villard, grandson of William Lloyd Garrison and publisher of the New York *Evening Post*, and the former Columbia University professor and famous literary critic Joel Spingarn.

Essentially, the NAACP, chartered under the laws of the state of New York, was a self-perpetuating Board of Directors of thirty members which employed a national staff and established local branches over which it possessed strict legal control. In theory, the annual meeting of the Association held in New York City, open to all dues-paying members, was the highest policy-making body of the organization, and it elected the Board of Directors. In actual fact, only a handful attended the yearly meeting of the corporation, and those present regularly endorsed the slate picked by the Board. The large annual conference, attended by delegates from branches across the country, was not a policy-making body but essentially an educational forum for the members and the general public. The NAACP's strategy of litigation in the federal courts and lobbying in Congress for favorable legislation accentuated the importance of the national organization and the New York headquarters. The branches for their part performed three major functions— attacking discrimination at the local level, providing test cases which the national office pursued in the higher courts, and raising money to finance the national program.

CORE began in 1942 as the Chicago Committee of Racial Equality, which was composed primarily of students at the University of Chicago. An offshoot of the pacifist Fellowship of Reconciliation, its founders were middle-class intellectuals, younger, much less prominent and considerably more alienated from the mainstream of American society than were the founders of the NAACP. Like the Association's founders, they were all college-educated people; but unlike them, none came from distinguished or wealthy family backgrounds, and none had achieved any degree of national prominence. Where only one or two of the original NAACP leaders were pacifists, all of the early CORE leaders were, and in fact three of the six persons most active in founding CORE served terms in jail or in CPS camp during World War II. Regarding the NAACP's legalism as too gradualist and ineffective, they aimed to apply Gandhian techniques of nonviolent direct action to the problem of race relations in the United States. In view of the radical pacifist outlook of its founders and early leaders and the unorthodox nature of their sit-in tactics, it is not surprising that for nearly two decades CORE was a relatively obscure agency of civil rights protest. On the other hand, the NAACP, with its elite leadership and its use from the beginning of traditional reformist tactics, was regarded as the preeminent vehicle for black protest.

In 1943, a year after its founding, Chicago CORE joined with half a dozen other groups that had emerged across the country, mostly under the encouragement of the Fellowship of Reconciliation, to form a federation known as the Congress of Racial Equality. Thus, in contrast to the NAACP, which started with a national committee and a national office, CORE began as a federation of local groups, jealous of their own autonomy. In one respect, it is true, CORE was more elitist than the NAACP. For whereas in the NAACP a simple annual payment of a dollar membership fee entitled one to all the privileges of membership, in CORE full—and voting—membership went only to those who worked actively in direct-action projects. CORE chapters thus remained small (generally between twenty and thirty members, and seldom over fifty). They consisted of a band of dedicated activists, for whom CORE tended to become a way of life.

From the point of view of internal structure, CORE was far more decentralized and democratic than the NAACP. Within local CORE affiliates, decisions tended to be made by the chapter as a whole, rather than by the local executive board, as in the NAACP. Again, in contrast to the NAACP, the CORE National Action Council (the counterpart to the NAACP Board of Directors) was elected directly by the annual conventions. In the early years, the decision to affiliate and disaffiliate CORE chapters was generally made by a vote of the groups rather than by the national body, while the annual convention itself selected such staff as there was: the volunteer or subsistence field representatives, and the unpaid national executive secretary.

The CORE groups were extremely reluctant to establish a strong national secretariat, and for years the executive secretary worked on a volunteer part-time basis. The affiliates deliberately rejected the idea of financing the national organization through memberships as practiced by the NAACP, where about half the membership fees went to the national organization. Again, unlike the NAACP, where most of the special fund-raising was the responsibility of the branches, the CORE groups refused to make significant contributions of any sort to finance the national organization. While most of the money flowing into the NAACP national office was raised by the branches, in CORE almost all of the national organization's income came through special fund-raising conducted by the national office. Given this situation, it is not surprising that only in 1957, fifteen years after CORE's founding, did a salaried secretariat appear.[3]

The years produced changes in both organizations, though the basic structure of each was not affected. The NAACP, which had begun as an interracial (and at first a largely white-dominated) organization, soon became overwhelmingly black in both membership and leadership. During its first decade, as it expanded by establishing branches across the country, the Association found its constituency in the black community. As early as 1914, 80 percent of the members were Negroes, and by 1920 the proportion was over 90 percent. In the process the NAACP established close ties with the two dominant institutions in the black community—the fraternal orders and the churches—a tie symbolized by the long tenure as Board chairman of Bishop Stephen Gill Spottswood. At the top the leadership remained interracial longer; not until 1920 was the first black secretary, James Weldon Johnson, appointed. Most of the influential Board members were whites until the 1930's; but even before then, power had largely passed from the Board into the hands of the black secretariat. And by 1935, when the legal work and the key position of Board chairman both passed into Negro hands, black control of the organization was complete. The minority of whites on the national Board and holding offices in the branches were almost always symbolic figures rather than wielders of significant influence in the Association. These changes had flowed quite naturally from the fact that the NAACP's base was in the black community, and from pressures for black control originating in that constituency. They came gradually and without formal changes in the organization's structure.[4]

However, as a result of both criticism by intellectuals outside the NAACP during the 1930's, and periodic internal demands for reform, the Association's method of governance underwent several significant modifications in the following decades. In practice, the annual convention became the highest legislative body, its resolutions establishing the policies and programs for the ensuing year. Although the Board and staff retained considerable discretionary power in implementing these resolutions, the Convention now set the basic policy for the Association. The national Board, which by 1961 had grown to sixty members, was chosen by a complex procedure. Members were elected for three years as previously, with one-third retiring each year—a fact which in itself promoted stability. Of the sixty, twenty-one were elected by the seven regions (three from each region), three by the youth division (as the result of pressures from the young activists in 1960 and 1961), eighteen by the Board, and eighteen at-large. The nominating committee for the at-large candidates consisted of three chosen by the Board and four elected by the convention. The nominating committee's slate, and the names of those nominated by petition, were then submitted to a vote of the branches.[5]

Meanwhile, over the years the NAACP had developed a well-organized and specialized bureaucracy. Experienced executives were placed in charge of branch work, youth work, church work, public relations, branch membership drives, and life memberships. Specialists had been added to the staff since the 1930's through the creation of a legal department, and after World War II there were housing, education, and labor secretaries. At the same time the field staff expanded markedly. Finally, after the NAACP Board consulted a management firm in 1964, the structure was further rationalized, with a strict hierarchical organization, and with much of the authority for internal operations resting in the hands of an assistant executive director, thus freeing the executive director for the larger planning and relationships with outside organizations.[6]

In practice an informal structure evolved, meshing with this formal structure, making for stability in the organization. In theory, the branches and the convention ultimately set policy; in practice, the staff and especially the secretary (since 1964 called the executive director) were the main source. In part this situation was a product of a long tradition of strong secretaries, who worked very closely with the leadership on the Board; in part it was due to the fact that the dynamic nature of the civil rights movement required critical day-to-day decisions by the national secretariat—within the broad framework of NAACP policy, of course. But even though legally the NAACP national office and the Board had control over the branches, in practice the branches acted autonomously in setting their own specific programs and exercised considerable constraints on the policy of the national staff. The fact that the most important function of the branches was to raise money for the national office through annual memberships and special financial appeals in itself required the national office to retain the support of its branches. Thus the power over the branches was clearly subject to serious limitations.[7]

Yet there were also ways in which the national office could influence the situation at the local, state, and regional levels, and thus ultimately in convention voting and elections. Critics of the NAACP's national administration charged that the field secretaries exercised an informal but potent influence at the grass roots in the selection of delegates and candidates.[8] Certainly field secretaries could often channel the program and activities of the branches. Suggestions and advice on policy from national leaders were, naturally, considered seriously by state and local leaders.

Thus there developed a complex web of relationships—between branches and state and regional conferences, between branches and national staff, between state and regional conferences and national staff, between staff and national Board—a network of mutual obligations and constraints and influences that served to promote stability, to prevent any sudden change. The complex system of elections to the Board also prevented sudden change; this body, while less important than the executive secretary in day-to-day policy decisions, still exercised a constraining role—especially when dissident elements were able to articulate their dissatisfactions through a minority faction on the Board. Finally, interlacing and underpinning the whole structure was a deep sense of tradition among NAACP staffers, branch leaders, and Board members. NAACP leaders, especially above the branch level, were almost always people of long experience with the Association, steeped in its traditions and philosophy.[9]

Changes in CORE's structure came about through a series of crises in the organization's history. In the middle 1950's, for a number of reasons which space prevents us from discussing, CORE had declined nearly to the point of extinction. A vigorous fund-raising campaign, followed in 1957 by the creation of a paid full-time executive secretary and field worker, paved the way for extensive growth and development. The organization's extraordinary expansion in the early 1960's and the challenge created by the events of the period led to growth in the power of the National Action Council and in the size and functions of the national staff. Nevertheless, CORE's bureaucracy must be regarded essentially as incipient, rather than fully developed. For one thing, CORE's method of nonviolent direct action meant that dedication, a long record of activism, arrests, and time in jail were often more important as job qualifications, particularly for field staff, than technical knowledge or expertise. Moreover, though new positions were created as CORE expanded, the national staff remained relatively unspecialized,[10] there was a tendency for individuals to shift from one office to another, and there were serious cases of overlapping jurisdictions that sometimes led to conflict. Unlike the NAACP, where growth and specialization of the staff were an orderly process, in CORE there was much instability, frequent reshuffling of positions by the National Action Council, and considerable experimentation in an effort to create a more efficient mechanism to meet the challenges posed by the rapid developments of the 1960's.

Meanwhile the local chapters remained as autonomous as before, and had, if anything, less to do with the national affairs of the organization. Without any financial responsibility for national interests, the chapters almost entirely pursued local ones. The National Action Council, however, did grow in influence. Constitutionally, it, instead of the convention, now selected the national director; to it had been delegated the major responsibility regarding affiliation of chapters.

Officially, of course, the convention remained the highest policy-making body of the organization; but in fact the chief locus of authority rested in the National Action Council. CORE's anti-bureaucratic sentiments and the weakness of the bureaucracy itself meant that the National Action Council was far more influential in shaping the ongoing policy of the organization than its counterpart, the NAACP Board of Directors. On the other hand, fewer constraints were actually placed on the national organization by the chapters than in the case of the NAACP. For example, the failure of the CORE chapters to contribute significantly to the financial support of the national office meant that the latter was less dependent upon the local affiliates. The chapters as such were not consulted in the election of any of the National Council and officers, all of whom were elected directly by the convention. This situation was exacerbated by the fact that the convention was less representative of the chapters than the NAACP convention; many CORE chapters did not bother to send delegates, and some delegates were seated from essentially inactive chapters without rigorous examination of their credentials. Ironically, in fact, the very autonomy of the chapters contributed to the lack of constraints which they exercised upon the national organization.[11]

Thus, although both organizations had oligarchic tendencies, various structural factors combined to make CORE potentially far less stable than the NAACP: the National Action Council, annually elected directly by the convention, and therefore more likely to be swayed by new fashions than the NAACP Board; the weakness of the national bureaucracy; and the relative paucity of mutual constraints between national and the locals.

This situation was accentuated by the contrasts between CORE and NAACP leadership and membership. CORE not only remained a small band of intensely involved individuals, but until 1964 it was majority white. Unlike the NAACP, nearly half of whose branch membership resided in the South, CORE's constituency was almost exclusively northern and western, even in the 1960's. Given CORE's tactic of street demonstrations and the risk of arrest, it is not surprising that its personnel tended to be young—mostly in their late teens and twenties; in contrast, NAACP activists were, aside from the youth councils and college chapters, generally middle-aged people. Finally, CORE's membership and leadership—at both the national and local levels—changed rapidly over time. While the data at our disposal do not permit any generalizations concerning the average NAACP members who paid their dues but never actively participated in the Association, there was striking continuity among the individuals who carried out the work of the branches over the years. It was not unusual for a branch president to remain in office for a decade or more. In contrast, CORE people aptly described the turnover among their leaders and active members as resembling a revolving door. This situation is epitomized by the top executive officers. Where three people held the post of NAACP secretary in the fifty-five years following 1920, CORE has had three national directors in the decade and a half since 1961. Similarly, while the turnover among NAACP board members was, as we have observed, a slow process, the composition of CORE's National Action Council underwent rapid changes, with very few people serving as long as four or five years.[12]

From such differences in the characteristics of participants flowed important differences in perspective. Youthful CORE people were often in rebellion against the methods and expectations of older people like those who dominated the NAACP. When significant improvements in the black man's status did occur during the early 1960's, southern blacks, who benefited most from these victories and who comprised such an important part of the NAACP constituency, were more impressed with these gains than were northern black activists. In addition, NAACP personnel, with long years of experience in a movement that had fought patiently but doggedly for these improvements, reacted favorably to the advances which the youthful and less experienced CORE people typically considered minimal and tokenistic.

The fluidity of CORE's membership and leadership and the resultant contrasts between the two organizations were further accentuated as CORE's membership expanded rapidly in the 1960's. CORE always remained a tiny organization which never exceeded 5,000 members, in contrast to the 500,000 reached by the NAACP. Yet CORE, consisting of no more than 400 members in January, 1960, mushroomed more than tenfold by the time it hit its peak in 1963–64. This expansion was accompanied by an extraordinary turnover of personnel. The pacifist nucleus which had founded the organization and which had declined in importance during the 1950's was now virtually wiped out. White liberals who had largely replaced the pacifists among CORE's white majority probably reached their maximum activity in CORE in 1961–62. By then there was an influx of various types of white radicals, and, even more important, an increasing number of blacks, both of whom were drawn to CORE not by its philosophy of nonviolence, but by its reputation for militance. This turnover in membership was reflected in the leadership of the local chapters, in the field staff, and on the National Action Council. Such rapid changes in personnel meant that CORE was characterized by recent arrivals who were not well socialized in the organization's traditions and philosophy. Moreover, the kind of commitment required of CORE activists meant that the organization typically attracted intense, highly dedicated types, "true believers" prepared not only to spend endless hours in CORE activity, but willing to risk arrests or even personal violence and death in the South. Such commitment often carried with it very high expectations of what could be accomplished by CORE's method, a millenarian spirit that led to profound disillusionment when the pace of social change proved frustratingly slow. Of course, there was a wide range of personality types in CORE, and actually the real "true believer" was far more characteristic of SNCC. But the point to be made here is that members of CORE typically differed from those in the NAACP in their impatience with the Association's traditional methods, and in the sense of commitment that made so many of them willing to undergo the sacrifices which participation in CORE often meant. Thus CORE both experienced a rapid turnover in leadership and attracted a high proportion of intense people likely to strike out in new directions if dissatisfied with the accomplishments achieved.

The contrasts between the two organizations were epitomized by the very different styles of their chief executives and spokesmen during the early 1960's—Roy Wilkins for the NAACP and James Farmer for CORE. Wilkins was a superb bureaucratic leader. His effectiveness in the NAACP stemmed not from personal magnetism or abilities as a public speaker, but from administrative talents, careful attention to detail, and an extraordinary control of the organizational mechanism. At the same time he displayed a talent for selling the Association's program to important elites in white America, building on the connections with civic leaders, political figures, progressive trade unionists, and prominent white liberals which the NAACP had forged over the decades. Farmer, in contrast, was, next to Martin Luther King, the most nearly charismatic of the civil rights leaders. A gifted and compelling speaker and an individual who displayed impressive personal courage by risking jail and even his life in protest demonstrations in the Deep South, Farmer was an inspiration and symbol of militance for

CORE members, a man who could stir people to action. At the same time, he was a superb interpreter of CORE and its program to the larger public, projecting in the mass media an image of militance tempered with responsibility. On the other hand, Farmer was anything but a bureaucrat—a fact well known to the people who, valuing his other talents, brought this founder of CORE back into the organization as national director at the end of 1960. He was reluctant to make decisions and inefficient as an administrator. His control of the organizational machinery was never as firm as that of Wilkins. In fact, once in 1964 and again in 1965 the National Action Council strongly criticized and in effect censured Farmer—an action unthinkable in the NAACP, despite the presence of a dissident minority on the Association's Board. Farmer at times did make pivotal decisions that strongly affected CORE's future; but typically he sought less to control CORE's direction than to relate effectively to CORE's changing constituency, to reflect and articulate its ever more militant temper.[13]

CORE's shift from interracialism to black separatism began in 1964, just after the high tide of success in the direct action phase of the civil rights movement. As CORE had moved into the northern cities and begun to articulate the problems of the northern ghettos in the winter of 1963–64, it had become evident that the millenarian expectations of 1962–63 were premature. Recalcitrant southern resistance to the voter registration campaigns produced a similar effect. In both areas there was a growing skepticism of the philosophy of nonviolence, and a rising feeling that black Americans would have to depend for their advancement more upon black community organization than upon the action of white allies.

The thrust for change in CORE came chiefly from individuals in some of the northern chapters that had sprouted as the organization turned its attention from public accommodations to the socioeconomic problems of the slum dwellers. Job campaigns had been successful against retail stores, but demonstrations for employment in the building trades, the rent strikes, and the school integration campaigns had failed. Both the influx into CORE of youthful and impatient militants, black and white, and the dashing of high expectations produced a tendency toward ever more extreme tactics, such as blocking building entrances and threatening highway "stall-ins," and, tentatively at first, a tendency toward black nationalist sentiments among some Negro members. These trends in CORE were reflected in the elections to the National Action Council in 1964. At the convention that summer, many of the more moderate chapters were virtually unrepresented, and the elections to the National Action Council directly reflected the new emerging currents. The number of old-line blacks and whites on the Council declined, and they were replaced with newer people who had entered CORE in the preceding two or three years. The ranks of the Council now included individuals with a point of view very different from the old CORE orientation. Without effective checks upon the National Action Council from the local chapters, the more moderate views prevailing in many of them were not reflected in its deliberations. With CORE increasingly emphasizing militance rather than its tradition of nonviolent interracialism, and with the breakdown of the organization's efforts to provide new members with formal training in CORE philosophy, there was no longer a strong ideological commitment that could act as a brake upon the change. And the Council (which, as we have noted, was more influential in shaping policy than the NAACP Board) at this juncture faced a bureaucracy weakened by a factional dispute. This struggle, which occurred in the spring and early summer of 1964, had led to the resignation of several staff members, chiefly black. Like their opponents, they were deeply committed to attacking the problems of the black poor in the ghetto, but they had also been firmly dedicated to interracial action and the goal of integration.

By the end of the year CORE was in a state of real crisis and was beginning a long-range decline. Income dropped off precipitously, placing the organization in unprecedented financial difficulties. Although the number of officially affiliated chapters was at its peak, the active membership was rapidly falling off. In addition, CORE, like the other civil rights organizations, was, in A. Philip Randolph's words, facing a crisis of victory. The movement had secured major triumphs, but enormous problems still remained unsolved. The crisis of victory was, in effect, a crisis of confidence, as activists searched for methods to bring about sustained and rapid progress. At the same time, the earlier victories, combined with dismay at the realization that white America was still a long way from according full equality to blacks, produced among many militants increasing skepticism and hostility toward all whites, including those whites who were active in the movement. Under the circumstances, with a national leadership strongly desiring to relate more closely to the problems of the northern ghettos and searching for new and more effective strategies to deal with them, and with the absence of a consensus within the organization as to what these new strategies should be, the nationalists on the Council were able to push their views. This became dramatically evident in the discussion and actions concerning white officeholders.

Since 1963, as CORE chapters grappled with the challenge of organizing ghetto communities to struggle against their myriad problems, there had been increasing support for the view that only blacks could carry out this task effectively; it was believed that the black poor would reject whites who functioned in leadership positions. Black-white tensions also arose from a variety of other causes, such as differences in education and in verbal and organizational skills: CORE's whites were drawn from a highly educated upper-middle-class group, while the organization's blacks came from a much broader spectrum and included many from modest incomes and educational levels. As blacks became more self-confident and more desirous of controlling the struggle for their own freedom, there was growing skepticism about the value of white participation, and resentment at the important role whites often played. Moreover, as CORE declined, it experienced the internal feuding that characteristically besets organizations going through such a crisis. One manifestation of this tendency to blame others in the organization for CORE's problems was increasing criticism of the role of white co-workers. Consequently incidents of overt black-white hostility became fairly common in many chapters, and steps were taken to oust whites from leadership. These trends were also reflected at the national level. Thus the number of whites on the staff declined rapidly in 1965–66. When a white official who held the second-highest post in the national staff resigned at the end of 1964, the race of his successor became an important issue at the meeting of the Council, and a decision was made to employ a Caucasian only on a temporary basis until a suitable Negro could be found. The question of whites holding office in the local chapters was raised vigorously at the 1965 convention, and the new constitution officially declared that most of the officers in the chapter must be black.

Symbolically and practically, this change was of momentous importance—it flew directly in the face of the explicit ideology of CORE's founders that only an interracial movement could achieve racial equality in the United States. As these decisions over white leadership in CORE indicate, the year 1965 was a turning point. Basically the stage had been set for the acceptance of the Black Power slogan in 1966, for the total exclusion of whites from active membership in 1968, and for the adoption of a black separatist program.[14]

The internal challenge to the NAACP in the middle 1960's came from a group known as the Young Turks, and basically the Association handled it as it had handled similar challenges to its program in the past. To some extent it accommodated itself to pressures, but its basic ideology and goals remained intact. For example, there had been much agitation in the 1930's, especially from younger black intellectuals, to compel the organization to democratize its structure and shift its emphasis from constitutional rights to a program attacking the economic problems of the masses. The NAACP Board did provide for the election of some at-large Board members under procedures described earlier. It adopted in principle an economic thrust as part of the program of the Association, and by the time the United States entered World War II the Board had cemented a close alliance with the interracial, industrial, CIO unions. Yet the NAACP program retained its former emphasis on attacking franchise restrictions, segregation, and mob violence, while the Board, with the staff, still remained in basic control of policy.[15] Again in the early 1960's, pressed by the dramatic direct action campaign of competing civil rights organizations, and by internal pressures, especially from its youth, the Association had endorsed and, especially on the part of the college and youth chapters, often participated in nonviolent direct action projects. Pressed by the younger people, it also gave the youth councils a degree of autonomy from the adult chapters in their communities, and provided them with representation on the national Board. On the other hand, the leadership—and large segments if not the majority of the adult membership—maintained that the older program and tactics were still vital and important.[16]

The Young Turks were a small group of men, chiefly lawyers, businessmen, and doctors in their thirties and forties,[17] who during the early 1960's were among those challenging the NAACP orientation toward legalism, and urging greater emphasis on direct action. They did not disagree with NAACP goals, but were concerned about tactics. For example, they wanted the executive director to go South and directly challenge the competitive threat posed there by Martin Luther King, who was receiving national publicity while NAACP accomplishments were largely ignored in the press. In this the Young Turks were supported by certain members of the national staff.

Subsequently, in the mid-1960's, their emphasis was on combatting the deep-seated social ills of the northern ghettos. At the same time, beginning in 1964 their attacks upon the national leadership grew sharper. They openly advocated the removal of the executive secretary and of the older black and white Board members, including the national Board chairman. They demanded the replacement of the white president with a black. They criticized the Association's dependence upon white liberal allies in the national government and in the labor unions, particularly in the United Auto Workers, whose president sat on the NAACP Board of Directors.

While their suspicion of many whites actively associated with the NAACP cause was thus evident as early as 1965, and while they urged community organization in the ghettos to meet the needs of the slum dwellers, they did not advocate an explicitly separatist program until the convention of 1968. At that time, calling themselves the "National Committee to Revitalize the NAACP," they demanded "a black approach" for the organization rather than old-style interracialism. The Turks insisted that the Association become "relevant to the black community" and denied "the very relevance of racial integration as a prime goal." They proposed the establishment of several convention committees, including one on "the Survival of Black Americans," evidently referring to armed self-defense of black communities. They also urged the creation of convention committees on African-American Culture, Afro-American and Non-White World Affairs, and Building Black Economic and Political Institutions. This proposal was defeated by a vote of 444 to 272, with the majority of northern delegates favoring it, while the Southerners overwhelmingly rejected it.[18]

Thus, while slower to move to a separatist position, the Young Turks paralleled their CORE counterparts in first being advocates of more militant direct action, then becoming disillusioned with the limited results of direct action after emphasis shifted to the ghettos' economic and social problems, and finally, as a consequence of their frustration, turning to a separatist program. Their challenge first took the form of verbal criticism, then an attempt to dominate the annual convention proceedings,[19] and most dramatically a campaign to gain control of the national Board.

The national office used a variety of techniques to repulse the challenge of the Young Turks. For example, when the Turks attempted to eliminate a white labor leader and a black bishop from the Board, the national staff denounced them for an anti-labor and anti-church stance, and union as well as religious groups rallied to the cause of the established NAACP leadership. Again, when the Young Turks, exploiting technicalities in convention procedures, secured control of the nominating committee in 1964 and 1966, candidates supporting the NAACP administration were nominated by petition and in most cases won election over the Young Turk candidates on the nominating committee's slate.[20]

At their high point in 1966–67, the number of Young Turks on the Board was not more than twelve. The largest number of votes they ever obtained on a particular issue was seventeen on a Board of sixty.[21] Similarly, at the dramatic 1968 convention, they mustered only about one-third of the votes.[22]

In the aftermath of this convention, the two top leaders of the Young Turks resigned from the Board. Even though the challenge of the Turks and their separatist position had been repulsed, the Association had modified its program to some extent. From 1965, in part seizing the opportunity presented by War on Poverty funds and foundation grants, the NAACP encouraged branches to become more actively engaged in organizing community action programs in the ghetto. It also paid more attention to aspects of black consciousness, such as Negro history. It developed a program to help black businessmen, specifically by organizing Negro contractors to pool their resources in order to qualify for substantial federal contracts.[23]

Finally, though insisting on retaining a white man in the ceremonial position of president of the Association until 1976, the NAACP leadership permitted the proportion of white members of the Board to decline from 22 percent in 1963 to 12 percent in 1969.[24] Actually, the decline in white membership on the Board came about for two reasons. It was partly due to the fact that many well-qualified Negroes who deserved recognition for their long service and many contributions to the Association were anxious to fill the vacancies. However, the pressure from the insurgents was also a significant factor. In any case, it no longer seemed feasible to elect to the Board whites who had national prestige but had not given years of service to the Association. And since the organization had for a long period been overwhelmingly black in its local membership (more than 90 percent), eligible whites were scarcely likely to rise from the ranks.

Nevertheless, the Association consistently and forcefully reaffirmed its traditional ideology and goals. The Board, meeting at the time of the 1968 convention, condemned its critics and resolved "that the historic policies of the Association should be and are hereby reaffirmed."[25] Four years later, when the tide of black nationalist sentiment reached its crest at the time of the Black Political Convention in Gary in 1972, the NAACP explicitly rejected "the concept of separate nationhood for black Americans." Instead, it defended its commitment "to a practical policy of accomplishment, utilizing the system as we find it in the conviction that its own processes provide the mechanism for needed changes" to "achieve equality and to make a reality of the doctrine of 'all men' enunciated in the Declaration of Independence."[26]

What brought about the contrasting ways in which the NAACP and CORE responded to the separatist surge represented by Black Power? First, it seems evident that the strong, bureaucratic, centralized nature of the NAACP, including its complex system of elections, acted as a brake upon the internal and external pressures pushing for a reorientation of goals. In contrast, the loose, decentralized nature of CORE, with its weak bureaucracy and relatively simple organizational structure, made it easy for such pressures to express themselves successfully. Yet structure by itself explains little, and ultimately we feel that one must look at an analysis of leadership and constituency.

By 1964–66 the CORE leadership, which no longer had a strong ideological commitment to the organization's original philosophy and which deeply desired to relate to the black masses in the ghettos, tended to move in the direction of the strongest pressures. In contrast, the NAACP leadership stood firmly on its commitment to the organization's traditional ideology, using all the legitimate instruments at its disposal to oppose the dissidents.

Even more important was the striking difference between the constituencies of the organizations. The NAACP, with an overwhelmingly black membership for more than six decades, has been firmly rooted in the black community, with strong ties to the churches and fraternal orders. It represents a better cross-section of the Negro community than any other national racial advancement organization, and comes closer than any of the others to representing the majority voice of that community. Certainly the mass of its membership, especially in the South,* favored its traditional integrationist position. In con-

*The NAACP's southern members, who had directly experienced the gaining of constitutional rights during the 1960's, displayed overwhelming support for the traditional program of the national organization, while the chief internal criticism of the NAACP's integrationist position came from certain northern branches. It is interesting to note in this connection that almost all of CORE's members were located outside the South, and that the thrust toward Black Power within the organization in 1965–66 came from certain members and leaders in a number of northern and west coast chapters. Similarly, one might also note that during this crucial transitional period the Southern

trast, CORE has had a rapidly changing membership. Predominantly white since its inception, CORE had become predominantly black by 1964. Moreover, there was a rapid turnover among its black members, who were typically activist types and therefore less representative of the total Negro community than the NAACP.

In CORE the loose structure facilitated and probably made possible a more complete shift than would otherwise have occurred. Changes in constituency were very rapidly reflected in the National Action Council; neither the Council nor the staff were responsible to the chapters in the way the Board and the secretariat were in the NAACP. In a situation where the leadership was desperately searching for new methods to attack the problems facing the black poor, and where the organization was becoming demoralized by signs of decline and by internal factional fighting, the active minority of Black Power–oriented people on the National Action Council were able to rather quickly change the thrust of the organization. In the NAACP, on the other hand, with a constituency that, especially in the South, remained committed to integration; with a complex structure in which the Board, staff, regions, and branches were all mutually responsible to each other in a complex network of relationships; where because of election procedures it was difficult to change the composition of the Board radically; and where the national leadership knew what it wanted and had the constitutional power and informal structural resources to assert itself, change was slower and less radical, and the basic commitment to the original ideology remained.

Viewed in the larger context of social theory, the contrasting

Christian Leadership Conference retained its faith in nonviolent direct action and in the possibilities of creating the "beloved community" of "black and white together." This consistency in SCLC's position was undoubtedly rooted in two factors: its southern base, and the commitment of its leadership to the nonviolent philosophy of the organization's charismatic founder, Martin Luther King. At first glance the Student Nonviolent Coordinating Committee, which began as a southern black student organization expressing Gandhian nonviolence, might appear to be an exception disproving these generalizations. Actually in the course of a few years SNCC changed from a group of college campus organizations to what was essentially a staff of highly dedicated activists that developed projects in local communities in various parts of the South but did not form local affiliates. Many on the SNCC staff were northern Negroes, and while the evidence at our disposal is incomplete, it would appear that the nationalist thrust came largely from this northern group. The southern leaders, particularly those who had been most profoundly imbued with philosophical nonviolence, were more likely to retain the original SNCC ideology.

roles of the policy-making elites in the two organizations are significant. As is evident from the preceding discussion, both the NAACP and CORE, like other voluntary organizations, have exhibited oligarchic tendencies. But these tendencies have taken strikingly different forms in the two racial advancement organizations. In the case of the NAACP, the corporate structure, the complicated elections procedures, the well-developed bureaucracy, and the complex machinery of branch, state, and regional organizations all facilitated the creation of an elite which was highly stable in terms of its personnel and ideology. Entrance of new members into this elite was constantly occurring, but only after a lengthy process of acculturation in the NAACP tradition as one climbed the ranks through years of active service. In the case of CORE, on the other hand, the simple structure and the policy of direct annual election of members to the National Action Council, as well as its anti-bureaucratic ethos, all facilitated a rapid circulation of the decision-making elite. Essentially it was this fluid and changing membership in its national governing elite which, reflecting changes in the larger society, brought a sharp shift in ideology, program, and goals in the Congress of Racial Equality.

1. See David Sills, *The Volunteers: Means and Ends in a National Organization* (Glencoe, Ill., 1957), p. 3.

2. The following discussion of the early leadership and organizational structure of the NAACP and CORE is based chiefly upon our own extensive research on the history of both organizations. On the NAACP see also Charles Flint Kellogg, *NAACP: A History of the National Association for the Advancement of Colored People, Volume I, 1909–1920* (Baltimore, 1967), and esp. the very perceptive analysis in B. Joyce Ross, *J. E. Spingarn and the Rise of the NAACP, 1911–1939* (New York, 1971), pp. 16–20, 49–59. On CORE, see August Meier and Elliott Rudwick, *CORE: A Study in the Civil Rights Movement, 1942–1968* (New York, 1973), chs. 1, 2.

3. CORE people were very conscious of the contrasting structures of the two organizations, and in fact seem to have deliberately sought to avoid the NAACP model. As one of CORE's leaders put it: "The structure of CORE is quite different from that of the NAACP. First of all, we are a federation of local semi-autonomous groups. These local groups function through the use of non-violent direct action on local projects. Secondly, instead of having the local groups support the national organization, we operate the other way around. That is, the Congress of Racial Equality exists primarily to build and aid our local chapters." Gordon Carey to I. Diane McClure, Oct. 7, 1960, CORE Archives, Wisconsin State Historical Society, Madison.

4. On these developments, see our "The Rise of the Black Secretariat in the NAACP," in this volume.

5. Confidential interviews; *Constitution of the National Association for the Advancement of Colored People* (New York, 1968); *The Crisis*, 70 (Feb., 1963), 107–8; *ibid.*, 73 (Feb., 1966), 100; *ibid.*, 68 (Aug.–Sept., 1961), 411. See also Wilson Record, *Race and Radicalism: The*

NAACP and the Communist Party in Conflict (Ithaca, 1964), pp. 142–43. In 1968 the Board was increased to 64 members, to permit seven youth representatives, one from each of the seven regions. NAACP Board Minutes, June 27, 1968, NAACP National Office, New York; and NAACP, "Summary Minutes, 59th Annual Convention, 1968," copy in possession of the authors.

6. Ross, *Spingarn and the NAACP*; confidential interviews. For administrative reorganization of 1964, see NAACP Board Minutes, Apr. 13, Sept. 14, 1964, NAACP National Office. In 1964 the title of the executive secretary was changed to executive director.

7. Confidential interviews.

8. Louis E. Lomax, *The Negro Revolt* (New York, 1962), p. 130.

9. Confidential interviews. On awareness of NAACP officials that the system of choosing the Board was a stabilizing influence, making it "proof against a coup d'état," see Report of a Special Committee to the Board of Directors entitled "Tenure of National Officers and Directors," NAACP Board Minutes, Apr. 12, 1966, NAACP National Office.

10. CORE's community relations director—the most important post after that of the national director—handled a broad range of functions, including both public relations and fund raising, and often took on other duties as well.

11. This discussion on CORE is a brief summary of the detailed analysis to be found in Meier and Rudwick, *CORE*.

12. One West Coast leader who figured prominently among the CORE advocates of Black Power and exclusion of whites from office in the organization in 1965 had been elected to the National Action Council only the year before, about two and a half years after he had first become active in CORE.

13. The foregoing discussion is based upon numerous interviews, Meier's personal observations as a participant in the civil rights movement of the 1960's, and the research for *CORE*.

14. For details, see Meier and Rudwick, *CORE*, chs. 10–12.

15. Resolutions of the Second Amenia Conference, 1933, Box C 229, NAACP Archives, Library of Congress; Report of the Committee on Future Plan and Program of the NAACP (The Harris Committee), 1935, Box A 28, *ibid.*; Ross, *Spingarn and the Rise of the NAACP*, chs. 6, 7, and 8.

16. On NAACP support for direct action (including direct action on part of NAACP branches in the late 1950's), see, *e.g.*, *The Crisis*, 67 (Mar., 1960), 162; *ibid.* (May, 1960), 313, 315, 319; *ibid.*, 70 (June–July, 1963), 347; *ibid.* (Aug.–Sept., 1963), 389, 400; *New York Times*, July 6, 1963; and NAACP "Summary Minutes, 54th Annual Convention, 1963," copy in possession of the authors. On NAACP youth acquiring greater autonomy, see esp. *The Crisis*, 70 (Aug.–Sept., 1963), 399; and Board Minutes, July 3, 1966, NAACP National Office.

For a typical defense of NAACP legalism, see *New York Times*, July 11, 1961, quoting NAACP Board chairman Bishop Stephen Gill Spottswood as supporting Freedom Rides, but calling them a mere "signal flare," compared to the NAACP's "barrage." Spottswood added, "We are too old in the ways of the long struggle that has engaged our fathers not to realize that wars are won by using every available military resource and not by the employment of raiding parties." For discussion of whole matter of changes in the NAACP from 1960 to 1963, see August Meier, "Negro Protest Movements and Organizations," *Journal of Negro Education*, 32 (Fall, 1963), 437–50.

17. Confidential interviews; *New York Times*, July 16, 1961. One, a veteran of a generation of civil rights activity, was actually in his sixties.

18. Confidential interviews; *New York Times*, Jan. 4 and July 16, 1967, for criticism of NAACP's alliance with white liberals, esp. the UAW; *New York Times*, July 2, 1968, and NAACP "Summary Minutes, 59th Annual Convention, 1968" (for events at 1968 convention). See also "Statement Presented to National Committee to Revitalize the N.A.A.C.P. at N.A.A.C.P. National Convention . . . June 23, 1968, from Chester I. Lewis . . ." (copy supplied by Chester I. Lewis), and leaflet circulated by Young Turks, "Goals of the NAACP 'Young Turks' " [1968], copy in possession of the authors.

19. The Young Turks' attempts to control the annual convention took several forms. In 1964 and 1965 they exploited the unit rule, which was repealed at the 1966 convention. (See NAACP "Summary Minutes, 57th Annual Convention, 1966," copy in possession of the authors.) The unit rule provided that the vote of each region would be cast as a bloc, with the votes of four of the seven regions needed to carry a motion. Strong in three of the regions, the Young Turks by means of astute politicking and horse-trading were able to gain enough support in other regions to win on critical issues, and, most important, to win a majority of the places on the nominating committee. Similarly, by securing a majority of seats on the committee on time and place, they were remarkably successful in arranging to have the conventions meet at locations where many of their supporters would attend; by controlling the committee on convention procedure and rules, they were often able to have their candidates selected as chairmen of the important legislative sessions where the resolutions establishing NAACP's official policy were debated and passed (confidential interviews).

It should also be noted that through their representatives on the "Committee on Evaluation for a Dynamic Program," appointed by the Board in 1962, the Young Turks also sought to accomplish their goals by a structural reorganization of the NAACP. Some important structural changes were accomplished, but they did not aid the cause of the Young Turks. Interview materials; "Report of Committee on Evaluation for a Dynamic Program," Jan., 1963, in Board Minutes, NAACP National Office; "Organizational and Procedural Survey of the National Association for the Advancement of Colored People, Adopted by the Board of Directors at Its Meeting April 13, 1964," Board Minutes, Sept. 14, 1964, *ibid.*

For other evidences of the Young Turks' challenge in the Board Minutes, see, *e.g.*, Minutes of Executive Committee, Dec. 14, 1965; and Board Minutes, Apr. 11, 1968, NAACP National Office.

20. Confidential interviews; *New York Times*, Oct. 5, Dec. 8 and 17, 1964, Jan. 6, 1965; Sept. 20, 1966; *The Crisis*, 71 (Dec., 1964), 693; *ibid.*, 73 (Nov., 1966), 489; and *ibid.*, 74 (Jan.–Feb., 1967), 17.

21. Usually only one of the three youth members on the Board voted with them. The whole question of the relationship of the youth to the Young Turks is one that deserves research. On the whole, the youth did not ally themselves with the Young Turks; their thrust was aimed less at modifying the program of the Association than at achieving more representation and autonomy for youth within the NAACP structure. At the 1966 convention the repeal of the unit rule, which the Young Turks wanted to retain, was initiated by the youth division. However, at the 1968 convention many youth, in a dramatic demonstration, walked out with the Young Turks. Undoubtedly the Turks drew most of their youth support in the North and were weak among the youth in the South (confidential interviews).

22. Actually even one-third of the convention delegates is an overrepresentation of their real strength. Because the key votes concerned non-ideological issues, the Turks picked up many more votes than they would have obtained if the ideological issue had been clearly joined (confidential interviews).

23. Confidential interviews; see also Roy Wilkins' speech at Annual Meeting, Jan., 1965, reported in *The Crisis*, 73 (Feb., 1965), 82.

24. The allegation of white dominance in the NAACP has been made. In 1963 Congressman Adam Clayton Powell mounted the most publicized attack prior to the Young Turks. See *New York Times*, Apr. 1, 1963; *The NAACP and Adam Clayton Powell*, NAACP pamphlet, Apr., 1963; Board Minutes, Apr. 8, 1963, and Report of Secretary of the Board of Directors for Mar., 1963, dated Apr. 8, 1963, NAACP National Office.

25. For reaffirmation of NAACP traditional ideology and goals, see keynote address of Roy Wilkins to 1966 NAACP convention, attacking Black Power, *The Crisis*, 73 (Aug.–Sept., 1966), 353–54, 361; "Time to Speak Up," *The Crisis* editorial, Nov., 1968 (reprinted as leaflet); Roy Wilkins, *The State of the NAACP, 1968: Report of the NAACP Executive Director to the Association's Annual Meeting*, Jan. 13, 1969 (New York, 1969); and pamphlet, *Common Sense Anyone?* (New York, 1969). The Board, meeting at the time of

the 1968 convention, condemned its critics, resolving "that the historic policies of the Association should be and are hereby reaffirmed, the recently encountered pressures to abandon democratic processes are rejected, and sowers of discord and advocates of threats and terror within our ranks are repudiated" (*New York Times*, June 29, 1968).

26. John A. Morsell, NAACP Assistant Executive Director, Memorandum to the NAACP's Black Convention delegates, May 10, 1972, quoted in Washington *Post*, May 11, 1972; and "The NAACP and the Black Political Convention," text of a letter from Roy Wilkins to Charles C. Diggs, Jr., co-chairman of the National Black Political Convention, May 3, 1972, in *The Crisis*, 79 (Aug.–Sept., 1972), 230.

On the History of Nonviolent Direct Action

The essays in Part III flow from the comprehensive research into the history of the twentieth-century civil rights movement in which we have been engaged for some years. Tactics that since the early 1940's have been called nonviolent direct action, it is now clear, have a long history in Afro-American protest. But their use has been episodic and for the most part quite completely forgotten. Later activists were rarely aware of what their predecessors had done or attempted. Moreover, it is one of the ironies of historical scholarship that, in this era of oral history, interviewers seem quite oblivious to the survivors of the many direct action campaigns of the 1930's; their efforts, lost to social memory, are ignored. The essays which appear here are based chiefly upon intensive use of black and white newspaper sources; however, for the events since the 1920's, they have been considerably enriched by interviews with surviving participants.

The first two of these articles—dealing with southern streetcar boycotts at the turn of the century and a northern school boycott of the 1920's—represent some of our detailed case studies of nonviolent direct action campaigns in the first part of the twentieth century. The final essay, "The Origins of Nonviolent Direct Action in Afro-American Protest: A Note on Historical Discontinuities," written especially for this volume, pulls together existing scholarship on the use of direct action in the nineteenth and early twentieth centuries and incorporates the results of fresh research, particularly for the period beginning in the 1930's. In the course of this enterprise, we have unearthed data which have led us to revise certain of our earlier conclusions on the subject, most notably in our discussions of the significance of A. Philip Randolph and the early work of CORE. Surveying the employment of direct action tactics over the sweep of Afro-American history, the article seeks to analyze the circumstances that from time to time prompted Negroes to employ what was in most periods a highly unusual method of combatting racism.[1]

1. The research for this essay has certainly not uncovered every instance of black utilization of direct action tactics. Indeed, while this book was in page proof we learned of additional rent strikes in Detroit in the late 1930's and another school boycott at Washington in midcentury. These events of course reinforce the conclusions we have reached.

TWELVE

The Boycott Movement against Jim Crow Streetcars in the South, 1900–1906

BY AUGUST MEIER AND ELLIOTT RUDWICK

The prelude to the civil rights revolution of the mid-twentieth century was the dramatic eighteen-month bus boycott in Montgomery, Alabama, led by Martin Luther King, Jr. Unknown at the time was the fact that Montgomery had witnessed a two-year boycott by its Negro citizens over a half-century before, when the city council enacted a trolley-car segregation bill. Like the bus boycott of 1955–56, the streetcar boycott of 1900–1902 was part of a larger regional Negro protest against Jim Crow urban transit. The boycotts in Montgomery, Birmingham, and Tallahassee during the late 1950's had their counterparts in more than twenty-five southern cities between 1900 and 1906. This earlier, forgotten movement was especially remarkable, for, unlike the Montgomery boycott which occurred in a period of rising Negro militance and increasing nothern sympathy for the Negroes' cause, the boycotts at the turn of the century came at a time when southern white hostility and northern white indifference were reaching their peak and when, as a result, a philosophy of accommodation had achieved ascendancy in Negro thought and action.

These protests arose in response to the Jim Crow streetcar laws passed at the height of the wave of segregation legislation enacted in southern states two generations ago. Georgia passed the first such law in 1891,[1] but it required segregation only "as

From *The Journal of American History*, 55, no. 4 (Mar., 1969), 756–75. Reprinted with permission from *The Journal of American History*. © 1969 by the Organization of American Historians.

much as practicable"; thus, it left implementation to the erratic discretion of the traction companies. Then, beginning about 1900, a number of southern cities passed municipal segregation ordinances. In that year, Atlanta,[2] Rome,[3] and Augusta[4] supplemented the state law with measures requiring segregation. Montgomery in 1900,[5] Jacksonville in 1901, Mobile in 1902, Columbia, South Carolina, and Houston and San Antonio in 1903,[6] all passed such ordinances. Meanwhile, states had begun to enact Jim Crow streetcar laws applicable only in certain localities. Thus a Virginia law of 1902 required segregation in Alexandria and in Fairfax County. An act of Arkansas in 1903 applied only to cities "of the first class," and one in Tennessee of the same year only to counties of 150,000 or more. The latter statute, which affected only Memphis, was never enforced.[7]

The first state to pass a mandatory statewide statute was Louisiana in 1902. Mississippi followed in 1904; and in the same year, Virginia authorized, but did not require, segregation in all cities. Tennessee and Florida required statewide segregation in 1905. The Florida law was declared unconstitutional, and the state did not enact another until 1909; but in the interim, Pensacola and Jacksonville had passed municipal ordinances which the high court sustained.[8] In 1906, Virginia finally made Jim Crow streetcars a requirement in all its cities; and the following year, Texas, Oklahoma, and North Carolina joined the list. In South Carolina and Alabama, city ordinances and streetcar company regulations provided a substitute for state action.[9]

Nearly everywhere, the streetcar companies opposed enactment of the Jim Crow laws by citing the expense and difficulty in enforcement, and the fear of losing Negro customers. Often the companies were able to defeat such bills or postpone their enactment. Sometimes, however, faced with an aroused public opinion, the companies endorsed the Jim Crow regulation— even at the cost of reversing their earlier position.[10]

Neither the streetcar segregation which emerged at the turn of the century nor the Negro boycotts against it were without precedent. There had been successful protests against Jim Crow horsecars during Reconstruction in Richmond, New Orleans, Charleston, and Louisville; but Savannah was evidently the only city of the period where a boycott was reported.[11] However, in every state and in many of the cities which passed segregation laws between 1891 and 1906, their enforcement precipitated Negro boycotts. There were at least three successful ones in Georgia during the 1890's, when attempts were made to implement the law of 1891: Atlanta in 1892–93,[12] Augusta in 1898,[13] and on the line from Savannah to the resort of Warsaw in 1899.[14] Thereafter, only five boycotts were even temporarily successful: Jacksonville in 1901, Montgomery and Mobile in 1902, and Jacksonville and Pensacola in 1905; and of these, the victory in the two Florida protests of 1905 was achieved by court action rather than by the boycott itself.

Boycotts have been identified in the following cities: Atlanta[15] and Rome,[16] Georgia, 1900; Augusta, Georgia, 1900–1903;[17] Montgomery, Alabama, 1900–1902;[18] Jacksonville, Florida, 1901;[19] Mobile, Alabama, 1902;[20] New Orleans[21] and Shreveport,[22] Louisiana, 1902–3; Little Rock, Arkansas,[23] and Columbia, South Carolina,[24] 1903; Houston, Texas, 1903–5;[25] Vicksburg and Natchez, Mississippi, 1904;[26] San Antonio, Texas,[27] and Richmond, Virginia,[28] 1904–5; Memphis,[29] Chattanooga,[30] and Knoxville,[31] Tennessee, and Pensacola[32] and Jacksonville,[33] Florida, 1905; Nashville,[34] Tennessee, 1905–6; Danville, Lynchburg, Portsmouth, and Norfolk, Virginia, 1906;[35] Newport News, Virginia,[36] and Savannah, Georgia,[37] 1906–7.

This listing is probably an underenumeration, for there are serious lacunae in the surviving evidence.[38] The limitations of the sources notwithstanding, it is evident that the boycott movement was an extensive one. Protests occurred in all the states of the former Confederacy. Most of the major cities in Georgia, and every major city in Virginia and Tennessee had one. As the Mobile *Daily Register* observed in 1905: "In every city where it has been found advisable to separate the races in the street cars the experience has been the same. The negroes . . . have invariably declared a boycott."[39]

Negro protests through mass meetings, petitions to city councils and legislatures, and even an occasional boycott, often began while the segregation bills were being considered. In

Savannah, for example, in 1901 a bill before the city council was defeated by the overt opposition of the streetcar company and by the more covertly expressed "conservative feeling of the leading white citizens," whose aid the Negroes had marshaled. Five years later, however, sentiment for segregation was much stronger among whites, and the Savannah Electric Company's president reversed his position. A Negro mass meeting urged defeat of the bill. The mayor, however, termed this protest inflammatory; the city council refused even to hear the Negro delegation and enacted the ordinance unanimously. In San Antonio, where the city council did permit a Negro committee to speak, an ordinance was also passed unanimously. In Jacksonville, after the city council in 1901 had passed a bill over the articulated opposition of the Negro community and its two Negro councilmen, colored people angrily stayed off the cars in an attempt to pressure the mayor into vetoing the bill. This boycotting proved futile, as did a similar step by Pensacola Negroes four years later, when they tried to force the city's streetcar company to lobby against the Avery streetcar-segregation bill, then before the legislature.[40]

Negroes resented these laws as a humiliating disgrace. The Nashville *Clarion* editorially condemned this effort "to humiliate, degrade, and stigmatize the negro." Several Lynchburg Negroes circulated a call for a boycott and termed the law "a gratuitous insult . . . to every one with a drop of Negro blood. . . . Let us touch to the quick the white man's pocket. 'Tis there his conscience often lies." In 1905, after the Avery bill had passed the Florida legislature, Jacksonville Negro ministers urged a boycott of this "unjust, barbaric and . . . cowardly measure" "in order to retain our self-respect." As the Savannah *Tribune* said: "Do not trample on our pride by being 'jim crowed,' Walk!"[41]

For Negroes the new order was startling, even shocking. One report spoke of the "mingled disgust and bewilderment" among Memphis colored people arising from the "obloquy and shame" imposed after forty years of unrestricted travel.[42] To men like John Mitchell, Jr., editor of the Richmond *Planet*, former city councilman, president of the Mechanics Savings Bank, and grand chancellor of the Virginia Knights of Pythias, the whites who demanded streetcar segregation represented a new and different Richmond. Mitchell maintained that since the Civil War no act had aroused "a more bitter feeling of racial antagonism." He deplored the passing of the "traditional harmony" between the races, survivals of which still existed in such events as the recent funerals of an "old mammy" and a church sexton who were buried from the churches and homes of the white Richmond patricians they had long served.[43]

Beyond this desire to preserve a status quo that in retrospect appeared to belong to a golden age of "harmonious," if paternalistic, race relations, there was the fear of physical maltreatment at the hands of "poor white trash"—conductors and motormen. The *St. Luke Herald* of Richmond predicted that "the very dangerous [police] power placed in the hands of hot headed and domineering young white men," already universally hated for their overbearing and insulting conduct, would "certainly provoke trouble."[44] Jacksonville Negroes also vigorously objected to the provision giving police power to conductors as "bound to bring about a strife and possibly bloodshed."[45] In fact, one of the reasons urged for boycotting was the belief that by keeping off the cars Negroes would avoid occasions for friction and disorder.[46]

Although in some cities the white press either ignored or attempted to minimize the extent of the boycott, generally, where the daily newspaper reported the protests, the editors commented upon the boycott's singular effectiveness. Universally the effect was startling to the white population. In Augusta, where the streetcar company instituted segregation on Sunday, May 20, 1900, about two weeks before the city council enacted its ordinance, the *Chronicle* reported: "It was noticeable that the negroes did not take to the cars as usual on Sunday. On about every fourth car passing one or two could be seen. . . ." The Mobile and New Orleans laws both went into effect early in November, 1902. The Mobile *Daily Register* admitted that "Nearly all of them are walking." In New Orleans, with its vast distances, the boycott was necessarily less marked. But there were so many empty seats in the Negro compartment that the whites bitterly resented having to stand. Little Rock conductors observed that very few Negroes used the lines most patronized by the race, "less than five percent as compared with the usual 60 percent." The day after the boycott started in Columbia, a white paper reported that "the absence of negroes was noted by everyone." In San Antonio, their presence on the vehicles was pronounced "a rarity." The Savannah *Morning News* commented that the colored clergy had been most effective in organizing the people. For example, the paper reported that Thomas Gamble, secretary to the mayor, had given his Negro maid carfare to carry his two heavy suitcases to City Hall. When she belatedly arrived, soaked with perspiration, Gamble discovered that she had walked to town because her minister had admonished everyone to keep off the trolley cars.[47]

The colored weeklies proudly carried similar reports. The Atlanta *Age* declared "that you can stand on the streets all day and never see a Negro riding . . . unless he is going to Decatur, Edgewood, or the River."[48] A Negro visitor in Houston was surprised at "the completeness" of the boycott,[49] while one in Montgomery, nine months after the local Negroes began walking, marvelled at this "universal boycott."[50]

The boycotts were easily sustained in their early stages because they were a natural reaction to the humiliation and fears associated with riding the Jim Crow cars. However, informal pressures were also used. In San Antonio, a few days after the movement began, six Negroes were arrested for pulling a youth off a trolley car. In Columbia, the few who rode "were 'guyed' when the cars passed groups of negroes on the streets." In Savannah, those who opposed the boycotts were publicly denounced at mass meetings as "demagogues and hypocrites." The city's police quickly took to arresting Negroes who stood on downtown street corners, heckled riders as they got off, and urged those ready to board the trolleys to take a hack instead.[51]

The traction companies were undeniably hard hit. In April, 1908, the president of the Savannah Electric Company informed the city council that the boycott had resulted in a 25 percent decline in business and had cost about $50,000. He estimated that in 1906, when the movement was at its height, the company's loss was over $32,000. The Houston Electric Company, about five months after the boycott began, decided that it was no longer possible to disguise the fact that the protest was "crippling" its receipts.[52]

In three cases, the companies temporarily capitulated to the protesters. Jacksonville city officials, undoubtedly acting at the request of the traction company, ceased enforcing their ordinance after a few months and quietly asked the Negro ministers to inform their congregations.[53] In Montgomery, after two years, the company was so hard hit that it simply suspended enforcement of the law.[54] The president of the Mobile Light and Railroad Company, in the face of the Negroes' financially ruinous action, decided to test the ordinance in the courts; and he directed employees to permit passengers to sit anywhere. A conductor was convicted in city court for doing this, and the company announced that it would appeal.[55] There was no further mention of the case, however. Apparently, in both Mobile and Montgomery, Jim Crow arrangements were quietly reinstated after a brief period.

In addition to walking, Negroes pressed private carriages, drays, and hacks into service. It is doubtful that the boycotts could have occurred at all except for the Negro hackmen and draymen, who in that period still dominated these two occupations in a number of southern cities.[56] In Jacksonville[57] and Savannah,[58] and undoubtedly elsewhere, the hackmen reduced their fare for boycotters from twenty-five to ten cents. In Savannah, the authorities became so concerned that the police began to look for overworked horses and to arrest unlicensed hackmen.[59]

In Houston, Negro hackowners lowered the price to five cents.[60] A Negro visitor reported that the protesters had developed an informal transit system of passenger vans, wagons, and carriages.[61] As the boycott entered its eighth month in June, 1904, a streetcar strike forced Houston whites to walk for a few days. The Houston *Post* noted the amusement of the boycotters and the advantage they had by virtue of their "crude omnibus lines."

> [I]n some instances the whites were hurrahed good-naturedly by acquaintances among the blacks. One well known businessman tells this on himself: "I live away out in the South End and having neither a horse nor carriage was forced to foot it to town. A conveyance came along driven by a negro and I asked him for a lift. Looking at me and grinning, he said: 'Boss, Ise bliged ter fuse yer de favor. De city council won't let de white folks and de

black folks ride together, and I ain't got my compartmint sign up yit,' and with that he drove on." The negroes seemed to enjoy the predicament of the whites hugely, and along toward noon many of their conveyances could be seen driving about the streets with a space in the rear some two feet in length blocked off by a piece of cardboard bearing the legend, "For Whites Only."[62]

The step from these arrangements to actual transportation companies was not a long one, particularly in view of the trends in Negro thinking of the period. Because of deteriorating conditions, there had been a shift in emphasis from agitation and politics to economic advancement, self-help, and racial solidarity, often coupled with a philosophy of accommodation. The development of transportation companies, therefore, functioned in three ways: as a means of protesting against discrimination, as a fulfillment of the dream of creating substantial Negro businesses by an appeal to racial solidarity, and— hopefully—as a practical solution to the transportation problems faced by the masses of boycotting Negroes.

In several cities Negroes talked about forming a transit company, and in Savannah two were actually organized, though there is no evidence that either put vehicles on the streets.[63] Only the Virginia and Tennessee boycotts of 1905 and 1906 produced functioning transportation lines.[64] Portsmouth Negroes obtained a "double horse wagonette" which seated about thirty passengers and made regular trips. Inspired by this example, members of the race in Norfolk formed the Metropolitan Transfer Company, which placed a yellow herdic on the streets—the first of a fleet of eight scheduled to arrive. Soon afterwards, however, the white daily newspaper noted that few Negroes were patronizing the vehicle, since by then most had returned to the streetcars.[65] In Chattanooga, where the boycott started on July 5, 1905, some unnamed "enterprising negroes" formed a hack line by the end of the month. After creating a stock company, they leased three carriages which made a regular schedule between downtown and a Negro section known as Churchville. Apparently this line did well, for in late August it was reported that, with the boycott continuing in "full force" and with the colored hackmen having "more business than they can handle," some "well known negroes" of the city had applied for a charter for the Transfer Omnibus Motor Car Company. A week later, however, there was evidence of a crackdown on the hack line. Charging that the Negroes were "working old, worn-out animals from early morning until late at night and are only half-feeding them," the county humane officer announced that he would prosecute the operators of the company.[66] While further evidence is lacking, it appears that harassment by the public authorities forced the Negro entrepreneurs out of business.

The most impressive attempt to develop a Negro-owned alternative to the Jim Crow trolley cars occurred in Nashville. There the boycott began July 5, and by the end of the summer the leaders formed the Union Transportation Company. Its incorporators included the elite of Nashville's business and professional community: the president was Preston Taylor, an undertaker and the pastor of the Lea Avenue Christian Church; its treasurer was a Fisk University official, George W. Henderson; and its purchasing agent was the Reverend Richard Henry Boyd, general secretary of the National Baptist Publishing Board.[67] For the first few weeks, the company used horses and wagons. By September 21, $7,000 worth of stock had been sold, another $18,000 worth subscribed, and five motor buses purchased. The buses arrived on September 29, and during the day large numbers of race-proud Negroes eagerly inspected them. According to the Nashville *Banner*, "the cars are on the steam wagonette style, and have a large front seat with two long seats running backward, band wagon style. They have a capacity for fifteen persons."[68]

The line began operations early in October. For at least a brief time, it invigorated the boycott, but the buses never fulfilled their expectation. The few vehicles naturally kept infrequent schedules. To remedy this problem, the company's inexperienced officers overpaid for nine more buses. These lacked sufficient power for Nashville's hills. Arrangements for boosting power were made with the local electric company, but either the results were unsatisfactory or the company reneged on its promises; in any event, the bus operations were constantly hampered. Little improvement resulted from a new generator installed at the National Baptist Publishing Board, and battery trouble repeatedly incapacitated the vehicles. Passengers became tired of waiting and increasingly used the Jim Crow streetcars. Two years later, W. E. B. Du Bois described this enterprise as one that cost its shareholders $20,000 for a few months of service.[69]

Legal efforts proved as futile as the transportation companies and, though not entirely eschewed, played a distinctly minor role. In a few cities Negroes seriously discussed going to court, but only in Florida did they actually undertake a legal attack. This litigation was directed by city councilman and attorney J. Douglas Wetmore, who twice carried test cases to the state supreme court. Arguing that the state law of 1905 was "vague and uncertain," that it violated the equal protection clause of the Fourteenth Amendment, and even that it discriminated among classes of Negroes by providing that Negro nurses accompanying whites could sit in the white section, Wetmore persuaded the court to hold the law unconstitutional. The judges did so, however, on the narrow ground that to allow Negro servants to sit in the white section was class legislation. Negro jubilation over the victory and the temporary end of segregation was shortlived. Jacksonville and Pensacola authorities quickly passed municipal ordinances. This time there was no general boycott. Negroes in both cities again resorted to the courts, but early in 1906 the high court upheld both city laws.[70]

The boycott leaders, where they can be identified, were uniformly an elite group which consisted of prominent business and professional men, with at times a sprinkling of federal employees or a rare politician. Jacksonville, Savannah, Nashville, and Richmond provide the most complete information. In Savannah, the leadership included the outstanding Baptist and African Methodist Episcopal ministers, two physicians, an attorney, an undertaker, a prosperous barber with white patronage, and an insurance executive. The pattern in Jacksonville was similar, except that it was unique in including the city's two Negro councilmen. In Nashville, the prime movers were the Reverend E. W. D. Isaac, editor of the Nashville *Clarion* and the *National Baptist Union*, and the Reverend R. H. Boyd, president of the One Cent Savings Bank, as well as secretary of the Baptist Publishing Board. Supporting them were prominent citizens like J. C. Napier, former city councilman, cashier of the One Cent Savings Bank, and later register of the treasury under William Howard Taft; Bishop Evans Tyree of the African Methodist Episcopal Church; the Reverend William D. Chapelle, secretary-treasurer of the African Methodist Episcopal Sunday School Union; and professors at Meharry Medical School and Fisk University. In Richmond, the most dynamic force behind the movement was John Mitchell, Jr. Working with him were two or three professors at Virginia Union University, most notably J. R. L. Diggs, who was later president of Kentucky State College; Benjamin Jackson, grocer and former city councilman; and most important of all, the officials of the leading benefit societies and fraternal orders and their affiliated banks. Besides Mitchell himself, these included Maggie L. Walker, head of the Independent Order of St. Luke; and the Reverend W. P. Burrell, president of the Richmond Baptist Sunday School Union and general secretary of the United Order of True Reformers—the outstanding non-secret mutual benefit order among Negroes of the period.[71]

Especially important was the role of the newspaper editors. Mitchell of the Richmond *Planet* and Sol Johnson of the Savannah *Tribune* clearly played leading parts in initiating and sustaining the boycott. W. A. Pledger of the Atlanta *Age* and Isaac of the Nashville *Clarion* evidently played comparable roles, although copies of their papers are not extant. The Chattanooga *Daily Times* denounced the Negro press of the city, especially the Chattanooga *Blade*, for stirring up "heresy" and disturbing racial harmony.[72] All six of the Richmond Negro newspapers supported the boycott there. In Augusta, W. J. White of the Georgia *Baptist* was nearly lynched for his denunciation of the Jim Crow law.[73]

The role of the ministers, in contrast, is a complex subject. The relationship of religion to Negro protest has always been paradoxical. The Negro church has played mainly an accommodating role, and its ministers have preached sermons about rewards in heaven for the meek on this earth. Yet Christian ideology has also served as a wellspring of protest from antislavery days down to Martin Luther King, Jr.[74] Ministers often represented the Negro community in dealings with whites, especially in the South. Such clergymen were influential among Negroes because they could obtain small favors from the white community. They were influential not because Negroes chose them, but because they were selected by prominent whites who utilized the clergy to control the Negro community.[75] A common dilemma was faced by the Reverend C. R. Dinkins, a minister in the Colored Methodist Episcopal Church and the principal leader of the boycott in Columbia, South Carolina. One-third of the cost of his church had been contributed by white people of Columbia. He was a man "in whom we have much confidence," said the Columbia *State* when it advised Negroes to drop the boycott.[76]

Ironically, because of this pattern of using the ministers to influence the Negro community, southern whites assumed that whatever happened there was the work of the "preachers." Clergymen were, in fact, often pictured as the provocateurs of the boycotts. As the Mobile *Register* said, wherever segregated streetcars had been inaugurated, invariably the Negroes had initiated a boycott, "backed by the exhortations of their religious leaders."[77]

It is true that often ministers were among the chief supporters of the streetcar protests. They were prominent in Pensacola, Jacksonville, and Savannah; they were the principal leaders in Montgomery and Columbia; and elsewhere, as in Memphis and Nashville, individual ministers were named as key figures. Yet the individuals who stood out most prominently among the opponents of the boycotts were certain African Methodist Episcopal and especially the Baptist ministers. The Natchez movement was in its third month when it was drastically undermined by a religious conference which was sponsored by the prominent African Methodist Episcopal minister, W. H. Jernagin. The delegates freely used the streetcars in getting to and from the sessions. The Reverend T. O. Fuller of Memphis, principal of the Howe Institute and later a chronicler of Baptist church history, wrote a letter to the *Commercial Appeal* and advised Negroes that "Law-abiding citizens can do nothing else but respect" the provisions of the state law and obey the conductors.[78] In Atlanta, African Methodist Episcopal Bishop Henry M. Turner helped to break the boycott by ostentatiously riding on the Jim Crow cars.[79] In Savannah, the ministers first actively supported the protest movement. But later, in the spring of 1907, the boycott began to break when influential men among the Baptist clergy and the faculty at Georgia Industrial College rode the streetcars.[80] In Richmond, the situation was the most extreme of all. There, even before the boycott began, an open split developed in the Negro leadership. The powerful Baptist Ministers Conference, consisting of the pastors of three-fourths of the Negro churches of Richmond,[81] opposed the movement and thereby seriously weakened it. United against the clergymen were the businessmen, the editors, the bankers, and the leaders of fraternal and insurance societies. Some of the most important individuals in this group were also Baptist ministers, but they did not serve churches and their identification was with the business community rather than with the religious leadership.[82] In Nashville, however, a comparable cleavage failed to develop. There, preacher-businessmen such as R. H. Boyd were able to obtain support from important clerics like Bishop Evans Tyree who were not businessmen. Thus, Boyd led a united community.

The elite leaders who headed the protest were known as impeccably respectable men, rather than as radicals or firebrands. Some, indeed, were close friends of the noted accommodator Booker T. Washington, whom contemporaries described as "conservative" in contrast to the "radical" minority of intellectuals that led the opposition to him and his philosophy of accommodation. Moreover, it should be emphasized that this widespread boycott movement occurred in an era when accommodation was in the ascendancy. One wonders, in fact, how it was that this protest movement occurred at all, given the context of race relations in which it took place.

The trolley-car boycotts can best be described as a "conservative protest." First, this movement was conservative in the sense that it was seeking to preserve the status quo—to prevent a change from an older and well-established pattern. Second, it is also noteworthy that the boycotts avoided a direct confrontation with the laws, such as would have occurred if Negroes had insisted on sitting in the white section. There were instances of Negroes being arrested for occupying seats assigned to whites, but these were rare incidents and, except for the Florida test cases, not part of the organized protest movements.[83]

Third, the statements of the boycott leaders themselves were often remarkably moderate or "conservative." This was true even of the editors, who formed the most militant segment of the movements' spokesmen. The Nashville *Clarion* vigorously supported the boycotters, yet added: "Their protestations are mild and peaceable however. They exhibit no spirit of anarchy or revenge, neither do they make any threatening demonstrations."[84] Mitchell, one of the most militant southern editors, described a meeting called to plan the Richmond protest: "The discussion was conservative and it was the opinion of the body that the colored people should do all in their power to promote peace and avoid any clash or disorder on the streetcars." The Richmond *Times-Dispatch* took a similar view of Mitchell's activities. In reporting a mass rally, it stated: "There was no turbulence, no fierce denunciation and no fire-eating, as many had feared. On the contrary, conservatism was urged. . . ." The paper noted that Mitchell advised Negroes "to be conservative and law-abiding, but to walk." Sternly, he warned his listeners to refuse to be provoked into confrontations with conductors which would lead to a race riot: "Then you will see their guns, their Winchesters. But we don't want guns, we want peace, and the way to keep it is to let the white people have their cars." Mitchell repeatedly urged Negroes who did board the streetcars to obey the law and sit in the rear; he emphatically declared: "Do not get on the streetcars to assert your rights."[85] Similarly, in Little Rock, boycotters were advised to "be obedient to the law. Let no one get on the cars and attempt to undo what the legislature of the great state of Arkansas has done. . . . Never mind about framing resolutions or arguing the merits or demerits of the affair with anyone. Simply stay off the cars." In Columbia, Dinkins told the press that the Negroes would do nothing intemperately and that they regretted hurting the Columbia Electric Street Railway Company, since its officials were among the Negroes' "safe and trusted friends." Dinkins justified the boycott because "there was no occasion for this ordinance. . . . Everything was going along pleasantly and preachers here have always avoided discussion of racial issues, preferring to try to inspire their congregations with faith in their own race and to encourage them to trust and to depend upon the southern white people."[86]

Perhaps the most conservative of the protest leaders were those associated with the National Negro Business League, which Washington had founded in 1900. Indeed, Washington organized the overwhelming majority of leading Negro clergymen and businessmen into what was widely recognized and publicly labeled as a "conservative" clique. Boyd, president of the Nashville Business League, in a letter to the evening newspaper, pointed out that it was at the request of traction officials that Negro leaders had decided not to protest against the bill in the state legislature. They had then vainly begged the company to attach separate trailers and hire colored fare collectors on the routes where there was the most Negro patronage. Since the company had "denied [them] even serious consideration," he continued, the colored people felt that actually it was the streetcars which had boycotted them. It was in view of this situation, Boyd concluded, that the Negroes of Nashville had decided that this would be a good time for "stimulating the cause of the automobile as a common carrier." As this letter suggests, a secondary motivation behind Boyd's actions was the vision of Negro enterprise built on the Negro market, of Negro "captains of industry," to use Washington's phrase. Men like Boyd may have been as much interested in the possibility of business enterprise as in protesting discrimination. As he said at the meeting of the National Negro Business League in 1903: "These discriminations are only blessings in disguise. They stimulate and encourage rather than cower and humiliate the true, ambitious, self-determined Negro."[87]

Another leading Nashville businessman who backed the boycott and the bus company and who, like Boyd, was given to accommodating utterances was J. C. Napier. He was a man of whom Washington once said, "I have never heard Mr. Napier express a narrow or bitter thought toward the white race." The two men were so close that Washington once offered Napier the presidency of the National Negro Business League.[88] In Richmond, also, prominent League people were active in the boycott movement. Attorney Giles Jackson, secretary of the

Virginia League, proved to be an exception when he sided with the Baptist ministers who opposed the boycott. But others, most notably Dr. R. E. Jones, president of the Richmond League, were the movement's ardent advocates.[89]

Although Washington did not personally involve himself with the streetcar boycotts, he had publicly approved the first one in Atlanta in 1892–93.[90] In contrast, it is interesting to note that the anti-Washington "radical" Niagara Movement, founded by Du Bois when the boycotts were at their height, paid no attention to them and failed to recommend this type of protest, even though two of its prominent members—J. R. L. Diggs of Richmond and the Reverend J. Milton Waldron of Jacksonville—were connected with the boycotts in their home cities. Indeed, the only public reference to the boycotts that came from the prolific pen of Du Bois concerned the transportation companies, which he discussed as exemplifying business enterprise rather than protest.[91]

Clearly, then, the streetcar protests were almost entirely led by conservative business and professional men. Their weapon was the boycott, a multifaceted response to oppression that protested and yet avoided confrontation with the discriminating whites. As the social psychologist Thomas F. Pettigrew has written, boycotts as a protest tactic have "the distinct psychological advantage" of appealing to all "three major types of responses human beings can make to oppression. . . . Such campaigns move toward the oppressor by seeking to achieve desegregation; they move against the oppressor by encouraging group unity and aggressively upsetting the white-controlled economy; and they move away from the oppressor by requesting the participators merely to avoid the scene of conflict."[92] By attacking and yet withdrawing, the boycotters—like the founders of the Negro churches a century before—were both protesting against race prejudice and accommodating to it.

It should be emphasized that, although the boycott was a tactic adopted by many conservative leaders, partly because it avoided confrontation and overt racial friction, it was, nevertheless, a genuine protest weapon. It was so considered by the whites and by those accommodating ministers who opposed its use. But as the least aggressive kind of protest, the least militant variety of what today is called nonviolent direct action, it fitted the conservatism of Negro leaders in southern cities during a period of accommodation. Even in such a time, the boycotts were a natural and spontaneous response, for they sought to preserve dignity in the face of a humiliating social change.

The streetcar boycotts varied considerably in length. The nature of the evidence is such that in most instances it is not possible to give a definite date for the conclusion of a boycott. After the first few days or weeks, the white press usually ignored the movement. Exchanges and other items from distant cities in the Negro weeklies were not ordinarily dated; and, thus, even for the victories in Jacksonville in 1901 and Montgomery in 1902, the Negro press failed to note the precise date.[93]

In Savannah, where the evidence is the most complete, the boycott began on September 13, 1906, and continued through the winter. As spring approached, the *Tribune* and the Chatham County Emancipation Association were urging Negroes not only to keep off the cars but also to refrain from patronizing the suburban Lincoln Amusement Park, owned by the transit company. Yet, as the *Morning News* observed a month earlier, "there has been a gradual tendency on the part of the negroes to resume riding on the cars." The last notice of a mass meeting published in the *Tribune* was for one scheduled for March 24, 1907. Actually, the boycott began to break down as important clerics and professors openly rode the streetcars. Some continued to walk, even though the majority slowly returned to the streetcars. In April, 1908, the president of the streetcar company indicated that it was still suffering to some extent; he put the return of colored patrons at 80 percent. As late as the following September, a few, like Johnson, were still boycotting the cars. But by then even the *Tribune* editor conceded defeat.[94]

The boycotts ranged in length from a few weeks to as long as two or three years. The Mobile *Daily Register* generalized that it took "about two months" to convince Negroes that they might as well use the cars again.[95] Yet some clearly lasted a good deal longer. The Montgomery boycott was entering its third month when the Atlanta *Constitution* marveled at its "surprising persistency. . . . The company reports that the receipts of the line have fallen off fully 25%. All efforts heretofore made in Alabama to organize strikes among the negro miners . . . have proved unsuccessful and it has been believed that no considerable number of negroes could be organized for any length of time . . . they have almost entirely refrained from riding."[96] The New Orleans and Nashville boycotts lasted at least eight months, the Atlanta boycott at least ten months, the Savannah boycott six to ten months, and the Newport News boycott fourteen months. The white press in San Antonio indicated the boycott there was going on three months after it began, and the daily paper in Houston reported the local boycott as still strong eight months after it started. A July, 1905, report in the Charleston *News and Courier* indicated that both were still in existence—making their length fifteen months and twenty-two months respectively. And in June, 1903, three years after the Augusta boycott began, the manager of the Columbia traction company reported that this movement was so effective that Negroes arriving on excursion trains from Augusta refused to ride the trolley cars even in Columbia.[97]

In some cities, like Atlanta, Memphis, Natchez, Richmond, and Savannah, leadership cleavages undoubtedly hastened the demise of the protests. But more than anything else, what undoubtedly caused their decline was a feeling of discouragement—a realistic pessimism—that must in time have come over the demonstrators as they saw that their withdrawal of patronage produced no results. Some, like editors Johnson and Mitchell, might continue to walk, but gradually a sense of futility set in.

It is not surprising that, in the end, the boycott movements against Jim Crow trolleys failed in all of the cities where they were initiated. They occurred at a time when southern racism was reaching its crest and when the white South had gained a respectful hearing in the North. With the Supreme Court endorsing the separate-but-equal doctrine and with Negroes in most places virtually disfranchised, the boycotts were the only way of protesting realistically open to them. In retrospect, it is easy to see that their failure was inevitable. The remarkable thing is not that the boycotts failed, but that they happened in so many places and lasted as long as they often did.

1. *Acts of Georgia*, 1891, pp. 157–58.

2. Atlanta *Constitution*, Feb. 6, 1900.

3. New Orleans *Southwestern Christian Advocate*, July 5, 1900; Cleveland *Gazette*, July 7, 1900.

4. Augusta *Chronicle*, June 5, 1900.

5. Montgomery *Advertiser*, July 3, 10, 24, Aug. 7, 1900.

6. Jacksonville *Florida Times-Union and Citizen*, Nov. 14, 1901; Mobile *Daily Register*, Oct. 17, 1902; Columbia *State*, June 24, 1903; Houston *Daily Post*, Sept. 29, 1903; San Antonio *Express*, Oct. 13, 1903.

7. *Acts of Virginia*, 1901–2, pp. 639–40; *Acts of Arkansas*, 1903, pp. 178–79; *Acts of Tennessee*, 1903, p. 75; Memphis *Commercial Appeal*, Mar. 27, Apr. 26, May 30, June 8, 1903; *Memphis Street Railway Co. v. State*, 110 Tenn. 602 (1903).

8. *Acts of Louisiana*, 1902, pp. 89–90; *Laws of Mississippi*, 1904, pp. 140–41; *Virginia Laws*, extra session of 1902–3–4, pp. 990–92; *Acts of Tennessee*, 1905, pp. 321–22; *Acts of Florida*, 1905, pp. 99–100; *ibid.*, 1909, pp. 339–40. On the Pensacola and Jacksonville municipal ordinances, see note 70.

9. *Acts of Virginia*, 1906, pp. 92–94; *General Laws of Texas*, 1907, pp. 58–60; *Public Laws of North Carolina*, 1907, pp. 1238–39; *Oklahoma Laws*, 1907–8, pp. 201–4; Gilbert Thomas Stephenson, *Race Distinctions in American Law* (New York, 1910), p. 229.

10. Savannah *Tribune*, Sept. 23, 1899; Augusta *Chronicle*, May 15, 17, 19, 20, 21, 1900; Richmond *Planet*, Mar. 15, 1902, May 7, June 18, 1904; Richmond *Times-Dispatch*, Apr. 17, 1904; Richmond *News-Leader*, May 9, 1904; Savannah *Morning News*, July 10, 1902, Aug. 31, 1906.

11. C. Vann Woodward, *The Strange Career of Jim Crow*, 2nd rev. ed. (New York, 1966), p. 27; Alrutheus A. Taylor, *The Negro in the Reconstruction of Virginia* (Washington, 1926), pp. 52, 214; Roger A. Fischer, "A Pioneer Protest: The New Orleans Street-Car Controversy of 1867," *Journal of Negro History*, 53 (July, 1968), 219–33; Joel Williamson, *After Slavery: The Negro in South Carolina During Reconstruction, 1861–1877* (Chapel Hill, 1965), pp. 281–83; Marjorie M. Norris, "An Early Instance of Nonviolence: The Louisville Demonstrations of 1870–1871," *Journal of Southern History*, 32 (Nov., 1966), 487–504; Savannah *Tribune*, Aug. 27, Oct. 22, 1892, Sept. 16, 1899.

12. Savannah *Tribune*, Nov. 5, 1892; Booker T. Washington, "Taking Advantage of Our Disadvantages," *African Methodist Episcopal Church Review*, 10 (Apr., 1894), 480; Clarence A. Bacote, "The Negro in Georgia Politics, 1880–1908" (Ph.D. dissertation, University of Chicago, 1955), p. 18.

13. Augusta *Chronicle*, Aug. 31, Sept. 10, 13, 1898; Savannah *Tribune*, Sept. 23, 1899.

14. Savannah *Tribune*, Sept. 16, 30, Oct. 7, Nov. 18, 25, Dec. 2, 9, 1899; Savannah *Morning News*, Sept. 10, 11, 1899; Augusta *Chronicle*, Sept. 13, 1899.

15. Washington *Colored American*, Mar. 17, Nov. 10, 1900; Atlanta *Age*, n.d., quoted in Richmond *Planet*, Apr. 7, 1900; Savannah *Tribune*, Sept. 15, Dec. 8, 1900; New York *Age*, July 5, 1900, in Hampton Institute Clipping Collection, Hampton Institute. Whether because of the vagueness of the ordinance or the pressure of the Negro boycott, until 1906 the Atlanta streetcars exhibited a flexible system of segregation, with mixed smoking sections at the back of the cars, and some Negroes sitting with whites in the middle part. Agitation in 1906 led the company to institute a rigid system of segregation. Charles Crowe, "Racial Violence and Social Reform—Origins of the Atlanta Riot of 1906," *Journal of Negro History*, 53 (July, 1968), 245–46.

16. New Orleans *Southwestern Christian Advocate*, July 5, 1900.

17. Augusta *Chronicle*, May 21, 1900; Washington *Colored American*, Nov. 10, 1900; Columbia (S.C.) *State*, June 28, 1903.

18. Atlanta *Constitution*, Aug. 16, Sept. 20, 1900; Montgomery *Advertiser*, Aug. 18, 1900; Cleveland *Gazette*, Mar. 16, 1901; New Orleans *Southwestern Christian Advocate*, June 12, 1902, and Mobile *Weekly Press*, quoted *ibid.*, Sept. 4, 1902.

19. Jacksonville *Florida Times-Union and Citizen*, Nov. 11, 1901; Savannah *Tribune*, Nov. 16, 1901; New Orleans *Southwestern Christian Advocate*, Jan. 30, 1902.

20. Mobile *Daily Register*, Nov. 4, 5, 11, Dec. 2, 1902.

21. New Orleans *Times-Democrat*, Nov. 4, 6, 9, Dec. 4, 1902; New Orleans *Southwestern Christian Advocate*, Nov. 6, 1902, Mar. 26, Apr. 23, June 12, Dec. 3, 24, 1903; New Orleans *Daily Picayune*, Nov. 4, 5, 9, 1902.

22. New Orleans *Southwestern Christian Advocate*, Dec. 3, 1903.

23. Little Rock *Daily Arkansas Democrat*, June 2, 1903; Little Rock *Arkansas Gazette*, May 28, 1903.

24. Columbia *State*, June 28, 29, 1903.

25. Houston *Daily Post*, Nov. 1, 2, 3, 23, 1903, Mar. 8, 15, June 3, 1904; Charleston *News and Courier*, July 4, 1905; *African Methodist Episcopal Church Review*, 20 (Apr., 1904), 409.

26. Vicksburg *Daily Herald*, June 2, 5, 1904; Vicksburg *Light*, July 4, 1904, quoted in St. Louis *Palladium*, July 30, 1904; Natchez *Daily Democrat*, Aug. 23, 25, 1904.

27. San Antonio *Express*, Mar. 16, 17, 20, June 16, 1904; Kansas City (Mo.) *Rising Son*, May 20, 1904; Charleston *News and Courier*, July 4, 1905.

28. Richmond *News-Leader*, Apr. 20, May 20, 1904; Richmond *Times-Dispatch*, Apr. 21, 1904; Richmond *Planet*, Apr. 23, 30, May 7, June 4, July 23, Aug. 20, Oct. 15, 1904, June 10, 1905; Baltimore *Afro-American Ledger*, June 11, 18, 1904; James H. Brewer, "The War Against Jim Crow in the Land of Goshen," *Negro History Bulletin*, 24 (Dec. 1960), 53–57.

29. Nashville *American*, July 31, 1905; Cleveland *Gazette*, July 29, 1905.

30. Chattanooga *Daily Times*, July 17, 25, 26, Aug. 13, 1905; Memphis *Commerical Appeal*, Sept. 7, 1905.

31. Knoxville *Journal and Tribune*, July 6, 7, 9, 1905.

32. Pensacola *Journal*, May 7, 14, July 2, Aug. 1, 2, 4, 1905.

33. Richmond *Planet*, June 10, 1905; Jacksonville *Florida Times-Union*, July 1, 3, 24, 1905.

34. Nashville *Banner*, July 6, Aug. 1, Sept. 22, Oct. 17, 1905, Mar. 16, 1906; "Fighting 'Jim-Crowism' in Nashville," *Literary Digest*, 31 (Oct. 7, 1905), 474–75; Richmond *Planet*, Aug. 12, 1905; Indianapolis *Freeman*, Oct. 7, 1905.

35. Danville *Register*, June 20, 1906; Lynchburg *News*, June 15, 1906; Norfolk *Ledger-Dispatch*, June 15, 26, 1906; Norfolk *Virginian-Pilot*, July 15, Aug. 24, 29, 1906.

36. Newport News *Daily Press*, June 15, 1906; New York *Age*, Aug. 1, 1907.

37. Savannah *Morning News*, Sept. 14, 15, 17, 23, 1906, Feb. 3, 1907; Savannah *Tribune*, Sept. 15, 22, 29, 1906, Jan. 12, Mar. 9, 23, May 18, June 1, 1907.

38. Since the boycotts were not illegal, court records are not helpful. The Booker T. Washington Papers contain a few references to boycotts. The W. E. B. Du Bois Papers contain nothing on the subject (interview with Herbert Aptheker, Nov. 22, 1968). Inevitably, one is compelled to depend upon contemporary newspapers. Local white papers had every reason to deemphasize—even ignore—the boycotts. Neither in Memphis nor in Atlanta did the daily press even mention the ones in their own cities. And where the local dailies reported the beginnings of a boycott, almost invariably the editors seem to have decided, after a certain point, that continuing discussion was no longer in the public interest. Unfortunately, of the cities in which boycotts occurred, only for Richmond, Savannah, and New Orleans are there extant copies of Negro newspapers. Since the Negro weeklies were marginal operations which lacked an efficient national network of communication until the rise of the Associated Negro Press in the 1920's, news of events in distant cities necessarily came irregularly through correspondence and "exchanges." Yet these "exchanges" and, more rarely, letters which travelers wrote to editors, provided helpful information about the boycotts in a number of cities. Moreover, the Richmond *Planet* and the Savannah *Tribune* published unusually complete accounts of the respective boycotts in which their editors played prominent roles. Also, in a few cases, most notably in Jacksonville and Pensacola, and—during the early part of the boycotts—in Nashville, Richmond, and Savannah, the accounts in at least one of the local white newspapers are remarkably full.

All non-southern papers cited are Negro weeklies. In every case but three, when a Negro paper unequivocally reported a boycott in a major city, corroborating evidence was found in southern white newspapers and almost always in the local dailies of the cities where the various boycotts occurred. The boycotts in Atlanta and Rome, Georgia, and in Shreveport, Louisiana, were mentioned in the Negro press but not in any white newspapers consulted. In the Rome and Shreveport cases it was not possible to obtain copies of the local papers either on microfilm or at the Library of Congress. Both the Atlanta and Memphis papers carried news of boycotts in other cities, but failed to report such protests in their own.

This is a conservative enumeration. A boycott certainly occurred in Wilmington, North Carolina, but it has not been possible to ascertain its dates. (See references to it in Charlotte *Daily Observer* and Raleigh *News and Observer*, both Apr. 3, 1907.) There were hints in the Negro press of a boycott in Macon in 1899 and in Austin in 1906 and suggestions in the white press of boycotts in Asheville, North Carolina, in 1907 and in Galveston in 1906. These have not been included because of a lack of firm evidence.

39. Mobile *Daily Register*, May 17, 1905.

40. Savannah *Morning News*, July 10, 1902, Sept. 12, 13, 1906; Savannah *Tribune*, July 12, 1902, Sept. 8, 1906; San Antonio *Express*, Sept. 15, 29, Oct. 13, 1903; Jacksonville *Florida Times-Union and Citizen*, Oct. 2, Nov. 6, 8, 9, 14, 1901; Pensacola *Journal*, May 7, 1905.

41. Nashville *Clarion*, n.d., quoted in "Fighting 'Jim-Crowism' in Nashville," p. 474; Lynchburg *News*, June 9, 1906; Jacksonville *Florida Times-Union*, July 26, 1905; Savannah *Tribune*, Sept. 15, 1906.

42. Cleveland *Gazette*, July 29, 1905.

43. Richmond *Planet*, Apr. 16, 1904.

44. Richmond *St. Luke Herald*, n.d., quoted in Washington *Colored American*, Apr. 16, 1904.

45. Jacksonville *Florida Times-Union and Citizen*, Nov. 6, 11, 1901.

46. Savannah *Tribune*, Sept. 15, 1906; Jacksonville *Florida Times-Union and Citizen*, Nov. 8, 1901; Richmond *Times Dispatch*, Apr. 16, 1904.

47. Augusta *Chronicle*, May 21, 1900; Mobile *Daily Register*, Nov. 4, 11, 1902; New Orleans *Times-Democrat*, Nov. 4, 6, 1902, and New Orleans *Southwestern Christian Advocate*, Nov. 6, 1902; Little Rock *Arkansas Gazette*, May 28, 1903; Columbia *State*, June 29, 1903; San Antonio *Express*, Mar. 16, 1904; Savannah *Morning News*, Sept. 15, 1906.

48. Atlanta *Age*, n.d., quoted in Richmond *Planet*, Apr. 7, 1900.

49. New Orleans *Southwest Christian Advocate*, Dec. 17, 1903.

50. Cleveland *Gazette*, Mar. 16, 1901.

51. San Antonio *Express*, Mar. 20, 1904; Columbia *State*, June 29, 1903; Savannah *Morning News*, Sept. 14, 16, 17, 23, Oct. 1, 2, 1906.

52. Savannah *Morning News*, Apr. 29, 1908, and Savannah *Tribune*, May 2, 1908; Houston *Daily Post*, Mar. 8, 1904; Henry H. Proctor to Booker T. Washington, Apr. 18, 1900, Booker T. Washington Papers, Manuscript Division, Library of Congress; courtesy of Louis Harlan.

53. New Orleans *Southwestern Christian Advocate*, Jan. 30, 1902; Indianapolis *Freeman*, Mar. 22, 1902.

54. New Orleans *Southwestern Christian Advocate*, June 12, 1902; Mobile *Weekly Press*, n.d., quoted *ibid.*, Sept. 4, 1902; Cleveland *Gazette*, July 5, 1902.

55. Mobile *Daily Register*, Dec. 2, 12, 1902.

56. The role of the Negroes in the transportation system of southern cities in the late nineteenth century is illustrated by the fact that the drivers on the Savannah horsecars were Negroes until the system was electrified and white motormen were substituted in 1892. Savannah *Tribune*, Sept. 3, 1892.

57. Jacksonville *Florida Times-Union*, July 25, 1905.

58. Savannah *Morning News*, Sept. 14, 1906; Savannah *Tribune*, Sept. 22, 1906.

59. Savannah *Morning News*, Sept. 17, 18, 24, 1906.

60. Houston *Daily Post*, Nov. 1, 1903; *African Methodist Episcopal Church Review*, 20 (Apr., 1904), 409.

61. New Orleans *Southwestern Christian Advocate*, Dec. 17, 1903.

62. Houston *Daily Post*, June 3, 1904.

63. Savannah *Tribune*, Sept. 22, 29, Oct. 27, Nov. 3, 1906; Savannah *Morning News*, Dec. 13, 1906.

64. Contrary to a widely held view at the time, the most noted of the Negro transportation companies, the North Jacksonville Street Railway, was not really a Negro-owned enterprise, nor was it organized as part of the 1901 boycott. Actually, its founder was an accommodator who had opposed the boycott; and at all times, most of the stock was owned by whites.

65. Norfolk *Ledger-Dispatch*, July 26, 1906; Norfolk *Virginian-Pilot*, June 26, July 15, Aug. 24, 29, 1906.

66. Chattanooga *Daily Times*, July 26, 28, 1905; Nashville *American*, Aug. 30, 1905; Memphis *Commercial Appeal*, Sept. 7, 1905.

67. Nashville *Banner*, Aug. 29, 1905; Indianapolis *Freeman*, Oct. 7, 1905.

68. Chattanooga *Daily Times*, Sept. 18, 1905; "Fighting 'Jim-Crowism' in Nashville," p. 475; Nashville *Banner*, Sept. 22, 30, 1905.

69. Nashville *Banner*, Oct. 17, 1905, Mar. 16, 1906; W. E. B. Du Bois, ed., *Economic Co-Operation Among Negro Americans* (Atlanta, 1907), p. 164.

70. Jacksonville *Florida Times-Union*, July 20, 21, 26, 29, 30, Oct. 18, Nov. 15, 25, Dec. 6, 7, 8, 1905, Feb. 7, 1906; Pensacola *Journal*, Aug. 1, 2, 4, Oct. 15, 17, Nov. 22, 25, Dec. 6, 1905, Jan. 11, Feb. 11, 1906; *Florida v. Andrew Patterson*, 50 Fla. 127 (1905); *Andrew Patterson v. Isham Taylor*, 51 Fla. 275 (1906); *L. B. Crooms v. Fred Schad*, 51 Fla. 168 (1906).

71. In the few other instances in which specific individuals are named in the press, they are of the same type: Dr. Charles Shelby and attorney J. T. Settle of Memphis; Dr. W. E. Atkins of Hampton, the most prominent Negro physician in Virginia; William H. Thorogood, a politician in Norfolk; and attorney I. L. Purcell of Pensacola.

Occupational information was gleaned from a variety of sources: the newspaper reports of the boycotts; city directories; and, for the major figures, from earlier research in the period. See August Meier, *Negro Thought in America, 1880–1915: Racial Ideologies in the Age of Booker T. Washington* (Ann Arbor, 1963); Elliott Rudwick, *W. E. B. Du Bois: A Study in Minority Group Leadership* (Philadelphia, 1960). The role of the fraternal and mutual benefit orders in the development of Negro business is discussed in Abram L. Harris, *The Negro as Capitalist: A Study of Banking and Business Among American Negroes* (Philadelphia, 1936), pp. 20, 21, 47–48; W. J. Trent, Jr., "Development of Negro Life Insurance Enterprise" (Master's thesis, University of Pennsylvania, 1932). On True Reformers and their importance, see esp. W. P. Burrell, *Twenty-five Years History of the United Order of True Reformers* (Richmond, 1909); Harris, *Negro as Capitalist*, pp. 62–67; and an editorial by W. E. B. Du Bois in *The Crisis*, 3 (Nov., 1911), 9.

72. Chattanooga *Daily Times*, July 25, 1905.

73. Augusta *Chronicle*, June 3, 1900; Washington *Bee*, June 9, 1900.

74. On accommodating role of ministers, see esp. Ralph J. Bunche, "Conceptions and Ideologies of the Negro Problem," unpublished memorandum prepared for the Carnegie-Myrdal Study of the Negro in America, 1940, pp. 135–36, 147, Schomburg Collection, New York Public Library; Benjamin Elijah Mays and Joseph William Nicholson, *The Negro's Church* (New York, 1933); Meier, *Negro Thought in America*, pp. 218–24. On the ambivalent relationship of religion to Negro protest, see Vincent Harding, "Religion and Resistance Among Ante-Bellum Negroes, 1800–1860" (Paper presented at the Organization of American Historians convention, Chicago, 1967); Gary T. Marx, "Religion: Opiate or Inspiration of Civil Rights Militancy among Negroes?" *American Sociological Review*, 32 (Feb., 1967), 64–72.

75. For numerous examples of this, see Ralph J. Bunche, "An Analysis of Negro Leadership," unpublished memorandum prepared for the Carnegie-Myrdal Study of the Negro in America, 1940, Schomburg Collection.

76. Columbia *State*, June 28, 29, 1903.

77. Mobile *Daily Register*, May 17, 1905.

78. Natchez *Daily Democrat*, Aug. 23, 24, 25, 26, 27, 1904; Memphis *Commercial Appeal*, July 4, 1905.

79. Bacote, "Negro in Georgia Politics," pp. 302–6; Savannah *Tribune*, Sept. 15, Dec. 8, 1900; Atlanta *Independent*, Jan. 23, Feb. 6, 1904. Bishop Henry M. Turner was known as a militant colonizationist who denounced American racism in colorful phrases (Edwin S. Redkey, "Bishop Turner's African Dream," *Journal of American History*, 54 [Sept., 1967], 271–90). Yet he was actually a highly complex personality, not easily classifiable as either a protester or an accommodator. Thus, he urged Negroes to vote for southern white Democrats and engaged in political deals with Hoke Smith, while his colonization efforts were supported by the white supremacist senator from Alabama, John Tyler Morgan. Moreover, Negroes generally—even many Negro colonizationists—regarded the American Colonization Society, which Turner served as vice-president, as dominated by racists and as hostile to the welfare of the race. Finally, it should be pointed out that, as in the case of the more recent Marcus Garvey and Black Muslim movements, separatist nationalism, even when associated with militant rhetoric, actually is a form of escape that avoids a confrontation with the white society and thus really functions as a form of accommodation.

80. Savannah *Tribune*, May 16, 18, June 1, 1907.

81. *Hill's Directory of Richmond*, 1904, pp. 1084–85.

82. Richmond *News-Leader*, Apr. 9, 15, 20, 25, June 4, 1904; Richmond *Times-Dispatch*, Apr. 20, 21, 1904; Richmond *St. Luke Herald*, n.d., quoted in Baltimore *Afro-American Ledger*, June 11, 1904; Richmond *Planet*, Apr. 23, 1904, June 10, 1905.

83. Memphis *Commercial Appeal*, July 16, Aug. 7, 1905; Chattanooga *Daily Times*, July 7, 1905; Richmond *News-Leader*, June 10, 1904. On Florida cases, see above.

84. Nashville *Clarion*, n.d., quoted in "Fighting 'Jim-Crowism' in Nashville," p. 475.

85. Richmond *Planet*, Apr. 16, 1904; Richmond *Times-Dispatch*, Apr. 20, 1905; Richmond *Planet*, Apr. 9, 1904.

86. Shorter College, Arkansas, *Voice of the Twentieth Century*, n.d., quoted in Little Rock *Arkansas Democrat*, June 23, 1903; Columbia *State*, June 28, 1903.

87. Nashville *Banner*, Sept. 27, 1905; *Report of the Fourth Annual Convention of the National Negro Business League* (Wilberforce, Ohio, 1903), p. 24.

88. Booker T. Washington, *My Larger Education, Being Chapters From My Experience* (New York, 1911), p. 65; Washington to J. C. Napier, July 7, 1903, Washington Papers.

89. Richmond *News-Leader*, Apr. 15, 1904. See also W. E. Mollison of Vicksburg in Memphis *Scimitar*, Sept. 9, 1904, clipping in Washington Papers; courtesy of Louis Harlan.

90. Washington, "Taking Advantage of Our Disadvantages," p. 480.

91. Du Bois, *Economic Co-Operation Among Negro Americans*, pp. 164–65. The Niagara Movement was steeped in the tradition of middle-class reform tactics and failed to see the boycott as a strategy for social reform.

92. Thomas F. Pettigrew, *A Profile of the Negro American* (Princeton, 1964), p. 200.

93. In Jacksonville, where the white press gave unusually full coverage to the protests, it carried no indication that the 1901 boycott had been successful until four years later when, during the election campaign of 1905, the mayor's opponent charged that the mayor had failed to enforce the 1901 Jim Crow law. See *Florida Times-Union*, May 3, 16, 20, 30, June 6, 7, 1905.

94. Savannah *Morning News*, Sept. 14, 1906, Feb. 3, 1907; Savannah *Tribune*, Mar. 9, 16, 23, May 18, 1907, May 2, Sept. 19, 1908.

95. Mobile *Daily Register*, May 17, 1905.

96. Atlanta *Constitution*, Sept. 20, 1900; Cleveland *Gazette*, Mar. 16, 1901.

97. For New Orleans, see note 21; for Nashville, see note 34; for Atlanta, see note 15; for Newport News, see note 36; for Houston and San Antonio, see notes 25 and 27; for Augusta, see note 17.

THIRTEEN

Early Boycotts of Segregated Schools: The Case of Springfield, Ohio, 1922–23

BY AUGUST MEIER AND ELLIOTT RUDWICK

Recent agitation over *de facto* segregation in northern cities is not simply a product of the civil rights revolution of the 1960's. Actually, it is a continuation of the struggle against Jim Crow schools which many Negroes have waged throughout the nineteenth and twentieth centuries.

During the antebellum period those northern communities which offered Negroes an elementary education generally created separate schools.[1] Negroes sought integrated education by petitioning the public authorities, conducting litigation in the courts and working to secure anti-discrimination legislation.[2] In the most famous of these campaigns, Boston Negroes, having failed in their appeals to the Massachusetts judiciary, transferred their efforts to the legislature which, in 1855, made it illegal to refuse a Negro child admission to his neighborhood school.[3] Ohio Negroes were less successful. The Black Laws of 1829 excluded them from public schools entirely. Not until 1848 was legislation passed creating public schools for Negroes, and then they were segregated schools, for which the state never provided adequate financing.[4]

After the Civil War, other northern Negroes followed the example set by those in Massachusetts, and took the initiative in securing the passage of laws barring public school segregation in most of the northern states. In Ohio agitation and litigation by Negroes and their friends proved unsuccessful for two decades, and the colored schools remained clearly substandard in-

From *American Quarterly*, 20 no. 4 (Winter, 1968), 744–58. Reprinted with the permission of *American Quarterly*. © 1968 by the Trustees of the University of Pennsylvania.

stitutions; finally in 1887 the legislature, pushed largely by the militancy of both blacks and whites in the Western Reserve, passed the Arnett Bill requiring mixed schools.[5] Although the statutes were often flouted in areas bordering the South,[6] Negroes in most major northern and western cities attended integrated schools by the opening of the twentieth century.[7] In the wake of the Great Migration of Negroes to the North that began during World War I, however, numerous boards of education actively promoted policies that resulted in racial segregation, and Negro opposition generally proved incapable of reversing the trend.[8]

Not only is protest against school segregation in the urban North very old, but the use of what today we call "nonviolent direct action" also has a long, if sporadic, history. As early as 1865 Chicago Negroes initiated a boycott that led the board of education to eliminate Jim Crow schools soon after they had been established. Two years later, Buffalo colored people for a couple of weeks staged a school sit-in and boycott, which ended in failure. At the turn of the century Alton, Illinois, and East Orange, New Jersey, witnessed prolonged though unsuccessful boycotts in response to the inauguration of Jim Crow classes.[9] In the 1920's the boycott technique was used again in a handful of communities during the wave of proscriptive regulations enacted by northern school boards. Of this group of boycotts the longest and most dramatic occurred in Springfield, Ohio.

Prior to 1887, when the state legislature repealed the law authorizing educational segregation, Springfield had three Jim Crow schools. In response to the 1887 statute the school board integrated the pupils and summarily dismissed all the Negro teachers.[10] Records at the turn of the century show that, although about half of the colored children were concentrated in three schools, there was not a single institution in the entire city which did not have some Negro students.[11]

However, two segments of the Springfield population, one white and the other Negro, favored and from time to time agitated for the resegregation of the schools. In 1898 it was reported that "a few misguided Afro-Americans who profess to be lovers of the race are seeking to reestablish the separate school system in our city, in order, they say to get [Negro] teachers." Four years later a group of white mothers protested to the board of education alleging that their children were out-numbered by Negroes in the Fair Street school.[12] School integration was maintained, however, until 1922, even in the face of a prejudiced milieu which produced the Springfield race riots of 1904 and 1906.[13]

Some Springfield whites averred that the riots were caused by an increase in the Negro population. Census figures, however, indicate that its growth was negligible until the Great Migration that began with World War I, when the vast demand for unskilled labor brought many Negroes from the South to Springfield and other northern cities. In the decade 1910–20, the Negro population climbed from less than 5,000 to somewhat more than 7,000—an increase of 40 percent. Actually this gain was small in absolute numbers, and the white population also rose rapidly, with Negroes forming around 11 percent of the city's population in both years. The whites' impression of a sizable increase in the Negro population was of course heightened by the tendency of the migrants to settle in the southwestern portion of the city served by the Dibert (later the Fulton) elementary school. There the proportion of Negroes in the student body rose from about 35 percent at the turn of the century, to about 45 percent in 1912–14, and to 62 percent in 1920–21. This white awareness of a "Negro influx" helped to bring on a third riot in 1921, and renewed efforts to resegregate the schools.[14]

Early in 1920 the board of education, in anticipation of the opening of three new schools in 1922, redistricted the school zones.[15] A report later published by the National Urban League noted that soon after this action of the board, the school superintendent George E. McCord interested a few selected Negroes in the establishment of separate schools. According to the League, "These Negroes represented a wide diversity of personal interests: some with political aspirations, some cherishing the notion of independent educational development, and some with the more immediately practical hope of employment as teachers either for themselves or for their children."[16] Mrs. John Collins, Mrs. Forest Speaks, and Mrs. Jane Lee, three socially prominent Negro ladies who wanted to teach and were fully qualified applicants, informed by the board of education that it could not hire them because there were no Negro schools, thereupon obtained the signatures of over 300 colored women to a petition urging the creation of a segregated elementary school. The petition was presented to the board by Mr. Forest Speaks, a clerk at a local printing company, and state grand secretary of the Negro Oddfellows. A group known as the Progressive Civic League countered with its own petition signed by 1,200 people who urged the board to select all teachers in the "regular way," without discrimination or segregation. The Springfield branch of the NAACP held a mass meeting to discuss the question and appointed a committee to take steps against the move to establish segregated schools. The committee was composed of the physician Dr. Richard E. Peteford, who had served as branch president for the year 1918–19, and two attorneys: George W. Daniels and Sully Jaymes, the president of the Great Lakes District Conference of the NAACP. In a statement addressed to the superintendent and board of education, these men applauded the idea of hiring Negro teachers, but voiced their fear that the request might "be used as an excuse to fasten upon this community that outrageous, un-American, undemocratic and unchristian institution of Separate, Segregated and Jim-Crow Schools," to the "possible temporary financial and political benefit" of "a few self-serving people," but an "everlasting moral detriment to . . . the entire community."[17]

In May, 1922, by a vote of three to two, the board decided to make Fulton an all-Negro elementary school. Fulton was situated in an old, middle-class neighborhood which contained many Negroes, but which, in the recollections of old residents, was also "full of whites"—a situation which suggests that it was not unusual at that time for Negroes to have white neighbors. The school also served an adjacent subdivision popularly known as "Needmore," so named because it was an impoverished ghetto inhabited chiefly by recent southern migrants. There was more need of decent housing, paved streets, and sidewalks here than in any other part of town. Some of its residents were so poverty-stricken that they took sheets of tin from a neighboring city dump to construct their hovels.[18] The board planned to create a segregated institution at Fulton by transferring all the white pupils and filling their places with Negroes from other schools.[19]

Meanwhile, for the first time in almost forty years, the school board had authorized the employment of Negro teachers. By the end of August it had secured twelve Negro teachers and a principal, R. W. Bullock, a graduate of the Presbyterian institution, Knoxville College, in Tennessee.[20] Although it had been argued that the separate school would provide employment for Springfield Negroes, only two local persons were appointed.[21] One was Jane Lee, who had helped circulate the petition for a separate school.[22]

The board justified its actions in the name of the expressed will of the Negro community and cited the support of the two leading Negro clergymen—Elmer W. B. Curry of the Second Baptist Church, and T. D. Scott of the North Street African Methodist Episcopal Church.[23] Both pastored churches which, in the words of an old Springfield resident, "catered to all the educated and cultured Negroes in the city." In these two churches were the few professionals, the skilled laborers, and "those who worked in service for the very wealthy whites."[24]

The leadership of both the supporters and the opponents of separate schools appears to have been drawn primarily from these two churches. The local NAACP branch was also led by the elite of the community and was likewise split on the issue of school segregation. In the face of the cleavage, the NAACP was practically immobilized for effective protest. Old residents recalled that the branch had "turned pink tea," that "every time there was a crisis here, we couldn't get the local NAACP to help us," that "as a working organization the NAACP went flop."[25]

The NAACP's national office, it is true, was very much interested in the case, and encouraged the local branch to support actively the protest effort. Reviewing the matter in a report to the national board some months later, the executive secretary asserted that in May, 1922, the local branch had presented a petition against the segregation plan, signed by 900 Negroes of the Fulton School District; that late in September, 1922, an attorney speaking at a mass meeting had pledged the NAACP's assistance in the fight; and that the national office had sent field staff members to Springfield to lend what aid they could.[26] Nevertheless, effective protest action was clearly organized outside of the NAACP, and all in all the local branch seemed incapable of making itself relevant to the situation in Springfield. Characteristically, a 1922 meeting[27] consisted of the reading of a paper on "The Disarmament Conference and What It Means to All American Citizens." This is all the more surprising because among the branch's officers were four outstanding leaders in the protest movement: the physician T. W. Burton, the dentist Clarence F. Keller, the attorney George W. Daniels, and most notably the branch president, Sully Jaymes.

In part, the split in the Negro community over the school segregation issue appears to have been associated with a political cleavage. In spite of the fragmentary evidence that survives concerning Negro participation in local politics at the time, two things, at least, are clear. One is that, as will be shown below, the Clark County Republican leadership was segregationist in its attitude. The second is that Negroes with political aspirations in Republican-dominated Springfield took their cues from the white Republican chieftains and were therefore obliged to support the proposal for separate schools.[28]

Two of the leading Negro politicians of the city, both of whom held quasi-political patronage jobs, were George W. Eliot, school board janitor and president of the Center Street YMCA, and Olie V. Gregory, librarian of the Springfield Bar and Law Library Association. Both were unwilling to speak out against the segregation at Fulton because of their political loyalties.[29] Forest Speaks, the Oddfellows leader who had promoted separate schools, and the two elite ministers, Curry and Scott, were also political types who spoke for the Republicans.[30] It is not possible today to ascertain the rewards which these Springfield leaders personally received from their political connection. Yet as Ralph Bunche has pointed out, it was a common pattern at that time for Negro religious and fraternal leaders to be closely allied with the Republican party, and to receive for their support small favors, such as an occasional minor job and small amounts of money and political patronage.[31]

On the other hand, the leaders in the protest against school segregation, men like Daniels and especially Jaymes, were

Democrats and advocates of the view that Negroes should be "independent" and "divide their vote," rather than remain unswervingly loyal to the Republicans who had deserted them. It would appear likely that just as the stand-patters were identified with the local Republican machine, so many of the leaders and participants in the protest movement were supporters of the Democratic party. Moreover, Democratic strength among the protesters grew in the course of the controversy.[32] Since Negroes were generally Republican in this period, very likely it was the prejudiced attitudes of the local Republican influentials that caused this sharp political cleavage in the Negro community.

With the Springfield NAACP immobilized because of the split within the Negro community, the Negroes who wished to combat the plans of the school board accordingly established the Civil Rights Protective League about the middle of July.[33] In fact, the appeal for aid made to the NAACP national office came from this group, rather than from the NAACP branch.[34] The League's leaders were a distinctly elite group of Negroes. The president was Charles L. Johnson, reputedly the relative of a prominent local white businessman, and manager of the Champion Chemical Company plant.[35] The dentist, Dr. Keller, was vice-president of the League. Other important leaders were James W. Leigh, a coal and ice dealer; Mrs. Arthur Riggs, whose husband was a chemist at the Champion plant; David Wilborn, an undertaker; Charles Green, a postman; and attorneys Daniels and Jaymes. Some laboring-class people were also active in the League: Mrs. Minnie Clark, its recording secretary, was listed in the City Directory as a helper's wife. Of thirty-two members arrested in November, 1922, during a picketing incident, ten were in the professional and business class, three others were also in white-collar occupations, two were college students, nine were skilled workers, and eight were in the unskilled laboring class.[36]

Among the ministers, the League's staunchest support came from the Reverend Pleas P. Broughton of the Mt. Zion Baptist Church, a "hell-fire" church whose members were mainly recent southern migrants with limited schooling, living in Needmore. The Reverend Mr. Broughton opened Mt. Zion for the League's weekly meetings.[37] At the first mass meeting there, a "deafening applause" greeted the suggestion of David Wilborn, the undertaker, that preachers who refused to take Sunday collections for the League "should be run out of town." League president Johnson condemned conciliatory Negro leadership, telling the audience that Negroes in Dayton and Columbus lost their battles to prevent school segregation because "their leaders threw them down." The assembled citizens of the Fulton district voted not to send their children to the school when it opened on September 5, and they agreed to set up a picket line in order to increase the boycott's effectiveness. The League's strategy was to use this form of what would now be called direct action as a device to force the school segregation issue to the attention of the courts. In an effort to involve the courts, the leaders promised legal aid to boycotters arrested for violating the compulsory attendance law, and Johnson even stated that if the school authorities failed to prosecute the boycotting parents, the League would file a taxpayers' suit compelling the board to obey the state law. It was also announced that three attorneys would handle the legal work: George W. Daniels, Sully Jaymes, and A. N. Summers, formerly a judge on the state supreme court. Judge Summers had been identified as a friend of the Negroes from the time he had first run for city solicitor in 1885 on a ticket that included two Negroes running for township office.[38]

Superintendent McCord at first warned Negroes against using pickets to keep children from school,[39] and he promised that the state truancy law would be strictly enforced.[40] League officials defiantly distributed handbills announcing, "If you don't want jim crow schools, keep your children home."[41] When school opened on September 5, pickets surrounded Fulton and, though estimates varied, press reports made it clear that less than half the colored students attended that day.[42] League leaders recorded the names of children crossing the picket line and planned home visitations. Johnson begged truant officers to arrest parents who participated in the boycott. By the end of the first week the League was publicly branding its Negro opponents as traitors to the race. Picket lines of over fifty persons greeted the Negro teachers with such signs as "They Teach in Jim Crow Schools," and "We Will Not Sell Out

For A Job." A contingent picketed the home of the Reverend
Mr. Curry. When the police chief refused to grant a permit for
a parade at the school, League members defiantly marched
nearby with their banners. At a mass meeting celebrating the
success of the first week of the boycott, Johnson claimed that
about 75 percent of the Fulton children remained absent—a
figure in substantial agreement with that of the school superintendent.[43]

At the start of the second week of picketing, the League
opened headquarters in an abandoned Baptist church directly
opposite the Fulton School and made arrangements to serve
hot lunches to the pickets. At the weekly mass meeting held on
September 14, Johnson reminded the League members that,
regardless of the sacrifice, integration was essential since it was
crucial for Negro and white children to "get to know each
other." He recalled that to end Jim Crow schools in 1887 Negroes had sacrificed Negro teachers, and in 1922 they were prepared to do it again: "If we cannot have colored teachers except
in segregated schools we do not want them at all." The next
mass meeting drew a capacity crowd that overflowed into the
street and contributed $103.50 toward legal expenses.[44]

For over two months the school board failed to prosecute
those who kept their children out of school. Reluctant to
summon the boycotting parents into court, it tried to undermine
the movement by placing pressures on the poorest and most
vulnerable of the boycotting parents. Before the end of September, League leaders reported that the loyalties of some parents in the Needmore area wavered after the school board's
business manager visited their homes. Accordingly, League
representatives went from house to house countering his arguments.[45] On one occasion two League workers called upon a
poor widow whose children continued to attend school despite
her promise to keep them out. In the middle of their talk with
the lady, the Reverend Mr. Curry's son appeared with a gift of a
sack of flour—and this occurred at the very time that the minister was disclaiming participation in the controversy.[46] The following month protest leaders charged that the Springfield Social Service Bureau had denied assistance to a needy widow for
insisting that she would keep her four children out of the illegal
Jim Crow school.[47]

Morale remained high and few children attended the school, despite these covert pressures from local authorities. Even in the rain and mud of late October weather, from ten to fifteen demonstrators, mostly women, lined the street daily and watched the Negro teachers drive up to school in city automobiles and be escorted inside by the policeman on duty there. When Principal Bullock left for Kentucky to visit his sick mother, a committee of "lady-pickets" was at the railroad depot to see him off, urging him not to return.[48]

Prominent visitors from out of town like Harry C. Smith, editor of the Negro weekly, the Cleveland *Gazette*, and a former state senator, and R. B. Barkus, grand chancellor of the Negro Knights of Pythias of Ohio and special counsel in the state attorney general's office, encouraged the demonstrators in their activities.[49]

Since it was an election year, League leaders tried to use the Negro vote as a weapon in their struggle. They sent questionnaires to Republican candidates asking if they belonged to the Ku Klux Klan and if they believed in separate schools.[50] William Copenhaver, chairman of the Clark County Republican executive committee and father of H. C. Copenhaver, one of the school board members who voted for the segregated schools, informed a Negro leader that whites were running the city, and that it was the Negro's place to vote for the Republicans but not to question their policy in regard to the race's interests.[51] League officials sponsored a boycott of a Republican rally, and Charles L. Johnson declared, "If necessary we should defeat the entire county ticket."[52] Although state Republican leaders indicated concern about Negro dissatisfaction,[53] there is no evidence that local party officials were disturbed.

From the beginning, however, the League had placed its chief hope in litigation. Anxious to get the case into the courts, where they were confident of victory, in September Charles Johnson and James Leigh filed suit in the court of common pleas, requesting that the board be enjoined from keeping white students out of Fulton. On October 30, Judge Frank W. Geiger granted a temporary injunction, but the board made no efforts to reassign the white children.[54] With the injunction going unenforced, and no other progress evident, by November signs of sagging morale became clear to League leaders, who envisioned disintegration of their movement if the controversy were not settled before the arrival of winter weather.[55] Moreover, school authorities continued to refuse to arrest parents for the truancy of their children. Thus more dramatic steps seemed required to compel a real confrontation in the courts. On the morning of November 7, therefore, the demonstrators arrived at the school, 150 strong, prepared to block the entrance of the teachers, even at the risk of arrest. When the automobile arrived with Bullock and several teachers, the crowd surged into the street, and some pickets jumped on the running board. In the melee a few rocks were thrown, and it was reported that one hit Bullock and the policeman on duty. More police arrived and the crowd broke up. But no pupils whatsoever reported for school that morning. Next day thirty-two persons, including several leaders of the League, were arrested.[56]

Other arrests followed, for the board now took sterner measures and intensified its campaign of intimidating lower-class parents by threatening them with prosecution for the truancy of their children. Five parents—all unskilled working-class people—were charged in magistrate's court with violating the compulsory attendance law. The courts, however, took a more sympathetic view than did the school authorities. On November 28 the case against Laura Jackson, a Negro laundress, was dismissed after she testified about her unsuccessful efforts to register her children at a school other than Fulton. The magistrate took the remaining cases under advisement, awaiting the decision on the lawsuit which the League had instituted for a permanent injunction against the school board.[57] A couple of weeks later, proceedings against Waldo Bailey, a laborer accused of rioting and assaulting the teachers in the November 7 demonstration, resulted in an even more significant victory for the Civil Rights Protective League. Defense attorneys admitted that Bailey had jumped on the car but denied that he had committed an assault. The jury found him not guilty and subsequently the police prosecutor dropped the other cases.[58]

The picketing and the boycott continued throughout the fall and winter of 1922–23. Negroes claimed that of more than 250 Negroes assigned to the school, daily attendance never exceeded fifty.[59] Meanwhile the proceedings on the Negroes' request for an injunction against the school board were taking their course. In testimony submitted in January, school officials denied that they had established segregation at Fulton, claimed that white children were in fact enrolled as pupils there, and contended that race had nothing to do with the assignment of teachers.[60]

On January 31, 1923, Common Pleas Judge Frank N. Krapp, who had defeated Frank Geiger in the November election, granted a permanent injunction restraining the local school board from transferring children on the basis of race or color to or from the Fulton school. Krapp dismissed the board's contentions as "pure sophistry." He declared that except for the first day of the school year, when three white children appeared at Fulton, not a single white child had attended and that neither the superintendent nor the board of education expected any to enroll. Krapp offered the board two alternatives: 1) close Fulton until the start of the following school year, and meanwhile transfer the pupils to other schools; or 2) reopen Fulton immediately, giving all children the choice of attending there or any other school. The judge ruled that to prevent hardship, the white children who formerly attended Fulton could remain where they were for the remainder of the school year, but he stressed that, beginning in the fall, no school assignments were to be based on race.[61] The board ignored his specific directives and simply authorized its attorney to appeal the decision.[62] Negroes discovered that the principals of nearby schools were still refusing to admit Fulton children.[63]

In May, the board began deliberations about the Negro teachers at the Fulton school. All were graduates of colleges or normal schools and had some previous teaching experience before coming to Springfield. The board regarded their work as "very satisfactory." Nevertheless, the superintendent postponed recommending their reappointment. By the end of the summer, with no decision from the appellate court and with Fulton therefore scheduled to reopen on an integrated basis, McCord dismissed every one of the Negro teachers and replaced them with whites.[64] Almost a quarter of a century would elapse before any Negroes were again hired as teachers in the Springfield public schools.

Two weeks after Judge Krapp's ruling, evidence surfaced

which implied that leading officials in the school system were connected with the Ku Klux Klan. On February 14, the Springfield police department raided the Klan's local headquarters and confiscated its membership rolls. Listed among the 681 names were several teachers; the school board architect; two school board members, including H. C. Copenhaver, son of the chairman of the Republican executive committee of Clark County; and Superintendent McCord. Some issued denials; others remained silent. McCord, who had permitted a Ku Klux Klan meeting in the local high school auditorium a week before the exposé,[65] at first called it "one of the prettiest frameups I have ever seen."[66] A week later, however, he not only admitted membership in the Klan, but added, "I'm mighty glad of it. I think it is the best 100 percent American organization in the country today."[67]

Although the Klan supported the pro-McCord slate in the school board election of 1923, the Negroes were unable to make the Fulton school controversy a campaign issue. Neither McCord's connection with the KKK nor his role in the Fulton controversy hurt his prestige as much as the fact that for his own political reasons he had fired several popular white teachers. These dismissals made him the "main issue" in the school board election of 1923.[68] Thus the Fulton school matter was not a significant campaign issue. Indeed, though the board candidates endorsed by the Klan were defeated by over 3,500 votes, the KKK emerged victorious in contests for the city commission and the post of police judge.[69]

Shortly after the election McCord resigned under pressure as superintendent,[70] and the board of education authorized its attorney to withdraw the Fulton case from the appellate court.[71] It is not known to what extent the new board of education abided by Judge Krapp's decision. In its annual reports the board no longer supplied information about school boundaries and the number of Negro pupils. Interviews with Springfield Negroes suggest that whites residing in the Fulton district were soon able to transfer their children to other schools, while Negroes were denied that privilege. By 1936 the board's *Annual Report* once again contained data on race and boundary lines. At that time the neighborhood was still a mixed one. Nevertheless, the Fulton school district, its borders substantially changed, was 97 percent Negro.[72]

Thus, despite the support of the courts, despite the exposure and defeat of the Klan candidates for the school board, the Springfield educational officials were able by various tactics to retain essentially the system of segregation. As in other places—like Alton, Illinois, in 1908, East Orange, New Jersey, in 1906, and Dayton, Ohio, in 1926—where the boycott was also employed as a device to resist the introduction of school segregation, the victory of the Springfield Negroes was an empty one.

In retrospect, the defeat of the Springfield demonstrators would appear to have been almost inevitable. Given the increasingly racist social context in which they lived, even a more unified Negro community could not have stemmed the rising tide of segregation that accompanied the Great Migration of Negroes to the northern cities. The Negroes' position was further weakened by their political impotence and the hostility of the leaders in the party which had traditionally assisted them. The remarkable thing is not that school segregation was successfully introduced in Springfield during the early 1920's, but that some Negroes were able to resist this effort as effectively as they did.

1. Leon F. Litwack, *North of Slavery: The Negro in the Free States, 1790–1860* (Chicago, 1961), pp. 114–16, 131–35; Leslie H. Fishel, Jr., "The North and the Negro, 1865–1900" (Ph.D. dissertation, Harvard University, 1954), pp. 30–40; Horace Mann Bond, *Education of the Negro in the American Social Order* (New York, 1934), pp. 372–82.

2. Litwack, *North of Slavery*, pp. 142–51.

3. *Ibid.*, pp. 143–50; Leonard W. Levy and Harlan B. Phillips, "The *Roberts* Case: Source of the 'Separate but Equal' Doctrine," *American Historical Review*, 56 (Apr., 1951), 510–18.

4. John Hope Franklin, *From Slavery to Freedom*, 2nd rev. ed. (New York, 1961), p. 226; Fishel, "The North and the Negro," pp. 34–35, 232–34; Litwack, *North of Slavery*, pp. 114, 115; Bond, *Education of the Negro*, pp. 379–80.

5. Fishel, "The North and the Negro," pp. 234–36, 321–22.

6. For cases of this in Oxford, Xenia, and Yellow Springs, Ohio, see *ibid.*, pp. 323–24.

7. *Ibid.*, pp. 324–44.

8. Emma Lou Thornbrough, "Segregation in Indiana During the Klan Era of the 1920's," *Mississippi Valley Historical Review*, 47 (Mar., 1961), 594–618, is an excellent case study of this trend.

9. Harold Baron, "History of Chicago School Segregation to 1953," *Integrated Education*, 1 (Jan., 1963), 17; Arthur O. White, "School Segregation and Its Critics in a Northern City: A Case Study, Buffalo, New York, 1837–1880" (unpublished MS); August Meier and Elliott Rudwick, "Early Boycotts of Segregated Schools: The Case of Alton,

Illinois, 1897–1908," *Journal of Negro Education*, 36 (Fall, 1967), 394–402; Meier and Rudwick, "Early Boycotts of Segregated Schools: The East Orange, New Jersey Experience, 1899–1906," *History of Education Quarterly*, 4 (Spring, 1967), 22–35.

10. *Report of the Public Schools of Springfield*, 1886 (Springfield, 1887), pp. 20–21; *Report . . . Public Schools of Springfield*, 1887–88 (Springfield, 1889), p. 8; *Champion City Weekly Times* (Springfield, Ohio), Sept. 8, 1887.

11. *Annual Report of the Springfield Board of Education*, 1898, pp. 27–28; 1899, pp. 26–29; 1903, pp. 17–20.

12. Cleveland *Gazette*, Aug. 6, 1898, Sept. 20, 1902. Interviews with Dr. Clarence Keller and Mrs. Grace Myers of Springfield, Ohio, Oct. 26, 1966. Dr. Keller was an NAACP leader and the vice-president of the boycott movement; Mrs. Myers was an active civic worker in Springfield for almost half a century.

13. WPA Federal Writers' Program, *Springfield and Clark County, Ohio* (Springfield, 1941), pp. 55–56.

14. *Twelfth Census of the United States, 1900*, I: Population, Pt. 1 (Washington, D.C., 1901), cxxi; *Thirteenth Census of the United States, 1910*, III: Population (Washington, D.C., 1913), 418; *Fourteenth Census of the United States, 1920*, III: Population (Washington, D.C., 1922), 784–85. *Annual Report of the Springfield Board of Education*, 1898, pp. 27–28; 1899, pp. 26, 29; 1903, pp. 17, 20; 1912, pp. 26, 33; 1913, pp. 12, 20; 1914, pp. 26, 32; 1921, pp. 32, 34. On riot, see Federal Writers' Program, *Springfield and Clark County, Ohio*, pp. 55–56; Springfield *Daily Sun*, Mar. 12, 1921; Benjamin F. Prince, *A Standard History of Springfield and Clark County, Ohio* (Chicago, 1922), I, 374–75.

15. Springfield *Daily News*, Aug. 24, 1922; Address of Board of Education President on Dec. 31, 1920, in *Annual Report of the Springfield Board of Education*, 1921, pp. 7–8.

16. "The School Strike in Springfield," *Opportunity*, 1 (Feb., 1923), 27. *Opportunity* was the official organ of the National Urban League.

17. Springfield *Daily News*, Sept. 3, 1922; Chicago *Defender*, Sept. 23, 1922; Cleveland *Gazette*, Sept. 16, 30, Nov. 4, 1922; George W. Daniels, Richard Peteford, and Sully Jaymes, "A Petition to Superintendent George McCord and to the Honorable Board of Education of Springfield, Ohio" [1920?], located in Clark County, Ohio, Courthouse, Court of Common Pleas, Case No. 24366, *Johnson and Leigh* v. *Board of Education*; "School Strike in Springfield," p. 27. Springfield Bd. of Ed. *Minutes*, May 25, 1922. On Peteford as NAACP president, see Beatrice Jackson to John R. Shillady, Mar. 15, 1918; for role of Sully Jaymes as president of Great Lakes NAACP Conference, see Sully Jaymes to Mary White Ovington, May 17, 1920, both letters in NAACP Archives, Branch files, Library of Congress Manuscript Division.

18. Interviews with Mrs. Myers, Oct. 26, 1966, Feb. 9, 1967, and with Dr. Keller, Feb. 9, 1967.

19. Springfield *Daily Sun*, Sept. 1, 1922; Board *Minutes*, May 10, 1923.

20. Board *Minutes*, May 25, 1922; Springfield *Daily Sun*, Sept. 1, 6, 1922.

21. "School Strike in Springfield," p. 27.

22. Cleveland *Gazette*, Sept. 30, 1922.

23. Springfield *Daily Sun*, Sept. 8, 27, 1922; Cleveland *Gazette*, Sept. 16, 23, Oct. 7, 1922; Interview with Mrs. Myers, Oct. 26, 1966. The Rev. Mr. Curry used the columns of the local papers in an effort to convince the people of his innocence. See Cleveland *Gazette*, Sept. 17, 1922.

24. Interviews with Mrs. Myers, Oct. 26, 1966, and Dr. Keller, Feb. 9, 1967. It should be noted that because of limited economic opportunities, the criteria for membership in the middle and upper classes of the Negro community have differed from the criteria employed among whites. This was even more true half a century ago than it is today. At that time a respectable, bourgeois style of life, service in prominent white families, employment in the skilled trades, or ownership of a prospering business accorded one upper-class status along with the tiny handful of physicians, schoolteachers, and well-educated ministers.

25. Interviews with Mrs. Myers, Oct. 26, 1966, and Dr. Keller, Feb. 9, 1967.

26. "School Strike in Springfield," p. 27; Cleveland *Gazette*, Sept. 30, 1922; *The Crisis*

(organ of the NAACP), 26 (May, 1923), 25, and (Sept., 1923), 200; Robert W. Bagnall to Sully Jaymes, Sept. 18, 1922, Jan. 16, 1923, NAACP Archives, Branch files; "Report of the [Executive] Secretary," *Minutes* of the Executive Board of the NAACP, Mar., 1923, NAACP Archives.

27. Prince, *Springfield and Clark County*, p. 375.

28. "School Strike in Springfield," p. 27.

29. Interviews with Mrs. Myers and Dr. Keller, Feb. 9, 1967. Occupational data were confirmed in the city directories.

30. *Ibid.*; Chicago *Defender*, Sept. 23, 1922.

31. Ralph J. Bunche, "A Brief and Tentative Analysis of Negro Leadership," Unpublished Memorandum for the Carnegie-Myrdal Study of the Negro in America, 1940, Schomburg Collection, New York Public Library.

32. Interviews with Dr. Keller and Mrs. Myers, Feb. 9, 1967. On Jaymes's activities on behalf of Democrats, see also Dayton *Daily News*, Oct. 29, 1924.

33. Springfield *Daily Sun*, Sept. 1, 1922.

34. George W. Daniels, telegram to W. E. B. Du Bois, Sept. 18, 1922. Robert W. Bagnall, NAACP Director of Branches, in replying to Daniels's telegram, strongly urged cooperation on the matter with the local NAACP branch; at the same time he wrote to Sully Jaymes that he hoped the branch would take the initiative in the fight (Bagnall to Daniels, Sept. 18, 1922). Jaymes in turn claimed that the League had been formed by the Springfield branch of the NAACP in order to raise funds for the fight, and that the two organizations worked closely together on the case. However, the evidence in the local sources does not substantiate this claim (Jaymes to Bagnall, Oct. 4, 1922, Jan. 7, 1923; Bagnall to Jaymes, Oct. 9, 1922). All the foregoing in Legal files, NAACP Archives.

35. Cleveland *Gazette*, Sept. 16, 1922; "School Strike in Springfield," p. 27. The Champion Chemical Co. employed about 125 Negroes and 50 whites, and among its colored personnel were a number of white-collar and professional people.

36. For names see Springfield *Daily Sun*, Sept. 1 and Nov. 9, 1922; occupational data derived from interviews and city directories.

37. *Ibid.*, Sept. 7, 1922.

38. *Ibid.*, Sept. 1, 1922. For information on Summers, see B. F. Prince, ed., *Centennial Celebration of Springfield, Ohio* (Springfield, 1901), pp. 106, 150, 159, 163; James G. Johnson *et al.*, *Memorial of the Life, Character, and Public Services of Augustus N. Summers* (n.p., n.d.), pp. lxix–lxxii; Springfield *New Era*, Mar. 5, 1885; interviews with Mrs. Myers and Dr. Keller, Feb. 9, 1967.

39. Springfield *Daily News*, Sept. 3, 1922.

40. Springfield *Daily Sun*, Sept. 5, 1922.

41. Springfield *Daily News*, Sept. 5, 1922.

42. *Ibid.*; Springfield *Daily Sun*, Sept. 16, 1922.

43. Springfield *Daily Sun*, Sept. 6, 7, 8, 9, 10, 1922.

44. *Ibid.*, Sept. 12, 15, 23, 1922.

45. *Ibid.*, Sept. 28, 1922.

46. Cleveland *Gazette*, Oct. 28, 1922.

47. *Ibid.*, Nov. 25, 1922.

48. *Ibid.*, Oct. 28, 1922.

49. Springfield *Daily Sun*, Sept. 9, 23, 1922.

50. Cleveland *Gazette*, Sept. 30, 1922.

51. *Ibid.*, Oct. 7, 1922.

52. *Ibid.*, Oct. 21, 1922.

53. *Ibid.*, Oct. 21, 28, and esp. Nov. 4, 1922.

54. *Ibid.*, Nov. 4, 1922; Springfield *Daily Sun*, Sept. 24 and Nov. 10, 1922; "School Strike in Springfield," p. 27.

55. Interview with Dr. Keller, Oct. 26, 1966.

56. Springfield *Daily Sun*, Nov. 8, 9, 1922; New York *Times*, Nov. 10, 1922; Springfield *Daily News*, Dec. 15, 1922; "School Strike in Springfield," p. 28.

57. Springfield *Daily Sun*, Nov. 29, 1922; presumably the charges against the other four parents were later dropped.

58. Springfield *Daily News*, Dec. 15, 1922; Cleveland *Gazette*, Dec. 23, 1922; "School Strike in Springfield," p. 28.

59. Cleveland *Gazette*, Dec. 9, 30, 1922. Enrollment figures issued by the board tend to bear out this assertion. Even the school superintendent never claimed an average daily attendance of more than 72 between Oct., 1922, and Jan., 1923. See *Annual Report of the Board of Education*, 1923, p. 48.

60. *Johnson and Leigh* v. *Board of Education:* Affidavits of McCord, Jane Lee, and Charles H. Deam, all dated Jan. 5, 1923; and Defendant's Answer to Plaintiff's Petition, Jan. 5, 1923; Springfield *Daily Sun*, Jan. 13, 21, 1923; Springfield *Daily News*, Jan. 20, 1923.

61. Springfield *Daily Sun*, Feb. 1, 1923; Springfield *Daily News*, Feb. 1, 1923.

62. Springfield *Daily Sun*, Apr. 13, 1923.

63. *Ibid.*, Mar. 12, 1923.

64. Board *Minutes*, May 10, 1923; Springfield *Daily Sun*, Aug. 31, 1923.

65. Springfield *Daily Sun*, Feb. 15, 1923.

66. Springfield *Daily News*, Feb. 15, 1923.

67. Springfield *Daily Sun*, Feb. 22, 1923.

68. Springfield *Daily News*, Sept. 8, 9, Nov. 2, 1923; Springfield *Daily Sun*, May 27, Sept. 8, Oct. 19, Nov. 3, 5, 1923.

69. Springfield *Daily Sun*, Nov. 7, 1923.

70. Board *Minutes*, Dec. 20, 1923.

71. *Ibid.*, Dec. 27, 1923.

72. *Annual Report of the Springfield Board of Education*, 1936, pp. 21, 25.

FOURTEEN

The Origins of Nonviolent Direct Action in Afro-American Protest: A Note on Historical Discontinuities

BY AUGUST MEIER AND ELLIOTT RUDWICK

Stirred by the dramatic boycotts, sit-ins, and mass marches of the civil rights revolution, historians have been gradually discovering that blacks employed direct action tactics for over a century before the rise of Martin Luther King.* This essay, drawing both upon the work of other scholars and upon our own research, will trace the history of such tactics in black protest. As will become evident, these techniques played a considerably more significant role than scholars have realized. Yet ironically our search for the origins of the direct action which flowered in the "black revolt" of the 1960's has led us to the unexpected conclusion that its roots lay not in any past tradition of nonviolent direct action, but in the changing context of race relations which had emerged by the middle of the twentieth century.

The term "nonviolent direct action" did not enter the vocabulary of civil rights activists until about thirty-five years ago, when CORE's pacifist founders used it to describe their adaptation of Gandhian techniques to attack racism in America. The phrase synthesized Gandhi's "nonviolent resistance" philosophy with the concept of "direct action" derived from the sit-down strikes of the 1930's. Gandhi's methods, unlike those historically employed by blacks, were rooted in pacifism and

*In the following pages we have sought to avoid overstating the extent to which direct action tactics were used. Accordingly we have limited ourselves to actions undertaken by groups and have omitted incidents involving only an individual or a single family. (For the earliest and one of the best examples of individual nonviolent resistance, see discussion of Paul Cuffe's arrest for refusing to pay a tax because he was denied the right to vote, in Henry Noble Sherwood, "Paul Cuffe," *Journal of Negro* sought to convert an oppressor from immoral ways through a step-by-step escalation of tactics. When negotiations failed, agitation to arouse public opinion was used. Next came mass marches, then picketing, strikes, boycotts, and sit-downs, and finally, if all else failed, outright civil disobedience. Throughout, Gandhi and his followers sought to love their opponents and refrain from violence even in the face of death. Such an ideology was absent from American civil rights activism before 1941, achieved salience for only a brief period beginning in the late 1950's, and declined rapidly when direct action became a major strategy in the 1960's. Yet, except for civil disobedience, none of the specific tactics that Gandhi employed were novel features in Afro-American protest.*

I

Antebellum Massachusetts, where militant blacks and their white abolitionist allies sought to attack discrimination at home while they fought slavery in the South, was the site of the earliest direct-action campaigns. First came a concerted drive in 1841 against railroad lines which had introduced Jim Crow cars. Black abolitionists like David Ruggles and Frederick

History, 8 [Apr., 1923], 163–64; and Sheldon H. Harris, *Paul Cuffe: Black America and the African Return* [New York, 1972], pp. 35–36.) Except for important movements like the 1941 March on Washington, we do not mention threats of direct action where there is no evidence that these were actually carried out. With a few exceptions we have excluded brief protest actions really designed as part of a legal strategy. We have however, included certain school boycotts, where the line between legalism and direct action was hard to draw. Finally, we do not discuss occurrences, like the activities of the sharecroppers unions in the 1930's, that can more appropriately be regarded as a form of labor activism.

*"Direct action" was originally a Syndicalist term introduced in the United States in the early twentieth century by the Industrial Workers of the World (IWW), who used it, along with a rhetoric of violence, to describe their advocacy of strikes, sabotage, and mass demonstrations. The IWW was never a model for protest activity among American blacks, who did not use the term "direct action" until years later, when it was coupled with "nonviolent." The pacifists who founded CORE were much impressed with the CIO sit-down strike strategy which, though lacking a nonviolent ideology, was identified in their speeches and publications as a form of "nonviolent resistance." Gandhi himself never spoke of "nonviolent direct action," and in fact used the term "direct action" only sparingly. "Nonviolent direct action" entered the American pacifist vocabulary through the writing of the Indian scholar and former associate of Gandhi, Krishnalal Shridharani. His *War Without Violence: A Study of Gandhi's Method and Its Accomplishments* (New York, 1939), which strongly influenced CORE founders, explicitly translated Gandhi's *satyagraha* as *non-violent direct action*. The first printed use of the phrase by the pacifists who inspired the founding of CORE seems to have occurred in the pages of *Fellowship Magazine* in 1941.

Douglass, often aided by white abolitionists traveling with them, refused conductors' orders to move to the Jim Crow car and were dragged from their seats. When these actions helped arouse public opinion and generated pressure for anti-segregation legislation, the railroads rescinded their segregation policy in 1843. Soon after, blacks in Salem (1843), Nantucket (1844–45), and Boston (1844–55) protested against Jim Crow public schools by inaugurating the first known school boycotts. In each case the blacks, having capitalized upon the sentiments of sympathetic white abolitionists and politicians, achieved victory.[1]

The next cluster of direct action occurred during the heightened militance of the late Civil War and Reconstruction period, when northern blacks returned to the school segregation issue and southern Negroes fought Jim Crow on urban streetcar lines. In 1863 some Chicago Negroes angrily responded to the creation of a separate school by keeping their children home. Blacks in Buffalo and Lockport, New York, weary from years of petitioning, inaugurated boycotts in 1867 and 1871. In these two cities, moreover, black students appeared at the white classrooms in an early version of the sit-in. The Chicagoans were victorious when Republicans regained control of the city council in 1865, but in the western New York communities the elimination of the Jim Crow schools came only several years later, under circumstances quite extraneous to the black protests.[2]

Meanwhile in New Orleans, Richmond, and Charleston in 1867, Louisville in 1871, and Savannah in 1872, blacks won their fight against Jim Crow horsecars. Usually they initiated confrontations with white passengers and police by blocking the streets or boarding vehicles reserved for whites. In Savannah, however, they utilized the more moderate boycott tactic that hurt the traction company economically, but avoided overt physical conflict with hostile whites.

Mixed seating in southern streetcars remained the rule for more than a quarter-century. Boycotts quashed segregation attempts on Georgia traction lines during the 1890's. Then, beginning in 1900, municipalities and states enacted laws that soon made trolley-car segregation the rule across the South.

This rash of legislation produced a wave of defensive protests. But unlike the Reconstruction era, when blacks boldly entered the white cars, the repressiveness of the South at the turn of the century made them rely entirely on the boycott. Such boycotts, lasting from a few weeks to three years, erupted in every state of the former Confederacy and in nearly all the principal cities of states like Georgia, Virginia, Tennessee, and Louisiana. In the end this widespread movement, a rear-guard action against the rising crest of southern racism, failed everywhere.[3]

Other incidents of direct action were rare in this era of black accommodation. But in the North there were four school boycotts, protesting the introduction of segregation in previously integrated schools. These actions, forming a tiny proportion of the widespread opposition to the growing trend toward educational segregation, were all in small communities and usually accompanied by litigation in the courts. There was a brief one at Wichita, Kansas, in 1906; another at East Orange, New Jersey, in 1905–6 and one at Oxford, Pennsylvania, in 1909, each lasting several months; and finally one at Alton, Illinois, that continued for eleven years (1897–1908) and included several days of sitting-in at the white schools. A few years later at Roslyn, Long Island, blacks introduced a new tactic when sixty children marched to the white school demanding admission. All these demonstrations failed, although success came in Wichita (1907) and Roslyn (1915) from court decisions.[4]

Blacks still did not believe that direct action might be practicable in attacking exclusion or segregation at theaters or restaurants. In fact, it was unique and unprecedented when Louisville Negroes in 1913 boycotted a new theater that restricted them to a side entrance and the second balcony. Faced with financial loss, the owners acceded to the blacks' desire to use the front entrance and first balcony.[5]

Although the New York *Age* contrasted this "object lesson" with the futility of petitions and indignation meetings, these remained the strategy almost universally employed. Such was the case, for example, with attempts to halt performances of the racist play *The Clansman* in 1906–7 and its movie adaptation, *The Birth of a Nation*, in 1915–16; sometimes the traditional kinds of protests were successful. Nevertheless, amid the wave of appeals and mass meetings, direct action did on occasion occur in cities with particularly militant black groups, though only after all other methods had failed.

Thus in Philadelphia in 1906 the city's most distinguished Negro leaders, rebuffed in their appeal to the mayor, sponsored a "peaceful demonstration" at the theater. Ministers spread the word in Sunday sermons, and a crowd of at least 2,000 blacks showed up on opening night to "make a moral protest." After police manhandled a Negro for throwing a rotten egg at the movie screen, and the mood of both blacks and onlooking whites outside became ugly, the crowd was dispersed. But the demonstration proved successful, for the mayor, following a meeting with seventy-five leading black citizens, banned the play.[6] Nearly a decade later, *The Birth of a Nation* produced demonstrations in Philadelphia and Boston that involved thousands and established several firsts: the first picketing, the first mass protest march, and the first arrests for nonviolent direct action tactics. In Boston the campaign lasted for months. With the mayor refusing to halt the show, 500 blacks led by the militant editor William Monroe Trotter arrived at the theater demanding admission. When the management declined to sell them tickets, Trotter adamantly remained in the line, from which he was repeatedly ejected by police. Forcibly clearing the lobby, the law officers arrested Trotter and ten others. Stink bombs exploded inside the theater and a rotten egg splashed across the screen, while black spokesmen lectured to interracial crowds outside. Next day nearly 2,000 blacks, singing "Nearer My God to Thee," marched up Beacon Street to the statehouse; Trotter and others conferred with the governor, who agreed to ask the legislature to create a board of censors. When this new body refused to bar the film, Trotter organized a "promenade protest" at the theater, where eight were arrested for violating a newly enacted picketing ordinance. Thus completely stymied, the campaign expired.[7]

Following the slaughter of thirty-nine blacks in the East St. Louis race riot of 1917, the NAACP made even more impressive use of the tactic of a mass protest march than had Trotter's group in Boston. To publicize the horror of mob violence, the

Association held a "Silent Protest Parade" in New York. Nearly 10,000 blacks marched down Fifth Avenue to the sound of muffled drums. Five years later, in 1922, the NAACP again employed this tactic as part of its campaign against mob violence. Thousands of blacks marched through the business districts of New York, Washington, and Worcester, Massachusetts, to dramatize the Association's efforts on behalf of the Dyer Anti-Lynching Bill.[8]

In general, however, direct action tactics were used only sparingly in the decade following World War I, appearing in the form of an occasional protest against *The Birth of a Nation*, a rare attack on discrimination in public accommodations,[9] and, somewhat more often, in school boycotts.

The school boycotts, which continued sporadically through the Depression and beyond, arose principally from the growing school segregation that accompanied the migration of Negroes to the northern cities.* While some Negroes welcomed the chance to control their own institutions and the jobs which separate schools provided, black resistance in many communities was vigorous and at least fourteen experienced school boycotts in the 1920's and 1930's. (See Table I.) Except for the struggles against school board gerrymandering at Philadelphia in 1925 and Chicago in 1933, these boycotts were all in smaller places, since the extensive ghettos of the large cities precluded mixed schools in most neighborhoods. Typically the boycotts, lasting from a few weeks to as long as two years in Berwyn, Pennsylvania, were accompanied by picketing, even though that practice then lacked the legitimacy which it acquired under the New Deal. A few communities employed more dramatic tactics. In Springfield, Ohio, where the city's reluctance to sue the parents under the compulsory attendance law thwarted their strategy, thirty-two protesters landed in jail after they deliberately courted arrest by physically preventing teachers from entering the black school. At Toms River, New Jersey, the students not only went "on strike," but conducted a march to the superintendent's office. In Berwyn, after parents were arrested in 1933 for violating the attendance law, several refused to pay

*In two cases (Monrovia, California, and the Lilydale section of Chicago) the protests were directed at the poor physical state of the existing separate schools.

TABLE I

School Boycotts, 1922–1940

Springfield, Ohio, 1922–1923	Montclair, N.J., 1933–1934
Dayton, Ohio, 1924–1925	Monrovia, Cal., 1933–1935
Philadelphia, Pa., 1925	Chester, Pa., 1934
Beachwood-Shaker Heights, Ohio, 1925	East Orange, N.J., 1936
Toms River, N.J., 1927	Chicago, Ill. (Lilydale School), 1936
Blythe, Cal., 1928	Lockland, Ohio, 1937
Berwyn, Pa., 1932–1934	Abington Township, Pa., 1940
Chicago, Ill. (Betsy Ross School), 1933	

small fines; in an early instance of what activists of the 1960's would call a jail-in, they chose to dramatize their position by serving a five-day sentence.

Legal action accompanied nearly all of these boycotts. The NAACP with its strategy of litigation was involved in the overwhelming majority of them; either parents received NAACP support after the boycott had started, or occasionally, as in Philadelphia and Shaker Heights, NAACP leaders suggested the boycott in the first place. At Dayton, where the local branch was split over helping the protesters, the national office stepped in with aid; at Toms River, parents spontaneously initiated the boycott but quickly obtained support from the national NAACP; at Berwyn, where 200 students withdrew from school, a suit was filed simultaneously by the Bryn Mawr NAACP. Clearly these boycotts occurred because blacks felt the courts would uphold their contention that separate schools were illegal; their use of more militant tactics revealed anger, bitterness, and a willingness to risk jail.

Strikingly enough, although most of these campaigns proved successful, victory came either through threatening court action or going to court, rather than through the boycott tactic. Admittedly, in the Ohio boycotts of the 1920's the Springfield and Dayton authorities later emasculated the judicial victories, and in Lockland the courts actually sustained the school officials. In East Orange, where the issue was a separate class for retarded black pupils, the Negroes reluctantly returned to school when the board switched the classroom from the basement to the first floor. In Montclair, where a group of middle-class black parents were protesting the assignment of their children to an inadequate, predominantly black school while wealthy white children from the same district were allowed to attend a superior school, the NAACP case was lost when the state office of education ruled that the school board had not violated the New Jersey anti-segregation law. But elsewhere blacks won a partial or complete victory. The Philadelphia authorities backed down in the face of a lawsuit and allowed most of the protesting students to return to the mixed school. In Toms River the blacks, with an NAACP lawyer, convinced the state supreme court to overrule the board of education. In Berwyn, however, a political decision resulted. With the litigation bogged down in the courts because of the state attorney general's disinterest, the NAACP found its legal tactics under criticism from Communist proponents of "mass action" who involved themselves in the campaign and undoubtedly were the ones to suggest the jail-in tactic. But in 1934, nearly two years after the boycott began, the Republicans faced a difficult election campaign, and black threats of defection had a decisive effect. Governor Gifford Pinchot finally spoke out against the school board, the attorney general started proceedings on the case, and the city's school officials reluctantly gave in.[10]

These school boycotts of the 1930's were but a minor aspect of the large volume of direct action that erupted during the Depression. Indeed, direct action during the Depression contrasted sharply both quantitatively and qualitatively with the history of such tactics during the entire preceding century, and achieved a salience in black protest that would not be equaled or surpassed until the late 1950's and 1960's.

II

The prominence of direct action in Afro-American protest during the 1930's was due to several interrelated factors. The crisis in which blacks lost much of their precarious economic foothold, the activities of the Communist party, the legalization of picketing by the Norris–La Guardia anti-injunction act of 1932, and the general leftward drift of American society, together created an environment in which direct action could flourish.

The exact role of each of these factors is hard to measure. Clearly the greater legitimacy accorded picketing by the surge of labor union activity and the Norris–La Guardia Act influenced black activism. Yet the impact of organized labor should not be overestimated, since the real flowering of black direct action took place around 1933–34, well before the famous sit-down strikes seized the headlines in 1936–37. In fact, labor's sit-down tactics received much criticism in the Negro press, even from editors supportive of black direct-action campaigns.[11] The work of black and white Communists in the ghettos supplied a significant militant component. However, the earliest and most widespread direct-action movement during the Depression, the "Don't-Buy-Where-You-Can't-Work" campaigns, were indigenous to the black community and were regarded with considerable ambivalence by the Communists. As Joseph D. Bibb, a prominent leader in the first of these campaigns, recalled later: "The men back of the effort were believers in rugged individualism, free competition. . . . There were no Communists, no Norman Thomas Socialists, no parlor pinks . . . among them."[12] The Communists in their criticism of the "misleaders" who headed these local movements virtually conceded the point.

These job campaigns, the most important and sustained of the black direct-action demonstrations during the 1930's, were the fruit of a long-term resentment at the failure of white-owned ghetto stores to employ blacks as clerks. The issue had been growing in salience during the late 1920's.* In 1925 the New York *Amsterdam News*, for example, was urging readers to spend money only where black clerks were employed, and by the end of the decade Urban League affiliates were devoting considerable effort to persuading firms with heavy black patronage to hire Negroes.[13]

During the Depression, blacks desperate for jobs mounted boycotts and picket lines against retail establishments in at least thirty-five cities across the country. (See Table II.) Most such attacks were short lived and limited to a few stores. The bulk of

*Curiously, small-scale selective-buying campaigns had opened a few jobs at clothing and department stores heavily patronized by black women in St. Louis and Cleveland in 1920. But these were isolated incidents and were not followed up. See St. Louis *Argus*, Mar. 19, 1920, and Cleveland *Gazette*, Feb. 1, 1930, both referring to 1920 events.

TABLE II

"Don't-Buy-Where-You-Can't-Work" Campaigns, 1929–1941

Chicago, Ill., 1929–1930; 1938–1941	Durham, N.C., 1936
Toledo, Ohio, 1930; 1932	Pittsburgh, Pa., 1937
Cleveland, Ohio, 1931; 1935–late 1940's	New Orleans, La., 1937
Detroit, Mich., 1932; 1941	St. Louis, Mo., 1937–1941
New York (Harlem), N.Y., 1932; 1934–1935; 1938–1941	Newark, N.J., 1938
	Dayton, Ohio, 1938
New York (Brooklyn), N.Y., 1933–1934; 1937–1941	Youngstown, Ohio, 1939
	Corona, Long Island (N.Y.), 1939
Washington, D.C., 1933–late 1940's	Evansville, Ind., 1939
Baltimore, Md., 1933–1934	Houston, Tex. 1939
Los Angeles, Cal., 1934–1935; 1937; 1940	Memphis, Tenn., 1939
Camden, N.J., 1934	Kansas City, Mo., 1939
Richmond, Va., 1934	Berkeley, Cal., 1940
Columbus, Ohio, 1934	Oakland, Cal., 1940
Cincinnati, Ohio, 1934	Jackson, Tenn., 1940
Philadelphia, Pa., 1934; 1936–1939	Rock Hill, S.C., 1940
Boston, Mass., 1934	Lockland, Ohio 1941
Atlanta, Ga., 1935	Newport News, Va., 1941
Gary, Ind., 1936	Alliance, Ohio, 1941

the black community often seemed indifferent and was in some places divided, with critics fearful that the tactics would result in the dismissal of blacks employed outside the ghetto. Yet in more than a half-dozen cities there were sustained campaigns ranging from several months to six or eight years, and involving major segments of the community's leadership.

First appearing in Chicago in 1929–30, this form of activism flickered and petered out in Toledo, Detroit, and Cleveland during 1930–32, and then in 1933–34 flowered in a series of major demonstrations in New York, Washington, Baltimore, and Richmond, with smaller efforts in at least six other cities. In 1935 a new movement began in Cleveland that would last for years. Subsequently, in 1938, after the Supreme Court legalized these picketing campaigns, "Don't-Buy-Where-You-Can't-Work" movements blossomed in St. Louis and revived in New York, Washington, Philadelphia, and Chicago. Lesser campaigns appeared in at least twenty-one other places between 1935 and 1941.

Only a few occurred in the South. Generally limited to one or two stores, they were, except for Richmond and Newport News, characteristically defensive actions that arose originally not to create new jobs, but to protest violence by white clerks or the replacement of black workers with whites. For example, at Atlanta in 1935 after an A & P clerk assaulted a youth, angry blacks picketed and boycotted the ghetto store for about a week. Demanding that all the white clerks be dismissed and blacks hired instead, they involved the NAACP and the Urban League in the struggle, but the A & P remained adamant in preserving its white-only policy. Shortly afterwards in Durham, several hours of picketing succeeded in restoring the jobs of two Negroes who had been fired from a Kroger store to make room for whites. Similarly at Rock Hill, South Carolina, in 1940, blacks boycotted Coca-Cola when the distributor dismissed his black drivers. But in all three cities after these incidents there were no further reports of activism.[14] Clearly "Don't-Buy-Where-You-Can't-Work" campaigns, especially sustained ones, were practicable only where white public opinion and the authorities were sufficiently permissive for blacks to anticipate no serious interference and some prospect of success. Even in northern cities the demonstrators were sometimes harassed by police and stymied by court injunctions. One reason for the flourishing campaigns in New York was the attitude of Mayor La Guardia, who sought to prevent police brutality against black pickets and street speakers.[15]

In Chicago the first "Don't Buy" drive was inaugurated in late 1929 by a small group who picketed a chain grocery store. Enthusiastically taken up by the Chicago *Whip*, the project succeeded, and the newspaper promoted an even more impressive Woolworth boycott the following summer. These demonstrations and threats of similar ones against other stores brought as many as 300 white-collar jobs. Nevertheless the campaign, though championed by the NAACP, lacked wide community support. The city's leading black journal, the *Defender*, ignored it; pickets had to be paid, and after one firm obtained an anti-picketing injunction in 1931, the movement disintegrated.[16]

The Chicago demonstrations created a stir across the country,[17] although the boycott and picketing tactics did not quickly take hold elsewhere. Bibb, for example, journeyed to New York, where, speaking under Urban League sponsorship, he described in detail the *Whip*'s "non-violent" campaign. But the Harlem committee for jobs which formed soon after his presentation declared that, unlike Chicago, "We are using conservative methods in our campaigns and do not countenance picketing."[18]

Nevertheless, over the next couple of years direct action did occur in three Great Lakes cities. The most substantial attack was in Toledo; there in 1930 the NAACP branch's most successful effort, a six-week boycott and picketing against Kroger stores, obtained an agreement to employ six black clerks and one manager. Two years later another successful campaign was staged when Kroger's violated its commitment to employ a black manager. The movements in Detroit and Cleveland in 1931 and 1932 were briefer affairs, sponsored by local ad hoc groups that had some victories but soon petered out. In none of these cities was there massive community support. Like Chicago, pickets in Toledo had to be paid, and the women's clubs in Detroit, fearing a boomerang effect that would result in blacks losing jobs outside the ghetto, opposed the demonstrations.[19]

In New York, the first of the East Coast cities to experience jobs demonstrations, the achievements were particularly substantial. There the impetus came from very diverse segments in the black community. Consequently the campaigns were beset by serious internal conflicts as various factions, including two lower-class nationalist organizations, the Communists, and rival cliques among the established leadership groups vied for dominance. With the more prominent Harlem residents originally reluctant to use direct action, the first demonstrations came from the nationalist Industrial and Clerical Alliance headed by Sufi Abdul Hamid, a former Chicago cultist. Influenced by the *Whip*'s example, Hamid's group began picketing Woolworth's on 125th Street early in 1932. Generally ignored by the New York black weeklies and enjoying little support, this effort disintegrated after four months when the police discouraged further demonstrations by arresting Hamid and fourteen followers. Accordingly, the first successful New York campaign did not occur until the summer of 1933 in Brooklyn, after the elite Crispus Attucks Council called for a boycott. Picketing, however, was carried out by an organization of working-class war veterans, headed by a real estate salesman who maintained cordial relations with Sufi Hamid. By the end of the summer a few clerks had been placed, but, foreshadowing subsequent developments in Harlem, the demonstrations collapsed amid infighting between the two Brooklyn groups, the veterans charging that they did all the picketing but received none of the credit.[20]

In May, 1934, Hamid's organization once more led the way on Harlem's 125th Street, picketing retail stores and making headlines when the Reverend Adam Clayton Powell, Jr., joined the marchers at Woolworth's. Meanwhile at the urging of a women's group the Reverend John Johnson of the prestigious St. Martin's Episcopal Church had created the Citizens' League for Fair Play, a broad-based coalition that inaugurated a boycott of Blumstein's Department Store in June. The League consisted of a wide range of organizations, from elite civic groups to the Garveyite African Patriotic League; the latter provided the leadership and manpower for the coalition's picket committee. After six weeks of boycotting and demonstrations, Blumstein's capitulated and hired five black clerks. Other stores quickly added black salespersons and by fall about a hundred jobs had been obtained. Nevertheless, Harlem was far from united. Thus the New York *Age* was an active ally of the Citizens' League, but the rival *Amsterdam News* opposed the campaign and tried to ignore it. There had been friction between the picket committee and Hamid's demonstrators; after the Blumstein agreement, Hamid denounced it and continued picketing the department store. In September the Citizens' League split wide open amid charges that jobs at Blumstein's went to light-skinned bourgeois women, rather than to the dark-skinned lower-class people who had done the picketing. The picket committee broke away, mounted its own demonstrations, and forced some stores to replace the recently hired clerks with its own members.

By then the Harlem campaigns reverberated in Brooklyn, where the Crispus Attucks Council renewed its demonstrations in September. Activities in Harlem, however, were seriously hurt in October when a shoe company, rejecting the picket committee's demand to fire the light-skinned employees, obtained an injunction from New York Supreme Court Justice Samuel I. Rosenman, who ruled that the picketing was not covered by the Norris–La Guardia Act. With leaders of both the Citizens' League and the "renegade" picket committee named in the injunction, only sporadic demonstrating followed, led by the Hamid group for a brief period, and more frequently by two interracial Communist organizations, the League of Struggle for Negro Rights (LSNR) and the Young Liberators.[21]

The Communists had at first been hostile—and then ambivalent—about the "Don't Buy" campaigns. These demonstrations were militant protests which they wished to exploit. Yet wedded to the principle of interracial workingclass solidarity, the Communists feared the divisive effects arising from dismissing whites to hire blacks. Their first response was to criticize. Maintaining that white and black workers should "stick together and demand the right of Negroes to all jobs with equal pay," they had denounced the leaders of the 1931 Cleveland demonstrations as "Negro reformists" who "mislead the Negro masses" by "exploiting race discrimination for their own benefit. . . . Their real object . . . is to create a jim crow market for Negro business." By 1934, however, the LSNR had decided to capitalize on the job issue, and in February it inaugurated campaigns against New York's Fifth Avenue Bus Company and certain chain stores in Boston and Philadelphia. In all cases the Communists' interracial demonstrations were peripheral to the mainstream of the "Don't Buy" movement and had no discernible influence on the black protest groups. Thus, although the Fifth Avenue Bus Company's substantial patronage from Harlem riders made it an ideal target, the LSNR was unable to mobilize support from other organizations. Insisting that openings for black bus-drivers come from shortening the work week rather than from firing whites, and enlisting a few black and white sympathizers, the LSNR inaugurated interracial picketing at the 125th Street terminal. Several whites and blacks were arrested the first day; thereafter the picketing and boycott continued with diminishing force, and an effort to revive it in July failed.[22]

The Communists revealed their ambivalence when the Citizens' League seized the spotlight that summer of 1934. "The boycott method," averred the *Negro Liberator* (LSNR organ), "is very good, because it is essentially a mass movement. . . ." On the other hand, Hamid and Johnson were simply "quarreling over the best way to continue the misleadership of the Negro masses." The Citizens' League was "a hodge-podge of self-seekers" barring sincere whites from picket lines and "taking advantage of the nationalist feelings of the much oppressed Negro people" in order to gain security for themselves.[23] Upstaged by the Citizens' League and failing to revive the Fifth Avenue bus boycott, the Communists in September sponsored their own successful job protest against a Harlem cafeteria. A few weeks later the Young Liberators mounted an interracial picket line at a variety store in Brooklyn; as if to underscore Judge Rosenman's recent hostile decision, a black and a white picket were sentenced to ten days in jail. Overall, with the combined pressures of the Communists and the Crispus Attucks Council, several Brooklyn stores hired blacks that autumn. But although the Communists promoted picketing in Harlem again in the spring of 1935, even attracting to their lines several prominent non-Communists like the Reverend William Lloyd Imes and Adam Clayton Powell, Jr., the momentum behind the local boycott was gone, and was not revived again until after the Supreme Court legalized the picketing in 1938.[24]

In no other city did such antagonistic and quarreling groups simultaneously sponsor demonstrations. Yet New York revealed in microcosm the strikingly diverse sources of support for the job campaigns that flourished across the country in 1933–34, and at a diminished pace into 1935–36. The members of the New Negro Alliance of Washington, formed in August, 1933, were a distinctly elite group of young, college-educated people, including a sprinkling of lawyers and professors. Rebelling against the gradualist methods of their elders in the NAACP, they galvanized support from among the city's black bourgeoisie and presented the unusual case of upper-class Washingtonians on the picket lines. In Baltimore the campaign was initiated in September, 1933, by an associate of Hamid, a faith healer named Kiwah Costonie. Local ministers were skeptical of his leadership, but he quickly gained the assistance of the Baltimore *Afro-American* and formed a chiefly middle-class coalition which included the lodges and two groups led by dynamic women: Lillie Jackson's Housewives' League, and her daughter Juanita's Young People's Forum. In the enthusiasm, many of the preachers fell into line. In contrast to both Washington and Baltimore, the Richmond campaign that began in March, 1934, was spearheaded by the NAACP, with the support of prominent ministers and fraternal leaders and the Richmond *Planet*. Once the boycott was under way, the Communist International Labor Defense (ILD) volunteered assistance which was accepted reluctantly. Communists were active in a few other cities as well. In the sustained Los Angeles campaign the *Sentinel* and its publisher Leon H. Washington worked in alliance with the Communist party's Young Men's Progressive League. In Cincinnati, where Baptist ministers had inaugurated a boycott, and where several young blacks had been arrested for "intimidating" storekeepers, the preachers came under criticism from the LSNR for not picketing and for limiting their targets to small grocers, rather than the major chain stores. The Camden, New Jersey, campaign was a project of a YMCA-sponsored Negro History Club, consisting of middle-class youth. The movement in Columbus, Ohio, led by a WPA street gang foreman, consisted of unskilled and unemployed workingmen, whose sporadic picketing produced a few jobs at Woolworth's and Kroger's. The unusually successful Cleveland Future Outlook League, organized by an Alabama-born shipping clerk, James O. Holly, drew chiefly from a lower-class constituency and at first faced opposition from the more conservative, established leaders. But from the beginning it had the unstinting backing of the black weekly, the Cleveland *Call and Post*; the paper's influential editor-publisher William O. Walker was largely responsible for the League's durability and its broad community support.

All of these jobs campaigns employed the twin direct-action tactics of boycotting and picketing, and in a majority of cities the street demonstrations produced one or more arrests on charges of disturbing the peace. Some groups, notably the Future Outlook League, spent little time negotiating and moved quickly to staging demonstrations in the streets. Others, particularly in Washington and Richmond, moved with considerable deliberation, making thorough investigations of retail trade patterns to strengthen their hand in negotiations, and turned to direct action only as a last resort. The impatient Future Outlook League tended to couch its demands more in the form of threats, and over time even the New Negro Alliance put less emphasis on negotiation and greater stress on action in the streets.

Despite differences, the movements appear to have generally been imbued with a petit bourgeois black business philosophy emphasizing not only job opportunities but upward economic mobility and the development of black enterprise as well. As a practical matter all of these organizations devoted their efforts to securing jobs for blacks in white-owned firms, yet ideologically they often placed equal or even primary emphasis on creating "bigger and better Negro business." As the Future Outlook League officially advised: "First, patronize your own group and second, patronize the business that will give you employment." Similarly, the New Negro Alliance declared: "We must organize our purchasing power behind a demand for equal opportunity to work and also in support of those businesses in which Negroes can do work without discrimination. The support of businesses owned and operated by Negroes is of course an essential part of such a program." Black entrepreneurship would in fact be helped, partly because training in successful white-owned firms would prepare blacks to establish their own companies. The nationalist spirit exemplified by this kind of economic separatism characterized most of the jobs movements in greater or lesser degree. Only in New York did one find the full-blown nationalism of the old Garveyites; but in Baltimore, for example, Costonie conducted classes in black history and race pride for the youth of the community. Furthermore, the Future Outlook League expressed what was undoubtedly a widespread viewpoint when it declared that one of its principal aims was "to advocate a closer union as a race, regardless of religion, politics, or economic status in life."

The New Negro Alliance was divided. For example, one prominent member sought to discount the importance of creating more black entrepreneurs when he observed that, practi-

cally speaking, Negro business for the foreseeable future would
be unable to furnish significant employment for the masses.
Moreover, the Alliance, which was severely criticized by the
well-known Howard University professors Ralph Bunche and
Abram L. Harris for a narrow "racialism" and a failure to
understand that the race's economic salvation lay in an alliance
with white labor, modified its ideology. Denying that its primary interest was to create a black capitalist class, the organization's leaders declared that their aim was to "better integrate
the Negro into the economy which exists and whose corporate
nature has excluded him, not further to separate [the] black
and white economy." Eventually it even cultivated a working
alliance with local CIO unions. But like the other "Don't-Buy-
Where-You-Can't-Work" movements, the New Negro Alliance
depended upon the power derived from a self-conscious racial
unity. As this successful organization's journal declared editorially in responding to the criticisms of Bunche and Harris:
"Uncontrolled and fanatic racialism is undoubtedly bad. But
worse even than that is lack of unity. . . . We believe in intelligently controlled racialism as an approach to the problem of
the eradication of racial lines."[25]

In almost every city, chain grocery stores—especially the
A & P—were favorite targets which often proved vulnerable to
the demonstrations; in some places, especially Washington and
Baltimore, smaller, independent merchants were also attacked.
Most of these movements achieved some early victories. The
New Negro Alliance obtained concessions from several small
firms, and most notably from the A & P; six months after or-
ganizing they had secured thirty-five openings. In Baltimore
the A & P and American stores not only opened up fifty sales
jobs, but also agreed to train blacks for managerial positions.
Elsewhere in the North the story was similar—in Columbus
sporadic picketing produced a few jobs at Woolworth's and
Kroger's; in Los Angeles there were victories at several ghetto
stores, most notably at Kress, that secured twenty-six openings.
More substantial were the results in Cleveland, where the Future
Outlook League's picketing and boycott projects brought jobs
at A & P and other grocery chains, movie theaters, and a dairy;
by the end of 1936 the League announced that it was responsi-

ble for the fact that slightly over 300 people were holding positions which had been previously closed to blacks. The Richmond NAACP also hopefully concentrated on the A & P chain, which in that southern city, felt no need to budge; yet fear of a possible boycott made some smaller Richmond stores hire about fifty Negroes.

Only a few campaigns—Washington, Baltimore, Richmond, and Cleveland—enjoyed a broad base of support. In Los Angeles, where the demonstrations lasted eighteen months, the NAACP branch publicly opposed the picketing, and the California *Eagle*, originally sympathetic to the *Sentinel*'s project, became very critical after a year. Even in Baltimore, Washington, and Richmond, after several months the campaigns encountered difficulties that effectively undermined them. In Baltimore, when the protesters turned from the chain stores to the smaller owner-operated businesses on Pennsylvania Avenue, an injunction was issued that halted the direct action. With the aid of the NAACP, the fight was taken to the courts; the leaders, capitalizing on the high pitch of enthusiasm, raised $1,200 in nickels and dimes from the Depression-ridden community. But the higher courts in the state sustained the injunction, and with Costonie's leadership already seriously damaged because of complaints that he had misappropriated funds, the local jobs movement was permanently destroyed. About the same time that Baltimore blacks were confronted with the injunction, the New Negro Alliance became embroiled in litigation with a department store, whose sales had plummeted because of an extraordinarily effective boycott. By mid-1934 this court case and a couple of others brought an end to direct action in Washington. Two years later demonstrations were revived, but they quickly stopped again when the Sanitary Grocery Company secured still another anti-picketing injunction. In Philadelphia sporadic but victorious campaigns conducted by coalitions in both North and West Philadelphia in 1936–37 came to a halt with the arrest of seven leading activists. In Richmond, although the A & P declined to bring the demonstrators into court, its firmness was very debilitating. Despite the impressive black unity there, community support soon collapsed; even a dramatic torchlight parade in

June, 1934, failed to revive the flagging campaign. Cleveland, however, proved an exception. Having been twice enjoined, the League in 1936 suspended picketing but was hardy enough to continue its successful activities solely through calling boycotts. Elsewhere even the strong campaigns tended to be short lived because of community apathy, disunity among the protesters, and adverse court decisions. None of these factors was individually decisive, though the vigorous support of at least one influential black newspaper was essential for a viable movement. Thus in Chicago, where the boycott was ignored by the *Defender*, a court injunction snuffed out an already declining campaign after financial reverses forced the *Whip*'s demise. Yet in Richmond the skillful waiting game played by A & P led to community apathy and sapped the NAACP, even though the demonstrations were supported by the city's influential black newspaper. Court injunctions did have a crushing effect, as in both the solidly organized Baltimore movement and the highly factionalized one in New York. On the other hand, the Future Outlook League and the New Negro Alliance remained intact despite adverse court decisions.[26]

The Alliance's 1938 Supreme Court victory in the Sanitary Grocery case upheld the right of a racial group to picket against job discrimination, and it was correctly assessed by black leaders as a landmark decision.[27] This ruling encouraged direct action across the country, bringing a renaissance of job campaigns in Washington, New York, Philadelphia,[28] Chicago, and Cleveland, and a major new drive in St. Louis.

In Washington, though the Sanitary Grocery chain continued its resistance, the Alliance negotiated a settlement with Kaufman's department store. Utilizing contacts in the local labor movement, it also prevailed upon a brewery workers' union to allow the employment of some blacks as truck drivers. By 1940 the Alliance, which moved against one ghetto store after another, could claim that on upper Seventh Street there was now scarcely a store that did not employ at least one Negro clerk.[29]

Closely akin in style to the New Negro Alliance was the Urban League–inspired St. Louis Colored Clerks Circle, composed of youthful high school and college graduates. The St.

Louis Urban League was itself an adept proponent of direct action and had used boycotts to open up jobs as milk, bakery, and coal-truck drivers. In its search for white-collar employment the Circle made detailed surveys of retail trade patterns, lined up support among the ministers, and (with the Urban League's help) conducted training sessions in clerking for its members. Direct action was used only "as a last resort." Taking to the streets after the New Negro Alliance decision, the Circle picketed and boycotted Kroger's for several weeks and won a favorable agreement. Moving on to other targets, it secured 140 sales and clerical positions in less than a year. Active until World War II, the Circle consistently enjoyed the cooperation of the Urban League—and indeed, the success of its drives came largely through support from a network of forty-five block clubs which the League had organized in the ghetto.[30]

In Chicago the revived job campaigns were the work of two groups: the Council of Negro Organizations, a coalition in which the Urban League was dominant; and the more militant Negro Labor Relations League, a small group composed mainly of young blue-collar workers. The two organizations in 1938 attacked the dairies that had long resisted hiring black drivers. The Negro Labor Relations League prevailed upon some South Side restaurants and residents to switch to the few companies which employed Negro drivers, and the Council twice sponsored a "milkless day" against discriminatory firms. Simultaneously with this futile campaign, the Labor Relations League called a successful movie theater boycott for jobs as projectionists. Mass demonstrations forced one major theater to capitulate; other similar protests led to the arrest of three pickets in a near riot when the demonstrators resisted police orders to disperse. By mid-November management and the union had given in and ten blacks were hired in south side theaters. The following year the organization's attempt to change Illinois Bell Telephone's employment policies fizzled when only a few black subscribers heeded a plea to cancel their phone service, but the picketing of south side realty offices produced jobs for several black clerks in 1940. Generally the League found Chicago blacks unenthusiastic about boycotting and picketing. Even in the case of their successful theater project they were reduced to using stink bombs to discourage movie-goers from crossing the picket line.[31]

This sporadic effort in Chicago was in marked contrast with the hard-hitting, sustained work of Cleveland's Future Outlook League and the complex and fruitful movement in New York. Following the Supreme Court decision the Cleveland group returned to the streets with greater frequency, most notably in the April, 1938, Woolworth demonstrations that produced a minor riot but a quick capitulation by the company, and the 1941 demonstrations at Bell Telephone's offices that opened jobs to blacks downtown. On the latter occasion the League introduced an innovative disruptive tactic when thousands of housewives simultaneously dialed "O" and jammed the switchboards. The League's militancy produced several arrests; in 1941 Holly himself served a brief jail sentence for picketing in violation of a court injunction. Undoubtedly the League's increasing influence owed a good deal to the city's political milieu. Blacks had five representatives on the thirty-three-member city council (including *Call-Post* publisher William O. Walker himself) who possessed a certain amount of political clout. Indeed, the intervention of Walker and other politicians in the telephone company case was undoubtedly a major reason for the quick victory. By the end of the decade the activities of the highly successful Future Outlook League had opened up over a thousand positions in white-owned establishments.[32]

In New York the revival of direct action actually preceded the Supreme Court decision, commencing in 1937 when two rival Brooklyn groups—a middle-class, interracial Citizens Civic Affairs Committee, and an offshoot of the African Patriotic League—chalked up modest successes. The following year open feuding broke out between them; in 1939 the Civic Affairs group split into Communist and anti-Communist factions, and by 1941 the banner of the Brooklyn jobs campaign had passed to the National Negro Congress, which was picketing Woolworth's.[33]

In Harlem three major groups sprang into action directly following the Supreme Court decision: the Harlem Labor Union (HLU), established by the African Patriotic League after Judge Rosenman's injunction; Adam Clayton Powell's Greater

New York Coordinating Committee for Employment; and the Harlem Job Committee, created by the *Amsterdam News* with the support of A. Philip Randolph. The Harlem Job Committee, after negotiating a weak, unenforceable agreement with the 125th Street merchants, soon faded away. Powell's group, a large coalition ranging from the ILD to the Urban League, moved into the vacuum, and in May, 1938, began picketing on 125th Street. Three months later the merchants agreed to hire blacks for at least one-third of the white-collar jobs in their stores, and by October over 300 positions had opened up. But the Harlem Labor Union, unhappy because its members were not hired, continued the street demonstrations which often forced the storekeepers to replace new black employees with HLU people. In the end, the two organizations divided responsibilities. The HLU concentrated on Harlem, where it won many victories, and Powell's group dealt with large downtown companies. In 1939 the Coordinating Committee attacked the World's Fair Corporation, and although few white-collar positions resulted, 400 blacks were added to the Fair's payroll. The picketing of Fair headquarters at the Empire State Building and the appearance of 500 black pickets at the fairgrounds on opening day were unprecedented mass demonstrations outside of the ghetto.[34]

The Powell Committee's most important achievement was the 1941 bus boycott conducted in cooperation with the HLU and the National Negro Congress. Communist influence was especially evident in this renewal of a campaign which the LSNR had sponsored in 1934. The National Negro Congress, the Committee's executive secretary, the supportive Transport Workers Union president Mike Quill, and Powell himself were all closely identified with the Communists at that time. For four weeks Harlemites boycotted the vehicles of the Fifth Avenue Bus and the New York Omnibus companies, both of which barred blacks as drivers. Thus pressed, the two corporations pledged to recruit 100 blacks as drivers and 70 as mechanics, and thereafter to hire blacks and whites on a 50-50 ratio until Negroes reached 17 percent of the blue-collar skilled work force. This kind of agreement was unprecedented and would not be seen again until the 1960's.[35]

Nowhere did these campaigns[36] make a significant dent in mass unemployment—a fact that is not surprising, since the bulk of the job market lay outside the ghetto. Yet in terms of the patterns of employment within the ghettos, the stronger local movements wrought marked changes. The more successful campaigns were responsible for placing hundreds of blacks in white-collar jobs. Others benefited indirectly, as many employers hastened to head off possible boycotts by changing their hiring practices. By the time the Depression ended, the presence of black clerks in the ghetto stores of major cities had ceased to be a rarity, and the changes were accentuated by the wartime manpower shortages. Not only could the New Negro Alliance assert that every store on upper Seventh Street now employed blacks, but by 1944, a dozen years after the first pickets appeared on Harlem's 125th Street, the majority of sales personnel there were black.[37]

On the other hand, most of the "Don't-Buy-Where-You-Can't-Work" movements were short lived, obtaining only modest victories; overall they collapsed with the coming of World War II. Only Cleveland's Future Outlook League, Washington's New Negro Alliance, and Chicago's Negro Labor Relations League survived into the postwar era, and their activities were sharply curtailed. Indeed, nowhere were the campaigns revived on a significant scale following the war. There are probably several reasons for this. For one thing, as we have suggested, changing employment patterns in black neighborhoods meant that the issue lacked its earlier salience. Moreover, despite the Future Outlook League's success with the phone company and the Greater New York Coordinating Committee's victory over the bus companies, black protest leaders did not regard direct action as a viable tactic against major corporations outside the ghetto. As one leader observed after the New York bus boycott, similar campaigns were not feasible in other large cities, since Harlem was unique in being served by an extensive subway system which provided satisfactory alternative transportation. In general, events bore out the 1933 prediction of the well-known commentator Kelly Miller, who suggested that boycotts "can be used only in densely segregated areas and cannot be extended to the downtown business districts where the great volume of business is transacted."[38] Not until the 1960's, when changing urban demographic patterns made downtown businesses more dependent on black patronage, did economic pressures against them become a significant part of black protest strategies.

It is a striking fact that the NAACP, the leading black protest organization, had only a minimal role in these campaigns. Indeed, the Urban League was far more supportive. Du Bois commented favorably on them in *The Crisis*, but NAACP branches were only occasionally involved, and the national office was cautious, if not ambivalent. In 1931, at a time when the Chicago campaign was widely talked about, NAACP Secretary Walter White simply advised the branches to meet with storekeepers and ask for jobs. At the NAACP's 1933 annual conference, in the midst of rising pressures on the Association to do something on the economic front and Communist criticisms of its failure to engage in "mass action," there was intense debate over whether the Association should "shift its lines of attack to meet the needs of the day." A representative of the Toledo branch told the delegates about its picketing of ghetto stores, but the convention decided not to endorse direct action and instead recommended a vaguely worded resolution urging blacks to "exercise their collective power as consumers."

By the following year the national office displayed somewhat greater involvement in direct action tactics. It gave substantial financial assistance to the Baltimore citizens' struggle against the injunction there. A few months later White, alarmed at Rosenman's decision in New York, personally discussed the matter with the judge and even considered an appeal to higher courts. Yet the Association was still not ready to openly endorse the jobs campaigns. Symbolically, *The Crisis* published a debate on the subject entitled "To Boycott or—Not to Boycott." Four years later, when the Supreme Court handed down its decision in the New Negro Alliance case, the NAACP enthusiastically publicized it but did nothing to stimulate further demonstrations, and in New York the national office was stand-offish toward the Greater New York Committee. Not until 1941, at the very tail end of the "Don't-Buy-Where-You-Can't-Work" campaigns, did Walter White publicly identify himself with them. At that time he had *The Crisis* print a picture of him marching outside a grocery store on a picket line sponsored by the Washington NAACP and the New Negro Alliance.[39]

By then the Association had made a calculated decision to become involved more directly in labor matters. Not long after, Walter White assisted the UAW in its organizational struggle with the Ford Motor Company, personally circling the plant in a sound truck and urging black workers to join the strike. This event marked a turning point in the NAACP's relations with organized labor, and the beginning of a period of close cooperation with the CIO. Yet the NAACP had long been concerned with Jim Crow practices in trade unions and at least once had employed a direct-action tactic—in 1934 the national office picketed the AFL's annual convention.[40] Actually, direct action was rarely used to fight union discrimination, although occasionally local organizations like the St. Louis Urban League, the Chicago Communists, and the American Consolidated Trades Council of Chicago picketed construction sites in black areas, demanding skilled jobs and the ending of union barriers.[41] All in all, direct action tactics were not utilized to gain jobs for blacks in the skilled trades or in major industry, but were pretty much limited to obtaining positions in ghetto retail establishments.

III

Like the NAACP, the Communists were essentially at the periphery of the "Don't-Buy-Where-You-Can't-Work" campaigns, and except for New York's bus boycott, they had not been responsible for innovative tactics. On the other hand, when it came to using direct action to tackle other problems of the black poor, Communist organizations were in the vanguard, inspiring a widespread series of demonstrations ranging from mass marches to sit-downs. Such "mass action" was especially intense in New York and Chicago, but occurred also in cities across the country from Los Angeles to Philadelphia and even in cities of the Upper South like Norfolk and Richmond.

In the early years of the Depression, blacks formed a large proportion of participants in the hunger marches which generally were Communist-inspired and often precipitated bloody confrontations with police. On March 6, 1930, Communist-sponsored International Unemployment Day demonstrations across the country included blacks among the marchers and speakers. At the one in Washington, Negro workers made up the bulk of the marchers in front of the White House. At Charlotte, North Carolina, the protest marked "the first time Negro and white workers openly demonstrated under the Communist banner in the South." Blacks figured prominently among those who marched on city halls and state capitols in the next few years—in Chicago, where they participated in several hunger marches between 1931 and 1933; in Pennsylvania, where a Negro miner was a prominent spokesman among the 400 marchers to the state capitol; in Richmond, where 6,000 demonstrators, mainly blacks, marched on city hall demanding larger relief payments; and elsewhere.[42]

The Communist-sponsored Unemployed Councils also brought workers from across the country to Washington for mass hunger marches, and in fact originated the phrase "March on Washington."[43] A quarter of the 1,600 who arrived for the one in December, 1931, were blacks; the "spokesman and leader" of the delegation that sought to see President Hoover was an unemployed black from Indianapolis. Both then and on the march held a year later, the protesters fought discrimination against black participants and insisted on sleeping and eating together. In 1932, when southern hunger marchers on their way to Washington were barred from Richmond's municipal auditorium and from housing accommodations in the city's white sections, they were quartered in the black-owned Johnson's Auditorium and held their mass meeting at the True Reformers' Hall. Black non-Communist observers were impressed, and a *Courier* columnist who witnessed the first march reported: "A large number of Negroes were in the lineup, and the whites saw to it that the Negro leaders as well as the followers, were treated fairly even in the southern city of Washington."[44]

After government relief agencies were created, they also became targets for mass demonstrations. These actions were generally Communist-inspired and interracial, even when they took place in Negro ghettos. Many such protests were held, especially in New York and Chicago; for example, Chicago police in January, 1932, battled more than 300 people who threatened to storm the offices of the relief commission.[45] In St. Louis two days of mass parades and demonstrations, involving thousands, were held at City Hall, demanding food and other assistance for those cut off the rolls of relief agencies. Blacks were prominent among the speakers and marchers, who sang to the tune of the old radical song "Solidarity Forever": "We're for interracial solidarity; we would rather fight than starve in slavery," with the refrain, "Solidarity forever, our Union makes us strong." On the second day, with the mayor still refusing to meet with the delegation of the protesters, a mixed crowd sought to force their way past the police into the city hall and were dispersed by tear gas. Even as far south as Greensboro, North Carolina, the interracial Unemployed Councils staged a strike of workers on federally funded relief projects, because blacks were discriminated against in the wage scale.[46]

Such demonstrations subsided after 1934, but in the aftermath of cutbacks in WPA jobs and relief appropriations the protests erupted again in the late 1930's.[47] Occasionally they were staged by non-Communists, as when a Brooklyn Baptist minister, Thomas S. Harten, led a mass march from his church to the relief station. Sometimes violence broke out, as in Cleveland in 1934, when police fired on black and white demonstrators at the Cuyahoga County relief office, killing two. Even in Atlanta the Workers' Alliance flouted custom when, early in 1939, it defied police with interracial picketing at WPA headquarters, demanding jobs and more relief for the unemployed; at the end of the year there were further mass demonstrations involving hundreds of whites and blacks at WPA headquarters and city hall, protesting cutbacks in WPA rolls.[48] This wave of demonstrations, influenced by the sit-down strikes, often exhibited a radicalization of tactics. In New York the Alliance and other organizations sponsored sit-downs both at Harlem's relief bureau and at the welfare office downtown. An interracial group led by the Workers' Alliance occupied a WPA office in Cincinnati for two weeks until removed by police. In Cairo, Illinois, a two-day sit-in at relief headquarters, staged by the Workers' Alliance, similarly ended when the protesters were evicted by National Guard troops and sheriff's deputies. Chicago experienced similar sit-in demonstrations at relief stations in black neighborhoods, and not long afterward a hundred whites and fifty blacks held a sit-down at the Illinois state capitol to press for passage of a relief bill. In Ohio an interracial group representing the state-wide Workers' Alliance sat in at the governor's office to emphasize problems involving relief allocations; one black was among the six arrested. At St. Louis in 1939 a group of nearly seventy mothers, one-third black, cut off from their WPA jobs, occupied the gallery in the aldermen's chambers. Vowing to remain until the alderman "decide to do something about it, even if it takes weeks," the women passed the time by singing "We Shall Not Be Moved," and spirituals in which the blacks led. The women remained in the gallery until threatened with arrest twenty-four hours later.[49] Perhaps the most unusual demonstration of the period involved several young black women who had been selling to the Chicago Health Department breast milk for orphaned babies. Demanding an increase from a paltry four cents an ounce, they held a sit-down strike right on the benches at the Board of Health office in 1937.[50]

Communists were in the forefront of the struggles with landlords, particularly in eviction protests early in the Depression, and less prominently in the rent strikes that came later. As the Depression deepened, landlords evicted tenants behind in their rent. Communist organizations—usually Unemployed Councils and the League of Struggle for Negro Rights—sought to move back the tenants' furniture that had been dumped on the sidewalk. In 1930 one such Harlem demonstration produced several arrests. The following year these protests were stepped up, and in Cleveland and Chicago violence erupted. Most striking were the confrontations in Chicago, where many evictions occurred in the summer of 1931. While members of the interracial Unemployed Councils hauled household goods back into the buildings, fiery speakers outside denounced landlords and the ruling class. These demonstrations reached a climax in August: police shot into a large crowd that was returning the furniture, killing three blacks. Two days later thousands of mourners (one-third white) marched in the funeral procession, and frightened city officials temporarily halted these evictions.[51]

Meanwhile demonstrations took place in cities like Philadelphia; Charlotte, North Carolina; Paterson, New Jersey; Baltimore; Detroit; and Los Angeles.[52] Outside of Chicago, the most substantial activity occurred in New York, and in both places during 1933 a large increase in the number of evictions produced a renewed round of demonstrations. These continued sporadically into 1935. In an especially dramatic instance in Philadelphia, neighbors of an evicted family rained bottles and stones on the police, who broke down the door and opened fire, killing the unemployed father. The protesters then picketed city hall, demanding an end to evictions.[53]

Rent strikes, which were most prominent in New York, Philadelphia, and Chicago, appeared in far fewer cities than anti-eviction demonstrations. These strikes nearly always involved middle-class tenants, and although Communists were often influential they were by no means dominant. Indeed, the strictly Communist-inspired rent strike movements among poorer people during the early 1930's never really got off the ground.

In New York, scene of the most sustained rent strikes, tenant organizations had developed among both races during the 1920's to cope with escalating rents in the era of prosperity. As early as 1920 a Harlem Tenants and Lodgers League had paraded 200 strong, denouncing profiteering landlords, and in 1926 black tenants in two Harlem apartment houses had apparently staged a successful rent strike. The Harlem Tenants League, formed in 1928 and headed by a leading black Communist, Richard B. Moore, widely publicized the idea of a mass rent strike the following year, when the New York Supreme Court invalidated the state's rent control law. Yet the organization was not strong enough to employ this tactic.[54]

Surprisingly enough, the first black rent strike of the Depression was conducted not in Harlem but in Norfolk, Virginia. There in late 1932 the Unemployed Council persuaded many black families to withhold their rent and demand a 25 percent reduction, as well as a halt to evictions. Though the leaders were arrested and some tenants fined, the Council claimed that evictions had "practically stopped" because of the strike. The first Harlem rent strikes in 1933 were similarly organized by the

Unemployed Council, with tenants in two 111th Street buildings protesting unsanitary conditions and exorbitant rents.[55]

These protests petered out, and although New York proved to be the leading center of rent strike activity, when the tactic was revived in 1934 it appeared in the elite Sugar Hill neighborhood of northern Harlem. In August over 200 families in four apartment houses organized into a United Tenants League and went on strike, picketing the buildings and withstanding eviction efforts. In a matter of weeks, they won significant rent reductions. The Communist functionary Benjamin J. Davis was active in that strike, which was supported by the LSNR. But after a settlement was reached, the Communists denounced the Tenant League's leaders as "Uncle Toms" who had "sold out" by accepting an unsatisfactory compromise; the Communist faction seceded and organized the rival New York Tenants' League. Despite this split, the movement gained momentum during September as more buildings joined the strike. At the end of the month Mayor La Guardia urged a truce that was accepted only by the United League. Moreover, by October the Communists were also assisting rent strikes in Lower Harlem. Nevertheless, soon afterwards the two tenant groups merged into the Consolidated Tenants League, and the strikes subsided. Not until the 1960's would the use of this tactic equal or surpass what it had been in 1934.

There is no evidence that La Guardia's intervention reduced rents, but the Consolidated League shifted its focus to lobbying in Albany for remedial legislation. By April, 1935, disgusted at the legislature's inaction, the organization, now claiming 5,000 members, announced a city-wide rent strike. The Communists, who had previously criticized the Consolidated League's willingness "to let the Mayor handle everything," now "pledged unstinting support." What followed, however, was a small flurry of middle-class rent strikes. Despite some successes, direct action again subsided until a year later, when there was another round of rent increases. Tenants in the affected buildings rushed to join the League, which sponsored a protest parade of 4,000 people through Harlem's streets. La Guardia again intervened and arranged a compromise in which a number of landlords agreed to reduce rents. Thereafter rent strikes occurred only sporadically. The Consolidated Tenants

League had entered upon a period of decline. The organization was torn by dissension; the chairman, forced from office, blamed a Communist faction for his downfall. Though occasional strikes followed, sponsored by the weakened League and the National Negro Congress, the rent strike movement by 1938 was basically finished in New York, the victim of landlord intransigence, La Guardia's well-meaning compromises, and conflicts among the tenant organizations.[56]

In Philadelphia and Cleveland less prosperous people were involved in the rent strike movements. During 1937 there was a surge of tenant organizing and strikes in North Philadelphia's black section which stimulated a similar movement among whites. Over an eight-month period nearly 200 black tenants in a half-dozen apartment houses struck. Through the mayor's mediation, negotiations with the real estate board produced lower rents in some cases and promises of repairs in others. In Cleveland two years later the Future Outlook League's threat of a city-wide rent strike prompted the mayor to mediate between the landlords and the blacks. Although no direct action occurred after he announced that the eviction laws would be strictly enforced against anyone refusing to pay rent, some landlords made small reductions while the City Council enacted a strengthened housing code. Stimulated by the FOL, the Detroit NAACP Youth Council made a similar threat which produced improvements in that city.[57]

In Chicago there was no significant rent strike activity until 1940–41, with earlier agitation on the issue having resulted in only "a few sporadic rent strikes" in 1937. Joe Jefferson, the leader of the Negro Labor Relations League, had organized the tenants of his apartment house in a successful action against a rent increase; in the spring of 1937 he created the Consolidated Tenants Association. The new organization, chaired by Alderman William Dawson, had ties with black politicians and other established leaders. It used the rhetoric of rent strikes, but its deeds were limited to protest parades and mass meetings at which ward politicians spoke militantly of attacking "rent hogs." No strikes took place, and while the Association went to the courts on behalf of some individual tenants, it undoubtedly served less to articulate black protest than to defuse it. The organization soon disappeared. In 1940 a wave of rent increases prompted a new surge in strike sentiment. As in New York, the action came from the black bourgeoisie, rather than from the poor. In April one apartment house had won a fight against a new rent hike, and over the next year further strikes were reported, nearly all led by the National Negro Congress' Tenants League. Few victories were won, but the organization managed to survive, experiencing a limited revival in 1942, and even staging occasional protests after World War II.[58]

Communists supplied the chief initiative for direct action against discrimination in places of public accommodation and recreation during the 1930's. Nearly all such demonstrations in the North were Communist-inspired, but this was rarely true of the few protests occurring in the border states and upper South. Seldom did the Communists develop a sustained campaign; typically their efforts were isolated "mass action" episodes that lacked followup and failed to disturb basic Jim Crow patterns. In practice these dramatic incidents, usually interracial, functioned as proof of Communist commitment both to the solidarity of white and black workers and to "mass action," which they disdainfully contrasted with the NAACP's legalistic techniques.

Yet beginning in 1929, when direct action against places of public accommodation was virtually unknown, the Communists, carrying out the Sixth International's recent mandate to give special attention to black grievances, held demonstrations at restaurants, hotels, pools, and beaches. Early in the year an interracial group from the American Negro Labor Congress, denied service in a New York restaurant, indignantly set up a picket line and were promptly arrested. Several months later a New York City youth group picketed a resort swimming pool which excluded them. At a mass meeting protesting this incident, Communist party congressional candidate Richard B. Moore denounced black leaders who relied on lawsuits instead of "mass action." And at conventions of Communist organizations in Cleveland and Pittsburgh in 1930, when black delegates were barred from hotels, white Communists dramatically moved to accommodations in the black community. In Pittsburgh 500 whites and blacks picketed the offending hotel.[59]

These protests set the pattern for the Depression years. During the early 1930's the Communists demonstrated at restaurants, pools, and beaches and at least once sponsored mass picketing at a Pittsburgh theater which Jim Crowed blacks. One of the most striking incidents took place in Cleveland: after an ILD attorney and the mother of two Scottsboro Boys were thrown out of a restaurant, the ILD organized a demonstration of hundreds of blacks and whites who descended upon the establishment, forcing the manager to serve the black protesters. Subsequently the city council passed an ordinance against restaurant discrimination. Sometimes the police used coercion and violence to counter this "mass action." In 1931, after two black workers were roughly ejected from a Detroit delicatessen and the LSNR had promptly marched on the place, the police broke up the demonstration and arrested several pickets. In Chicago, where rigid Jim Crow customs prevailed on the lakefront beaches, mixed LSNR groups sought to integrate them in 1934. Following one police attack, the LSNR called for a citywide campaign, but after the police did not harass the next LSNR testers, the project fizzled and the Jim Crow pattern continued. As usual, the Communists disdained legal tactics. For example, in Denver, when mixed ILD groups were attacked by hoodlums and the police while using the white beaches in 1932, the NAACP went to court and had the "colored" signs removed. But because the judge strongly urged the blacks not to insist on their legal rights, the *Liberator* witheringly criticized the NAACP for defusing mass action by "rely[ing] on the 'fairness' and 'impartiality' of the courts." Litigation, editor Benjamin J. Davis asserted, was valuable "only if . . . backed by mass protests."[60]

By mid-decade direct action against places of public accommodation subsided, except for protests against hotels during conventions of Communist organizations.* The most dramatic

*Similar incidents involving other groups also occurred occasionally. For example, during a Socialist-sponsored Continental Congress of Workers and Farmers, meeting in Washington in 1933, delegates picketed and withdrew from a hotel that would not accept a black conferee, and later secured service for a Negro delegate at a discriminatory restaurant by refusing to order meals or to leave the establishment until the black person was served. (See esp. Edward Levison to Walter White, May 12, 1933, Box C-379, NAACP Archives.) The following year 250 delegates to an ILGWU convention in Chicago moved en masse to other hotels when one hostelry would not allow blacks to

of these occurred during a 1937 conference of the American League Against War and Fascism in Pittsburgh. White delegates entered the city's largest and finest hotel dining rooms, demanding service for black delegates and picketing places that refused. In an action reminiscent of the 1929 demonstration in the same city, a taxicab caravan of 500 indignant sign-bearing pickets, black and white, "stormed" the William Penn Hotel and blockaded its entire front.[61] Communists also undoubtedly spearheaded a campaign in Los Angeles in 1938, protesting Jim Crow signs in the washrooms and recreation buildings of the Bureau of Power and Light's construction camps. Following the *Sentinel*'s exposé, the local National Negro Congress picketed the Bureau's headquarters and sponsored a "Dark Night" when ghetto residents turned off their lights at eight P.M.[62]

Occasionally groups staged direct-action attacks on Jim Crow public accommodations in the border states and even in the upper South. Unlike the ones in the North, these were black-inspired, included no white participants, and were unconnected with Communists.* The protests occurred principally in theaters and auditoriums; their objective was usually not desegregation, but a fairer allocation of the separate arrangements.

In 1932 Raleigh's black ministers refused to participate in the dedication of the new War Memorial Auditorium, and the Negro community boycotted the ceremony because blacks were confined to a small section of the balcony. In Richmond, where blacks had been shunning the Mosque Theater for eight years following the management's refusal to admit them except by a side door, the boycott ended in 1935 when the theater, suffering badly from the Depression, lifted its ban. Thousands of blacks returned to the balconies. Later in the decade, when the St. Louis municipal auditorium relegated blacks to undesirable locations for an appearance of Benny Goodman and his racially mixed band, the Colored Clerks' Circle and the Urban League

use the elevators (Baltimore *Afro-American*, June 3, 1934), and in certain instances overwhelmingly white religious organizations acted in the same way. See, *e.g.*, Atlanta *Daily World*, May 18, 1934, for YWCA convention in Philadelphia, and Norfolk *Journal and Guide*, July 16, 1938, for religious group meeting in Columbus.

*An exception was a Communist mass meeting held in the Norfolk City Auditorium, where an interracial group, half black, defied the law requiring segregated seating (Norfolk *Journal and Guide*, Oct. 22, 1932).

circulated handbills urging, "Let's have a sit-down at home—turn on the radio and hear them without being there and taking insults." Few blacks attended the dance concert.[63] Meanwhile the nation's capital witnessed the first of a long series of efforts to end the exclusion of blacks from downtown theaters. As early as 1933 prominent black Washingtonians picketed the National Theater when an all-black show played to white-only audiences; seven years later the Washington Civil Rights Committee, grasping a good symbolic occasion, picketed the film premiere of *Abe Lincoln in Illinois*. Rarely were frontal assaults made on the issue of segregation itself. But at the Alexandria, Virginia, public library, which excluded blacks, five youths were arrested for staging a "sit-down strike" in 1939.[64]

The decade was punctuated by occasional protests against revivals of *The Birth of a Nation*; such demonstrations were generally conducted by Communists and sometimes by NAACP branches.[65] There was also sporadic picketing over racial stereotyping in *Gone with the Wind*.[66] In a most unusual action, black college students in Greensboro, North Carolina, disturbed when the state theater-owners' convention condemned "the appearance of colored people in scenes with whites on an equal basis," started a theater boycott that spread to other cities where even white students became involved.[67]

Police brutality was a serious problem, and in the South it was compounded by frequent cases of white store clerks assaulting blacks. Although this type of violence was not very amenable to attack, direct action was occasionally used. As noted earlier, a few southern "Don't-Buy-Where-You-Can't-Work" boycotts began as protests against such incidents. Even in Memphis, with its Deep South mores, after a white clerk assaulted a black girl, blacks mounted a rigid boycott of a store that had long enjoyed heavy Negro patronage. In another Deep South town, Warren, Arkansas, blacks boycotted a theater when police kicked a Negro woman for standing in the white ticket line. The best-organized protests against police brutality occurred in Washington, D.C.; in 1938 and again in 1941 Communist organizations arranged mass parades, condemning wanton killings by white police and demanding reforms in the law enforcement system.[68]

Both the Communists and the NAACP utilized direct action

in national campaigns against inequities in the administration of justice, making the mass march a major instrument in the struggle for Negro rights. The Communists led the way, dramatizing the Scottsboro case through numerous marches that began in May, 1931, with a parade of 5,000 blacks and whites in Harlem. Two years later there was a call for a "March on Washington," and 3,000 blacks and 1,000 whites marched in front of the White House demanding release of the Scottsboro Boys. About the same time in Chicago, 20,000 marched through the streets of the south side.[69]

Over the next several years the NAACP adopted direct action in its campaign to secure a federal anti-lynching law. Scoring the indifference of the attorney general, the Association in 1934 picketed the Justice Department's National Crime Conference in Washington, and Assistant Secretary Roy Wilkins was among the four pickets arrested for carrying signs without a permit. Two days later Howard University professors and students, joined by a few leading black clergymen, appeared at Justice Department headquarters in a novel demonstration—to circumvent police rules against picketing, the demonstrators quietly stood several feet apart, each with a noose around his neck.[70]*

Beginning in 1936 the NAACP vigorously renewed its campaign for federal anti-lynching legislation. Walter White and Roy Wilkins led the picket line when presidential contender Senator William F. Borah, who had been largely responsible for the failure of the NAACP's previous efforts, spoke in New York. On Lincoln's birthday in 1937, NAACP branches and youth councils "staged the first nation-wide youth demonstration against lynching." Mass meetings were held in key cities and on black college campuses. The Chicago Youth Council staged a big parade through the Loop; in New York, where the NAACP operated through the United Youth Committee Against Lynching, the parade was followed by a large mass meeting addressed by Walter White and Adam Clayton Powell. The next year there were more NAACP-sponsored Lincoln's Birthday demonstrations demanding an end to the filibuster in

---

*Participants who later became internationally famous were student Kenneth Clark and Professor Ralph J. Bunche.

the Senate. The United Youth Committee, which had recently
marched through Times Square protesting the stalling tactics,
paraded through Harlem with Negroes and whites "marching
side by side wearing black armbands as a sign of mourning for
the eight victims lynched in 1937."[71]

These mass marches notwithstanding, the NAACP had not
embraced direct-action tactics as a basic part of its strategy. As
already mentioned, its relationship to the jobs campaigns had
been cautious. Criticisms from the Communists and pressures
on Walter White from advisors like the prominent civil rights
lawyer Charles H. Houston had little effect on the Association.
At the height of the Communists' denunciations on this score,
James W. Ford, recent Communist party candidate for vice-
president, appeared at the 1933 Annual NAACP Conference
and spoke vigorously for mass action. The delegates conducted
an intense debate, yet sidestepped the issue with a watered-
down resolution that urged blacks to concern themselves with
economic problems but failed to endorse direct action. Essentially the conclave reaffirmed the NAACP's traditional emphasis on legalism.[72] The Association's picket line at the 1934
AFL convention was a unique event. The organization eschewed rent strikes and public accommodations demonstrations. At a time when the NAACP was engaged in major litigation to open the doors of southern universities, the sole instance
of direct action on this issue occurred when the St. Louis Colored Clerks Circle in 1939 picketed the inferior Jim Crow law
school set up by the state of Missouri after the NAACP's Supreme Court victory in the Gaines case.[73] In short, except for
the sporadic school boycotts and mass marches supporting the
lobbying for the Wagner-Costigan anti-lynching bill, direct
action did not form a significant part of NAACP tactics.[74]

IV

All this direct action of the Depression years has been virtually
forgotten, and almost totally ignored by historians. Ironically,
what the informed public remembers and what historians have
treated as a precedent-making departure was a mass march that
never took place—A. Philip Randolph's March on Washington

of 1941. World War II was, of course, a period of heightened black militance, and the theme of direct action achieved a salience in black *thinking* that it never possessed before. Yet the March on Washington Movement was actually the culmination of developments that occurred during the Depression years. The really innovative elements in the history of direct-action strategies during the early 1940's came not from Randolph, but from the Gandhi-inspired pacifists who founded the Congress of Racial Equality.

In January, 1941, Randolph proposed a mass march on Washington of 10,000 blacks "to wake up and shock official Washington as it has never been shocked before," and thus to press Roosevelt to end discrimination in the armed forces and defense industries.[75] Randolph, of course, was not alone in his protests as the nation rearmed and moved closer toward war. Indeed, perhaps motivated at least partly by his dramatic proposal, others staged direct-action projects in the spring of 1941. In April, at the urging of the NAACP's national office, branches in New York, Chicago, and a number of other cities picketed companies with defense contracts, and National Negro Congress affiliates occasionally sponsored similar demonstrations.[76] But it was Randolph who really captured the popular imagination; speaking in the name of the black masses, it was he who prevailed upon Roosevelt to create the Fair Employment Practices Commission.

Randolph believed that "broad, organized mass action" was required to put pressure on the political authorities. The day of speeches, petitions, and conferences between black and white leaders had passed. As organized labor recognized, "Nothing stirs and shapes public sentiment like physical action. Mass demonstrations against jim-crow are worth a million editorials and orations." Since the government was an amoral "organism . . . constantly balancing pressures from conflicting social forces," blacks must "build a mammoth machine of mass action with a terrific and tremendous driving power" that would force the president to outlaw discrimination in government, the armed services, and defense industries.

While white allies like liberals and trade unionists were useful, "There are some things Negroes must do alone. This is our fight and we must see it through." Power to force change lay in all-black unity across class lines. The elites and intellectuals, he averred, could be effective only with the organized power of the masses behind them. "Not only must the chasm between the uneducated and the educated Negro be abolished . . . but the 'little Negro' must be drawn into the fight by actual participation and given a sense of his importance. . . . The fact is the Negroes' cause cannot win without the masses." Indeed, "Only the masses possess power. Only the voice of the masses will be heard and heeded—Negro America has never yet spoken as a mass, an organized mass."

In Randolph's view, a display of mass action by unified blacks would dramatize the Negroes' grievances and bring pressure on the government. As he once said, because the world "is used to big dramatic affairs," blacks "must develop huge demonstrations . . . to put our cause into the mainstream of public opinion and focus the attention of world interests." He called for a march on Washington, synchronized with "monster" mass meetings and marches on city halls across the country: "An all-out thundering March on Washington, ending in a monster demonstration at Lincoln's Monument will shake up white America." At the same time, Randolph carefully kept his movement as legitimate as possible in the eyes of whites by explicitly counseling against violence and disorder.[77]

Firmly rooted in protest tactics of the 1930's, Randolph's approach flowed from his past as a radical Marxist and trade unionist.[78] In explaining his MOWM strategy of mass action, he constantly alluded to the example set by the trade unions. More to the point, his proposals strikingly resembled certain tactics of the Communists, who had sponsored many marches on city halls and even marches on Washington. Three of Randolph's favorite expressions—"mass action," "monster mass meetings," and "march on Washington"—had been part of the Communist vocabulary of the 1930's; and the notion of mass action itself came not from Randolph's Socialist associates, but from the extreme left wing of American radicalism—the IWW and the Communists.[79] On the other hand, like the essentially petit bourgeois "Don't-Buy-Where-You-Can't-Work" movements, the MOWM was an all-black enterprise, indigenous to the black community; and in his outspoken insistence that blacks depend on "their own power for self-liberation,"[80] Randolph differentiated his movement from the deliberately interracial activities of the Communists. Moreover, the 1941 MOWM was clearly a new departure from the Communist demonstrations, both in the breadth of Randolph's conception of a mass movement encompassing all strata in the black community, and in his ability to marshal support from all the major race-advancement organizations.

Ironically, the ambitious rhetoric notwithstanding, the principal march actually staged by the MOWM was a poorly attended demonstration modeled on the NAACP's 1917 Silent Protest Parade, and held in 1942 after the execution of Odell Waller, a sharecropper who had killed his white landlord in self-defense.[81] Ironically also among Randolph's greatest admirers was a small interracial band who soon afterward took the first steps that led to the formation of the Congress of Racial Equality (CORE). Like Randolph, those who established the first CORE group in 1941–42 were committed to direct action, but unlike him they were dedicated pacifists who consciously sought to apply Gandhian methods and believed strongly that only blacks and whites struggling together could solve the race problem in America. It was they who introduced the phrase "nonviolent direct action" into the vocabulary of Negro protest; and although committed to confrontations with racists, they embraced strict nonviolence for both ideological and pragmatic reasons. Although CORE's founders greatly admired the CIO's mass action tactics of the 1930's—they termed their first sit-in a "sit-down," after the famous sit-down strikes—both their inspiration and specific methods were rooted in the Gandhian movement in India.[82]

Previously Gandhism's influence on Afro-American protest had been negligible. Articulate blacks had been impressed by the struggle against caste and colonialism in India, and they spoke admiringly of Gandhi's leadership of a united people.[83] A handful of Baptist theologians connected with the black colleges—most notably William Stuart Nelson of Shaw University, and Howard Thurman and Benjamin Mays of Howard University—were deeply impressed with Gandhi's message and philosophy,[84] but seldom did black leaders seriously consider applying Gandhi's methods to America's racial problem. James Weldon Johnson, who was unusual in the way he systematically examined alternative strategies, wrote in 1922: "It will be of absorbing interest to know whether the means and methods advocated by Gandhi can be as effective as the methods of violence used by the Irish. . . . If non-cooperation brings the British to their knees in India, there is no reason why it should not bring the white man to his knees in the South." Such sentiments were rare in the black community, and indeed there were those who considered Gandhian tactics irrelevant or even inappropriate for the United States. Thus the noted sociologist E. Franklin Frazier predicted that if a Gandhian type of movement ever emerged in the South, "I fear we would witness an unprecedented massacre of defenseless black men and women in the name of Law and Order."[85]

Gandhism's influence on the black protest movement came largely through a predominantly white source—the interracial pacifist Fellowship of Reconciliation (FOR). The FOR supplied the impetus for CORE, and in 1942–43 certain black FOR and CORE leaders infused Randolph's March on Washington Movement with a Gandhian thrust.* Under their influence Randolph, searching for a way to revive the flagging MOWM, decided to espouse Gandhian tactics. By the autumn of 1942 he enthusiastically referred to the Gandhian mass movement in India as a model for black Americans, and at year's end proposed a week-long civil disobedience campaign against Jim Crow public accommodations. Asserting that "a citizen is morally bound to disobey an unjust law," Randolph even urged southern blacks to persistently enter white railroad coaches and waiting rooms. Because many blacks considered this civil disobedience too dangerous, Randolph softened his proposal, substituting, for example, a boycott of southern railroads for the original sit-in tactic; by June, 1943, he had watered it down

*This group consisted of three individuals: James Farmer, Bayard Rustin, and a white leader in early CORE, Bernice Fisher. Of the three, Rustin was closest to Randolph. Interviews with Farmer and Rustin, Dec. 2 and 3, 1975, indicated that these three often spoke with Randolph in the 1942–43 period, and it was their influence that explains the shift. A letter from Rustin written at the time lends further support to the information we obtained from interviews. (See Rustin to A. J. Muste, Feb. 23, 1943, Fellowship of Reconciliation Archives, Swarthmore College Library.)

further, to the point of vaguely describing his plan as "constitutional obedience" and "nonviolent good-will direct action." Prominent FOR and CORE leaders appeared at the MOWM conference early in July, explaining their direct-action techniques and the philosophy behind them. But by then Randolph, discouraged at his inability to gain much support in the black community, had shelved his mass campaign of civil disobedience and instead endorsed small action projects conducted by carefully trained interracial groups along CORE lines.[86]

The MOWM soon faded away, and it was tiny CORE, virtually unknown in the black community, which carried the banner of nonviolent direct action as a conscious philosophy and strategy. Even though Randolph had briefly espoused their method and would embrace it again in the fight against a Jim Crow army after World War II, CORE represented something essentially new in the struggle against racism. Its founders had developed their organization and program independently of other black and interracial direct-action groups of the 1930's. CORE knew something of the "Don't-Buy-Where-You-Can't-Work" campaigns, yet all but ignored employment problems until much later. It articulated a radical pacifist and socialist ideology that contrasted markedly with the petit bourgeois job movements, and CORE based its strategy upon an explicitly interracial and anti-nationalist position. Even though CORE was founded in Chicago, its leaders were ignorant of the substantial history of direct action there, knowing about neither the Negro Labor Relations League nor the Communist and Communist-front organizations. Although similar to the Communists in being philosophically dedicated to interracialism, in other ways the two groups were antithetical. In its commitment to nonviolence, in its use of carefully indoctrinated small groups rather than untrained masses of people, and in its painstakingly planned public accommodations campaigns, CORE was the direct opposite of the Communists. CORE founders were unaware of the Communists' pioneering work in public accommodations. Moreover, CORE was ideologically anti-Communist and hoped that strict adherence to nonviolent discipline would keep out Communists without resort to Red-baiting, much as Randolph's MOWM hoped to minimize Communist participation by limiting membership to blacks.* CORE would have liked to become a mass movement, but given the fact that even Randolph could not marshal the masses into the MOWM, it is not surprising that CORE projects involved very few people.

Thus Randolph had dramatized direct-action methods, while CORE's black and white pacifist founders brought a new dimension through imparting the philosophy and techniques of Gandhi. However, there was less actual use of direct-action tactics during World War II than in the 1930's: the war, although stimulating black militance,[87] simultaneously created a milieu not conducive to direct action. The full-employment economy blunted grievances on the job front; the Communists, who placed support for the war and Russia above everything else, soft-pedaled their championship of black causes; and wartime social pressures undoubtedly militated against large-scale or disruptive direct-action tactics.

Action on housing problems was minimal. The serious shortage of dwellings, rent control, and higher wages all combined to dampen protest tendencies. In addition to the Chicago Tenants League activities mentioned earlier, there were a few successful rent strikes in Harlem and Brooklyn and occasional strikes against rent increases in public housing projects.[88]

In employment there were several cases of black workers in war plants[89] waging strikes against prejudiced foremen, Jim Crow cafeterias, and similar types of discrimination. There were also some struggles against job exclusion in war industries and in public transit and utilities, where employers flagrantly

---

*A word of explanation is required concerning the role of Bayard Rustin, the one early CORE leader who had been a Communist. As a Young Communist League organizer at CCNY he had been active in the New York bus boycott and (with Randolph unaware of his political affiliation) had played a minor part in the MOWM. After Russia entered World War II and the American Communists soft-pedaled the race issue, Rustin converted to pacifism and became active with the Fellowship of Reconciliation, simultaneously moving closer to Randolph. Interestingly enough, however, Rustin's experience with "mass action" as a Communist had no impact on CORE or on his advice to Randolph; rather, under the stimulus of his conversion he developed a passionate commitment to Gandhian tactics. What endured from his Communist experience was an organizing expertise that later served nonviolent direct-activism well when he became associated with Martin Luther King and coordinated a series of mass demonstrations at the nation's capital, culminating in the March on Washington of 1963 (interviews with Rustin, Mar. 28, May 29, 1974; Dec. 4, 1975; Feb. 3, 1976).

ignored FEPC directives. In 1942, after FEPC hearings found the District of Columbia's transit company guilty of barring Negroes as motormen and conductors, an interracial group briefly sponsored parades and picketing.[90] The Cleveland Future Outlook League and its branches in Akron and Canton, as well as the St. Louis March on Washington Committee picketed certain defense plants early in the war to protest anti-Negro hiring policies. Subsequently the St. Louis group—probably the only MOWM affiliate engaged in significant local activity—picketed the telephone company in a drive that led to the hiring of several black operators. In Baltimore, however, a Total War Employment Committee demonstrated at the phone company offices for nearly a year without achieving any victory.[91] Finally, in Los Angeles and New York blacks picketed stadiums protesting major league baseball's white-only policy. Mayor La Guardia barred such a demonstration at Ebbets Field and the Polo Grounds in the fall of 1945, and protestors were compelled to use the streets of Harlem instead. But soon after that demonstration the Brooklyn Dodgers signed up Jackie Robinson.[92]

Most numerous of the wartime projects were those against segregation in public accommodations. These generally differed from the ones of the 1930's in being sustained efforts instead of isolated demonstrations; besides picketing, they also included the more militant sit-in tactic. CORE chapters and college campus organizations in the North and West staged direct action against restaurants, theaters, and barber shops; these groups were interracial and ordinarily had white majorities. In one such project white students from Antioch College and blacks from Wilberforce University broke down the segregated seating policy at a Yellow Springs movie theater. In a carefully planned demonstration, blacks and whites sat together all over the theater; the manager, finding that the activists had substantial support in the community, gave in.[93] The most notable campaigns were in two border cities, Washington and St. Louis; there, unlike in the North, the activists' demands lacked the legitimacy provided by state civil rights laws. Both of these campaigns resulted from black initiative, although in St. Louis Negroes secured the participation of sympathetic whites. In Washington during the school year

1942–43 three Howard University undergraduates from the North, shocked at conditions in the capital, took to testing and sitting in at lunch counters. On at least one occasion they were arrested. Deciding to broaden the campaign, they organized a Civil Rights Committee under the campus NAACP. In 1943 and 1944 their group used the sit-in to desegregate a cafeteria near the university, and then it coordinated similar demonstrations at a downtown restaurant until the university administration stopped the students. In St. Louis a committee carried out a half-dozen lunch counter sit-ins at the major department stores in 1944. As a result, one store opened its basement cafeteria. Neither group in starting its demonstrations knew of the activities of CORE. Both campaigns were fresh, spontaneous inventions born of the new mood of the war era.[94]*

During the heightened militance of World War II, black men and women in the armed services occasionally employed nonviolent resistance against racist policies.† In one case in 1944 a company of black soldiers, protesting the policy of promoting junior white officers over more qualified blacks, refused to leave their barracks and were charged with mutiny.[95] Early the following year a thousand Seabees in a construction battalion at Port Hueneme, California, went on a two-day hunger strike in protest against their white Mississippi commander who engaged in various discriminatory practices, most notably his refusal to promote blacks while bringing in whites as petty officers. Resulting publicity led to his removal, but the battalion was shipped back to the Pacific under armed guard.[96] Later in the year, ninety-six black WAC medical technicians, objecting to being assigned menial jobs, went on a "sit-down" strike in Massachusetts. Four leaders were court-martialed and convicted, but, following an NAACP appeal, the secretary of war

---

*There was one pacifist prominent in the NAACP Civil Rights Committee at Howard University—Pauli Murray, a law student who as early as 1940 had served a three-day jail sentence for refusing to move to the back of a Virginia bus and subsequently had worked at the MOWM on the Odell Waller March. Murray became an inspiration to the Howard undergraduates, but their first sit-ins had occurred before she was involved, and the impetus for their campaigns had nothing to do with pacifism, Gandhi, or Randolph. Although they practiced a pragmatic nonviolence, neither pacifism nor Gandhism entered their discussions.

†We have excluded from our discussion strikes against prison segregation which were staged by white and black conscientious objectors in a half-dozen federal penitentiaries during the war.

reversed the decision.[97] Finally, in 1944–45 black officers of the 477th Bombardment group protested their exclusion from the white officers' clubs at three Air Force bases in the Midwest by persistently entering the clubs, which closed temporarily rather than serve them. In April, 1945, an attempt to use the white facilities at Indiana's Freeman Field led to the arrests of 101 officers. However, the court-martial board headed by General Benjamin O. Davis acquitted the men.[98]

V

Thus, although direct action continued here and there during the war, blacks did not perceive such tactics as a major weapon; indeed, the two principal groups identified with this strategy, MOWM and CORE, were small and weak. The decade following the war, although an era of rising black activism that included the development of black voter registration leagues in the South and a formidable expansion in the scope of NAACP work, was similarly a period in which direct action remained a distinctly minor weapon.

The most highly publicized episode involving direct-action techniques in the immediate postwar period was Randolph's proposed civil disobedience campaign against military segregation in 1948. Testifying before the Senate Armed Services Committee, which was then considering a peacetime draft bill, Randolph warned that if segregation in the military services were not abolished, he would lead "a mass civil disobedience movement along the lines of the magnificent struggles of the people of India against British imperialism": "I personally pledge myself to openly counsel, aid and abet youth, both white and Negro" to violate the new law. Other leaders like Walter White disavowed this civil disobedience but used the opportunity to reemphasize the blacks' unalterable opposition to Jim Crow in the armed forces. Randolph stepped up his agitation and headed a picket line at the White House. When the draft bill was passed, he organized the interracial League for Non-Violent Civil Disobedience against Military Segregation, whose members were prepared to face prison rather than submit to segregation in the armed forces. In violation of the law Ran-

dolph openly urged draft resistance, stating that he was prepared to "oppose a Jim Crow Army until I rot in jail." In August President Truman, responding to all the agitation by Randolph and others, issued an executive order "aimed at the eventual end of segregation." Bayard Rustin and others associated
with Randolph in this battle distrusted Truman and wished to
continue the fight. But Randolph, faced with the opposition of
the black newspapers and Negro leadership, realizing that he
lacked mass support for his radical proposal, and having received personal assurances from the President, decided to dis-
solve the League. Characteristically Randolph, while threatening massive civil disobedience, had backed away from the
brink—a decision justified by later events.[99]

Less publicized but at least as significant were the attacks on
places of public accommodation and recreation which, as during the war, continued to be the principal focus of direct-action
projects. CORE chapters, still largely on college campuses, continued to devote their main efforts to such campaigns; actions
were also staged by independent groups and occasionally by
NAACP branches as well as Communist-related organizations.
As northern hotels and restaurants came to generally obey civil
rights laws, more demonstrations occurred at amusement
parks, bowling alleys, skating rinks, and swimming pools. Most
of these demonstrations in the northern states were conducted
by interracial groups, with all-black ones most likely in the more
southerly counties.[100] In spite of the obvious model that the
original sit-ins of CORE supplied, few of the participants in
these projects were pacifists. Rather, nearly all of them viewed
their nonviolent tactics simply as a useful strategy.

By the late 1940's, as the public accommodations issue moved
toward solution in the North, the major border cities became
the leading sites of direct action. Here the campaigns were first
initiated against legitimate theaters that either excluded blacks
entirely (as did Washington's National Theater and Baltimore's
Ford Theater) or restricted them to an upper balcony (as in St.
Louis's American Theater). Early in 1947 a Washington interracial committee and the Baltimore NAACP simultaneously
began picketing the National and Ford theaters, which were
controlled by the same chain. Sustained picketing went on sea-

son after season; in 1948 the National closed its doors to plays rather than submit to the demands of Actors Equity who, allied with the demonstrators, refused to appear before all-white audiences in the nation's capital. Finally in 1952 both theaters capitulated. A few months later the American Theater also integrated, thus bringing to a successful conclusion six years of intensive picketing—mainly by the NAACP, but also with some rival demonstrations from the Communist-front Civil Rights Congress. (Even earlier a four-year NAACP campaign that included considerable picketing had desegregated the Kansas City, Missouri, Music Hall.[101])

By then CORE's most active chapters were located in the same three cities, where they attacked black exclusion from lunch counters in downtown variety stores, pharmacies, and department stores. Step by step, one store at a time, they gradually broke down the barriers. In Baltimore the changes came partly through sit-ins and picketing by Morgan State College students, while in Washington progress was expedited by the rival and Communist-influenced Coordinating Committee for the Enforcement of D.C. Antidiscrimination Laws, which staged its own demonstrations and won a 1953 Supreme Court decision outlawing discriminatory public accommodations in the nation's capital.[102] Somewhat earlier, direct action had also been employed in Washington to attack a problem that had rankled blacks for forty years—segregation of employes at the Bureau of Engraving and Printing. Much of the segregation in federal offices had ended about the time of World War II, but the Bureau, among the first to institute Jim Crow early in the century, was now one of the last holdouts. In June, 1949, under the sponsorship of an interracial coalition, 500 people set up a picket line, and other picket lines followed. By midsummer Jim Crow had finally ended in the Bureau.[103]

In the South, of course, protests against segregation remained extremely rare. In the guarded optimism that followed the war and accompanied the stirrings which the Supreme Court's 1944 white primary decision encouraged, Negroes in Columbia, South Carolina, staged a "Jim Crow Sunday" in March, 1946, boycotting segregated buses and theaters. Most of the city's blacks participated in this unique "day of silent, nonviolent and passive resistance." Yet the necessarily cautious character of the episode was very evident. Sunday was chosen over Saturday, since a demonstration on the latter day would have inconvenienced too many shoppers, and although blacks in other southern cities expressed considerable interest in the project, it was never replicated in Columbia or anywhere else.[104] The following year CORE made its first foray into the South, when a small interracial group challenged segregation in interstate bus travel in Virginia and North Carolina. This Journey of Reconciliation resulted in road-gang sentences in North Carolina for four participants. To CORE and its friends, the Journey remained an important symbol of what courageous black and white activists could do, but it did not change transportation practices, and was not reported widely even in the black press.[105] Indeed, CORE did not seriously attempt further activity in the South for another decade. On the other hand, by the early 1950's southern blacks in the less repressive cities, undoubtedly stimulated by what was happening in the border states, did start to use direct action to protest theater segregation. Perhaps the first theater picketing in the Deep South occurred in 1949 when the Young Progressives of Austin, Texas, briefly demonstrated at a white-only theater. Two years later the Richmond NAACP, as part of its prolonged campaign to completely eliminate Jim Crow at the Mosque Auditorium, boycotted performances there by Marian Anderson and other black artists. In December, 1952, the Nashville NAACP organized an almost "100% successful" boycott of a Christmas passion play to protest the segregated seating in the city's Ryman Auditorium.[106]

Given the fact that this was the era of new FEPC laws in some northern states and agitation for a permanent national FEPC, it is hard to account for the paucity of direct-action projects for jobs. This situation was of course in marked contrast to the 1930's, when employment campaigns were the preeminent form of direct action. The three surviving organizations from the 1930's were far less active than before, although the Future Outlook League staged demonstrations at East Cleveland stores that retained their lily-white employment policies even after the neighborhoods became black.[107] CORE only rarely initiated such projects; occasionally NAACP branches and Communist-front organizations sponsored some,[108] but typically they were run by ad hoc coalitions that disintegrated when the project was over. Sustained efforts were the exception; more characteristically the campaigns were sporadic, short-lived affairs that either foundered or ended with minimal gains.

Occasionally demonstrations accompanied lobbying for FEPC laws.[109] The most frequent objects of attack were still firms doing business in the ghettos, though nowhere did these efforts reach the scope of the 1930's. Ordinarily they involved a single chain store or theater and subsided after one or two jobs had been secured.[110] The 1949 campaign in San Francisco, where a community-wide coalition secured fourteen positions after picketing Fillmore Street stores for twenty-three days, was unusual. Also unusual was the first and most fruitful of the few attacks on manufacturers with large sales among black consumers, the Chicago fight with Wonder Bread to obtain jobs as driver-salesmen. The coalition initiated by the Negro Labor Relations League sponsored a year-long boycott and picketing that ended the white-only policy and won jobs for five blacks. In contrast, direct action was almost totally useless in the strongly unionized beer industry, as disappointing experiences in Harlem and Chicago showed.[111]

Seldom did blacks stage direct-action job projects outside the ghettos. Yet there was a significant new departure in the occasional demonstrations against large downtown department stores. In Pittsburgh the Urban League–dominated campaign of two years concluded in 1947 with a written promise to hire blacks. At the new Santa Monica Sears store that year another coalition, this time headed by the NAACP, finally secured a retailing job after two months of boycott and picketing. In Chicago a similar united effort, initiated at CORE's suggestion, against Goldblatt's department store in the Loop disintegrated when the company, maintaining that its record was superior to that of its competitors, charged anti-Semitism.[112] Rarest of all were actions against powerful utilities and transit companies, but among them was a precedent-setting boycott that the San Francisco NAACP launched in 1955 against the Yellow Cab Company for refusing to hire Negro drivers. Accompanied by periodic picketing demonstrations, this project lasted about two years.[113] In Omaha the interracial De Porres Club of Creighton University, which had earlier won several job projects, waged a year-long fruitless drive, including picketing, for black drivers on buses and streetcars.[114]

Employment campaigns were virtually absent in the South, of course, but there were a few demonstrations in the less repressive cities. In Atlanta in 1946 the United Negro Veterans Organization marched a hundred strong on the city hall to protest the failure to appoint black police; the NAACP and other organizations declined to endorse this type of tactic. As earlier, Norfolk proved to be among the most important sites of what little direct action there was. In 1948, after three weeks of picketing staged by a black ad hoc committee with some NAACP support, a Woolworth ghetto store promoted two black women to sales positions and promised to hire only blacks thereafter. The following year the local Progressive party used interracial picketing in a successful attempt to obtain a black manager at a theater in the ghetto.[115]

Housing projects in the postwar decade were weak and almost entirely confined to Chicago and New York. In both cities tenants' leagues surviving from the 1930's did little. The National Negro Congress was still talking of rent strikes in Chicago, but only one was actually reported. In New York the Consolidated Tenants League in 1954 proposed a community-wide rent strike against building code violations, but it never got off the ground. There were a few demonstrations in each city for a couple of years after the war. The most significant one in New York occurred in 1953, when a black family who had sublet an apartment in the Metropolitan Life Insurance Company's all-white Parkchester development was evicted. Hundreds of blacks and whites demonstrated at the company's downtown headquarters; using techniques prefiguring the 1960's, six people shackled themselves with chains inside the building. The largest demonstrations were in Chicago, protesting the failure of city officials to protect black families violently assaulted after they had moved into the previously lily-white Trumbull Park housing project. In March, 1954, an interracial group of 1,500 marched on city hall under the aegis of the Chicago Negro Chamber of Commerce; the following year, led by the NAACP, 5,000 demonstrators again picketed city hall to denounce continued in-action in the face of two years of violence.[116]

Preeminently CORE was the organization identified with the sit-in at places of public accommodation; various ad hoc coalitions dominated the sporadic employment campaigns, and specialized tenant groups typically were at the heart of rent strikes. But in the school boycotts it was the NAACP that generally took the lead. Direct action was employed occasionally by college students demanding an end to their inferior segregated education, as when students from Langston University in Oklahoma, the North Carolina College at Durham, and several Texas colleges picketed their state capitols in 1949.[117] More important, although boycotts remained a seldom-used weapon in the struggle against educational segregation, this tactic was employed in at least seventeen communities in the decade before the *Brown* decision—one during World War II and nearly all the others between 1946 and 1951. (See Table III.) As earlier, these protests occurred mainly in small and medium-sized places, leaving segregation in big-city school systems untouched; and, as in previous years, these were almost entirely initiated and sustained by blacks.* On the other hand, these demonstrations differed from the ones of the preceding century. Except for Hempstead, where the boycott and related legal action stemmed from a newly instituted gerrymander, these protests were not defensive actions to preserve an older policy of integrated schools; rather, they were part of a militant black offensive to improve long-existing Jim Crow systems or to abolish them entirely. Moreover, for the first time school boycotts appeared in border and southern states; in Lumberton, North Carolina, and St. Louis they were accompanied by dramatic downtown mass marches of hundreds of students—an unprecedented tactic for school protests in a border city or a small southern town.†

This new stance reflected both the rising militance of blacks

*The leadership of the Long Branch boycott was interracial; the one in Mt. Holly was supported by the Seventh Ward Interracial Association; the boycott in Hempstead enjoyed the assistance of the American Labor party and American Jewish Congress; a white woman was prominent in the Merriam campaign.

†Actually, what may have been the first use of a mass march in southern school struggles occurred in 1939, when hundreds of Norfolk school children marched to protest the dismissal of a black teacher who was the plaintiff in a suit against racial salary differentials. See Norfolk *Journal and Guide*, July 1, 1939.

TABLE III

School Boycotts, 1943–1953

Hillburn, N.Y., 1943	Alton, Ill., 1950
Chester, Pa., 1946	Kinston, N.C., 1951
Lumberton, N.C., 1946	St. Louis, Mo., 1951
Long Branch, N.J., 1947	Farmville, Va., 1951
Fairhaven, N.J., 1947	Washington, D.C. (Payne School), 1951,
Merriam, Kan., 1948–1949	1953
Kansas City, Mo. (Bruce School), 1949	Kansas City, Mo. (Booker T. Washington
Hempstead, Long Island, N.Y., 1949	School), 1952
Mt. Holly, N.J., 1949	West Point, Va., 1952–53
East St. Louis, Ill., 1949	Lafayette, La., 1953

in this period and the growing salience that NAACP activities had given to the school issue. Since the mid-1930's the Association had engaged in much successful litigation compelling southern states to equalize teacher salaries and school facilities as a first step in a long-range program to secure school desegregation. Then in 1948 the NAACP decided that henceforth it would accept only cases directly challenging segregation.[118] The Association was involved in eleven of the seventeen communities, either instigating the boycott or lending assistance after local parents had inaugurated their own protests. Even in the other six places, demonstrations undoubtedly reflected the well-publicized NAACP efforts.* CORE, interestingly enough, was not involved in any boycott, and it did not use this tactic in school projects until the 1960's.

With the educational struggle in transition and the southern efforts still principally geared to upgrading black schools, rather than integrating them, both demands were involved in the postwar wave of school boycotts. The protests in North Carolina, Louisiana, Kansas City, St. Louis, and Washington dealt solely with relieving inferior, unsanitary, and overcrowded facilities. The first of the two Kansas City boycotts, for example, attacked a dilapidated elementary school whose four wooden buildings were heated by pot-bellied stoves and served by outdoor privies; the second boycott protested dangerously

*The NAACP was involved in Hillburn, Chester, Lumberton, Long Branch, Fairhaven, Merriam, Hempstead, East St. Louis, Alton, Farmville, and West Point.

overcrowded conditions. However, except for the Lumberton case, which occurred before the NAACP's shift in strategy, the Association's involvement always meant that school integration became the issue, even when it had not been the original goal of the protesters. In all the northern places except Chester, Pennsylvania, integration was demanded from the start; there, as well as in Farmville and West Point, Virginia, integration became the goal after the NAACP convinced the parents to attack the more basic problem.

The demonstrations were brief in most instances, lasting no more than a few days or weeks; but several continued longer— eight months in Chester, and a year or more in Merriam and West Point. Three places experienced more than one demonstration: Kansas City, where there were boycotts in two elementary schools; Washington, where the Payne school was boycotted twice; and St. Louis, where one-day walk-outs, mass marches, and picketing occurred over several months. In localities where the segregation violated state law (East St. Louis, Alton, and Hillburn) the NAACP at times encouraged the boycott as one tactic in an essentially legal campaign. But in most instances the direct action was the heart of the protest, even though legal action frequently followed.

The majority of these postwar school protests were successful. The blacks won clearcut victories in thirteen of the seventeen communities. Almost always this came through a combination of direct action and litigation. A boycott was solely responsible only in Fairhaven, New Jersey, where the officials quickly ended the segregation, and in Lafayette, Louisiana, where they met the black protesters' major demands for bus service and other improvements. In both Lumberton and Kinston the authorities, afraid of the legal action, provided new school buildings. The Long Branch, New Jersey, school board, facing a similar threat, integrated the schools. In Chester, the working-class group that withdrew their children from the unsanitary firetrap finally succeeded, with the assistance of NAACP lawyers, in integrating previously all-white schools in their neighborhoods. In Merriam and Hempstead the courts forced compliance with the state law. In Washington, after nearly two years of agitation, the school board finally relieved the overcrowding by assigning an under-utilized white school to the black children. In Kansas City and St. Louis, however, the protest was less successful. Missouri's Supreme Court sustained the school board's refusal to alleviate the situation at the Bruce School; and, as in Washington, the authorities in both cities moved slowly and reluctantly to grant even some relief. In the two Virginia integration cases—West Point and Farmville—white opposition proved intransigent; Farmville, in fact, became one of the NAACP cases on which the U.S. Supreme Court ruled school segregation unconstitutional in 1954. Even after that decision the recalcitrant Prince Edward County commissioners mounted a program of "massive resistance" to the black demands, while in West Point the officials refused to waive the thirty-day jail sentences that eight parents received for violating the compulsory attendance law, until the Virginia Supreme Court of Appeals reversed the convictions in 1957. Yet the significant point about the fruits of this postwar group of demonstrations is that, in contrast to earlier school boycotts that usually ended in failure, the majority of these later protests proved successful.[119]

Reviewing the war and postwar period it is evident that, despite the publicity which Randolph gave to direct action and the diligent work of the CORE chapters, demonstrations had declined sharply compared to the 1930's. It is true that public accommodations projects claimed more attention than ever before, that school boycotts continued to occur sporadically, and that the immediate postwar years had witnessed mass marches to protest lynchings in the South,[120] as well as picketing of the White House and the 1948 Republican national convention to demand passage of civil rights legislation.[121] Yet, overall, the amount of direct action was minor compared to the Depression era. Moreover, in the early 1950's direct action almost reached the vanishing point.

It is difficult to account for this decline in the postwar decade. One might have anticipated that the new state and municipal FEPC laws would raise expectations and generate considerable direct action for jobs. Yet blacks still did not feel that they had the leverage to attack downtown retail stores. Enormous work was required even against manufacturers with major sales in the ghettos, and even these efforts produced only a minuscule number of jobs. Paradoxically, the postwar decade was also a period when gradually improving conditions in the North and West encouraged blacks to believe that if they prepared themselves they could capitalize on the expanding economic opportunities. In the case of rent strikes, which had never occurred in more than a very few cities anyway, housing shortages and rental laws protecting landlords encouraged a feeling of futility. Yet success was also a factor in explaining the decline of direct action, since as the public accommodations issue was solved in the North, sit-ins ceased there. Ironically, once these victories had been achieved, CORE chapters often disappeared because of an inability to use direct action against other kinds of discrimination. Finally, changes in the broad climate of public opinion had a bearing on the lower volume of demonstrations. Nearly all of them had occurred during the era of liberalism associated with the Roosevelt-Truman administrations—before the conservatism of the early 1950's. The temporary ascendancy of McCarthyism, while not impeding the NAACP's progress in the courts, did have an inhibiting effect upon direct action, which to a large extent had been fueled by interracial and largely white radical groups. It ended the work of the Communist-front organizations, and it even seriously weakened a non-Communist group with a radical image like CORE. Whatever the precise explanation, the early 1950's was a period in which direct action had nearly ceased to be a weapon in the black protest struggle.

VI

When direct action revived during the latter half of the 1950's, the principal theater of activity shifted dramatically from the North to the South. A new mood of black militance had emerged in Dixie in the wake of several Supreme Court cases. Following the White Primary decision of 1944, the number of registered black voters rose, particularly in peripheral states like Texas, Virginia, and North Carolina, and black voters' leagues sprang up across the South. Black expectations were further heightened by a series of anti-segregation decisions won by the NAACP Legal Defense Fund. The most famous of these was the 1954 ruling on public schools; in addition, the following year the Supreme Court outlawed racial exclusion at tax-supported golf courses and beaches, the ICC barred segregation in interstate rail and bus travel, and a federal court of appeals declared segregated intrastate bus transportation illegal in Columbia, South Carolina.[122] Angry white Southerners responded by forming White Citizens Councils, resisting school desegregation, purging voter registration rolls, and harassing the NAACP even to the point of barring it from Alabama, Louisiana, and Texas. But these actions further heightened black militance, and there was a surge of nonviolent direct action in the Deep South beginning in 1955. Given the southern context in which physical confrontation with whites would have meant violence, imprisonment, and probably defeat, blacks not surprisingly selected the boycott tactic to battle whites seeking to keep them in Jim Crow schools, in the back of buses, and out of political power.

In many places white Southerners fought school integration by taking economic reprisals against parents who tried to enroll their children in all-white schools. In Orangeburg, South Carolina, the blacks counterattacked with a notable campaign. In mid-summer in 1955, after the Orangeburg newspaper published the names of people who had petitioned the school board for integration, a White Citizens Council soon appeared; white businessmen harassed individual signers by canceling charge accounts, dismissing employees, and refusing to supply black retailers. Among the leading anti-Negro wholesalers was the mayor, who owned both the Coca-Cola franchise and the major local bakery. Within six weeks nearly half the petitioners had withdrawn their names, and NAACP Secretary Roy Wilkins was denouncing the reprisals before the Senate Judiciary Committee.

By then the black community, counterattacking vigorously, had set up its own boycott with twenty-three merchants on the first list. The national NAACP assisted by contributing thousands of dollars to the beleaguered blacks. With the white merchants beginning to suffer, state authorities decided to bar

NAACP members from public employment and to investigate NAACP activities at the South Carolina State College in Orangeburg. Thoroughly aroused, the students boycotted the bread which the school bought from the mayor's bakery, and at one point even stayed out of the cafeteria altogether because its milk came from a dairy that had cut off deliveries to signers of the petition. At neighboring Claflin College a boycott of the Coca-Cola machines led to their removal. In April, 1956, supporting a strongly worded faculty and staff protest against the NAACP investigation, the South Carolina State College students went on a strike which was ended nearly a week later by threats of severe disciplinary measures. Five faculty members were dismissed and about twenty-five students expelled. With both the local businessmen and the state officials standing firm, the black boycott gradually petered out.[123]

While the Orangeburg movement received little notice, the Montgomery bus boycott of 1955–56 became known around the world. Montgomery got the headlines, but there were four other southern bus boycotts; the first of these, although virtually ignored, had actually occurred in 1953 at Baton Rouge.

In both Montgomery and Baton Rouge, Jim Crow patterns on the buses were particularly galling. Not only were blacks required to sit in the back, but if the bus became filled they would also have to give up their seats to whites. In Baton Rouge, where black voting began to signal the broader changes that were slowly undermining the southern race system, the city council acceded to Negro demands and modified the seating arrangements. The new ordinance, while maintaining segregation, provided for seating on a strictly first-come-first-served basis. The incensed bus drivers went on strike, returning to work only after the state attorney general declared that the new city law conflicted with the state segregation statute. But the blacks, clearly well organized, responded under the NAACP's leadership with a 100 percent effective boycott demanding both the new seating plan and the hiring of black bus drivers. Operating as the United Defense League, a broad coalition that produced solid unity in the community, the blacks created a "free lift" auto service of 150 private cars and taxis. The local white daily reported: "a steady stream of cars and trucks pass in front of the Old State Capitol picking up Negro passengers from the large crowd gathered there. Dispatchers facilitate the movement of the 'free ride' vehicles and passengers are grouped together according to their destinations." During the boycott the bus company, which had derived most of its revenues from black riders, lost $1,600 a day. Victory came a week later. The city council enacted a new ordinance which, while staying within the technicalities of the state law by reserving two front seats for whites, was essentially the bill passed earlier in the year.[124]

The Baton Rouge boycott did not inspire similar demonstrations in other cities. However, blacks were becoming increasingly impatient, and in a growing number of instances individuals challenged seating arrangements on the buses. Some of these went to the courts, and it is perhaps no coincidence that the favorable federal court decision in the Columbia, South Carolina, case in the summer of 1955 came only a few months before the Montgomery bus boycott began. Montgomery blacks, who had in recent months witnessed at least two arrests stemming from the bus segregation law, were unwilling to wait until the Supreme Court adjudicated the issue. Indeed, leading Montgomery citizens had been considering a boycott for some time; when Rosa Parks was arrested, they seized upon her protest as the opportunity they were looking for to galvanize the black community.

Although the original demands of the Montgomery boycott were identical with those of the earlier Baton Rouge protest, the Montgomery movement was an entirely independent, autonomous development. Indeed, none of the four leaders responsible for initiating the Montgomery boycott knew about the one in Baton Rouge. After their campaign was getting underway and Martin Luther King, who had previously been uninvolved, assumed the leadership, it was he who recollected the Baton Rouge boycott and contacted friends there for information about the "free ride" car pool which became the model for Montgomery. But both boycotts in their origins were independent inventions arising out of the new mood of blacks in the South.[125]

Montgomery blacks were taking practical steps to alleviate an intolerable situation. They were nonviolent of necessity, but originally did not articulate an ideology of nonviolence. Absent from the outlook of the boycott's initiators were any thoughts of Gandhism or pacifism, ingredients which were supplied later by Glenn Smiley of the FOR staff and Bayard Rustin of the War Resisters League, whose respective organizations sent them in February, 1956, to assist King. Upon arriving in Montgomery, Rustin found guns in King's home, to be used if necessary in self-defense. Yet King, familiar with Gandhi's philosophy from divinity school, was soon combining pacifist doctrine with Christianity in his speeches and became convinced that violence, even in self-defense, was wrong. As he pointed out at the time, "We have discovered a new and powerful weapon—nonviolent resistance. . . . Face violence if necessary, but refuse to return violence."[126]

Actually it was not the boycott, but a Supreme Court decision[127] that desegregated the buses at the end of 1956, a year after the movement began. Generally unperceived by the public was the decisive role of the high tribunal, which would certainly have invalidated bus segregation even without the boycott. Instead the campaign was viewed as a signal victory for nonviolent direct-action tactics. Although it is impossible to measure the precise influence of the Montgomery movement on the course of black protest, clearly the campaign itself—and, more important, the charismatic leader it produced—made an extraordinary impression on Afro-Americans across the country. As a staff writer for the St. Louis *Argus* reported several weeks after the boycott started: "The passive resistance movement currently underway in Montgomery is easily the most revolutionary thing to occur in the South since the Civil War."[128]

The Montgomery protest both articulated and further stimulated the growing militance among southern blacks. Even in the repressive Mississippi Delta, where Negro leaders faced extreme economic and psychological pressures that stymied their efforts to increase voter registration, interest was expressed in the possibilities of direct action.[129] While this was premature for Mississippi, blacks in nearby Memphis, who for years had unsuccessfully urged the *Commercial Appeal* to cease handling news in a racist way, in mid-1957 finally resorted to a boycott. Thousands stopped buying the newspaper, and in a few weeks most of their demands were met.[130]

More important were the bus protests inspired directly by Montgomery, notably at Tallahassee, Birmingham, and Rock Hill, South Carolina. The Tallahassee campaign that began in May, 1956, was spearheaded by C. K. Steele, a Baptist minister and NAACP president who promoted community unity through an umbrella group, the Inter-Civic Council. The determined blacks maintained their informal transportation system even after twenty-one leaders were arrested and fined for running a car pool without a license. Following the Supreme Court decision that outlawed segregation in Montgomery, the Tallahassee city commission circumvented it by giving bus drivers authority to assign seats. Defiantly the blacks tried to maintain the protest, but in the face of considerable violence the boycott petered out, and the buses remained segregated until the end of the decade.[131]

In Birmingham the bus protests were sponsored by the Alabama Christian Movement for Human Rights which NAACP leader Fred Shuttlesworth founded in 1956 after the NAACP had been enjoined from operating in the state. The Reverend Mr. Shuttlesworth articulated the same amalgam of Gandhian nonviolence and Christianity that had formed the ideological rationale for both the Montgomery and Tallahassee movements. But disunity among Birmingham's leaders and the large size of the Birmingham metropolitan area militated against a viable bus boycott. On December 26, 1956, the night after his home was bombed and his children injured, Shuttlesworth courageously led a mass bus ride that brought the arrests of twenty-one persons. Nearly two years later he and a dozen others challenged transportation segregation again, and their jailing finally precipitated a bus boycott. Not nearly as effective as the ones in Tallahassee and Montgomery, it dissipated after the first surge of anger had subsided. The buses were not desegregated until a federal court voided the seat-assignment law late in 1959.[132]

Elsewhere, following Montgomery's bus desegregation, ministers in Atlanta and Shreveport tested the Jim Crow policies by sitting in the front of the vehicles. But with the authorities intransigent, the blacks resorted to the courts in both cases.[133] More direct action would have undoubtedly occurred, except for the fact that in many places bus companies without any public announcement simply dropped their Jim Crow rules.[134] The final bus boycott—an NAACP-led one in the small community of Rock Hill—was begun in July, 1957. Under the inspiration of the Presbyterian minister C. A. Ivory, the city's blacks organized their own car pool and bus line that drove the local traction company out of business in December. Ivory, though crippled and confined to a wheelchair, would make Rock Hill an important center of southern direct action in the early 1960's.[135]

The other major boycott of the 1950's—at the predominantly black town of Tuskegee, Alabama—was precipitated not by the example of Montgomery and Martin Luther King, but by the repression of whites afraid of black voters. For years the Tuskegee Civic Association headed by Professor Charles G. Gomillion had worked with modest success to increase the number of blacks on the voting rolls. As early as 1953 blacks had boycotted local merchants for several weeks, hoping to put pressure on the board of registrars to cease their discrimination. In 1957 fears that the number of black registrants in Tuskegee would soon threaten the status quo led the Alabama legislature to redraw the town's boundaries so that virtually all blacks were excluded. Within a week Tuskegee blacks had mounted a highly effective boycott against the merchants. A number of small businesses, dependent on Negro patronage, were driven into bankruptcy; however, the community's most influential people, personally unaffected by the boycott, remained firm. The gerrymander was ended only in 1960 by a Supreme Court decision.[136]

It is a striking fact that as effective as were these boycotts, with solid black support behind them everywhere except in Birmingham, in no case did the direct action itself secure redress of black grievances. Black protesters lost their battle in Orangeburg, Tallahassee, and Rock Hill. They were victorious in Montgomery, Birmingham, and Tuskegee only because of the decisions handed down by federal judges. Although these courageous campaigns were impressive and inspiring to blacks and sympathetic whites across America, the fact is that in the repressive context of the Deep South such tactics had only a slim chance of success. Bus companies and merchants, squeezed to the wall, might urge acquiescence to black demands, but politicians responsive to white voters would nevertheless stand firm.

Not surprisingly, therefore, except for the half-dozen campaigns we have considered, the Deep South was not yet a viable milieu for nonviolent direct action. This was certainly the conclusion of ranking NAACP officials. King, speaking at the Association's 1956 convention amid the excitement generated by the Montgomery boycott, urged the delegates to commit their organization to a substantial program of direct action. Enthusiastically they recommended that the Board and national staff carefully consider using "non-violent resistance" along the lines of the southern bus boycotts "in our expanding program for civil rights." But the Board did not feel that this strategy was realistic. Despite their own rhetoric, King and his associates also understood the enormous difficulties in staging direct-action projects in the South. Indeed, in setting up the Southern Christian Leadership Conference in 1957 they announced that its program would consist of voter registration.[137] Similarly, when CORE first penetrated the Deep South that same year, sending a field secretary into South Carolina, it engaged in voter registration work.

Of course CORE-style sit-ins were far harder to stage than boycotts, which avoided physical confrontations with hostile whites. This was even true in the more moderate areas of the Upper South. In a rare and probably unique instance, a small group in Durham in 1957, led by a young Methodist minister named Douglas E. Moore, were convicted for trespassing after seeking service in the white section of an ice cream parlor. Similarly, in states like Tennessee and Virginia CORE eschewed confrontation campaigns. The affiliate in Nashville in 1957, unable to mount sit-ins, devoted its energies to helping black parents who, in a climate of severe intimidation, were sending their children to schools recently desegrated by court order. As late as 1958–59 efforts to establish viable CORE groups in Virginia fizzled; the principal project there also revolved around school integration, with CORE and the state NAACP co-sponsoring a "Pilgrimage" to the state capitol on

New Year's Day 1959, protesting the governor's "massive resistance" program.[138]

With both school desegregation and the direct action movement stymied in the South by white recalcitrance, the black activists decided to press an indifferent president and a slow-moving Congress for federal enforcement of the southern Negroes' constitutional rights. Early in 1957 King called for a "Prayer Pilgrimage" to Washington. The proposal came originally from Shuttlesworth, who felt that, with the bombings, arrests, and other forms of intimidation in Birmingham and throughout the Deep South, something was needed to force intervention by the national government: "We had to do something. We had to get the attention of the nation—to let them know what was happening in the South." Rustin, who worked closely with King, secured Randolph's backing for the Pilgrimage and handled the logistics from Randolph's New York office. Soon after, Roy Wilkins agreed to NAACP co-sponsorship. Support for the Pilgrimage also came from black fraternal, professional, and civic organizations, and it was endorsed by liberal white churchmen and union leaders. On May 17, 1957, the third anniversary of the *Brown* decision, a predominantly black group of 25,000 held their demonstration at the Lincoln Memorial, appealing to the conscience of the nation. King's memorable "Give Us the Right to Vote" speech addressed itself to the newly formed SCLC's area of chief concern.

As Randolph and others said at the time, there were significant similarities between this "Prayer Pilgrimage for Freedom" and the 1941 March on Washington, yet contemporaries also realized that the differences were even more important. The very word "pilgrimage" used by King and his Baptist associates in SCLC was, in the Pittsburgh *Courier*'s view, a "softer term implying a more peaceful approach . . . more persuasion than force." Quite likely this demonstration reflected not only the religious style of Southern Baptist preachers, but also the fact that it took place in the shadow of McCarthyism. Certainly its tone was not one of "shaking up America" with "mass action." In 1957 the word "March" was deliberately rejected in favor of "Prayer Pilgrimage" because the organizers believed that rhetoric which sounded too militant would be counter-productive. Rather than make "demands," they made "an appeal to the conscience of the nation"—the demonstration's mood was one "of black people appealing to white people." "We wanted," recalled Shuttlesworth, "to emphasize love, nonviolence, we wanted to emphasize prayer, pleading to the nation." To allay the anxieties of white Washingtonians about a pilgrimage in their midst, King announced beforehand that there would be "no picketing or posterwalking" and that the program would be confined "solely" to the Lincoln Memorial. The speeches delivered on that occasion reflected this suppliant tone. Pointedly stressing the gulf between the black man's struggle and the aims and methods of the Communists, both King and Randolph called upon federal officials for help. As King explained to the crowd, "We come to Washington today pleading with the President and the Congress to provide a strong, moral and courageous leadership. We come humbly to say that the civil rights issue is an eternal moral issue. . . . Give us the ballot," he pleaded, "and we will quietly and nonviolently, without rancor or bitterness, implement the Supreme Court's Decision."[139]

This Pilgrimage was part of the extensive agitation that preceded passage of the Civil Rights Act of 1957, the first such federal law since Reconstruction. Ironically the Act, with its tepid enforcement clauses, heightened black expectations rather than providing remedies for grievances. Randolph, now choosing to focus on the highly salient school desegregation issue, initiated two youth marches in the nation's capital, in October, 1958, and April, 1959. Coordinated by Rustin and endorsed by a wide range of civic, labor, and black advancement organizations, including SCLC and NAACP, these Youth Marches for Integrated Schools were billed as interracial demonstrations. In fact, however, the 10,000 high school and college youth who marched down Pennsylvania Avenue in 1958 and the 25,000 marchers of 1959 were overwhelmingly black. Both demonstrations turned out to be essentially symbolic gestures that produced no concrete accomplishments.[140]

Meanwhile it was in the border states, where the gradual shift in white public opinion made conditions ripe for successful demonstrations, that most of the campaigns of the latter part of the decade occurred. Significantly, black participation in these movements grew markedly, and while CORE work revived, more and more campaigns tended to involve NAACP people, particularly youths dissatisfied with legalism.

CORE in the late 1950's tried simultaneously to establish a base in the Deep South, rekindle its activities in the North, and push forward in the border areas. Its efforts in Kansas were abortive, but successful all-black chapters were founded in 1958 in East St. Louis, Illinois, and Charleston, West Virginia. The interracial St. Louis CORE experienced a renaissance, although its viability actually depended on a close alliance with NAACP youths led by the future Congressman William Clay. Without the initiative and manpower supplied by the St. Louis NAACP, neither the intensive large-scale picketing at a Howard Johnson restaurant that produced some arrests, nor the very successful job campaigns during 1958–59 would have been possible. In Baltimore, where the CORE chapter was also weak, the banner of direct action passed to black student activists at Morgan State College, who assumed the major burden of the struggle to desegregate places of public accommodation.[141]

In Kansas City, Missouri, a group of black clubwomen spearheaded the campaign that desegregated department store lunch-counters in 1958–59. They enlisted the cooperation of several ministers; having thus assured themselves of substantial community support, they also obtained endorsement and financial help from a reluctant NAACP branch that was trying to solve the problem by lobbying for a civil rights ordinance. Ministers and housewives led the picket lines for several months, until all the stores changed their policy. Although their sit-in tactics resembled those used earlier by St. Louis CORE to desegregate the department store lunch-counters, actually the Montgomery bus boycott was the inspiration. As one of Kansas City's leading ministers put it, "If they walked in Montgomery, surely we can stop buying in Kansas City."[142]

Elsewhere the NAACP adult leadership was also reluctant and cautious. Although direct action in the border states became increasingly all-black, with considerable NAACP involvement as in St. Louis, the NAACP youth councils, rather than the adult branches, were in the militant vanguard. Despite the skepticism of adult leaders, the Wichita NAACP Youth Council sat in at lunch counters as early as 1956; two years later their campaign succeeded in desegregating the counters of one major drugstore chain throughout the city.[143] Similarly, the most substantial of the border-state demonstrations—those in Oklahoma City in 1958—were also carried out by the NAACP Youth Council and were inspired by the work of Martin Luther King. The sit-ins quickly desegregated lunch counters at four drug and variety stores; impressed by this campaign, another thirty-five businesses promptly opened their eating facilities. The impetus for the project came from the Youth Council's adult advisor, Clara Luper, a dynamic history teacher who, although aware of CORE's work, had actually been stimulated by the drama and successes of the charismatic Martin Luther King.[144] Finally, impressed by developments in Kansas City and Oklahoma City, the NAACP branch in Louisville undertook sit-ins at downtown drugstores early in 1959. The adults quickly became discouraged, but the Youth Council staged demonstrations at lunch counters and restaurants for two more months, and at the end of the year it was picketing a downtown movie theater that excluded blacks.[145] Desegregation of public accommodations in Louisville would not occur until the mass demonstrations of 1961, but these sit-ins of 1959 revealed the changing mood of southern Negroes.

So also did CORE's ability to inaugurate direct action in Kentucky and further south. During 1959 interracial chapters staged sit-ins in Lexington, Kentucky, and Miami, and a predominantly black affiliate was formed in Tallahassee. By then even the CORE affiliates in South Carolina, previously limiting themselves to voter registration, had begun occasional sit-ins. Members in Columbia, the state capital, had successfully tested the airport restaurant, the public library, and the front section of buses as early as the fall of 1958. A year later the Greenville group, with the NAACP's support, had desegregated the local airport; and in Sumter CORE teenagers were testing the drugstore lunch-counters.[146]

As the pace of activism quickened in the border and southern states, boycotting and picketing for jobs also occasionally occurred. Indeed, the most substantial and successful employment campaign in the country during the late 1950's, and one reminiscent of the jobs movements of the Depression, was the sustained St. Louis NAACP-CORE effort in 1957–58. The demonstrations won agreements to hire blacks from a leading downtown department store, from two major chain stores in the ghetto, and (after a year of agitation and boycott) from the Taystee Bread Company. Washington blacks staged a one-day boycott of the downtown department stores during the Easter shopping season of 1958 to dramatize the demand for equal employment opportunity. The following year the Jacksonville NAACP picketed the Sears Roebuck store for weeks because it refused to hire qualified Negroes for responsible positions. In Norfolk at year's end the interracial CORE demonstrated against a supermarket until enjoined by court action, and in South Carolina the Sumter and Greenville CORE affiliates were both contemplating job boycotts.[147]

In the North, despite the rising militance of black Americans, there was still far less resort to direct action. CORE, for example, hoped to develop techniques to attack housing and employment problems; but, lacking a significant base in the black community, it had no leverage to accomplish anything by itself. Moreover, even all-black organizations remained for the most part unconscious of the latent potential of boycotts and picket lines. Only sporadic campaigns foreshadowed the kinds of tactics that flowered during the 1960's. In Chicago, for example, a leading center of black direct action during the Depression, the close alliance between the Daley machine and organizations in the Black Belt inhibited the development of militant strategies. Even in New York, where the liberal milieu and the highly factionalized politics gave blacks considerable leverage and thus provided the context in which direct action flourished more than anywhere else in the North, demonstrations were relatively few.[148] Characteristic of the occasional jobs projects scattered across the country[149] were the weak ones that cropped up in New York in 1959, after several years in which no employment demonstrations had occurred there. The Bronx NAACP's four Saturdays of picketing at a Sears store with a large black and Puerto Rican clientele produced only a promise to consider the two racial minorities for future vacancies.[150]

More impressive was the New York NAACP's picketing and boycotting of white-owned Harlem liquor stores in 1959, demanding that the owners no longer deal with wholesalers who refused to hire black salesmen. Within weeks twenty stores had signed agreements with the NAACP. Unfortunately, however, the picketing, which was suspended when the city's Commission on Intergroup Relations intervened, was not resumed after that body's ineffective report was issued.[151]

Important as the *Brown* decision was in stirring the consciousness of southern blacks, rarely if ever was direct action used to secure its implementation.* In the immediate aftermath of that decision, the few southern school boycotts, although successful, demanded not integration but new and better separate school facilities.[152] There was slightly greater direct action in the North, even though the impact of *Brown* was as yet very limited there. In Michigan a small school district precipitated a futile two-week black boycott after it established a Jim Crow school in 1955.[153] In at least three other places blacks were motivated by the Supreme Court ruling to aggressively combat long-standing separate schools by resorting to direct-action tactics. At Hillsboro, a small community near Dayton, Ohio, twenty Negro pupils boycotted for nearly two years. The national NAACP took up their fight, and in March, 1956, the Supreme Court required an immediate end to the black elementary school.[154] At New Rochelle three years later an extended campaign of litigation against the gerrymandering of black children into a dilapidated Jim Crow school included a two-day boycott.[155]

The most important school demonstrations occurred in New York City, where activists began an attack on de facto segregation that prefigured the militant northern school boycotts of the 1960's. Black leaders in both Brooklyn and Harlem pressed the Board of Education almost immediately following *Brown*. Their intensive and sustained efforts in 1958 and 1959 included mass street demonstrations and small-scale boycotts in which parents demanded the right to transfer their children to better schools

---

*King, speaking at a press conference, did once propose boycotting southern schools to secure enforcement of the Supreme Court's desegregation mandate, but the proposal was not carefully developed, and nothing ever came of it. See Louisville *Defender*, July 5, 1956.

outside the ghetto. Pickets—as many as 500 at a time—
appeared periodically before city hall and the board headquarters. The longest and bitterest boycott involved nine parents
who kept their children out of three Harlem schools for 156
days, until the youngsters were transferred. About the same
time there was a similar, shorter boycott in Brooklyn. Under
such pressures the school board ultimately acceded to these
specific demands, but it failed to deal with the basic problems of
de facto segregation and the inferior education at slum schools.
Again at the beginning of 1960, twenty-five children were
transferred to schools outside Harlem only after a lengthy
boycott involving 200 children and the arrest and conviction of
four parents.[156]

New York was also the site of the only significant use of direct
action to attack housing problems during the late 1950's. The
protests attempted to end discrimination in sale and rental of
residential units and to correct the outrageous conditions in
slum tenements. In 1957 at CORE's instigation an interracial
coalition, pressing for an anti-discrimination ordinance, held a
mass demonstration at city hall; enacted in December, this ordinance became the first municipal fair-housing law in the
country.[157] The Consolidated Tenants League was now devoting itself to numerous court cases,[158] and when rent strikes
reappeared in 1959 they were sponsored by a new group, the
Lower Harlem Tenants Council. Headed by Jesse Gray, "a
long-time radical expelled from the National Maritime Union
for his left-wing associations," the Council gave its attention to
organizing poor people. By the end of the summer residents of
twenty-two apartment houses were striking to correct such
problems as lack of heat and hot water. While the Department
of Housing and Buildings was thus pressured to haul some
slumlords into court, little was accomplished. But these efforts
did foreshadow the dramatic rent strikes that would break out
in the fall of 1963.[159]

As the New York *Amsterdam News* observed in the summer of
1959, the mood of Harlem's residents was "the most hostile" it
had been since the Depression—a mood of "revolution" and "of
stern but stubborn defiance of the status quo."[160] Events in
New York, like the demonstrations on the fringes of the South

during 1958 and 1959, were atypical. But they did reflect the growing militance among American Negroes and constituted a rising tide of direct action spawned by the revolution in black expectations. No one anticipated the revolt that commenced in 1960. Yet the stage had been set for the southern college sit-ins and the momentous events, South, West, and North, that followed.

VII

As the evidence in this study indicates, the use of direct action in Afro-American protest extends far back in black history. One is struck by the varied times and circumstances under which it occurred, the diverse targets and tactics involved, the different racial composition of the demonstrators, and the range of ideologies employed to justify the demonstrations.

Direct action only seldom achieved a major role in black protest, and there was a tendency for these tactics to cluster at certain periods. Thus such clusters appeared in antebellum Massachusetts, during Reconstruction, and at the turn of the century. Thereafter direct action was more likely to occur sporadically, as in the intermittent and widely scattered school boycotts spanning the entire twentieth century. Nevertheless, direct action still tended to achieve salience in certain periods, with high points during the Depression and again in the decade following the Montgomery bus boycott.

Jim Crow schools were the most persistent target of these campaigns, though confined to the North until the mid-twentieth century. The boycotts and other demonstrations were directed solely at segregated schools and transportation facilities throughout the nineteenth and early twentieth centuries. Except for the Massachusetts confrontations, the transportation demonstrations all took place in the South.* And aside from the Journey of Reconciliation in 1947, the South experienced no direct action against transportation segregation for nearly a half-century after the streetcar boycotts collapsed in the early 1900's. During the decade preceding World War I, the remarkably modern demonstrations against Negrophobic theatricals were a major tactical innovation, but the mass

*Even though Jim Crow horsecars appeared in cities like New York and Philadelphia in the mid-nineteenth century, there is no evidence that protesting blacks employed direct action in those cities.

media's treatment of blacks never became a major focus of subsequent campaigns. Not until the Depression did direct action in employment and housing, as well as Jim Crow restaurants, hotels, theaters, and similar places of public accommodation and recreation, become significant.

During the nineteenth century the principal technique was the boycott; blacks were using it even before the word entered the English language after 1880. Confrontations and sit-in type tactics were much rarer, cropping up periodically in transportation and school demonstrations during the antebellum and Reconstruction periods. Picketing and mass marching were introduced around the time of World War I, but blacks did not use either tactic widely until the 1930's. The Depression decade marked the first time that boycotts, sit-ins, picketing, and mass marches—along with a new weapon, the rent strike—were all simultaneously employed.

The era of the Depression marked a watershed in Afro-American direct action in other ways as well. Until the 1930's white participation was extremely rare. The principal exception was in antebellum Massachusetts; there, following the blacks' initiative, white Garrisonians lent encouragement to the school boycotts and joined blacks in the railroad car confrontations.[161] Later a few whites participated in the protests against *The Birth of a Nation* in New York and Boston.[162] Although these demonstrations and the early twentieth-century black school boycotts sometimes received support from certain whites, all were black inspired and black led. The period of the Depression and World War II, with the self-conscious interracialism of first the Communists and then CORE, thus spelled a significant new departure. Despite the enormous differences between CORE and the Communists, the whites in both groups were radicals outside the mainstream of American reform who regarded their interracialism and direct-action tactics as militant innovations. In both CORE and the Communist organizations, moreover, whites were not merely participants, but played crucial policy-making roles. This white activism was most evident in public accommodations projects, although whites were also involved in a few job campaigns and in the majority of the Communist demonstrations, particularly in New York City.

The Depression era and World War II also marked a new

departure in the ideological justification for direct-action tactics. The basic motivation underlying direct action and black protest generally has always been a fervent belief in the equality of all citizens in a democratic society. Beyond this, blacks who employed direct action had been essentially non-ideological, basing their tactics on very practical considerations. Prior to the 1930's blacks had boycotted and picketed not from any theory of mass action or belief in philosophical nonviolence, but because such techniques seemed logical means for obtaining citizenship rights.

However, many of the campaigns during the Depression had ideological overtones. In the "Don't-Buy-Where-You-Can't-Work" movements, some groups articulated a petit bourgeois entrepreneurial philosophy, often with a significant nationalist component. Much of the other direct action of the 1930's and early 1940's was at least partly a product of the radical Marxist theory of mass action, an idea that entered the general reform vocabulary and was advocated by many non-Communists as well. Then in the early 1940's CORE founders, inspired by pacifism, Gandhi, and the CIO's sit-down strikes, brought a new dimension to direct action; for the first time, the ideology of nonviolent resistance became a justification for civil rights protests.*

No one summed up these developments of the 1930's better than A. Philip Randolph. First and foremost a black militant dissatisfied with traditional forms of protest and the moderation of the major race advancement organizations, Randolph from the beginning of his career found in Marxism and trade unionism certain strategies that would be helpful to black protesters. The March on Washington Movement, while black inspired and black led, clearly drew upon his background and experience as a Socialist and labor organizer. Although Randolph had been a militant Socialist, not a Communist, his con-

---

*There is no evidence that antebellum theories of passive resistance and noncooperation had any influence on the Massachusetts protests (interview with Louis Ruchames, Dec. 13, 1975). Our interpretation here is thus at variance with the thrust of the presentation in Carleton Mabee, *Black Freedom: The Nonviolent Abolitonists from 1830 Through the Civil War* (London, 1970). Similarly we believe that Marjorie M. Norris's view that the Louisville streetcar demonstrations of 1870–71 expressed a nonviolent philosophy is unsupported by the evidence (Norris, "An Early Instance of Nonviolence: The Louisville Demonstrations of 1870–1871," pp. 503–4).

ceptualization of direct action revealed the impact that Communists had upon social activism in the 1930's. His vocabulary of "mass action," "monster mass meetings," and "marches on Washington" had all been popularized by the Communists. In addition, as Randolph's strategy evolved during the 1940's it showed the influence of CORE pacifists like James Farmer and Bayard Rustin. Randolph was never a pacifist any more than he was a Communist. He was essentially a militant and radical black man appropriating militant tactics from other sources.

Yet most of the direct action that followed during the 1940's and 1950's was not related to ideologies of mass action or Gandhism. This was certainly true of the school boycotts, job campaigns, and non-CORE public accommodations demonstrations. Moreover, most CORE members were not pacifists or Gandhians; in fact, the early CORE pacifist leaders, whose commitment was first and foremost to the advancement of racial equality, quickly sought to shed CORE's pacifist image, and to appeal to liberal whites and blacks on purely practical grounds. It is, of course, tempting to perceive a chain of development from Randolph and CORE to King and the Montgomery bus boycott and ultimately to SNCC, and historical connections do indeed exist. After all, Rustin helped provide King with a philosophical rationale and linked King's SCLC to Randolph in the 1957 Prayer Pilgrimage and the subsequent youth marches. King's success in Montgomery helped revive a dying CORE. In addition, King inspired those involved in the sit-ins of the Oklahoma City NAACP Youth Council in 1958 and the SNCC youth in 1960. Yet the origins of the Montgomery boycott owed nothing to CORE, Randolph, or Gandhi. SNCC's founders, although impressed with the early King and at first couching their official ideology in Gandhian terms, mostly viewed nonviolent direct action pragmatically as a useful tool. Thus it would be an oversimplification to describe the "black revolt" of the 1960's as the consequence of the earlier activism of Randolph and King.

Surveying the history of black protest, it becomes clear that the use of direct-action tactics has not characteristically emerged out of an explicit ideology of nonviolence. What, then, are the sources of the blacks' use of nonviolent direct action? Is the more than 125 years of boycotts, sit-ins, and other demonstrations a manifestation of a continuous tradition, indigenous to the Afro-American community from which generations of black protesters have drawn ideas and inspiration? Have these tactics been largely borrowed from other movements of social protest? Or were they the result of repeated spontaneous invention by black groups and organizations seeking effective tools to attack the myriad problems they faced?

While there has been a sustained tradition of black protest throughout American history, the use of direct-action tactics has been episodic and marked by sharp discontinuities. Not only did these tactics cluster in certain times and places, but until the mid-twentieth century there were also long gaps between one series of campaigns and another; even the school boycotts were isolated, sporadic, and geographically scattered. Only rarely were leaders of direct-action movements in one historical period aware of similar movements in an earlier period.

For example, except for Savannah, there is no evidence that leaders in the streetcar boycotts at the turn of the century knew of the Reconstruction campaigns. Even more striking was the fact that the instigators of the Baton Rouge and Montgomery bus boycotts of the 1950's had never heard of the streetcar boycotts in the same cities half a century earlier. Similarly, except where motivated directly by the national office of the NAACP, the concerned parents who began the school boycotts were responding to local problems and had no relationship with similar movements elsewhere.* The 1955 Montgomery bus boycott provides the most dramatic illustration of this tendency toward autonomous invention of the same direct-action tactics in different times and places: this famous campaign was inaugurated with no knowledge of the 1953 movement in Baton Rouge. Similarly, the first lunch-counter sit-ins conducted by Chicago CORE and the Howard University NAACP occurred almost simultaneously but without any connection

---

*It is, of course, not surprising that in Chester, where two boycotts occurred a decade apart, leaders of the second were quite aware of the first; in fact, at least one had participated as a student in the first boycott. On the other hand, in East Orange, where the two boycotts took place thirty years apart and involved different schools, there is no evidence of any interrelationship.

with each other. The St. Louis department store sit-ins a year later were likewise initiated independently. This is not to suggest that direct-action tactics were not diffused from one city to another during "waves" or clusters of demonstrations that occurred within a relatively brief span of time. Almost certainly the leaders of campaigns in neighboring communities, as in the Massachusetts school boycotts of the 1840's or the southern Ohio ones in the 1920's, were in touch with each other. The "Don't-Buy-Where-You-Can't-Work" campaigns of the 1930's provide the clearest example of diffusion. The Chicago movement received considerable attention around the country, and its leaders actively propagandized their strategy in visits to other cities. The national office of the Urban League encouraged such campaigns, and they were discussed on the program of the NAACP's 1933 national convention. Moreover, the instigators of the Harlem and Baltimore campaigns came from Chicago and proudly referred to participation in the *Whip*'s projects there, while the Cleveland Future Outlook League was inspired and influenced by a careful study of the Chicago campaign.[163]

A more complex case is posed by the wave of southern street-car boycotts at the turn of the century. Black elites in the different cities interacted regularly at national, church, fraternal, and race advancement conferences; they corresponded frequently, and undoubtedly exchanged information concerning the protests against streetcar segregation. Yet there is virtually no documentary evidence for this.[164] The published reports of neither the Afro-American Council nor the Niagara Movement—the two important protest organizations of the period—mentioned the boycotts. Moreover, the prolific writings of the protest leader W. E. B. Du Bois contain only the rarest references, and these are discussions of the occasional black transportation companies that grew out of the boycotts, not of the protests themselves. Rather than being a response basically dependent on borrowing, the streetcar boycotts appear in the surviving sources to be more like spontaneous and angry reactions precipitated directly by the passage of state or municipal Jim Crow laws. Thus even the editor of the Richmond *Planet*, who displayed an unusual amount of interest in boycotts elsewhere, failed to refer to them when encouraging his readers to support their own local boycott. Probably, knowing of their general futility in other cities, he could hardly have used them as a rallying symbol. Moreover, it is a striking fact that the black press's references to these protests were scattered and usually brief, and readers of a single paper would have been unaware of the broad extent of these local movements.[165] Even a militant editor like Sol Johnson of the Savannah *Tribune*, who was a boycott leader in his own city, paid almost no attention to such protests occurring elsewhere. In short, even in a wave of protests like these streetcar boycotts, the case for diffusion is hard to prove.

It is important to note that in the more distant past the diffusion of information about black protest activities in various cities was far less marked than during the 1960's, when the white mass media played an extremely important role in spreading news of the demonstrations among both blacks and whites. Indeed, before the Montgomery bus boycott, reporting of such events in the white dailies and weekly newsmagazines was negligible. The black press, of course, did better; but even here, with only a few exceptions, the attention which any newspaper gave to direct-action movements in distant cities was usually slight. Not only had references to the streetcar boycotts of the early 1900's been scattered, but over forty years later the Journey of Reconciliation was scarcely reported. Even more to the point, boycotts of the 1950's at Baton Rouge, Orangeburg, and Rock Hill were seldom discussed in most of the black papers across the country. These omissions by the black press and the Negro editors' limited attention to direct action reinforce our thesis that there was nothing in the Afro-American experience that could be called a tradition of direct action. The absence of a sustained tradition of direct action is illustrated by events in St. Louis in the 1940's. Not only were the women who started the department store sit-ins in 1944 unaware of recent sit-ins in Chicago and Washington, but when St. Louis CORE was begun three years later and sought to integrate the same department stores, its leaders had no knowledge of the earlier local movement.[166] Similarly, the substantial history of direct action in Chicago had no influence on the pacifists who founded

CORE there in 1941–42, and they were unaware of the Communists' pioneering direct action against places of public accommodations. Finally, the fact that Martin Luther King's associates could assert (as they often did without contradiction) that a new technique was born in Montgomery in 1955 epitomizes the absence of such a tradition.*

If there was no continuous tradition of black direct action, could blacks have borrowed tactics from other movements of social protest in various periods of American history? The trade union movement comes readily to mind, but its influence was essentially peripheral. As already noted, blacks were employing the boycott and even occasional sit-down type tactics long before such words were invented. Moreover, black use of the phrase "direct action" was not borrowed from the radical industrial unionists; although the Wobblies had employed the term, it did not enter the language of black protest until introduced by CORE pacifists in 1942 as "nonviolent direct action." Blacks did not engage in picketing until the time of World War I, and they adopted that tactic only rarely before the 1930's, when the Norris–La Guardia Act gave it legitimacy. It can be argued that the general increase of labor activism and the growing sympathy for labor's cause among the general public served to encourage black use of a trade union tactic like picketing. Yet blacks were essentially charting an autonomous course, and their use of direct action did not closely parallel labor's. Thus the most substantial direct action by black demonstrators in the Depression took place in the early 1930's before organized

*Interestingly enough, our findings have their parallel in the history of the labor movement's sit-down strikes. These were regarded as a new tactic when they swept the country in 1936–37, but such strikes had actually been invented many years earlier and periodically reinvented by workers who possessed no knowledge of previous sit-downs. In the United States the strategy had been employed during a brewery strike in Cincinnati in 1884 and by the Wobblies at General Electric's Schenectady plant in 1906. More to the point, in the early 1930's there was a series of short, unconnected factory sit-downs. Among them was the earliest sit-down in the Akron rubber industry—the brief demonstration that erupted at the General Tire Company in 1934, two years prior to the famous Goodyear strike which precipitated the wave of CIO sit-down strikes across the country. Significantly, this seminal General Tire strike had been invented by a local leadership unaware of similar sit-downs that occurred a few months earlier at the Hormel Packing Company in Austin, Minnesota, and even at the White Motor Company in nearby Cleveland. Daniel Nelson, ed., "The Beginnings of the Sit-Down Era: The Reminiscences of Rex Murray," *Labor History*, 15 (Winter, 1974), 90–97; interview with Rex Murray of Canal Fulton, Ohio, Jan. 15, 1976; Sidney Fine, *Sit-Down: The General Motors Strike of 1936–1937* (Ann Arbor, 1969), pp. 122–23.

labor's largest and most dramatic strikes and mass actions, and the revival of the "Don't-Buy-Where-You-Can't-Work" campaigns was prompted not by any action of organized labor but by the Supreme Court's 1938 decision in the New Negro Alliance case. Furthermore, black protesters at the time only very rarely saw the applicability of the sit-down tactics to their cause. Although CORE would later introduce an adaptation of the sit-down tactics and Randolph often referred to organized labor's methods as a justification for his March on Washington strategy, it seems clear that labor exercised only slight influence on black activism.

Even more marginal to direct action among blacks was the women's suffrage movement. However, the protest march up Beacon Street led by Trotter in 1915 bore marked similarities to the contemporary demonstrations of the suffragists, and in one instance the latter probably supplied a specific model. This was the Silent Protest Parade of 1917, which strikingly resembled the quietly impressive annual Fifth Avenue parades sponsored by the New York feminists.[167]*

The case for Communist influence is stronger, in view of all the interracial unemployment marches, anti-eviction demonstrations, and Scottsboro parades, not to mention the origins of the rent strike movement. Yet the blacks' most important and extensive demonstrations of the 1930's, the "Don't-Buy-Where-You-Can't-Work" campaigns, were clearly indigenous to the Afro-American community, tended ideologically to have petit bourgeois and black nationalist overtones, and constituted a movement that the Communists joined only when they became aware of its appeal among Negroes. Moreover, whatever the Communists' precise role in the complex history of rent strikes, these were clearly a non-Communist enterprise, found characteristically among middle-class blacks rather than those of the working class. Nor, except for the Berwyn campaign, did the Communists play an active role in the school boycotts of the period. Finally, although Randolph's March on Washington

*It is probably no accident that the Silent Parade tactic was suggested to the NAACP by one of its leading founders, treasurer Oswald Garrison Villard, who had wide-ranging reform interests, whose mother was active in the feminist movement, and whose grandfather, William Lloyd Garrison, had, of course, been a champion of women's rights.

Movement employed a mass-action vocabulary reminiscent of the Communists, his activism was of long standing and was generated by strictly black concerns.

A fairly strong case can also be made for the influence of Gandhism, but in the history of black activism, Gandhian ideology appeared late. For nearly fifteen years after this philosophy was introduced into black protest in the early 1940's, its importance was slight. Even Randolph received scant support among blacks for his civil disobedience proposals, and he never seriously tried to carry them out. CORE did attempt to work more systematically along Gandhian lines, but its activities gained little attention in the black press. During and after World War II, direct-action tactics declined; even when used, they were typically unconnected with either CORE or Gandhism. It was Martin Luther King who really projected Gandhism as a philosophy of black protest—but, as noted earlier, this thrust came only after the Montgomery boycott was well underway.

Thus the evidence indicates that direct action neither formed a continuous tradition in black protest, nor owed much to the strategies of other protest movements. Rather, we would argue that such tactics and strategies were continuously reinvented by blacks in response to shifting patterns of race relations and the changing status of blacks in American society. Both the clusters or "waves" of direct action as well as the isolated instances of such tactics occurred when blacks were experiencing critical changes in their status. During the 1840's in Massachusetts and during Reconstruction, as well as in the mid-twentieth century, there was a period of improvement in certain key respects, of increased white support for black aspirations, of rising expectations and therefore of heightened Negro protest. This militance was reflected in the direct-action campaigns aimed at either eliminating or preventing segregation in transportation and schools. Conditions at the turn of the century were different: racism was becoming more extreme. Both the southern streetcar boycott movement and the attacks on school segregation in the North were defensive actions aimed at preventing a loss of status. So were the northern school boycotts of the 1920's and 1930's. Similarly, the picketing and demonstrations against *The Clansman* and *The Birth of a Nation* were attempts to fight the increasingly virulent racism of the mass media. In contrast, the direct action of the 1940's and 1950's accompanied a gradual improvement in race relations and the black's status in America. In the case of the public accommodations campaigns, for example, they occurred first in the North and then, as the climate of race relations slowly changed, they cropped up in the border states and the Upper South. More recently, the nonviolent direct-action movement of the 1960's arose not so much because of the earlier work of Randolph and CORE, not so much because of King's charismatic appeal, but because blacks were growing impatient with techniques of legal and legislative action. Impressive victories notwithstanding, these now appeared gradualist and of limited effectiveness. This rising black militance reflected a new sense of confidence in the future that was rooted in the new laws and court decisions. Paradoxically, it was the NAACP's very victories in the legislatures and courts that more than anything else produced this revolution in expectations, this dissatisfaction with the limitations in the NAACP's program, and this rising tempo of direct action which culminated in the student lunch-counter sit-ins and the subsequent mass demonstrations of the early 1960's.

Historically, direct-action demonstrations tended to occur in two different contexts: 1) when Negroes faced a serious loss of status; and 2) when they experienced a rising set of expectations. In the former situation, blacks were seeking to resist social change and preserve a more favorable status quo; in the latter, they were trying to promote social change and destroy the status quo. Both kinds of situations converged to produce the direct-action campaigns of the 1930's. On the one hand, the loss of jobs was serious; on the other, the currents set loose by the New Deal and the general radicalization of American society led blacks, like dispossessed whites, to struggle with greater vigor for improvement in their status.

Clearly, then, the nonviolent direct action in the era of the civil rights revolution was neither dependent on a pacifist-Gandhian ideology, nor the fruit of any long-standing tradition of black direct action. Rather, direct action consisted of various tactics which blacks adopted at times and under circumstances that made them seem appropriate. Whatever the historical connections with the women's suffrage movement, the labor movement, the Communists, or the pacifists, the fact is that black direct action was essentially an indigenous creation of the Negro community. This is indisputable for the nineteenth-century protests, for the early twentieth-century streetcar boycotts, for the school boycotts, and for the "Don't-Buy-Where-You-Can't-Work" campaigns. Even with the complexities of the period since the Depression, it is clear that most black direct action came from within the Negro community and was not inspired by outside models. Indeed, nothing better illustrates both the indigenous nature of black direct action and the tendency for Negro protesters to continually reinvent specific direct-action tactics than the Baton Rouge and Montgomery bus boycotts. Not only were these boycotts independently invented by local citizens in the 1950's, but it was only after the Montgomery movement had started that the Gandhian pacifist ideology was adopted as a philosophical framework for southern black protest. Finally, the essentially extraneous role played by Gandhian nonviolence in the explosion of direct action of the 1960's is suggested by the marked tendency of most activists to slough off the Gandhian and Christian reconciliatory aspects of their strategy.

It would of course be hard to overstate the role of philosophical nonviolence in legitimizing the direct-action campaigns of the 1960's in the minds of the white public and political leaders, particularly as articulated in the oratory of Martin Luther King. Nevertheless, the evidence of history suggests that even if Gandhi's revolution had not developed in India, even if CORE and Randolph's 1941 March on Washington Movement had never existed, even if a conscious philosophy of nonviolent direct action had not emerged among Afro-Americans, the sit-ins and other demonstrations of the 1960's would still have occurred. The white public might have been slower to accept their legitimacy, although a Christian rhetoric and ideology unquestionably would have substituted for the Gandhian philosophy. But the general shape of black protest in the 1960's, its extent, its accomplishments, and its transformation, would undoubtedly have been pretty much as we have known them.

1. Louis Ruchames, "Jim Crow Railroads in Massachusetts," *American Quarterly*, 8 (Spring, 1956), 61–75; Arthur O. White, "Salem's Antebellum Black Community: Seedbed of the School Integration Movement," *Essex Institute Historical Collections*, 108 (Apr., 1972), 110–11; discussions of Nantucket in White, "Black Parents for Desegregation in Nineteenth Century," *Integrated Education*, 10 (Nov.–Dec., 1972), 38, and in White, unpublished, untitled MS on the antebellum Massachusetts school boycotts; Carleton Mabee, "A Negro Boycott to Integrate Boston Schools," *New England Quarterly*, 41 (Sept., 1968), 341–61; Arthur O. White, "The Black Leadership Class and Education in Antebellum Boston," *Journal of Negro Education*, 42 (Fall, 1973), 512–13; White, "Antebellum School Reform in Boston: Integrationists and Separatists," *Phylon*, 24 (June, 1973), 203–17. These accounts stress the role of blacks and the boycott in the agitation. Stanley K. Schultz, *The Culture Factory: Boston Public Schools, 1789–1860* (New York, 1973), and Donald M. Jacobs, "While the Cabots Talked to God: A History of the Boston Negro from the Revolution to the Civil War" (Ph.D. dissertation, Boston University, 1968), emphasize the white abolitionists' role, and Schultz gives scant attention to the boycott. On the whole issue of school discrimination in antebellum Massachusetts see Arthur O. White, "Blacks and Education in Antebellum Massachusetts: Strategies for Social Mobility" (Ph.D. dissertation, SUNY at Buffalo, 1971).

2. Michael W. Homel, "Race and Schools in Nineteenth-Century Chicago," *Integrated Education*, 12 (Sept.–Oct., 1974) 40–42; Arthur O. White, "The Black Movement against Jim Crow Education in Lockport, N.Y., 1835–1876," *New York History*, 50 (July, 1969), 265–82; and White, "The Black Movement Against Jim Crow Education in Buffalo, New York, 1800–1900," *Phylon*, 30 (Winter, 1969), 375–93. Jim Crow schools ended at Buffalo in 1872 and at Lockport in 1876.

3. Roger A. Fischer, "A Pioneer Protest: The New Orleans Street-Car Controversy of 1867," *Journal of Negro History*, 53 (July, 1968), 219–33; Marjorie M. Norris, "An Early Instance of Nonviolence: The Louisville Demonstrations of 1870–1871," *Journal of Southern History*, 32 (Nov., 1966), 487–504; William C. Hine, "The 1867 Charleston Streetcar Sit-Ins," *South Carolina Historical Magazine*, 77 (Apr., 1976), 110–14; August Meier and Elliott Rudwick, "A Strange Chapter in the Career of 'Jim Crow,' " in Meier and Rudwick, eds., *The Making of Black America* (New York, 1969), II, 14–16; and Meier and Rudwick, "The Boycott Movement against Jim Crow Streetcars in the South, 1900–1906," in this volume. For the Baton Rouge boycott, an addition to those we uncovered earlier, see Baton Rouge *Daily Advocate*, Nov. 7, 1902.

4. Meier and Rudwick, "Early Boycotts of Segregated Schools: The Alton, Illinois Case, 1897–1908," *Journal of Negro Education*, 36 (Fall, 1967), 394–402. Meier and Rudwick, "Early Boycotts of Segregated Schools: The East Orange, New Jersey, Experience, 1899–1906," *History of Education Quarterly*, 4 (Spring, 1967), 22–35. For Oxford, Pa., see Oxford *Press*, Sept. 2, 16, 30, 1909, March 3, 1910; *Lincoln University Herald*, 13 (Sept., 1909), 4; Cleveland *Gazette*, Sept. 11, 1909; Oxford *News*, July 4, 1934. On Wichita, see Wichita *Searchlight*, Sept. 8, 15, Oct. 13, 27, 1906, July 13, 1907; Wichita *Eagle*, Sept. 11, 13, 18, 21, 23, Oct. 13, 24, 28, 1906, July 6, 1907. On Roslyn, see *The Crisis*, 7 (Nov., 1913), 322, and 11 (Aug., 1915), 165; *Afro-American Ledger* (Baltimore), June 19, 1915.

5. Lester A. Walton, "An Object Lesson," New York *Age*, Jan. 29, 1914.

6. Baltimore *Afro-American*, Oct. 27, 1906; Washington *Bee*, Nov. 3, 1906; Chicago *Broadax*, Nov. 10, 1906; Philadelphia *Inquirer*, Oct. 23, 24, 25, 26, 1906; Philadelphia *Evening Bulletin*, Oct. 23, 24, 25, 1906.

7. Boston *Herald*, Apr. 18, June 3, 8, 1915; Boston *Sunday Globe*, Apr. 19, 1915; Boston *Daily Globe*, June 3, 4, 5, 8, 1915; Chicago *Defender*, June 19, 1915; Stephen R. Fox, *The Guardian of Boston: William Monroe Trotter* (New York, 1971), pp. 191–97. For Philadelphia, see the exaggerated account in the Chicago *Defender*, Sept. 25, 1915; Philadelphia *Tribune*, Sept. 4, 1915; Philadelphia *Evening Bulletin*, Sept. 7, 1915.

8. New York *Times*, July 29, 1917; James Weldon Johnson, *Along This Way* (New York, 1933), pp. 320–21; James Weldon Johnson to Shelby J. Davidson, May 31, June 5, 1922, and Davidson to Johnson, telegram, June 14, 1922, Box G-34, NAACP Archives; clippings from *Christian Science Monitor*, June 4, 1922, New York *Age*, June 10,

1922, Washington *Post*, June 15, 1922, New York *World*, June 15, 1922, in Box C-249, NAACP Archives; Butler Wilson to Johnson, Aug. 8, 1922, Box C-245, *ibid.*

9. St. Louis *Argus*, May 20, 1921, and esp. NAACP, *Annual Report for 1921* (New York, 1922), pp. 65–66. (Title for the NAACP annual report varies; we have adopted a short form here.) In a highly unusual action for this period, Detroit blacks in 1929 withheld patronage from a White Tower restaurant in the ghetto because the chain's other branches refused to serve them. See Pittsburgh *Courier*, Nov. 16, 1929.

10. For Springfield, see Meier and Rudwick, "Early Boycotts of Segregated Schools: The Case of Springfield, Ohio, 1922–1923," *American Quarterly*, 20 (Winter, 1968), 744–58.

For Dayton, see account in Meier and Rudwick, "Negro Boycotts of Jim Crow Schools in the North, 1899–1925," *Integrated Education*, 5 (Aug.–Sept., 1967), 8–10.

For Beachwood–Shaker Heights, see Cleveland *Gazette*, Oct. 24, 31, 1925; *The Crisis*, 31 (March, 1926), 230; NAACP, *Annual Report for 1925* (New York, 1926), p. 12; Harry E. Davis to James Weldon Johnson, Oct. 30, Dec. 7, 1925, Box G-151, NAACP Archives.

For Philadelphia, see Philadelphia *Tribune*, Sept. 12, 19, Oct. 10, 1925, Feb. 26, 1926; *The Crisis*, 31 (Mar., 1926), 230; NAACP Board of Directors Minutes, Sept. 14, 1925, Box A-2, NAACP Archives, Library of Congress; NAACP, *Annual Report for 1925*, p. 11.

For Toms River, N.J., see Pittsburgh *Courier*, Mar. 19, Apr. 2, June 27, 1927; Kansas City *Call*, July 15, 1927; NAACP Board of Directors Minutes, Mar. 14, 1927, Box A-2, NAACP Archives; Report of the Secretary to the Board, Apr. 7, 1927, NAACP National Office, New York.

For Blythe, Calif., see *California Eagle*, Aug. 31, Sept. 14, 21, 28, Oct. 5, 1928.

For Berwyn, Pa., see Philadelphia *Tribune*, Nov. 24, Dec. 29, 1932; Jan. 26, Feb. 2, 16, Apr. 6, 13, 20, 27, May 4, 18, 25, June 1, Aug. 17, 31, Sept. 7, 14, 21, 28, Oct. 5, 12, 16, 26, Nov. 16, 23, Dec. 7, 14, 1933; Feb. 15, Mar. 15, 29, Apr. 19, 26, May 3, Sept. 18, 1934; Pittsburgh *Courier*, esp. Mar. 18, June 3, Aug. 19, Sept. 30, Oct. 28, Nov. 4, 1933; Apr. 21, May 12, 1934; *Harlem Liberator*, Oct. 21, 1933, Mar. 24, Apr. 7, 1934; *Negro Liberator*, Aug. 11, 18, 1934; NAACP, *Annual Report for 1933* (New York, 1934), pp. 19–20, and *Annual Report for 1934* (New York, 1935), p. 20; Memoranda and correspondence on the case in Box D-48, NAACP Archives.

For Chester, Pa., see Pittsburgh *Courier*, Sept. 16, 1933, Feb. 10, 17, Mar. 3, June 16, 1934; Philadelphia *Tribune*, Sept. 14, 21, 1933; Feb. 23, July 19, 1934; interviews with boycott leaders Mr. and Mrs. Cecil Bond of Chester, July 30, Aug. 3, 1975.

For Montclair, N.J., see Norfolk *Journal and Guide*, Oct. 27, 1933, Apr. 28, 1934; Montclair *Times*, July 15, Oct. 27, 1933; Feb. 9, Mar. 9, Apr. 20, June 9, Aug. 24, Sept. 26, 1934; Newark *Evening News*, Apr. 17, 18, 19, 20, 1934.

For Betsy Ross School, Chicago, see Chicago *Defender*, Feb. 4, Sept. 23, 30, 1933.

For Monrovia, Calif., see *California Eagle*, Oct. 26, Nov. 16, 23, Dec. 21, 1934; Jan. 18, Feb. 1, Mar. 1, Apr. 26, May 10, 17, 1935; *The Crisis*, 42 (Apr., 1935), 119–20, and (July, 1935), 215.

For East Orange, N.J., see Norfolk *Journal and Guide*, Aug. 8, 22, 1936; New York *Age*, Sept. 19, 1936; East Orange *Record*, Sept. 11, 1936; Newark *Evening News*, Sept. 10, 22, 30, Oct. 6, 1936.

For Lilydale School, Chicago, see Michael W. Homel, "The Lilydale School Campaign of 1936: Direct Action in the Verbal Protest Era," *Journal of Negro History*, 59 (July, 1974), 228–41.

For Lockland, Ohio, see Cleveland *Gazette*, Oct. 30, Nov. 13, 1937; Cincinnati *Times-Star*, Sept. 20, Oct. 8, 1937; interviews with movement leaders Mrs. Claude Grace of Lockland, Aug. 8, 1975, and with Herman Roberts, now of Chicago, Aug. 11, 1975.

For Abington Township, Pa., see Philadelphia *Tribune*, Aug. 15, Sept. 26, 1940; Pittsburgh *Courier*, Oct. 12, 1940.

11. *E.g.*, *California Eagle*, May 14, 1937; Kansas City *Call*, Jan. 15, 1937; Richmond *Planet*, Mar. 20, 1937.

12. Joseph D. Bibb column in Pittsburgh *Courier*, July 6, 1946.

13. Arvarh E. Strickland, *History of the Chicago Urban League* (Urbana, Ill., 1966), pp. 93–95; New York *Age*, Nov. 20, 27, 1926; New York *Amsterdam News*, June 3, 1925, Dec. 11, 1929; Robert W. Bagnall to Walter F. White, Dec. 27, 1929, Box C-321, NAACP Archives; George S. Schuyler, "A Deadly Boomerang," *The Crisis*, 41 (Sept., 1934), 259.

14. Atlanta *Daily World*, Nov. 17, 19, 20, 21, 23, 24, 1935; Richmond *Planet*, Feb. 29, 1936, for Durham; Pittsburgh *Courier*, Apr. 27, 1940, and Rock Hill *Evening Herald*, Aug. 8, 1957.

15. See speech of the Reverend Ross D. Brown reported in Baltimore *Afro-American*, Oct. 20, 1934.

16. Oliver Cromwell Cox, "The Origins of Direct-Action Among Negroes," unpublished manuscript, 1973 (microfilm copy available from Bell & Howell Microphoto Division); St. Clair Drake, *Churches and Voluntary Associations in the Chicago Negro Community*, mimeographed (Chicago, 1940), pp. 248–51; *California Eagle*, May 9, Oct. 17, 1930; W. E. B. Du Bois, editorial, "The Boycott," *The Crisis*, 38 (Mar., 1930) 102; T. Arnold Hill, "Picketing for Jobs," *Opportunity*, 8 (July, 1930), 216; interviews with Archibald Carey, Jr., Mrs. Joseph D. Bibb, and Dr. Arthur G. Falls, of Chicago, Apr. 11, 1973, and with Metz Lochard of Chicago, Nov. 4, 1975. See also Chicago *Defender*, Sept. 13, 1930, for letter critical of *Whip* tactics, and Baltimore *Afro-American*, Oct. 20, 1934, for participant in the Chicago movement recalling lack of community support.

17. See esp. Hill, "Picketing for Jobs," p. 216. For examples of interest stirred by Chicago campaign, see New York *Age*, Nov. 1, 15, 1930, for New York, and *California Eagle*, June 20, Aug. 8, 1930.

18. New York *Amsterdam News*, Apr. 30, 1930; Pittsburgh *Courier*, Aug. 25, 1930. No concrete campaign seems to have been undertaken in New York at the time. An example of a successful attempt to press for jobs without an actual boycott occurred in Los Angeles in 1930–32. See *California Eagle*, 1929–32, *passim*.

19. For Toledo, see Pittsburgh *Courier*, Dec. 27, 1930; *California Eagle*, Sept. 30, 1932; *The Crisis*, 40 (Jan., 1933), 17; Lillian Upthegrove, "Chain Store Jobs," talk at NAACP Annual Conference, 1933, Box B-10, NAACP Archives; interview with movement participant Clarence Smith of Toledo, Aug. 11, 1975; and particularly the following correspondence in Box G-168, NAACP Archives: W. Payne Stanley to Walter White, Oct. 23, 1930, Stanley to Robert Bagnall, Dec. 10, 1930, Toledo Branch Annual Report for 1931, Ivan C. McLeod to White, Aug. 9, 1932, Bertha Irvin to Bagnall, Aug. 10, 1932, Bagnall to White, Aug. 15, 1932, White to Irvin, Aug. 18, 1932, J. M. Howard to Bagnall, Aug. 29, 1932, and Stanley to Bagnall, Oct. 25, 1932. For Detroit, see *California Eagle*, Jan. 29, 1932; Norfolk *Journal and Guide*, Feb. 6, 1932; and Chicago *Defender*, March 5, 1932. For Cleveland, see Cleveland *Gazette*, Nov. 7, 21, 1931; *The Liberator*, Oct. 10, 1931; Christopher G. Wye, "Merchants of Tomorrow: The Other Side of the Don't Spend Your Money Where You Can't Work Movement, Cleveland 1935–1945," unpublished paper, 1974; interview with Mrs. Milton G. Roberson of Cleveland, widow of one of the movement's leaders, Nov. 1, 1975.

20. Pittsburgh *Courier*, Feb. 20, Oct. 1, 1932; Chicago *Defender*, June 25, 1932; New York *Age*, June 25, 1932, June 17, July 29, Aug. 12, 1933; New York *Amsterdam News*, June 22, 1932; Apr. 26, June 14, 21, Aug. 2, Sept. 6, 1933; interview with Mrs. Elvin Sullinger, widow of the Brooklyn veterans' leader, Dec. 24, 1975.

21. New York *Amsterdam News*, May 26, June 30, July 21, Aug. 4, 11, Sept. 15, 29, Oct. 20, Nov. 3, Dec. 29, 1934; New York *Age*, Feb. 24, June 2, 9, 16, 23, 30, July 7, 14, 21, Aug. 4, 25, Sept. 15, 22, 29, Oct. 6, Nov. 10, 1934, Feb. 2, July 6, Aug. 17, 1935.

22. *The Liberator*, Oct. 10, 1931; *Harlem Liberator*, Feb. 10, 17, Mar. 17, 24, 1934, for Boston; *ibid.*, Feb. 3, 17, Mar. 10, 17, 31, Apr. 7, 21, May 19, 26, June 2, 9, July 7, 1934, and New York *Amsterdam News*, Feb. 7, Mar. 10, 1934, for Fifth Avenue bus boycott.

23. *Negro Liberator*, Aug. 4, Sept. 15, 1934.

24. New York *Age*, Sept. 8, 15, Oct. 20, Nov. 10, Dec. 8, 1934; *Negro Liberator*, Sept. 8, 15, 22, Oct. 27, 1934, Apr. 15, June 15, 1935.

Published accounts of the Harlem movement of the early 1930's, with varying degrees of distortion, are: Claude McKay, *Harlem: Negro Metropolis* (New York, 1940), pp. 185–205; McKay, "Labor Steps Out in Harlem," *Nation*, 145 (Oct. 16, 1937), 399–402, and debate between Adam Clayton Powell, Jr., and McKay in New York *Amsterdam News*, Oct. 30, Nov. 4, 1937; William Muraskin, "The Harlem Boycott of 1934: Black Nationalism and the Rise of Labor-Union Consciousness," *Labor History*, 13 (Summer, 1972), 361–73; Roi Ottley, *'New World A-Coming': Inside Black America* (Boston, 1943), pp. 112–18. See also Melville J. Weiss, "Don't Buy Where You Can't Work: An Analysis of Consumer Action Against Employment Discrimination in Harlem, 1934–1940" (M.A. thesis, Columbia University, 1941).

25. Cleveland *Call and Post*, Nov. 28, 1935, and Charles H. Loeb, *The Future Is Yours: The History of the Future Outlook League, 1935–1946* (Cleveland, 1947), pp. 24, 36; *New Negro Opinion*, Dec. 16, 1933, Oct. 13, 1934, Mar. 16, 23, 1935, and John A. Davis, "We Win the Right to Fight for Jobs," *Opportunity*, 16 (Aug., 1938), 230 37. On Harris's views, see also his *The Negro as Capitalist* (Philadelphia, 1936), pp. 180–81.

26. On Washington, see *New Negro Opinion*, Dec. 16, 1933–Apr. 13, 1935, *passim*, courtesy of Judge William H. Hastie; Davis, "We Win the Right to Fight for Jobs," pp. 230–37; *Baltimore Afro-American*, Sept. 9, 16, 23, 30, Oct. 21, Dec. 23, 1933; Pittsburgh *Courier*, Oct. 7, 14, Nov. 18, Dec. 2, 30, 1933, Jan. 13, 27, May 5, Aug. 25, 1934, April 25, May 9, 1936; Washington *Tribune*, Aug. 31, Sept. 7, 14, 28, Oct. 5, Oct. 12, Nov. 16, 30, Dec. 7, 21, 28, 1933, Jan. 11, 18, Apr. 26, July 5, Aug. 4, Oct. 13, Dec. 8, 1934, Dec. 10, 1935; Norfolk *Journal and Guide*, Sept. 16, Oct. 7, 14, 21, 1933, and June 9, 1934; Ralph J. Bunche, "The Programs, Ideologies, Tactics, and Achievements of Negro Betterment and Interracial Organizations," unpublished memorandum prepared for the Carnegie-Myrdal Study of the Negro in America, 1940, pp. 380–92. Interview with Judge William H. Hastie, a leader of the New Negro Alliance, Dec. 30, 1975.

On Baltimore, see Baltimore *Afro-American*, Sept., 1933–Apr., 1935, *passim*; extensive correspondence between NAACP national office and Baltimore branch, 1934, Box D-85, NAACP Archives. See also very fine accounts in Pittsburgh *Courier*, Dec. 23, 1933, Apr. 29, 1935, and Roy Wilkins's column in Kansas City *Call*, Apr. 19, 1935.

For Richmond, see Richmond *Planet*, Mar. 17, 24, Apr. 14, 21, 28, May 5, 12, 19, June 23, July 7, 14, Oct. 20, 1934; Rosa E. Walton to John A. Hartford, May 18, 1934, and J. M. Tinsley to Walter White, June 8, 1934, Box G-211, NAACP Archives; Norfolk *Journal and Guide*, Sept. 9, 1933, Mar. 3, Apr. 14, 21, May 12, 19, June 9, 1934, Nov. 2, 1935.

For Los Angeles, see *California Eagle*, Jan. 26, Apr. 20, 1934, Apr. 19, 26, May 10, 1935; *Harlem Liberator*, Feb. 10, Sept. 29, 1934.

For Columbus, see Pittsburgh *Courier*, Apr. 7, 1934; Baltimore *Afro-American*, Apr. 7, 1934; Atlanta *Daily World*, July 6, 1934; interviews with Harrison Bridges and Edna Evans of Columbus, children of the movement leader, Nov. 2, 1975.

On Cincinnati, see Cincinnati *Enquirer*, Aug. 28, 29, 30, 1934; *Negro Liberator*, Sept. 29, 1934; *New Negro Opinion*, Sept. 29, 1934.

On Camden, see Philadelphia *Tribune*, July 12, Aug. 2, Oct. 4, 1934; Baltimore *Afro-American*, Oct. 6, 1934; interview with the Negro History Club's president Carl Egerton, now of San Francisco, Dec. 9, 1975. For general outlook of the club's program, see accounts in Richmond *Planet*, Nov. 24, 1934, May 18, July 6, Oct. 5, Nov. 9, 16, Dec. 14, 1935.

For Cleveland, see Loeb, *The Future Is Yours*; Cleveland *Call and Post*, 1935–41, *passim*; *Voice of the League*, Nov. 16, 1937–June 21, 1941, *passim*; Kenneth M. Zinz, "The Future Outlook League of Cleveland: A Negro Protest Organization" (M.A. thesis, Kent State University, 1973); interviews with Charles H. Loeb, Jan. 27, 1976, and William O. Walker, Jan. 26, 1976, both of Cleveland.

For Philadelphia, see Philadelphia *Tribune*, Feb. 27, Mar. 19, May 28, Oct. 15, Nov. 19, 1936, Jan. 21, Feb. 25, May 6, June 3, July 1, 22, Aug. 5, 12, 19, 26, Sept. 23, 1937.

In addition, for citations to pre-1938 movements which are listed in Table II, but not discussed in the text, see *The Crisis*, 43 (Nov., 1936), 345, for Gary; New York *Age*, June 26, 1937, for Negro Youth Congress activity in Pittsburgh; Pittsburgh *Courier*, Sept. 4, 1937, for New Orleans; and *ibid.*, July 31, 1937, for Los Angeles.

27. *E.g.*, Kansas City *Call*, Apr. 1, 8, 1938; New York *Amsterdam News*, Apr. 2, 1938;

Washington *Afro-American*, Apr. 2, 1938; Norfolk *Journal and Guide*, Apr. 9, 1938; New York *Age*, Apr. 9, 1938; Davis, "We Win the Right to Fight for Jobs," p. 230.

28. The Philadelphia campaigns, which resumed in the summer of 1938, continued to be sporadic affairs. See Philadelphia *Tribune*, Aug. 4, 25, Sept. 1, 8, 1938; Baltimore *Afro-American*, Oct. 8, 1938, Feb. 4, Sept. 3, 1939, Dec. 30, 1941.

29. Washington *Afro-American*, May 14, 21, July 9, 16, 30, Sept. 16, Dec. 31, 1938, Aug. 26, Sept. 16, Nov. 4, 1939, Apr. 19, 26, May 24, 1941; Davis, "We Win the Right to Fight for Jobs," p. 231; Bunche, "Memorandum," pp. 384–87; Norfolk *Journal and Guide*, Dec. 2, 16, 1939.

30. St. Louis *Argus*, Apr. 1, 15, May 20, June 3, 10, July 1, 1938, Feb. 2, Mar. 1, 15, 22, Oct. 4, 1940, Apr. 4, 1941, June 19, 1942, Oct. 14, 1955; Kansas City *Call*, Feb. 24, 1939; Pittsburgh *Courier*, Apr. 22, June 24, 1939, Jan. 27, Apr. 20, 1941; St. Louis *Post-Dispatch*, editorial, n.d., reprinted in Savannah *Tribune*, July 7, 1938; and William Jones, "Trade Boycotts," *Opportunity*, 18 (Aug., 1940), 240.

31. Chicago *Defender*, Aug. 13, 27, Sept. 3, 10, 17, Oct. 1, 8, 15, 29, Nov. 5, 1938, Jan. 7, May 13, 20, June 10, July 1, Aug. 26, 1939, Apr. 20, June 29, July 27, Aug. 3, 10, 1940; St. Clair Drake and Horace Cayton, *Black Metropolis* (New York, 1945), p. 254; Strickland, *History of the Chicago Urban League*, pp. 130–32; Drake, *Churches and Voluntary Associations in the Chicago Negro Community*, p. 252; interview with Joe Jefferson of Chicago, head of Negro Labor Relations League, Feb. 13, 1976.

32. Loeb, *The Future Is Yours*; Cleveland *Call and Post*, 1938–41, *passim*. Interview with William O. Walker; Jones, "Trade Boycotts," p. 240.

33. New York *Amsterdam News*, Aug. 14, Oct. 30, 1937, May 14, June 11, 1938, Sept. 9, 1939, Feb. 22, 1941; New York *Age*, Aug. 28, Sept. 25, 1937, May 14, Aug. 20, Sept. 17, Oct. 8, 1938, June 24, 1939, Jan. 11, 1941.

34. New York *Amsterdam News*, Feb. 26, Apr. 2, 16, 23, 30, May 7, 21, June 4, 1938, Apr. 29, May 6, 20, 27, Oct. 21, 28, Dec. 16, 23, 1939; New York *Age*, Apr. 9, 23, 30, May 7, Aug. 13, Oct. 29, Nov. 5, 19, 1938, Dec. 9, 1939, Apr. 5, 1941; New York *Times*, Apr. 29, 1938; Pittsburgh *Courier*, Oct. 29, Nov. 5, 1938, June 24, 1939, Dec. 21, 1940; Meier and Rudwick, "Negro Protest at the World's Fair, 1939–1940," *New Politics*, 3 (Fall, 1964), 62–68. See also materials on the struggle against job discrimination at the Fair in Box C-418, NAACP Archives.

35. New York *Age*, Mar. 22, 29, Apr. 12, 26, May 10, 1941; New York *Amsterdam News*, Mar. 22, Apr. 5, 12, 26, May 3, 1941, Jan. 17, 1942; interview with Professor Mark Naison of Fordham University, July 18, 1975; interview with Bayard Rustin, Aug. 5, 1975.

36. Citations for movements, 1938–41, listed in Table II but not discussed are as follows: for Newark, New York *Amsterdam News*, Apr. 9, 30, 1938, Pittsburgh *Courier*, Apr. 23, 30, 1938, and inverview with Mrs. J. Otto Hill of Newark, leader of the campaign, Dec. 25, 1975; Cleveland *Call and Post*, May 19, 1938, and Pittsburgh *Courier*, Aug. 13, 1938, for Dayton; Cleveland *Call and Post*, Aug. 10, 1939, and Cleveland *Gazette*, Oct. 7, 14, 1939, for Youngstown; New York *Amsterdam News*, Apr. 1, 1939, for Corona; Houston *Informer*, Oct. 21, 28, 1939, for Houston; St. Louis *Argus*, Sept. 22, 1939, for Evansville; Pittsburgh *Courier*, July 15, 1939, for Memphis; Kansas City *Call*, Nov. 24, 1939, for Kansas City; Chicago *Defender*, Apr. 6, 1940, for Berkeley; *California Eagle*, Apr. 4, May 2, 1940, for Oakland; *ibid.*, Nov. 28, 1940, and Savannah *Tribune*, May 16, 1940, for Los Angeles; Pittsburgh *Courier*, July 6, 1940, for Jackson, Tenn.; Norfolk *Journal and Guide*, Oct. 11, 18, Nov. 1, 1941, for Newport News; Detroit Branch, NAACP, press release, Oct. 18, 1941, in folder, "Labor, 1941," NAACP Archives, for Detroit; Cleveland *Call and Post*, Dec. 6, 1941, for Alliance; *ibid.*, Nov. 14, 1942, and interview with Walter Hueston of Lockland, Dec. 13, 1975, for Lockland.

37. New York *Amsterdam News*, July 8, 1944.

38. Arthur Huff Fauset column in Philadelphia *Tribune*, May 1, 1941; Kelly Miller column in Pittsburgh *Courier*, Dec. 23, 1933.

39. *The Crisis*, 38 (Mar., 1930), 102, and 40 (Nov., 1931), 393; NAACP, *Annual Report for 1931* (New York, 1932), p. 33; Walter White, Memorandum to Branches, Oct. 30,

1931, Box C-321, NAACP Archives; "Resolution[s] Adopted by the 24th Annual Conference of the National Association for the Advancement of Colored People," Box B-10, *ibid.*; Walter White, "The Chicago N.A.A.C.P. Conference," July 6, 1933, *ibid.*; White to Arthur B. Spingarn, Nov. 3, 15, 1934, Box 7, Spingarn Papers, Library of Congress; NAACP's bitter public attack on the decision in New York *Amsterdam News*, Nov. 3, 1934; Vere E. Johns and George S. Schuyler, debate, "To Boycott or — Not to Boycott," *The Crisis*, 41 (Sept., 1934), 258–60, 274; NAACP press release printed in several papers, *e.g.*, Kansas City *Call*, Apr. 8, 1938; notation by Walter White on letter to him from Coordinating Committee executive secretary Arnold P. Johnson, Nov. 24, 1939, and Roy Wilkins, telegram to A. Clayton Powell, Jr., Nov. 28, 1939, in Box C-323, NAACP Archives; Gertrude B. Stone to Walter White, May 19, and White to Stone, May 21, 1941, and the New Negro Alliance leaflets, all in folder, "Labor, 1941," Box 234, NAACP Archives; *The Crisis*, 48 (May, 1941), 165, and (July, 1941), 226.

40. *The Crisis*, 41 (Nov., 1934), 342; Baltimore *Afro-American*, Oct. 13, 1934; and materials in Box C-413, NAACP Archives. For NAACP and the Ford Motor strike of 1941, see *The Crisis*, 48 (May, 1941), 161, 171, 173, and extensive materials in folder, "Ford Strike," 1941, NAACP Archives.

41. Pittsburgh *Courier*, Aug. 27, Oct. 2, 1937, for St. Louis; Atlanta *Daily World*, June 30, 1932, for Chicago Communists; Chicago *Defender*, Apr. 21, 1934, and Drake and Cayton, *Black Metropolis*, p. 743, for Consolidated Trades Council.

42. *The Liberator*, Mar. 15, 1930; Chicago *Defender*, Feb. 14, 1931, Mar. 26, Nov. 5, 1932, Mar. 11, 1933; *The Liberator*, May 30, 1931; Norfolk *Journal and Guide*, Nov. 12, 1932; for another Richmond march, see *ibid.*, Feb. 11, 1933. For other such interracial hunger marches in southern cities, see Atlanta *Daily World*, July 1, 1932, and Norfolk *Journal and Guide*, Dec. 3, 10, 17, 1932. For marches on statehouses in border states, see Pittsburgh *Courier*, Apr. 11, 1931 (for Maryland) and *The Liberator*, Oct. 24, 1931 (for Missouri). See also *The Liberator*, Mar. 14, July 4, Oct. 24, 31, 1931, for such marches on northern statehouses and city halls.

43. See headline, "Prepare March on Washington for December 7," in *The Liberator*, Oct. 24, 1931.

44. *Ibid.*, Dec. 19, 1931, Dec. 15, 1932; Pittsburgh *Courier*, Dec. 19, 1931; Kansas City *Call*, Dec. 16, 1932; Norfolk *Journal and Guide*, Dec. 10, 1932.

45. Chicago *Defender*, Jan. 16, 1932. On Chicago, see also *ibid.*, Dec. 10, 1932, Feb. 11, 1933. On New York, see *The Liberator*, Nov. 14, 1931; *Harlem Liberator*, May 27, June 3, July 15, 1933. For Newark, see New York *Amsterdam News*, July 19, 1933. For Philadelphia, see Philadelphia *Tribune*, Sept. 22, Oct. 27, 1934. For Washington, see Baltimore *Afro-American*, Dec. 1, 1934. For Los Angeles, see *California Eagle*, Jan. 20, 1933.

46. St. Louis *Post-Dispatch*, July 9, 11, 12, 1932; Norfolk *Journal and Guide*, Apr. 22, 1933. See also Atlanta *Daily World*, Jan. 15, 1934, for picketing in protest against anti-black discrimination by the CWA.

47. See Philadelphia *Tribune*, July 22, 1937; Chicago *Defender*, July 10, 1937, Aug. 24, 1940; Philadelphia *Tribune*, Aug. 26, 1937, for Washington; New York *Amsterdam News*, Nov. 6, 1937, for Newark; *California Eagle*, Mar. 3, 1938, for Los Angeles; Baltimore *Afro-American*, Jan. 9, 1940; and, for Cleveland demonstrations protesting discrimination against hiring blacks on WPA projects, see Cleveland *Call and Post*, Sept. 30, 1937.

48. Norfolk *Journal and Guide*, Aug. 8, 1936, for Brooklyn; Cleveland *Call and Post*, July 21, 1934; and, for Atlanta, Kansas City *Call*, Jan. 20, 1939, and Atlanta *Daily World*, Jan. 4, Oct. 18, Nov. 2, 1939.

49. New York *Amsterdam News*, Dec. 4, 25, 1937; Philadelphia *Tribune*, Mar. 11, 1937, *California Eagle*, Mar. 12, 1937, and esp. Norfolk *Journal and Guide*, Mar. 13, 1937, for Cincinnati; New York *Age*, Dec. 18, 1937, and esp. Anna Caplow to Roy Wilkins, Apr. 23, 1937, Box C-382, NAACP Archives, for Cairo; Chicago *Defender*, Jan. 15, Feb. 26, June 4, 1938; Kansas City *Call*, June 24, 1938, for Illinois capitol; Columbus *Citizen*, Apr. 9, 10, 12, 13, May 7, 10, 12, 1937; St. Louis *Argus*, Jan. 20, 1939, and St. Louis

Post-Dispatch, Jan. 13, 14, 1939. See also sit-in over relief problems reported in St. Louis *Argus*, May 21, 1937, and Workers' Alliance protests in Washington reported in Pittsburgh *Courier*, Aug. 7, 1937, and Washington *Afro-American*, June 29, 1940.

50. Chicago *Defender*, Mar. 20, 1937; Chicago *Daily Tribune*, Mar. 16, 1937.

51. *The Liberator*, Oct. 11, 1930, for Harlem; *ibid.*, Oct. 10, 17, 1931, for Cleveland; *ibid.*, Aug. 8, 15, Oct. 10, 24, 1931, Chicago *Defender*, Aug. 1, 8, 29, 1931, Apr. 30, 1932, and Drake and Cayton, *Black Metropolis*, p. 87, for Chicago.

52. *The Liberator*, May 30, July 4, Nov. 14, 1931, Jan. 16, Mar. 18, 1932; and for Los Angeles, *California Eagle*, Jan. 20, 1933, and *Harlem Liberator*, Sept. 16, 1933.

53. For Chicago, see *Harlem Liberator*, June 3, 1933; for New York, see *The Liberator*, Nov. 19, 1932, Jan. 3, 1933, *Harlem Liberator*, May 20, 27, 1933, *Negro Liberator*, Dec. 8, 1934; for Philadelphia, see *ibid.*, Aug. 18, 1934. For later ones in New York, see *Harlem Liberator*, May 19, 1934, and *Negro Liberator*, May 1, 1935.

54. Richmond *Planet*, Mar. 27, 1920; New York *Age*, June 5, 1926, and Ted Poston's recollections in New York *Amsterdam News*, Aug. 18, 1934; *ibid.*, Nov. 27, 1929, Jan. 8, 1930; *The Liberator*, Dec. 7, 14, 1929, Apr. 19, June 7, 1930.

55. *Ibid.*, Dec. 15, 1932, and Norfolk *Journal and Guide*, Oct. 22, Nov. 12, Dec. 10, 1932; *Harlem Liberator*, July 22, Aug. 5, 1933.

56. *Negro Liberator*, Aug. 18, 25, Sept. 1, 8, 29, Oct. 13, 1934, May 1, Oct. 1, 1935; New York *Age*, Sept. 15, 29, 1934, Oct. 17, 1936, Apr. 5, 19, 26, 1941; New York *Amsterdam News*, Aug. 18, 25, Sept. 1, 8, 22, 29, Oct. 6, 1934, Mar. 30, Apr. 20, Aug. 24, 1935, Oct. 3, 17, 1936, Jan. 16, Apr. 3, 24, Oct. 2, 16, Nov. 13, 20, 27, 1937, Feb. 4, 25, Apr. 15, May 6, 13, 27, June 3, Sept. 16, Oct. 21, 1939, Apr. 12, 19, 1941.

57. Philadelphia *Tribune*, June 3, 17, 24, July 15, Aug. 5, Sept. 2, 9, 30, 1937, Feb. 17, 1938; Zinz, "The Future Outlook League of Cleveland," ch. 3; Cleveland *Gazette*, July 8, 22, 1939; Norfolk *Journal and Guide*, Sept. 22, 1939; Loeb, *The Future Is Yours*, pp. 61–63. On Detroit, see *ibid.*, p. 63, and interview with Gloster Current, leader in the Detroit movement and currently Director of Branches for the NAACP, Dec. 28, 1975.

58. Horace R. Cayton, "Negroes Live in Chicago," *Opportunity*, 15 (Dec., 1937), 369; Chicago *Defender*, Feb. 20, Mar. 27, Apr. 3, 10, 17, 24, May 1, 29, Nov. 6, 27, 1937, Apr. 27, Nov. 23, 1940, Apr. 12, 26, May 3, 17, July 5, 12, 19, Aug. 9, 1941, Apr. 25, May 2, 9, 16, June 13, July 25, 1942; interview with Ishmael Flory of Chicago, local leader of National Negro Congress, Jan. 29, 1976.

59. Savannah *Tribune*, Feb. 7, 1929; Pittsburgh *Courier*, Sept. 21, 1929; *The Liberator*, Jan. 4, 1930, and New York *Amsterdam News*, Jan. 1, 1930.

60. *Harlem Liberator*, Apr. 28, 1934, for Pittsburgh; Cleveland *Call and Post*, Apr. 21, 28, Dec. 8, 1934, *Harlem Liberator*, Apr. 21, 1934, *Negro Liberator*, Dec. 15, 1934, and interview with Christopher Wye of Washington, D.C., Dec. 10, 1975, for Cleveland; Pittsburgh *Courier*, Jan. 31, 1931, for Detroit; *Negro Liberator*, July 28, 1934, for Chicago; *The Liberator*, Oct. 20, 1932, for Denver. For other similar demonstrations in Cleveland, Newark, Chicago, Minneapolis, and New York, see *The Liberator*, Apr. 15, 1930, Dec. 5, 1931; *Harlem Liberator*, June 2, Dec. 23, 1933, Feb. 17, 1934; *Negro Liberator*, Aug. 11, 1934, July 15, 1935; New York *Age*, July 13, 1935.

61. Pittsburgh *Courier*, Dec. 4, 1937, Richmond *Planet*, Dec. 4, 1937. For lesser incidents in Philadelphia and New York, see Philadelphia *Tribune*, Oct. 21, 1934, Pittsburgh *Courier*, Oct. 23, 1937, and Kansas City *Call*, Apr. 18, 1941.

62. *California Eagle*, Sept. 7, 14, 1939.

63. Atlanta *Daily World*, Aug. 24, 1932, for Raleigh; Norfolk *Journal and Guide*, Nov. 2, 1935, for Richmond; St. Louis *Argus*, Sept. 23, 1938. For an incident in Kansas City similar to the one in St. Louis, see Chicago *Defender*, Mar. 6, 1937.

64. Pittsburgh *Courier*, Mar. 4, 1933, *The Crisis*, 57 (Apr., 1940), 25, Washington *Afro-American*, Jan. 27, 1940, and "Crossing the Picket Line," editorial in *Opportunity*, 18 (Feb., 1940), 34–35, all for Washington; Norfolk *Journal and Guide*, Sept. 2, 1939, for Alexandria.

65. See Chicago *Defender*, Dec. 24, 1932, Mar. 9, 23, May 25, 1940; *The Liberator*, Aug. 15, 1932, for Kansas City; Washington *Afro-American*, Feb. 26, 1938, for

Washington; New York *Amsterdam News*, May 7, 1938, and Savannah *Tribune*, Oct. 3, 1940, for New York.

66. Chicago *Defender*, Feb. 3, 1940; Washington *Afro-American*, Mar. 16, 1940.

67. Norfolk *Journal and Guide*, Jan. 22, Feb. 19, 1938.

68. Pittsburgh *Courier*, May 28, 1932, for Memphis; Kansas City *Call*, Oct. 16, 1941, for Warren; Washington *Afro-American*, July 16, 1938, Sept. 20, 1941, and Norfolk *Journal and Guide*, Sept. 27, 1941, for Washington.

69. *The Liberator*, May 30, 1931; Philadelphia *Tribune*, Apr. 20, 1933; New York *Amsterdam News*, May 10, 1933; Baltimore *Afro-American*, May 13, 1933; Washington *Afro-American*, May 27, 1933; Chicago *Defender*, April 22, 1933.

70. Atlanta *Daily World*, Dec. 11, 12, 19, 1934; *The Crisis*, 42 (Jan., 1935), 26, and (Aug., 1935), 233; Norfolk *Journal and Guide*, Dec. 22, 1934; Washington *Afro-American*, Dec. 22, 1934; Washington *Tribune*, Dec. 22, 29, 1934. See also documents in Box C-231, NAACP Archives.

71. Pittsburgh *Courier*, Feb. 8, 1936; materials in folder on "William E. Borah, 1936–37," Box C-394, NAACP Archives; *The Crisis*, 43 (Mar. 1936), 88, and 44 (Mar., 1937), 89, and 45 (Sept., 1938), 289; New York *Amsterdam News*, Jan. 22, 1938. Unfortunately there is not much material on the youth marches of 1937 and 1938 in the NAACP Archives, and in fact most of the "demonstrations" staged in various cities in 1938 consisted simply of mass meetings. See folders on "Anti-Lynching Demonstrations" in Youth Files, Box E-1, NAACP Archives.

72. "Resolution[s] Adopted by the 24th Annual Conference of the National Association for the Advancement of Colored People," Box B-10, NAACP Archives; Norfolk *Journal and Guide*, July 8, 1933; Baltimore *Afro-American*, July 8, 1933; Walter White, "The Chicago NAACP Conference," July 6, 1933, Box B-10, NAACP Archives.

73. St. Louis *Argus*, Sept. 22, Oct. 6, 13, Dec. 29, 1939; *Missouri ex rel. Gaines* v. *Canada*, 305 U.S. 337 (1938), 823.

74. See also Ralph J. Bunche's evaluation in his "The Programs, Ideologies, Tactics, and Achievements of Negro Betterment and Interracial Organizations," p. 48.

75. Washington *Afro-American*, Jan. 25, 1941.

76. Pittsburgh *Courier*, Jan. 4, 1941; Kansas City *Call*, Apr. 18, 1941; New York *Amsterdam News*, May 3, 1941; Chicago *Defender*, May 3, 10, 17, June 7, 1941; *The Crisis*, 48 (May, 1941), 184; for National Negro Congress, see, *e.g.*, Pittsburgh *Courier*, May 10, 1941.

77. "Call to Negro America to March on Washington," *Black Worker*, May, 1941; Editorial, "Let the Negro Masses Speak," *ibid.*, Mar., 1941; statements of Randolph quoted in *California Eagle*, Nov. 6, 1941, and Kansas City *Call*, Jan. 31, 1941; articles by Randolph in Chicago *Defender*, June 19, July 3, 17, 1943; Randolph, "Keynote Address to the Policy Conference of the March on Washington Movement," 1942, reprinted in August Meier, Elliott Rudwick, and Francis L. Broderick, eds., *Black Protest Thought in the Twentieth Century* (Indianapolis, 1971), p. 230.

78. Interview with Bayard Rustin, Dec. 3, 1975.

79. Theodore Draper, *American Communism and Soviet Russia* (New York, 1950), pp. 13–15.

80. "Call to Negro America to March on Washington," *Black Worker*, May, 1941.

81. Herbert Garfinkel, *When Negroes March: The March on Washington Movement in the Organizational Politics for FEPC* (Glencoe, Ill., 1959), pp. 98–102.

82. Meier and Rudwick, *CORE: A Study in the Civil Rights Movement, 1942–1968* (New York, 1973), pp. 4–6, 9–10; interviews with early CORE leaders: James Farmer, Dec. 2, 1975; James R. Robinson, Dec. 2, 1975; Bayard Rustin, Dec. 3, 1975.

83. *E.g.*, Chicago *Defender*, May 10, 1930; Pittsburgh *Courier*, July 19, 1930, Feb. 28, 1931, Oct. 1, 1932, Nov. 4, 18, 1939; Savannah *Tribune*, Mar. 5, Sept. 29, 1930, Jan. 7, 1931.

84. See esp. Howard Thurman, *Jesus and the Disinherited* (New York, 1949), and references to his work in Atlanta *Daily World*, Sept. 22, 1935, May 6, Nov. 4, 1936; series

of columns by Benjamin Mays in Norfolk *Journal and Guide*, May 22, 29, June 5, 1937; interview with Mrs. William Stuart Nelson, Mar. 1, 1976.

85. James Weldon Johnson, column in New York *Age*, Mar. 25, 1922. Only rarely does one find comparable suggestions—but see, *e.g.*, editorials in Kansas City *Call*, Jan. 15, Feb. 12, 1932. E. Franklin Frazier, "The Negro and Non-Resistance," *The Crisis*, 28 (Jan., 1924), 59; see also George S. Schuyler's cynical evaluation of the Gandhian movement in Pittsburgh *Courier*, Sept. 19, 1931.

86. Randolph, "Keynote Address to the Policy Conference," pp. 231, 232; *Black Worker*, Dec., 1942, Jan., Feb., 1943; interview with Bayard Rustin, Dec. 3, 1975; reports in black press, *e.g.*, Chicago *Defender*, Jan. 9, 23, Feb. 6, 1943; articles by Randolph, *ibid.*, June 26, July 3, 17, 1943; reports on July, 1943, conference in Baltimore *Afro-American*, July 6, 1943, and New York *Age*, July 10, 1943. On FOR involvement in the 1943 MOWM Conference, see also the following materials in the FOR Archives, Swarthmore College Library: Randolph to A. J. Muste, Apr. 30, May 25, 1943; Muste to Randolph, May 21, 28, 1943; and esp. J. Holmes Smith to Muste, July 8, 1943.

87. Richard M. Dalfiume, "The 'Forgotten Years' of the Negro Revolution," *Journal of American History*, 55 (June, 1968), 90–106.

88. New York *Amsterdam News*, Aug. 22, 1942, Dec. 25, 1943, Jan. 8, 1944, for New York. On public housing rent strikes, see Baltimore *Afro-American*, Oct. 27, 1942, for Philadelphia; Cleveland *Call and Post*, Aug. 29, Sept. 5, 12, 19, Oct. 10, 1942, for Columbus; *ibid.*, Oct. 31, Nov. 7, 21, 28, Dec. 5, 12, 26, 1942, Jan. 16, 1943, for Toledo. For a postwar public housing rent strike in Toledo, see *ibid.*, Aug. 24, 1946.

89. St. Louis *Argus*, Mar. 17, June 30, Aug. 4, 11, 1944; Chicago *Defender*, July 8, 1944.

90. [Bayard Rustin], "Project No. 5," in papers for San Francisco Institute of Oct.– Nov., 1943, Fellowship of Reconciliation Archives, Nyack, N.Y.

91. Cleveland *Call and Post*, May 9, 16, July 11, Sept. 5, Oct. 10, 1942, June 12, 26, July 17, 1943; St. Louis *Argus*, June 26, 1942, Sept. 1, Nov. 17, 1944, and Dec. 17, 24, 1945; Baltimore *Afro-American*, June 29, July 6, 13, 20, 27, Oct. 3, Dec. 21, 1943, Apr. 18, 1944.

92. Baltimore *Afro-American*, June 1, 1943, Apr. 21, 1945; New York *Amsterdam News*, Apr. 28, Aug. 25, Nov. 3, 1945.

93. Meier and Rudwick, *CORE*, pp. 15–16, 26–29; for Yellow Springs demonstration, see esp. Cleveland *Call and Post*, Jan. 9, Feb. 13, 1943.

94. Pauli Murray, "A Blueprint for First Class Citizenship," *The Crisis*, 51 (Nov., 1944), 358–59; various materials in the Pauli Murray Papers, 1943–44, Moorland Foundation Room, Howard University Library; Philadelphia *Tribune*, May 1, 1943; Baltimore *Afro-American*, May 23, 1944; interviews with three leaders in the Howard University group: Pauli Murray, Feb. 3, 1976, Ruth Powell, Feb. 3, 1976, and Marian Musgrave, Feb. 9, 1976; St. Louis *Argus*, May 19, July 14, 21, Sept. 1, 8, 15, Nov. 3, 17, 24, Dec. 1, 1944; interview with Mrs. Pearl Maddox of St. Louis, leader of the sit-in movement there, Dec. 4, 1975. On Murray's bus demonstration, see Pittsburgh *Courier*, Apr. 13, 1940; on her work with the MOWM, see Garfinkel, *When Negroes March*, p. 100.

95. Chicago *Defender*, Feb. 17, 1945.

96. *Equality*, Apr., 1945; Pittsburgh *Courier*, Mar. 10, 1945; Chicago *Defender*, Mar. 10, 1945; *The Crisis*, 52 (Apr., 1945), 110–11; (May, 1945), 142; (June, 1945), 174.

97. Report of the Secretary to the NAACP Board of Directors, Apr. and May, 1945, NAACP National Office, New York; Chicago *Defender*, Mar. 17, 24, Apr. 7, 1945.

98. St. Louis *Argus*, Apr. 20, July 6, 1945; Chicago *Defender*, Apr. 28, June 30, July 7, 1945; *The Crisis*, 52 (May, 1945), 142, (June, 1945), 174, and (Aug., 1945), 232.

99. Randolph's testimony before the Armed Services Committee, printed in Meier, Rudwick, and Broderick, eds., *Black Protest Thought in the Twentieth Century*, pp. 274–80; New York *Times*, Apr. 1, 8, May 1, June 27, July 18, Aug. 19, 1948; Chicago *Defender*, Apr. 3, May 1, Aug. 7, 21, 1948; New York *Amsterdam News*, Apr. 3, 10, July 31, Aug. 21, 1948; Cleveland *Call and Post*, Aug. 28, 1948.

100. For college-based activities against restaurants and barbershops, other than actions of CORE chapters, see St. Louis *Argus*, June 7, 1946, for University of Illinois; Pittsburgh *Courier*, Aug. 14, 1948, for UCLA; Chicago *Defender*, Dec. 18, 1948, for Pennsylvania State University; New York *Amsterdam News*, Mar. 1, 8, 1947, for Williams College; and Philadelphia *Tribune*, Feb. 5, 1952, Apr. 4, 1953, for Lincoln University, Pa. For examples of demonstrations by Communist-front organizations, see Cleveland *Call and Post*, Aug. 10, Sept. 7, 1946; Philadelphia *Tribune*, July 23, 1946, Aug. 6, 1948; Pittsburgh *Courier*, Oct. 1, 1949, an early example of sitting in at *downtown* variety store lunch-counters (East St. Louis). Bowling alleys were a popular object of demonstrations on the part of Communist-oriented, trade union, and NAACP groups, until the American Bowling Congress rescinded its white-only membership rule in 1950. See, *e.g.*, Baltimore *Afro-American*, Mar. 30, 1946, Aug. 21, 1948, Feb. 19, 1949, for demonstrations in various cities, including one by NAACP-CIO at bowling convention in 1949 at Atlantic City. For examples of NAACP youth council projects, see, *e.g.*, Chicago *Defender*, Jan. 1, 8, Feb. 5, Nov. 19, 1949, Philadelphia *Tribune*, Sept. 22, 1953. On other local groups, see, *e.g.*, St. Louis *Argus*, June 21, 1946, and Kansas City *Call*, Dec. 16, 1949, both for Des Moines; and *ibid.*, Nov. 21, 1947, for interracial group of federal employees picketing a Washington cafeteria that would not serve Negroes.

101. The Washington demonstrations were rather widely reported. See esp. Baltimore *Afro-American*, Nov. 2, 9, 16, 23, 1946, Apr. 21, 1947, July 3, 1948, and May 6, 1952. For Baltimore, see *ibid.*, 1947–52 *passim*; for St. Louis, see esp. St. Louis *Argus*, 1947–53, *passim*; for Kansas City, see Kansas City *Call*, Jan. 3, 10, 17, 24, 31, Feb. 28, Mar. 21, 1947, Feb. 27, 1948, and Chicago *Defender*, June 16, 1951.

102. Meier and Rudwick, *CORE*, p. 51; Washington *Afro-American*, Mar. 4, June 3, 10, Aug. 12, Oct. 7, 14, Dec. 30, 1950; Mar. 10, Apr. 21, May 26, June 9, 30, Aug. 25, Sept. 22, Oct. 6, 1951; Jan. 5, 19, May 3, June 7, 28, Aug. 30, Sept. 6, Oct. 18, 1952; Jan. 24, Mar. 14, Apr. 11, June 13, 1953. The titular head of this committee was the venerable and well-known Mary Church Terrell.

103. Philadelphia *Tribune*, July 2, 30, 1949; Baltimore *Afro-American*, Aug. 20, 1949; Cleveland *Call and Post*, Aug. 3, 1949; Washington *Post*, June 24, 1949.

104. Atlanta *Daily World*, Mar. 2, 8, 1946; St. Louis *Argus*, Mar. 22, 1946; interview with John McCray, now of Talladega, Ala., chairman of the boycott's steering committee, Oct. 7, 1975.

105. Meier and Rudwick, *CORE*, pp. 34–39.

106. Philadelphia *Tribune*, Aug. 9, 1949, for Austin; *ibid.*, Jan. 23, 30, 1951; Washington *Afro-American*, Feb. 10, 1951, Baltimore *Afro-American*, Nov. 10, 1951, and Kansas City *Call*, Feb. 9, July 13, Oct. 5, 1951, for Richmond; Pittsburgh *Courier*, Dec. 20, 1952, for Nashville.

107. For Future Outlook League, see Cleveland *Call and Post*, June 8, 1946, May 10, July 5, Sept. 27, Oct. 4, 25, Nov. 1, 29, 1947, Mar. 5, July 23, Aug. 20, 1949. For New Negro Alliance, see St. Louis *Argus*, May 28, 1948; Philadelphia *Tribune*, May 29, 1948; and Rolandus H. Cooper to Gentlemen, June 12, 1948, in Washington Interracial Workshop Papers, State Historical Society of Wisconsin, Madison. For Negro Labor Relations League, see below.

108. For examples of Communist-related organizations' activities, see reference in Joseph D. Bibb's column in Pittsburgh *Courier*, July 6, 1946, to Los Angeles; Kansas City *Call*, Oct. 21, 1949, regarding Boston; Philadelphia *Tribune*, Feb. 8, 15, 1949; St. Louis *Argus*, Sept. 5, 1952, June 5, 1953, Jan. 1, 1954, regarding lengthy campaign against Sears. For examples of NAACP-sponsored campaigns, see Kansas City *Call*, Nov. 18, 1949, regarding Richmond, Calif., chain-store grocery project; and boycott of Yellow Cab Company in San Francisco described below. Future Outlook League branches in Cincinnati and Akron also engaged in some direct action—see Cleveland *Call and Post*, July 12, Aug. 16, Oct. 25, 1947.

109. For campaigns in St. Louis and Philadelphia led by ad hoc coalitions, see St. Louis *Argus*, March 29, 1946, and Philadelphia *Tribune*, June 4, 1946.

110. For examples of such campaigns sometimes lasting as long as 6–9 months to get

one or two clerks, see Philadelphia *Tribune*, Apr. 17, 1948, regarding New York; *ibid.*, Feb. 8, 15, 1949, regarding Philadelphia; Kansas City *Call*, Nov. 18, 1949, and Chicago *Defender*, May 20, 1950, regarding Richmond, Calif.; St. Louis *Argus*, July 18, 1947, for San Francisco; and two instances in Brooklyn, reported in New York *Amsterdam News*, Aug. 9, 1947, and July 17, 1948.

111. St. Louis *Argus*, Oct. 7, 1949, for San Francisco; Chicago *Defender*, Apr. 27, May 4, June 8, 22, 1946, Jan. 25, Feb. 8, Mar. 29, 1947, for Wonder Bread in Chicago; *ibid.*, Nov. 13, 1948, and Philadelphia *Tribune*, Nov. 7, 1951, and Apr. 12, 1952, for beer campaigns.

112. New York *Amsterdam News*, Dec. 14, 1946, and Pittsburgh *Courier*, Feb. 8, 1947, for Pittsburgh; Philadelphia *Tribune*, Dec. 30, 1947, Feb. 21, 1948, and St. Louis *Argus*, Oct. 24, 1947, for Santa Monica; Meier and Rudwick, *CORE*, p. 59, for Chicago.

113. Kansas City *Call*, Aug. 5, 1955; Pittsburgh *Courier*, Sept. 3, 1955; San Francisco *Chronicle*, June 26, 1956; *The Crisis*, 62 (Oct., 1955), 496, and 63 (May, 1956), 267; interview with NAACP attorney Terry Francois, of San Francisco, Dec. 11, 1975.

114. Meier and Rudwick, *CORE*, p. 60; Kansas City *Call*, Nov. 2, 1951.

115. Atlanta *Daily World*, Mar. 3, 5, 1946, and interview with E. G. Boddie of Atlanta, leader of the March, Dec. 8, 1975; Norfolk *Journal and Guide*, Dec. 11, 1948, Aug. 20, 27, 1949. For a Louisville campaign against the telephone company, see Louisville *Defender*, Sept. 16, 23, 30, Oct. 14, 28, Nov. 25, 1954; for Mobile boycott of Coca-Cola for dismissing 21 black drivers, see Chicago *Defender*, May 5, 1951.

116. For Chicago, see Meier and Rudwick, *CORE*, p. 22, and Chicago *Defender*, June 30, 1945, May 11, June 22, Nov. 9, 1946, July 19, Aug. 2, 16, 1947, Aug. 27, 1949, Mar. 27, 1954, Oct. 22, 29, 1955; for New York, see New York *Amsterdam News*, Aug. 25, 1945, Jan. 4, 1947, May 14, 1949, May 2, 9, 1953, Dec. 18, 1954, and, for description of the chaining episode, Pittsburgh *Courier*, May 30, 1953.

117. St. Louis *Argus*, Jan. 14, 1949, for Oklahoma, including participation of white University of Oklahoma students; Norfolk *Journal and Guide*, Apr. 9, 1949, for North Carolina; Kansas City *Call*, May 9, 1949, for Texas, including the participation of several white University of Texas students.

118. NAACP, *Annual Report for 1948* (New York, 1949), p. 29.

119. For Hillburn, see New York *Age*, Oct. 9, 16, 23, 1943; New York *Amsterdam News*, Oct. 2, 16, 1943; NAACP, *Annual Report for 1943* (New York, 1944), pp. 9–10.

For Chester, see Philadelphia *Tribune*, Apr. 6, June 1, 4, 8, 11, 29, July 27, Aug. 27, 31, Sept. 7, 10, 14, 24, 28, Oct. 5, 1946; Chester *Times*, May 28, June 18, Aug. 27, Sept. 20, 1946; interviews with Cecil and Frinjela Bond of Chester, Aug. 4, 1975.

For Lumberton, see Pittsburgh *Courier*, July 12, 1947; NAACP, *Annual Report for 1947* (New York, 1948), p. 26; interview with Mrs. L. S. Stephens, Jr., of Lumberton, Aug. 4, 1975.

For Fairhaven, see New Jersey *Afro-American*, Sept. 13, 27, 1947.

For Long Branch, see *ibid.*, Sept. 6, 13, 20, 27, Oct. 11, 18, Nov. 1, 1947; interview with the Reverend Stanford Welcker of Birelle, N.J., former president of the Long Branch NAACP, Aug. 6, 1975.

For Merriam, see Kansas City *Call*, July 22, Sept. 16, 1949; *The Crisis*, 56 (Jan., 1949), 28–29; NAACP, *Annual Report for 1949* (New York, 1950), p. 35.

For Hempstead, see New York *Amsterdam News*, Sept. 24, Dec. 3, 1949; Philadelphia *Tribune*, Sept. 27, Oct. 11, Nov. 18, 1949, June 6, 1950; Savannah *Tribune*, Aug. 23, 1951, Jan. 10, 1952; NAACP, *Annual Report for 1949*, p. 34.

For Mt. Holly, see Philadelphia *Tribune*, Sept. 10, 1949; New Jersey *Afro-American*, Sept. 17, 1949.

For East St. Louis, see St. Louis *Argus*, Dec. 17, 31, 1948, Jan. 21, Feb. 4, 1949; NAACP, *Annual Report for 1949*, p. 34; Resolution of East St. Louis NAACP Branch, Dec. 18, 1948, in East St. Louis Branch Archives, and other local sources cited in Elliott Rudwick, "Fifty Years of Race Relations in East St. Louis: The Breaking Down of White Supremacy," *Midcontinent American Studies Journal*, 6 (Spring, 1965), 6–7.

For Bruce School, Kansas City, see Kansas City *Call*, Sept. 16, 1949, May 2, June 20,

1952; Kansas City *Times*, June 10, July 8, 1952; Kansas City *Star*, Sept. 12, 13, 1949, Jan. 3, 1951; interviews with the following Kansas City participants: attorney Harold L. Holliday, Sr., Oct. 17, 1975, Mrs. Gertrude Hobby, Oct. 17, 1975, and Thomas A. Webster, Oct. 5, 14, 1975.

For Alton, see Kansas City *Call*, Feb. 3, 1950; NAACP, *Annual Report for 1952* (New York, 1953), p. 47.

For Kinston, see Kansas City *Call*, Nov. 30, 1951; Philadelphia *Tribune*, Dec. 1, 1951; Pittsburgh *Courier*, Feb. 16, 1952.

For St. Louis, see St. Louis *Argus*, Sept. 7, 14, 21, 28, Oct. 5, Nov. 30, 1951, Jan. 25, Feb. 1, 8, Nov. 14, 1952; interview with movement leader Hubert L. Brown of St. Louis, Aug. 15, 1975.

For Farmville, see Baltimore *Afro-American*, May 8, 15, 1951; Pittsburgh *Courier*, Mar. 22, 1952; NAACP, *Annual Report for 1951* (New York, 1952), pp. 41–42. See also account in Richard Kluger, *Simple Justice* (New York, 1976), pp. 466–71, 475–78.

For Washington, see Washington *Post*, Dec. 7, 8, 10, 11, 12, 13, 1951, Jan. 11, Feb. 5, Mar. 20, Sept. 3, Oct. 10, Nov. 1, 1952, Jan. 18, 29, Feb. 3, 4, 5, 6, 9, 12, 13, 16, 17, Mar. 6, 14, 20, 25, June 16, 1953; Washington *Afro-American*, Dec. 8, 15, 22, 1951, Jan. 5, Mar. 22, 1952, Feb. 7, 14, 21, Mar. 21, June 20, July 4, Aug. 8, 1953; interviews with movement leaders James A. Thalley, Aug. 10, 1975, and Mrs. Vernice Waters, Aug. 10, 1975, both of Washington, D.C.

For Booker T. Washington School, Kansas City, see Kansas City *Call*, Sept. 26, Oct. 10, 24, Nov. 7, 14, Dec. 5, 12, 19, 1952, Jan. 23, Mar. 27, Aug. 14, 1953; Kansas City *Times*, Sept. 19, 23, Oct. 17, 20, Nov. 12, 1952, Jan. 17, Mar. 20, Aug. 1, 1953; Kansas City *Star*, Sept. 20, Nov. 3, Dec. 11, 1952, Jan. 11, 1953; interviews with Thomas A. Webster, Oct. 5, 14, 1975.

For West Point, see Kansas City *Call*, Sept. 19, 26, Oct. 10, 1952, Jan. 13, Feb. 20, July 10, Oct. 2, 1953; Pittsburgh *Courier*, Jan. 24, Feb. 21, 1953; NAACP Legal Defense and Educational Fund Monthly Reports for June 1–15, 1953, and Jan., 1954, NAACP National Office, New York; interview with Wilbra Billups of West Point, daughter of a boycott leader, Aug. 18, 1975.

For Lafayette, see Pittsburgh *Courier*, Mar. 7, 1953; Chicago *Defender*, Mar. 14, 1953; interview with movement leader Eva Reynolds Domingue, of Lafayette, Dec. 10, 1975.

120. See, *e.g.*, Baltimore *Afro-American*, Aug. 3, 10, 1946, for demonstrations in Washington, and Cleveland *Call and Post*, Aug. 17, 1946, for NAACP-sponsored one in that city. See also Washington *Afro-American*, Feb. 3, 1951, for Civil Rights Congress interracial picketing of White House for the "Martinsville, Va. 7," sentenced to die for assaulting a white woman.

121. Baltimore *Afro-American*, Aug. 14, 1948, for Civil Rights Congress and Progressive party picketing White House, and Philadelphia *Tribune*, June 22, 1948, for nonpartisan committee picketing Republican convention.

122. *Smith* v. *Allwright*, 321 U.S. 649 (1944); *Brown* v. *Board of Education*, 347 U.S. 483 (1954); *Holmes* v. *City of Atlanta*, 350 U.S. 879 (1955), and *City of Baltimore* v. *Dawson*, 350 U.S. 877 (1955); *Fleming* v. *South Carolina Electric & Gas Co.*, decided July 14, 1955.

123. Howard W. Quint, *Profile in Black and White* (Washington, 1958), pp. 51–54; "Dateline: Orangeburg, S.C.," *Fellowship Magazine*, 22 (Feb., 1956), 7–10; Baltimore *Afro-American*, Sept. 13, 20, Oct. 11, Nov. 1, 1955, Apr. 10, 17, May 22, June 19, July 10, 24, Sept. 4, 25, Oct. 2, 1956, Feb. 12, May 7, 1957; Orangeburg *Times and Democrat*, July 31, Aug. 12, 13, 29, 31, Sept. 4, 7, 10, 11, 14, 16, 18, 22, 25, Oct. 10, 13, 15, 18, 26, Nov. 24, 1955, Jan. 25, Feb. 26, Mar. 17, 18, 27, 29, Apr. 10–16, 26, 1956; see also excellent material in Pittsburgh *Courier*, Sept. 24, Oct. 8, 1955; New York *Amsterdam News*, Oct. 22, 29, Nov. 26, 1955; Savannah *Tribune*, Apr. 5, 1956; confidential interviews with local citizens, Apr. 17–18, 1969.

124. Baton Rouge *State Times*, June 16–20, 22–26, 29, 1953; Pittsburgh *Courier*, June 27, July 4, 11, 1953; St. Louis *Argus*, July 3, 1953; interview with T. J. Jemison of Baton Rouge, the boycott leader, Dec. 11, 1975.

125. David Lewis, *King: A Critical Biography* (New York, 1970), pp. 49–50, 63; King, *Our Struggle* (New York, 1956), unpaged pamphlet, reprinted from *Liberation*, Apr., 1956; interviews with the following individuals who were central to the initiation of the boycott: Jo Ann Robinson (now of Los Angeles), Dec. 16, 1975; Mary Burks (now of Princess Anne, Md.), Dec. 17, 1975; attorney Fred Gray, Dec. 20, 1975; E. D. Nixon, Jan. 10, 1976; T. J. Jemison of Baton Rouge, Dec. 11, 1975. See also discussion in L. D. Reddick, *Crusader without Violence: A Biography of Martin Luther King, Jr.* (New York, 1959), pp. 113, 126.

126. Lewis, *King*, p. 72; interview with Bayard Rustin, Mar. 28, 1974; Lerone Bennett, *Confrontation: Black and White* (New York, 1965), pp. 197–99; King, *Our Struggle*; King, "Walk for Freedom," *Fellowship Magazine*, 22 (May, 1956), 5–7.

127. *Gayle* v. *Browder*, 352 U.S. 903 (1956).

128. Buddy Lonesome, column in St. Louis *Argus*, Mar. 2, 1956.

129. Report of Rustin's trip to Mississippi, in *WRL News* (published by War Resisters League), Nov.–Dec., 1956; interview with Rustin, Dec. 10, 1975.

130. St. Louis *Argus*, Aug. 30, 1957; "Civil Rights [U.S.A.] Justice 1963," unpublished report, U.S. Civil Rights Commission, ch. 4: "Memphis, Tennessee," pp. 11–12, copy in possession of authors.

131. The Tallahassee bus boycott received fairly wide attention in the black press. For other summary accounts, see Tampa *Tribune*, Dec. 30, 1956; Charles U. Smith and Lewis M. Killian, *The Tallahassee Bus Protest* (New York, 1958), and the analysis in Robert M. White, "The Tallahassee Sit-Ins and CORE: A Nonviolent Revolutionary Submovement" (Ph.D. dissertation, Florida State University, 1964), esp. pp. 46, 105–6.

132. Kansas City *Call*, Jan. 4, 1957; interview with Fred Shuttlesworth, now of Cincinnati, Dec. 4, 1975; Baltimore *Afro-American*, June 12, 1956, Oct. 28, Nov. 4, 11, 18, 1958; Pittsburgh *Courier*, Jan. 5, 1957, Nov. 8, 1958, Jan. 24, 31, Feb. 14, Sept. 12, Dec. 5, 19, 1959; Jacquelyne J. Clarke, *These Rights They Seek* (Washington, 1962). On disunity among Birmingham's black leadership, see James T. McCain to James R. Robinson, Feb. 26, 1956, CORE Archives, and Louisville *Defender*, May 28, 1959. On size of the city as a factor in the viability of the boycott, see Shuttlesworth's statement in Louisville *Defender*, May 3, 1959.

133. For Shreveport, see St. Louis *Argus*, June 28, 1957; Pittsburgh *Courier*, Dec. 28, 1957. For Atlanta, see New York *Amsterdam News*, Jan. 12, 1957; Savannah *Tribune*, June 1, 15, 1957; Chicago *Defender*, Jan. 24, 1959. The Atlanta citizens finally achieved victory in federal district court in Jan., 1959.

134. Pittsburgh *Courier*, May 5, 1957. Miami Negroes threatened a boycott at one point in 1956, but the issue was actually settled in court a year later. See St. Louis *Argus*, June 15, 1956, Aug. 30, 1957.

135. Pittsburgh *Courier*, Sept. 14, 1957; Rock Hill *Evening Herald*, Aug. 1, 3, 4, 6, 8, 9, 13, 14, 20, Sept. 3, Oct. 1, 15, Dec. 18, 1957, Feb. 26, 1960.

136. Robert E. Hughes, director of Alabama Council on Human Relations, "First Report on Tuskegee," July 9, 1957, in Glenn Smiley files, FOR Archives; interview with Charles G. Gomillion of Tuskegee, Dec. 7, 1975; *Gomillion* v. *Lightfoot*, 364 U.S. 339 (1960); Clarke, *These Rights They Seek*; Charles V. Hamilton, *Minority Politics in Black Belt Alabama* (New Brunswick, N.J., 1960). The Tuskegee boycott also received good coverage in the black press, too extensive to make citing appropriate here.

137. NAACP, *Annual Report for 1956* (New York, 1957), p. 67; New York *Times*, June 28, July 1, 1956; Chicago *Defender*, July 7, 1956; New York *Amsterdam News*, July 7, 1956; Pittsburgh *Courier*, Aug. 17, 1957.

138. Durham *Morning Herald*, June 24, 25, July 17, 18, 1957; Durham *Sun*, June 24, July 17, 1957, Jan. 10, 1958; Kansas City *Call*, Aug. 2, 1957; interview with Douglas E. Moore, leader of the demonstration, now of Washington, D.C., Jan. 4, 1972; Meier and Rudwick, *CORE*, pp. 85, 86.

139. Interview with Fred Shuttlesworth, Jan. 14, 1976; interviews with Bayard Rustin, May 29, 1974, Dec. 10, 1975; New York *Amsterdam News*, May 4, 25, 1957; Pittsburgh *Courier*, Apr. 6, 20, 27, May 11, 18, 1957; Baltimore *Afro-American*, Feb. 19, Apr. 16, 30, May 21, 1957; Washington *Post*, May 17, 18, 1957.

140. Pittsburgh *Courier*, Sept. 13, 27, Nov. 1, 1958, Apr. 25, 1959; Baltimore *Afro-American*, Oct. 21, 28, 1958, Mar. 10, Apr. 14, 1959; New York *Amsterdam News*, Nov. 1, 1958, Apr. 25, 1959; Washington *Post*, Oct. 23, 26, 1958, Apr. 18, 19, May 2, 1959; interviews with Bayard Rustin, May 29, 1974, Jan. 18, Feb. 3, 1976.

141. See Meier and Rudwick, *CORE*, pp. 92–94, 74. In addition, on NAACP's role in St. Louis, see *Annual Report for 1959* (New York, 1960), p. 36.

142. Kansas City *Call*, Dec. 5, 26, 1958, Jan. 2, 9, 23, 30, Feb. 20, Mar. 6, Apr. 3, 1959; Dorothy H. Davis, "Changing Discriminatory Practices in Department Store Eating Facilities in Kansas City, Missouri" (M.A. thesis, University of Kansas, 1960), esp. p. 44; interviews with Mr. and Mrs. Kenneth Kerford of Kansas City, Apr. 4, 1968. Mrs. Kerford was a leader of the boycott.

143. Ralph O. Blackwood to Lula Farmer, Aug. 28, 1956, CORE Archives; Blackwood to Lula Farmer, Nov. 27, 29, 1956, Lula Farmer Papers, courtesy of Lula Farmer, Washington, D.C.; Kansas City *Call*, Aug. 15, 22, 1958; NAACP, *Annual Report for 1958* (New York, 1959), p. 33.

144. Barbara Posey and Gwendolyn Fuller, "Protest Drug Counter Discrimination," *The Crisis*, 65 (Dec., 1958), 612–13; NAACP, *Annual Report for 1958* (New York, 1959), pp. 32–33; Alan Saxe, "Protest and Reform: The Desegregation of Oklahoma City" (Ph.D. dissertation, University of Oklahoma, 1969), pp. 162–69; interview with Clara Luper, Nov. 14, 1975; Oklahoma *Black Dispatch*, Aug., 1958–July, 1959; Carl R. Graves, "The Right to Be Served: Oklahoma City's Lunch Counter Sit-Ins," unpublished seminar paper, University of Kansas History Department, 1974, copy courtesy of the author. See Kansas City *Call*, Sept. 5, 1958, for drugstore sit-ins in Enid, Okla., stimulated by the Oklahoma City campaign.

145. Louisville *Defender*, Jan. 22, Feb. 5, 12, 19, 26, Mar. 5, 12, 26, Nov. 12, Dec. 31, 1959, Jan. 7, 1960.

146. Meier and Rudwick, *CORE*, pp. 82, 89–92.

147. Kansas City *Call*, Apr. 11, 1958, for Washington; Pittsburgh *Courier*, Oct. 10, 1959, for Jacksonville; Meier and Rudwick, *CORE*, pp. 93–94, 90, for the CORE chapter projects.

148. For suggestive discussions on the relationship between politics and racial protest activity in the two cities, see James Q. Wilson, *Negro Politics: The Search for Leadership* (Glencoe, Ill., 1960), esp. pp. 23, 26, 32–36, 53–54, 63–64, 82, 97–99, 111, 113, 114, 117, 121, 151, 153, and Wilson, "Two Negro Politicians: An Interpretation," *Midwest Journal of Politics*, 4 (Nov., 1960), 364–69.

149. See Kansas City *Call*, Mar. 21, 1958, and interview with Joe Jefferson, Feb. 13, 1976, for Negro Labor Relations League project in Chicago; Pittsburgh *Courier*, June 27, 1959, for Buffalo; Meier and Rudwick, *CORE*, p. 95, for Los Angeles; Kansas City *Call*, Dec. 6, 1957, for Kansas City; and Chicago *Defender*, Jan. 3, 1959, for Gary.

150. New York *Amsterdam News*, Jan. 3, 10, 17, 1959; *The Crisis*, 66 (Mar., 1959), 173.

151. New York *Amsterdam News*, July 4, 11, 18, Oct. 31, Nov. 21, Dec. 12, 1959; Kansas City *Call*, Aug. 7, 1959; Baltimore *Afro-American*, Sept. 15, 1959.

152. Baltimore *Afro-American*, June 4, 1957, for Surry, Va.; Chicago *Defender*, Feb. 21, 1959, for Snow Hill, N.C.; *ibid.*, Mar. 7, 1959, for Hollister, N.C.

153. Pittsburgh *Courier*, Jan. 29, 1955; Benton Harbor *News-Palladium*, Jan. 5, 15, 17, 18, 19, 21, 1955; interview with James Griffin of Benton Harbor, a leader in the boycott, Oct. 14, 1975; NAACP Legal Defense Fund, Monthly Report, Jan., 1955, NAACP National Office.

154. The U.S. Supreme Court denied a writ of *certiorari*, thus allowing to stand the federal circuit court decision requiring an end to the black elementary school. St. Louis *Argus*, Apr. 20, Oct. 8, 1956; Kansas City *Call*, Mar. 9, Apr. 6, 1956; series of articles on the Hillsboro situation by Julian Krawcheck in Cleveland *Press*, Mar. 20, 21, 22, 23, 1956; NAACP Legal Defense Fund, Monthly Reports, Sept., Oct., Nov., 1954, Jan., Feb., Oct., 1955, Mar., 1956, NAACP National Office.

155. New York *Amsterdam News*, Oct. 10, 1959.

156. *Ibid.*, Sept. 28, 1957, May 24, Sept. 13, 20, Oct. 11, 18, Nov. 22, Dec. 13, 20, 27,

1958, Feb. 14, 1959; Irving Goldaber, "The Treatment by New York City Board of Education of Problems Affecting the Negro, 1954–1963" (Ph.D. dissertation, New York University, 1964), pp. 112, 136, 139, 142, 145–46, 163–73; David Rogers, *110 Livingston Street* (New York, 1968), pp. 22–23.

157. Meier and Rudwick, *CORE*, p. 94; New York *Amsterdam News*, Nov. 16, 1957.
158. *E.g.*, New York *Amsterdam News*, Feb. 25, 1956.
159. Mark D. Naison, "The Rent Strikes in New York," *Radical America*, Nov.–Dec., 1967, reprinted in Fred Cox *et al.*, eds., *Strategies of Community Organization* (Itasca, Ill., 1970), p. 227, for quotation; New York *Amsterdam News*, July 4, 18, Aug. 8, Sept. 5, 19, Dec. 5, 12, 1959.
160. New York *Amsterdam News*, July 4, 1959.
161. Interview with Professor Louis Ruchames, University of Massachusetts (Boston), Dec. 13, 1975.
162. For the New York demonstration, see New York *Times*, Apr. 15, 1915, and Indianapolis *Freeman*, April 24, 1915.
163. Interview with William O. Walker, Jan. 26, 1976.
164. For a rare example, see *Proceedings of the Fifth Annual Convention of the National Negro Business League, 1904* (Pensacola, Fla., 1905), pp. 63–68.
165. Of the extant newspapers only the Cleveland *Gazette*, Richmond *Planet*, and *Southwestern Christian Advocate* (New Orleans) reported as many as one-third of the streetcar boycotts we have discovered, and even these references tended to be brief and scattered.
166. Interviews with Marvin Rich of New York, Dec. 20, 1975, and Marian and Charles Oldham of St. Louis, Dec. 20, 1975, founders and leaders of early St. Louis CORE.
167. For description of suffragist parades on Fifth Avenue, see Eleanor Flexner, *Century of Struggle* (Cambridge, Mass., 1959), p. 259. Our colleague at Kent State University, Professor James P. Louis, also shared with us his intimate knowledge of the New England feminist movement, providing the basis for our statement about the march led by Trotter.